THE IMAGE OF THE JEW IN AMERICAN LITERATURE

LOUIS HARAP

THE IMAGE OF THE JEW IN AMERICAN LITERATURE

SECOND EDITION

FROM EARLY REPUBLIC TO MASS IMMIGRATION

SYRACUSE UNIVERSITY PRESS

To
Evelyn

Copyright © 2003 by Syracuse University Press, Syracuse, New York 13244
First edition copyright © 1974 by The Jewish Publication Society of America
Second edition, 1978

All Rights Reserved

First Syracuse University Press Edition 2003
03 04 05 06 07 08   6 5 4 3 2 1

Second edition originally published in 1978 by The Jewish Publication Society of
America. Reprinted by arrangement with the Estate of Louis Harap.

The paper used in this publication meets the minimum requirements of
American National Standard for Information Sciences—Permanence
of Paper for Printed Library Materials, ANSI Z39.48-1984.∞™

Library of Congress Cataloging-in-Publication Data
Harap, Louis.
The image of the Jew in American literature : from early Republic to mass
immigration / Louis Harap.—2nd ed.
p. cm.
ISBN 0-8156-2991-5 (pbk. : alk. paper)
1. American literature—History and criticism. 2. Jews in literature. 3.
American literature—Jewish authors—History and criticism. 4. Judaism
and literature—United States. 5. Judaism in literature. I. Title.
PS173.J4 H3 2003
810.9'35203924—dc21
2002032757

Manufactured in the United States of America

CONTENTS

PART V: TOWARD THE AMERICAN JEWISH NOVEL

HONORING LOUIS HARAP

ELLEN SCHIFF

I am surprised," confessed a flushed eighty-seven-year-old Louis Harap, "that the work is judged to be of greater importance than I had originally conceived." The setting was the 1991 conference of the Association of Jewish Studies. Six scholars had just presented critical evaluations of the Harap oeuvre. All had agreed with Lewis Fried's introductory statement that "Harap's work is both a summa and a summary of Jewish contribution to American life." However, while the warm assessments of Harap's accomplishments did him great honor, this was hardly a love feast. The six widely ranging appraisals demonstrated how Harap's life work continues to provoke thought and prompt spirited discussion.

No two scholars even identified Harap in the same way. Fried characterized him as a civic writer; R. Barbara Gitenstein, as a literary critic. For Stanley Chyet, he was a social historian; for Sanford Marovitz, a Jewish humanist and scholar; for Daniel Walden, an astute cultural interpreter. Jules Chametzky called him "the author of the first full systematic and laudable treatment of the Jew in American literature."

Chametzky was of course referring to *The Image of the Jew in American Literature.* In fact, each of the AJS speakers acknowledged in some way this work's unique grounding in history, society, and politics. Daniel Walden emphasized its "awareness of the social and cultural milieu in which the authors lived." Marovitz was attracted to the "moral understanding and intellectual tolerance" with which, for example, *The Image* discusses, inter alia, Melville's uneven representation of Jews. Chametzky, contemplating how to read negative depictions of Jews in high modernist writers like Fitzgerald, Hemingway, and Cather, noted the wisdom of Harap's judging writers' anti-Semitic attitudes in the light of their historical context.

Chyet, for whom Harap's sociological sensitivity places him in the company of such giants as Salo Baron, Moses Rischin, and Jacob Marcus, noted how that perspective illuminates, for instance, Hawthorne's Judeophobia. The book's final chapter on Abraham Cahan prompted two speakers to praise Harap's wide-angled view of Cahan as literary writer and *Forverts* editor, but to disagree about the extent to which autobiography informs *The Rise of David Levinsky*. Still another window onto *The Image* was opened by Gitenstein, whose specialty is poetry. She cited as exemplary of the study's broad compass its chapter on the Fireside Poets, remarking that "they're not usually thought of in this kind of discussion."

It is precisely the scope of *The Image* that leaves the book open to multiple interpretations. Sanford Marovitz accurately designated the work "an essential source and guide for future scholars in American-Jewish letters no less than it has proved over more than fifteen years for most of us here today"—an affirmation with which it would be hard to quarrel.

Harap was an assured pathfinder. In the preface to the first edition of his magnum opus (1974), he rightly notes that it was "the most comprehensive yet to appear on the image of the Jew in American literature from its beginning up to the fiction of Abraham Cahan." Then, in what became his signature approach, he promptly supported that claim by detailing the social, historical, and literary reasons his subject had not been studied sooner. That account is one of the pleasures in store for readers of this new edition.

Harap's attention to literature "not usually thought of in this kind of discussion" is precisely the phenomenon that first captured my attention. I was researching the depiction of Jews in American dramatic literature, a subject routinely ignored not only in American Jewish literary history and criticism, but in any scholarship that investigates the image of the Jew in American life. One day I came upon *The Image* and discovered chapter 9, "The Drama," with delight and gratitude.

Harap's treatment of drama goes well beyond his giving literature written for the stage its due place in the literary canon. Rare among critics, he never loses sight of what he had famously called the social roots of the arts and of the history that profoundly influences them. Here, as everywhere, Harap keeps us mindful that literature not only reflects society, but is also shaped by all manner of nonliterary forces. Nowhere is that truer than in the public arena of theater.

Chapter 9 illustrates Harap's approach beautifully. He is about to discuss some three dozen early plays. But first he addresses the unfindability of the hundreds of scripts he suspects must have existed. Their disappearance, he discovers, resulted from lopsided copyright laws and the unscrupulous practices of actor-managers who bought script they promptly hoarded so no one else could perform them. The American theater, Harap shows us, has been from the start a domain where plays are regarded as properties, where art has to wrestle with commercialism.

As I tucked the dust jacket into the last page of chapter 9, I caught sight of its author's photograph—a literary leprechaun with a smile that suggested his joy in uncovering treasures. Under the photograph was the information that Harap lived in Belmont, Vermont, a hamlet I finally located on a very large map. Within minutes, Harap and I were deep into what grew into a series of substantial telephone discussions. Not long after, I made the first of many visits to Louis and his wife, Evelyn. Louis was then finishing the three volumes that brought his study of Jewish images well into the twentieth century.[1] One day, Louis shyly asked if I would agree to serve as his literary executor. It has been a joy to transfer his papers to the American Jewish Archives in Cincinnati and to shepherd *The Image* to this paperback reprint.

Like the academics who honored Harap at AJS, former Syracuse University press director Robert Mandel recognized Louis Harap as a pioneer and *The Image* as a classic. In scholarship as in life, however, noblesse oblige. Louis was enormously pleased with the consensus that "the work is judged to be of greater importance" than he had assumed it would be. He would surely have valued as keenly the appearance of this new edition, which provides substance and model for ongoing investigations of the ever-enlarging image of the Jew in American literature.

---

1. *Creative Awakening: The Jewish Presence in Twentieth-Century American Literature, 1900–1940s; In the Mainstream: The Jewish Presence in Twentieth-Century American Literature, 1950s–1980s;* and *Dramatic Encounters: The Jewish Presence in Twentieth-Century American Drama, Poetry, and Humor and the Black-Jewish Literary Relationship.* New York and Westport: Greenwood, 1987.

AS I REMEMBER LOUIS HARAP

MORRIS U. SCHAPPES

I knew and worked with Louis Harap from June 1947 to the day he died on May 12, 1998—and he has been continually in my mind since then. I am therefore most gratified by this Syracuse University Press reissue of his *magnum opus* of 1974, *The Image of the Jew in American Literature: From Early Republic to Mass Immigration.* And I say this not only because he honors me at the close of his preface by recording that "For his close reading of the entire manuscript, I am deeply indebted to Morris U. Schappes, who also generously gave me access to some of his research materials on several authors," but also because, more important, he was a Marxist scholar, thinker and activist.

In 1936, Louis helped to found the Marxist publication *Science and Society,* and he joined the Communist Party in 1937. My own close association with him began ten years later, when he joined the editorial board of *Jewish Life* (as *Jewish Currents* was originally named). He contributed an enormous amount of writing to our pages, so much so that he was obliged to adopt a pseudonym, Jeremiah Lesser, to keep his own name from appearing as a byline more than once in an issue. Become managing editor in November 1948, he was the man at the helm when the magazine weathered the greatest crisis in its history. Two months after Nikita Khrushchev's "Secret Speech" in February 1956, the *Morning Freiheit* reprinted an article from the Warsaw Communist Yiddish *Folks-Shtimme* about Stalin's previously unmentioned murders of the Soviet Yiddish writers. "The world fell out from under me," Louis Harap said. In a seven-page editorial entitled "Why Did We Not Suspect?" in our May 1956 issue, we began the agonizing reappraisal of our previous ideological rigidity.

Wanting to devote more time to his writing and research, Louis resigned as managing editor of *Jewish Life* in late 1957. In 1961, he moved to Vermont with his wife, Evelyn, but remained on the editorial board, and continued to contribute prolifically to the magazine, known since 1958 by its present name, *Jewish Currents*. His series on the Jewish Labor Bund, which ran from February through June in 1974, occasioned much comment, as did his unflinching review of Aleksandr Solzhenitsyn's *Gulag Archipelago* in November of that year. His three articles on "The Zionist Movement Revisited" were reprinted as a pamphlet.

In 1974, when the magazine hailed his forthcoming seventieth birthday at its annual luncheon, he responded to the greeting by demanding, "Why do you people ask, 'How old are you?' Why not, 'How young are you?' " He went on to assert that vitality was "no less likely to be found in the chronologically old than in the chronologically young. And that is why my three score and ten seem so incredible to me. I don't feel like that at all." In 1984, when another luncheon celebrated his eightieth birthday by printing in its *Souvenir Journal* a complete bibliography of his writings for the magazine, it took more than three full-sized pages of small type to do it.

Amazingly, during these same thirteen years Louis not only completed his *Image of the Jew in American Literature* but also added three small volumes updating it to the present: *Creative Awakening* and *In the Mainstream,* dealing with fiction, and *Dramatic Encounters,* covering drama, poetry, and humor, as well as the literary relationship between Blacks and Jews (all three published by Greenwood Press, Westport, Conn., 1987).

Louis's contribution to both this magazine and American literary scholarship in general, in a word, was immense, and it is ongoing. The meticulousness and passion with which he served *Jewish Life/Jewish Currents* will continue to be a part of his legacy to us. When, upon attaining his ninetieth birthday on September 16, 1994, he retired from our editorial board, we hailed his contribution by declaring, as he assumed the status of Editor Emeritus, "The technical expertise and intellectual energy that he gave to our magazine cannot be measured. . . . We hail his contribution both for the gift it was and the inspiration it will continue to be."

In 1996, its fiftieth anniversary year, *Jewish Currents* honored Louis and myself, the sole survivors of its original editorial board, with its annual M. S. Arnoni Award, named after the Dutch Jewish journalist Menahem Samuel Arnoni (1921–1985). Characteristically, Louis's acceptance speech included commentary on what he felt the magazine had still to do, even beyond its already substantial achievements. After recapitulating briefly the critical events of 1956 in the USSR, he declared, "In my opinion, we have never undertaken a sufficiently deep and comprehensive analysis of the mistakes of the past," suggesting that such an undertaking was still timely, as it would identify "problems that still plague us."

Louis then asked why the magazine had not done more to establish relations with the progressive Arab community in this country, deploring the almost complete absence of any Arab writers in our pages. At the same time, he noted that the magazine's longstanding call for Arab-Israeli negotiations, a conspicuously minority viewpoint in the American Jewish community for many years, had finally been vindicated by reality "in the context of the post-1989 world." Similarly, he hailed the magazine's work in promoting black-Jewish relations, noting its simultaneous challenge to anti-Semitism among some blacks and to racism among some Jews.

But self-congratulation was never Louis's mode. "The fact that we have tenaciously maintained a critical and self-critical attitude on issues and persons does, I think, go far toward explaining how we managed to survive." He said. And he reminded us that more urgent than anything else was the need of the magazine to attract "younger generations," in order to guarantee the continuation of that survival. He concluded, "We have been through hard times in the past and survived them, and must persist in a difficult present. . . . We may at the very least, at this time, celebrate our achievements. They should encourage us to overcome obstacles to a forward path."

Our steps along that path will be illuminated by the memory of Louis's dedication and example.

PREFACE TO THE SECOND EDITION

This new edition provides the welcome opportunity to correct an error in the first edition pointed out by Milton Hindus ("Edward Smith King and the Old East Side," *American Jewish Historical Quarterly*, Vol. XLIV, No. 4 (June 1975), 321–30). Hindus clears up once and for all the widespread confusion, even among seasoned scholars, of two contemporaneous Edward Kings, one the author of *Joseph Zalmonah* (1893), and the other a New York labor organizer and friend of Abraham Cahan. The former died in 1896, the latter in 1922. The pertinent passages of the present book are now purged of this confusion. In addition, typographical and other errors have been corrected and the Index revised and expanded to serve reference needs more usefully. My thanks are owing to Morris U. Schappes for conveying to me many typographical and other errors caught by his sharp, scholarly eye.

Belmont, Vermont   L. H.
June 1977

PREFACE TO THE FIRST EDITION

When one considers the central position that the Jew has held in the past few decades both as author and subject in the mainstream of American literature, one may be brought up short by the question of how the Jew fared as author and subject from the beginning of the Republic. It is surprising that no comprehensive study of this aspect of American literature has yet been published, especially in light of the proliferation of American studies in the post-World War II period. Monographs and essays on individual pre-twentieth-century authors and works dealing with attitudes toward the Jew have appeared, and even more books and monographs and articles have been published on authors, works, and periods of the present century. But only three studies that even purport to cover the whole of pre-twentieth-century American literature in relation to the Jews have appeared: Joseph Mersand's *Traditions in American Literature: A Study of Jewish Characters and Authors* (New York, 1939) is most fragmentary on early authors and is given over mainly to twentieth-century writers; Leslie Fiedler's pamphlet *The Jew in the American Novel* (New York, 1959) is necessarily brief and touches on only a few authors earlier than our century; and Sol Liptzin's *Jew in American Literature* (New York, 1966), which, though the most inclusive of the three, omits vast areas of the subject. In addition, two doctoral dissertations at New York University have explored the drama and novel, respectively: J. Stephen Bloore's "Jew in American Dramatic Literature, 1794–1930" (1950), which is far from exhaustive; and Abraham H. Steinberg's "Jewish Characters in the American Novel to 1900" (1956), which is not quite exhaustive. The present work, which considers poetry, fiction, and the drama, is the most comprehensive yet to appear on the image of the Jew in American literature from its beginnings up through the fiction of Abraham Cahan. Although further research undoubtedly will unearth additional works containing Jewish characters, it would surprise me if the general outlines of attitudes toward the Jew as revealed in the present study are materially altered.

Why has a study like the present one been so long in coming? Although it is true that ethnic studies (except for those relating to the blacks) have not greatly occupied our literary historians and scholars, there is an additional, reinforcing reason. In American literature before our own century there was an absence of any Jewish characters that seized the imagination of readers with any force. Contrast this with the situation in English literature. No fewer than five books have appeared—and all of them in the United States— on the Jew in English literature. Three pioneer works were all written by rabbis: the Rev. Dr. David Philipson's *Jew in English Fiction* (Cincinnati, 1889, rev. eds. in 1902 and 1911); Rabbi Harry Levi's Chautauqua study guide, *Jewish Characters in Fiction: English Literature* (Philadelphia, 1903); and Rabbi Edward N. Calisch's *Jew in English Literature as Author and Subject* (Richmond, Va., 1909). The most inclusive study, *The Jew in the Literature of England* (Philadelphia, 1939), was written by Montagu Frank Modder, a non-Jewish Englishman working in the United States. Edgar Rosenberg's *From Shylock to Svengali: Jewish Stereotypes in English Fiction* (Palo Alto, Cal., 1960) is a brilliantly written, highly selective study. An English writer, J. M. Landa, published a comprehensive survey of *The Jew in Drama* (primarily, in fact, in English drama) (Port Washington, N.Y., 1968 [c1926]). In addition, there have been a veritable library of books and articles on Shylock and innumerable studies of Fagin, George Eliot's *Daniel Deronda,* and other individual authors and works with Jewish characters.

Why the discrepancy between the attention paid to this topic in English literature and the peripheral attention to it in American? The basic reason is the number of memorable Jewish characters in English literature who have caught the popular imagination. There is no one in American literature comparable to Shylock, Jessica, Sheva, Rebecca, Daniel Deronda, Fagin, Svengali, or a host of other characters less generally known. In all of nineteenth-century American literature there is not a single Jewish character who can match any of these in popular appeal, symbolic value, or influence on the popular mind. In the absence of such characters, it has not occurred to scholars and critics to concern themselves with a survey of the phenomenon, less striking artistically than in English literature, throughout the span of our national life. I venture to say that the question, "How were Jews treated in our literature," if posed to specialists in American literature, would produce the reply, "I never thought of it." Jewish participation in the national life during the first century of our history has remained in the penumbra of general American history, and the Jew's place in the context of American literature before our century has been even further from the literary historian's awareness and concern.

Nor has the problem of the Jew as literary stereotype in our literature as a whole drawn their concentrated attention. The present study shows that the Jew was a minor, if not peripheral, element in the work of most major American writers before our century. It is equally apparent that any study of the Jew as a literary stereotype requires that one explore beyond the major, enduring works. While Edgar Rosenberg was able to make a significant analysis of the stereotype by examining only works of high literary value in English literature, it would be far more difficult in American literature because of the paucity of important Jewish characters in the work of major writers. The present study is therefore quite inclusive, embracing the works not only of major authors, but also of minor and even subliterary ones.

The present study is by no means strictly literary in intent, since we are mainly interested in discovering the image of the Jew as a social phenomenon and as an indicator of the real status of the Jew in the United States throughout its history. If some authors seem to receive far more attention than their literary quality merits, it is not because literary value or lack of it is misapprehended, but rather because their work is valuable in revealing attitudes toward the Jew. By the same token, it is our hope that this study will lay to rest the euphoric view of the Jew in pre-1900 American literature to which Oscar Handlin has given currency.

The reader will observe that I have used quotations from original sources generously. In the course of my research it was borne in upon me that no more striking evidence of prevailing attitudes could be adduced than the *ipsa verba* of the authors themselves, which were often so expressive and perhaps unconsciously revealing. In addition, ample citation was necessary because so much of the material is unfamiliar not only to the general public, but even to students of literature.

A special problem faced by this study was the treatment of the Jew in the religious novel, a very popular genre in the last two-thirds of the nineteenth century. Our primary interest in this genre was to derive from its exemplars the attitude of the author—and persons of whom the author was representative—toward contemporary Jews.

For instance, condemnation of the Jews as the deicide people carried with it a belief in the "tribe" as "accursed" even down to these authors' own time. There is also a marked tendency among these authors—but not all—to depict Jews who convert to Christianity as "good" characters and Jews who refuse to recognize Jesus as Savior as "bad" characters in the stories. Traditional religious anti-Semitism is operative in many of these novels, as I believe our examination shows. Since such stories exhibit an attitude toward contemporary Jews, they belong in our survey.

The copious literature in Yiddish written in the United States, like the literature in other non-English languages, is not within the scope of our study.

In organizing the variegated material we have compromised between organization by chronology and by literary type, although our divisions are by no means watertight. Part I deals with poetry and fiction between the earliest days of the national life and the Civil War. Some of the authors treated in this section survived until late in the century, but their formative period and usually the creation of their most significant work occurred before the Civil War. We pause in Part II to follow the theme of the Wandering Jew as it was rendered throughout the century in religious literature, the historical novel, and the drama. Part III traces the self-image of the Jew as rendered by Jewish authors through most of the century. We then return in Part IV to postbellum literature to the end of the century in the popular novel, the West Coast writers, the aristocrats Henry Adams and Henry James, the realists, led by William D. Howells, and the utopian novelists. In Part V we trace the beginnings of the American Jewish novel and the feeble efforts of some Jewish fiction writers, the earliest examples of the American Jewish novel from Henry Harland to Edward King, and the climax of this trend in the work of Abraham Cahan. We leave the proliferation of literature by and about Jews in our own century to other, younger hands.

Thanks are owing to more individuals and institutions than I can record here. Professor Sidney Kaplan, of the University of Massachusetts, by his direct suggestion that I undertake this study, was the catalytic agent for an idea that I had secretly harbored for some time. For their helpful reading of parts of the manuscript and for their suggestions, I wish to thank Angus Cameron, Dr. Annette T. Rubinstein, and Joyce Adler. For his close reading of the entire manuscript, I am deeply indebted to Morris U. Schappes, who also generously gave me access to some of his research materials on several authors. My special thanks go to Dr. Abraham H. Steinberg, who generously loaned me a copy of his unpublished dissertation, "Jewish Characters in the American Novel to 1900." It is doubtful if the present study could have been made if Dr. Steinberg had not with enormous industry done the spadework of ferreting out a few hundred nineteenth-century American novels that contained Jewish characters. Mrs. Devorah Abramovitz's editorial skill helped make the manuscript more readable. Permission to reprint parts of my previously published articles was kindly given by the *American Jewish Historical Quarterly,* the *Jewish Spectator,* the *American Jewish Archives,* and *Jewish Currents.* Use of manuscript material in the Houghton Library is by permission of the Harvard College Library. My debt to several libraries is great indeed: to the New York Public Library, Harvard College Library and its various branches, the Dartmouth College Library; to Dr. Nathan Kaganoff of the Library of the American Jewish Historical Society for unstinting help, and to Mrs. Barbara Eniti, Head of the Reference Services Unit of the Vermont Department of Libraries for her extreme helpfulness in obtaining for me books on interlibrary loan from many parts of the country. My thanks go out also to my wife, Evelyn, for first draft typing of a near-illegible manuscript.

A grant from the Louis M. Rabinowitz Foundation was of great assistance in several parts of the work. My thanks are owing to its Advisory Board.

Belmont, Vermont
April 1974

THE IMAGE OF THE JEW IN AMERICAN LITERATURE

INTRODUCTION

Seldom in their history have the Jews been more fervent in their devotion to a country than they were during the founding of the United States. This devotion was expressed in the letter addressed to President Washington by the Newport Congregation on August 17, 1790: "Deprived as we have hitherto been of the invaluable rights of free citizens, we now, (with a deep sense of gratitude to the Almighty Disposer of all events) behold a Government, (erected by the Majesty of the People) a Government . . . which to bigotry gives no sanction, to persecution no assistance—but generously affording to All liberty of conscience, and immunities of citizenship—deeming every one, of whatever nation, tongue, or language equal parts of the great governmental machine."[1] Indeed, at that time fewer barriers—legal, economic, and social—were raised before the Jews of this country than of any other country. The national Constitution guaranteed such equality, even though federal authority over the states had not yet been fully asserted, and some disabilities remained against Jews in some states. Nevertheless, in its treatment of the Jews the United States was the most advanced country in the world.

It would be a profound error, however, to assume that anti-Semitism had in actuality been dispelled by the Bill of Rights. The more we learn about relations between Jews and their fellow countrymen in the early days of the nation, the more evidence emerges of mutual feelings of both tolerance and hostility.

It is remarkable that we do not even yet have a full history of anti-Semitism in the United States, only intensive monographs concerning individuals or periods. Since we have not as yet gained a perspective fully fleshed out as to both the positive and negative attitudes toward Jews, how much more is this the case with respect to the view of the Jewish character as expressed in American literature? Thus a teacher of American literature who has published a number of articles on the Jew in literature can write in a Jewish magazine: "Literary anti-Semitism does not rear its head until later in the nineteenth century. . . . Indeed, it is one of the most enduring glories of American literature that it was left for the most part untouched by this contagion."[2]

Examination of American literature since the revolution to discover precisely what treatment was, in fact, accorded the Jewish character shows that the "contagion" was no less prevalent in our literature than in English literature. Indeed, the history of the Jewish character in American literature is also a chapter in the history of anti-Semitism in the United States. For until our own century, with only a few exceptions (and some were important), presentation of the Jewish character in American literature was in its essentials taken over from the English. Yet an American historian who has also written extensively on the history of the Jew in the United States, Oscar Handlin, writes as if the literary stereotype of the Jew took on negative definition only in the 1890s. The stereotype, he writes, became delineated in the course of the nineteenth century as the number of Jews in the country increased; the stereotype became "distinct" by the 1890s.

To bring out the allegedly still-indeterminate conception of the Jew and indistinctness of the stereotype, Handlin adduces (among others) the "Leedle Yawcob Strauss" poems of the New Englander Charles Follen Adams, which appeared in periodicals of the 1870s. Yet the untenability of Handlin's thesis can be demonstrated by this very example. Handlin implies that Yawcob is Jewish, but "not recognizably different from any other German," and that he "was pictured in a wholly kindly light."[3] It is true that the heavily accented Yawcob was cast in a friendly light, but there is no internal evidence in the poems for supposing that Adams specifically intended him to be Jewish. It is true that the German Jew was at the time not always distinguished from the non-Jewish German. At the same time, it is clear that Adams did have a conception of the Jew as such, as appears in a poem, "A Tale of the Nose," in the very same volume with the "Leedle Yawcob Strauss" poems. In this poem the Jew is explicitly differentiated from the German:

> 'Twas a hard case, that which happened in Lynn.
> Haven't heard of it, eh? Well then, to begin,
> There's a Jew down there whom they call "Old Mose,"
> Who travels about, and buys old clothes.
>
> Now Mose—which the same is short for Moses—
> Had one of the biggest kind of noses:

It had a sort of an instep in it,
And he fed it with snuff about once a minute.

One day he got in a bit of a row
With a German chap who had kissed his *frau,*
And, trying to punch him *à la* Mace,
Had his nose cut off close up to his face.

He picked it up from the ground,
And quickly back in its place 'twas bound,
Keeping the bandage upon his face
Until it had fairly healed in place.

Alas for Mose! 'Twas a sad mistake
Which he in his haste that day did make;
For, to add still more to his bitter cup,
He found he had placed it *wrong side up.*

"There's no great loss without some gain";
And Moses says, in a jocular vein,
He arranged it so for taking snuff,
As he never before could get enough.

One thing, by the way, he forgets to add,
Which makes the arrangement rather bad:
Although he can take his snuff with ease,
He has to stand on his head to sneeze![4]

Handlin would then have us believe that it was only "by then"—
by the 1890s—that the Jew was identified "as a peddler, as an
old-clothes dealer, and as a pawnbroker." He further asserts that
"the American stereotype involved no hostility, no negative judgment." The reader may himself judge the accuracy of this assertion
from the evidence assembled in the present study of the Jew in early
American literature. Handlin is so impressed with the new quality
of anti-Semitism in the United States, similar to that in Europe,
which developed in the first few decades of the twentieth century,
that he underestimates the quality and quantity of prejudice present
before this. He asserts that the rendering of the Jew on the stage and
in vaudeville and comic magazine caricatures were not meant as
"anti-Semitic insults" and "were not taken as such at the time."[5]
Comments in the English Jewish press of the time, as we show in this
study, demonstrate the opposite. In the 1850s Rabbi Isaac M. Wise
stated that one reason for publishing his Jewish magazine, *The Israelite,* was to counteract the current stream of abusive Jewish stereotypes. "A rascally Jew," he explains, "figured in every cheap novel,
every newspaper printed some stale jokes about Jews to fill up space,
every backwoodsman had a few such jokes on hand for use in public
addresses; and all this called forth not one word of protest from any
source."[6]

Moreover, in retrospect we may judge that to the extent that the demeaning nature of these caricatures of Jews was not recognized as such, whether by Jews or non-Jews, it can be explained only as evidence of insensitivity as to the real nature of such caricature.

In view of the freedom before the law enjoyed by the Jew in this country, how can we account for the persistence of the stereotype in most works of American literature? Several reasons can be suggested. First, there is the inertial power of the conception of the Jew that was formed in the Middle Ages. Enmity toward the Jews for their alleged deicide, draconic exclusion of Jews from most acceptable occupations and their resort, of necessity, to moneylending and trade, and the effect on family and community life of segregation in a ghetto produced a profound mutual sense of alienation between Jews and Christian society. For centuries the Jews had been aliens wherever they lived. The stereotype was the product of this alienation and at the same time a self-justification by the Christian world for its attitudes. If the Jews were regarded as evil, money-obsessed haters of Christians who were strange in their religious and social customs, it was obviously their own fault that they were not and could not be accepted as equal and eligible members of Christian society. They had only themselves to blame for their obstinate differentness and refusal to see the light of Christianity.

This tradition of the anti-Semitic stereotype is rooted in the condemnation to eternity of the Jews as the deicide people, recently modified by the Vatican Council. Rulers exploited this popular hostility to their advantage. Segregation of the Jews and the restriction of their economic activities, as well as the all-consuming taxation to which they were subjected, formed the basis for the hardy secular prejudices against them. These prejudices and misconceptions about the Jews were perpetuated not only in the oral traditions of the people, but also in the sophisticated arts as well, from the medieval tendency to associate the Jew with the devil to the more modern literary convention of the Jewish pawnbroker. Before our own century nearly all European writers, major and minor, shared these prejudices and projected the Jewish stereotype in their art. It was not until late in the eighteenth century, with Lessing's *Nathan the Wise* (1779), that the Jew was treated in the arts as a human being with human possibilities and characteristics.

The deepest impression on both the sophisticated and the popular mind was made by Shylock, the archetype of the stereotype. The transcendent artist in Shakespeare could not help but endow Shylock with an articulateness that gives him humanity, though the violence of Shylock's hatred passes the boundaries of human behavior. But it was not the human aspect of Shylock that became rooted in the literary tradition, it was his preoccupation with money and his inhuman hatred of the Christian. The narrowest interpretation of the Shylock character is the one on which the anti-Semitic convention was based, and this was the core of the literary conception of the Jew until our own century. Its grip on the literary mind was not loosed until laissez-faire doctrine penetrated to all areas of thought in the Enlightenment in the latter half of the eighteenth century.

But for over a century and a half most writers continued to resort to the stereotype, and some of the most virulent, such as Fagin and Svengali, were created during this latter period. When Sheva, the counter-Shylock image, was presented in Cumberland's *Jew* (1794), he was a reverse image of the negative stereotype, an essentially absurd character of unintelligent, unmotivated "goodness." In any case, the Jew was almost invariably presented in literature in connection with money. Whether the Jewish type is "bad" or "good," whether a Shylock or a Sheva, his relationship to the other characters is pecuniary.[7] This is one central feature of the stereotype, from which all others flow.

Though it would be accurate to assert that obsession with money is the predominant feature of the stereotype, other traditional traits are occasionally added, such as the red hair of the medieval Judas-devil figure, which is imposed on the Jews, or repellent physical characteristics such as an extremely heavy beard, greasy hair and skin, and a humpback. The vengefulness of Shylock is sometimes attributed to the Jewish character and designated as an inherent Jewish trait since biblical times. Another extremely widespread feature is "Jewish eyes," an idea probably derived from the "evil eye" attributed to the Jews during the Middle Ages. Another traditional stereotype is the Wandering Jew, including not only perpetual wandering and endless existence, but their concomitants of universal knowledge of events, past and present, and even supernatural or diabolical powers.

In the last few centuries, since emancipation, other stereotypes have developed as some Jews have emerged into society as possessors of musical talent or extraordinary, perhaps sinister, intellect. By the end of the nineteenth century there was a new set of stereotypes: the Jew as flaming revolutionary or as manipulator of political power through his command of money. Popular imagination, from which many minds of high intellect were not immune, seized upon the careers of Jews who achieved fame or notoriety in music, finance, or politics and assigned the talents thus displayed to the Jews as a people.

The persistence of the stereotype, once it made its appearance, suggests to some that treatment of the Jew in literature was completely static and was essentially unaffected by the changes in the Jewish situation in society as that society itself changed. Some light can be shed on this central question by examining the opposing views presented in the two most comprehensive studies of the Jew in English literature, one by Montagu Frank Modder and the other by Edgar Rosenberg. Modder asserts that history shows "that invariably the poet, the novelist, and the dramatist reflect the attitude of contemporary society in their presentation of the Jewish character, and that the portrayal changes with the economic and social changes of each decade." More specifically, Modder adds that "one must note the relation which it [the history of the Jewish character in literature] establishes between social prejudice and social change, between diminishing ignorance and diminishing hostility, between the growth of humanitarianism and the growth of human freedom. Anti-Jewish feeling is here proved to be a symptom of existing social ills."[8] Modder thus emphasizes what must be true of all human expression, that it arises out of existing economic, social, and intellectual conditions.

Two decades later Edgar Rosenberg's *From Shylock to Svengali: Jewish Stereotypes in English Fiction* acknowledged that "much may be said in favor of this approach" of Modder's. But Rosenberg warned that

The principal objection to the historical rationale is that it is apt to slight the massive durability of a stereotype. . . . The historical argument . . . is likely to leave unexplained some of the simple and obvious points of identity: the persistence of the Jew-villain in the popular novels that a supposedly enlightened constituency devoured in the palmy days of the Reform Bill; the depressingly uniform presentation of the Jewish paragon as a moralizing apologist, a tolerant and educated bore, long after the apologies had become supererogatory; the portrayal of the Jew as black priest centuries after the Jews stopped being suspected of poisoning the municipal water works and accused of cutting up babies for Passover.[9]

Rosenberg shows with considerable cogency that the "good" stereotype, of which Cumberland's Sheva is the prototype, is essentially the other side of the coin of the Shylock stereotype. For both revolve about money, the one to accumulate it greedily, the other to dispense it with absurd "goodness." In neither case is the character anything like a real human being with a full range of interests and interactions, but only an agency for the generation or distribution of money.

Rosenberg has raised a real question that may easily slip through Modder's broad generalizations if one is not careful. There is even some justification for Rosenberg's extreme-sounding statement: "A study of the Jew in English fiction is fundamentally a study in the stasis of thought." For we shall see in our study of American literature, as Rosenberg found in English, that the stereotype survived with a desperate kind of stubbornness. However, despite Rosenberg's concessions to the limited utility of the "historical rationale," his emphasis on "stasis" throughout his book tends to discount the historical aspect altogether. Indeed, he indicates his lack of sympathy with the social approach by indicating his agreement with the psychologistic interpretation of anti-Semitism that was extremely influential during the 1950s, when he was writing his book. "The whole question of private race prejudice," he writes, "has come to be recognized as less and less of a socioeconomic problem and is increasingly left in charge of the psychiatrists, who are sworn to professional secrecy."[10]

The vulnerable point in Rosenberg's view is that he construes socieconomic influence too narrowly. He asks, quite properly, why the anti-Semitic literary convention persisted during a period of emancipation and enlightenment. Does he therefore mean to imply that the use and enjoyment of such literary conventions are ahistorical? He has not taken into account that the middle-class Jew became an economic competitor, and that the stereotypes of the deicidal and money-obsessed Jew were useful weapons in this competition. It is a sad fact of history that some social attitudes persist beyond the time in which they are historically appropriate. When Rosenberg assigns this kind of ahistoricity to the Jewish stereotype, he ignores certain facts of history: until quite recently, the Jew was still widely considered a member of the deicidal people among many sectors of the population; until quite recently the Jew was a strange, exotic, altogether alien being to most segments of the population and was thought to be characterized by sharp practice and preoccupation with money. While the law recognized the Jew as equal and without disabilities of any kind, and growing numbers of the general population became convinced that Jews had neither horns nor a universal and insatiable hunger for money, there were—and are—many others who have not entirely thrown off acceptance of these beliefs.

In other words, prejudice against and ignorance of Jews, which are at the foundation of the stereotype and make possible its persistence, are still very much a part of history and have been even since the emancipation of Jews became worldwide. Anti-Semitism and the stereotypes it engenders still meet with acceptance and are still useful for diversionary purposes. Delusions about Jews are obsolete only in the more knowledgeable segments of the population; they persist in the backwaters, which still form a considerable part of the landscape. Indeed, the recurrence of the Jewish stereotype in literature is itself one index of the continued presence of anti-Semitism in its audience.

While the stereotype is static, as Rosenberg has said, in that its various features have recurred in literature since the Middle Ages, the image of the Jew has nevertheless undergone a variety of alterations in accordance with the currents of social conditions and religious ideas. For instance, the specific religious experience of the American people during the nineteenth century brought forth hundreds of novels dealing with the Jew of biblical and early Christian times; this reached a climax with *Ben-Hur* in 1880. Even in this fiction the anachronistic stereotype of the money-obsessed Jew appears occasionally. But the religious attitude toward the ancient Hebrews as forerunners of Christianity generated a stereotype of the patriarchal pre-Christian, biblical Jew. Those Jews of the Christian era who are won over to Christianity are usually depicted as noble, saintly, and strong in character, while those who refuse conversion and the mass who remain faithful to Judaism are accursed for deicide. Usually the women are good and virtuous and possess a dark, exotic, "Jewish" beauty—especially those who acknowledge Jesus as Savior. Judaism is almost invariably compared unfavorably with Christianity, as a less spiritual religion, lacking in inwardness and dominated by vengefulness.

But even in the rendering of the modern or contemporary Jew, the concept is static in only a limited sense. For the image of the contemporary Jew undergoes a variety of individuations in accordance with the Jew's economic and social position in society. The Jew in literature varies in social position and even in vocation from time to time, a point we will elaborate on in our study. For example, during the years when the United States was emerging as a nation, Barbary piracy was a prominent national issue. The fact that Jewish bankers in North Africa served as negotiators between the Barbary rulers and Americans explains the inclusion of Jewish characters in that capacity in the drama of the period. Also, we may perhaps account for the paucity of contemporary Jewish characters in the literature of the first half century of the Republic by the fact that very few Jews lived in the U.S.—they constituted about one-tenth of one percent of the population. When a contemporary Jew did appear in fiction he was usually met with in a foreign country, where many Americans in the early years did, in fact, meet their first Jew.

When the Jew became a commercial competitor on the frontier he was mercilessly caricatured, as in the frontier novels of John Beauchamp Jones in the 1850s, which were intended to instruct the aspiring merchant in the opening lands. In the middle years of the century the Jew in fiction was often portrayed as a pawnbroker or secondhand clothes dealer on Chatham Street in New York, where he often was found in reality, although most of the fiction rested on the assumption that this was the Jew's only vocation. As the century wore on and the Jew became more fully integrated in American life, he began to appear in literature in a greater variety of vocations, such as musician, theater manager, or doctor.

With the mass immigration at the end of the century, and the increasing caricaturization of immigrants of the several nationalities, the vaudeville Jew, along with the stage Negro, Italian, and Irishman, gained currency in drama, and a fictional literature of the immigrant Jew arose. While features of the stereotype persisted through all these changes of locus, the variations did reflect changes in the Jew's economic and social position in American society. Both the "static" and the varying aspects of the Jewish image were equally manifestations of socioeconomic life. For despite all professions of equality, prejudice and discrimination continued to exist, and they were expressed, consciously or unconsciously, by the stereotyping of Jewish characters.

If the Jews of the United States were emancipated, in terms of both social equality and acculturation, it does not necessarily follow that American novelists and dramatists knew the Jews sufficiently to render them as credible human beings. For nearly a century there were so few Jews in the country that many Americans could grow to adulthood without ever having known one. Even those who had met Jews or encountered them in trade could be said to have only a casual knowledge of them. The lives of literary figures through two-thirds of the nineteenth century shows little if any contact with Jews. Therefore it is not to be wondered at that Jews introduced in fiction, poetry, and drama turned out to be conventional stereotypes taken over from English literature. In the most significant exception to this, Herman Melville's treatment of Jewish characters in his long poem *Clarel*, their individuation, is the result of the author's personal experience in the Levant and his intense study of the Jewish history of Palestine. No other American author before the 1890s brought to bear a comparable depth of insight into his Jewish characters. On the contrary, most writers were content to reach for the obvious literary conventions of the Jew. Basically, then, the persistence of the stereotype was owing to the fact that the Jew as Jew remained as alien to most Americans, essentially unknown as a human being, and hence was identified in terms of the ingrained clichés of Western civilization.

There are those who challenge the view that a writer who introduces the Jewish literary stereotype is thereby manifesting anti-Semitism, whether conscious or unconscious. Is the stereotype, then, a literary convention that has esthetic but not necessarily social import? Rosenberg cites Louis Kronenberger's observation on this point. Within the literary tradition, writes Kronenberger, "Barabas and Fagin involve not how anti-Semitic but *only* how antirealistic a Marlowe and a Dickens are."[11] Obviously, the stereotype is by definition anti- or nonrealistic, for it reduces the individual character to a mold that is outside any concrete time and place—a convention, in short. But is the stereotype *"only"* antirealistic? Does not its use by the writer and acceptance by the reader also presuppose anti-Semitic attitudes? Lest the charge of parochialism or paranoia be hurled at this position, it is clear that "anti-Semitism" is not a sharply defined quantity of anti-Jewish prejudice, but occurs within a continuous range of intensity, from passive acceptance of the convention to articulate, intense belief in it.

In any given instance of the use of the stereotype, the degree of intensity of anti-Semitism needs to be judged within the entire context of the social milieu, personal history of the writer, and context of the work in which it appears. In our study we shall frequently find that contrary tendencies occur within the same writer and sometimes in the same work. Ambivalence toward the Jew is strikingly illustrated by Lafcadio Hearn. During the 1880s in New Orleans and the 1890s in Japan he manifested considerable sympathetic interest in the Jews. He wrote about them in the New Orleans *Item* and the *Times-Democrat*. In 1881 he wrote an article on Lassalle in which he chides "Christians" and "freethinkers" who ignore the fact that Lassalle and Heine were Jews. The next year he wrote an admiring article on the Talmud; in 1884 he described in detail the ritual of a Jewish funeral he attended. In 1886 he called attention to the founding of the Société des Étude-Juives in Paris in 1880, and summarized the salient points of dramatist Abraham Dreyfus's article in the society's *Revue* on the Jew on the French stage. He obviously concurs in Dreyfus's condemnation of the stage Jew, and agrees with the Frenchman that the "Jewish type proper disappeared with the demolition of the old *ghettos,*" and that the Jew is no longer any different from his fellow citizens.[12] In Japan his sympathetic interest in the Jew continued, for in his letters of 1893 and 1894 we find enthusiastic recommendations of the Jewish author Sacher-Masoch; "I am very fond of the Jewish novelists," he adds. He praises Leopold Kompert's *Scenes of the Ghetto,* saying that "all of Kompert is good. . . . [He is] the greatest Jewish story-writer of the age."[13]

On the other hand, he was not above disparaging the Jews when they annoyed him in his personal life. When he was in Grand Isle, an island resort near New Orleans, in the 1880s, he wrote his friend Marion Baker that the weather was bad and that his fellow guests at his hotel were mostly Jews; more were expected, "so we shall soon have a Jerusalem Street." Later he wrote that he was "disgusted": "Whereas the Jews pay nothing, the fury of the waiters and other employees is turned upon us Christians—hands stretched from all points for quarters, fifty cents, dollars. . . . If I want to sit *here,* I am sternly shunted away *there;* if I do not like Abraham Levi, Abraham Levi is placed beside me. . . . Abraham poketh his elbow in my eye." The letter ends in a postscript: "*Damn* the island and the Jews and the Gentiles, and the sea and the infinite face of the earth!"[14] More serious was Hearn's editorial on the Jews for the *Times-Democrat* in 1885, probably written under the temporary influence of the French anti-Semitic publicist Edouard Drumont; this piece never appeared because the editor found it too abusive.[15] How hard it was for the non-Jew to keep his attitude toward the Jews on an even keel is evident in Hearn's ambivalence, despite his interest in and predominant goodwill toward the Jews.

The fact that Jews are not depicted as human beings but as stereotypes can be ascribed either to a lack of skill on the part of the writer, who avails himself of a handy convention, to the deliberate indulgence of a writer's anti-Semitic feelings, or simply to a writer's lack of familiarity with the Jewish people. In any case, the stereotype implies an anti-Semitic attitude because in its origins, and most of its uses, it was generated by hostility toward Jews. In its perpetuation that hostility is carried forward, for the convention is unfavorable. It would have us believe that all Jews are like this, or at least share some of these quite unpleasant or antisocial traits. Jews are not given credit for being a people like any other, with a range of traits and a variety of talents and moral characteristics. This is not to say that Jews do not have a national character, do not have distinctive national characteristics, or are no different from others, but only that its members have individual characters like any individuals of any people. The anti-Semitic nature of the stereotype consists in the denial of an individual nature to Jews, whether the stereotype is positive or negative, and in the tenacious belief in the dominance of Jews in the world of money.

It would be excessive to maintain that certain features of the stereotype were absolutely irrelevant to the Jews. True, in the Middle Ages quite extraneous traits such as red hair or an evil eye or a special odor were imposed on the Jews, and certain notions about the devil were transferred to the Jews. Mythical activity, such as murder of Christian children whose blood is then mixed into unleavened bread at Passover, and the like, was also attributed to the Jews. But the association of Jews with money was not without foundation. As is generally known, the exclusion of Jews from agriculture, the professions, and the trades, and the imposition of crushing taxation forced Jews into either moneylending or trade. By the time of emancipation the tradition of Jewish engagement in trade and banking had become well established, so that a disproportionate number of Jews were involved in these occupations. Even today the occupational distribution of the Jews is not "normal," that is, similar to that of the surrounding population, except in Israel. While perhaps a majority of Jews are in the working class, they are disproportionately represented in the professions and trade.

In the latter half of the nineteenth century Jews in the United States moved into a prominent place not only in banking, but also in several areas of manufacturing and trade, the clothing industry, retail merchandising, finance, and the professions. Chatham Street was a reality, as was the preponderance of Jewish proprietary signs along lower Broadway. Wall Street had its Jewish banking houses; Jewish managers controlled a good part of theater productions; the enrollment of Jews at the free municipal City College was disproportionately high. Many of these vocations found their way into post-Civil War fiction. But as our study shows, most of these figures in fiction and the drama were so burdened with stereotyped features that they lacked individuality, and the writer's animus was sometimes ill-concealed. What is more, until the immigrant novel came along there was a tendency to ignore the fact that from 1890 to 1920 the Jews were concentrated among the poor. Literature during this period did justice to neither the broad spectrum of Jewish roles and identities in American life nor the richness and complexity of individual characters within the spectrum.

When one confronts a documented history of the ill will toward the Jews manifested in most literature through nearly the entire gamut of writers, from the great to the untalented, there is a danger that one's perspective may be skewed. Are not the great ones thereby diminished in stature? Is not our admiration misplaced for minds that could not rise above vulgar prejudices against a persecuted people? At the very least, anti-Jewish prejudice hardly enhances their stature. Perhaps one is tempted to depreciate hitherto venerated literary figures, but such a response to the treatment of the Jews in literature would be itself ill-considered and lacking in perspective. For most writers, the Jews lay at the periphery of their interest and attention, and they uncritically accepted the current lore about the Jews. Most writers lacked any real acquaintance with Jews and did not know them as full human beings. When writing about Jews, therefore, they resorted to the familiar stereotype and often fell into current anti-Jewish locutions as if they were figures of speech—as indeed they were. Such pejorative phrases virtually had the status of idioms, and their propriety was scarcely questioned in the general community.

Traditional prejudice is implanted in language as an index of popular attitudes, and writers, whether major or minor, are not exempt from this form of prejudice. It is no extenuation to hold that, in resorting to the stereotype, the writer is only using a literary convention, not necessarily expressing personal views. In an article on the Negro characters in Melville, Eleanor E. Simpson has argued that the Negro stereotypes in his fiction are merely literary conventions used for literary purposes, and therefore cannot be taken to represent personal convictions of the artist.[16] If explicit or implicit rejections of such attitudes are lacking in the work of art, however, the artist must bear responsibility for them. It is usually possible to determine from the context whether such expressions are made by the character in his own person as distinguished from the author, and whether the author has dissociated himself from them. Where stereotypes do occur, it is often clear from the context that the author has unconsciously accepted them. Use of a stereotype that does injustice to a people is evidence either that the artist accepts the hurtful popular notion or that he is insensitive to the harm to which he is contributing. In either case the artist leaves himself open to criticism.

Resort to a pejorative cliché is symptomatic of the conscious or unconscious attitude of the artist using it. As F. O. Matthiessen has written: "An artist's use of language is the most sensitive index to cultural history, since man can articulate only what he is, and what has been made by the society of which he is a willing or unwilling part."[17] The fact that an artist does not rise above the conventional wisdom in certain respects does not absolve him of responsibility, though he may not be aware of what he is doing.

In any case, sensitivity on the Jewish question was not as highly developed as it is today. We shall also find many instances of ambivalent attitudes toward the Jews, with an author adopting anti-Jewish clichés but in the same work also expressing positive attitudes. For instance, when Herman Melville finally focused attention on the Jews in *Clarel,* he left us humane portraits of several Jewish characters, yet in the same work he also uses anti-Jewish locutions. The ambivalence of many authors is symptomatic of the transition from the universally accepted stock image of the Jew in literature before the eighteenth century to the human conception of the Jew as evinced in much recent literature.

In other words, judgment of writers for their attitude toward the Jews must be made in terms of the historical context. This is not to condone prejudice or to absolve writers of their responsibility. To the extent and degree to which prejudice is manifested in his writing, an author is diminished. But such negative aspects of his work do not cancel out the elements of greatness, and in many cases are so peripheral that they may be omitted without essential damage to the literary work. In any case, it is not remotely my intention to deflate the reputation of great figures of American literature, even if I could do so, because their attitude toward the Jew was less than exemplary. It is rather my aim to open up a window on an aspect of American literature that has largely been neglected; although in many cases this does not reflect particular credit on writers, it sheds its modicum of light on their times and on their relationship to their age.

PART ONE

FROM EARLY REPUBLIC TO CIVIL WAR

1

POETRY AND FICTION TO 1830

How great an advance toward freedom was the creation of the United States, as crystallized by the American Revolution, can be gathered from the political and social status of its Jews. Religious prejudice had not magically disappeared; on the contrary, prejudice continued to be directed against Jews, Protestant dissenters, and Catholics, and the institution of slavery was tragic evidence of how far the country had yet to travel to achieve true equality. Anti-Jewish discrimination was only one aspect of a general pattern of intolerance toward religious dissenters. Protestant dissenters, concludes Jacob Rader Marcus, "had no political equality in ten colonies; Catholics and Jews, none in thirteen colonies."[1] Even so, Jews were better off than other dissenters. While Quakers and Baptists were even beaten for their dissent, Jews were untouched—perhaps because they did not compete with the established religion, as dissident Protestants did. At any rate, in practice Jews enjoyed unrestricted economic rights of land ownership and were generally accorded civil liberties. Despite all the limitations inherent in the status of the Jews, they were better off here than anywhere else in the world at the time.

With the promulgation of the Declaration of Independence and the adoption of the Constitution, political equality for the Jews and all dissenters was affirmed—though the slave was declared constitutionally to be but three-fifths of a man. The gap between profession and reality in the case of the slaves was eloquently condemned by George Buchanan on July 4, 1791, before a meeting of the Maryland Society for the Abolition of Slavery: "Deceitful men! Who could have suggested that American patriotism would at this day countenance a conduct so inconsistent; that while America boasts of being a land of freedom, and an asylum of the oppressed of Europe, she should at the same time foster an abominable nursery of slaves to check the shoots of her growing liberty? Deaf to the clamors of criticism, she shows no remorse."[2]

At a time when Jewish emancipation was only beginning to stir in Europe, the Jews of the United States gained complete equality before the law, and Jewish citizens participated fully in the national life, even as public officials. As Hannah Adams wrote with pride in 1812: "The United States is perhaps the only place where the Jews have not suffered persecution, but have, on the contrary, been encouraged and indulged in every right as citizens."[3] As a matter of fact, however, federal sovereignty had not yet been fully achieved, and discriminatory legislation persisted in some states, despite the categorical provision in the Constitution that "no religious test shall be required as a qualification to any office or public trust under the United States." Only after several decades of debate, for instance, did Maryland in 1826 rescind its statutes prohibiting Jews from practicing law and holding public office. As late as 1840 the constitutions of five states—Connecticut, New Hampshire, New Jersey, North Carolina, and Rhode Island—still had discriminatory legislation on the statute books. Discriminatory laws against Jews and Catholics remained in the North Carolina constitution until 1868. Nevertheless, both in principle and practice Jews throughout the United States enjoyed an unprecedented measure of freedom.

There was far more than rhetoric in the sentiments expressed by a succession of presidents from Washington to Madison strenuously affirming equality for the Jews. Each one stated his lively awareness of the equal status of his Jewish fellow citizens. Thus when the Jewish congregations of Philadelphia, New York, Charleston, and Richmond sent a joint letter of congratulation to George Washington on his election to the presidency, he warmly responded that "the liberal sentiment towards each other which marks every political and religious denomination of men in this country stands unrivalled in the history of nations." In his reply to a letter from the Newport congregation on the same occasion, Washington asserted that our government "gives to bigotry no sanction," a phrase he echoed from the congregation's letter.[4]

John Adams, the second president, went beyond affirmation of Jewish equality in this country when he wrote, in response to a letter from Mordecai M. Noah in 1818: "I wish your nation may be admitted to all the privileges of citizens in every country in the world." And Thomas Jefferson, the third president, who was largely responsible for inclusion of the principle of separation of church and state in the Constitution, said in a letter to the Danbury Baptist Association in 1802 that he advocated "building a wall of separation between church and state," and that "religion is a matter solely between man and his God."[5] When the fourth president, James Madison, acknowledged receipt of Jacob De La Motta's discourse at the consecration of the Savannah synagogue he wrote: "Among the features peculiar to the political system of the United States is the perfect equality of rights which it secures to every religious sect." A picture of that equality is given in the *Pennsylvania Packet* on July 9, 1788, in its account of the Fourth of July celebration in Philadelphia. In the parade, it reports, marched "the clergy of different Christian denominations, with the rabbi of the Jews, walking arm in arm."

The Jews, for their part, were acutely aware of the freedom they enjoyed. Their spokesmen gave expression to this awareness on many occasions. For instance, in a sermon at the Synagogue of New York in 1798, Rabbi Gershom Mendez Seixas spoke for all Jews in the United States when he described them as being "established . . . in this country where we possess every advantage that other citizens of these states enjoy."[6]

But it was inevitable that anti-Jewish feeling should persist, in view of the centuries during which the Christian world had despised and persecuted the Jews, and that such prejudice should be exploited for political advantage. The remarkable thing was not the continuation of such prejudice, but rather the degree to which it had diminished, and indeed the national recognition of equality as a goal. The anti-Jewish clichés and stereotyped attitudes that hardly persisted were amply attested to in the literature of the country, and there were occasional overt outbursts of anti-Semitism. A flagrant example is offered by the printer and editor James Rivington, a loyalist during the revolution and Federalist thereafter. In 1795 he reprinted in New York the anti-French, antidemocratic novel *The Democrat,* by English poet laureate Henry James Pye. In his preface to the novel the American editor writes that the French "democrat" in the novel, Jean Le Noir, serves as a subversive agent for "the Metropolitan See of Sedition and Murder at Paris, to propagate these principles in a neighboring country." Rivington then goes on to draw a parallel with the activities of the Democratic Society in New York: "This itinerant gang will easily be known by their physiognomy; they all seem to be like their *Vice-President,* of the tribe of Shylock: they have that leering underlook, and malicious grin that seem to say to the honest man—*approach me not."*[7] The "Vice-President" was Solomon Simpson, a Jeffersonian radical, a Jewish merchant who became president of the Democratic Society in 1797 and had been president of the Congregation Shearith Israel.

The anti-Semitic attack was anonymously answered in two letters in Thomas Greenleaf's *Argus*. In the second letter, the writer censures Rivington's preface for the "invidious and personal remarks that it contains, not only upon a worthy individual, but also upon a numerous class of citizens, who are certainly, at least, more sincere in their attachment to the interests of America than yourself."[8]

During William Cobbett's sojourn in New York as a journalist, writing under the name Peter Porcupine he vented anti-Jewish prejudice as well as anti-Jacobin invective. One instance was his attack on Moses Levi, one of the lawyers arguing the libel case of Dr. Benjamin Rush in 1800 against Cobbett. To an argument of Levi's, Cobbett replied: "Such a diabolical thought never could have been engendered but in the mind of a Jew! . . . he did not believe a word that he said; he vash working for de monish, dat vash all."[9]

Another attack on the Jews occurred in 1790, during the intense debate on Hamilton's proposal that the government fund debts incurred during the war, a plan that would fantastically enrich speculators. A satirist writing in the *Pennsylvania Gazette* charged that such funding would require imposition of taxes so that "spies and Jews may ride in coaches."[10] Yet not a single Jew was named among the large speculators.

But on balance the United States was without doubt a comparative haven of freedom for its Jews. Basic socioeconomic and ideological forces were at work that explain this situation. The libertarian principles of the Enlightenment took deep root in the United States because socioeconomic conditions—a fluid and expanding social order, with its unexampled horizon of development—put up little resistance to their practice. The fact that Jews were not numerous at the time, and hence offered little economic competition to the rest of the population, minimized the potentialities for prejudice. There are no exact figures, but it is estimated that in 1800 there were from twenty-five hundred to three thousand Jews in a total population of 5 million persons—roughly about one-twentieth of one percent. By 1830 the number had grown to about six thousand in a population of 13 million. For the most part Jews lived in the cities. When the revolution broke out, there were organized Jewish communities in New York, Newport, Philadelphia, Lancaster, and Charleston, and some Jews lived in remote settlements. A few decades after the revolution Jews were largely concentrated in the port cities of New York, Philadelphia, Baltimore, Charleston, and Savannah. The largest Jewish community in 1800, about five hundred families, lived in Charleston. There were only a few families in the New England cities of Boston, Newport, and New Haven.

The Jews earned their living as brokers, auctioneers, merchants, shopkeepers, traders for the westward migration, Indian agents, customs inspectors, artisans, and even as public officials. For instance, in New York in 1800, forty-five were brokers and fifteen, shopkeepers; in Philadelphia, ten were brokers and commission agents, forty were merchants, and five, shopkeepers. Unlike Europe, where Jews were excluded from craft guilds, Jews in America worked without restriction as artisans and craftsmen of various kinds. From the beginning of the westward movement, Jews served as provisioners for pioneers moving westward from Lancaster.

A comparison of attitudes among European and American men of the Enlightenment is the clearest evidence of the decrease in traditional anti-Jewish attitudes in America. Practically all of them, both in Europe and America, poured scorn on the ancient Hebrews and their religion as the fount of Christian superstition. On the other hand, the toleration and libertarianism that they espoused logically led to equality and the emancipation of modern Jews. This concrete logic worked itself out slowly in Europe, more rapidly and surely in America. Yet the situation presented a strange anomaly. Many of the men of the European Enlightenment were intensely anti-Semitic. One student of the situation writes that "ill-will toward the Jew was far more common than goodwill" among the European Enlightenment figures.[11] But on the whole their American followers did not manifest this hostility.

The denunciation of the Bible and ancient Hebrews initiated by Spinoza and the early English deists received its most influential expression in Voltaire's philippics. "Over and over again," writes Arthur Hertzberg, "Voltaire insisted that the Jews borrowed everything in their culture from others, that they were certainly not the teachers of the Greeks, that they were ignorant of the arts and sciences, and that their morality was inferior to that of the Greeks and Romans."[12] Moreover, Voltaire charged that in the Bible the ancient Hebrews had tried to palm off Egyptian writings as their own, and that they were cruel and ruthless barbarians. These themes were echoed by American deists, who followed their European fellow deists' condemnation of the ancient Hebrews. Yet the Americans did not regard contemporary Jews with unfriendliness, to say nothing of venomous anti-Semitism like Voltaire's.

Thomas Jefferson denounced the ancient Jewish codes in a letter to John Adams in 1813: "What a wretched depravity of sentiment and manners must have obtained, before such corrupt maxims could have obtained credit!" Adams, although an Enlightenment man in important respects, maintained a conservatism in his latter days permeated by the Calvinistic view of human nature, and consequently he had a more sympathetic view of the biblical models revered by the Puritans. So in his reply to Jefferson he rose to their defense. "The Hebrews," he wrote, "have done more to civilize man than any other nation."[13] Both men, however, were champions of equality for their Jewish fellow citizens, and Adams, as we saw earlier, universalized his sentiments for Jewish equality.

Thomas Paine was an ardent deist who, in *The Age of Reason* and elsewhere, rivals Voltaire in the intensity of his denigration of the Bible and the ancient Hebrews. The Bible, he thought, far from being the "word of God," was an immense fraud, a thesis that he tried to prove by the methods of higher criticism taking shape in his time. The Bible narrative, he held, was a collection of Arabian stories that was not even entertaining. He disputed the Hebrew authorship of the Bible, asserting that it must be taken as anonymous except where Egyptian authorship was indicated. He polemicized against a leading contemporary Jewish Bible scholar, David Levi, whose defense of the Bible he considered full of "ignorance." The Hebrews, Paine asserts, were a "restless bloody-minded people."[14]

Viewing them from a distorted anthropological and historical perspective, Paine thought the ancient Hebrews guilty of the worst atrocities ever committed by any people. Further, in line with his Enlightenment predecessors he repeated that nowhere is it written that the Jews "were the inventors or the improvers of any one art or science."[15] He thought Moses a drastically overrated figure. "The character of Moses as stated in the Bible," he writes, "is the most horrid that can be imagined. If those accounts be true, he was the wretch that first began and carried on wars on the score or on the pretense of religion; and under the mask, or that infatuation, committed the most unexampled atrocities that are to be found in the history of any nation."[16]

There is no evidence, however, that Paine shared Voltaire's personal hatred of contemporary Jews. He made no exception of the Jews in his advocacy of the rights of man. Harry Hayden Clark has observed that "needless to say, Paine, the champion of tolerance, was not anti-Semitic toward contemporaries."[17] More typical of his attitude is his versified tale "The Monk and the Jew," published in the *Pennsylvania Magazine* of March 1775, which Paine adapted from the same tale in British magazines. "An unbelieving Jew," skating on the ice, breaks through and falls into the water; another skater, a "papist," comes to his rescue. Since it is "heresy to help a Jew," the papist insists that the Jew must first promise to embrace the church before he can be drawn from the water. To this Paine has the Jew reply in conventional dialect: "For swear mine fait! No! Cot forbid!/ . . . Come tink agen, how cold and vet,/ And help me out van little bit." The papist refuses, for "the Church forbids it." The Jew then promises to comply, but the papist suspects that the Jew will renege once he is saved. So, says the papist, " 'This was a happy fall for you:/ You'd better die a Christian now,/ For if you live, you'll break your vow.'/ Then said no more, but in a trice,/ Popp'd Mordecai beneath the ice." Obviously Paine's target here is religious intolerance. The Jew is hardly a sympathetic figure in this bit of macabre humor, but in the satire Paine's basic principle of religious tolerance is affirmed, not only in general, but for the Jews as well.

On one hand, the United States offered unprecedented affirmation of equal rights for the Jew and iteration of this principle by the nation's greatest men. On the other, official discrimination against Jews continued in some states, and anti-Semitic sentiments appeared in the public press. This ambivalence is reflected in the literature of the early days of the Republic.

Allusions to the ancient Hebrews are frequent in the early literature, but any reference to contemporary Jews is rare. The people were steeped in the Bible, and biblical allusions were the common coin of the language. Indeed, Puritanism marked a return to Old Testament religion. The Puritans, accepting literally the sacred books of the Hebrews, regarded themselves as modern Israelites and their contemporary situation as a latter-day version of Old Testament history. When the Puritans came to this country, they thought of George III as Pharaoh and looked on America as the promised land, to which they were led by their own Moses and Joshua, personified in their elders John Winthrop and William Bradford. To them, the heretic Anne Bradstreet was Jezebel.[18] As Mordecai M. Noah wrote to Daniel Webster in 1849: "I cannot but call to mind that your Puritan ancestors lived, a hundred years ago, under the Mosaic laws and flourished under the same government to which David and Solomon added power, glory and splendor." The occasion for this letter was an invitation to Webster to address the Hebrew Benevolent Association of New York City. Webster declined, but assured Noah that "I feel, and have ever felt, respect and sympathy for all that remains of that extraordinary people who preserved, through the darkness and idolatry of so many centuries, the knowledge of one supreme being, the Maker of Heaven and Earth. . . . *

The Hebrew scriptures I regard as the fountain from which we draw all we know of the world around us, and of our own character and destiny as intelligent and responsible beings."[19]

When Timothy Dwight composed his epic poem celebrating the American Revolution, published in 1785, he called it *The Conquest of Canaan,* and described the revolutionary struggle in biblical terms, with Joshua standing for George Washington. Yet despite the frequent introduction of biblical Jews in his writing, the contemporary Jew is absent from Dwight's poetry, as it is from that of all his fellow poets among the Hartford Wits.

In one respect, however, Americans who were theologically inclined did have a deep interest in the Jews of their time. The Puritans ardently believed in the Second Coming, an event that must be preceded by the Jews' acknowledgment of Jesus as their Savior. They tried to evangelize any Jews at hand. Cotton Mather urged conversion of the Jews, but success was meager. The most famous conversion of that early period was that of Judah Monis in 1722; indeed, his adoption of Christianity was the condition for his appointment as teacher of Hebrew at Harvard College.

Efforts at conversion were motivated by benevolence in many cases. The case of Ezra Stiles (1727–95), president of Yale, is instructive in this respect. Perhaps no eminent Christian of this period had more cordial personal relations with Jews than Stiles. In his lifetime this learned man was acquainted with six visiting rabbis, occasionally engaging them in New England theological discussion. So close was he to the Jewish merchant Aaron Lopez, of Newport, that he wrote an English inscription for Lopez's tomb when he died in 1782. In his diary Stiles refers to Lopez as "my intimate friend and Acquaintance" and, epitomizing the attitude toward conversion in that period, he adds: "Oh! how often have I wished that sincere, pious and candid mind could have perceived the Evidences of Christianity, perceived the Truth as it is in Jesus Christ, known that *Jesus* was the *Messiah* predicted by Moses and the Prophets."[20]

The close link between efforts at conversion and a sympathetic attitude is apparent from the remarks of Rev. Abiel Holmes, father of Oliver Wendell Holmes, in his *Life of President Stiles* (1798):

This civility and catholicism [of Stiles] toward the Jews is worthy of imitation. It is to be feared that Christians do not what ought to be done towards the conversion of this devoted people. While admitted into most countries for the purposes of trade and commerce, instead of being treated with that humanity and tenderness which Christianity should inspire, they are often persecuted and condemned as unworthy of notice or regard. Such treatment tends to prejudice them against our holy religion, and to establish them in infidelity.[21]

The same attitude is manifested by the great physician Benjamin Rush. Writing to his wife in 1787, he described in sympathetic detail the Jewish wedding ritual he witnessed at the marriage of the daughter of his friend Jonas Phillips to Michael Levy, of Virginia. During the ceremony his mind wandered back to the ancient Hebrews, and then forward to the hope for a return of the Jews to "divine favor." "I was led forward into futurity and anticipated the time foretold by the prophets when this once hallowed race of men shall again be restored to the divine favor when they shall unite with the Christians with one heart and one voice in celebrating the praises of a common and universal Saviour."[22]

Another outstanding proponent of this attitude was Hannah Adams, the first professional woman writer in the United States and author of the first history of the Jews written in this country. She was deeply influenced in her attitude toward and interest in the Jews by the Abbé Grégoire, with whom she corresponded. A friend said of her: "If you want to know Miss Adams, you must talk to her about the Jews."[23] Her history of the Jews, published in 1812, is informed with profound sympathy for their suffering and pride in the fact that this country was the only one in which Jews were free from persecution and were granted equal rights. Yet she deplores their stubbornness in refusing to embrace Christianity:

The history of the Jews exhibits a melancholy picture of human wretchedness and depravity. On one hand we contemplate the lineal descendants of the chosen people of God, forfeiting their inestimable privileges by rejecting the glory of Israel, and involving themselves in the most terrible calamities; condemned to behold the destruction of their city and temple; expelled from their native country; dispersed through the world; by turns persecuted by Pagans, Christians and Moslems; continually duped by imposters, yet still persisting in rejecting the true Messiah.[24]

Miss Adams's convictions, like those of earlier American religious proselytizers, were to have a long career in the world of popular American fiction throughout the nineteenth century. The fervent Miss Adams acted on her beliefs. Inspired by the example of the London Society for Promoting Christianity, which was founded in 1809 by the converted German Jew Joseph S. C. F. Frey (born Joseph Samuel Levy), in 1816 she gathered a group of women around her to found the first society in the United States for the conversion of the Jews. This organization, which survived until 1843, was called the Female Society of Boston and Vicinity for Promoting Christianity among the Jews. In 1820 the American Society for Meliorating the Condition of the Jews—"melioration" meant accepting Jesus as Savior—was founded. This most important of the many conversion societies of the nineteenth century had the support of such eminent men as John Quincy Adams, who was vice-president in the society's early years, and De Witt Clinton. Its main purpose in the first few decades of its frustrating, futile existence was not to convert American Jews, but to settle converted Jews from Europe in the United States. The active missionary of this society was Frey, who came to this country in 1816 after a morally checkered career in England working for the London society. He had been a missionary for the short-lived (1816–18) American Society for Evangelizing Jews before he instigated the establishment of the longer lasting society, which expired in 1870.

The Jews were somewhat perturbed by these efforts at conversion, notwithstanding their futility. In 1820 an anonymous "Israelite" published a book in New York, *Israel Vindicated,* charging that the stigmatization of Judaism as an inferior religion violated the Constitution. "If Judaism is regarded as inferior," he writes, "and the Jews are living in a degraded and uncultivated state, . . . it is impossible that this persecuted people can ever obtain their rights."[25] In light of the numerous schisms among Christians, he continues, and the intolerance of one sect for another, how can they "meliorate" the condition of the Jews? The first Jewish periodical in the United States, *The Jew,* published in New York in 1824 and 1825, was exclusively given over to refuting the arguments of the conversionists.

A few poems of this period reflect the zeal for conversion of the Jews. Continuing Hannah Adams's well-meant desire to relieve Jewish persecution by promoting their conversion, an unidentified poet, probably a woman, published a poem in the *Christian Spectator* for February 1823, "On the Depressed State of Jewish Females, and the Recent Efforts for Their Relief, through the Medium of Female Charitable Societies." The author exalts Hebrew women of the Bible and those around Jesus, and contrasts their state with that of the modern Jewish woman: "How are ye fall'n! How is the 'most fine gold/Dim,' and defac'd." She invokes the contemporary charitable Christian women, "Like angel spirits, clad in mortal robes,/ Rising to comfort you." The poem ends with the implied hope of conversion. These charitable Christian women,

> seek the peace of Zion, they behold
> With sister's love the persecuted seed
> Of Abraham, "Friend of God." Haste then, arise
> Shine forth, O Zion! for thy light hath come,
> And *He* who is thy glory shall disperse
> The cloud that covers thee, invest thy brow
> With its forgotten diadem, and bid
> The lyre no more reluctant, swell the song
> Of Earth's Salvation.[26]

For the most part, however, poetry of the period contains few allusions to the contemporary Jew.

The case was otherwise for biblical Jews. During the first few decades of the nineteenth century, interest in Palestine as the land of Jesus was growing, and many poems were written about it. One of the earliest of these was the popular "Airs of Palestine," by John Pierpont, written in 1816 and intended by the author to be performed in "an evening concert of sacred music for the benefit of the poor." Under the influence of both Thomas Gray and Chateaubriand's *Génie du Christianisme,* Pierpont bathes the Palestinian scene in a romantic and mystic haze through which a pilgrim wanders. The poet summons up a series of ancient figures like Moses, Elijah, and finally Jesus. In search of faith, the pilgrim wanders through Florida, Rome, and Scotland. The poem ends with an affirmation of the Christian doctrine of faith, hope, and charity. In another poem, "Jerusalem," Pierpont wishes he had seen that city and gives an idyllic description of the places he would visit. But now, he says, Jerusalem is a suffering city because the Jews have rejected Jesus. "His blood is on thy head," he writes, and "*thy* cross thou bearest now!/ . . . The crescent is thy cross!"[27]

A more strictly contemporary use of the Moses story is made in one of Pierpont's "Hymns for Temperance," written for the opening of the Marlborough Hotel as a temperance house in 1837.

> Had Moses built a still,
>   And dealt out to that host,
> To every man his gill,
>   And pledged him in a toast,
> Would cooler brains,
>   Or stronger hands,
>   Have braved the sands
> Of those hot plains?[28]

Another widely read biblical poem of the period was "Noah," published in Baltimore in 1821, an example of a form too much used in the eighteenth century: rhyming iambic pentameter. This verse retelling of the Noah story gives special attention to Japheth, son of Ham, as the ancestor of the Negro slave.

Of special interest is the eulogy to a contemporary Jew by the reigning postrevolutionary poet of Boston, Robert Treat Paine, Jr.[29] The poem bemoans the death in 1805 of Paine's friend Moses Michael Hays, a prominent Jewish merchant of Boston. No reference whatever is made to Hays's Jewishness, but Paine eulogizes his charm, wit, friendship, generosity, and vigor of mind. The poem is significant for what it implies about the equality enjoyed by the Jews at that early date. Much is conveyed by the fact that a Jew could be described in these human terms by the most highly regarded Boston poet of the time.

The work of the most gifted poet of the period, Philip Freneau, contains little reference to the contemporary Jew, but nevertheless has relevance to the image of the Jew current at the time. Like his coevals, Freneau frequently alludes to the biblical Hebrews in his themes and illustrative figures. While a sophomore at Princeton in 1768, the sixteen-year-old Freneau tried his hand at heroic couplets in a paraphrase of a biblical story in "The History of the Prophet Jonah." "The Pyramids of Egypt: A Dialogue," written two years later, shows the influence of the Enlightenment; and the militant democrat in "Genius" deplores the labor expended by slaves:

> To raise this mighty tomb—and but to hide
> The worthless bones of an Egyptian king,—
> O wretch, could not a humbler tomb have done?
> Could nothing but a pyramid inter thee!

In "The Deserted Farmhouse" (1772) the desolation of a deteriorating, abandoned farmhouse arouses philosophical thoughts of the decline of Rome, "once mistress of the enslaved," and of Palestine:

> So sits in tears on Palestina's shore
>   The Hebrew town, of splendour once divine—
> Her kings, her lords, her triumphs, are no more;
>   Slain are her priests, and ruin'd every shrine.[30]

Together with his college friend, the novelist H. H. Brackenridge, Freneau wrote the Princeton commencement poem in 1771. In the 1809 edition of his poems, he published a revised version of his own lines of this poem as "The Rising Glory of America," in which national expansion is hailed:

> And time anticipates when we shall spread
> Dominion from the north, and south, and west,
> Far from the Atlantic to Pacific shores.

He foretells a great future for the nation. In the course of the poem he contributes to the current speculation that the Indians originated as the Ten Lost Tribes. Perhaps, he writes, "the hardy tribes/ Of banished Jews, Siberians, Tartars wild" wandered across Greenland, and "Came over icy mountains, or on floats." Or perhaps—"another argument more strange"—the biblical theory of Genesis 10:25 that in Peleg's day the earth was "cleft in twain—'divided' east and west" with the Atlantic rolling in between is correct. As for the theory that the Wandering Jews inhabited America, it is, he says, "the flimsy cobwebs of a sophist's brain."[31]

By 1775 the poet had become a full-fledged Jeffersonian and iconoclastic deist, and expressed himself in bluff American style. Why, he asks with pragmatic irreverence, spend years in learning ancient languages, "Latin, and Hebrew, Chaldaic, and Greek," when they "To the shades of oblivion must certainly sneak;/ Too much of our time is employed on such trash/ When we ought to be taught to accumulate cash." The scornful Enlightenment attitude toward Judaism is expressed in his poem "Sketches in American History" (1784). In Columbus's delusion about just where he had landed, writes Freneau, he "resembled old Moses, the Jew," who led "his wrong-headed crew."[32] He goes more deeply into deistic condemnation of Judaism in an essay, "Epic Poetry" (1790), which satirizes Timothy Dwight's *The Conquest of Canaan.* An epic poet seeking a theme with which to achieve fame, he says, will "turn to ancient Jewish history" for there the poet will find the "*butchering* work" so necessary to the epic "displayed to perfection in the annals of the Hebrew butchers." Such a poet may read in Josephus "authentic accounts of now and then, eighteen or twenty thousand young children having been cut to pieces of a morning by order of the Supreme Being (*alias* the Priests)."[33]

But as with Tom Paine there is no evidence that he applied his adverse judgment of the ancient Hebrews to contemporary Jews. On the contrary, as an Enlightenment man, his satirical treatment of both church and synagogue was directed against religious intolerance— for instance, in his prose piece "The Philosopher of the Forest" (1781). The first section purports to be the autobiography of a descendant of William Tell. The hero of the satire travels to discover his vocation. While in Egypt he decides, "by the advice of a trading Jew, to embrace the profession of travelling *pilgrim.*" In the course of his travels Freneau's hero ridicules categorization of any people by presumed ethnic identification. He relates how in China he was taken to be a Spanish Jesuit, in Europe, a traveling philosopher, "but have ever been considered in America as a rabbinical Jew, collecting contributions for the distressed of that nation residing in or near Jerusalem."[34]

Freneau pours withering scorn on intolerant, dogmatic Christianity in several letters signed with one of his numerous pseudonyms, Robert Slender, O. S. M. ("One of the Swinish Multitude"), in the character of a wily pretended innocent. In one letter (1799) he recounts a purported conversation with a parson who complains that Slender has not been seen in church lately. In extenuation Slender replies that he is confused by the evanescence of orthodoxies. While the "true Calvinistic Presbyterian religion" is the current orthodoxy, he says, he disagrees that "it is neither agreeable to Judaism or Christianity." To illustrate his point, he tells the story of a great man who is suffering from leprosy. The unfortunate one is told that "in the land of Jewry" there is someone who can cure him by laving him in the waters of Palestine. At first he protests that the water of his own country is better than that of Palestine, but in desperation he goes to Palestine and is cured. Which, then asks Slender, is the superior religion? To reinforce his point, Slender adds that while antipapism was once orthodox, it is now heterodox, and Calvinists are now defending Catholicism in France as an antirevolutionary force. Poor Slender is confused by all these contradictions in the concept of orthodoxy.[35]

In another letter (1800) in the same vein, Slender opposes an anti-Jeffersonian preacher who insists that Slender accept the preacher's doctrine even if he disagrees. How dare an "illiterate" like Slender dispute with a learned minister? But, Slender shyly asks, has not a man "a right to his own judgment"? Indeed, he adds, there would never have been any Christians at all if such a practice had not been followed. Why do Presbyterians criticize Catholics, who, after all, have the same authoritarian attitudes? Oh, that's different, replies the preacher, for "the Jews and Papists are advocates for a false belief." But these sectarians say the same of the Presbyterians. The innocent Slender is still confused.[36]

None of the evidence thus far shows any anti-Jewish feelings toward contemporaries. On the contrary, the evidence points to a vigorous advocacy of universal religious tolerance. This conclusion is strengthened, strangely enough, by Freneau's pejorative use of the term "Shylock." This invidious word is used in a number of poems, but in no case does it have the traditional connotation of the money-obsessed Jew. In every case Freneau uses the word for political satire. In his work of the 1780s and 1790s, "Shylock" usually is an epithet against political antagonists. When Freneau revised his poems for later publication, "Whaccum's canker'd hoof" became "Shylock's canker'd hoof" in an anti-Federalist satire. In other poems with similar intent, "dunces" became "Shylock"; "Oswald's scribblers" became "Shylock's poems"; "Oswald's rancorous page" was changed to "Shylock's rancorous page"; "Fallon, the priest" became "Shylock, their bard"; and "Timon with malicious spirit" was rewritten as "Shylock with malicious spirit."[37] To Freneau, "Shylock" signifies a *politically* reprehensible person.

In addition, during the 1780s and 1790s Freneau used the title "Shylock Ap-Shenkin" in six satirical poems. The significance of "Ap-Shenkin" is obscure. "Ap" is the Welsh patronymic, but a search for the identity of "Shenkin" (a Welsh name) has thus far been fruitless. Since all the poems with that title are satirical attacks upon printers, publishers, and editors, one might suppose Shenkin to have been one of these who had a bad reputation, but no such actual personage has been identified. Freneau's targets in several of these poems were the Federalist printers Fenno and Oswald, who exchanged versified abuse with him. One of the liveliest of the "Shylock Ap-Shenkin" poems is Freneau's reply to Hamilton, who charged in Fenno's *Gazette of the United States* that Freneau and his paper, the *National Gazette* (founded in 1791 to combat the Federalists and particularly Fenno's journal), were Jefferson's hired creatures and that Freneau had received money from Jefferson to publish his magazine. Writes Freneau:

> What is my crime, that thus Ap-Shenkin raves?
>   No secret-service-money have I had
> For waging two years' war with fools and knaves.
> Abus'd at court, unwelcome to the Great—
>   This paper of mine no well-born aspect wears:
> On honest yeoman I repose its fate,
>   Clodhopper's dollar is as good as theirs.

The titles of several of the poems that duel verbally with Oswald were changed: from "To a Concealed Royalist, on a Violent Attack" to "To Shylock Ap-Shenkin, an abusive court writer"; from "To the Foe to Tyrants" to "To Shylock Ap-Shenkin."[38]

These numerous uses of "Shylock" are totally lacking in the usual anti-Jewish imputation, let alone money obsession. Freneau drained

the epithet of its specific anti-Jewish content and used it as a generalized term of abuse. While the traditional connotations of the word
must have occurred to some readers (and the usage was in this sense
unfriendly to Jews), Freneau's use of the term minimizes any anti-
Jewish animus.

Very few contemporary Jews are depicted in American novels of
the first decades of the United States. The first known mention of
a modern Jew in American fiction occurs in Royall Tyler's *The
Algerine Captive* (1797), which was concerned in part with the problem of the Barbary pirates. For some decades after its establishment,
the United States was plagued with this problem. From the seventeenth century on, corsairs had preyed on commerce in the Atlantic
and the Mediterranean. They captured ships and enslaved their
crews and passengers, holding both ships and people for ransom.
After the United States achieved independence, it inherited from
Britain the responsibility to protect American ships and citizens.
American consuls in the Barbary States were in almost constant
negotiation to try to reach agreements, however precarious; free
captured ships; and ransom enslaved citizens. In return for "protection," the Barbary rulers were paid tribute in money, naval stores,
regalia, and jewelry. These negotiations often involved Byzantine
intrigue in which British and French consuls schemed to put Americans at a disadvantage in the lucrative Mediterranean trade.

It was in response to piracy that the United States Navy was
created in 1794. Soon after William Eaton, an aggressive, adventur-
ous Yankee who was interested in expanding United States commerce in the Mediterranean, was sent to the Barbary States in 1797
as one of three consuls, he became convinced that diplomacy was
futile and that the issue could be resolved only by force of arms. He
bombarded the Department of State with memorandums urging
force rather than bribery. His importuning was finally rewarded; in
1803 a fleet was sent to Barbary, and he himself was put in command
of a land force to capture Tripoli and enthrone the brother of the
ruling dey as an American puppet. Eaton led a victorious march, but
before he could reach Tripoli a naval bombardment of the city
frightened the dey into capitulation. It was not until 1816, however,
after a naval force led by Stephen Decatur forced the dey of Algiers
to surrender, that the hazard to American shipping and citizens was
finally ended.

Throughout this period two powerful Jewish banking families in
Algiers, the Bacris and Busnachs, served as mediators in these
negotiations. By their skill in finance and diplomacy they had be-

come virtual partners of the deys. They held a monopoly on banking, were dominant in trade with Europe, helped supervise the
piracy, and were the diplomatic channel to the deys. Joel Barlow,
who was sent to negotiate the release of captives in 1796, reported
that Bacri negotiated for the United States with great diplomatic
skill. In spite of protection by the dey, however, the personal situation of these bankers was precarious under the intrigue-ridden state
structure of Algiers. Busnach was assassinated in 1805; a pogrom
engineered by the government followed, and warehouses were pil-
laged. Competition for power between Bacri and the rising Jewish
house of David Duran led to the decapitation of Bacri by order of
the dey in 1811. Later the same year Duran was himself decapitated
by order of the dey.[39]

Consular reports to the Department of State make it clear that the
Jewish bankers were indispensable to the operations of the American
consuls. The Jews were not only diplomatic go-betweens, they also
loaned money for consular expenses and for ransom. Their un-
popularity with the consuls, however, is not hard to understand—
William Eaton's reports, especially, exhibit intense hostility toward
the bankers. He was certain that they were working against American interests in collusion with the French and were trying to prevent
peace in order to prolong their profitable dealings as brokers. On
December 6, 1799, Eaton complained that negotiations were being
hampered by "French intrigue and Jewish infidelity." In desperation
he reported on September 5, 1800, that, although he was "destitute
of funds, . . . happen what will, I shall have no resort to Jews."[40]
Louis B. Wright and Julia H. MacLeod observe: "Reading their
dispatches out of context, one might assume that the consuls were
three anti-Semitic Americans heaping insults upon the Jewish race.
Actually these diatribes were directed at a particular group of Jewish
bankers and not the race as a whole."[41]

Whatever the consuls' personal views on Jews in general may have
been, their relation with the bankers was obviously very trying. A
bizarre example of what they had to contend with is given in a report
by a man named Reynal Keene in 1814. Jacob Bacri, who was
negotiating for the dey, told Keene that Algiers demanded $2 mil-
lion as the price for a treaty. Keene protested that this was too much:
it was more than any other nation was paying. Bacri blandly replied
that in a war the American navy would be completely destroyed by
the British, and that a new navy would have to be built to protect
trade. It would be cheaper for the United States to pay tribute than
to build a new navy to protect its ships![42]

In these circumstances the Jewish bankers easily slipped into the stereotype and lent it a certain credence. A firsthand view of them has been left to us by Mordecai M. Noah, probably the most prominent Jew of the period, a playwright, editor, and politician. He served as American consul to Tunis from 1813 to 1815, and writes in his book of travels that one motive in seeking this post was to obtain "the most authentic information, in relation to the situation, character, resources and numerical force of the Jews in Barbary." His candid estimate of the Jewish bankers is pertinent:

The Jews are the leading men, they are in Barbary the principal mechanics, they are at the head of the custom-house, they farm the revenues; the exportation of various articles and the monopoly of various merchandise are secured to them by purchase, they control the mint and regulate the coinage of money, they keep the Bey's jewels and valuable articles, and are his treasurers, secretaries, and interpreters; the little known of arts, science and medicine, is confined to the Jews. . . . They are ever in the presence of the Bey, every Minister has two or three Jewish agents, and when they unite to obtain an object, it cannot be prevented. These people, then, whatever may be said of their oppression, possess a very controlling influence, and their friendship is worthy of being preserved by public functionaries, and their opposition is to be dreaded. The intrigues which the Jewish merchants set on foot, to obtain for me the prize goods at their own evaluation, I could not, with all my efforts, effectually destroy, as I discovered that the Bey, his brother, two sons, and several of his officers, were interested in the result. Their skill in business, and the advantage which they take of Christians and Moors, have been the subject of severe and just animadversion; they will, if not narrowly watched, avail themselves of opportunities to overreach and defraud.[43]

In the many works of fiction and drama* dealing with this subject, the Jew is pictured as rich. True, these characters are based on real models, the Bacris and Busnachs, who were indeed ruthless traders and bankers. But there is no hint in any work that not all Jews in Barbary were bankers and brokers. Noah had observed that while many of the Jews are "possessed of great wealth, many are poor."[44] He himself had written a play on the Barbary theme, *The Siege of Tripoli* (1820). Since there are no Jewish characters in it, we may conclude that Noah thought it the better part of wisdom to refrain from mentioning them. Even in a chapter by Tyler on the Jews of Algiers there is no mention of poor Jews. Besides being bankers and merchants, the Jews of Algiers engaged in a full range of occupations and the majority of them were steeped in poverty.

*   *   *

*See chapter 9.

Tyler's *Algerine Captive* was originally published in Walpole, New Hampshire, in 1797. Tyler was born in Boston in 1757, fought in the revolution, participated in the suppression of Shays's Rebellion, and ended his years as chief justice of the Vermont Supreme Court and law professor at the University of Vermont. In addition to several contemporary plays, he wrote three plays in blank verse— "sacred dramas" he called them—on the Old Testament stories of Esther and Haman, Joseph, and Solomon.[45] He had a keen sense of a separate American ethos and urged a national literature independent of England's. In the preface to *The Algerine Captive* he pleads "that we write our own books of amusement, and that they exhibit our own manners."

His novel, which is representative of Enlightenment thought, relates the picaresque career of a young New Englander, Updike Underhill. The book, which satirizes classical education, the medical profession, and Puritanism, still affords amusement to the modern reader. After an apprenticeship with a doctor, the young Yankee hero unsuccessfully tries to practice medicine in several states, and finally goes to sea as a ship's doctor. His vessel takes on slaves in Africa, giving Tyler the occasion to express his intense antislavery views. Underhill describes the inhumanity of the slave trade and concludes: "I execrated myself for even the involuntary part I bore in this execrable traffic: I thought of my native land and blushed." For these scruples he is derided by his shipmates. He describes a hunger strike by the slaves that ends only when the women and children are threatened with whipping. Underhill vows that upon his return home "every moment of my life shall be dedicated to preaching against this detestable commerce."[46]

He himself is enslaved when his ship is captured by Algerian pirates, but his wretched lot is alleviated when he is sold to be an aide in a medical clinic in Algiers. Taking advantage of his freer situation, he frequents the Jewish quarter. There he is approached by a Jewish merchant, who has heard of his medical skill and asks him to attend his ailing son. The conventional description of the wealthy Jew's living quarters follows: the exterior of the house is shabby and ramshackle, but behind the façade of poverty is an apartment of oriental splendor where the merchant, Adonah Ben Benjamin, reappears richly clothed. Adonah (who speaks without an accent) explains that the outward show of poverty is necessary to avert the dangerous suspicion of wealth, and he tells Underhill that he is protected by the dey. Adonah's son recovers under the doctor's care, and a friendship springs up between Adonah and Underhill, who frequently visits the house. In gratitude for his son's recovery, Adonah agrees to have letters transmitted to Underhill's parents through the American chargé d'affairs in Madrid. When no reply comes, Underhill concludes that "from the known humanity of that gentleman [Adonah], my letters miscarried."[47]

The "friendly Jew" then proposes that Underhill earn his ransom money by performing medical services. The "benevolent Hebrew" offers to hold the money as it is earned, and promises to make up the needed balance after Underhill's earnings have reached nine hundred dollars. Adonah says that then he too will go to the United States and set himself up in commerce through a Jewish friend, a Mr. Lopez, who lives in Rhode Island or Massachusetts, to whom he will send his money. He wishes to live in a country, he says, "where no despot should force from him his honest gains."[48] The whole plan meets with disaster when Adonah suddenly dies of apoplexy.

Adonah's services to Underhill are reasonable and adequately motivated. He does not exhibit the fatuous goodness of a Sheva, although Tyler may have derived his conception of the "good" Jew from Richard Cumberland's *The Jew* (1794). But Tyler was too sensible to carry Adonah's goodness to the absurd extreme of Sheva's. Yet Adonah remains a stereotype because his function revolves wholly around money. It is true that Tyler has a friendship develop between the two men, but this is a perfunctory aspect of the relationship; the substantial aspect is financial.

Tyler's attitude toward the Jews is revealed in passing comments and in a chapter on the Jews of Algiers. Like so many American writers before this century, Tyler deplores the failure of Jews to adopt Christianity. They were, he writes, "too wilfully blind to see the accomplishment of their prophecies in the person of our Saviour, in the midst of exile were ready to contemn those prophecies which had so long deluded them with a Messiah who never came." The chapter briefly describes the dey's exploitation of the Jewish bankers in financial and diplomatic manipulations, in return for which the dey gives them protection. Tyler notes that "popular prejudice is generally against" the Jews and that the dey exploits this prejudice by large exactions of money for protection when the Jews are menaced by a pogrom. When a case of ritual murder was charged against the Jews in 1690, the author relates, the pogrom that followed was halted by the dey. "The dey," writes Tyler, "who desired nothing less than the destruction of so useful a people, was soon appeased by a large present, and declared them innocent." The enlightened Tyler characterizes the ritual murder charge as "a horrid tale, which should have been despised for its absurdity and inhumanity." While Tyler exhibits sympathy for the Jews, he nevertheless describes them as "that cunning race . . . [who] now solace themselves with a Messiah whose glory is enshrined in their coffers."[49]

After Adonah's sudden death, the story goes on to tell about Underhill's relationship to Adonah's son. When asked to return the money deposited with Adonah, the son refuses, professing total ignorance of the transaction. The epithets used by Tyler to describe the good Adonah become phrases such as "the artful Jew" and "the wily Israelite" when he characterizes the son. The son again falls ill and regards this as a judgment for his deceit. He promises to return the money, and Underhill restores him to health. The son's contrition is short-lived, however, and he again embarks on a monstrous deception. "You think," he tells Underhill, "a Jew will always deceive in money matters; you are mistaken." He gives Underhill several thousand dollars and purportedly arranges to smuggle him on board a ship leaving Barbary. Instead, Underhill is robbed by the son's agents, sold into slavery, and placed on board a ship bound for Tunis. When the ship is captured by a Portuguese frigate, Underhill is liberated and returns home, to the "freest country in the world."[50]

The second mention of the Jew in the American novel occurs in James Butler's *Fortune's Football* (1797–98). Two Jews enter the story briefly, one of whom never actually appears on the scene. The story opens in England, where the hero, Mercutio, is ordered by his father to marry a girl of his father's choice. Since he loves another, he refuses. When Mercutio petitions the father of his beloved for her hand, he is again rebuffed. Mercutio must cease seeing his daughter, says her father, because "my daughter is to be married in a few days to Mr. Ephraims, of the old Jewry, a wealthy broker." Mercutio leaves, "pronouncing the words *damned avarice*"[51] on the well-founded assumption that the father is marrying his daughter to Ephraims for his money. We get no inkling of the character of Ephraims or his attitude toward the girl. He simply serves as a symbol of the extrusion of finer values by money. The rest of the book is a picaresque novel. Mercutio, driven from home by his father and from his beloved by her father, has a series of adventures in France, Italy, and elsewhere, his travels taking him all the way to Persia.

We meet the second Jew in the novel as a result of Mercutio's friendship with the British Wilcox family, who have been captured by pirates and put up for sale in Constantinople as slaves. A stranger signs the bond for their ransom and invites them to his home. The stranger turns out to be a Jewish merchant, Aaron Levi, who bears a close resemblance to the first "good" stereotype of the Jew in English literature, Joshua Menassah of Smollett's *Adventures of Ferdinand Count Fathom* (1753). Aaron Levi puts up the money to save Mercutio's friends from slavery, just as Menassah advances the money (and refuses interest) to extricate Fathom's friend Melvil from a desperate financial situation. Levi is not so exaggeratedly benevolent as Menassah—at least he has a motive for his goodness, for he had received financial aid years earlier from the man he now saves from slavery. Butler comments: "Levi's conduct on this occasion deserves our warmest approbation, and his manner of performing this disinterested action, enhanced the value of the favor in a ten fold degree."[52]

Levi is "distressed" by his guests' expression of gratitude and entreats them "to desist," saying he is only discharging his debt to the man who saved his life. Levi invites his guests to remain at his house until they sail for Holland, and urges them to accept "what money will be necessary to defray your expences, as I have enough of it, and you shall partake of it to the last ducat." Somewhat later Mr. Wilcox tells his story to the British consul, who then sends for Levi and commends him, saying: "A good man I revere, be his name, country or religion what they may." The consul pays Levi the money due on the bond, whereupon Levi responds: "I wish it was in my power to replace all the Pirates have deprived you of—you should then see with what cheerfulness I would serve you." When the financial dealings are ended, Levi excuses himself promptly every time on the grounds of "urgent business,"[53] thus relieving everyone of any social relations with him. His place in the fiction, in accordance with the stereotype, positive or negative, revolves exclusively around money.

Both Tyler and Butler depicted foreign Jews; the first *American* Jew was introduced by Charles Brockden Brown in his novel *Arthur Mervyn,* the first part of which was published in 1799 and the second in 1800. In his delineation of a central character in the second part Brown not only portrayed a Jew, Achsa Fielding, in America, but also transcended the conventional stereotype in his portrayal—perhaps the earliest breakaway from the stereotype in all literature in English. Brown depicts her as having arrived from England a year and a half before the action of the novel. She is a wealthy widow of twenty-six, six years older than the titular hero, whom she marries.

She is represented as a fully developed character in her own right, and except for one feature, discussed below, she lacks the female Jew's salient traits in the literary convention. Contrary to the stereotype, Achsa is not an appendage to an avaricious and money-obsessed father, nor does she lack a living mother. In fact, both loving parents are no less tender after Achsa's marriage to a Christian.

Nor is there any hint that her origin is a barrier to that marriage. The text does not support Leslie Fiedler's statement in *The Jew in the American Novel* (New York, 1959) that at the moment of Achsa's revealed Jewish origin "the promised Happy Ending trembles in the balance" (pp. 6–7). When doubts about the marriage are discussed by Mervyn with his friend, Dr. Stevens, Achsa's Jewishness is not even mentioned. Instead, they raise the questions of Achsa's age and Mervyn's poverty.

Fiedler further mentions the displeasure of the poet Shelley, a great admirer of Brown's, at the novelist's having married off Mervyn to Achsa, instead of the fifteen-year-old farm girl Eliza Hadwin, whom he loves but rejects as not conforming to his ideal. "Shelley," writes Fiedler, "could never forgive him for allowing the hero to desert an Anglo-Saxon 'peasant' girl for a rich Jewish widow." Thomas Love Peacock, who reported Shelley's disappointment, had written: "The transfer of the hero's affections from a simple peasant girl to a rich Jewess displeased Shelley extremely." Shelley's objection was based on class considerations rather than on "racial" grounds, as implied by Fiedler. Fiedler corrects the matter in his *Love and Death in the American Novel* (New York, 1960), where he drops the phrase "Anglo-Saxon" and writes more accurately that "Shelley could never forgive him for marrying off his hero to a sedate and wealthy Jewess instead of a poor 'peasant girl' " (p. 138). (Incidentally, Fiedler is also in error when he designates Achsa as the "first Jewish character in American Fiction" [*The Jew in the American Novel,* p. 6]. As we have seen, Jewish characters had already appeared in the novels of Tyler and Butler.)

Perhaps the most striking departure from the stereotype is the fact that Achsa is not exotically beautiful, as the established convention would have dictated. On the contrary, she is quite plain physically. Dr. Stevens, who is modeled after Dr. Elihu Hubbard Smith, Brown's most intimate friend in real life, describes her as lacking in physical beauty, though she does radiate spiritual beauty, grace, intelligence, and cultivation. "A brilliant skin is not hers," says Dr. Stevens, "nor elegant proportions; nor majestic stature; yet no creature had ever more power to bewitch. Her manners have grace and dignity that flow from exquisite feeling, delicate taste, and the quickest and keenest penetration. She has the wisdom of men and books. Her sympathies are enforced by reason, and her character regulated by knowledge."[54] In short, Achsa is the perfect mate for an Enlightenment man of the eighteenth century.

There is additional support for the view that Achsa is a departure from the stereotype: we have indications that in some respects Achsa was created in the image of the woman Brown wanted to marry—"the type after which my enamored fancy has modelled my wife," as Mervyn says of Achsa.[55] In 1797 Brown had fallen in love with Susan A. Potts, of Philadelphia. In the fall of 1798, however, Brown's mother had forbidden the marriage, probably because Susan was not a Quaker and marriage outside the sect was prohibited. In November 1800, after the second part of *Mervyn* had been published, Brown met Elizabeth Linn, a non-Quaker, married her in 1804, and was duly read out of the Quaker meeting. It is altogether probable that Susan Potts was very much on Brown's mind while he was writing the second part of *Mervyn,* which was completed in April 1800.[56] Achsa's resemblance to Susan is suggested by the description of Susan in a letter by Brown's friend Elihu Smith. "Without being beautiful," wrote Dr. Smith, "she was very interesting."[57] In the novel Mervyn characterizes Achsa thus: "Never saw I one to whom the word *lovely* more truly belonged: and yet, in stature she is too low; in complection dark and almost sallow."[58] Like Susan, Achsa was not imposing in looks but had spiritual beauty.

There is no documentary evidence that Brown had much to do with Jews, although we may assume that he observed them during his residence in Philadelphia and New York. The record shows probable acquaintance with one Jew, Solomon Simpson, a politically active New York merchant—the same man who was the target of Rivington's Jew-baiting in 1795—who was a member of the American Mineralogical Society, of which Brown was also a member during his stay in New York in 1798. We do not know whether the as yet unidentified I. E. Rosenberg, to whom Brown dedicates his *Ormond* (1799) and whom he describes there as a recent immigrant from Germany, was Jewish, nor whether a man or woman. Since *Ormond* was written just before *Mervyn,* and since we know of no reason why Brown should have made Achsa Jewish, it is possible that his attention was drawn to the Jews by his current friendship with a Jewish person named Rosenberg.

In any event, Brown's treatment of Achsa shows no more than a superficial acquaintance with Jewish life. He was probably as free from anti-Jewish prejudice as could be expected of any non-Jew in his time. Arthur Mervyn expresses the author's own equalitarian convictions when he says of Achsa: "I have heard her reason with admirable eloquence, against the vain distinctions of property and nation and rank. . . . Her nation has suffered too much by the inhuman antipathies of religious and political faction." Although Brown was deeply influenced by the Enlightenment, he does not share the strong anti-Jewish attitudes of leading European spokesmen of the movement like Voltaire. He was closer in this respect to eminent American followers of the Enlightenment.

But Brown was not entirely free from preconceptions about Jews. Achsa is probably echoing his own views when she tells Mervyn that she supposes there is "some justice in the obloquy that follows them [the Jews] so closely." She is at pains to dissociate her father from the traits commonly accepted as Jewish. Her father was, she says, a wealthy Portuguese who had come to London as a boy and had "few of the moral or external qualities of Jews." He was "frugal without meanness, and cautious in his dealings, without extortion."[59]

Underlying these disclaimers must have been Brown's own wish to make Achsa and her family as sympathetic as possible to the reader —and to Arthur Mervyn—despite their Jewishness. The indications point to Brown's acceptance of some traditional beliefs about Jews but his rejection of overt anti-Semitism. Total freedom from anti-Jewish attitudes was rare in those days, even among militant non-Jewish advocates of Jewish rights. The most glaring example of Brown's acceptance of popular beliefs is his use of the surviving medieval notion of the special quality of "Jewish eyes." It is through this feature that Achsa's Jewish origin is discovered. One day Mervyn notices that Achsa's eyes have "a vague resemblance to something seen elsewhere the same day"—presumably a Jew. He says to her: "Those eyes of yours have told me a secret . . . and I am not less amazed at the strangeness than at the distinctness of their story. . . . Perhaps I am mistaken. . . . But let me die, if I did not think they said you were—*a Jew.*"[60]

Achsa, who confirms his guess, is very much upset by the revelation. But it is clear that the "deepest sorrow and confusion" brought on by the disclosure stem from the memories it arouses of an unhappy past rather than from her Jewishness. "Connected with that word [Jew]," she replies, "are many sources of anguish, which time has not, and never will dry up; and the less I think of past events, the less will my peace be disturbed." She then tells Mervyn the story of her girlhood. She was the "darling" of her parents and was brought up "in the most liberal manner." She received a secular English education, moved easily in English society, and was indifferent to religion, which her parents did not impose on her. "Except frequenting their church and repeating their creed, and partaking of the same food," she adds, "I saw no difference between them and me. Hence I grew more indifferent, perhaps, than was proper to the distinctions of religion."[61]

Achsa's untroubled youth and relaxed parental care, she adds, made her impressionable and excessively trusting of people. At sixteen she fell in love with the son of a wellborn English official, who consented to the marriage, as she later realized, because he had a very large family and was not affluent; hence he was not unwilling to marry off his son to a Jew in order to acquire for him, as he thought, a rich father-in-law. Since she had "abjured my religion" and was indifferent to the "disrepute and scorn to which the Jewish nation are everywhere condemned,"[62] Achsa easily yielded to the one condition to her marriage made by the father of her betrothed: that she join the Church of England. Her own father removed any objections he may have felt on religious grounds in deference to her inclinations, and also because he wished her to be married before his impending but as yet secret bankruptcy was disclosed.

After her marriage and the birth of a child, she had been beset by those calamities that cause her distress when Mervyn opens the subject of her past. Her father committed suicide because of bankruptcy, her mother's mind became unhinged by the event, her child died, and her husband ran off with another woman. But Achsa recovered her fortune and came to America to begin a new life. The book ends with her marriage to Mervyn. It is true that Achsa's assimilationism makes it easy for Mervyn to marry her, but nowhere does her Jewish origin create in Mervyn's mind any doubts about the marriage.

Although the most significant fiction before Brown's work, Hugh Henry Brackenridge's *Modern Chivalry,* contains no Jewish characters, it does contain clichéd allusions to Jews. The novel grew by accretion: first published in 1792, this satirical polemic against demagogy in electioneering, abuses of democracy, and slavery went through several enlarging editions, until it reached final form in 1815, a year before the author's death. To judge from the slender evidence in the book, this friend of the common man exhibited a conventional attitude toward Jews. On one hand, he uses the exam-

ple of the ancient Hebrews, especially the critical function of the
prophets, to expound contemporary problems: "I have often
thought," he writes, "that if the president of the United States in our
time has a *Jewish prophet* to denounce the people, their *political trans-
gressions;* that is to say, the swerving from the true faith; in other
words, his *own party;* how much more secure his standing would be;
how much less vexed by the calumny of editors, and paragraphs in
gazettes." On the other, he uses anti-Jewish clichés. A ballad singer,
who mocks the romanticizing of frontier life, says he is "too lazy"
to trap beaver with the people from town "because I have just
enough 'f it;/Don't like to be as rich as a Jew." When the author
sums up the meaning of the book on the last page, he writes: "Your
philosophers may teach you to catch crabs in a new way, or to open
oysters; I look to what will establish the government and render it
vigorous; taxation, and no borrowing from Jew brokers, like minors
who have their states in expectancy."[63]

Nor does the even more important novelist Washington Irving
concern himself with Jews. In all of his work only a few references are
found. One is a passing allusion to the Wandering Jew in *Salmagundi*
(1807–8).[64] The other is a whimsical contribution to the speculation
about the origin of the Indians in his *Knickerbocker's History of New
York* (1809). After the deluge, writes Irving,

[Noah,] becoming sole surviving heir and progenitor of the earth, in
fee-simple, after the deluge, like a good father, portioned out his
estate among his children. To Shem he gave Asia; to Ham, Africa; and
to Japhet, Europe. Now it is a thousand times to be lamented that he
had three sons, for had he had a fourth, he would doubtless have
inherited America . . . and thus many a hard-working historian and
philosopher would have been spared a prodigious amount of weary
conjecture respecting the first discovery and population of America.

Some pages later he offers one of the "theories" of writers who:

insinuate that the Canaanites, being driven from the land of the Jews,
were seized with such a panic that they fled without looking behind
them, until, stopping to take breath, they found themselves safe in
America. As they brought neither their national language, manners,
nor features with them, it is supposed they left them behind in the
hurry of their flight—I cannot give my faith to such opinions.[65]

In sum, except when they were used in a totally unthinking, static
manner, references to the Jews from the beginning of the nation
through 1830, though infrequent, reflected the tolerance that was
a conscious national goal.

2

ANTEBELLUM POPULAR FICTION

Beginning with the 1830s, a change in the social visibility of the Jews took place in accordance with the nature and numbers of the new immigration from Germany. Until that time the Jewish community had been relatively very small, and was predominantly Sephardic in ritual, but already mostly Ashkenazic in origin. It constituted a stable, established part of the American people and had achieved a high degree of economic, social, and cultural integration. Discriminatory treatment of the Jews in Germany, however, impelled thousands of them to emigrate to this country, and the stream was swelled after the crushing of the 1848 revolution. The figures tell the story: in 1830 there were about three thousand Jews in the United States. By 1850 the number had grown to about fifty thousand, almost three-fifths of them from Germany. Of the total immigration of three million between 1850 and 1860, about one hundred thousand were Jews. By 1860 about fifty cities had organized Jewish communities, and others had unorganized ones. New York had about forty thousand Jews; Cincinnati, six thousand; and there were several thousand in New Orleans. In 1861 about 15 percent of all United States Jews lived in the South. Immigrants from all nations were rapidly integrated in the expanding economy—agriculture, industry, and transportation—which was growing in all parts of the nation.

In this fluid social situation the condition of Jews in society was freer, and access to the economic and social life of the general community less impeded, than anywhere else in the world. There was no pattern of discrimination backed by ideology, if we exclude negative theological dogmas about Jews and the Shylock image reflecting economic ideology. This does not mean that discrimination and anti-Jewish attitudes did not exist. "A distinction should be drawn," writes John Higham, "between actual social relations and stereotypes in ideas; the prevalence of good relations does not mean that American attitudes toward Jews were ever wholly favorable. Behavior and belief do not necessarily coincide in any area of life. . . . American conceptions of Jews in the abstract at no time lacked the unfavorable elements embedded in European tradition."[1] Theological condemnation of the Jews for their refusal to accept Christ persisted strongly, and the economic stereotype of the money-obsessed, grasping Jew began to assume a dominant place in the American "mythology" with the increasing visibility of Jews and their broader involvement in the economic life of the nation.

As early as the 1840s Jews lived in and owned small shops in the slums of lower New York City and were the object of interested description, as the East Side was to become later. Chatham Street was lined with secondhand stores and pawnshops. A story by Cornelius Matthews, written in 1845, gives a naturalistic description of Chatham Street:

The Jews were as thick, with their gloomy whiskers, as blackberries; the air smelt of old coats and hats, and the sideways were glutted with dresses and over-coats and little, fat, greasy children. There were country men moving up and down the street, horribly harassed and perplexed, and every now and then falling into the hands of one of these fierce-whiskered Jews, carried into a gloomy cavern, and presently sent forth again, in a garment, coat or hat or breeches, in which he might dance, and turn his partner to boot.[2]

The Jew often entered the literary scene at those points where he entered the social scene, that is, where he became socially visible. For the most part the portrayal in fiction was far from flattering. This is true of one of the most widely read novels of the antebellum period, George Lippard's *The Quaker City*. It first appeared as a ten-part serialization in the *Saturday Evening Post* beginning in September 1844, under the title "The Monks of Monk Hall," and was published in book form in the next year. The book was so popular that thirty editions appeared within four years. George Lippard was an early example of that strange American phenomenon: the Populist, whose concern for the poor was joined to intense antiforeign prejudice and anti-Semitism.

Born in Philadelphia in 1822, Lippard began his career as a theological student, but abandoned this study because he believed Christianity to be hypocritical. He became a law clerk, but quickly gave up the law on the ground that it did not serve justice. Then at the age of twenty he turned to journalism. He was a police reporter in 1841, and wrote short stories and magazine pieces for six months at such a rate that he became ill from overwork. The loss of a ten thousand dollar legacy through a bank failure intensified his hatred of the rich. He was passionately convinced that the poor were exploited by the rich, that the rich were never honest toward their employees, and that the higher echelons among official, economic, and social Philadelphia were riddled with corruption and immorality. He devoted himself to a superheated, sensationalized exposure of the vices of the rich and powerful.

A notorious murder on the Camden ferry in 1843 provided him with a ready-made plot for a full-scale exposure. A prominent Philadelphian had shot another member of his class for violating his sister, kidnaping her, and placing her in a brothel. The jury acquitted the murderer in half an hour. Lippard's novel, based on this sensational case, poured hatred and anathema on the rich and powerful of his city. When a dramatic production based on the novel was announced, a thrill of fear ran through the officials and the elite of Philadelphia for fear they might be personally represented in the play. The mayor banned the play on the ground that it would provoke the mob to violence. In the five months after the play was suppressed, forty-eight thousand copies of the book were sold. Lippard continued to write novels, became a lecturer, and founded a nativist fraternal organization, The Brotherhood of the Union, whose ideas he incorporated in several books. He was a friend of Poe's, and helped the sick, unhappy poet on his last journey to the South in 1849. Lippard died of tuberculosis in 1854 at the age of thirty-two.[3]

In *The Quaker City,* Lippard declares his intention "to lift the cover from the Whited Sepulchre."[4] The book is a reductio ad absurdum of the Gothic novel, "probably the most extravagant compound of Gothic terror, intense melodrama, and social invective ever written on this continent," as Alexander Cowie has written.[5] It is cluttered with Gothic claptrap: lushly decorated rooms, underground vaults, skeletons, death pits, a ghost room, and eerie lighting; lubricious descriptions of women about to be seduced add a touch of pornography. "Monk Hall" is a brothel and the "monks" are the respectable professional men and businessmen of the city who repair to the hall to indulge their vices. Interwoven with the background of murder and moral corruption is a scheme to forge letters of credit and embezzle $200,000. The forger is, of course, the Jewish character of the book, Gabriel Van Gelt (sic), a "hump-back" from Charlestown who has "rather a Jewish twang to his tongue"[6] and speaks in dialect.

He is to receive ten thousand dollars for forgery and facilitating an embezzlement for the highly respectable "abbot" of Monk Hall. Van Gelt is a virtual caricature of a man. His head is like a

horse's head affixed to a remnant of a human body . . . his shoulders arose on either side, as high as his ears, and his back protruding in a shapeless hump, was visible above the outline of his head. . . . "Jew" was written on his face as clearly and distinctly as though he had fallen asleep at the Temple at Jerusalem, in the days of Solomon, the rake and moralist; and after a nap of three thousand years, had waked up in the Quaker City, in a state of perfect and Hebraic preservation.

Van Gelt goes to the house of the widow Smolby, where a payment of ten thousand dollars is deposited for him. After murdering the widow he takes not only his money, but also three thousand dollars of the widow's savings. Arriving at her house, he says: "Bi-Gott! . . . I smellsh te goodt already." When the chest with the widow's money is found, he exclaims: "Toubloonsh! Toubloonsh!" while thrusting his hands eagerly into the chest. He tries to blackmail his employers, and they in turn attempt to kill him at Monk Hall. He escapes, but Luke Harvey, hero of the book, catches up with him and demands that he surrender the forged documents, allowing him to keep the ten thousand dollars. "As for the *'murder,'* " Harvey adds, "you can turn 'State's Evidence'; it will suit you, being a Jew."[7] However, the plotters, suspecting that Van Gelt has informed to the police, hang him.

In another novel by Lippard, *The Empire City* (1853), a Jewish financier appears briefly. The Jew in this exposure of vice and corruption in New York fares better than Van Gelt, but he is no less evil. Despite his swindling, writes Lippard, he "still lives and prospers, a chosen favorite of the Prince of Darkness."[8]

Contemptuous treatment of the Jew and the blatant economic stereotype are also to be found in the novels of Charles F. Briggs, a well-known New York editor. In *The Adventures of Harry Franco,* published in 1839, an innocent country boy is cheated by a Mr. Isaacs. Young Harry Franco comes to New York to make a career. He wanders into an auction store on Broadway, where he is advised by Mr. Isaacs to bid for a rosewood casket decorated with jewels. Mr. Isaacs has "a nose both high and long, and his eyes were very black, but large and heavy; his hair was black and crispy; and he had a stoop in his shoulders." Isaacs advises Franco in his bidding and promises "upon his honor as a gentleman"[9] to buy back the casket the next day at twice the price Franco paid for it. Franco buys the casket for fifty dollars. But when he returns the next day Isaacs cannot be found; apparently he is an agent for the auction house. In desperation Franco sells the casket back to the auctioneer for five dollars.

The Jew in Briggs's *Haunted Merchant,* published in 1843, is a more extended and even more malicious caricature that so closely resembles Van Gelt in Lippard's *Quaker City,* which was written a year later, that one suspects that Lippard took the idea from Briggs's book. Jacobs is hired in a plot by Tom and Fred Tuck to drug their uncle and steal his latest will, in order to claim their inheritance in an earlier will. A drug overdose administered by Jacobs kills the uncle. But Jacobs steals the wrong will, as well as another man's watch. After these mischances the nephews bribe Jacobs to leave town. Before Jacobs can flee, however, he is arrested and sent to jail, where he is visited by Tuck, who asks: "And what is the nature of the complaint for which you are arrested? Is it murder, or house-breaking? or some of your low Chatham-Square practices?" Jacobs answers that it is "something about a watch," and "a suspicion of breaking your uncle's house."

Tom Tuck arranges to kidnap the witnesses against Jacobs, and the charges are dropped. When Tuck later hears that Jacobs is trying to extort money, he exclaims: "Curse him, the Iscariot wretch; I wish there was an Inquisition for his sake and that I was Grand Inquisitor. I would tear his dog's flesh with hot pincers for this."[10] The nephews send Jacobs a check on an overdrawn account. Jacobs, who is also a member of a counterfeiting ring, is caught passing a bogus bill and is imprisoned again. Maneuvers to get him out of jail are foiled, and Jacobs threatens to turn state's evidence. An effort by the nephews to bribe Jacobs to keep quiet also fails because the law catches up with them; they are imprisoned and tried with Jacobs, and all are found guilty of murdering the uncle. Jacobs is hardly an innocent victim. The vicious caricature of the Jew occurs in a highly melo-dramatic context and is permeated with ill will for the Jew.

Briggs continued his stereotyped, unflattering picture of the Jews in his next novel, *Working a Passage* (1844), "published for the benefit of young Travellers."[11] A young man, Jack Plaskett, is sent to England as a seaman to escape the cholera epidemic in New York in 1832. He jumps ship in Liverpool and meets a servant girl, "a pretty, black-eyed Jewess" named Antoinette. "Her father," explains the author, "was a wealthy jeweller, with a house at Everton, and she had been turned out of doors for joining the established church," and compelled to become a servant for want of training for anything else. Young Plaskett and Antoinette fall in love, but Plaskett is drowned on his next voyage.

"The pretty Christianized Jewess" is a pathetic, homesick creature, who steals home by the back door to see her brothers and sisters. Her father sees her on one of these visits, and "thrusts her rudely into the street." (It must be granted that the unrelenting father is no stranger to actual Jewish life; and one recalls Sholem Aleichem's Tevye, who steadfastly renounces his daughter for converting and marrying a non-Jew.) No more is known of her: "Perhaps she is in Heaven."[12] Antoinette exhibits the traits of one variant of the female Jewish stereotype—beauty, conversion, and the love of a Christian—and being a converted Jew she is treated with sympathy.

An economically based anti-Semitism is transparent in a series of novels by John Beauchamp Jones, a fervent Christian and traditional southerner. He puts Jewish competition for the trade of pioneer western communities in the worst possible light. In his *Western Merchant* (1849) Jones purports to give instruction, in fictional form, to easterners who plan to go into business in the opening West. The story conveys an intensely hostile response to the Jewish merchant, Moses Tubal, who has opened a store in Hannibal, Missouri, where Luke Shortfield, the hero, is a rival merchant. Moses is depicted as totally unscrupulous and described as having "a prominent nose, high cheek bones, and sparkling eyes . . . a cunning Jew, in quest of a location to cheat his neighbors and spoil the regular trader's business." His speech is heavily accented. He is suspected of starting a rumor that his store is stocked with stolen goods, which are therefore cheaper than Luke's. This stratagem, notes Luke, "was characteristic of the peddling Jews. Success is their motto, and they pursue it with indomitable perseverance, and with a total indifference to reputation. They have no credit themselves, and they credit nobody. They trade upon the productions of others (they never create or produce anything), and cheat the Christians with their own wares." Luke adds that his hostility to these Jewish merchants "may not have been altogether unmixed with unfounded prejudice," but later experience has given little ground for modifying this opinion. "The Western Jews," Luke concludes after much of his trade has gone to Moses, "are extremely vindictive, and most pertinacious in their efforts to cripple their Christian competitors."[13]

The trade war between the two merchants goes back and forth, as each resorts to tricks to lure the other's customers away. Luke finally gets the best of Moses, who decides to move on after fraudulently declaring himself bankrupt. "The Jews," says Luke, "are proverbially a restless, roving class. . . . The Shylocks prefer to be on navigable streams, where it is always convenient for them to take passage for 'parts unknown,' should their necessities or indications render it expedient to do so."[14] In the last scene Luke meets Moses on the dock at Saint Louis, where Moses is transporting fifty boxes of goods to set up a store in Jefferson City.

The invidious conception of the Jewish merchant in the new towns of Missouri was continued by Jones in his *Life and Adventures of a Country Merchant* (1854). The theme is the same as that of the earlier novel. Two Kentuckians, Jack and Nap, set up a store in Missouri set against a backdrop of events typical of the opening of the West: a camp meeting and a temperance lecture, political campaigning, hunting, speculation in land, the purchase of goods from the East and their transportation to and sale in Missouri. Once the store is established, the Jewish competitor, Moses Rhine, a "double-purple, madder-dyed Jew,"[15] enters the tale.

The storekeepers complain that Moses undersells them, and a rumor of mysterious origin has it that Moses is selling smuggled goods, which are therefore cheaper. Not to be outdone, Nap sets going counterrumors that deflect the business from Moses. "Chopfallen, the Jews generally show their feelings in their faces," Nap observes. Moses hires a clerk "just imported from Germany," and complains that the clerk is not good for his business because he does not understand English. When Moses's store is partially destroyed by fire, he receives full damages, although he is suspected of having set the fire himself.* He sells the remaining stock, closes down the store, and moves away without paying his creditors.

A new note is added: two competitors take the place of Moses, but the proprietors of the original store are not discouraged, since the newcomers are not Jewish. "They were Christians, however," writes Jones, "and Jack was satisfied, while Nap consoled himself with the reflection that the more business there was done in the place, and the greater the number of inhabitants, the more valuable would become his unimproved lots." As for "the Jews in the West," they "rarely have any real estate, until they have grown rich, when they

---

*This is an early example of the stereotype of the Jew as arsonist to collect insurance. After the Civil War many insurance companies refused to insure small Jewish businesses owing to the prevalence of this stereotype.

find honesty is the best policy."[16] While the basic attitude toward the Jewish competitor had not changed in the second novel, the sneering derision in the first is softened to humorous disdain in the second.

Jones abandons the theme of Jewish competition in the new West in two subsequent novels, and returns to the image of the money-lending pawnbroker. In *The Winkles* (1855), set in Philadelphia, a few students from Princeton and the South in search of amusement decide to pretend they wish to pawn a diamond at Abraham Laban's shop. After a little bargaining, Laban—who is said to be an "American Israelite" and does not, for a change, speak with an accent—suspects that they are not serious: "I should not be surprised if you came here purely for amusement." Thus far the treatment of the Jew has been relatively benign, but the mood changes when a poet, Pollen, comes in offering to dedicate a poem to Laban for payment. Exhibiting crass philistinism, Laban asks the monetary value of the poet's reputation. Men of genius, he says, lack common sense and are improvident, and more, would importune for money if he should set a precedent with Pollen. Laban offers five dollars for the poem; Winkle counters with a price of ten dollars and Laban buys the poem.

Pollen later returns to "the den of Abraham Laban, the Jew" to borrow money. In the course of the negotiations Laban defends himself against the traditional slanders. "It is astounding," he says, "that so many hundreds rely upon me for fortunes, and at the same time condemn me for my gains. Yet, how could I furnish so many with money, if I did not derive it from others? If I did not keep my profits, my purse would soon be exhausted, and then the Jew could assist no one. Blind, ungrateful fools!" To which Walter Winkle replies: "And that's as true as any speech Shylock ever made." Nevertheless, Jones will not let go. The "cormorant Jew" offers "a pitiful sum" for the "portfolio and copyrights" of the poet. When they are reclaimed, "the interest had accumulated to such a geometrical absurdity that it required all my funds to satisfy the smiling rascal."[17]

The next time Jones expatiates on the Jews is in *Border War* (1859), in which he returns to the theme with his earlier venom. The novel is an anticipated version of the Civil War that was actually to break out two years later. Early in the story an auction of "stocks and real estate" is described, in which "Jews, mostly, were the purchasers. They seemed like greedy vultures, snatching, scrambling for the scattered remnants of ruined fortunes. They were incessantly bargaining, chaffering, quarreling." A swashbuckling southerner, Sergeant Binns, having gambled away his pay, goes to an old tenement in Washington, D. C., where he has hidden a chest of treasure. There he finds that his chest has been claimed and is guarded by a starving Jewish broker. Binns exclaims: "Why, you are that infernal little, old, bill-broking, sharp-faced, screw-flint Jew, Solomon Mouser."

Solomon remonstrates that he has been robbed of his own trunk by a boy he hired to carry it for him. The sergeant charges that this is a lie, and adds: "I was glad to hear you lost your money—no, not *your* money . . . but the earnings of poor men and women you had shaved from them. Begone, you lying varmint! Go, I say, or I'll make mince meat for the rats, and that's all you are fit for." When the sergeant offers to pay Solomon for guarding the chest, Solomon tries to knife him, but Binns turns the knife on Solomon, who agrees to continue to guard the gold. "I'm not afraid you'll spend it," says Binns; "No doubt you counted it a thousand times."[18] At the end of the book Binns, now a colonel, returns to the attic for the gold. After Binns persuades Mouser to sell his stocks at fifteen dollars a share, he tells Mouser that he knows someone who will pay twenty-five dollars a share—whereupon Mouser faints.

The spirit and letter of the fictional delineation of the Jewish pawnbroker hardly differs from purported actual descriptions of Chatham Street pawnbrokers and storekeepers and their milieu. A malignant account is given by George G. Foster in his widely read book, *New York by Gaslight* (1850), in which Foster takes his readers on a tour of the underside of New York life. The chapter on the "Five Points" includes the Jewish section. There can be found "the 'fences,' or shops for the reception and purchase of stolen goods. These shops are of course kept entirely by Jews." Thieves sell their loot at a low price, "but then, you know, 'de peoplish ish very poor in dis neighborhood, and we can't kif much—and besides we don't really want 'em at all.' " The shopkeepers live in back of the stores and have many children, "the descendants of Israel being as celebrated for fecundity as cats or Irish women." Foster finally pulls out all the stops:

However low the grade or wretched the habitation—and the latter are generally filthy to abomination—of the Jew, the race always retains the peculiar physical conformation constituting that peculiar style of beauty for which his tribe has been celebrated from remotest antiquity. The roundness and suppleness of limb, the elasticity of flesh, the glittering eye-sparkle—are as inevitable in the Jew or

Jewess, in whatever rank of existence, as the hook of the nose which betrays the Israelite as a human kite, formed to be feared, hated and despised, yet to prey upon mankind.[19]

Foster's description hardly differs from that in Peter Hamilton Myers's lurid melodrama, *The Miser's Heir* (1854). The hero, in financial straits, goes to see a "sallow and bearded Jew, who hides his soiled bags of gold in the darkest basements of Chatham." The hero goes to a "Chatham Street cellar, the entrance to which was hung with well-scoured suits of second hand clothing, while the interior was similarly decked on all sides with huge piles of resuscitated garments." The "old clothes man," David Hakes, who speaks with the usual accent, pretends he has no money, but finally agrees to lend the hero one thousand dollars to be repaid tenfold, a deal to which the hero agrees. Hakes's "features and occupation proclaimed him a Jew, and his speech told that he was a German . . . sitting, spider-like, in the back part of his den, watching for his prey."[20]

Myers's novel was one of a mass of cheap melodramatic fictions that flooded the immense new market opened up by greater literacy among the working class, and the increased production made possible by the radical technological changes in printing and in the manufacture of paper and ink. An author could turn out novels with incredible speed and frequency. Often the stories would first run serially in newspapers and then be published complete in cheap, paper-covered editions.

One of the authors who most successfully exploited these new possibilities was Joseph Holt Ingraham. He was born in Portland, Maine, in 1809, and became a Protestant Episcopalian priest in 1852. He served his church thereafter in several places in the South, and died in Holly Springs, Mississippi, in 1860. The impression he made early in his career is evident from a letter that Longfellow wrote on October 22, 1838: "A new American novelist has arisen; his name is Professor Ingraham. He is the author of The Pirate of the Gulf,—dedicated to me, but without permission. . . . He is tremendous—really tremendous. I think I may say that he writes the worst novels ever written by anybody. But they sell; he gets twelve hundred dollars a piece." Eight years later he notes that Ingraham had visited him and reports that "he has written eighty novels, and of these twenty during the last year; till it has grown to be merely mechanical with him. These novels are published in the newspapers. They pay him something like three thousand a year."[21] These remarks were made before Ingraham published his enormously popular trilogy of religious novels, which we shall discuss later. When Ingraham became a priest, a scornful, indignant note in *The Knicker-bocker,* a New York general monthly, said: " 'Professor Ingraham,' who has within the last ten years written more immoral books than any other of the many penny-a-line scribblers . . . has taken to the Church for a 'living!' "[22]

Not unexpectedly, Ingraham introduced the surefire Jewish stereotypes in some of his stories, no doubt more than the three we here record. His *Moloch, the Money-Lender; or, The Beautiful Jewess,* first published in 1845, was often reprinted. Ingraham makes such complete and fulsome use of the stereotype that one can set up a catalog of clichés from this story. It is set in London and concerns a yacht commander, Tudor Dauling, the illegitimate son of a duke, who is hard put to pay his gambling debts to the moneylender Moloch. Dauling tries to evade imprisonment for forging a note on his father's bank account.

When Dauling first comes to the old-clothes shop of Enoch Moloch (who is also a jeweler and moneylender) eyes receive their usual notice: a youth tending the shop has "black eyes shining like stars through the clouds of tobacco"; Moloch has "large, full, piercing black eyes" and at other times "dark Syrian eyes" and "dark Arabian eyes." His young niece Rachel is beautiful (of course!) and has "fine Jewish eyes." Business is transacted in the rear part of the house in a room richly furnished in oriental style. Moloch speaks with a strong accent, but Rachel speaks a pure English.

Dauling, the gambler and forger, often expresses his contempt for and virtuous indignation at the usurer. When Moloch asks Dauling for security against a loan, the gambler replies: "I was not so ignorant of the cold avarice of thy own heart or of thy race. . . . As I know you have no principle or conscience where gold is concerned, I am assured what I am about to propose will meet your peculiar view of things." Moloch is "wholly unmoved by the insulting words and manners" of Dauling, who wants Moloch to help him pay back a check forged with his father's name. Moloch replies, in a manner reminiscent of Shylock's reply to Antonio: "Te Christian plead humbly to te Jew ven he would have money, and curses him ven he no more needs him. Vat can a Jew do? Show me how I can let you haf money?" When Moloch offers to lend the money at exorbitant interest, Dauling cries: "Accursed Jew! Do you dare propose such a thing to me?"[23] and he threatens Moloch with exposure for infraction of the usury laws. Moloch, however, replies he can expose Dauling for forgery, and they reconcile their differences.

Another cliché is the attraction of the Jewish woman. As Rachel ushers Dauling out, Ingraham falls back on the formula: Dauling's "courteous manner set ill with the haughty and sinister expression that was upon his features, as if he despised the race to which the young girl belonged, while he admired her physical beauty." He does not realize that he is a pawn in Moloch's plot to vent his hatred of Christians in general, and revenge upon Dauling's father in particular. Many years before, at Oxford, Dauling's father, the duke, had struck Moloch because of his refusal to obey the duke's order to take off his hat to a guidepost and say, "Jesus is the Christ." Moloch vowed that in revenge he would contrive to marry the duke's son to a Jew. When Moloch suggests to Rachel that she marry Dauling but not live with him thereafter, Rachel replies: " 'There is nothing I would shrink from to serve you and do injury to the Christian!' As she spoke her dark eyes flashed and her lip curled with the proud hatred a beautiful Jewish woman only can express when she speaks of the persecutors of her race."[24]

Moloch blackmails Dauling into marrying Rachel. "The insult stung him to the soul," writes Ingraham. Although the threat of arrest and exposure hangs over Dauling, "to purchase exemption from it by sacrificing himself to the Jew's niece, he felt would be paying too dear a price"; but he finally agrees. He is so affected by Rachel's beauty that "were she not a Jewess, he would not be making so great a sacrifice" after all. When the marriage is finally revealed to the duke he disinherits his son, "for he who stoops so low as to marry a Jewess, has no honor worth possessing!" But when the duke's objections are finally overcome, Dauling reforms, and the couple lives happily ever after. Rachel is even presented at court, where "the grace and beauty of the Jewess was the theme of every tongue."[25]

The Jew makes a brief appearance again as an avaricious merchant in Ingraham's *Romero.* Most of the action of the story takes place in Spain, where the Cordovan Jew Osias holds a mortgage on a church. On the last day before the mortgage expires, the abbot and the ex-buccaneer Romero, now a monk, go to redeem the mortgage. At the door to Osias's shop Romero jingles money as an inducement for Osias to open the door, whereupon the latter says: "I hears te monies,"[26] and lets them in. Osias refuses the money for the mortgage, saying that the year has just elapsed. Romero overpowers Osias, binds him, and helps himself to the deed. Under the circumstances, the holy men regard their acts as just.

A third novel by Ingraham containing a modern Jewish character was the fruit of his ministry in the South, where he swallowed the southern ideology whole. *The Sunny South* (1860), which purports to be a series of letters, the last written in 1856, from a young northern governess in the South, is an apology for slavery. The aim of the work, says Ingraham in his preface, "is to do justice to the Southern planter." Early in the work the governess writes that she is "already getting reconciled to slavery, since I find that it does not, in reality, exhibit the revolting horns I was taught in the North to discover on it. . . . The African is happier in bondage than free!"[27]

Several encounters with Jews on the way to and from the South set off extended ruminations on the Jews that on the surface are inconsistent with the evil stereotype in Ingraham's other novels. It is likely that these remarks were triggered by the deep impression made on him by the fame of Judah P. Benjamin, the senator from Louisiana who was later to become the secretary of state of the Confederacy. On board a ship to New Orleans the governess meets the newly elected Senator Benjamin. She finds that he is a friendly and charitable man with great talent for politics. She then goes into a long comment on the significance of his elevation to high office.

Mr. Benjamin [she writes] is an Israelite. His election, therefore, is a practical illustration of the free institutions of our happy land, where theological disabilities are not known. It is surprising how the Jews, I mean the educated and talented, place themselves in the highest rank of society always. There is inherent in them an element of greatness that irresistibly finds its noble level. We see in them the blood of David and Isaiah, of Abraham and Solomon, of Joseph and the Maccabees; their princely lineage is not extinct. How odd it would be if we should have a Jew to be President of the United States. And why not? Mr. Benjamin is a Senator. He is a rising man. He may one day hold the highest office in the gift of the nation. Would any man refuse to vote for him *because* he is a Jew?[28]

Again, on a boat headed for New York the governess meets "a handsome young man who was a Jew!" This leads once again into thoughts about Jews.

Has the Jew a nation [she asks herself]? . . . How extraordinary that one can always tell a Jew! or rather, let me call them "Israelites," which is the honorable name conferred on them by Jehovah, and by which they like to be distinguished—the term "Jew" being quite as repulsive to them as "Yankee" to the New Englander. That this wonderful people bear the impress of their Oriental origin to this day, after seventeen hundred years of exile and dispersion, is a continual miracle. The Jew of Chatham Street, in this city, is, in every lineament, the Jew of Jerusalem today, and of the Jews of the days of Jesus. In what this peculiarity consists, it is difficult to determine precisely, though an artist, who studies closely the characteristics of feature, might be able to explain.[29]

She then constructs a minute design for that ubiquitous cliché "Jewish eyes."

It is chiefly in the style and expression of the eyes, I think. It is not because the eye is black—for thousands of Americans have black eyes, which are wholly different in expression from the peculiar Jewish eye. The Israelite eye is very slightly almond-shaped, the upper lid droops over almost one-seventh of the iris of the eye, and gives an indescribable expression; while the lashes curve backwards, and have the effect of a fringe, more than any other lashes of any other people's eyes. The expression of the whole eye is sad, yet sparkling—dewy, yet brilliant—a sort of April-sky eye.[30]

She goes on to dithyrambic speculation on the glorious future of Israel, when the Jews will foregather in Palestine from the four quarters of the earth as prophesied in the Bible:

How wonderful the presence of their people among us and other nations! A *people,* yet without a country! a religion, yet without altar, priest, or temple! a God, yet punished by Him with a dispersion of one thousand seven hundred years! Their present state is a living testimony to the truth of the Bible, wherein it is predicted, as well also, their future restoration to their own country! . . .

For what is this remarkable and *careful* preservation of the Israelite? Ever dwelling among the Gentiles—yet never commingling with them, they never lose their nationality. . . . The Jews are being preserved so they can, at Divine counsel, return to Jerusalem. And what a spectacle will be presented when they arise as one man to obey the voice of Jehovah! It will be a second march, like that forth from Egypt. Every land, every city, every town, almost every hamlet, where men trade and do commerce with men, will give up this people among them—and this "nation of merchants," laden with gold and silver, the spoils of the Gentiles, shall direct their way toward Jerusalem, the city of their love and pride. From every sea-port will sail ships laden with the sons of Israel, steering for Palestine, and from every inland town go forth wealthy caravans taking the road towards the City of David. The present exodus to California and Australia, for gold of the Gentiles, in a thousand ships, will give a faint idea only of the mighty movement that shall draw the eyes of the world when Israel shall arise in her numbers, and elevating the standard of the "Lion of the Tribe of Judah," gather her outcasts beneath its shadow for the march.

And when the land of Canaan shall once more shake with the tread of returning Israel—when the thousand cities of her green vales shall be rebuilt—when Jerusalem shall lift up her head from the dust of centuries and dazzle the world's eye with her regenerated splendor—when the ports of Tyre, Jaffa, Sidon, and Caesarea shall once more extend their marble piers into the sea to embrace the commerce of the world—then will the Israelite take his true place among the nations, and, from his geographical position, command the avenues of the earth's commerce. . . . She will sit enthroned in the true commercial center of the earth, and, from the vast wealth that her people will carry to her from the nations wherein they have been dispersed, they will be able to control the commercial empire of the whole globe. . . . And this is no visionary speculation. It is to come to pass in the years that are before us, for prophecy has spoken the wind. It is from many hours' conversation with the youthful Israelite, our fellow-passenger, that I have become so interested in his nation —hence my enthusiasm in the foregoing people.[31]

Also phenomenally popular was Mrs. E. D. E. N. (Emma Dorothy Eliza Nevitte) Southworth, who was born in 1819, ten years after Ingraham, and lived until 1899. A great part of her life was spent in the Washington, D. C., area. After a few years of marriage she was separated from her husband. A prodigious worker, she gained her livelihood by teaching school and writing. One Christmas Eve in 1844, having put her children to bed, she wrote "The Irish Refugee" for Dr. Snodgrass's *Baltimore Daily Visitor.* The story was well received, and she continued to write. She was also principal of a school of eighty pupils. In 1847 or 1849 Harpers published her first novel, *Retribution.* In the late 1850s she signed a contract to write stories exclusively for serial publication in the *New York Ledger,* after which they were published in book form with enormous success. The dramatization of her novel *The Hidden Hand* (1859) rivaled *Uncle Tom's Cabin* in popularity on the stage. Before she died, she had authored fifty to sixty novels, some still in print in the 1930s, and a 42-volume uniform edition of her works was published in 1872. She was for many years a friend of Whittier's; he thought her a great novelist, and she received critical acclaim, though there were dissenting voices, too.

For humor she relied a great deal on crude dialect speech by Negro, Scottish, Irish, German, and Jewish characters, which often impeded the narrative. At least five of her novels contain Jewish characters. Two of them, both set in England, record brief encounters with pawnbrokers. In *The Bridal Eve* (1864) Laura pawns a ring worth a hundred guineas, for which she receives five pounds. " 'Eh, mine shole, vere did you get dish?' exclaims old Issachar, pouncing down upon the jewel, and glaring upon it with ravenous eyes"; he hoped the ring "would yet revert to himself."[32] More of the same is found in *Allworth Abbey* (1865), when a character visits the "shop of a Jew dealer in second-hand clothing." "How mush do you wantsh?" asks the Jewish salesgirl; on being told, she replies: "You must be jokinsh." After the bargaining was over, writes Mrs. South-worth, the seller "was cheated"[33] by the Jew.

An elaborate argument as to the immorality of revenge, a motive often assigned to the fictional Jew, is at the center of *Miriam, the Avenger,* published serially in 1854–55. Miriam, the Jewish offspring of a mixed marriage, is pledged by her Christian mother, Edith, not to marry until she has brought the supposed murderer of her Jewish father's half sister, Marian, to the scaffold. But Marian was not killed after all, it turns out, and at the end of the book she admonishes Miriam that the role of avenger "is never to be assumed by an erring human creature. 'Vengeance is mine, and I will repay, saith the Lord.' " When Edith Lance married the Jewish Michael Sheilds, she had been disinherited by her wealthy uncle because her husband *"was* an Israelite"; and "friends and relatives on either side were everlastingly offended by their marriage." Michael's half sister, Marian, who is half Jewish, is described as being beautiful but there is no reference to characteristic "Jewish" beauty. Edith and Mi-chael's daughter, Miriam, on the other hand, has a "fine dark Jewish beauty" and from childhood wears "a prevailing expression of im-passioned melancholy." A Jewish medical student, Solomon Weiss-man, appears several times in a peripheral role.

The Jewish aspect of the three important Jewish characters, Mi-chael, Marian, and Miriam, is not mentioned after the first quarter of the novel, and there is no suggestion that any of them affirms his or her Jewish identity. In fact, the author specifically mentions that Marian, whose mother was a Christian, attends a Protestant church. Despite Mrs. Southworth's use of the stark negative stereotype in other books, in this novel she throws the burden for intolerance toward intermarriage on both sides, and she retains a certain objec-tivity concerning contemporary Christians—"there were many good conservative Christians in this age, who, had they lived in the days of Christ, would, from their temperament and dispositions, have been very conservative *Jews,* and been among the first to cry, 'Crucify Him! Crucify Him!' "[34]

Her greatest success was *Ishmael* (1864) and its sequel, *Self-Raised* (1865). Indeed, Frank Luther Mott observed in 1947—before the paperback era—that Mrs. Southworth was "the most popular autho-ress in the annals of American publishing." Her *Ishmael* and *Self-Raised,* he notes, sold two million copies each.[35]

Ishmael is the son of Herman Brudnell and Nora Worth, who conveniently dies in childbirth. For Mrs. Southworth is thus relieved of the problem of dealing with a bigamous situation, since Herman had previously married Bernice D'Israeli in England. (She is a Jewish heiress who has survived a railway accident in which Herman has supposed her killed.) Ishmael is devotedly reared by Nora's maiden sister, Hannah. Bernice, a fascinating beauty, has meanwhile married an old nobleman, Count Hurstmonceaux, with whom Bernice's father "forgot his religious prejudices" and "coaxed" her "to sacrifice herself" in marriage in his ambition to obtain a title for his family. The old count dies, leaving Bernice penniless, but she still is "the sole heiress of the wealthy old Jew, Jacob D'Israeli."

Bernice comes to America, but Brudnell will have none of her since he believes that she was unfaithful to him when they were married. She wishes to claim Ishmael, for, "to the Jewish woman, the child of her husband, even if it is at the same time the child of her rival [Nora], is as sacred as her own." Nora's sister will not surrender the boy, and Bernice realizes "how apart were the ideas of the Jewish matron and the Christian maiden [Hannah]." For, says Bernice, Ishmael is "my husband's son, and so, his mother being dead, he becomes mine." She tells Hannah that her father was an "apostate to his faith. My nation cast me off for being his daughter and marrying a Christian."[36] But Brudnell repudiates Bernice, and Hannah succeeds in keeping Ishmael. Bernice then retires to Brudnell Hall, where, though she is the object of prejudice in the community, she leads a blameless life full of generosity to the poor. Brudnell refuses to be reunited with her and travels abroad. The remainder of the narrative is devoted to the self-education of Ishmael (he is thought to have been modeled on William Wirt, a brilliant Virginia lawyer of the first third of the century), and his career as a rising young lawyer.

The story is continued in *Self-Raised*. Brudnell returns from his travels. Ever since he discovered that Bernice was alive, he tells Ishmael, "I have been a lonely, homeless, miserable wanderer over the wide world! The fabled Wandering Jew was not more wretched than I!" Ishmael has fallen in love with Claudia, but she marries the villainous Lord Vincent, a relative of Count Hurstmonceaux's. When Claudia discovers her husband's character, she begs her father, Judge Merlin, to come to her rescue in England, and Ishmael joins the judge to help effect the rescue.

Claudia has meanwhile taken refuge in England with Bernice, that model of virtue and goodness. She is made even more acceptable to the reader when she explains to Claudia: "You thought that I was a Jewess! . . . But it is now many years, Lady Vincent, since I embraced the Christian religion!" Claudia joyfully replies: "1 am very glad! I am very, very glad! Ah! I am but a poor, unworthy Christian myself, yet I do rejoice in every soul converted to Christ."[37] It turns out that Ezra Isaacs, a relative of Bernice's who speaks with a heavy Jewish accent, helped spread the slander that defamed Bernice and caused her to be estranged from Brudnell. Ishmael succeeds in exposing the falsity of the slander, and Bernice and Brudnell are brought together.

This extremely sentimental, plot-ridden tale is a paradigm of the Victorian moral code and lacks any depth of characterization. The popularity of Mrs. Southworth's fiction is accounted for by the speed and facility of narrative and dialogue and the multiplicity of incidents; the whole drips with sentimentality. She spices her story with the clichés of Jewish exoticism, but her treatment of Bernice and her strictures on the prejudice against this long-suffering woman reveal the author to be, if not intellectually sophisticated, at least softhearted. After all, Bernice does finally become converted to Christianity.

We next meet the modern Jew in "The Diamond Lens," first published in the *Atlantic Monthly* in 1858, by that dashing Irishman Fitz-James O'Brien, who was born in Ireland in 1828 and immigrated to the United States at the age of twenty-four, and in 1862 was killed fighting for the Union in a skirmish with the rebels. In a spare narrative style he tells the story of Linley, a New Yorker who has been enthralled with the microscope since boyhood and now passionately devotes himself to making a powerful instrument, a "universal lens" for which a 140-carat diamond is required. In search of such a rare diamond, Linley goes to a Jew, Jules Simon, who "had many traits of Jewish character: a love of jewelry, of dress, and of good living." Simon is ostensibly a seller of objets d'art and seems to have plenty of money. Linley speculates that Simon's business might be a front for a slave-trade operation.

During a drinking bout Simon reveals to Linley that he has a great diamond, which he stole from a slave in Brazil. Linley decides to kill Simon to obtain the diamond, for, he ruminates, "after all, what was the life of a little peddling Jew, in comparison with the interests of science? . . . Simon was by his own confession a criminal, a robber, and I believed in my soul a murderer. He deserved death quite as much as any felon condemned by the laws: why should I not, like government, contrive that his punishment should contribute to the progress of human knowledge?"[38] The murder is cleverly accomplished without detection and Linley gains the diamond, which he grinds into the powerful lens. Its powerful magnification of a drop of water reveals an idyllic microcosm, complete with a beautiful young woman whom Linley falls in love with. But he carelessly allows the drop of water to evaporate, and with the death of his beautiful animalcule, he goes mad.

The Jew as criminal of a different kind is set forth in Joseph A. Scoville's novel *Vigor* (1864). Scoville was a financial journalist and a historian of New York business firms who praised the success and probity of Jewish business houses in his books. It is therefore curious that in his novel he introduces a Jewish villain who is "not much of a business man," but is the nonworking partner in a New York firm in which he supplies inherited money and international connections through his family in Holland (a non-Jewish partner actually runs the business). Ferdinand Nordheim is about forty, "of small stature, with dark, piercing, oriental sort of eyes, and a nose that clearly told his Hebrew origin. He spoke English with great purity," although raised in Holland.

His main occupation is that of "the worst of libertines."[39] He buys a sixteen-year-old non-Jewish wife, pays five hundred dollars for a sixteen-year-old mistress, and indulges in many debauches in his frequent out-of-town trips. But about a third of the way through the novel he gets his comeuppance. At the opera one evening he finds the lovely South Carolina belle who is seated in front of him irresistible and he pinches her. The girl's brother assaults Nordheim, who dies in the hospital—but not before he repents of his past wickedness, apologizes to his assailant for the insult, and wills his entire fortune to his wife.

One may conjecture that Scoville does not project Nordheim as a businessman to avoid sullying the favorable picture of the Jewish businessman that he sets forth in his books on New York merchants. Later in the novel he introduces a pawnbroker modeled on the honest Jews of his business histories; he is obviously a Jew, though not named as such. "Mr. Simpson, of Chatham Street," writes Scoville, "ought to be regarded as an institution in New York. He is supposed to work for a large percentage. Grant it. He ought to get a much larger one," for he relieves pain and anguish. "The worthy Simpson" is pictured as a man of integrity. Elsewhere in the novel Scoville is at pains to advise a young man about to enter business:

Could all the young men who have gone into business upon their own account in New York City before they reached twenty-five years, be traced out, it would be found that they have failed where, had they been content to gain experience as clerks until they were thirty years of age, their success would probably have been certain. The Jews are a sensible people in this regard. Their children don't take upon themselves the responsibilities of men until they are thirty. Our blessed Lord and Savior did not separate himself from parental control until he was thirty.[40]

Scoville thus curiously reverses the stereotype: the "good" Jew is the businessman; the "bad," criminal Jew does not occupy himself with business.

When American writers tried to picture the contemporary Jew in foreign lands, their attitude was generally no different from that toward the American Jew. Nathaniel Parker Willis indulges his contempt for the Jew in his novella "The Gypsy of Sardis" (1836), the story of a platonic love affair between an American on tour in Asia Minor in 1834 and a beautiful fifteen-year-old Gypsy girl, whom the American and his friend espy at a Gypsy encampment. They are asked by a Gypsy mother to take her and her son—who turns out to be the girl in protective disguise—to Constantinople with them, which they do. The American falls in love with the girl.

They take along as interpreter "an obsequious Jew," who is also "officious." He is never given a name, but is designated only as "our Jew" and is generally a pathetic creature. In their travels the Americans urge rowers of their skiff to hurry, thus endangering other skiffs. When the other rowers swear at them, writes Willis, "the Jew laughed, as do Jews since Shylock, at the misfortunes of their oppressors; and in the exercise of his vocation, translated the oaths as they came in right and left."[41] In Constantinople they lose and then find the girl; her American lover gives her the choice of coming with them or returning to her people, and she conveniently decides to go back to her Gypsy group. The story is not impressive; though Willis had facility he lacked depth. Much of his poetry, which deals with both Old and New Testament themes,[42] is, like his prose, "shallow," as Lowell called it.

A more extended stereotype of a foreign Jew occurs in the historian John Lothrop Motley's youthful novel *Morton's Hope*, published in 1839. The novel was the fruit of Motley's student life at Göttingen. At a tea party the hero, Uncas Morton, meets Miss Judith Potiphar, a "Jewish Juno," who, in accordance with the stereotype, has no mother. She is dancing with "a fat, vulgar-looking man," Maccabäus, a "little, sneaking, bald-headed" moneylender, described as a "blackguard." Maccabäus is "a friend of her father,

. . . the large greasy looking plebian." Morton's friend Count Trump von Toggenburg, an unpleasant character, is courting Judith for her money. He vows to marry her despite the objections of her father and "the whole synagogue." Although Judith's features are "very Jewish," she is a handsome woman with eyes "large and black as death." Her figure is "superb," and "the majestic fulness of the whole development accorded well with her Eastern origin." To all these charms fifty thousand dollars a year is added, "a sufficient inducement to Trump to mix his pure Gothic blood with that which formerly flowed in the veins of the Maccabean kings."[43]

Judith's father refuses to consent to the marriage, and the unscrupulous Trump decides to elope with her. This plan is frustrated, but Trump finally succeeds by engaging a rogue named Skamp to force Potiphar's consent by blackmail, for Skamp knows about Potiphar's illicit business dealings.

Motley's treatment of the Jew is purely in the stereotype tradition. There was probably no basis in his German experience for his rendering of the Jews, since his letters from Germany contain no reference to them. Where Motley falls back on his own intimate experience as an American student in Germany, the novel is vivid and perceptive. But for humor and melodrama he draws unimaginatively on literary conventions.

Some short stories of the period utilize the Jews for exotic color; occasionally they are central to the story. An example is S. B. Beckett's "Jewess of Cairo," which appeared in the *Ladies Home Companion* in 1840–41. Although the story is better left buried in the files of the magazine, we have resurrected it to illustrate further the exploitation of the literary conventions relating to Jews. Francis Wingate, an American traveling in Cairo, rescues a Jewish girl, Naomi, from a soldier who is attempting to abduct her for the pasha. Naomi and her father, Abraham, urge Wingate to flee to escape being murdered for his good deed. They tell him to meet them at night at a pyramid, where they will help arrange his flight. But at the pyramid Wingate is seized by the pasha's men and imprisoned. He reflects bitterly that his plight is "owing to my accursed folly in trying to rescue the daughter of a worthless Israelite, who doubtless has shielded himself by betraying us." But he is mistaken. Having bribed her way into the jail, Naomi appears at his cell door, guides him to freedom, and directs him to escape. Meanwhile, of course, he has fallen in love with Naomi, the exotic Jewish woman who, as usual, lacks a mother.

Wingate travels on but is recaptured by the pasha's band. Again
he is miraculously saved by Naomi and her grateful father, who
explain that they had not betrayed him to the pasha earlier. Still
pursued by the pasha's men, he goes to Jerusalem in search of
Naomi. There he meets an old man, who turns out to be Abraham.
Abraham leads Wingate through a dilapidated building to a room
of oriental splendor. "Although belonging to a race from whom
God has for a long time averted his face—who are scattered and
oppressed in every land on the face of the earth, still the Jew has
wealth—he can imitate something of the royal magnificance of his
forefathers, and that, too, in the very haunt of the lion." Again we
have the convention of the voluptuous mode of living of the wealthy
Jew.

Abraham reveals that he comes not from Cairo, but from Charleston and that Naomi was born and educated there. They have come
to Cairo to help restore the Jews to their "former greatness." Naomi
appears, richly attired. "The rich Jews of Syria," comments the
author, "surpass all other people in the costliness of their apparel."[44]
Wingate proposes marriage, but Abraham refuses his consent, and
the next day Wingate discovers that they have left. Failing to find
Naomi he returns to New York, where his lawyer tells him that
Abraham has bequeathed railroad stocks to him. Then, to no one's
astonishment, he finds that Naomi is in America and that she is his
sister's friend. Since her father has died in Aleppo, a marriage is now
arranged and all ends happily. The Jews in this story are "good" and
totally without individuality.

A beautiful exotic Jewish woman in Egypt also figures in Sylvanus
Cobb's trashily melodramatic *The Mameluke,* published in 1852 under the pseudonym of B. Parley Poore. Judith Fezenzac, the "only
child of a wealthy Jewish merchant of Smyrna" (and no mother in
evidence!), has been abducted and taken to the bey's harem at
Alexandria. She prays for deliverance before the bey has his pleasure
with her and is saved by Osmanli, a Mameluke warrior in Napoleon's army. When Judith sings before Napoleon, he offers her a
place in the Paris opera. Osmanli, now in love with Judith, proposes,
but his offer of marriage is not acceptable without her father's blessing.

Meanwhile, Judith's father, Mordecai, is full of grief and bitterness at her disappearance. He is "bowed down by the weight of
tyranny and the everlasting sin of his race." His house in Smyrna is
described in the conventional manner as splendid with lush oriental
richness. His search for his daughter ends in the opera house in

Paris, where Judith is singing on stage. Mordecai tries to drag her off the stage and away from these abominable "heathen mummeries." He refuses to allow the marriage with Osmanli and takes her to the house of a relative, again described in the usual manner: "The main apartment was fitted up in true Hebrew style, a magnificent seven-branched chandelier of solid silver, illuminating the rich damask curtains and velvet-covered furniture."[45] After Mordecai is stabbed to death in the streets of Paris, Osmanli marries Judith—at Notre Dame Cathedral. Not only is she now conveniently a Christian, but Osmanli turns out to be the son of an English mother and an American father. The happy pair immigrate to Savannah and live happily thereafter.

The treatment of the Jew is no less conventional in two novels by Theodore Sedgwick Fay. His *Countess Ida* (1840), set in Berlin at the end of the eighteenth century, contains the sinister figure of a Polish Jew who is an assassin hired by a Jewish businessman. The murderer is dressed in gabardine lined with fur, "and a long beard descended to his breast, . . . one of those Polish Jews who are not infrequently seen in the streets of Berlin." The rapacious Jewish businessman tries to gain possession of the estate of the hero, but the law finally catches up with him. When he is "brought to punishment and transported"[46] he confesses to having hired the assassin. The Jews in the novel, who are peripheral to the plot, are unrelieved villains.

More central to the story, because they are involved in the downfall of the villain, are the Jews in Fay's *Sidney Clifton* (1839). Early in the story Fay expounds his theory of the modern Jewish character. He first contrasts the situation of the Jew in the Old World and the New: "Under the despotic governments of the old world, his political and personal rights have been the football of tyranny and cupidity," but in the United States, "in the letter and spirit of the Constitution, he enjoys these privileges which are dispensed with an equal hand to all." But even now the Jew is "powerless to effect total emancipation from the dominion of individual and national prejudice." For he is bowed "beneath the weight of that anathema, which has gone forth against his race, and reverberates through the earth with fearful destructiveness, the lofty spirit that of old swept as with an eagle's wing the realms of literature and science, and with prophetic gaze pierces the arcana of futurity." As for Fay himself, he condescendingly writes, he "deem[s] the lonely descendant of God's chosen people not unworthy the sympathy and admiration of the Christian and the philanthropist." Through the centuries, the Jew has remained "self-isolated from the multitude that surrounds him" and is deaf to Christian voices. He has been "constant to his faith amid the mutations of centuries" and "presents an image of stern and melancholy grandeur—towering in its pride of place, unshaken by the moral convulsions whose mighty throes the less stable monuments of human will are overthrown."

Fay also explains, as he sees it, the current view of the Jews. The centuries have taken their toll of the Jews, he holds:

> The holy zeal, which sustained his ancestors in the wilderness, has long been quenched— . . . the genius which poured forth the language of inspiration now wastes its energies upon the details of petty traffic,— . . . the sublime conceptions of an Isaiah and a Jeremiah no longer glow in the bosoms of their successors. Still over all the halo of former glory sheds the undying lustre, and around the brow of the most insignificant scion of the once noble race, yet lingers the shadow of that beauty whose perfections were concentrated in the features of the Redeemer.[47]

Fay's Jewish character is the exemplar of a people which "now wastes its energies upon the details of petty traffic." The Wall Street moneylender Isaac Samuel is described with most of the grotesque features of the stereotype. He is "a striking illustration of the fearful inroads that ironhearted avarice makes upon the frame and spirit of its worshippers." At sixty he has been consumed by the anxieties of his vocation—"the tremulous nerves prematurely shattered by continual apprehension of pecuniary loss," an effect of his "inordinate pursuit of gain." In his "long wasted fingers" and the "tremulous helplessness of his manner" he appears to be one who could benefit from philanthropy, instead of being the "envied possesser of millions in the funds." Samuel has been lending money to the villain, DeLyle, who now appeals for an additional loan. In a gratuitous heaping up of Samuel's avarices, DeLyle pays Samuel one hundred dollars for a watch that is "worth perhaps ten dollars." The indignant villain is then described as astonished "at this exercise of the usurer's cupidity, notwithstanding his previous knowledge of the man." Samuel is, after all, "the votary of the yellow gold."[48]

Enter the "lovely Jewess," Samuel's daughter, Rachel, the educated, shy, protected, romantic, sublimely innocent victim of DeLyle's villainy. She is "tall and dark-eyed, with bold and striking features, cast in the Roman mould of the finest order; and the voluptuous outline of her well-turned limbs, the swelling bust and exquisitely rounded neck and shoulder indicated high health, while the free and lively expression of her handsome countenance attested the absence of all care and anxiety." DeLyle courts her in the hope of so compromising her that her father will be compelled to permit the marriage, thus giving him access to Samuel's fortune. Fay allows that "Isaac Samuel loved his child with an affection as ardent as his grasping nature could conceive for *any* object." But Fay is unrelenting in his characterization, for Samuel's "cupidity forbade her entertaining female visitors, and the usurer possessed no friends except those who clung to his skirts from stern necessity, and who, of course, never intruded on his notice except at his counting room."

After DeLyle insinuates himself into Rachel's affections—without her father's knowledge of course—he absents himself from her for a while, and she pines away. Her father suggests that she take medicine for her indisposition, but she insists that exercise alone will do; he is glad, for "this was the *cheaper* remedy." Rachel falls hopelessly in love with DeLyle, who is exposed as the seducer of a friend's servant. When his relationship to Rachel is discovered by her father, DeLyle escapes and flees to England. Rachel sickens and dies, and her father at last realizes that he has been so intent on "the pursuit of gain, that he was not sensible of the hold his daughter retained on his affections." He is seized with "remorse at the maddening reflection that for filthy lucre he had ministered to the depraved appetites of DeLyle, and thus indirectly been the instrument of her misery."[49] He follows DeLyle to England, bent on revenge. He plans to convert the twenty thousand dollars DeLyle owes him into a debt of honor so that he may challenge him to a duel. When Samuel finds DeLyle he shoots him and then turns the gun on himself.

That the anti-Jewish attitudes implicit in these literary images were by no means universal is indicated in the memoirs of Jews during this period. Indeed, such documents would lead to quite the opposite view. Joseph Jonas, who settled in Cincinnati in 1817 and was probably the first Jew to reside there, published his memoirs in *The Occident,* a Philadelphia Jewish monthly, in 1844. He recounts the participation of non-Jews in the founding and consecration of "this first Temple west of the Alleghany Mountains" in 1835. He writes that fifty-two Christians contributed twenty-five dollars each toward construction of the temple. And at the consecration, he records, "the crowd of our Christian friends was so great that we could not admit them all. We therefore selected the clergy, and families of those gentlemen who so liberally had given donations toward the building."[50]

A similar account of cordial relations between Christians and Jews in the 1850s comes from an early settler of Chicago, Leopold Mayer, who recorded his recollections of those days half a century later. He relates that Jews were members and officers of political and fraternal organizations, and a young Jew was even captain of the fire engine company. Jews, he writes, often attended "balls and festivities," and "were never in the least looked upon as undesirable."[51]

In the Far West during the days of the Gold Rush the same story is true. Jews were among the first to come to San Francisco to participate in that economic bonanza. They met with little intolerance and many became public officials. In the 1850s almost the whole clothing industry in the city was in Jewish hands. When the building of a Jewish synogogue was started, the San Francisco *Evening Picayune* of March 15, 1851, welcomed the event, affirming that "we are glad for them that they have chosen to cast their lot with us under a government that gives them the fullest protection in the exercise of their faith . . . and which affords them equal opportunities with all other citizens to develop to any extent of their aspirations, their political, social, religious and civil interest."[52]

The invidious stereotype of the pawnbroker and businessman we have found in so many novels, however, would appear to contradict these firsthand accounts. Doubt may then be cast on John Higham's assertion that "the praise of Jewish enterprise considerably outweighed the jibes at Jewish avarice in the early nineteenth century. . . . The Shylock idea [was] sufficiently mild and impersonal before the Civil War."[53] The novels reveal attitudes and not necessarily behavior, of course, and probably actual relations were less acerbic than those reflected in the novels. However, the reality must have been ambivalent at best.

Not that friendly expressions were lacking in the period. A judicious article on the Jews in the *North American Review* in 1856, for instance, comes to their defense. "The Jews are too recently established here," says the article, "to have attained much influence in politics or much distinction in science." The writer acutely counters the popular notion of Jewish obsession with money-making by remarking that they "find a more congenial sphere in that which is our national business, money-making, and in this they rival the sons of the Pilgrims." He protests "the fashion of 'change to couple the name of Jews with scandalous epithets,—a fashion, as we believe, most unjust and unwarranted." In direct contradiction to the economic stereotype, he asserts that "it is not the Hebrew merchant in our cities who most resembles the portrait of Shylock. The commercial integrity of the race of Israel stands, on the whole, as fair in New

York or New Orleans, as that of any race; and according to their means, their sympathy is as quick and their benevolence as genuine."[54] These sentiments, however, found little expression in the literature of the time.

Strong sentiment against intermarriage was felt on both sides, and Christian opposition might well be accompanied by Jew-baiting. In an early literary appearance of the problem in Charles Brockden Brown's *Arthur Mervyn,* as we saw, Jewishness was not a barrier to intermarriage, and the situation was free from anti-Jewish animus. Some years later a literary discussion of the problem was precipitated by Maria Edgeworth's *Harrington* (1817), published in England. In that novel the hero falls in love with the supposed daughter of a Jewish banker. Edgeworth then proceeds to skirt the issue by revealing that the girl is only an adopted daughter and is a Christian after all, a conventional evasion that is also employed in Lessing's *Nathan the Wise.*

A minor American writer, Mrs. Sarah Hall, though tolerant of Jews, argues the issue as set forth in *Harrington.* Mrs. Hall disagrees with a critic who charged that Edgeworth had destroyed "the moral of her tale" by making it "pretty plain that she does not think a Hebrew damsel a proper helpmate for a John Bull." On the contrary, says Mrs. Hall, the author has made a strong moral affirmation by perceiving that, while the Jews are no better or worse than other people, the difference in religion is an insurmountable barrier if religion is taken seriously enough. Edgeworth would have made her solution even more elevated if the girl had indeed been Jewish and the lovers had separated as "the sacrifice of their love to religion." She denies Edgeworth's assertion that intermarriage "frequently" takes place in America, usually without infringing on the faith of each partner. There are also cases, she says, where one partner adopts the faith of the other or where both are indifferent to religion. "We know of no uncharitable barriers between Jews and Christians in our happy community," adds Mrs. Hall, but the religious difference is unbridgeable. Intermarriage is undesirable from the Jewish viewpoint also, because the Jews "would have been long ago amalgamated," since abstention from intermarriage is "the principal means by which they are preserved in their separate state."[55]

A less benevolent but more extensive exploration of the problem appears in an anonymous short story, "Judith Bensaddi, a Tale Founded in Fact," in the Philadelphia journal *The Souvenir,* in 1828. When this story, expanded to novella length, was published in the *Southern Literary Messenger* in 1839, the author was identified in the journal's index as the Rev. Dr. Henry Ruffner, president of Washington and Lee University. The plot was essentially unchanged in the revised and rather verbose second version, and it is the latter form of the story that we shall discuss.[56] Set in the second decade of the century, the novella is based on an actual experience that was reported to Ruffner. On his way home to Lexington by boat from the South, a young man becomes friends with a cultured Jewish brother and his beautiful sister, who are from England. When the brother is accidentally drowned, the young man takes temporary charge of the grief-stricken sister, accompanies her to New York, and sees her to the boat to Liverpool. They agree to correspond and in fact do write one another; there the true story appears to end.

In "Judith Bensaddi" Ruffner fleshes out this true story. He makes it a sentimental tale of frustrated love arising from the problem of intermarriage, and reveals conventional hostility toward the Jews. The young man, William Garame, meets the nineteen-year-old Judith Bensaddi and her twenty-one-year-old brother, Eli, on a train. The siblings are "in the bloom of youth, with complexions between brown and fair, raven black locks, and eyes moderately large, not quite jetty black, but star-bright interpreters of intellect and feeling." Judith was "the most beautiful gem of humanity" Garame had ever seen, and he adds, as if in extenuation for his infatuation, that "her nose had no very marked character." They are English and speak the language perfectly, "but in their person," he notes, "differed from my notion of the Anglo-Saxon race."[57]

A discussion on slavery ensues, in which Judith argues against her brother's abolitionism. She recapitulates the southern arguments for slavery, presumably arising out of her own observations: English laborers are worse off than the slaves she has seen; on the whole, the slave loves his master; slavery removes worries over subsistence, in contrast with the wretched lot of free laborers. Judith observes that she previously had too dark a view of slavery, and that she will now tell people at home that the institution is not so bad as they had thought. Thus Ruffner, a slave owner, uses Judith as a vehicle for his views.

Garame falls in love with Judith, and the trio agree to travel together. He invites the others to visit his home in Kentucky (they never do). The invitation gives Ruffner occasion to launch into many irrelevant pages of description that help pad out the story. After a few days together in Charleston, they embark on the boat for Norfolk. Eli falls into the sea during a storm and drowns. Judith is wild with grief, and Garame comforts her, helping her become resigned to her loss. Ruffner makes a point of noting that Garame lets pass without notice Judith's cry, "O Jehovah, God of Abraham, teach me resignation." She accepts his offer to accompany her to Boston, where she will meet a relative.

A lucky fall from a horse keeps Garame in Philadelphia with Judith as his loving nurse. Both are now in love, and he proposes. Judith weeps. "You have looked upon me as a suitable companion for life; when you know all, you may think differently; you are a serious Christian; will you not shudder at the thought of marrying a Jewess?" "A Jewess! You a Jewess!" Garame exclaims with a start. "Oh (said she in a tone of sudden grief), my fears were true!" He denies this. She replies:

My heart is your's [sic]; the difference in our national descent and religious education, shall not prevent me from giving you my hand, if in full consideration, you and your friends think that these things will not prove fatal to your happiness. Some of my kindred have married Christians; my father has told me, that if I should meet with a Christian whose temper and character were suitable to mine, he would not refuse to own him as a son-in-law. I am no bigot. Though educated in the religion of my fathers, I have learned to respect the Christian religion; . . . and though I do not profess the Christian faith, I could easily live in concord with one who professes it mildly and sincerely as you do. But I am aware of the prejudices which many entertain against my nation, and what a horror they would feel at so intimate a connection with an Israelite. I know, too, that a serious Christian may feel conscientious difficulties in such a case.[58]

The bewildered Garame ponders the situation. "True," he says to himself, "I have never liked the character of the Jews, either ancient or modern; but she has charm enough to put all such prejudices to flight! Why not marry one who was of the same people as prophets and apostles of Jesus? But were the Jews never so vile or loathsome as a people, my Judith has sufficient personal merits to redeem her from all objection and to cover all her people's sins." She also has the virtue of leanings toward Christianity and may soon become a convert: "In spirit and feeling she is a far better Christian than nine-tenths of those who make the loudest professions. She loves the rules and the spirit of the Christian religion, and I have no doubt that she only needs to be placed in Christian society, and under Christian influence, to be soon persuaded to believe fully in Jesus of Nazareth."[59]

With Garame's reaffirmation of his proposal, she advises him to think further about it, to consult his kindred, and then to write her in England telling of his decision. Enter Judith's uncle from Boston,

Isaac Von Caleb, the "good" stereotype, and his friend, Simon Levi, the "bad" stereotype, whose "darling theme is money." Von Caleb tells Garame about the vast wealth of Judith's father and says that she is his heir. Garame is to send his decision to Judith through a letter transmitted by Levi.

On the train taking him back to Kentucky the word "Jewess" haunts Garame's mind and grates on him more and more. "That detestable word returns and troubles the sweet current of my feelings. . . . Am I really in love with the daughter of a Jew? Am I to connect myself with that accursed race?" When he brings her home, what will the neighbors say? His imagination summons up the awful picture: "My children are to be half-blooded Jews. My neighbors are to point at her, as we pass, and say, 'That is the Jewess. When we go to church—*we*, do I say? Perhaps she will not go to church; but be wishing for her Rabbi and her synagogue." And if she should go to church, the neighbors will ask: "Do you know whether she is likely to be converted?" Most horrible of all, the minister will then preach at her and "deal out anathemas against the unbelieving Jews." How can he make Judith "the mistress and the mother of my family. Oh, how can I do it?"[60]

Recalling the scriptural story, he is filled with

detestation of the very name of Jew. The Jews! The stiff-necked. hard-headed race . . . who provoked the patience of God, until by his prophets cursed and banned them out of his mercy and from the pale of human society, and made them a hissing and a curse among all nations! . . . And am I to marry one of them! Oh, why was so beautiful, so amiable a creature born of the accursed race? The miserly clannish race! The scorn and detestation of travellers in Poland, and wherever strangers are exposed to their knavish tricks and unprincipled exactions! Faugh! The squalid occupants of suburbs and streets, where a decent passenger is nauseated by their filth! The bearded vendors of old clothes! . . . Jew signifies miser and rogue.

Garame keeps his secret from his family. One day his father returns from town with the complaint that a merchant tried to "Jew me." Probably it was a Jew, but "if he was not a rogue of a Jew, he was a Jew of a rogue." A discussion ensues, and Garame's mother adds that "it is a happy circumstance that we have no Jews among us in the Valley. I should hate to have anything to do with them." His father replies: "They are not *all* so bad." But his mother is adamant: "Good or bad, a Jew is a Jew; and I should hate to have any of them about me." Garame tells his family of his marriage plans, and they finally agree to them, in light of "the symptoms of [Judith's] inclinations to Christianity, and the fact so generally agreeable to parents, that she was very rich." But Garame receives no reply to his letter to Judith, for Levi withholds Garame's letter in the hope that his own son, Joseph, will persuade the heiress to marry him, especially now that her uncle, Von Caleb, has also settled his wealth on her.

A year later Garame receives a letter from Judith in which she explains that she has not heard from him. Meanwhile, she has been converted to Christianity: "The eloquent and pious friend who won me finally to Christ" is now her betrothed, and "now my faith in Jesus of Nazareth is my chief consolation."[61] She offers her help if he is ever in need. Having lost his beautiful Judith and her money, Garame is naturally sorrow-laden.

Ruffner's story met with such success that he was unfortunately led to continue it in a sequel, "Seclusavel," published later in the same year.[62] It is an involved and contrived tale, far inferior to the earlier story. Garame, the owner of the great estate Seclusavel but still unmarried, is a highly successful lawyer, and since gold has been struck on land he has acquired, he is now rich. Through a series of contrived events he discovers that Judith, also unmarried, has lost her fortune and is a teacher in America. He finds her—she is now a devout Christian—and they are duly married.

This sequence of stories by Ruffner is negligible as literature but interesting in its revelation of social attitudes, especially those found in backwoods western areas, where almost no Jews lived and where the only Jew ever encountered was an itinerant peddler. In these communities traditional contempt for Jews, on both religious and social grounds, would appear to have been fairly general. Enlightened attitudes were probably more common in the cities or in areas closer to modern cultural currents. To countrymen in remote areas, Jews were exotics; knowledge of them was traditional rather than personal. Furthermore, fundamentalist religious beliefs probably played a large part in fixing hostility to Jews for their obstinate rejection of Jesus. Judith is acceptable to Garame and to most of the readership because the author treated her as not only according to the stereotype of the beautiful and exotic Jewish girl, but also as one inclined toward Christianity. Furthermore, the stories are significant in their exposure of the thoughts of the Christian of the time who contemplated marriage with a Jew. However much romantic sentimentality may pervade this fiction, it is at least faithful to reality in its anti-Jewish attitudes. On the other hand, it would be an error to suppose that the feeling toward Jews displayed in this story was universal in America, as the memoirs cited earlier attest. Though no figures are available, we know that there was a certain amount of intermarriage by the established Sephardic Jews.

It is interesting that one of the rare public evidences of Jewish discomfort in the face of the negative attitude in fiction in those early years occurs in connection with "Judith Bensaddi." In the *Richmond Compiler* for October 12, 1839, a review of "Seclusavel," the only known review that comments on the Jewish aspect of the stories, reports that

an intelligent Israelite complained much to us the other day against the author of Judith Bensaddi. He said that no writer in romance had done the Jewish character full justice—as with Professor Ruffner's tale, Jews are painted as angels before they are converted to become Christians, and turn away from "the chosen people." This he thought inconsistent with facts, unjust in the extreme, and said it seemed to argue that nothing pure and lovely could remain among the Jews.

A few days later, the paper reports a further comment by the "intelligent Israelite": Ruffner's "attempt to make the *perfection* of the Heroine, the more *perfect* by her abandonment of her faith . . . in his 'prejudiced' view,' as he says, 'tends rather to depress than exalt, and thus defeats the object of the talented author. . . . If she was an angel before her conversion, she was a "fallen angel" afterward.' "[63] That the general public tended to side with Ruffner, not the "Israelite," is apparent from the fact that the *Southern Literary Messenger* reprinted "Judith Bensaddi" in its August 1850 issue in response to insistent requests by readers.

In the decades before the Civil War, the Jew, very often the new German Jewish immigrant, was tending to displace the Yankee as itinerant peddler. This socially useful occupation was peculiarly available to them because peddling, as Maxwell Whiteman writes, "was a quick and natural step into the American economy. It required little or no investment and the fertile field plowed by the Yankee was open to the immigrant for the price of a peddler's license. Rural America was in need of goods of every description and the Jewish peddler continued to furrow the field now partly deserted by the Yankee."[64] By 1860 there were about 16,600 peddlers in the United States, most of them Jews.[65]

At the outset peddlers with pack on back scoured the countryside and small towns for customers. If they were successful they purchased a horse and wagon with which to ply their trade. The next stage was the establishment of a store in the new villages and towns. The progress of the Jewish merchant from peddler to storekeeper was reflected in a novel by Otto Ruppius, a non-Jewish refugee of the 1848 German revolution who had lived in Louisville and Milwaukee and had worked as a journalist in Saint Louis in the 1850s. He went back to Prussia in 1861, when an amnesty made it possible for him to return. *The Peddler, a Romance of American Life,* written in German and published in English translation in Cincinnati in 1857, is a presumably autobiographical account of a German immigrant's efforts to make a living. In 1849 August von Helmstedt, a lawyer, arrives in New York in flight from the failed revolution. After he has been robbed of all his money through the villainous scheming of one Seifert, he is offered help by Isaac Hirsch, whose "shrewd countenance with its conspicuously bent nose, was unmistakably that of a Jew." Helmstedt is suspicious of Hirsch's offer to help, "since a Jew never does anything without expecting to profit by it, you would say." Hirsch replies: "Well, so be it, perhaps I can see a profitable investment by giving you advice." Helmstedt accepts, and Hirsch obtains work for him and teaches him English. Hirsch, a peddler, is a benevolent, virtuous, "good" Jew.

The scene then shifts to a gambling saloon in the South; Baker, a partner of the gambler Seifert's, is cheating one of Hirsch's customers, Ashton. Hirsch, concerned that as a result of his losses Ashton will be unable to pay him for his goods, warns Ashton against continuing, and is railed at by Ashton: "Do you know, you damned Jew, that I ought to shoot you like a dog! for uttering slanders that would ruin any business man." He is nevertheless saved by exposure of the cheating gambler. Hirsch has obtained a bookkeeping job in an Alabama town for Helmstedt, who tries to thank Hirsch for his goodness to him. "I will take your thanks for granted," replies Hirsch. "But to remind you of your own words, remember, 'A Jew never does anything without expecting profit!' And a word of empty thanks would not profit me. We shall see if your thanks are negotiable."[66] He asks Helmstedt to serve secretly as his agent in judging the credit of local merchants, and Helmstedt accepts.

The plot thickens: Helmstedt falls in love with his employer's daughter, Ellen, who is also loved by the villain Baker. Baker ruins a girl, who commits suicide. Helmstedt is arrested for the murder of the girl because he refuses to jeopardize Ellen's reputation by admitting that he was in her room, albeit innocently, at the time of the murder. But at the last moment of the trial Ellen appears as a witness, and further testimony by Hirsch clears Helmstedt, who is released and marries Ellen. Hirsch returns to New York and sets up a business there, offers Helmstedt a partnership, and makes him executor of his estate. The Helmstedts go to New York to visit the ailing Hirsch, but he dies before they arrive. Throughout the story the peddler is shown to be the opposite of the negative stereotype. Helmstedt's assumptions about Jews are changed by Hirsch's kindness in saving Helmstedt at melodramatic and crucial junctures in his career, and in assuring his financial future.

The relationship of the Jews to the slavery question was little reflected in the literature of the period. After the Civil War, Nathan Mayer published a novel *(Differences)* on this theme, which we shall discuss later, but antebellum literature offered little. There were Jewish individuals, rabbinical and lay, on both the abolitionist and slavery sides; some were even militants. But no position was taken by Jews as a community either in the North or South. In the South, Jews appear to have had no difficulty in adjusting to the slave system, although some did manumit their slaves. Bertram W. Korn has observed that Jews manifested "almost complete conformity to the slave society of the Old South. . . . They participated in the buying, owning, and selling of slaves, and the exploitation of their labor, along with their neighbors. The behavior of Jews toward slaves seems to have been indistinguishable from that of their non-Jewish friends. This description also characterizes the opinions of Jews about slavery." Indeed, Korn has asserted that Jews in the South achieved a higher social and political station than in the North because of the "very presence of this large [Negro] mass of defenseless victims who were compelled to absorb all the prejudices which might otherwise have been expressed more frequently in anti-Jewish sentiment."[67] Nevertheless, Korn has granted that there was "a serious amount of anti-Jewish prejudice [in] both North and South."[68]

The two outstanding Jewish religious leaders, Isaac Leeser and Isaac Mayer Wise, declared their neutrality on the slavery issue, both during the fateful election of 1860 and after the outbreak of war. Just before election day Leeser wrote, in words that appear drastically wrongheaded a century later, that "our paper [*The Occident*] has no connection with politics, and we would consider it a degradation of the religious press . . . to wade into the pool of partisan warfare." A few months after the Civil War broke out, an article in *The Occident* affirmed that "it is not our purpose to write anything which any reasonable and intelligent man, whether he be a Union man or a secessionist, must consider a particular offense to his party."[69] A similar neutral attitude was expressed in *The Israelite* by Rabbi Wise, when he insisted that he had never discussed politics because "the pulpit is for higher than a political object."[70] As a matter of fact both Leeser and Wise tended to be prosouthern, and both had discussed politics when they defended Jews against instances of anti-Semitism. But the readership of the journals was national, and these rabbinical editors regarded it as their obligation to minister to both northern and southern Jews by not taking an open stand on the issue.

In New York, however, the *Jewish Messenger* published an editorial, "STAND BY THE FLAG!" in its April 26, 1861, issue, declaring its categorical support for the Union cause; it was the only Jewish periodical to do so. "The time is past for forbearance and temporizing," it says. "We are now to *act,* and sure we are, that those whom these words may reach, will not be backward in realizing the duty that is incumbent upon them—to rally as one man for the *Union and the Constitution.*"[71] There is no mention of slavery in the editorial. But individual Jews did take a stand against slavery—some were even abolitionists—and thousands fought on the Union side in the war.

A moving account of the modest contribution to the antislavery cause of the brothers Joseph and Isaac Friedman, of Tuscumbia, Alabama, is given in the biography of the ex-slave, Peter Still, who told his story to the abolitionist Kate E. R. Packard. His story was published in 1856 in *The Kidnapped and the Ransomed.* Mrs. Packard had been a teacher at the Friend's Seminary of Tuscumbia, and had known Peter Still and many of those who figured in his narrative. The Friedmans helped Peter Still buy his freedom at considerable risk to themselves. The story, as told to Mrs. Packard by Still, is simple, honest, and without pretense as to style but is nonetheless moving. When the freeman Peter Still is six he is kidnaped in Philadelphia and sold into slavery to a master in Tuscumbia, Alabama. There he grows up, marries, and has several children by his wife, Lavinia. He longs for freedom. When his master hires him out, he looks about for an employer he can trust to help him buy his freedom.

His attention is "mysteriously attracted" to the only Jewish merchants in town, Joseph and Isaac Friedman. In 1847 Still persuades his master to hire him out to the Friedman brothers, for he has heard Joseph Friedman utter "some careless sentence, which reveals his sympathy with the suffering, and his hatred of injustice and oppression." Whenever Still "was in their [the brothers'] presence, although no word respecting himself was uttered, he felt he was regarded as a *man.*" Confidence between Still and Joseph Friedman grows, and in the second year of his employment Still at last broaches his plan to Joseph, who readily agrees to buy Still, who will work off the purchase price of five hundred dollars.

At first Still's young mistress refuses to sell Peter, "especially to a *Jew* who had no higher wish than to make money."[72] But a year later the sale is made. The general opinion is that *"of course,* Friedman wanted to make money out of him." The children of the town express their distress: "Mr. Friedman bought him; and 'ma says he's a *Jew,* and she says Jews *will sell their own children for money.* Pa says he don't doubt that Mr. Friedman will sell him the very first chance he gets to make money out of him; and then, perhaps, he'll be taken off to the rice swamps." Mrs. Packard comments that this was the judgment passed upon "the noblehearted Jew by men and women who had bought and sold, and beaten, and oppressed the poor until their cry had gone up to heaven."[73]

By 1850 Still has earned his purchase money. Joseph Friedman charges no interest for the money he has advanced toward the purchase, and a document of sale is signed. At this point Friedman decides to move his business to Cincinnati. Amid outraged suspicions that Friedman will now sell Peter Still, and offers by townspeople to buy him if Friedman will put him up for sale, the Friedmans and Still travel north, where Still regains his freedom.

The contrast between those actual living Jews and the fictional image then prevalent is all the more striking because it is made in a contemporary account. The same contrast is suggested in an article on "The Jews" in the *Boston Journal* in 1837.

The Jews [writes the author] have been accused of crimes of which they were not guilty. . . . The Jews have been reproached with their avidity to acquire riches. . . . This, however, is probably more the effect of the contempt in which they are held by Christians than the cause; and perhaps may be more owing to their habitual industry, their business qualifications, and the thorough knowledge which they seem to possess of every brand of trade, than to a morbid wish to increase their hoards.[74]

3

THE FIRESIDE POETS

Poetry was a far more popular literary form among the general populace during the nineteenth century than it has been until recently. Of the many poets whose works were read by the family circle at the hearthstone, five stand out: Bryant, Whittier, Longfellow, Holmes, and Lowell, called the Fireside Poets. Their lives spanned the entire century. The oldest, Bryant, was born in 1794 and the youngest, Lowell, in 1819; Bryant died in 1878, and the last to die was Holmes, in 1894. Thus they lived through the radical changes in American society in its development from agrarianism to an expanding industrialism. Most of their best poetry appeared before the Civil War and they remained, basically, poets of an agrarian society. All were antislavery with varying degrees of militance, from Whittier, who was the poet of the abolitionist movement, to Holmes, who wrote no poetry on slavery and was hostile to militance of any kind except anti-Calvinism, being a militant Unitarian himself. But since their formative years had been spent in an agrarian America, they never fully grasped the new form of things in an industrial society. Unlike the great quintet of their contemporaries—Emerson, Thoreau, Hawthorne, Melville, Whitman—they failed to penetrate the depths of the dislocations of consciousness generated by the emerging industrial order.

The Fireside Poets had little contact with Jews and showed no particular grasp of Jewish issues. In their attitude toward the Jews they ranged from tolerance to ambiguity to Lowell's obsessive interest late in life. All held conventionally religious views of one liberal persuasion or another, and when they mentioned Jews in their poems, they did so from a Christian viewpoint—except for Holmes, as we shall see. Sol Liptzin has aptly and succinctly written that the poems about Jews by "the New England poets . . . were basically Christian in sentiment and not Jewish. They were the literary products of sensitive outsiders who looked in upon the Jewish scene, admired the Jewish past, tolerated the Jewish present, and were indifferent to the Jewish future."[1]

Bryant was exceptional among the group in that he wrote no poems at all on Jewish themes, whether modern or biblical, although he did write hymns and religious poetry. His attitude toward Jews is discernible in his prose writings, however, even though allusions to the Jews are so few that apparently they did not engage his interest very much. For instance, in his essay "American Society as a Field for Fiction" he writes that our free institutions permit of an "infinite variety of forms of character." Religious tolerance sets in motion a great variety of influences on the people, and in this connection he remarks that "the Jew worships unmolested in his synagogue."[2] In his writings on his travels in England in 1849 he notes the intense discussion on the issue of admitting Jews to Parliament. It is generally agreed, he states, that a majority favor lifting the religious barriers, and that Jews will be allowed to hold seats in Parliament. He predicts that Jews will become "adversaries of the Establishment making war upon it in the House of Commons. Nor would it be at all surprising," he adds, "if, after a little while one hears of Jewish barons, earls, and marquises in the House of Peers. Rothschild himself may become the founder of a noble line, opulent beyond the proudest of them all."[3] History has proved Bryant right on both counts.

Tolerant though he was, Bryant was not free from clichés about the Jewish character. In 1866 he wrote his most extended comments on the Jews in his article on Shylock as portrayed by Edwin Booth. Jews, he writes, are marked by an "unquenchable lust for lucre," and Shakespeare was following his best impulses in "execrating" it. But Bryant goes on to criticize Shakespeare for failing to show "that this passion was but the effect of that persecution which by crowding the Jew out of every honorable pursuit, and thus cutting off his nature from every sympathy with the world around, sharpened and edged the keen corners of his brain for the only pursuit left to him." While Jewish bankers are now received by the leaders of nations, "it is not so much that the prejudice against Jews has ceased, but that the love of money has increased; not that the Jews have become as Christians but that Christians have become as Jews."[4]

While Shakespeare was right in condemning the passion for money, Bryant goes on, he was wrong in ascribing to Jews "a craving for revenge," since "revenge is not a characteristic of the Jew." Bryant also asserts that Jessica's contempt for her father is "equally uncharacteristic of the Jew," since familial affection among the Jews is "universally admired." Bryant implies that he has visited with Jews: "No one can ever have visited the homes of Jews without having been struck by the glowing affection with which the daughter greets the father" on his return from business. But Bryant's description of the father is derived from the stereotype: on being greeted by his daughter, "these small, restless eyes, that sparkle and gleam like a snake's in search of prey, shine out a softened, loving lustre as they fall upon the face of Rebecca, Jessica, or Sarah, and now he stands no longer with crooked back, but erect and commanding as he blesses his household gods with an exultation as vehement as the prejudices which during the day have galled and fretted his nature."[5] Bryant was well aware that anti-Semitism was a common, daily experience.

Bryant's complaint is not against Shakespeare's condemnation of the "repulsive" character of the Jews, but his omission of their "grandeurs." One should present both sides, not only the "infamies," but also "that superiority of intellect which has survived all persecutions" and the great positive influences which "may be traced to the wonderful workings of the soul of the Hebrews and the supremacy of that spiritual nature which gave to mankind its noblest religion, its noblest laws, and some of its noblest poetry and music."[6] Thus Bryant's tolerance and intention to do justice to the Jews show him still bound by popular conceptions and stereotypes. He believes in the pair of extremes often associated with Jews: a malevolent lust for money and an extraordinary intellectual and spiritual quality. Few in the world had yet learned that Jews are a group of human beings and not an abstract type, good or bad.

The poetry of John Greenleaf Whittier is free of the Jewish stereotype. A dedicated Quaker, he was the poet of abolitionism and extended his ideal of freedom to all peoples. He stemmed from a line of Massachusetts farmers—the only Fireside Poet who was not a patrician—and was sensitive to the needs of the poor. However, his agrarian mentality inhibited him from applying this feeling to the trade union movement, which he opposed. In "King Solomon and the Ants" he seizes upon a story about Solomon to voice his humanitarian feeling for the poor. Solomon's procession out of Jerusalem with the Queen of Sheba comes upon an anthill. When the ants complain that the great king will crush them underfoot, Sheba responds that the lowly should be happy to perish under the foot of the great. But the wise Solomon demurs: "Nay . . . /The wise and strong should seek/The welfare of the weak," and he turns aside.

Sheba then acknowledges the wisdom of Solomon, saying the land must be happy "Whose ruler heedeth more/The murmurs of the poor/Than flatteries of the great." Whittier was explicit also in enjoining freedom of worship for all faiths. In "The Quaker Alumni," read at the Friends' School in Providence in 1860, Whittier offers thanks for the benevolence of the Quaker faith:

> For a sense of Goodness revealed everywhere,
> As sunshine impartial, and free as the air;
> For trust in humanity, Heathen or Jew,
> And a hope for all darkness
>   The Light shineth through. . . .
> Enough and too much of the sect and name.
> What matters our label, so truth be our aim?
> The creed may be wrong, but the life may be true,
> And hearts beat the same under the drab coats of blue. . . .
> So the man *be* a man, let him worship at will,
> In Jerusalem's courts, or on Gerizim's hill.

While preaching tolerance for other faiths, and decrying sectarian disputes, he adjures his hearers, with the conventional Christian view of Pharisaism, to cling to the Quaker faith: "The old paths we'll keep until better are shown." He further elucidates his meaning by warning against exclusiveness:

> No talk of our Lion as if we were Jews; . . .
> We need not pray over the Pharisee's prayer,
> Nor claim that our wisdom is Benjamin's share.
> Truth to us and to others is equal and one.
> Shall we bottle the free air, or hoard up the sun?

A similar injunction against Pharisaism of any kind is urged in "Lines from a Letter to a Young Clerical Friend," asking that God "teach him that the Christian man/Is holier than the Jewish priest." This statement expresses the Quaker doctrine of guidance by the Inner Light rather than by a minister. The contrast is essentially between man and priest, but why does Whittier contrast the Christian man with the Jewish rather than the Christian "priest"? Whittier also advises his young friend to "Unmask the priestly thieves and tear/The Bible from the grasp of hell!"[7]

In the first half of his life the deeply religious Whittier wrote a number of poems on biblical themes, usually with a Christian orientation. In "Ezekiel" he follows the prophet's lament with his own observation: "So it was when the Holy One / The garments of the flesh put on"—an obvious allusion to Christ. Even "The Wife of

Monoah to Her Husband," an encomium to Samson by his mother, has a christological overtone. After Samson's destruction of himself together with the Philistines, his mother says: "With me, as with my only son,/O God . . . Thy will be done!"—a veiled allusion to Mary and Jesus. At the same time, in his "Crucifixion," there is no mention of Jews or their part in the event, thus indicating that he did not strongly associate anti-Jewish feeling with the death of Jesus. His early poem "Palestine" is an idyllic evocation of the land of Jews. "What if my feet may not tread where he stood," says Whittier, for Jesus's "Spirit is near"; though "the outward has gone, . . . the spirit surviveth the things of an hour."[8]

No less christological are Whittier's two poems concerning rabbis. "The Rabbi Ishmael," a late poem (1881), derives from a talmudic story about Ishmael Ben Elisha to whom God speaks in the holy of holies. The rabbi pleads for mercy for man and asks that God's compassion prevail over anger at man's weaknesses. It seems to Rabbi Ishmael that God acquiesces, whereupon the rabbi blesses the Lord; God seems to acknowledge the blessing. But, as Sol Liptzin has pointed out, the Christian Whittier could not endure ending with man blessing God, so he has the face of the Lord vanish after he grants Ishmael's request, and the poem ends with Ishmael praising God for his mercy.[9]

The other poem, "The Two Rabbins," concerns the ancient Rabbi Nathan, who has lived without sin until the age of fifty and then succumbs to a great temptation. He goes to the Rabbi Ben Isaac in Ecbatana, in Media, for counsel. He confesses to Ben Isaac that he has sinned, and Ben Isaac replies that he too has sinned in thought, "if not in act." They console each other, "each made his brother's woe his own," and Rabbi Nathan later inscribes on his headstone the Christian sentiment that salvation lies in denying self "in love's service: Save thou a soul, and it shall save thine own!"[10]

This christianizing of the Jew and his tradition was lacking in Oliver Wendell Holmes, interestingly enough. He was a true son of his father, Rev. Abiel Holmes, in his tolerance for the Jew; but unlike his father, whose Calvinism he rejected in favor of a liberal Unitarianism, he was absolutely free of the proselytizing zeal of that gentle clerical worthy. The younger man manifested no desire to change the Jew, and he accepted the Jew as a Jew. He shared with his Puritan forebears the analogical comparison between the Jews as "the Chosen People" and the new American nation, and in his early poem "The Pilgrim's Vision," he writes that the Pilgrims were "the chosen tribe that sought this Western Palestine!"[11]

Holmes's amiable tolerance is illustrated by the tone of a poem he read at a dinner in 1843 to honor the two men whose donations of ten thousand dollars each had made possible the completion of the Bunker Hill monument—Boston merchants Amos Lawrence and Judah Touro:

> Amos and Judah! venerated names!
> Patriarch and prophet press their equal claims,
> Like generous coursers running neck to neck,
> Each aids the work by giving it a check.
> Christian and Jew, they carry out a plan,
> For, though of different faith, each is in heart a Man.[12]

There is no suggestion in his writing that the Jew could be saved by adopting Christianity or that the Old Testament was only a preparation for the New.

The inevitable references by Holmes to the Wandering Jew bear no weighty religious overtones, but are made with characteristic levity. In the "Old Man of the Sea," his satire on the "Ancient Mariner," he writes:

> O the dreadful Old Man of the Sea, of the Sea!
> He's come back like the Wandering Jew!
> He has laid his cold claw upon me, upon me,—
> And be sure he'll have it on you.

And in his fable "The First Fan," read before the Boston Bric-a-Brac Club in 1877, he relates how the fan was given to mortals. When paganism came to an end and "Jove's high palace closed its portal," the gods "sold out their frippery to a mortal"—to the Wandering Jew. "The bearded wanderer" then bargains with each god for some article of clothing in the manner of the comic Jewish stereotype. But as for Venus, "Her wardrobe, as I blush to tell,/Already seemed but quite too scanty." Her only resort was to make a fan of "one fan-tailed pigeon," she "bounds the glossy plumes together," and "the price she named was hard to stand,/But Venus smiled: the Hebrew paid it." Since then, "o'er the world The Wandering Jew/Has borne the Fan's celestial pattern," which may thus be traced "To Aphrodite's fan-tailed pigeon."[13] The adaptability of the concept of the Wandering Jew knows no limits.

Holmes's attitude toward the Jews was most explicitly brought out in the last few decades of the century, when anti-Semitism was taking on a more severe and discriminatory form in the United States. He was among the eminent authors who protested the exclusion of

Joseph Seligman from the Grand Union Hotel in Saratoga Springs in 1877. And he was among those prominent Americans to whom Philip Cowen, managing editor of the *American Hebrew,* addressed four questions concerning anti-Jewish prejudice: Did their personal experience justify anti-Semitism? Was Christian instruction the source of anti-Semitism? Was Jewish behavior any different from that of Christians of the same social status? What should be done to dispel prejudice?

The answers were published in the *American Hebrew* of April 4, 1890. The Rev. Edward Everett Hale made the interesting observation that "when I have seen it [anti-Semitism] mentioned in the press, it has been a subject of constant amazement to me. I do not think it existed in my boyhood or youth." As a matter of fact, it *had* existed earlier in the century, but its quality had latterly drawn closer to the explicit European mode. John Burroughs thought race prejudice inevitable and ineradicable. He placed the burden of dispelling prejudice on the Jews themselves; they had to become "more Americanized and modernized" and to get "more out of the channels of trade and . . . into the actual productive industries of the country." Thomas Wentworth Higginson said that he was not prejudiced and could find no justification for it. He agreed that prejudice was partly owing to "Christian traditions and teachings," but he thought that there were instances of "Jewish families, whose wealth was out of all proportion to their education and refinement and who made themselves unwelcome guests at hotels or boarding houses by selfish or boorish manners." The only solution was "through advancing civilization and the evolution of the human race." William Dean Howells's responses were categorical: "I.—No, indeed! II.—Certainly not! III.—No. The Jews vary according to their breeding and temperament, as Christians do. IV. Christianize the Christians."[14]

Holmes's response to the questions affirmed his freedom from prejudice. He had no recollection of prejudice in his religious education, except for the hymns and Sunday services. As to difference in standards of conduct between Jews and Christians, he replied: "I have not had experience enough in dealing with Hebrews to authorize me to draw any general conclusions." As to a remedy, he asserted that Christianity must learn "modesty and humility in its self-estimate," and that as a result "the Hebrew will partake of the general benefit that will accrue to humanity." Until then, the Jew "must expect to share the epithets and general condemnation which most of the Christian Churches bestow on the vast majority of mankind."[15]

It is true that Holmes had little contact with Jews, as one may gather from the special note he took of meeting Jews on several occasions. While he was studying in Europe in 1834, he wrote his parents that "one of the greatest pleasures of living abroad is to meet in such an easy, pleasant sort of way people from all quarters of the world. Greek and Barbarian, Jew and Gentile, differ much less than one thinks at first, and this you never learn from books—or never believe."[16] On another occasion, when Holmes was traveling in the South during the Civil War, his wagon companion was a German Jew, Phillip Ottenheimer, "whose features at once showed him to be an Israelite." When Holmes questioned him about his Jewish views, he heard "some answers that sound strange in Christian ears." The man opposed intermarriage; he thought Jesus "a right smart man and a great doctor"; he would regard with horror a reading of the New Testament by a young Jew, just as appalled, Holmes observed, as "one of our straitest sectaries would be, if he found his son or daughter perusing *The Age of Reason.*"[17]

Holmes elaborates his response to the *American Hebrew* questions in *Over the Teacups.* He reveals that in his youth he inherited "the traditional idea that they were a race lying under a curse for their obstinacy in refusing the gospel." He "walked in the narrow path of Puritan exclusiveness," which regarded Judaism as one of the many false religions. "The principal use of the Jews seemed to be to lend money, and to fulfill the predictions of the old prophets of the race." He agrees that the Jews "whom one found in our ill-favored and ill-flavored streets were apt to be unpleasing specimens of the race." But Jews eminent in many areas "forced the world to recognize and accept them" despite legal disabilities and religious prejudice. Christians have refused to allow Jews to differ about Jesus, and for the disagreement "have insulted, calumniated, oppressed, abased, outraged" the Jews. Holmes appeals for tolerance toward all religions: "The religion we profess is not self-evident. . . . We have no claim to take it for granted that we are all right, and they are all wrong."

Holmes then recalls that years earlier he wrestled with his attitude toward " 'the chosen people,'—chosen as the object of contumely and abuse by the rest of the world," and emerged with brotherly feelings.[18] He recounts this experience in the poem "The Pantomime," which he revised in 1874 from an 1856 version, "A Hebrew Tale." The poem is an interesting paradigm of how prejudice is overcome by experience. He is attending a performance on a hot August evening in an overcrowded hall, and his temper is short. He notes that many Jews are present, and he is wedged in by a "cursed unbelieving Jew." He becomes enraged and invokes the stereotype:

> I stabbed in turn with silent oaths
> The hook-nosed kite of carrion clothes,
> The sneaky usurer, him that crawls
> And cheats beneath the golden balls,
> Moses and Levi, all the horde,
> Spawn of the race that slew its Lord.
>
> Up came their murderous deeds of old,
> The grisly story Chaucer told.
> And many an ugly tale beside
> Of children caught and crucified;
> I heard the ducat-sweating thieves*
> Beneath the Ghetto's slouching eaves,
> And, thrust beyond the tented green,
> The lepers cry, "Unclean! Unclean!"

But he then looks at the faces of his crowding young neighbors, and sees reflected in them the human qualities of Jesus himself. The anger and dislike fall from him, and he ends: "Peace be upon thee, Israel!"[19]

Holmes's interest in Jews as a living, contemporary people was far greater than Longfellow's. John J. Appel has accurately observed that Longfellow was "concerned less with the particular situation of the relatively few Jews then living in the United States than with the role of their ancestors in the transmission of cultural traditions and literary productions."[20] This faint interest in the modern Jew is consistent with Longfellow's general lack of engagement with the problems of a nation in transition to industrialism, if we except the seven rather weak antislavery poems composed on board ship when he returned from England in 1842. Emma Lazarus observed acutely in her memorial address at the YMHA on April 8, 1882, following the poet's death, that he belonged

intellectually and artistically to the generation of Washington Irving, rather than to that of his actual contemporaries, Emerson or Walt Whitman; all his links are with the past; the legendary, the historic, enchanted him with an irresistible glamor; not only was he without the eyes of the seer, to penetrate the well of the future, but equally

*In *The Professor at the Breakfast Table*, Holmes had written: "I suspect the story of *sweating* gold was only one of the many odious fables got up to make the Jews odious and afford a pretext for plundering them" (*The Writings of Oliver Wendell Holmes* [Cambridge, Mass., 1871], 2:163).

without the active energy or the passionate enthusiasm of an inspired champion in the arena of the present.[21]

Longfellow's interest in contemporary Jews was slight. Like so many Americans born in the first half of the century who traveled in Europe, he made note of an encounter with a Jew as if he were an oddity hardly known in his own country. On a trip in Germany in 1835 Longfellow characterizes a fellow traveler, a Jew from Hamburg, in a conventional way: "He was a comical character, draped in gray, with the customary hooked nose and half-moon mouth of his tribe; though he could hardly be less than sixty years old he travelled night and day, so as to avoid paying for a lodging."[22] Conventional, too, is his treatment of the Jews in relation to the crucifixion. In the final section of *Hiawatha* (1855), when the hero is about to leave his people forever, he calls upon them to listen to the missionary, "the Black-Robe chief, the Prophet," who has related to the tribe the story of Christ, and

> of the Virgin Mary,
> And her blessed Son, the Saviour,
> How in distant land and ages,
> How he lived on earth as we do;
> How the Jews, the tribe accursed,
> Mocked him, scourged him, crucified him;
> How he rose from where they laid him,
> Walked again with his disciples,
> And ascended into heaven.[23]

In "The Divine Tragedy" (1871), the drama in verse that forms the first part of the *Christus* trilogy, he cleaves to the invidious New Testament account of the Jews' part in the drama of Jesus, and even dilates on Pontius Pilate's presumed perplexity at the intransigence of the Jews. Says Pilate:

> Wholly uncomprehensible to me,
> Vainglorious, obstinate, and given up
> To unintelligible old traditions,
> And proud and self-conceited are these Jews![24]

In the second part of the *Christus* trilogy Longfellow ridicules the ritual murder tale by retelling it in the words of a besotted monk.

His attitude toward the Jews as a people is best exemplified in one of his finest poems, "The Jewish Cemetery at Newport." He records that on July 9, 1852, he was led to the seventeenth-century Jewish burying ground by "a polite old gentleman who keeps the keys.

There are few graves. Nearly all are low tombstones of marble, with Hebrew inscriptions, and a few words added in English or Portuguese."[25] The once-flourishing Sephardic community was no more: all the Newport Jews had either been assimilated into Christian families or had left the city. "Closed the portals of their Synagogue,/Gone are the living, but the dead remain," he writes. This, however, does not account for the poem's conclusion: "dead nations never rise again." One may infer that Longfellow believed the Jews of his time to be a dying people and thought that there was no future for the Jews as a collective entity.[26] Longfellow also voiced his condemnation of past persecutions:

> How came they here? What burst of Christian hate,
>   What persecution, merciless and blind,
> Drove o'er the sea—that desert desolate—
>   These Ishmaels and Hagars of mankind?
>
> They lived in narrow streets and lanes obscure,
>   Ghetto and Judenstrass, in murk and mire;
> Taught in the school of patience to endure
>   The life of anguish and the death of fire.
>
> All their lives long, with the unleavened bread
>   And bitter herbs of exile and its fears,
> The wasting famine of the heart they fed,
>   And slaked its thirst with marah of their tears.
>
> Anathema maranatha! was the cry
>   That rang from town to town, from street to street;
> At every gate the accursed Mordecai
>   Was mocked and jeered, and spurned by Christian feet.[27]

It is indicative of the poet's aversion to politics that he deliberately excluded contemporaneity from the final version of the poem. In the first version he recognizes that persecution has not yet been ended in his own time:

> A sword still bars the gate of rest and peace;
>   A foot still breaks and grinds them like the grain!
> A voice still speaks the doom, that ne'er shall cease;
>   A hand still points to the deep mark of Cain!

He also deleted the following verse, which was present in the third and fourth versions, from his final draft:

> Is there no hope? no end to all their wrongs?
>   No rest—no Truce of God to intervene,

For those who gave the world its noblest songs,
The only perfect man this world hath seen?

Also rejected in the final version was his verse celebration of Jewish equality in the United States:

But here at length the Truce of God prevailed;
The oppression and the contumely ceased,
No more were they molested, nor assailed
By royal tax or malison of priest![28]

The political aspect of these omitted stanzas is so innocuous that one wonders why he chose to omit them. The ideas in them would surely be appropriate to an American poem. Perhaps the poet believed that contemporary allusions broke into the sadness caused by the dying of a great and suffering people and detracted from the unity of mood. In any case, the absence of current social and political interest makes the poem all the more characteristic of his work.

Viewing Longfellow's work as a whole, we find that his primary interest in the Jew was scholarly and cultural. The Talmud and the Hebrew language interested him as a scholar of language and comparative literature; though he probably never mastered it, he was acquainted with Hebrew. In "Elegiac Verse" he implies a knowledge of the language: "Wisely the Hebrews admit no Present in their language;/While speaking the word, it is already the Past."[29]

His interest was further stimulated by his association with Emanuel Vitalis Scherb, a German revolutionary refugee. In his journal entry for November 8, 1849, he notes that Scherb "came in at tea-time. In the evening he repeated to me some of the Psalms, in Hebrew; strange, mysterious language, building up poems with square blocks of sound. The same tongue in which Jeremiah prophesied, and David sang."[30] In 1857 Scherb also read to him from a German work, the talmudic legend that Longfellow made into the poem "Sandolphin" after consulting the account of the legend in John Peter Stehlin's *Traditions of the Jews* (London, 1732). In the legend Sandolphin is the angel of prayers who gathers the prayers of man into garlands of flowers, which shed their fragrance "Through the streets of the City Immortal." To the poet, the legend

is a part
Of the hunger and thirst of the heart,
The frenzy and fire of the brain,
That grasps at the fruitage forbidden,

The golden pomegranates of Eden,
To quiet its fever and pain.[31]

Scholarly interest also predominates in the poet's depiction of "a
Spanish Jew from Alicante" in *Tales of a Wayside Inn,* a series of tales
patterned on Boccaccio and Chaucer. Among the storytelling group
gathered around the fire at the Red Horse Inn in Sudbury are,
besides the venerable Spanish Jew, a Norwegian musician, a poet,
a Sicilian, and a student. "All the guests, as well as the Inn," writes
Longfellow in a note, "are real"[32]—but one can hardly call them
realistic. The original of the Jew was Isaac (called Israel in the poem)
Edrehi, who was born in Morocco and had immigrated to the United
States after living in Tangier, Jerusalem, Amsterdam, and London.
Edrehi's father, Moses, a scholar and lecturer who taught at a talmudic academy and at Cambridge University, was the author of a
cabalistic book on the history of the Ten Tribes that was first published in London in 1836. Isaac Edrehi solicited subscriptions in this
country for the book, which was reprinted in Philadelphia in 1853.
It is conjectured that Longfellow first became acquainted with Isaac
when Isaac solicited a subscription from him. Something of the
father's looks, known to the poet from a portrait in the book, must
also have entered the picture of the Spanish Jew in the poem.

Longfellow presents the old Jewish scholar as the nineteenth-
century stereotype of the Jew as patriarch—"Like an old Patriarch
he appeared," writes the poet.

A Spanish Jew from Alicant
With aspect grand and grave was there;
Vendor of silks and fabrics rare,
And attar of rose from the Levant.
Like an old Patriarch he appeared,
Abraham or Isaac, or at least
Some later Prophet or High-Priest;
With lustrous eyes, and olive skin,
And, wildly tossed from cheeks and chin,
The tumbling cataract of his beard.

As Longfellow goes on to describe the fragrant aroma hovering
about Edrehi, one wonders if the poet did not intend thereby to
counteract the medieval cliché of the Jews as ill-smelling because the
devil was in them: "His garments breathed a spicy scent/Of cinna-
mon and sandal blent." Later in the poem the theme returns. As the
"aromatic Jew" enters the room in the morning, "on the air/
Breathed round about him a perfume/Of damask roses in full

bloom,/Making a garden of the room." At the very least this picture of Edrehi contributes to his image as a patriarch and exotic scholar, and emphasizes, perhaps excessively, the poet's friendliness toward the character.

Edrehi's scholarly attributes are also described:

> All stories that recorded are
> By Pierre Alphonse he knew by heart,
> And it was rumored he could say
> The Parables of Sandabar,
> And all the Fables of Pilpay,
> Or if not all, the greater part!
> Well versed was he in Hebrew books,
> Talmud and Targum, and the lore
> Of Kabala; and evermore
> There was a mystery in his looks,
> His eyes seemed gazing far away,
> As if in vision or in trance
> He heard the solemn sackbut play,
> And saw the Jewish maidens dance.[33]

Of the four tales related by Edrehi, two are Jewish in theme. The first is a talmudic legend told to Longfellow by Scherb concerning Rabbi Ben Levi's encounter with the angel of death. The rabbi strikes a bargain with God and the angel of death that the angel will remain invisible to those he has come to take away; that is why the angel of death "walks on earth unseen forever more." The second, "Azrac" (also the angel of death), is seen as a ghostly form who follows Solomon when he walks forth with a visiting rajah from Hindustan; the rajah implores Solomon to order the wind to carry him back to Hindustan, so that he may evade the angel. Solomon complies, and the angel commends Solomon, for he was on the way to meet the rajah in Hindustan. The third story tells the legendary exploits of the Albanian hero Scanderbeg, and the fourth is the Tartar legend "Kambalu," whose moral is the unwisdom of miserliness and love of gold and treasure.

It cannot be by chance that the poet chose to have the Jew recount a moral tale urging against obsessive love of gold. Did he not here intend to counteract the cliché of the money-loving Jew? The wealth of the caliph was

> Heaped and hoarded and piled on high,
> Like sacks of wheat in a granary;
> And thither the miser crept by stealth
> To feel of the gold that gave him health,
> And to gaze and gloat with his hungry eye

> On jewels and gleamed like a glowworm's spark
> Or the eyes of a panther in the dark.

The returning conquering hero, Alan, reads his brother, the caliph, a lesson in the futility of gold lust:

> Thou art old,
> Thou hast no need of so much gold. . . .
> These grains of gold are not grains of wheat;
> These bars of silver thou canst not eat;
> These jewels and pearls and precious stones
> Cannot cure the aches in thy bones,
> Nor keep the feet of Death one hour
> From climbing the stairways of thy tower![34]

Although Longfellow's primary interest in the Jew was scholarly, in this instance it seems to have been the poet's gentle nature that led him, perhaps unconsciously, to present a portrait that ran counter to the popular conception of the Jew as money-obsessed.

The youngest of the Fireside Poets, James Russell Lowell, had a more complex relationship with the Jews than his fellow poets. His attitude may be regarded as transitional between the benevolence of the other poets and the intense anti-Semitism of intellectuals of the next generation like Henry Adams. While Lowell's mind was not primarily analytic, it was more so than those of other poets of the time; he exercised it in a bizarre way on his views concerning Jews. An ambiguous attitude toward them is manifested in his review of Disraeli's *Tancred,* written when he was in his twenties. Lowell remarks that "seldom has the inner life been so aptly symbolized in the outward as in the case of the Jews. That the idolators of ceremony and tradition should become the vendors of old clothes, that the descendants of those who, within earshot of the thunders of Sinai, could kneel before the golden calf, should be the money-changers of Europe, has in it something of syllogistic completeness." He then proceeds to apply his argument to a contemporary Jew: "The work by which the elder D'Israeli will be remembered is the old curiosity shop of literature. . . . The son, with his trumpery of the past, is clearly a vendor of the same wares, and an offshoot from the same stock." Yet in the same essay he keenly observes that in Europe the Jews were used to satisfy "this peculiar craving of the supreme Caucasian nature"[35] to establish superiority; in the United States, he observes, the Negro took the place of the Jew in gratifying this craving.

The Jew seldom appears in Lowell's poetry. There is the inevitable allusion to the Wandering Jew: "Humbugs never die, more than the Wandering Jew." In the single poem in which the Bible and the Jew figure importantly, "Bibliolatres" (1849), Lowell assumes the conventional Christian religious view that the Jews violate the prophetic aspect of the Bible and worship in an arid, ossified ritual.

> Yea, what are thou, blind, unconverted Jew,
> That with thy idol-volume's covers two
> Wouldst make a jail to coop the living God?

While the poem's condemnation of a closed and dogmatic adherence to the Bible may also be applied to rigid Christians, he places the burden on the Jews. Those who believe that "the cisterns of those Hebrew brains/Drew dry the springs of the All-knower's thoughts" are not aware that "the Bible of the race is writ" as "Each age, each kindred, adds a verse to it."[36]

Lowell's ambivalent feeling about the Jews became most marked in his later years. It is impossible to know whether his admiration and the exaggerated importance he ascribed to them stemmed from fear and unpleasant awe or was generous and genuine. At the same time that he praised them, he indulged in the unfavorable stereotype. In a letter of 1878 he wrote, in connection with French reformer León Gambetta's Jewish origin, that "the strength of his Jewish ancestors . . . [was] that they could supply you or me with an accommodation at heavy interest. Where would a Jew be among a society of primitive men without pockets and *a fortiori* without a hole in them?" In another letter in the same year he asserted that "a good deal of the prejudice against Beaconsfield is medieval like that which dictated the legend of Hugh of Lincoln."[37]

In Lowell's latter years, in the 1870s and 1880s, when the mass immigration of poor Eastern European Jews began to pour into the country, the Jews became an obsession with him. This period marked the development of Anglo-Saxon racism and a new quality of anti-Semitism that began to trickle into this country from Europe. An anonymous writer on Lowell, who had met the author in Paris in 1881, writes in the *Atlantic Monthly* in 1897 that the Jews were "almost a monomania with him."[38] But it could do gross injustice to Lowell to simplistically label him an anti-Semite. If his admiration for the Jews was ambivalent, he was quite explicit in condemning anti-Semitism past and present. In his famous essay "Democracy" (1884) he attacked those who resisted change, including those who would respond to mass immigration with exclusionist legislation, a movement that was just beginning.

One of the most curious of these frenzies of exclusion was that against the emancipation of the Jews. All share in the government was denied for centuries to perhaps the ablest, certainly the most tenacious, race that has ever lived in it—the race to whom we owed our religion and the purest spiritual stimulus and consolation to be found in all literature—a race in which ability seems as natural and hereditary as the curve of their noses, and whose blood, furtively mingling with the bluest bloods of Europe, has quickened them with its own indomitable impulsion. We drove them into a corner, but they had their revenge, as the wronged are always sure to have sooner or later. They made their corner the counter and banking-house of the world, and thence they rule it with the ignobler scepter of finance.[39]

Even in defending the Jews, Lowell cannot avoid falling into the stereotype of the Jew as financial ruler of the world.

Lowell's preoccupation with the Jews took the peculiar form of detecting Jewish ancestry in all sorts of improbable people by the scrutiny of their names. In 1892 Leslie Stephen notes Lowell's obsession with seeing concealed Jews everywhere through their names or physical features, so that "it was scarcely possible to mention any distinguished man who could not be conclusively proved to be connected with the chosen race." In the end, Stephen writes, the subject of the Jews was the only one on which "I could conceive Lowell approaching within measurable distance of [being] boring."[40]

Lowell even saw a Jewish strain in himself through the name Russell, and was proud of it because this derivation carried with it the Jews' presumed intellectual power. "He detected a Jew in every hiding-place and under every disguise," says the *Atlantic* writer, "even when the fugitive had no suspicion of it himself." He would talk of the insinuation of Jews into places of power by their intermarriage with ruling houses. "In short," the writer goes on, "it appeared that this insidious race had penetrated and permeated the human family more universally than any other influence except original sin." By their "talent and versatility" the Jews had won distinction in "literature, the learned professions, art, science, and even war." Lowell had asserted in a conversation with the writer that all bankers and brokers and most barons were Jews: they controlled the press, and were becoming influential in politics at the highest levels. While they had earlier lived in ghettos, they now had palaces, moved in aristocratic circles, and were buying up many English estates. Lowell mixed his speculations with humor, but ended upon a whispered note of alarm: "And when the Jews have got absolute control of finance, the army and navy, the press, diplomacy, society, titles, the government, and the earth's surface, what do you suppose they will do with them—and with us? . . . That is the question which will eventually drive me mad."[41]

In Lowell one finds the strangest image of the Jew, a mixture of the highest and lowest qualities, and an ambiguous estimate of both. They seemed to touch some sensitive nerve in him that threw his rationality off balance. But there was none of the viciousness and malignity that scarred the writings of intellectual figures of the next generation.

4

AMERICAN RENAISSANCE

While the ongoing changes in American life, the transition from an agrarian to an industrial society, found no penetrating expression in the Fireside Poets, it was quite otherwise with the literary artists who comprise what has come to be known as the "American Renaissance." Emerson, Thoreau, Hawthorne, Melville, Dickinson, and Whitman were almost exact contemporaries of the Fireside Poets, but they registered far more sensitively the deep effect on consciousness and social life wrought by the changing material conditions.

While all the Fireside Poets achieved wide popularity in their time, among the prose writers only Emerson and Hawthorne won contemporary favor; the stature of Thoreau, Melville, Dickinson, and Whitman was not recognized for decades. The popular poets themselves were hardly much in advance of the general public in this respect. Lowell, for instance, completely missed the point of *Walden*, seeing in it only an expression of egotism and overlooking Thoreau's profound critical insight into modern society. Nor could he, any more than Whittier or Longfellow, see much in Whitman. *Moby Dick, Walden,* and *Leaves of Grass* lay on barren ground for many years after publication. The refreshment of the American imagination in these works went unrecognized because, as so often happens, the absorption of new elements of consciousness required a gestatory period before a general awakening to a new state of affairs could occur. The unsettling effect of changing material conditions upon moral consciousness received probing exploration in this coming of age of American literature.

As with the Fireside Poets, the substance of their work was largely set down before the Civil War, and this may account for the glancing interest (with a few exceptions as we shall see) in the modern Jew in their work. There were relatively few Jews in New England before the Civil War, and many of its residents could grow up without ever having met a Jew. In some cases the educated New

Englander would meet his first Jew in his European *Wanderjahr*. In 1858 the young Henry Lee Higginson wrote his father from Vienna about his acquaintance with two Jews: his piano teacher, "a most captivating man, and a great artist," and a violinist, "a prime fellow." "I never saw a Jew before coming here," Higginson adds, "but those whom I have known in Vienna are very talented, true, liberal in views of life and religion, and free-handed to a marvellous extent." His father replied that he, too, had "met individuals of that race who seemed fitted in solid essentials for an intimacy of such character. I am thankful that really worthy ones have fallen in your way."[1]

Emerson encountered what may have been his first Jew during a European sojourn. At a party in Rome in 1833, given by a college friend, he met Gustave d'Eichtal of the French Jewish banking family.[2] The fact is that contemporary Jews figured peripherally, if at all, in the lives of the five great writers. This is not surprising in the case of Thoreau, considering that he spent most of his life in Concord. No allusion to contemporary Jews can be found in any of his works and journals. One reference to the traditional Hebrew does occur in his journals. Of his quiet search for "The Ineffable" he records on September 7, 1851, that it must be pursued without sadness. "These Jews," he writes, "were too sad: to another people a still deeper revelation may suggest only joy. . . . In the Hebrew gladness, I hear but too distinctly still the sound of sadness retreating. Give me a gladness which has never given place to sadness."[3]

The case is similar with Emily Dickinson. Far more sequestered than even Thoreau, there is no evidence of contact with any Jew whatsoever in her life. But she does mention the Jew in four poems, probably written during 1861 and 1862. In all cases the Jew begs for a smile—from one of those men whom she is said to have loved —in terms of a commercial transaction at a "counter." She would "buy a smile" in exchange for diamonds or rubies, "like a star!" The exchange would be a " 'Bargain' for a *Jew!*" In another poem she longs to see the face of a beloved, and bargains with his wife, presumably, for "*One hour*—of her Sovereign's face!" The poet offers stocks, bonds, money for the privilege.

> Now—have I bought it—
> "Shylock?" Say!
> Sign me the Bond!

In another poem Dickinson says of an orchard at the coming of day that it "sparkled like a Jew." And in a fourth poem she writes that she knows only "the names, of Gems," but if her lover's smiles could only be hers, she would "but be a Jew."[4] It is altogether likely that this exquisite mind had no immediate knowledge of the modern Jew, but was introducing the literary stereotype as she might any other established metaphor.

There is one episode in New England literary life of that period, however, in which a literary figure came to know a Jew intimately. In 1845, when Margaret Fuller was thirty-four, she met at the Horace Greeleys a prosperous German Jewish businessman, James Nathan, who had been a penniless immigrant in 1830. He was a cultivated man with a love of music who considered Miss Fuller "a foolish little girl," while she thought of him as a "personification of the romance of the East."[5] She fell in love with him, pressed the friendship, and wrote him passionate letters. "I have long had a presentiment," she wrote him, "that I should meet—nearly—one of your race, who would show me how the sun of today shines upon the ancient Temple—but I did not expect so gentle and civilized an apparition and with blue eyes!"[6] Whether he fled the insistent Miss Fuller or really preferred to move back to Europe, Nathan left the country after a four-month affair. Convinced that the affair was ended, Miss Fuller demanded the return of her letters, which Nathan refused to do. His behavior aroused bitterness in Miss Fuller, and she easily slipped into a characteristic generalization about Jews as a whole. To her diary she confided: "I understand more and more of the character of the *tribes*. I shall make a sketch of it and take the whole to account in a literary way, since the affections and ideal hopes are so unproductive."[7] As far as I know, this feeling never did reach literary expression.

But Miss Fuller's intimate acquaintance with a Jew was not typical. Longfellow's interest in his friend Edrehi was because of the talmudic lore of the Jews, not their present condition. The only modern Jew who was important enough to receive attention in the record of Emerson's life and career was Emma Lazarus. In his writing, allusions to modern Jews are few and rely on the conventional stereotype. In 1828 he wrote complainingly from Cambridge to his brother William, who was running a newspaper, that he does not write to him much; he suspects that "you are sunk into the vulgarest man of business who has no correspondence for any but the Jews with whom you have dealings." A few years later (1831) he again wrote William: "Do you not die of the Jews to whom you pay usance?"[8] Pejorative allusions recur in the following years. In a journal entry for July 3, 1839, he writes of a visit to an exhibit of

Washington Allston's paintings. Referring to several paintings of Polish Jews, he comments: "In the Allston Gallery the Polish Jews are an offense to me; they degrade and animalize. As soon as a beard becomes any thing but an accident, we have not a man but a Turk, a Jew, a satyr, a dandy, a goat. So we paint angels."[9] Later, in the essay "Fate," he echoes the conventional view of Jewish power. "A man must thank his defects," he writes, "and stand in some terror of his talents—a transcendent talent draws so largely on his forces as to lame him; a defect pays him revenues on the other side. The sufferance which is the badge of the Jew, has made him, in these days, the ruler of rulers of the earth"[10]—the popular stereotype of Jewish bankers who control the thrones of Europe by their financial power.

Like those of so many of his contemporaries, his personal comments on modern Jews are restricted to observations about Jews abroad. While in Italy in April 1833, he notes in his journal that he "did not go to the baptism of the Jew today. Usually it is a weary farce. 'Tis said they buy the Jews at 150 scudas the head, to be sprinkled." During the next month he records his visit to "Campo Santo passing through the Jews' quarter of whom there are 2800 who are shut up every night as in Rome like dogs." He does not betray any real knowledge of contemporary Jews, however, and his thinking about this people was largely limited to their religious significance in Western history and reflected the usual Christian viewpoint. But his views were riddled with inconsistencies. On one hand, he writes that "the Jewish Law answered its temporary purpose. It was set aside. Christianity is completing its purpose as an aid to educate man." The Jews adhered to an obsolete system of ethics and were superseded. "If ethics were an immovable science," he writes, "the primeval altar of the Jews might serve as a model of our holy place." But modern men, he adds, "are standing on a higher stage. . . . We leave the ritual, the offering and the altar of Moses, we cast off the superstitions that were the swaddling clothes of Christianity."[11]

Many years later, however, he was far from complacent concerning the superiority of Christianity as it was interpreted by the clergy. In a speech given in 1869, he decried the disparagement of wisdom in other faiths:

I find something stingy in the unwilling and disparaging admissions of these foreign opinions—opinions from all parts of the world—by our churchmen, as if only to enhance by their dimness the superior light of Christianity. . . . You cannot bring me too good a word, too dazzling a hope, too penetrating an insight from the Jews. I hail every one with delight, as showing the riches of my brother, my fellow soul, who could thus think and thus greatly feel.[12]

Yet in another lecture in 1853, as Philip L. Nicoloff points out, Emerson asserted that, in Nicoloff's words, "the Jews had flowered in Jesus and ended as a nation."[13] Considering the very lively and often tragic history of the Jewish people since Jesus' time, Emerson was here misled by his own rhetoric. Indeed, in his essay "Fate" he writes, as was obvious enough and more realistic, "we see how much has been expended to extinguish the Jew, in vain."[14] And in his *Journal* during 1867 Emerson calls attention to white Christian responsibility for what he calls the "base" condition of both Negroes and Jews. "You complain," he writes, "that the Negroes are a base class. What makes and keeps the Jew or the Negro base, who but you, who exclude them from the rights which others enjoy?"[15] Note Emerson's concession to popular opinion by his designation "base."

How peripheral the contemporary Jew was in the first century of the Republic is indicated by the absence of any valid consideration of their life in this country by Emerson and other major writers of the time. The Bible was central to American thought, but the *contemporary* descendants of the ancient Hebrews elicited little interest among these writers—until they became a problem after mid-century, when they rose in economic importance.

Although the Bible was of great importance, and sometimes central, to the work of most writers of the nineteenth century, to none was it more determinative of form than to Walt Whitman. He valued the Bible above all other literary works as a comprehensive expression of man's deepest and highest thoughts. While the Bible was "nothing in argument or logic," it was

unsurpassed in proverbs, in religious ecstasy, in suggestions of common mortality and death, man's great equalizers—the spirit everything, the ceremonies and forms of the churches nothing, faith limitless, its immense sensuousness immensely spiritual—an incredible, all-inclusive non-worldliness and dew-scented illiteracy (the antipodes of our Nineteenth Century business absorption and morbid refinement)—no hair-splitting doubts, no sickly sulking and sniffling, no "Hamlet," no "Adonais," no "Thanatopsis," no "In Memoriam."

For Whitman this ancient book exemplified the concept of poetry as an expression of the whole man, in which good and evil, the material and the spiritual, the individual and the "collectivity" were an organic unity. It may seem paradoxical that the poet who exalted self should assert about the greatest poetic expression of man, the Bible, that "nowhere else" does one find "abnegation of self towering in such quaint sublimity."[16]

But the paradox is only apparent, for it was really an affirmation of Whitman's basic belief that his own individuality was continuous with that of all others, that his empathy was so profound that no barriers existed between him and men of all colors, races, and creeds. He would say of himself what he wrote of the Bible: that he was "the finest blending of individuality with the universal." He was "The Answerer," the all-responsive one. He "answers for all." He was a brother to all men of history of whatever station in life or belief. "A Jew to the Jew he seems, a Russ to the Russ, usual and near, removed from none."[17] His conception of democracy extended beyond the narrowly political, for it embraced a brotherly feeling for the total life of all men in a universal sense of fraternity.

But the Bible meant just as much to him in the formal artistic sense, for it provided him with a source not only for form but also for substance, and was always an all-important cue for his poetic form. "Could there be any more appertane suggestion," he writes, "to the current popular writer and reader of verse, what the office of poet was in primeval times—and is yet capable of being, anew, adjusted entirely to the modern?" For the renewal of poetry, as well as the renewal of the spirit, he looked to the simpler, more elemental relationship of being expressed in ancient times, which was most fully exemplified, he thought, in the Hebrew Bible. The "spinal supports of the Bible are simple and meagre, . . . the eternal thread of the Deific purpose and power." The poets of the Hebrew Bible lacked the sophistication of rhyme and meter in the narrow sense; without these devices their statements were more immediate expressions of the relation of man to his own desires and aspirations, to nature, and to duty. Adopting this ancient formal, elemental naiveté, Whitman gave it life for modern man by clothing it with language intimately wedded to everyday life. He thus conceived of his poetry as making accessible to modern man, in form as well as content, an organic unity of sympathy with all men and all times, embodied in the illimitable empathy of the individual Walt: "I am an acme of things accomplish'd, and I [am] an encloser of things to be." To all men, past and present, Whitman's word is: "I am the man, I suffer'd, I was there."[18]

But there is no evidence that Whitman was much interested in the contemporary Jew. In a journalistic piece on Broadway he keeps a standoffish distance from his Jewish fellow New Yorkers. In describing the Broadway scene he writes, among other things, about "dirty-looking German Jews, with a glass box on their shoulders, [who] cry out 'Glass to mend,' with a sharp nasal twang and flat squalling enunciation to which most Yankee brogue is sweet music."[19] Horace Traubel, Whitman's Boswell in the last few years of his life, was Jewish. Though Traubel, an agnostic and socialist, was apparently hardly interested in his Jewish identity, it seems remarkable that in all four volumes of Whitman's memoirs of these final years there is no discussion of the Jew.

In Whitman's creative work there are a few references to contemporary Jews. There is a friendly though brief picture of a Jewish boy in one of his early stories, published in 1845 in the *Democratic Review,* "Revenge and Acquittal: A Tale of a Murderer Escaped." A murder that is committed in a "Jew pawnbroker's shop" on Chatham Street is witnessed by a Jewish youth with a "face of wonderful youthful beauty," who cries, upon seeing the uplifted knife, "Forbear! In Jehovah's name, forbear!" At the trial the murderer sees the face of the "young stranger,—the son of a scorn'd race," and fears he will be betrayed. But the youth, having heard the testimony revealing the wickedness of the murdered man and being struck with compassion for the accused, does not offer to testify. The murderer is acquitted, and Whitman asks: "Shall we applaud or condemn him? Let every reader answer the question for himself."[20] The moral dilemma is not, however, presented with significant insight.

In *Leaves of Grass* a few allusions to the contemporary Jew occur. Amid references to many peoples and lands in "Salut au Monde!" there is a conventional reference to "You Jew journeying in your old age through every risk to stand once on Syrian ground!/You other Jews waiting in all lands for your Messiah!" And in "Birds of Passage" the poet affirms: "I respect Assyria, China, Teutonia, and the Hebrews." But in all his works there is rarely a specific immediate awareness of the Jews of his time. In seventeenth-century America, he writes, "yes, the American Quakers were much persecuted —almost as much by a sort of consent of all other sects, as the Jews were in Europe in the middle ages."[21] The ancient Hebrews were central to his thinking and feeling; but he seemed hardly aware of the existence of the Jews of his own time.

5

HAWTHORNE AND
THE WANDERING JEW

Although Jews figured very little in Hawthorne's experience, they did engage his imagination and in important ways entered into his explorations of the moral dilemmas of man. The legend of the Wandering Jew particularly attracted him as literary material, and this theme of moral death in physical deathlessness runs through his fiction in direct and indirect ways. How the ideas he associated in his fiction with this legendary character are related to his personal feelings toward the Jews is a subtle question.

Hawthorne was no exception among his fellow writers in the scantiness of his immediate experience with Jews, a fact that can be explained in part by the relatively small number of Jews who lived in the United States during his lifetime. There are no references at all to the contemporary Jew in Hawthorne's American notebooks. He did, in 1836, note down "a modern Jewish adage" that reflects the stereotype of the overdressed Jewish woman: "Let a man clothe himself beneath his ability, his children according to his ability, and his wife above his ability."[1] As to his beliefs, he reveals a thoroughly conventional attitude on the issue of Jewish guilt for the death of Jesus in a poem, "The Star of Calvary," published in an annual of 1845:

> Behold, O Israel! behold,
>   It is no human One
> That ye have dared to crucify.
>   What evil hath he done?
> It is your King, O Israel!
>   The God-begotten Son!
>
> A wreath of thorns, a wreath of thorns!
>   Why have you crowned him so?
> That brow is wreathed in agony,
>   'Tis veiled in every woe:

Ye saw not the immortal trace
    Of Deity below.[2]

More frequent allusions to Jews occurred in the European notebooks, and, significantly, nearly all are infused with repugnance,
which even seems justified in some instances. In the Italian notebooks he describes a visit to a Jewish synagogue in Leghorn. "It
looked very like a Christian church," he writes, but the likeness
stopped with the form, for he adds, perhaps accurately, that "it was
dirty, and had an odor not of sanctity." And at the Barberini Palace
in Rome his attention was drawn to Dürer's "Christ Disputing with
the Doctors." He describes the repulsive figure at Christ's left as
"the ugliest, most evil-minded, stubborn, pragmatical, and conten-
tious old Jew that ever lived under the law of Moses."[3] In the same
tenor, in *The Marble Faun* (1860) he evokes the Roman ghetto as
"the foulest and ugliest part of Rome." In the ghetto, he writes,

thousands of Jews are crowded within a narrow compass, and lead
a close, unclean, and multitudinous life, resembling that of maggots
when they over-populate a decaying cheese. . . . There was a confusion of black and hideous houses, piled massively out of the ruins of
former ages; rude and destitute of plan, as a pauper would build his
hovel, and yet displaying here and there an arched gateway, a cor-
nice, a pillar, or a broken arcade, that might have adorned a palace.[4]

One misses any note of compassion in these expressions of disgust
and revulsion. Inferences about his feelings concerning Jews do not
have to be drawn from these passages alone, for others equally
betray a hostile attitude. There is an ironic overtone in *The Marble
Faun* when the author details rumors about Miriam's origin. One
rumor has it, he writes, that Miriam's father was "a great Jewish
banker" and that she left home to escape marriage with a cousin,
"the heir of another of that golden brotherhood."[5]

The fact is that Hawthorne simply did not like Jews. He said as
much quite plainly and unequivocally in a revealing passage in his
English Notebooks. In 1856 he was a guest at a formal dinner given
by the lord mayor of London, David Salomons, who was the first Jew
to be elected to that post. Sitting opposite Hawthorne were the lord
mayor's brother and sister-in-law; his charged description of these
two supplies the key to Hawthorne's opinion of the Jews. Underlying his words are the assumptions of the Rebecca and Shylock-
Iscariot stereotypes. These passages are so revealing that they warrant quotation in full. First, the Jewish woman:

My eyes were mostly drawn to a young lady who sat nearly opposite me, across the table. She was, I suppose, dark, and yet not
dark, but rather seemed to be of pure white marble, yet not white;
but of the purest and finest complexion, (without a shade of color
in it, yet anything but sallow or sickly) that I ever beheld. Her hair
was a wonderful deep, raven black, black as night, black as death;
not raven black, for that has a shiny gloss, and hers had not; but it
was hair never to be painted, nor described—wonderful hair, Jewish hair. Her nose had a beautiful outline, though I could see that
it was Jewish too; and that, and all her features, were so fine that
sculpture seemed a despicable art beside her; and certainly my pen
is good for nothing. If any likeness of her could be given, it must
be by sculpture, not painting. She was slender, and youthful, but
yet had a stately and cold, though soft and womanly grace; and,
looking at her, I saw what were the wives of the old patriarchs, in
their maiden or early married days—what Rachel was, when Jacob
wooed her seven years, and seven more—what Judith was; for,
womanly as she looked, I doubt not she could have slain a man, in
a good cause—what Bathsheba was; only she seemed to have no
sin in her—perhaps what Eve was, though one could hardly think
her weak enough to eat the apple. I should never have thought of
touching her, nor desired to touch her; for, whether owing to distinctness of race, my sense that she was a Jewess, or whatever else,
I felt a sort of repugnance, simultaneously with my perception that
she was an admirable creature.[6]

Note the elements of the female Jewish stereotype: she is beautiful,
idealized, yet essentially untouchable because of the barrier of
"race." Hawthorne's feeling is love-hate, the sexual attraction-
repulsion of a self-regarded superior for a female of an outcast
people. She was the model for Miriam, and we shall see how he
bent this original to his artistic purposes.

Then her husband is described:

But, at the right hand of this miraculous Jewess, there sat the very
Jew of Jews; the distilled essence of all the Jews that have been born
since Jacob's time; he was Judas Iscariot; he was the Wandering Jew;
he was the worst, and at the same time, the truest type of his race,
and contained within himself, I have no doubt, every old prophet
and every old clothesman, that ever the tribes produced; and he
must have been circumcised as much as ten times over. I never
beheld anything so ugly and disagreeable, and preposterous, and
laughable, as the outline of his profile; it was so hideously Jewish,
and so cruel, and so keen; and he had such an immense beard that
you could see no trace of a mouth, until he opened it to speak, or
to eat his dinner,—and then, indeed, you were aware of a cave, in
this density of beard. And yet his manners and aspect, in spite of all,
were those of a man of the world, and a gentleman. Well; it is as hard
to give an idea of this ugly Jew, as of the beautiful Jewess. . . . I
rejoiced exceedingly in this Shylock, this Iscariot; for the sight of

him justified me in the repugnance I have always felt towards his race.[7]

It is hard to credit the intensity of prejudice so explicitly brought to expression. As far as I can ascertain, this passage has been ignored in studies about Hawthorne. Even if the Jewish man *was* repulsive, Hawthorne was not satisfied to stop with the individual, but seized the occasion to attribute to the entire Jewish people the physical and moral ugliness he imputed to the individual. (Jewish women seem to be chivalrously exempt from these characterizations.) He is for Hawthorne the essential Jew, the "Jew of Jews." The "worst" type of Jew is "the truest type of his race." Hawthorne finally "rejoiced" that "this Shylock, this Iscariot . . . justified me in the repugnance I have always felt towards his race."

Hawthorne used no restraint in this shocking characterization of the Jews because these notes were not meant for publication. When he came to fashion the notes of his English sojourn into articles for publication, which he later gathered in *Our Old Home,* he rewrote these passages under the tutelage of his censor. All references to Jews and Jewishness are omitted. The beautiful woman in his rewritten version has for him an unexplained "strange repulsion and unattainableness in the very spell that made her beautiful." The invidious characteristics of her husband are muted, but he is called a "Bluebeard."[8]

In his fiction, Hawthorne's attitude toward the Jews finds expression in his variations on the legend of the Wandering Jew, which has a peculiar suitability for the exploration of his main themes. The legend had extremely wide currency in the nineteenth century. A number of novels based upon it were produced in England and America, but the most widely known was Eugène Sue's *Wandering Jew,* which became an immense best seller on its appearance in English translation in 1845. Perhaps it was in response to press reports of actual encounters with the Wanderer in Europe and New York and to credulous popular interest in the legend that Hawthorne treated the Wandering Jew with levity on one occasion. In "A Select Party" (1844) he gives the Wanderer short shrift as a commonplace. The Wanderer is among the fatuous types in the "Paradise of Fools" assembled in the story, and Hawthorne quickly dismisses him with a whimsical remark:

This personage, however, had latterly grown so common in min-
'ng in all sorts of society and appearing at the beck of every

entertainer, that he could hardly be deemed a proper guest in a very exclusive circle. Besides, being covered with dust from his continual wanderings along the highways of the world, he really looked out of place in a dress party; so that the host felt relieved of an incommodity when the restless individual in question, after a brief stay, took his departure on a ramble towards Oregon.[9]

But this humorous treatment is exceptional. In all other references to the Wandering Jew, Hawthorne is deadly serious.

His interest in the legend was probably aroused by his reading William Godwin's *St. Leon* when he was sixteen, an interest that persisted until the end of his life. His irresistible tendency to symbolize and allegorize found a ready vehicle in the legend, and it became a recurrent theme in his work. Hawthorne's concern with the Wanderer and the idea of eternal earthly life first appears in "A Virtuoso's Collection" (1842). In a museum the guide shows the story's narrator various artifacts and the likenesses of objects and people of past eras, of mythology, literature, and history; the guide speaks of them with intimate, seemingly firsthand knowledge. At the tour's end the visitor wonderingly asks the guide who he is. "My name," replies the guide, "has not been without its distinction in the world for a longer period than that of any other man alive. . . . Yet many doubt of my existence; perhaps you will do so tomorrow. This dart which I hold in my hand was once grim Death's own weapon. It served him well for the space of four thousand years; but it fell blunted, as you see, when he directed it against my breast." The truth dawns on the visitor: "You are the Wandering Jew!"[10]

The guide offers the narrator an elixir of life but the narrator declines, for to him death is a friend who, "in his due season, even the happiest mortal should be willing to embrace." In too long a life, he adds, "the spark of ethereal fire would be choked out by the material, the sensual." The offered elixir "would produce death while bestowing the shadow of life." But to the Wandering Jew "life —earthly life—is the only good." The narrator tries to persuade the Wanderer that the spirit becomes extinct if life continues indefinitely. But the deathless one is adamant: he only wants "what I can see, and touch, and understand, and I ask no more." He is a rationalistic materialist, the antagonist of the spirituality prized by Hawthorne. The narrator concludes that the Wanderer's "soul is dead within him."[11]

The Wandering Jew is once again the symbol for death of the soul in "Ethan Brand" (1850). In this instance he helps effect Ethan Brand's submission to the unpardonable sin: pride of intellect unsoftened by human warmth. Ethan Brand has undergone a "vast intellectual development" and acquires an overweening intellectualism, until at last he realizes that he has thereby committed the unpardonable sin. It is, he now knows, "the sin of an intellect that triumphed over the sense of brotherhood with man and reverence for God, and sacrificed everything to its own claims! The only sin that deserves a recompense of immortal agony!"[12]

The Faustian Ethan Brand must have his Mephistopheles, and here Hawthorne introduces the Wandering Jew as the satanic agent. Although the "old German Jew travelling with a diorama on his back" is not specifically designated as the Wandering Jew, he clearly functions as such. The pictures of scenes and events out of the past seen through the diorama, together with the old Jew's commentaries, suggest one of the conventional marks of the Wandering Jew: his role as universal witness of the past. As he expounds the meanings of the pictures, his hand is seen through the diorama as a "gigantic, brown, hairy hand,—which might have been mistaken for the Hand of Destiny." Ethan Brand looks into the diorama and withdraws in shock at what he sees there: "I remember you now," Ethan Brand mutters. The Jew answers "with a dark smile, . . . 'I find it to be heavy matter in my show-box,—this Unpardonable Sin.' "[13] It is apparent that the Mephistophelean Jew has directed Ethan Brand toward that deforming pride of intellect that has pushed out "the heart," the human fellow feeling, at the price of his soul. As in "The Virtuoso's Collection," the Wandering Jew is the symbol of —indeed the agency for—freezing the warm human heart, deadening the soul.

The legend is again involved in Hawthorne's inquiry into the fall from innocence and the educative nature of sin in *The Marble Faun* (1860). It is in this work that Hawthorne introduces his sole depiction of a Jewish woman in the character of Miriam. She is an artist, the daughter of a Jewish Englishwoman and an Italian nobleman. Miriam is the reincarnation in art of the beautiful Jewish woman who had made such a deep impression on Hawthorne at the lord mayor's dinner a few years before. He draws on the description in his notebook to depict her in the novel. Hawthorne describes the self-portrait Miriam has painted: she "had black, abundant hair, with none of the vulgar glossiness of other women's sable locks; if she were really of Jewish blood, then this was Jewish hair, and a dark glory such as crowns no Christian maiden's head. Gazing at this portrait, you saw what Rachel might have been, when Jacob deemed her worth the wooing seven years, and seven more." Miriam is not Jewish in her beliefs, however; on the contrary, one must assume that she is a Christian. For when her friends question her about her "infidel" tormentor, she replies—even though it is an evasion—that she hopes "to achieve the glory and satisfaction of converting him to the Christian faith."[14] Her sense of Jewish identification is limited to her maternal connection, when she entrusts the packet of family papers to the genteel Hilda for delivery to a relative in the Roman ghetto.

Why did Hawthorne portray Miriam as being only half Jewish? It was because he wished to lend an aura of mystery, which, in the literary imagination of the time, inhered in that "something in Miriam's blood, in her mixed race" which helps to raise the happenings of the tale above ordinary life. The Jew was felt to be somehow alien and apart from the prevailing culture, and this strangeness could be used as a literary device for mystification. The exotic flavor was deepened by the mixture of the familiar Christian strain with the Jewish. The fictional character whose origin was mixed was thus invested with ambiguous moral qualities in light of the deep-seated Christian feeling of the Jews' perverseness in rejecting Jesus. As one gazed at Miriam's self-portrait, Hawthorne writes, one could suppose that "she might ripen to be what Judith was, when she vanquished Holofernes with her beauty, and slew him for too much adoring of it."[15] Hawthorne also associates Miriam with Jael, who slew Sisera; Herodias, who was instrumental in causing John the Baptist's death; and Beatrice Cenci, who was implicated in the murder of her evil father. The Jewish strain in Miriam thus enhances the moral complexity of this version of the problem of sin.

Early in the novel Hawthorne hints at the moral problem that haunts Miriam. When she was young her father had contracted a betrothal for her with an Italian marchese. But Miriam has adamantly refused to go through with the marriage, a decision that Hawthorne attributes to her "mixed race . . . which had given her a freedom of thought and force of will."[16] Her decision has been fortified by the fact that her intended husband is a thoroughly evil man. At the same time, she is suspected of complicity in some unnatural crime, the precise character of which is never stated and of which she is actually innocent. She is tormented by the suspicions about her connection with the crime, as her self-portraits in her paintings of Judith and Jael attest. She leaves her family and lives in Rome under an assumed name. There she actually is an accessory to a murder committed by her lover, the innocent, faunlike Donatello, who receives her unspoken assent to the murder at a critical moment. The moral problem is similar to that of Beatrice Cenci, the subject of a much-admired portrait by Guido Reni.

Donatello's victim is Miriam's rejected suitor, the marchese, who is invested with features of the Wandering Jew. When Miriam strays from a party of friends on a tour of the catacombs, she encounters the marchese, who is variously described as an "apparition," "the Spectre of the Catacomb," "a nameless vagrant," "a demon." In his physical appearance there is a suggested resemblance to the brother of the lord mayor, described with such venom in Hawthorne's notebook: the marchese has a "dusky wilderness of mustache and beard." Kenyon, a sculptor friend of Miriam's, asks the stranger: "And how long have you been wandering here," whereupon the guide of the party mutters: "A thousand and five hundred years! . . . It is the old pagan phantom that I told you of, who sought to betray the blessed saints!" Here, then, is a variant of the Wandering Jew's archetypal offense against Jesus on the way to the cross, now changed to betrayal of saints. Hawthorne connects the marchese with the legend of Memmius, which belongs to the Wandering Jew family of legends. Memmius had spied on the Christians hiding in the catacombs and had rejected an opportunity to accept the cross and "the holy light of the soul." For this he was condemned to wander forever in the catacombs. When he was able to induce someone to guide him into the daylight, he would perpetrate some evil and then return to the catacombs. Manifesting another trait of the Wandering Jew—his knowledge of things long past—the "specter" offers to teach Miriam "a long lost, but invaluable secret of old Roman fresco-painting."[17]

Hawthorne uses the legend flexibly; for the character of Miriam's persecutor, who is taken out of the catacombs by her and thereafter dogs her footsteps, has some (though not all) of the traits of the Wandering Jew. He is related to the two crimes that place Miriam in an ambiguous moral position. While she is altogether innocent of the earlier crime, her life is shadowed by it. But her moral responsibility for the second, a subtler matter, forms the core of the predicament of the novel. Miriam and Donatello, whose identity combines aspects of the natural and supernatural (does he really have tufts on his ears?), are in love but are harassed by the marchese. They meet the spectral one at the edge of the Tarpeian Rock. The enraged Donatello grapples with the "demon," and interpreting the look in Miriam's eyes as assent—"a look of hatred, triumph, vengeance, and, as it were, joy at some unhoped-for relief"[18]—he hurls the marchese over the precipice to his death. The moral problem of guilt, earlier broached in the cases of Judith, Jael, Herodias, and Beatrice Cenci, is now confronted squarely by Miriam and Donatello.

The ethical function of sin in the universe, which has occupied theologians from time immemorial, is at the heart of Hawthorne's work. Miriam and Donatello are mired in the problem. By his act Donatello is transformed from the simple, gay, lighthearted creature, innocent of the "blackness" of the world, into an ethically mature man. He is now preoccupied with weighty moral problems:

The germs of faculties that have heretofore slept are fast springing into activity. The world of thought is disclosing itself to his inward sight. . . . Is sin, then,—which we deem such a dreadful blackness in the universe,—is it, like sorrow, merely an element of human education, through which we struggle to a higher and purer state than we could otherwise have attained? Did Adam fall, that we might ultimately rise to a far loftier paradise than his?[19]

Hawthorne here conjectures that sin—"blackness"—was deliberately placed in the universe as a means for man to rise to a higher moral plane than he would achieve if total innocence were to prevail. Confrontation with sin is for him a condition for wisdom, understanding, and a profoundly serious life aligned with the moral character of the universe. He does not argue that universal moral governance exists: to him this is an indisputable premise, indeed, an axiom. It follows that sin itself must therefore have a moral purpose, and this he sees in its educative and thereby elevating function. He thus drew upon the symbolical potentialities of the legend of the Wandering Jew to grapple with the problem in this story, and again the Wanderer is associated with the evil forces of the world.

In the last years of his life, which were marked by waning creativity, Hawthorne was preoccupied with giving imaginative shape to his thoughts about endless life. Perhaps the sense that his own end was approaching explains his absorption with the subject. In his last work, *The Dolliver Romance*, which he left incomplete, there is ambivalence in his approach to the question. The good Dr. Dolliver has discovered the elixir of life, and by taking the potion in very small doses he gradually reverses the process of aging. (His motive for tampering with nature is his concern for the welfare of his orphaned granddaughter, Pansie, who would be left destitute if he, her sole surviving relative, dies.) But when the arrogant Colonel Dabney takes a deep draft of the potion, he dies. How Hawthorne would have resolved this ambiguity we can only guess.

Hawthorne's arguments against the wisdom of endless life predominate in his work, and he dramatizes this view in his penultimate novel, *Septimius Felton*, which was also left unfinished, although it is more elaborated than *Dolliver*. In 1860 Hawthorne had returned from Italy and was living at "The Wayside," an old Concord house. Thoreau had once told him that an earlier occupant of the house had believed that he would live forever. Hawthorne joined this tale of the earlier resident with his own lifelong interest in the idea of eternal life, and in 1861 began to write *Septimius Felton* on this theme. As a young man at the outbreak of the American Revolution, Septimius is determined not to die, for he believes that "death was an alien misfortune, a prodigy, a monstrosity, into which man had only fallen by defect." He throws all his energies into finding the elixir of life. Like Miriam, he is of "mixed" origin, this time part Indian and part Anglo-Saxon. As in *The Marble Faun,* Hawthorne uses a mixed origin to mystify his tale and to account for extraordinary events. "There was something in Septimius," he writes, "in his wild, mixed nature, the monstrousness that had grown out of his hybrid race, the black infusions, too, which melancholic man had left there, the devilishness that had been symbolized in the popular regard about his family." Not only does Septimius have "ministerial blood," but also "the wild streams that the Indian priest [his ancestor] had contributed."[20] Here, Hawthorne uses popular suspicion of the Indian, as he uses popular feelings about the Jew in *The Marble Faun*.

Septimius proceeds in his search through a contrived network of coincidental occurrences. Like Ethan Brand, as he believes himself to be approaching his goal, "a stoniness . . . was gathering about his heart." At long last he believes he has found the missing ingredient for the potion and is now ecstatically ready to embark on eternal life. He persuades Sybil Dacey, the English girl who is mysteriously involved in his search, to share his deathlessness. When they are about to drink the potion, Septimius tells Sybil of his plans for centuries of life. At this point Hawthorne builds upon a suggestion of a story about the Wandering Jew that he had jotted down in 1845: "A disquisition, or a discussion between two or more persons, on the manner in which the Wandering Jew has spent his life;—one period, perhaps, in wild carnal debauchery; then trying over and over again to grasp domestic happiness; then [as] a soldier; then a statesman, etc.; at last realizing some truth."[21] Septimius proposes that they divide their lives into projects lasting one century each. For one century they will indulge in a life of evil in which they will experience everything possible to man, so that, having experienced everything, they will understand all; for another century they will delve into all philosophical systems and emerge with an ultimate system; for another century they will help society erect an ideal government;

for another, Septimius will become a religious prophet greater than Mohammed and make mankind holy and happy. But Sybil knows that the missing ingredient he believes he has found at last is really a poison. She loves him, and to convince him of the evil and futility of seeking endless life she drinks some of the potion, destroys the remaining liquid, and dies. Septimius abandons his quest.

We can now see how Hawthorne's private feelings of prejudice against the Jews received subtle expression in his fiction, in his treatment of Miriam, and in the place that the Wandering Jew held in his symbolic explorations into the nature of sin. He seized upon the beautiful Jewish woman at the lord mayor's dinner, a woman of a people alien to him, who obviously attracted him sexually and raised contradictory feelings of both attraction and repulsion, to create the morally complex Miriam. However, no sympathetic traits are emotionally necessary for the male of the Jewish species. The legend of the Wandering Jew is the product of centuries of hostility toward Jews, and it is this aspect of the legend that Hawthorne adopts, for the most part. It is true that in *Septimius Felton* both aspects appear: the desire for immortality is morally negative to Hawthorne because he does not believe it will result in an ethically superior life; on the other hand, Septimius's intentions to help mankind, illusory as they may be, expose a positive aspect of the legend. But in "The Virtuoso's Collection" the Wandering Jew is the spokesman for "materialism" and the death of the soul. In "Ethan Brand" the Wandering Jew is subtly identified with the devil, and in *The Marble Faun,* Miriam's spectral tormentor is a malicious and evil character, the personification of evil influence. Even though he is not Jewish, this character is linked to the blasphemous Wandering Jew who, Hawthorne barely suggests, resembles the lord mayor's brother (the epitome of Jewish odiousness for Hawthorne, as we have seen). There is nothing essential in Hawthorne's adaptations of the legend of the Wandering Jew to suggest any mitigation of this figure's association with the evil forces of the world: he is the protagonist of a life without soul or human warmth.

Hawthorne was both too civilized and too prudent to give public expression to the "repugnance" he felt toward Jews. But the literary convention of the Wandering Jew that was at hand peculiarly fitted in with his ethical speculations. For the most part, he has this legendary figure function in a morally negative manner. Was this negativity an expression of his actual feeling toward Jews? Though perhaps unconscious and unintended, the conjunction of his prejudice with his use of the Wanderer as a morally negative figure is an objective fact.

6

MELVILLE: THE TWO PHASES

An outstanding exception to the stereotyped representation of the Jewish character occurs in Melville's book-length poem *Clarel,* published in 1876. In symbolic significance, in variety, in awareness of Jewish matters, and in humanistic depiction this work is without parallel in all of American literature before our century.

The record of Melville's life before writing *Clarel* shows little interest in or acquaintance with contemporary Jews. The case is quite otherwise with respect to the biblical Jew, as any attentive reader of his fiction is aware. Nathalia Wright has documented the view that the Bible and Shakespeare were the two major influences on Melville's writing. He was repelled, she says, by modern textual criticism and was drawn to the Bible's "mythology, or its allegorical representation of metaphysical truth."[1] But that is a long story, and here we are concerned primarily with the image of the contemporary Jew in his writing.

The evidence shows that Melville had little contact with Jews. He may have been aware of them during his visits to and residence in New York City. They were growing numerous: from about ten thousand in 1842 to about sixteen thousand in 1850; and by 1860 they numbered about forty thousand. The Chatham Street episode in *Redburn* (1849) suggests personal observation.

During Melville's 1840 trip to Galena, Illinois, to visit his Uncle Thomas, he had occasion, Leon Howard reports, to take "casual notice of Jewish settlers who first came to Chicago in the summer of 1840."[2] A decade later, while visiting the National Gallery in London, for the second time he "spent an hour looking at Rembrandt's Jew," as he notes in his journal of that trip.[3] If the conjecture is correct that David Davidson, London agent for the publisher Wiley, was Jewish, Melville's brief but cordial relations with him both in London and New York would appear to be the closest he ever got to knowing a Jew. The record shows one late contact with a Jew, in 1876, when Melville called on Moses Polock, the noted Philadelphia bookseller and uncle of A. S. W. Rosenbach, perhaps concerning possible publication of *Clarel*.[4] And that is all, except for the journey to the Levant and Palestine that formed the basis for *Clarel*.

In his creative work Melville's attitude toward the Jews emerges in two phases. The first is the treatment in his fiction, all of which (except "Billy Budd") was completed by 1856. In this phase Melville's attitude was ambivalent: Jews are alluded to in some passages in stereotyped terms, in others with compassion for past suffering. The second phase emerges in *Clarel*, in which Jews are depicted with humanity and understanding.

In all of Melville's fiction only one novel, *Redburn*, contains Jewish characters: several pawnbrokers. Considering his scant contact with Jews this should not surprise us. For he wrote out of deeply felt experience, and in this instance the experience was lacking. It is plausible that the chapter in *Redburn* devoted to the fledgling sailor's encounter with pawnbrokers on Chatham Street, then lined with secondhand stores and pawnshops, reflects the young Melville's own attempt to pawn something on the eve of his departure as a sailor on his first voyage. Redburn goes to Chatham Street to sell his fowling piece before leaving. He is accosted by a pawnbroker, "a curly-headed little man with a dark, oily face, and a hooked nose, like the pictures of Judas Iscariot," in front of a "strange-looking shop, with three gilded balls hanging over it." The man is obsequious and speaks with "a peculiar accent, as if he had been over-eating himself with Indian pudding or some other plushy compound." The broker offers Redburn three dollars for the piece. Thinking that too little, Redburn goes to another "hook-nosed man," who offers him only a dollar. He returns to the first broker, who then offers him two dollars and a half, which Redburn reluctantly accepts.[5]

The physical traits and speech of the pawnbrokers are vividly and naturalistically described. But the association of the brokers with "the pictures of Judas Iscariot" is a perhaps unconscious reversion to the medieval fantasy of the Jew. Later in the novel another allusion also recalls a medieval survival, the "evil eye" of the Jew. Describing the "agents" soliciting on the Liverpool docks, Melville characterizes one type thus: "They nudge you with an elbow full of indefinite hints and intimations; they glitter upon you an eye like a Jew's or a pawnbroker's; they dog you like Italian assassins."[6]

All his other fiction, except the first and last, *Typee* and "Billy Budd," contain at least a passing reference to the Jews. With compassion and the light touch that distance allows, Melville occasionally alludes to the history of Jewish suffering to underscore the tribulations of shipmates. In *Omoo* he recounts the harassment to which veteran sailors subject the novice: "No sooner is his cleanliness questioned than they rise upon him like a mob of the Middle Ages upon a Jew; drag him into the lee-scuppers, and strip him to the buff."[7] In *Redburn* the vexation visited upon the forlorn singer Harry recalls to Melville the Hebrew captives of the Babylonians, who refused to sing for their captors. Harry, "too, many a night, was called upon to sing for those who through the day had insulted and derided him"; still he refused to sing.[8]

In *White Jacket* Melville comments on the several parts of the ship from which ordinary seamen are rigidly excluded: "I was as a Roman Jew of the Middle Ages, confined to the Jews' quarter of the town, and forbidden to stray beyond my limits." In the same book Melville pays the highest tribute to the ancient Hebrews in his fervent apostrophe to the United States: "And we Americans are the peculiar, chosen people—the Israel of our time; we bear the ark of the liberties of the world. . . . Long enough have we . . . doubted whether, indeed, the political Messiah had come. But he has come in *us.*"[9] Finally, a satirical allusion to medieval attitudes toward the Jew is made in *Moby Dick:* "The truth is, that living or dead, if but decently treated, whales as a species are by no means creatures of ill odor; nor can whale-men be recognized, as the people of the Middle Ages affected to detect a Jew in the company, by the nose."[10]

At the same time, pejorative stereotyped references crop up in the fiction. In *The Confidence Man* the Missourian satirically rails at the man from the "Philosophical Intelligence Office," for his scientific approach to the study of man: "I am of opinion you should be served like a Jew in the Middle Ages with his gold; this knowledge of yours, which you haven't enough knowledge to know how to make a right use of, it should be taken from you."[11] Epithets appear in other novels, such as, "tell that to the marines, say the illiterate Jews and the jewelers";[12] or, "some Jew clothesman, with a tea-canister on his head."[13]

The most striking evidence of the negative side of Melville's thought, however, is the unfriendly allusions embedded in passages exalting freedom from national prejudice. In *Redburn* Melville pays eloquent tribute to the United States as an international amalgam of immigrants. "There is something in the contemplation of the mode in which America has been settled," he writes, "that, in the noble breast, should forever extinguish the prejudices of national dislikes.

. . . You can not spill a drop of American blood without spilling the blood of the whole world." Then to reinforce his point he adds: "We are not a narrow tribe of men, with a bigoted Hebrew national-ity—whose blood had been debased in the attempt to ennoble it, by maintaining an exclusive succession among ourselves."[14] Melville here shows no awareness that separation and exclusiveness were forced upon the Jew by ghettoization, or that the Christian world was no less separatistic in relation to the Jews than the reverse. Nor does the passage betray any sensitivity to the fact that, in the land where Jews were freer than anywhere else in the world at the time, they were less separatistic and participated more fully in the national life than elsewhere. Melville's reference to the "bigoted Hebrew na-tionality" reveals that he accepts here without thought the deep-seated, prejudiced conception of the Jew.

A similar passage appears in *The Confidence Man*—paradoxically, in the chapter excoriating "Indian-hating":

It is terrible that one creature should so regard another, should make it conscience to abhor an entire race. It is terrible; but is it surprising? Surprising, that one should hate a race which he believes to be red from a cause akin to that which makes some tribes of garden insect green? A race whose name is . . . painted to him in every evil light; . . . now an assassin like a New York rowdy; . . . now a judicial murderer; . . . or a Jew with hospitable speeches cozening some fainting stranger into ambuscade, there to burk him, and account it a deed grateful to Manitou, his God.[15]

It would be a mistake to conclude from Melville's invidious refer-ences to Jews that he was a true anti-Semite. What is indicated is rather that his attitude was conventionally anti-Semitic.

Melville's relation to the Jews as artist and man is radically differ-ent in *Clarel* from what it is in his other works. The poem is based on a trip that Melville took to Palestine and the Levant from October 1856 to May 1857. The locus of the poem is Palestine, the theme is the quest for religious belief; one focus of the artist is therefore necessarily on the Jews, ancient and modern. Melville's observations of Jews encountered on his trip, pithily recorded in his journal, give evidence of this interest, which is echoed in *Clarel*. For years after his return he immersed himself in books on Palestine and the Jews. That his interest included modern as well as ancient Jews is indicated by his marginal markings in the Bohn edition of Heine's *Complete Poems* that he purchased in 1862 (now in the collection of the New York Public Library). In the introductory memoir on Heine by the translator, Edgar Alfred Bowring, Melville marked the following: "The Jewish descent and Jewish sympathies of the poet are plainly discernible in ["The Hebrew Melodies"], the most interesting of which, and probably the best of the whole collection contained in the 'Romancero,' is that which sets forth the life of Jehuda ben Halevy, the great Hebrew poet of the middle ages. Some critics rank this poem amongst Heine's very best productions."[16] The only passages that Melville marked in "The Hebrew Melodies" were in the ballad "Disputations," a characteristically irreverent tale of a thirteenth-century debate between a Capuchin monk and a rabbi on the merits of Christianity and Judaism. Melville marked two verses, each presenting the position of one side in satirically expressed opposition, indicating Melville's interest in Judaism in connection with the religious problems with which he was grappling.

So informed on Jewish matters is *Clarel* that Edward Sanford, Melville's cousin, wrote to a mutual cousin, Catherine Lansing: "How did friend Melville know so much about the Jews?"[17]

Melville's spiritual mood fused well with the religious, ethical, and social problems precipitated by a visit to the seeding ground of Western religions. The key to the meaning of *Clarel* can be found in the well-known conversation between Melville and Hawthorne at Southport, near Liverpool, on November 12, 1856, when Melville was en route to the Levant. Melville, writes Hawthorne in his notebook, "began to reason of Providence and futurity, and of everything else that lies beyond human ken. . . . He can neither believe, nor be comfortable in his unbelief; and he is too honest and courageous not to do one or the other."[18] *Clarel* is essentially an extended debate within Melville himself in which religious, ethical, social, and intellectual creeds of the day are examined with a view to arriving at a position that might make life tolerable both metaphysically and socially. Melville's being is absorbed in his effort to "Slip quite behind the parrot-lore/Conventional."

The religious and philosophical doubts that assailed Melville in the antebellum decades were not dispelled by the political and religious turmoil of the postbellum period. Popular indifference to his later fiction must have contributed to his dour view of the world. The travail of the postwar years, the political and social degeneration and corruption, and the failure of Reconstruction, as well as the country's frantic economic expansion, only reinforced his scepticism. A suitable atmosphere for his mood was provided by the deteriorated religious and social state of Palestine, and this mood pervades the poem. The argument sways back and forth for thousands of lines, and the poem contains probing insights, social and spiritual. Despite the remaining uncertainties, at the end Melville holds out for some vague, undefined hope:

> Then keep thy heart, though yet but ill-resigned— . . .
> That like a swimmer rising from the deep— . . .
> Emerge thou mayst the last whelming sea,
> And prove that death but routs life into victory.[19]

Millenarianism figures importantly in the poem because this belief in an imminent Second Coming was rife in the middle third of the century. The way for Christ's reappearance on earth was to be prepared by the return of the Jews to Palestine, and then earth would be turned into heaven. Melville voices the millenarian belief:

> That gate would open, yea, and Christ
> Thence issue, come into His own,
> And earth be re-imparadised. . . .
> Zion restore, convert the Jew,
> Reseat him here, and the waste bedew;
> Then Christ returneth.[20]

Melville had encountered in Palestine some of the American millenarian missionaries who had come to help prepare the way, by converting the Jews, and to witness the Second Coming. He observed the wretched conditions under which the Jews were living: "In the emptiness of the lifeless antiquity of Jerusalem the emigrant Jews are like flies who have taken up their abode in a skull," he notes in his *Journal*.[21] In *Clarel* he remarks on the help given the Jews of Palestine by the Jews of the outside world:

> In almost every country known
> Rich Israelites these kinsmen own:
> The hat goes round the world.[22]

He relates in the *Journal* how missionaries like Mr. and Mrs. Saunders and Mrs. Minot (Minor) had tried to set up agricultural schools for the Jews, partly to help prepare the land and partly as an indirect means to lure the Jews into conversion. But the effort was a pathetic failure. Melville was told by Mrs. Minor that after three or four years of effort, "not a single Jew was converted to either Christianity or Agriculture." Mrs. Saunders told him that Jews would pretend interest, receive clothing, and then disappear. Melville condemns these efforts as "this preposterous Jew mania . . . half melancholy and half farcical—like all the rest of the world."[23]

Toward Judaism itself Melville felt repugnance. In this respect he followed the Enlightenment tradition of scorning Old Testament religion. Though he personally disagreed with many of the ideas expressed by characters in *Clarel,* like those of the millenarian Nehemiah and the Anglican conformist priest Derwent, there is no reason to suppose that he would dissent from their critical allusions to "poor misled Jews" or "the Jews' crab-apple creed."[24] His feelings toward Judaism are explicitly expressed by his meditations on the pyramids in the *Journal.* They "oppressed" him with their awful, mysterious, inhuman magnitude. They were to him "something vast, undefiled, incomprehensible, and awful." And he speculates that Moses "conceived his idea of Jehovah" from the pyramids. Just as the "wise men" of Egypt could create out of the crude, unformed masses of earth a "transcendent," overpowering work of art in the pyramids, so Moses was inspired to organize "insignificant thoughts that are in all men" into "the transcendent conception of a God." The terror and giddiness he experienced at the top of the pyramids reminded him of Judaism. He felt a similar revulsion against the "extraordinary physical aspect" of Jerusalem. And the "diabolical landscapes [in a] great part of Judea must have suggested to the Jewish prophets their ghastly theology."[25] He clearly felt an antipathy for the "ghastly theology," to which his observations in Palestine gave imaginative support.[26]

The compassion and insight of the artist are brought to bear on the portrayal of the characters in *Clarel.* Melville is sensitive to the persecution and hardships of the Jews in Palestine, which he observed in the passing crowd at the Jaffa gate. Clarel, a theological student on a pilgrimage, notes the Jew-hating of his fellow travelers: "Nazarene Hebrews twain rode next,/By one of the escort slyly vexed." In rejecting the ritual murder slander, he gives it a pregnant social turn. Ungar, the radical, disillusioned Confederate veteran, is speaking:

> Old ballads sing
> Fair Christian children crucified
> By impious Jews: you've heard the thing:
> Yes, fable; but there's truth hard by:
> How many Hughs of Lincoln, say,
> Does Mammon in his mills, today,
> Crook, if he do not crucify?[27]

Of some thirty-odd characters of consequence in the poem, six are Jewish. None are as important to the poem as Clarel, the inquiring young theological student; Rolfe, who partially represents Melville himself; and Vine, a portrait of Hawthorne. The Jews described, however, cover a wide range of types: the American Jewish family of Nathan, Agar, and Ruth; Abdon, the black Jew from Cochin, India; the Lyonese, a young French salesman; and Margoth, the geologist. These characters vary in structural and thematic importance, but each symbolizes some human aspect that reflects a different facet in Melville's argument with himself. Unlike the allusions to Jews in his novels, they are not clichéd.[28] All of them—except Margoth—are treated in an appropriately human manner. Together they represent the most substantial treatment of the Jew in American literature before the 1890s.

The Jewish character most closely linked to the main theme of religious doubt is Margoth, an atheistic scientist. Melville participates in the current science-versus-religion controversy through the character of Margoth. New developments in geology had thrown doubt on the Genesis story of the origin, and therefore the age, of the earth; Darwin's *Origin of Species* (1859) had challenged the entire system of ideas about the origin and nature of man. Melville, riven with religious doubts, could get no help from science since he believed that the answers lay beyond science, and his treatment of Margoth shows that he was repelled by science. He has Margoth argue the case for science in a boorish, crude manner, and he makes Margoth personally unpleasant and insensitive. The very name Margoth is indicative of this contempt: the spoiling barbarian. At their first encounter, he shocks Clarel with his "gibe" at the desolate appearance of Jerusalem: "What city's this? town beautiful/Of David?"[29] His arrogance in advancing his scientific views repels the pilgrims. To him, Palestine is just another field of geologic investigation, and he mocks at all religious traditions and stories about the land in a personally offensive way. Melville argues his case ad hominem.

Melville admits that from science "much that's useful, grant, is won," but immediately adds, "but more's claimed." The portrait of Margoth emerges from a personal distrust of science, however, rather than a judicious weighing of arguments. Margoth is called "a kangaroo of science."

An especial butt of Margoth's is the saintly, simple-minded tract-dispenser Nehemiah. When Nehemiah calls himself the "chief of sinners," Margoth splenetically comments: "How I do loathe such lowliness." As the pilgrims bow their heads at the burial of Nehemiah, Margoth bends his head with "sulking reverence."[30] In the course of the last discussion before Margoth leaves the pilgrims, his words are echoed by the braying of an ass.

To add to the denigration of Margoth, Melville also depicts him as a philistine. We first make his acquaintance at the dung gate of Jerusalem, when he says:

> 'Tis heavy prices here must rule;
> Choice house-lot now, what were it worth?
> How goes the market?

Again, during a discussion about the sad state of Jerusalem, he remarks:

> Stale is she!
> Lay flat the walls, let in the air,
> That folks no more may sicken there!
> Wake up the dead; and let there be
> Rails, wires, from Olivet to the sea,
> With station in Gethsemane.[31]

Margoth proposes modernization that would mock the character and significance of the historic places.

In a poem that treats most of its characters with deep respect, the hostile rendering of Margoth stands out. Melville's antipathy for Margoth is not the result of anti-Semitism, as is quite clear from his explicit disclaimer; Christianity, he says, must acknowledge its debt to the Jews for its founder, and Melville has no intention of subscribing to Jew-baiting:

> For why disown the debt
> When vouchers be? Yet, yet and yet
> Our saving salt of grace is due
> All to the East—nor least the Jew.
> Perverse, if stigma then survive,
> Elsewhere let such in satire thrive—
> Not here. Quite other end is won
> In picturing Margoth, fallen son
> Of Judah.[32]

Margoth, as an apostate from Judaism—"fallen son of Judah"—on the very ground where Judaism and Christianity originated, is for Melville an effective countersymbol to Palestine as the symbol of spirituality. He is the Jewish foil to the problem of religion in the land of the Jews.

The pilgrims are arrested by the thought that Margoth is a Jew. Melville devotes an entire canto, entitled "Concerning Hebrews," to the pilgrims' discussion of religious dissent among the Jews, triggered by the knowledge of Margoth's apostasy. The canto opens with Vine's musing remark: "One can't forbear/Thinking that Margoth is—a *Jew*." At first the Anglican priest, Derwent, answers that it is strange to find this "geologic Jew" in the land of Judah so different from the traditional notion of the Jew. On second thought, he adds that history has known dissenting Jews. The group discusses other Jews to show how great a variety there is historically in this respect. Margoth's apostasy is not so queer after all. Derwent points to the sharp contrast between the "Houndsditch clothesman" and ancient seers like Aaron and Moses. Then, there are the

> Jew banker, merchant, statesman—these,
> With artist, actress known to fame,
> All strenuous in each Gentile aim.

Rolfe (Melville) disputes the "Gentile" characterization. Jews transplanted from their land of origin, he replies, change and adapt themselves to the new land; however, even these Jews may cling to their ancient religion. But there are also those, says Derwent, who would undermine Judaism, such as Uriel Acosta, and those who tried to shore up their faith with eclectic borrowings from Platonism. There have been others, too, who were never converted to Christianity in spite of doubts, like Moses Mendelssohn; and still others, like Neander, historian of Christianity, who abandoned Judaism. Yet, answers Rolfe, men like these retained their integrity, "The selfhood keep they pure and sweet." But not so Margoth, who is contrasted with Spinoza: both are dissenters from Judaism, yet are poles apart, "the blind man and the visionary."[33] Which of these Jews, each an admirable human being of integrity, holds the true view? No one can answer satisfactorily. The canto ends with the question unanswered. Clarel—and Melville—are left with their doubts.

The five other Jews in *Clarel* are treated with understanding and respect.

Nathan, the father of the Jewish family, is originally a Christian of New England Puritan stock who moves with his father and mother to Illinois—a region that Melville knew from his visit to his Uncle Thomas in 1840. Although Nathan outwardly conforms to the Protestant religion for his mother's sake, doubts have crept into his mind. He comes upon Paine's *Common Sense* and turns to deism. After his mother's death he moves to a lake port and falls in love with a Jewish girl, Agar, who converts him to Judaism and marries him. His conversion has awakened the Puritan strain in him—"a strain/ How evident, of Hebrew source"—and he is fired with zealotry. He sells his farm and takes his wife and two children to Palestine, "With seed and tillage help renew—/Help reinstate the Holy Land."[34] He buys a farm on the Plain of Sharon; although harassment and mortal danger from the Arabs force him to remove his family within the city walls, he himself stubbornly remains outside on the farm despite the tearful pleas of his wife. Melville notes in the *Journal* that "Jews dare not live outside the walled towns or villages for fear of malicious persecution of the Arabs and Turks."[35]

Nathan is modeled on Warder Cresson, whom, Melville notes in the *Journal,* he had met in Palestine: "An American turned Jew— divorced from (former) wife—married a Jewess, etc.—Sad."[36] Cresson was a Quaker and prosperous farmer who had become successively a Shaker, a Mormon, and a Millerite. In 1844 he went to Jerusalem in order to convert Jews and Muslims to Christianity. Gradually, however, he came to oppose the "soul-snatching" of the missionaries. In 1848 he converted to Judaism and was circumcised. He returned to Philadelphia to wind up his affairs with a view to settling in Palestine permanently, adopting for himself the name of Michael Boaz Israel. His Christian wife and son took him to court in 1849 on the division of his property and to have him declared insane. At the trial, which was widely publicized, the jury acquitted him. This legal precedent helped establish the principle that religious opinion cannot be a test of sanity. Cresson returned to Jerusalem and lived there as a respected member of the Sephardic community until his death in 1860. In order to frustrate missionary efforts, he set up a "Soup House" in Jerusalem. He also made a futile effort to set up a model agricultural settlement for Jews and generally worked to ameliorate their condition. In some of his ideas he anticipated nonstatist Zionism.[37]

The convert Nathan matches Cresson in the ardor of his Judaism and his zeal to return Jews to the soil. The canto devoted to Nathan's history (1.17) is the longest of the poem. Although Melville treats Nathan with deep respect, Nathan serves as an example of unreasoning zealousness and is a portrait of the Cresson type in American life.

Clarel comes to know Nathan's daughter, Ruth, and his wife, Agar. The young pair fall in love, and Clarel is a frequent visitor to Ruth's home. Ruth is a shadowy figure of virginal loveliness, "Hebrew the profile, every line." Is Ruth in the literary tradition of the beautiful Jewish daughter whom the gentile hero may love but never marry? This is an arguable point, but it is doubtful in this instance. As Walter Bezanson points out, Ruth is one of a line of Melvillian girls such as Yillah in *Mardi* and Lucy in *Pierre,* and "another instance of Melville's inability to write about heterosexual love, except allegorically."[38]

To Clarel, Ruth "looked a legate to insure/That Paradise is possible/Now as hereafter." Neither lover raises a bar to their relationship on religious grounds, nor does Ruth's mother. Melville offers no notion of Nathan's view, perhaps because Nathan is so obsessed with his mission that he is unaware of the relationship. Only the rabbi sternly disapproves: "But by the sage was Clarel viewed/With stony and unfriendly look," hoping to "make Clarel straight forgo/Acquaintance with his flock." Both mother and daughter are drawn to Clarel not only for his human warmth, but also because he renews their links to home. They long for their native country, especially after the second child dies: "With Clarel seemed to come/A waftage from the fields of home."[39] The idea of homesickness may have been suggested to Melville by his meeting with the Saunders family, whose little daughter "pines for home."[40]

Agar, whose name is a variant of Hagar, the mother of Ishmael, is a more clearly defined character than Ruth. She is the image of maternal feeling, which Melville can render more concretely because he is not inhibited by the prospect of carnal love. Though Agar is reluctant to come to Palestine, she acquiesces out of love for Nathan. Melville does not suggest that the Judaistic faith of Ruth and Agar is weakened by their harsh circumstances. Yet, to Agar,

> The student, sharing not her blood,
> Nearer in tie of spirit stood
> Than he she called Rabboni.

This would not be uncharacteristic of a Jew brought up in the United States. To Melville, Agar is the typical woman, living by feeling rather than intellect: " 'Twas not that Agar reasoned—nay,/She did but feel, true woman's way." It is entirely plausible that, as Bezanson suggests, Melville put something of his wife, Elizabeth, in Agar.[41]

The fate feared by Nathan overtakes him, and he is killed by Arab marauders. Clarel comes to comfort the bereaved mother and daughter but is barred from entering the house by the rabbi, because non-Jews are forbidden in the house of death by Jewish "modes." Clarel has meanwhile been asked to join a pilgrimage for ten days. He is reluctant to leave Ruth, but his exclusion from her house decides the issue for him, and he goes on pilgrimage after writing her a letter enclosing a ring. The remainder of the poem is devoted to the pilgrimage. Many times during the journey Clarel's thoughts return to Ruth, and he broods over the separation. On his return to Jerusalem he hastens to her house, but on approaching the Jewish cemetery he sees a funeral in progress and discovers that both Ruth and Agar are dead. He is told that both had died of grief over Nathan's death. Clarel rants at the graveside in a manner reminiscent of Hamlet at Ophelia's grave. He lingers in Jerusalem. His religious feelings are profoundly shaken, if not destroyed, but he finally clings to the hope that "stoics" may yet "be astounded into heaven."[42]

Melville's depiction of this family is unfailingly dignified and warm. There is not the slightest suggestion of prejudice or condescension in Melville's attitude. The same can be said of his portrayal of Abdon, the black Jew from Cochin, who owns the inn where Clarel stays in Jerusalem. Abdon is described as stemming from the Ten Tribes of Israel, who, according to tradition, went eastward from Palestine and were "lost." From colonial times onward, it was speculated that the American Indians were descended from the Ten Lost Tribes, and Anne Bradstreet, in her poem "The Four Monarchies," had questioned whether they might be found among the American or Asian Indians. Melville was thus continuing an American religioliterary tradition in placing a presumed member of the lost tribes in his poem. Abdon is described thus: "So strange his shade/Of swartness like a born Hindoo." He is reverently portrayed as a meditative old Orthodox Jew who has come to Jerusalem to die. Years earlier Abdon had gone to Lisbon with a Portuguese Jewish merchant, engaged in trade all over the world, and then settled in Amsterdam. After the death of his wife, he had come to Palestine "less to live, than end at home."[43]

On the doorpost of Abdon's inn Clarel observes a mezzuzah, "a slim vial set in bed/Of door-post all of masonry."[44] Melville notes in his *Journal* that at his hotel at Jaffa he has seen "a vial masoned in, and (visible) containing some text of Jewish scripture."[45] The idea of having a Jewish innkeeper was probably suggested to him by the fact that several of his innkeepers in Jaffa and Jerusalem were Jewish. But as a character Abdon was Melville's own creation, in whom he infused his profound respect for the genuinely religious person of gentle human qualities.

At the opposite end of the human spectrum is the Lyonese, a young French Jew who shares a hotel room with Clarel for one night in Bethlehem. He represents to Clarel the carefree, hedonistic life as an alternative to the inconclusive life of religious doubt. The

Lyonese is a traveling salesman for a Lyons luxury business; he has a "mobile face, voluptuous air"; he is a "toy of Mammon; but the ray/And fair aureola of youth/Deific makes the prosiest clay." For some reason Clarel feels impelled to engage the Lyonese in a discussion of the sad state of Jerusalem Jews and the Jewish question. But the replies of the Lyonese are evasive, and he tries, without success, to divert the conversation. Clarel is insistent, so the Lyonese leads the conversation into a panegyric of Jerusalem wine and Jewish girls. Judea does not depress him, he says lightly.

> There is no tress
> Can thrall like a Jewess's. . . .
> Earth's best,
> Earth's loveliest portrait, daintiest,
> Reveals Judaean grace and form.

He then turns to the general question: "Priests make a goblin of the Jew:/Shares he not flesh with me—and you?"[46] and adds that he has met all sorts of Jews. Clarel asks if he has not seen anything strange in the Jews and their fate. The Lyonese admits that they are dispersed like the Gypsies and "odd" like the Parsees. But people don't make a fuss about these, so why bother about the Jews? And with that he ends the conversation and goes to sleep. He leaves in the morning before Clarel wakes.

The next day Clarel meets a Russian who knows that Clarel had been the Lyonese's roommate. When the Russian asks what they talked about, Clarel replies that they discussed the Jews, but that the Lyonese had at first answered grudgingly. The Russian exclaims that his suspicions are confirmed: "Evade he cannot, no, not hide./ . . . His race supplied the theme: a Jew!" Clarel asks naively why he should try to hide his Jewishness. Because, answers the Russian,

> Society
> Is not quite catholic, you know,
> Retains some prejudices yet—
> Like not the singular; and so,
> He'd melt in, nor be separate—
> Exclusive. And I see no blame.[47]

The Lyonese is the assimilated Jew who is anxious to discard his identity and heritage because they are inconvenient in a hostile world and interfere with his pursuit of pleasure. Melville's own attitude toward assimilationism is unclear here, but his delineation of the type is vivid and acute.

*   *   *

We have seen how in his fiction Melville maintains a conventional attitude toward the Jews. Like most non-Jews of his day—and larger numbers today than we may suppose—on occasion he acquiesces almost reflexively to the prevailing stereotype. In his fiction "idiomatic" thinking about the Jews prevails, primarily because he thought about them only casually. The outcome is otherwise when, stimulated by his actual experience and preoccupied with Jews as an aspect of his theme, he writes *Clarel.* In this poem Melville's humanistic mind is at work in the creation of his Jewish characters. No other writer in our literature up to his own time created a comparable gallery of Jews as human beings.

PART TWO

SOME NINETEENTH-CENTURY GENRES

7

RELIGIOUS POETRY
AND FICTION

The nineteenth century was an era of fervent religious activity in which numerous evangelical Protestant sects made their appearance. In a country where church and state were constitutionally separated, where freedom of the individual was manifested in socioeconomic life, and where the ties to traditional denominations were easily loosened, religious life was in ferment. Under influence of the Enlightenment an unprecedented decline of organized religion occurred in the last quarter of the eighteenth century and deism was widespread, but this process was reversed by the end of the century. A wave of revivalism swept the nation, especially the frontier regions. Missionary activity among the Jews was particularly intense. Promotion of Bible reading generated the formation of the American Bible Society in 1816. An immense pamphlet literature devoted to popularizing Bible teachings was promoted by the American Tract Society starting in 1825. In 1826 the state missionary societies united to form the national American Home Missionary Society.

During the first half of the nineteenth century this current of emotional evangelism, reacting against rationalism and deism, generated secession from established denominations, like the breakaway of Unitarianism from its Congregational mother church. Inspirational and fundamentalist sects, the "come-outers," proliferated in the 1830s and 1840s. New "prophets" arose, like John Humphrey Noyes, the founder of the Oneida Community. Belief in the imminent Second Coming of Christ was widespread. In 1831 William Miller, the most sensational prophet of the imminent end of the world, informed all who would listen—and thousands did—that Christ would return in 1843, gather the faithful, living and dead, and destroy the unbelievers and the world in a holocaust. Despite the failure of his prediction, millenarianism continued to be a significant current in religious thought in the antebellum period. Typical of the poetry giving expression to the millennial sentiments of the day is "The Latter Day," a poem by Thomas Hastings, cofounder with Dr. Lowell Mason of the prevailing psalmody in the United States:

> Hail to the brightness of Zion's glad morning;
>   Joy to the lands that in darkness have lain;
> Hushed be the accents of sorrow and mourning;
>   Zion in triumph begins her mild reign!
>
> Hail to the lightness of Zion's glad morning,
>   Long by the prophets of Israel foretold;
> Hail to the millions from bondage returning;
>   Gentiles and Jews the blest vision behold![1]

One of the most significant of these religious developments was the establishment of the Mormon Church. Its "prophet," Joseph Smith, was an extraordinary figure, to whom secret divine records were allegedly revealed in 1827. He "transcribed" them into *The Book of Mormon,* a new Bible, published in 1829, and gathered about him a flock of disciples, the Latter-Day Saints. They were intolerantly driven westward and gradually moved from a small town in New York State, where they had originally settled, to Salt Lake City, where the now prosperous Mormon Church established itself.

Doctrinally, the Mormons went beyond the Puritans in directly equating present-day Christians with the ancient Hebrews. The Puritans had legislated their lives according to their interpretation of the Old Testament and had regarded themselves as latter-day Hebrews; but the Mormons actually traced themselves in lineal descent from the tribes of Israel that were dispersed after the fall of the Tower of Babel. According to the Mormon "revelation," the tribes made their way to America, fought exterminating wars with each other until only the prophet Mormon and his son Moroni were left. It was their gospel that was "divinely" revealed to Joseph Smith. The Mormons thus actually regarded their community as Israel, and America as the new Zion. America was only an interim Zion, however; the original Zion would be restored when the Jews returned to Palestine. The Mormons made no attempt to unite organically with contemporary Jewry.[2]

The identification of the Mormons with the ancient Hebrews found little expression in literature. There is some desultory poetry and one historical play. Edward W. Tullidge, a Mormon editor, published a play, *Ben Israel* (1875), which is concerned with the return of the Jews to England during the reign of Charles II. What is especially interesting is the author's patent identification with the Jews of the play.[3]

This pervasive emphasis on the Old Testament in American religious life, and the fervent evangelical sentiments surrounding belief in the return of the Jews to Palestine and the ensuing Second Coming, gave rise to a voluminous outpouring of travel books, fiction, and poetry after the 1830s. Interest in travel to Palestine was high, and many books describing Judea appeared. The stream of American travel books and guidebooks to Palestine was initiated in the 1830s and continued unabated into our century. It was largely from the descriptions in such books and in the Bible that authors writing of the land of the Jews and of early Christianity drew their local color, rather than from firsthand experience. Lew Wallace, for instance, wrote *Ben-Hur* some years before he actually visited Palestine. Indeed, of the major American writers, only William Cullen Bryant, Herman Melville, and Mark Twain actually traveled to Palestine.

Nearly all the writing on Palestine, whether descriptive or fictional, was Christian in orientation. It invariably exhorted the Jews to accept Jesus as Savior. The earnest hope of these writers was to bring the Jews closer to conversion. The attitude toward the Jews in the first half of the century was usually benevolent, as we saw earlier. This literature lamented the history of persecution, and in kindness offered the Jews the solution of conversion. "A Letter to the Jews of This Country," written in 1833 by "A Unitarian Christian" and published in a religious journal, expresses the typical attitude. The writer disavows the persecuting spirit, which he believes to be contrary to Christian teaching. If the Jew is deterred from accepting Christ because this would mean abandoning his persecuted brethren, he need not have any apprehensions, says the writer:

Here, the Christian cannot look down upon you, without violating the principle of his country's constitution, as well as the principles of justice, common sense, and the Gospel. Here you stand on the same level with your fellow-citizens of other sentiments; and if, in some cases, prejudices are still entertained against you, they are not stronger certainly than those which many denominations of Christians entertain against others.[4]

The benignity displayed by Hannah Adams earlier in the century was common among conversionists. Devout Christians' kindly attitude toward the Jews was typically expressed in an anonymous verse published in 1836:

> But, O Judea, there shall come
> For thee another glorious morn,
> When thy retreats shall be a home

For thousands pining and forlorn
In distant lands; no more to roam
The objects of disdain and scorn.[5]

The ever-present hope among the pious for conversion of the Jews
is signalized in "The Synagogue," a poem by William Croswell, an
1822 Yale graduate who was an Episcopalian minister and religious
poet. The minor place held by Jews in the consciousness of America
in the first half century is indicated by the fact that Croswell's poem
is the only one in Rufus Griswold's *Poems and Poetry of America*
(1842) that deals with the contemporary Jew, though allusions to
Palestine and biblical subjects are frequent. Croswell's poem describes a visit to a synagogue and is replete with an idealized description of the scene. It ends, as usual, with the hope that the film will
fall from the Jews' eyes, and that they will accept Christ as the
Messiah. The poem's precise description of the ritual makes it worth
quoting in its entirety.

I saw them in their synagogue,
    As in their ancient day,
And never from my memory
    The scene will fade away,
For dazzling on my vision, still
    The latticed galleries shine
With Israel's loveliest daughters,
    In their beauty half-divine!

It is the holy Sabbath eve,—
    The solitary light
Sheds, mingled with the hues of day,
    A lustre nothing bright;
On swarthy brow and piercing glance
    It falls with saddening tinge,
And dimly gilds the Pharisee's
    Phylacteries and fringe.

The two-leaved doors slide slow apart
    Before the eastern screen,
As rise the Hebrew harmonies,
    With chanted prayers between,
And mid the tissued veils disclosed,
    Of many a gorgeous dye,
Enveloped in their jewell'd scarfs,
    The sacred records lie.

Robed in his sacerdotal vest,
    A silvery-headed man
With voice of solemn cadence o'er
    The backward letters ran,
And often yet methinks I see
    The glow and power that sate

Upon his face, as forth he spread
    The roll immaculate.

And fervently that hour I pray'd,
    That from the mighty scroll
Its light, in burning characters,
    Might break on every soul,
That on their harden'd hearts the veil
    Might be no longer dark,
But be forever rent in twain
    Like that before the ark.

For yet the tenfold film shall fall,
    O Judah! from thy sight,
And every eye be purged to read
    Thy testimonies right,
When thou, with all Messiah's signs
    In Christ distinctly seen,
Shall, by Jehovah's nameless name,
    Invoke the Nazarene.[6]

A more realistic description of the synagogue of the time was offered in 1841 by the author and abolitionist Lydia Maria Child. Although there were a number of Jews in Boston at this time, she had never seen one there. When she came to New York in 1841 to edit the *National Anti-Slavery Standard,* she lost no time in visiting Rosh Hashanah services at the Crosby Street synagogue of Shearith Israel, the oldest congregation in the United States. She was "gruffly" ordered to take a front seat in the women's gallery. She reports that she was "gratified at being treated contemptuously as a Gentile and a 'Nazarene'; for I remembered the contumely with which *they* had been treated by Christendom." She notes the ritual dress of the worshipers, but thinks the service less solemn than the Catholic ritual, for the "ceremonies were shuffled through in a cold, undramatic style." Judaism bears to Christianity, she thinks, the relation of "shadow and substance, type and fulfilment." Yet, she adds, despite the Jews' "blindness and waywardness," they were after all the creators of monotheism. Notwithstanding their prosaic occupations and their "mechanical mode of perpetuating ancient forms," one cannot "divest them of a sacred and even romantic interest."[7]

In a later book on religious ideas Mrs. Child is more vehement in her condemnation of prejudice; the mistreatment of Jews by Christians, she writes, was "the darkest blot on their [the Christians] history. . . . Theological prejudice, that most hateful fiend of all the catalogue of Evil Spirits, has kept them under depressing influences in the countries called Christian. . . . They suffered persecution, relentless, universal and prolonged, beyond all precedent." But the Jews were not crushed by this: "Their constance and fortitude equalled their unequalled wrongs. They endured every form of deprivation, suffering, and death rather than abjure the faith consecrated to them by the teaching of ages." The heavy hand has not yet been wholly lifted from them by Europeans, where "the best that can be said is, they are beginning to do less injustice." Though she accepts the reputation of Jews for "artifice and cunning," she holds that the Jews were often driven to these practices by the "fiery ordeal through which they have been passing for ages." Unlike those who condemn the Jew for such alleged traits, she would "let the shame rest on those who left their disinherited brethren no other defense against the rapacity and violence of the powerful." But she does not accept the popular stereotype. The Jews, she concludes, "are everywhere a peaceable, industrious, and enterprising class of citizens."[8]

While the lament over Jewish persecution is common in the writing of the time, there is little dissent from condemnation of the Jews for their reputed role in the death of Jesus. When Jones Very, the mystical, heterodox "brave saint" (Emerson's term), needed a historical metaphor with which to condemn his orthodox ministerial tormentors in Salem, the story of the ancient Hebrews was at hand for the purpose. This friend of Emerson's deplored what he thought was the externality and emptiness of New England religion. For his part, Very zealously believed himself to be immured in divinity and divinely inspired, and the intensity of his identification with God was not unlike that of his contemporary Kierkegaard. In 1839 he addressed his critics in a sonnet, "The Jew," which draws a parallel between his situation and that of Christ:

> Thou art more deadly than the Jew of old,
> Thou hast weapons hidden in thy speech;
> And though thy hand from me thou dost withhold,
> They pierce where sword and spear could never reach. . . .
> Go, cleanse thy lying mouth of all its guile
> That from the will within thee over flows;
> Go, cleanse the temple thou dost now defile.[9]

The calamities that beset the ancient Hebrews are detailed in a prolix, bombastic "epic" poem by the western poet Johnson Pierson, in 1844. In this pseudo-Miltonic poem Jewish history from the exodus to the destruction of the Temple is versified. Pierson offers an elaborate apology for publishing his poem: "The events connected with the fortunes of the Jewish nation are of such a character as to

endear their history to every individual of the human family. . . . Nor
can we advert to the calamities which were poured down from God
to this stiff-necked people, for their disobedience, without shedding
the sympathetic tear to their misfortunes." English literature, he
writes, contains nothing more sublime than "the writings of the
Jewish bards," whose people are the "heaven-protected Jews."[10]

Of quite a different sort is William Wetmore Story's long poem
giving an antitraditional view of "the case of Judas." Story was born
in New England and was the son of Supreme Court justice Joseph
Story. He left a law practice in Boston and expatriated himself to
Italy, where he became a sculptor and poet. Before he left Boston
he expressed his contempt for the Jews in a letter to James Russell
Lowell, dated December 30, 1855. The noted French actress Rachel
had performed in Boston, and, he wrote, "she made a great sensation here; nobody understood what she said; but everybody thought
her wonderful. . . . Nobody cared for her character." As for her
fellow actors, "she was wretchedly supported by a set of dirty Jews,
and they were taken into the general admiration. She was jewier
than ever and tried to skin a flint in Boston, which created a little
reaction." After Henry James quotes this letter in his book about
Story, he feels constrained to comment on what he calls Story's
"subjective" response as the expression of "an alienated mind
. . . in a society which was fundamentally and superficially *bourgeois.*"[11]

It was this mind that sought to rehabilitate Judas by an ingenious
revision of the betrayer's case in the poem "A Roman Lawyer in
Jerusalem." Purporting to be a recently unearthed first-century manuscript written by a pagan Roman lawyer, the poem presents a view
of the case radically different from the accepted one through a
reexamination of the facts and the evidence. Did Judas in fact intend
to betray Jesus, or was he justified, asks the lawyer. Years after the
event the lawyer is given new evidence by Lysias, chief of the centu-
rions at the crucifixion. It is Lysias's opinion that Judas was brave,
noble, honest, fiercely loyal to Jesus, and, indeed, alone of all the
disciples "thought he [Jesus] was God." So great was his faith that
he believed that if any hand was raised against Jesus, God would
make Himself manifest, and Jesus would be vindicated before the
people. Judas believed that Jesus had wanted this test to be made,
and thus "prove/He was Messiah, God, the King of all." Jesus
wanted Judas to betray him, for did he not say: "What thou hast to
do,/Go and do quickly"? None of the other disciples attempted to

stop Judas because they, too, believed betrayal was Jesus' wish. When God did not liberate Jesus with a manifestation of His presence after all, Judas was stricken with agony. "What have I done?" Was it not impossible that Jesus could be crucified? "For he is a God!" Judas returns to Lysias, as if stung by a scorpion: "Take back thy purse!/It was not for that foul dross I did the deed."[12] Judas is discovered hanged, and the hanging proves his innocence, concludes Story, for if he were a betrayer he would feel no remorse.

A long companion poem, "A Jewish Rabbi in Rome," is set in the fifteenth century. Rabbi Ben Esdron comes to Rome to learn the truth about the Christian world. He regards Jesus as a "pure idealist" and visionary, whose criticism of the Jews was not entirely wrong. Had Jesus not been martyred, thinks the rabbi, he might have become a conventional leader, but "we lifted him above the rest" by taking his life. In contrast with the spirit of Story's anti-Jewish response to the actress Rachel and her troupe is his affirmation here, through the rabbi, that Christian love is not extended to Jews:

> They hold us rather like foul swine,—
> Abuse us,—lay great burdens on our backs,—
> Spit on us,—drive us forth beyond the walls,—
> Force us all slavish offices to do,—
> And if we join their sect, scorn us the more.
> If those are blessed, as he says, whom men
> Revile and persecute, most blessed are we!

The rabbi believes that Jesus was a thorough Jew and never renounced his Jewish faith, and his creed was:

> Be first a Jew, then poor. Renounce all wealth;
> Keep nothing back. These are conditions prime,
> Refusing which, your following I reject. . . .
> He was a Communist—denied the right
> Of private wealth; ordained a common purse
> To be administered for all alike,
> And all rejected who refused him this.[13]

But Christians do not abide by his doctrine; they make war, persecute others, live in luxury, impose class tyranny, trample on the poor, live in pride—"the devil's work done in the name of God." Ben Esdron would like to see some sect arise that would really live Jesus' doctrines. Rome is no less corrupt than Jerusalem: "Ah, my Jerusalem!/Thy sister here is Rome, and sins like thee." The Christian rich and Pope Sixtus live in luxury, while the poor starve. Yet

Bad as the Christian's lot is, ours is worse:
We are the football and scorn of all,—
Laden with taxes, tributes;—and forced to wear
An ignominious badge,—banned from the town,
And huddled in the Ghetto's filthy den,
No public office may we hold: our oath
Avails not in their courts against the word
Of any Christian; and more, worse than this,
In these last years one degradation more
Is cast upon us by this Christian court, . . .
We are but beasts that in the Carnival
Must race half-naked, clothed but round the loins,
A halter on our necks, as if we were dogs,—
Insulted, hooted, jeered at by the mob.

Ben Esdron is also offended at the response of the Jews—they do not submit proudly to this treatment but are debased by it, and "cringe and whimper" and "creep and crawl."[14]

There is some power in this indictment of both the Christians and Jews of the time, a power that Van Wyck Brooks suggests would have been "surprising" if these poems "had not been virtually written by Browning,"[15] with whom Story was very friendly in Rome and who was the predominent influence on his poetry.

"A Jewish Rabbi in Rome" probably reflects in poetic form what Story felt about the ghetto of Rome, which he describes in his *Roba di Roma*. He is pained by the cry of *"roba vecchia"*—"old clothes" —but adds that after refurbishing the clothing the Jew will sell the clothing "at a hundred times its cost, and twenty times its value." The ghetto is entered through the Piazza del Pinto—the Place of Weeping—

for sorrow and tears have been the heritage of the children of Israel ever since their splendid city was destroyed, and they were scattered to the four winds of heaven. . . . This Roman colony of Jews have lived more than eighteen centuries, despised and degraded—the pariahs of Europe and the Church. Through all the sad vicissitudes of these ages of ignominy, here they have clung with a pertinacity which is unaccountable . . . and obstinately resisted conversion. . . . There is something sublime in the loyalty of their allegiance.[16]

Story is repelled by the dirty, overcrowded streets, the manner of luring prospective buyers into the shops, and the hard bargaining. His description reminds us of his letter to Henry James. All the faces, he says are "unmistakably Hebraic, but very few are of the pure type." Only the "disagreeable" features remain: "the thick peculiar lips, the narrow eyes set close together, and the nose thin at the junction with the eyebrows, and bulbous at the end. Centuries of degradation have for the most part imbued their physiognomy, and all have a greasy and anointed look." This "May-fair of rags . . . is the great receptacle into which the common sewers of thievery and robbery empty." His disgust does not deprive him of indignation at their condition, however, which—echoing the poem—he regards as "shameful, intolerant and unchristian." The Jews are "branded with ignominy, oppressed by taxes, excluded from honorable professions and trades, and reduced to poverty by laws which belong to barbarous ages. Shut up in the Ghetto, and forced to earn a miserable livelihood by the meanest traffic, they are scorned as a filthy and dishonest people. . . . The favors granted them are hypocritical and visionary—the injuries alone are real."[17] If one can believe traditional writers, Story notes, the only remedy for their condition is the abandonment of their ancient faith; but conversions have been few.

Like all poets of the period, Story also wrote about Judea. In "The Desolation of Jerusalem" he laments the decayed state of the city, ending with the hope that Jehovah will once more reign there, calling: "Come back, O my people, come back, I will lift you up,/ And place on your heads the crown."[18] But his rebellious spirit did not urge conversion, in contrast to some others, like the genteel Mrs. Crawford; she writes in a pair of poems about a crusader who laments to his Hebrew lady love that they must part. But the lady replies that he must tell her of the "Christian God," and the poem ends with her exclamation: "Christian, I believe thy God!"[19]

By the last third of the century, millenarian hopes for a return of the Jews to Palestine were supported by secular political developments. Phoebe A. Hanaford, who in 1868 became the minister of the Universalist Church of Hingham, Massachusetts, the first woman to be ordained in that state, published a poem, "The Return of the Jews to Palestine" (1870). The poem was preceded by an excerpt from the *Philadelphia Press* that anticipated the reality of a century later: "The Sultan of Turkey is encouraging Jewish immigration to Palestine. . . . Some of the hills around Jerusalem have already become Jewish property; and it is by no means improbable that some in the present generation [she herself lived until 1921!] will see the entire city of Jerusalem again in the hands of its ancient owners." The *Press* article continues: "That mighty revolutions will follow in the wake of such an event is probably as certain as that the Jews will return at all; at all events, affairs in that immediate region of the East must ere long become an engrossing theme among the nations of the earth."

The poem itself eagerly greets the return. The "barriers" of "Roman soldiers" and "Moslem pride" are gone, and it will not be long before peace and brotherhood "shall soon the song of nations be":

> Partition walls shall crumble then,
>   And Jew and Gentile bend,
> With loving hearts, at one fair shrine,
>   Their offerings to blend.
> Then shall the bondman fling his chains
>   With joyful shout away;
> And every heart with praise shall hail
> Earth's bright millennial day.[20]

More voluminous than the poetry was religious fiction. The first few decades of the nineteenth century saw the reemergence of religious activity in the Second Awakening. Revival meetings and evangelical fervor swept through the entire country. By the 1830s the new religious feeling of the country was fairly well institutionalized. It is estimated that church membership grew from about one in fifteen in 1800 to about one in eight in 1835.[21] Beginning in the 1830s, and continuing throughout the nineteenth century and into the twentieth, a stream of religious novels set in the biblical or Christian periods appeared with the express purpose of propagandizing for the faith. Many of the authors were clergymen who regarded their writing as a function of their ministry. Harriet Beecher Stowe expressed a widespread belief when she said: "It has often seemed to me that no greater service could be done to a large class in the community than to reproduce the sacred narrative under the aspect which it presents to the imaginative mind with the appliances of geographical, historical and critical knowledge."[22]

James A. Hillhouse, an influential New Haven literary theorist of the period and author of the biblical epic *Hadad,* formulated a rationale for using the biblical period as the base for epic or tragedy. Adopting the classical models, he writes, would mean "the abandonment of finer and more appropriate materials." Instead, the model for his age is the biblical:

It is the blended history and poetry of a peculiar people. . . . It is the sacred and eternal witness of the faith of the Patriarchs, of the truth of the Prophets, of the valor of godlike Kings,—of the existence, agency and purpose of invisible Spirits,—of the power, providence, and immutable character of God, . . . its inspiration is the efflux of the Holy One. . . . The greatest masters have kindled their sublimity, and from the tender legacy of our Saviour, snatched their finest traits of disinterestedness and love.[23]

Specifically, said Hillhouse,

to congenial talents, the Old Testament offers matchless materials.
. . . The aim should not be to amplify, or in other words, modernize,
those tales and episodes which are finished with a grace and pathos
surpassing human imitation. . . . In developing the main conception,
the writer's mind will array it, without effort, in the colors and
splendid imagery of the Bible. . . . Under such an illumination, the
true moral aspects of things can scarcely fail to be preserved inviolate.[24]

His own biblical verse plays and poems are hardly inspiring to us—
in fact, they are quite dull.

In exalting the biblical theme Hillhouse was articulating the literary response to the widespread reawakened religious consciousness of the people. A whole literature grew up with a primarily missionary intention: to acquaint the readership with the Bible, and to do this in such a way as to awaken, reinforce or promote conversion to the Christian faith. The interest in Judaism and the Old Testament was almost invariably christological. Insofar as it was worthy of respect, the religion of the ancient Hebrews was seen as an early stage of and a prelude to Christianity. The Old Testament is the book in which the coming of Christ is prophesied.

One popular writer, Maria T. Richards, states her aim in terms that might apply to nearly all the works in this genre. Her series of Old Testament sketches, she writes in the preface to *Life in Israel* (1852), are links in "a chain of successive developments of one idea, —the coming of the Saviour." This idea, she continues, is "traced through the history of 'the chosen people,' from the dawn of the early promises, to the full establishment of the kingdom of heaven upon the earth, and the sending forth of its blessed evangels into all nations." The history of "the children of Abraham" provides in part

the sacred pages which God has given us as a revelation of his will
to the whole human race. They stand from age to age living monuments of the truth of its prophecies. . . . They have been singled out
"as a royal priesthood, a holy nation," to become the channels
through which the great mystery of the incarnation, and the grace
and glory of the atonement, should be communicated to the children
of man.[25]

The feeling toward the Jews within this restricted religious perspective, however, is inevitably contaminated by two thousand years of a largely hostile relationship. While many of the biblical characters in the religious fiction of the century are sage patriarchs living in whatever grace was available before Jesus came on the scene, we shall occasionally find an intrusion of the stereotypes that are a legacy of medieval and early modern times. In tales based on the times of Jesus, the good Jews tend to be those who follow him, while the bad Jews are those who scorn him and after the Resurrection persist in denying him and clinging to pre-Christian Judaism. Converts to Christianity are invariably saintly after their conversion, while the intractible Jews are generally not good human beings, especially in the fiction.

One prime target for religious propaganda fiction was, of course, the children. The interdenominational American Sunday School Union, founded in 1824, published a number of children's books to drive home their interpretation of the Bible. As might be expected, these books are moralistic and didactic. One of the earliest was the anonymous *Hadassah, the Jewish Orphan* (c1834), which tells the story of Esther and Mordecai. The virtue of Hadassah's, or Esther's, implicit obedience to her Uncle Mordecai is brought home: "Nothing is more amiable and praiseworthy in young persons than this childlike submission to those whose purity and wisdom they may safely trust." Toward the end of the story, when the king gives Mordecai the highest office in the land and he finds favor with the people, the author reminds the reader that these were the people who greeted "our beloved Redeemer" with hosannas, but later cried: "Crucify him!" The story ends with the moral that pride and ambition destroy happiness, that pride will eventually be put down, and that "the righteous are safe"[26] through God and Jesus.

Several juvenile books by the Reverend Jarvis Gregg were also published at about this time by the Sunday School Union. *Selumiel* (1833) is in the form of a narrative by a Sunday school teacher that is punctuated by questions from pupils. After the crucifixion the historic places in Jerusalem are pointed out on a tour of the city that is taken by the Jewish Christian Selumiel and two Roman Christian brothers: Jonathan and Simon. A Jew, Helah, is converted in the course of the narrative. Throughout the story presumed Jewish characteristics are contrasted with Christian. The Jew is intensely emotional, but the Christians exhibit "calmer and more liberal feelings"; the Jewish law is a heavy burden, but "the yoke of Christ is easy compared with that of the law";[27] the Jews are destined for a terrible doom unless they ultimately accept Jesus; Jewish national pride needs to be curbed by a sense of guilt for the wrong done to Jesus.

Two years later Gregg published another story, *Elisama*, using the same technique to tell a biblical story about the rebuilding of the Temple. Throughout, Christianity is asserted to be spiritially superior to Judaism. The prophecy about the coming of Jesus is revealed to Daniel, and Old Testament passages are said to presage Christianity. Again the Jewish religion is contrasted with the Christian: Jewish ritual is ostentatious and external, while Christian ritual is spiritual and warm. The Jews are stiff-necked in adhering to their beliefs in the face of ridicule from their idolatrous neighbors. Despite their achievements the Jews are not without wrongdoing, though this is by no means limited to the Jewish people.

In another Sunday School Union juvenile book, *Iddo* (1841), the story of the Maccabean wars for Jewish independence presents the contrast between those Jews who are faithful to the religion of their fathers and those Jews who practice heathen worship. The anonymous author conveys unstinting admiration for the warrior sons of Mattathias and those who defended the faith with them. Apparently the author did not think it necessary to warn against the "negative" effects of the Jews: he considered the piety, goodness, and courage of the faithful Hebrews example enough for his young readers. What is so remarkable about this story, in fact, is the absoluteness with which the author asserts that Judaism was the "true faith" before the time of Jesus. Those who cooperated with Antiochus Epiphanes in persecuting the faithful Jews are utterly condemned as "apostate Jews." Upon death of Antiochus, the author comments that thus "died one of the most relentless persecutors of the true faith that lived before the Christian era."[28]

Into her juvenile story, *Zerah, the Believing Jew* (1837), Mrs. Sarah Pogson Smith introduces the didactic device of interspersing her narrative with passages from the Gospels in italics. The story of the crucifixion is told through the eyes of the long-suffering witness, Zerah, a Jew converted to Christianity and an ardent believer. Life is a trial to him, and his only consolation is the beatitude of the life to come. His beautiful young wife, Rachel, is murdered by the jealous, evil, unconverted Jew Sanbellad. Zerah travels to Damascus and Alexandria, then to England, and finally to Rome, where he witnesses the persecution of the Christians there and is himself eventually killed by robbers. The unregenerate Jews are presented in a most unfavorable light, and the life of religious devotion is shown as hard, rewarding only in the afterlife. The need to establish a moral contrast between the converted and unconverted Jew does not arise in a juvenile story about pre-Christian times, *From Night to Light,* by Emma Elizabeth Brown (published under the initials B. E. E. in

1872). In the story, which is set in the time of Daniel, the antagonists are the invading Medes and Persians, but they are not monsters: both Jew and non-Jew share "a common nature."[29] The ancient Hebrews in the story are presented favorably, and the God of the Jews is benevolent and just.

The message intended in another juvenile story, *The Spell of Ashteroth* (1888), by Samuel Duffield Osborne, is not so clear, but the absolute loyalty demanded by a relentless, grim, all-powerful Jehovah is quite unmistakable. The twenty-year-old warrior Asdriel, who is with Joshua's army at Jericho, acquits himself heroically. But in the temple of Ashteroth (who was the Phoenician counterpart of Aphrodite and the Semitic goddess of love and fertility) he comes upon her votary, Elissa, and is immediately smitten by an unquenchable love. He has been betrothed to the Hebrew maiden Miriam, but he now abandons her and Jehovah as well, and embraces Ashteroth. Will Jehovah or Ashteroth prove the more powerful?

Meanwhile, Asdriel's father has been condemned for having appropriated loot meant for the treasury, and the penalty is death by stoning for his entire family. Asdriel, who has been away from his family, has lost sight of Elissa, but he finds her at the stoning; she is being roughly treated by guards, so he fights with them, and both lovers die by the sword. Osborne could not permit these illicit lovers to live happily ever after, so they are united in beatitude. Osborne no doubt meant to align his readers on the side of Jehovah, but perhaps unintentionally he makes out a case for the supremacy of love. Asdriel, he writes, "was under the spell of a power more present than the command of his God, more potent than the ties of race and kindred, and under which he passively resigned himself unto the bidding of a woman of the doomed race, and devoted his puny strength to thwarting, on her behalf, the express will of Jehovah." Romantic young readers must have been torn between sympathy for the lovers and the less attractive call to the severe demands of religion. But were the lovers damned eternally? Osborne leaves the reader in doubt at the very end. "Ashteroth," he writes, "had shed her blessing over their sleep, and had Jehovah cursed them to the uttermost? Who is he that dares say it?"[30]

Later in the century the Jewish Publication Society made its contribution to the genre, implicitly offering a nonchristological example of it, by publishing *Lost Prince Almon* (1898), by the non-Jewish author Louis Beauregard Pendleton. This is a story of the Old Testament exclusively and lays no claim to foreshadowing Jesus. The story relates the adventures of the handsome Prince Jehoash, the last surviving scion of the house of David. The wicked Queen Athaliah, a devotee of Baal, thinks that she had him killed in youth, but he survives. He sets out to regain the crown usurped by Athaliah, and after many adventures he becomes king, determined to defeat the worshipers of Baal. The story encourages its young readers to believe that good conquers all, and here good does not imply fulfillment in Christianity.

Nearly all these fictional renderings of Old and New Testament stories are essentially missionary efforts for the propagation and reinforcement of Christian faith among young and old. In many instances they are also stories of the conversion of Jews to the gospel of the Christians. The doctrine of the Second Coming was never far from the surface of religious consciousness. Since return of the Jews to Jerusalem and their acceptance of Jesus were conditions of the Second Coming, evangelical sects tried to accelerate this event by promoting conversion. Missionary societies flourished throughout the century, their efforts aimed at Jews abroad and at home. Not surprisingly, a number of religious stories about contemporary life centered on the conversion of Jewish neighbors, usually in an atmosphere of benign condescension. The actual results of Christian conversion efforts were quite meager, but one would never guess this from the succession of conversion novels in which Jews are easily won over and in turn bring their entire families into the fold.

A typical example is *The Jewish Twins* (1860), by Mrs. Sarah Schoonmaker (Tuthill) Baker, writing under the pen name of Aunt Friendly. Jacob Myers, storekeeper and occasional peddler, and his wife, Naomi, live in an eastern city with their twin sons, Muppim and Huppim, named after the sons of Benjamin in Genesis. They are grateful for their freedom in America. "What a blessing it is," writes Aunt Friendly, "to live in a country that is a safe refuge for the ancient people of God!"

Though Naomi lives in fear that her sons' devotion to Judaism will be weakened by his association with Christians, when their Christian playmate Charlie Fay is blinded by a firecracker, Naomi allows her sons to visit the boy. What ensues gives meaning to Aunt Friendly's observation that "the Jews who train their children in the scriptures of the Old Testament, are preparing them for good things. It is the Jew who is lost in the love of gain, who insures for his children the curse pronounced on his doomed nation." The twins' father is of the latter kind, for he "thought it no sin to talk of all his bargains in the synagogue between prayers."

But the twins have indeed been "prepared" for conversion—by their study of the Old Testament rather than the Talmud. They are also impressed with the forgiving and merciful character of Jesus, as exemplified in the life of the pious little Charlie and his "testimony to the truth of the Christian faith." Charlie proselytizes by example, not by direct teaching. "Muppim was beginning to understand something of the gentleness and mercy of God in Christ Jesus," writes Aunt Friendly, until at length, after assiduous study of the Scriptures,

Muppim had become in heart a Christian Jew. A Jew he must ever be by nation; he would not have renounced this privilege. He was of the same people as Moses and the prophets. The Virgin Mary and the twelve disciples were of that people to which the Blessed Saviour, as a man, had chosen to belong. Over that nation the Saviour has promised again to reign, and in their prosperity the Gentiles rejoice.[31]

When Muppim breaks the news of his conversion to his parents, his mother isolates him from his brothers, and his father whips him and sends him to another city.

After his baptism Muppim, now a successful businessman, resists suggestions that he change his name. "I am not ashamed of being a Jew!" he exclaims. His fondest wish is that his twin brother be baptized with him. When his father dies in a fire, the family is left destitute, but the prospering Muppim supports the family. Huppim, too, becomes a successful businessman, and the whole family, persuaded by Muppim's goodness, is converted to Christianity. Finally, "the happy time came at last when the Jewish Passover was once more kept at Jacob Myers'; as a Christian family, the mother and her sons knelt at the Christian communion."[32] Huppim's business ability brings prosperity to the family, and Muppim trains to become an evangelist to the Jews.

The conversion of a Jewish girl is the core of a story, *Into the Light; or, The Jewess* (1867), by Mrs. C. A. Ogden, which was printed as a volume in the "American Girl Series." The book's popularity is indicated by the fact that it was still in print after three decades. Of the several Jews in the book, one, the villainous and prosperous Joseph Fleming, is immune to the appeal of Jesus and remains unconverted at the story's end. Joseph unscrupulously courts Naomi Hammet, but he is unsuccessful. In his cupidity he discards a notice for renewal of his insurance because he mistakes it for a solicitation for charity, and so is without insurance when his business is burned out.

"His greatly reduced circumstances," writes Mrs. Ogden, "seemed to develop all the low cunning of his character. He became miserly in the extreme, and the pawnbroker's shop he afterwards opened proved a suitable field for the exercise of his peculiar talents."[33] Such are unregenerate Jews.

Naomi Hammet is finally won by the young minister Horace Vincent, who has saved her father, Reuben, from a fall on the ice. Reuben is a pious Jew, Naomi the "lovely scion of a despised race." Naomi and Horace are drawn to each other spiritually but do not marry until late in the story. In the meantime Reuben has become a Christian, as have his Jewish physician, Dr. Heber, the physician's wife, and Naomi. A discussion between the doctor and Rabbi Ben Zara on conversion leaves the rabbi at a great disadvantage. The doctor asserts that converts "are doubly Jews by virtue of their acceptance of the Holy One of Israel and their acknowledgement that David, Isaiah, and the prophets were Christians."

After Reuben's death Naomi and Horace are married. Naomi sings "I Know that My Redeemer Liveth" and exclaims: "I never sing those words that I do not feel a tenderness, mingled with compassion, for those of my own nation (sons and daughters of Israel) who are shut out from the light and blessing of that faith which I now consider the crowning glory of my life." Horace replies:

When we consecrate our new home to God,—when we bow before Messiah's throne, let us remember his chosen people, and plead for their speedy restoration to the land of their heritage, through faith in the Holy One of Jacob. One prophecy after another is rapidly being fulfilled, and the time is doubtless very near when their blindness shall be taken away, and thy people shall once more take a high position among the nations of the earth.

At the birth of a son they are enraptured with the "little immortal, who may one day swell the song of Israel's redeemed, singing glory to the King of Kings! The Hebrews' true Messiah!" Naomi says joyfully: "The ransomed tribes will soon return from all lands, bearing the Cross of Calvary in triumph, while the shadows of unbelief shall flee away before the splendor of the 'true Light' forever."[34]

Conversion of the Jews was obviously a preoccupation among many pious evangelical Christians of the time. In the dedication to *Lost but Found; or, The Jewish Home* (1866), Harriette N. W. Baker ("Aunt Hattie") exhorts the daughters of her friends to "labor and pray more earnestly that their [the Jews'] hearts may be turned to the Messiah promised their fathers."

We find that over and over again the dedications of these evangelical stories express hope for the conversion of the Jews. "Aunt Hattie"'s story relates the course of conversion of the wealthy Jewish Seixas family (Seixas is, in fact, the name of an old, established Sephardic family in the United States), and, as usual, the adherence to Judaism is broken first by the children and then by the parents. The Seixas's twin daughters become friends with Isaac, the son of Mrs. Duncan. She tells him that, although Mr. Seixas "regards Christians with contempt," Isaac should love the Jews "and pray earnestly for them that their eyes may be open to behold the true Messiah." The story attempts to reinforce strongly the idea that there is a curse upon the Jews for deicide. Mrs. Duncan reminds Isaac that at the crucifixion the Jews had cried out: "His blood be upon us, and on our children," and that "this was the awful curse they brought down on their own heads, which has clung to them ever since. . . . For it was foretold of them that, for their rejection of Christ, they should be scattered over the world; they are a down trodden people." She further ventures the opinion that perhaps Mr. Seixas hated Christians because "the suspicion that he himself is regarded with the contempt many feel for Jews, may prejudice him; or it may be that he is naturally of an envious, evil, sour temper." Nor does Mrs. Duncan have a high opinion of the Jews' devotion to their religion, for they "are extremely lax in their religious duties because there is no vitality in them."[35]

The story contains the familiar clichés of popular fiction: Mrs. Seixas is an invalid; Isaac saves the twins from a wild bull and turns out to be Mr. Seixas's nephew; while his own son Isaac, abducted some years earlier, is finally returned to his family. The proselytizing by nephew Isaac and Mrs. Duncan succeeds in converting the entire family, and the family rabbi, Rabbi Ben David, can only impotently protest. A great change comes over the once distant and haughty Mr. Seixas; he is now "kind and affable to all."[36] He teaches Sunday school and is so fervent in his zeal that he removes from his shop the evil influence of an infidel—who also happens to be his best workman—by discharging him.

In another story, *Rebecca the Jewess* (1879), Mrs. Baker reiterates in the preface her motive for writing: "The aim of the writer will be realized if a Jewish child should by it come to believe that Jesus Christ is indeed the Messiah, promised of old." Again, we are exposed to the change in character before and after conversion. Rebecca, a rich, orphaned heiress of ten, feels unhappy and abandoned by God. As she grows up she cares only for ostentatious jewelry and clothing. Her cousin Esther is converted to Christianity, and undertakes to convince Rebecca that Jesus was the Messiah. Rebecca reads the New Testament and passes through doubt to belief after reading *The Converted Jew* by Reverend Mr. Livermore, who also leads her personally to conversion. She laments that "so many of my people remain in ignorance . . . and I thought that I should like to devote my life to teaching them."[37] By the efforts of Rebecca and Esther, their surviving parents and relatives and Esther's fiancé are converted as well. Rebecca becomes ill and nearly dies, but she wins her struggle with death and marries Mr. Livermore. They go to Jamaica as missionaries to the Negroes. There she falls ill again with tuberculosis and dies with rapture at the prospect of going to the Lord.

In the 1870s another popular female author, Susan Warner, wrote a series of books which are climaxed by the conversion of a half-Jewish girl. Contemporary records indicate that this writer's *Wide, Wide World* was the first book by an American author to sell one million copies. She was also the author of a series of didactic stories interpreting the Bible. The ancient Hebrews are shown as patriarchs, but for all their virtues they lack the perfect goodness of Christians, especially because of their subsequent denial of Jesus as the Messiah. Two sequential juvenile stories, *The House in Town* (1871) and *Trading* (1872), center on Matilda and Norton, from Poughkeepsie, and their half-Jewish cousins, Judith and David, from New York. Norton is not pleased by his connection with the latter; he calls them "two Jew cousins. . . . Judith is a real little Jewess as black as dewberry and as bright; and David—well, *he's* a Jew. . . . Don't ever bring up the *New* Testament to him, unless you want stormy weather."

Matilda and Norton come to New York to live, and Norton taunts David about his Jewishness. Norton explains that "there is some old rabbi here in New York that is David's great uncle and makes much of him; and so David has been taught about Jewish things, and told, I suppose, that he must never forget he is a Jew; and he don't, I guess. Not often."[38] At school David is not liked and is isolated, but it is not clear whether he or his classmates are at fault. Before the book is over, however, David is shown to be a nice boy after all, while Judith is shown as arrogant and intolerant.

Matilda, who is an adopted daughter, is a pious Christian full of humanitarian sympathies for the poor. In *Trading* the story is carried forward, with Matilda growing in righteousness and charity toward the poor. David agrees with her, citing the Old Testament for support. He contrasts Matilda's goodness with the triviality and unfriendliness of his own sister, Judith, who remains unpleasant—and unconverted: unredeemed to the end. Under Matilda's influence David converts; he believes that his acceptance of Jesus is a fulfillment of his Jewishness.

The zealous campaign to convert the Jews persisted. In 1896 Annie Fellows Johnston preached conversion in a novel, *In League with Israel,* which possesses no merit as literature but is pervaded with a rare benignity toward the Jews. Frank Marion, local leader of the Epworth League's efforts at conversion, relates how ten years earlier he had been "blinded by a prejudice" that was "hereditary . . . and entirely without reason," and how he "took Fagin and Shylock as fair specimens of the whole race." He acknowledges that many church members "have the same inexplicable antipathy" toward Jews. He concludes that it is no wonder that the Jews "fail to recognize their Messiah in the distorted image that is reflected in the lives of his followers." He later asserts that "Pharaoh's cruelties were not a tithe of what was dealt out to them in the name of the gentle Nazarene. No wonder their children were taught to spit at the mention of such a name." If dedicated Christians want to convert Jews, he says, they must divest themselves of their prejudice and make an effort to understand them.

Missionaries to the Jews must also be aware that Christians of their own day are not immune to a flaw that they criticize Jews for: the observation of the form without the spirit. After attending a Yom Kippur service Marion comments on the cold, formal ritualism of "the great mass of the congregation." But he acknowledges that he has also been challenged about the "dead-heads in your Churches," to which he replies: "I have no harsher denunciation for the indifferent Jew than for the indifferent Christian," and says he deeply respects a spiritual Jew. He agrees with one of his friends that "Israel has some great part to play in the conversion of humanity. Anyone must see that nothing short of Divine power could have kept them intact as a race, and Divine power is never aimlessly executed."

But the Jew must first be converted, or rather, as Marion believes, he must claim his heritage of Christ as the Messiah as the fulfillment of Judaism. The church, he says, must apply itself to this task: "The Church will make sacrifices. . . . [It] will cross the seas, will overcome almost any obstacle to send the gospel to China or to Africa, anywhere but to the Jews at their elbows." So he convinces all those about him to train their missionary zeal upon the young lawyer David Herschel, who is finally converted. The benign author concludes this call for conversion of the Jew with a prayer: "God grant,

. . . this study of Israel, earnestly and honestly pursued, may turn all bitterness and prejudice into the broad sweet spirit of brotherhood!"[39]

An actual conversion that occurred in the first half of the century was recounted in the memoirs of S. Jane Picken Cohen in *Henry Luria; or, The Little Jewish Convert* (1860). The book, which is dedicated to the popular religious author Joseph Holt Ingraham, was written in Holly Springs, Mississippi, where Ingraham was a minister and where Mrs. Cohen was living with her married daughter. In 1806 Jane Picken, of Philadelphia, falls in love with A. H. Cohen, son of the local rabbi, who possesses "a highly cultivated mind, and polished manners." After a whirlwind courtship of three weeks, they marry. Jane has agreed to convert to Judaism, with whose ritual and practices she has become infatuated. She loses some of her Christian friends and relatives as a consequence. When her firstborn son dies in 1814, her Christian friends interpret this as a divine judgment on her for the sin of converting, and she agrees that this is so. Her husband succeeds his father as the rabbi of the city, and she has "access to the best society amongst the Jewish people."

But her conscience troubles her, and she goes through spiritual agonies over her sinful conversion. She confesses the source of her trouble to her husband and becomes mentally deranged. Finally she undergoes a mystical conversion back to Christianity and is at peace. "This," she writes, "was conversion—deep and heartfelt conversion —such as baffles the power of description; for language can give no idea of it; and such as can only be experienced once in our lives— a change of heart, a pure and holy offering to God."[40]

She tells her husband of the conversion and he "rent his clothes and called it blasphemy, . . . declaring if I adhered to such belief he would cast me off forever." But they agree to remain together if she keeps her own beliefs secret and lives outwardly as a Jew. By 1828 the Cohen family is living in Richmond. Their four-year-old son, Henry Luria, then shows signs of mysteriously, without instruction, embracing Christianity. He becomes ill with fever and happily preaches Christian sentiments; he prays, and angels hover about him; he shows a "heavenly smile," he calls on all those about him to be baptized; he prays to Jesus and manifests great happiness at his imminent entrance to heaven, then dies. "And he," writes Mrs. Cohen, "my cherub boy, was resting in the bosom of our blessed Saviour."

She then feels she must go forth and publicly acknowledge her faith. Her husband decides he must leave her, although they love one another. Mrs. Cohen then warns against intermarriage in her memoirs:

In regard to the union of Jew and Gentile, for the sake of both, may it never be! Take warning from what I write; let my example, my sufferings and sorrows, be the beacon-light to guard you from such danger. Not that I write this in any bitterness of feeling, for I have experienced all the kindness and affection from the Jewish people, and especially those of my husband's kindred, . . . and some holding high positions, an honor to their name, religion, and country.[41]

The decade in which the genre of the evangelical historical novel emerged, the 1830s, also saw its first best seller, a book by the Reverend William Ware. He was ordained a Unitarian minister in 1821, but after serving a congregation in New York City until 1836 he concluded that the minister's life was not for him, and turned to writing. His *Zenobia* (1837) was an immense success. He followed this with two less popular novels: *Probus* (1838), a sequel to *Zenobia*, and *Julian* (1841). The first two novels are set in the third century C.E., and the third during the lifetime of Jesus. The first two, which are in the form of a series of letters from a Roman, Piso, to and from Rome, should be looked upon as one story. The Roman Jew Isaac, one of the important characters, is remarkable in this genre in being an admirable character throughout, although he remains a devoted Jew. However, he is clearly projected as an atypical Jew.

Judaism itself is depicted in unflattering terms, though persecution of the Jews is repeatedly condemned. Isaac is introduced as "one of those travelling Jews, who infest all cities, towns and regions, and dwell among all people, yet mix with none." He meets Piso on a ship bound for Palmyra and soon finds himself competing with Probus, "a Jew-hating Nazarene." Isaac would convert Piso to Judaism, while Probus, a missionary, proselytizes for Christianity. Piso reports some of their disputations. Isaac warns that the Jews will not be suppressed forever.

The Jew is now but a worm, [says Isaac] writhing under the heel of the proud Roman. Many a time has he, however, as thou well knowest, turned upon his destroyer, and tasted the sweetness of brief revenge . . . but Rome beware! Small though we seem, the day will yet arrive when the glory of Zion shall fill the whole earth—and He shall come, before whom the mighty Emperor of Rome shall tremble in his palaces.

The exceptional character of Isaac as Jew soon appears. Probus acknowledges that "the very spirit of universal love, I believe, reigns in his soul. Would that all of his race were like him." Probus exempts Isaac from his general condemnation: "The Jew bears a deeper hatred toward us than toward you [Piso], and would sooner sacrifice us; for the reason, doubtless, that we are nearer to him in faith than you."[42]

Piso has come to the East to rescue his brother, Calpurnius, from the Persians and enlists Isaac's aid, because all believe Isaac to be "honest." When Piso goes to Isaac's house, Isaac greets him with the conventional claim of poverty: "A patrician of Rome in the hovel of a poverty-stricken Jew! That would sound well upon the exchange. It may be of account." Isaac at first thinks that Piso has come to discuss Judaism or to buy jewelry. When Piso relates his proposal, Isaac is reluctant at first: "How can an old man like me encounter such labor and peril? These unbelieving heathen think not so much of the life of a Jew as of a dog. Gentile, why goest thou not thyself?" In the ensuing discussion, Piso explains that Isaac's skill and connections would make the rescue possible, and Isaac finally agrees to help him, leaving instructions that if he does not survive the payment should be given to his "tribe." Isaac stresses his hatred of Rome for having subdued Jerusalem: "I bear thee, Piso, no ill-will; nay, I love thee; but wert thou Rome, and this wheaten straw a dagger, it should find thy heart!"[43]

After the rescue is brought about and Calpurnius returns from captivity, Piso is grateful to "this kind-hearted Jew": "May every wish of your heart, concerning your beloved Jerusalem, be accomplished," Piso tells Isaac. In the ensuing discussion with Piso, Calpurnius, and their friends, the family of Queen Zenobia, Isaac is prompted by their praise and gratitude to set forth his ideas on the condition of the Jew, some of which have an anachronistic ring:

The Gentile despises the Jew [says Isaac]. He charges upon him usury and extortion. He accuses him of avarice. He believes him to subsist upon the very life blood of whomsoever he can draw into his meshes. I have known these who have firm faith that the Jew feeds upon the flesh and blood of Pagan and Christian infants. He is held as the common enemy of man, a universal robber, whom all are bound to hate and oppress. . . . Believe me that in the Jew there is a heart of flesh as well as in a dog. Believe that some noble ambition visits his mind as well as yours. Credit it not—it is against nature— that any tribe of man is what you make the Jew.

He then contrasts his simple, almost beggarly mode of life and his wealth, and explains that "it is for Jerusalem. . . . Friends, the hour of our redemption draweth nigh."[44]

In the second book, *Probus,* Piso, now back in Rome, has been converted to Christianity by Probus. Although Isaac continues to deplore Christianity, he is still treated as a positive character. The emphasis in this volume is on the inferiority of Judaism to Christianity. The keynote is struck early in the story. The descriptions of the statues of Moses and Christ in Piso's house indicate the author's conceptions of the two. The expression on Moses is "one of authority and sternness," while Christ's is one "of gentleness and love." The contrast is again emphasized by Isaac's expressed hatred of Christians, despite the Christians' tolerance toward him. In this book Isaac reappears in Rome as a seller of jewels and precious objects. The diamonds he has for sale, says Isaac, "are rarer than humanity in a Roman, or apostasy in a Jew, or truth in a Christian."[45]

Despite his disappointed hope that Piso and his wife, Julia (daughter of the Jewish convert Queen Zenobia, who is now imprisoned in Rome), will convert to Judaism, Isaac comes to Piso to warn him of Emperor Aurelian's plan to repress the Christians. This persecution of the Christians, Isaac admits, makes the Jews glad. "Piso," says Isaac, "thou wilt despise me when I say that my tribe rejoices at this and laughs; that the Jew is seen carrying the news from house to house, and secretly feeding on it as a sweet morsel!" He offers a rationale for this vindictive feeling.

And why should they not? Answer me that, Roman! Answer me that, Christian! In thee, Piso, and in every Roman like thee, there is compacted into me the enmity that has both desolated my country and—far as mortal man may do so—dragged down to the earth her altars and her worship. Judea was once happy in her ancient faith; and happier than all in that great hope inspired by our prophets in endless line of the advent in the opening ages of one who should redeem our land from the oppressor, and give to her the empire of the world. Messiah, for whom we waited, and while we waited were content to bear the insults and aggressions of the whole earth— knowing the day of vengeance was not far off.

After the coming of the Messiah, the millennium, in a sort of Pax Judaica, was to ensue: "Peace was to be on the earth, and universal love. God was to be worshipped by all according to our law, and idolatry and error cease and come to an end." Instead of this, Isaac concludes, "this false prophet of Galilee" came, and "beguiled the people with his smooth words, and perverted the sense of the prophets, and sowed difference and discord among the people."[46]

Piso and Julia refuse to flee, and Isaac understands their stubborn courage from Jewish experience, for "rarely has the Jew been known to deny his name and faith." Moreover, there is a discrepancy between his generalized vindictive feelings as a Jew and his personal attitudes as a man. Though he hates Romans and Christians "as a Jew, . . . I cannot hate them as a man, or not unto death; and thee I do love. . . . The true love of God cannot exist without making us true lovers of man." Thus Isaac, of whom a character says, "All Rome holds not a man of larger heart than Isaac the Jew,"[47] is admirable *despite* his zealous belief in Judaism. When Aurelian's persecution of the Christians intensifies, Isaac again comes to warn Piso of his danger and offers to shelter him and his family, but Piso refuses. He is seized and condemned to death. Isaac, disguised as a jailer, offers to lead Piso and Julia to safety. They refuse but are saved by the opportune death of Aurelian and the subsequent edict of toleration for Christians; they are freed with the assistance of Isaac. Although he condemns Judaism as a religion for its refusal to acknowledge Christ, by simultaneously rendering Isaac as a zealous Jew and a man of high personal character, Ware also demonstrates his freedom from prejudice against the individual Jew as a man.

The third volume of Ware's trilogy, *Julian* (1841), is set three centuries earlier, during the life of Jesus; it takes the form of letters from a young Roman Jew, traveling to visit his highly placed uncle in Caesarea, to his mother in Rome. The narrative follows the stages of his change from assimilated Jew to believer in the Messiah, though he does not accept Christ. The idea of Judaism as vengeful and vindictive is continued from the earlier volumes. On his journey, Julian proudly reports: "I passed everywhere for a Roman of unadulterated Roman blood." Ware resorts to the stereotype of "Jewish eyes," for Julian continues: "But for something in my eye, they should not suspect me to be other than a Roman." A fellow passenger says to Julian: "You may be Roman born, but if so, your Hebrew blood wears well, for the Jew looks out at your eyes. . . . Never hope to play the Roman with those eyes in your head."

Anna, the daughter of the family with which he is staying in Caesarea, chides him for forgetting his origin; he counters by condemning the miserliness of his father: "Gold, gold was his only God; and he cared not for man." Yet Julian confesses that he still feels "a secret fondness to the land and stock, from which I had come," which is brought to the surface by his sojourn in Judea. While he is there Pontius Pilate orders the destruction of the synagogue, and the Jewish resistance, in which Anna's militant brother, Philip, takes part, causes Julian to "become a Jew in feeling, at least, as well as in name."[48] He observes the contrast between the compromising

position of the hellenizing Jews and the militants like Philip. Both
Anna and Philip are killed by the Romans during a confrontation.

Julian goes on to his Uncle Onias in Beth-Harem. It turns out that
Onias has already begun to be affected by religious unrest through
the prophesying of John the Baptist and the rumors of a child born
in Bethlehem under supernatural signs. Onias has no high opinion
of the Jews. They are, he exclaims,

a besotted and ignorant people! What hope is there of Judea? The
one part are slaves to Rome, another part are slaves to riches, and
another part are slaves to sin, . . . corrupted and stiff-necked as they
are. . . . They make distinctions between the worship of God, and
virtue; and consider these two things as not necessarily joined together. Not but what the same error is to be observed elsewhere,
but that here it appears to be more universal.[49]

Onias and Julian become active in a conspiracy against Rome that
would enthrone Herod in Judea. As do so many of the Jews converted to Christianity in the novels of the period, Julian at first
supposes the Messiah to be a conqueror over the Roman state, and
Herod is the Messiah in this sense. Julian and Onias gradually learn
about Jesus and accept him as a prophet, but not as the promised
Messiah.

Joseph Holt Ingraham's biblical trilogy had an even greater popularity than the books of William Ware. From the 1830s on, Ingraham
poured out many penny dreadfuls. However, following his 1852
ordination as a Protestant Episcopal priest in Natchez, Mississippi,
he wrote a trilogy of religious novels that were phenomenally successful. His grandson reported that he used some of the money
earned by the trilogy to buy back the copyrights of some of his early
thrillers. It has been asserted that his *Prince of the House of David*
(1855) was "the very best seller on record." It sold between four
and five million copies,[50] went into twenty-three editions, and in
1900 was still in demand. No fiction was to exceed it in popularity
until *Ben-Hur,* several decades later. Following the success of *The
Prince,* Ingraham published *The Pillar of Fire* (1859), which went into
nine editions, and *The Throne of David* (1860), which had twelve
editions. Each of the three is centered on a great figure from
the Bible: Moses (in *The Pillar*), David (in *The Throne*), and Jesus
(in *The Prince*).

So popular were Ingraham's novels that by the time he wrote his
religious trilogy he was said to be receiving ten thousand dollars plus

royalties for each novel, an immense sum for those days. His aim in these novels, he writes in his dedications, is strictly devotional. The stories were especially designed to bring the light of Christ's divinity to the Jews, as well as to reinforce this belief in the Christians. *The Prince* is dedicated to "the Daughters of Israel, the Country-Women of Mary, the Mother of Jesus" in the hope that "they as well as the unbelieving Gentile, may be persuaded . . . that 'This is the very Christ.' " In a later edition he reiterates the hope that the book might even "be the means of convincing one son or daughter of Abraham to accept Jesus as Messias, or convince the infidel Gentile that He is the very Son of God."[51] The next book, *The Pillar,* he dedicates to "the Men of Israel that you, of this generation who are dispersed in all the earth, may behold and follow the light of the Cross."[52] The third, *The Throne,* he inscribes to "the American Hebrews" to show them the direct line from David to the last prince of the house of David, Jesus Christ.[53]

Internally, the first of the series, *The Pillar,* is the least interesting. This interminable 600-page epistolary novel is generally sympathetic and favorably disposed to the Jews. For Ingraham, the leadership of Moses represented a new phase of Jewish history that started from the promulgation of the Tables of the Law from Sinai. Moses is, of course, a heroic figure. Jehovah is virtually a character in the book, giving out this or that pronouncement and performing this or that miracle.

But Ingraham warmed to his subject in the next, *The Throne of David,* for here he was on more congenial christological ground, since David was the founder of the royal house of which Jesus was said to be the last prince. Epistolary in form like the others, *The Throne* eulogizes the Jews. Ingraham expresses his own view when he has the Assyrian Arbaces write in a letter to King Belus of Assyria: "I was amazed, your majesty, at the audacity and boldness of speech of these Hebrews! They are a fearless race, saturnine in complexion, with brilliant black eyes, raven hair, and faces full of intelligence and genius. I like them much." The awesome power of their Deity is also described. After forty years of wandering in the desert, their sandals bear no signs of wear, showing "what a God of wonders and power must be the deity of the Hebrews! How extraordinary his acts!" Not only power, but also "surpassing Goodness, wondrous Patience, and perfect Love" are His qualities. The device, used by Ingraham in all three volumes, of having a foreign observer happen to witness crucial events or hear about them from eyewitnesses lends a synthetic objectivity to the narratives and observations. This technique provides Ingraham with innocent-appearing anticipations of the won-der-working of Jesus. In *The Throne* the foreign letter writer, Ar-baces, falls in love with the Hebrew Princess Adora and is converted to Judaism, which in this context is a stage toward ultimate accep-tance of Christ. The ancient Hebrews and their leaders are romanti-cized and idealized, though some faults are recognized in David, and Jehovah of course is especially solicitous of his chosen people. "How wonderful the God of this people!" exclaims Arbaces.[54]

A sharp difference in attitude toward the Jews is evident in *The Prince of the House of David,* the most popular of the series, which Ingraham wrote first. In this christological account of the era of Jesus, the old Judaism has lost its inspiration. It is literalistic and ripe for renewal in the form of Christianity, heralded by the appearance of the true Messiah, Jesus. This story is set forth in both narrative and epistolary form. The letters of young Adina to her father, the wealthy Alexandrian Jew Menassah Benjamin, are sent during her sojourn in Jerusalem, where she lives during the last four years of Jesus' life. She lives with a Jewish family that accepts Christ. Adina is interested in the new dispensation and looks into it, believing that "the worship of Israel fears nothing from inquiry"; she eventually converts. At one point she is rescued from a group of rough Roman soldiers by the centurion Aemilius, whom she later marries and who is himself finally converted. In letters to her father she describes the main events in the ministry of Jesus as witnessed by herself or through accounts of others. She is inclined to accept the preaching of Jesus, not as a new religion but as a fulfillment of Judaism. "Did I discover in this prophet any disposition to bring in a new faith, opposed to the ancient faith of Abraham, I should tremble to enter-tain it for a moment."[55]

She is ecstatic when she hears Jesus preach. She meets with some of the Twelve. At this time Judas is described as being "of good height" and "well-featured." But as betrayal approaches the descrip-tion changes: Judas now has a "sharp and unpleasing voice . . . was low in height, . . . ill-featured. . . . He had a suspicious air, . . . a cringing deference . . . that made me think he must be a hypocrite." Finally, after the betrayal, Judas becomes the medieval stereotype: "He was low in stature, broad-chested, with a stiff, reddish beard, narrow eyes, and a sharp, unpleasant visage." Adina finally accepts Jesus; he "is truly Messias, the Son of God," and she now believes herself all the more faithful to Judaism. "In believing Jesus of Nazareth to be the Messias of God, I do not make myself less a Jewess; but without believing it, my dear father, I could not be completely a Jewess."[56] Her faith is momentarily shaken by the crucifixion, but Jesus' resurrection and ascension revive her faith.

The Jews of Jerusalem are "good" or "bad" according to their acceptance of Jesus. The opposition to Jesus by Annas and Caiaphas is especially vicious, and bribery is used to get Jesus arrested. Avarice is a typical trait of those Jews who reject Jesus. The protracted account of the trial and crucifixion of Jesus pictures a vindictive, hate-filled Jewry pressing hard upon a reluctant Pontius Pilate. Only after Caiaphas tells Pilate that "his blood be upon us, and on our children" does the hard-pressed procurator agree to the crucifixion, with this disclaimer: "I am innocent of the blood of this just person."

The quality of the Jews' religious faith is denigrated by Adina early in the book. They worship *"nought,"* she exclaims. "We are worse off than our barbarian conquerors, for we have *no* God; while they at least have gods many and lords many, such as they are."[57] Furthermore, the appearance of the Jewish Christians differentiates them from other Jews: Adina's nose is straight, and Mary has blue eyes. Ingraham thus passes on without modification the traditional Christian conception of the Jews of Jesus' time, as distinguished from those who accepted Jesus. Pre-Christian Jewish life can be idealized because the Jews of that time did not reject Jesus, but rather, in the view of the author, foretold his coming. Hence, there is a consistency of outlook in Ingraham's trilogy.

Several decades were to pass before the prime best seller based on the early Christian period—*Ben-Hur*—appeared. In the meantime, fiction on biblical themes and the start of Christianity continued to be published: *Life in Judea; or, Glimpses of the First Christian Age,* published in 1854 by the American Baptist Publishing Association, is somewhat reminiscent of William Ware's novels and also includes elements of a Palestine travel book, a genre very popular at the time. The narrative, moving from Rome to Palestine, centers on conflict within the Jewish community through several generations: between assimilation and assertion of Jewishness, and between acceptance and rejection of Jesus. Ultimately, however, nearly all these tendencies are resolved in conversion to Christianity. The author's militant Jew of the first generation gives up the notion of the Messiah as temporal king of the Jews, becomes an Essene, and accepts Jesus. Even the wealthy, rigid, hard-bitten Pharisaic Zerah is converted on his deathbed.

An opposition is set up among some of the characters between Judaism as an upper-class religion and the new Christian dispensation as the faith of the poor. The view that the religion of Jesus does not negate Judaism is advanced by Nathan, who follows Jewish ritual scrupulously as a devout Christian. The author finds it hard to understand how a Jew can fail to recognize Jesus as the fulfillment of Hebrew prophecy. She explains through several characters that those who do not convert are simply stubborn to the point of madness. In the war with Rome, she writes, they were "a people rash, furious, and ungovernable, bidding defiance to all the rules and ordinances of war, and setting at nought every consideration of interest and mercy."[58] Their defeat by Rome, says the convert Mary at the end, is God's punishment of the Jews for their responsibility for the death of Christ.

In *Life in Israel* (1852) Maria T. Richards presents a series of sketches on the Hebrews' wandering in the desert, the era of Solomon, and the story of Esther. She is quite explicit in her intention to convey, especially to young people, "the chain of successive developments of one idea,—that of the coming of the Saviour." The history of the Jews, she writes, "occupies a large part of the sacred pages which God has given us as a revelation of his will to the whole human race . . . and from all the tribes of the earth they have been singled out 'as a royal priesthood, a holy nation,' to become the channels through which the great mystery of the incarnation, and the grace and glory of the atonement, should be communicated to the children of men."[59]

The biblical novel also was prey to the melodramatic and sentimental writing of the period. An exacerbated instance is Alfred Duke's *Fortunes of Esther, the Jewess* which was published as a serial in the *Southern Literary Messenger,* an influential periodical of the time, from June to November 1847. The basic conflict in the story emerges when Esther, handmaiden to Vashti, confesses that she is a Jew. Vashti replies:

You, an accursed Jewess, and dare obtrude your crafty visage within the walls of this palace? Your insolence is now explained—I wonder not—no! not at all at your impudence. Your hateful race living in exclusive usages and customs cultivate a system of misanthropy toward all other nations, sanctifying your infamy by pretended devotion to a God whom none know besides, and whose laws are but a fiction to gloss your crimes.

Esther replies, echoing the author's views, with the universalistic assertion that "the evil we do is in express violation of our God's demands. He is the God of righteousness and mercy, and beside him, there is no God. He is the God of the Persians, as well as the Jews, and of every nation and kindred under the sun."[60] The writing is dull, stilted, and prolix beyond endurance, with distended speeches. One wonders how reader interest was sustained through six months.

Of similar unreadability is *Athaliah: A Novel* (1869), by Joseph H. Greene, Jr. The work centers on the wars of King David's sons at the end of his reign, and reeks of blood and resounds with thunder.

Of some interest is Elizabeth Harriet Siddons Mair's *Mariamne; or, The Queen's Fate* (1859), because a chariot race early in the novel predates the similar celebrated event in *Ben-Hur.* The contrast between the faithful Jews and those who emulated the Romans at the time of Herod is set forth in the story of Mariamne, who is coerced into marrying Herod, though she loves Zerah. While the Romans are the villains of the piece, their Jewish retainers are among the negative characters. Mariamne is as nearly perfect as a Jewish woman could be before Christianity teaches her "religion of the heart, the knowledge that obedience is better than sacrifice, a contrite spirit than burnt-offerings." Her devotion to moral principle and her beauty comport with "that high and intellectual character which belonged to her lofty race."[61]

The peak of the religious novel, both in readability and popularity, was reached in 1880 with the publication of Lew Wallace's *Ben-Hur.* It is essentially a conversion story: the individual Jewish characters, Ben-Hur, his mother and sister, the merchant Simonides and his daughter, Esther, all become disciples of Christ eventually. The novel throws into relief then-current evangelical belief: that Judaism is a preparation for Christianity and that the Jews bear collective guilt for the crucifixion. The popularity and durability of the novel are attested to by the striking fact that in 1913, thirty-three years after its first appearance, the mail-order house of Sears, Roebuck brought out an edition of one million copies.

Wallace's attitude toward the Jews in this novel is kindly, except for the traditional anathema upon the Jews for collective guilt for the condemnation and crucifixion of Jesus. Even in this connection Wallace is at pains to convey that in addition to the Jews of many nationalities who lined the path of Jesus' last agonized walk, there were also "thousands not Jews—thousands hating and despising them—Greeks, Romans, Arabs, Syrians, Africans, Egyptians, Easterners. So that, studying the mass, it seemed the whole world was to be represented, and, in that sense, present at the Crucifixion." Yet the outbursts against Jesus—"Crucify him, crucify him!"—were incited by Jewish leaders, "prompters and directors." And when Jesus expired on the cross, the people "stared at each other aghast. His blood was upon them! . . . They beat their breasts and shrieked with fear. His blood was upon them!"[62]

Wallace presents his conception of Judaism in the course of the story. At about the time of Jesus' birth, he writes, the Romans had learned that "the Jew, with all his pride, could be quietly governed if his religion were respected." Wallace implies a contrast between the supposed changelessness of the Jew, as expressed by the anti-Semitic Roman soldier Messala—"All men and things, even heaven and earth, change; but a Jew never"—and the change brought about by the emergence of Christianity from Judaism. The Jew's inflexible devotion to religious law is exemplified by Ben-Hur's refusal to grant the tribune Arrius' request to kill him so he can avoid a disgraceful return to Rome. "As a thing of conscience," Ben-Hur replies, "I would rather die with thee than be thy slayer. . . . Thy Cato and Brutus were as little children compared to the Hebrew whose law a Jew must obey." In contrast to the "sensualism" of the East, writes Wallace, "there were in all earth but two peoples capable of exaltations of the kind referred to—those who lived by the law of Moses, and those who lived by the law of Brahma. They alone could have cried, Better a law without love than a love without law." So painful was the effect of the Law, that Ben-Hur's sister Tirzah, stricken with leprosy, "did not make an end to her sufferings. *The Law forbade her!* A Gentile may smile at the answer; but so will not a son of Israel."[63]

Yet a higher stage is still to be achieved. While Ben-Hur has reason enough to feel revengeful toward Messala, who confiscated his fortune and imprisoned him and his mother and sister, even though they were innocent, the inferiority of Judaism as a religion is implicit in Ben-Hur's defensive statement: "Revenge is a Jew's of right; it is the law." And Ben-Hur is believed to be a Jew because of "the intensity of his hate." It is only by the most strenuous spiritual exertion that the Jew can conceive of the Messiah in non-secular terms, Wallace would have us believe. Ben-Hur believes in the coming of the Messiah, as prophesied by Isaiah, Micah, Jeremiah, Daniel, and Zechariah. Under the influence of his steward, Simonides, Ben-Hur comes to believe that the coming king of the Jews will have secular as well as spiritual power, and will rule as a conqueror over all the world. Simonides holds out to Ben-Hur the vision of gathering legions of Jews from all nations and leading them in conquest in behalf of the Messiah. In time Ben-Hur comes to regard Jesus as the temporal king he will enthrone: "The King who was coming, to whom he was himself devoted, whose path he had undertaken to smooth, whose empty hands he dreamed of filling. . . . The day the new King should come to claim his own and take possession of it. . . . [He thought] of the millions of Israel [coming] to assemble with palm-branches and banners, to sing rejoicing because the Lord had conquered and given them the world."[64]

When Ben-Hur finally sees Jesus his earlier conception is undermined. "Who is this man?" he ponders. "And what? Messiah or King? Never was apparition more unroyal. Nay, looking at that calm, benignant countenance, the very idea of war and conquest, and lust of dominion, smote him like a profanation. . . . King he may be, but not of another and greater than Rome." But he is not yet convinced. When Jesus is condemned, Ben-Hur discovers that the legions of Jews he has assembled will not come to rescue the king of the Jews, but have already joined the mob crying for his death. At the crucifixion Ben-Hur comes to the realization that "he who hangs yonder is the Son of God." Within a short time Ben-Hur and all his family are devoted Christians, and Ben-Hur bestows his vast fortune on the church in Antioch, where they live; an additional fortune inherited by him is given for the building of the Roman catacombs: "Out of that vast tomb Christianity issued to supersede the Caesars."[65]

The novelty of Christianity as a belief emerges starkly from Wallace's account of the trial of Jesus. "In the opinion of the rabbis and the teachers, he [Jesus] is guilty of a great crime" because he has preached a religion of universalism. "In his eyes the uncircumcised Gentile is as worthy of favor as a Jew of the strictest habit. He preaches a new dispensation." Intimations of universalism have already come to Ben-Hur. He has lived an affluent life in cosmopolitan Rome for five years as the adopted son of Arrius, and there "he must have been visited by the thought that possibly there might be some branches of the family of man worthy divine consideration, if not mercy, though they were of the uncircumcised." The old Egyptian Balthasar makes a deep impression on Ben-Hur by his universalist conception of a God who can be known and worshiped without the intervention of a priesthood—"a Father to whom all his children were alike in love—Father, not more of the Jew than of the Gentile —the universal Father, who needed no intermediator, no rabbis, no priests, no teachers." In the end, Wallace is saying, Christianity is "better" than Judaism. When the leprous Tirzah receives a gourd of water directly from an apparently unafraid man, she exclaims: "Art thou a Jew?" He replies: "I am that, and better; I am a disciple of the Christ who teacheth daily by word and example this thing which I have done unto you. The world hath long known the word charity without understanding it."[66]

The physical appearance assigned to Jesus by Wallace is also symbolic of his new universalist religion. For he is not Jewish in appearance. All other Jewish characters are described in conformance with the convention. "Wherever on the land men go," writes Wallace, "and on the sea ships, the face and figure of the Jew are familiar. The physical type of the race has always been the same; yet there have been some individual variations." When Ben-Hur first appears in the story, "an observer skilled in the distinctions of race, and studying his features more than his costume, would have soon discovered him to be of Jewish descent. . . . The comeliness . . . of the Jew [was] rich and voluptuous." Like her brother's, Tirzah's features "were of the same Jewish type." But one could not determine from the features of Jesus if they were Greek or Jewish; "the delicacy of the nostrils and mouth was unusual to the latter type." Quite unconsciously, Wallace's description of Jesus is that of the manly beauty of the idealized Anglo-Saxon, with large "dark-blue" eyes and soft auburn hair.[67] This was not "Greek or Jewish" to Wallace, but universal. Despite Wallace's unconscious bias toward a "universal" spiritual beauty that is actually Anglo-Saxon, his intention is not anti-Jewish. His Jewish characters are noble and admirable, within his framework, but they are so because they are ultimately open to conversion. Wallace's approbation of the Jews is provisional. As long as they prepare for the coming of Jesus and acknowledge him when he comes, they are admirable. But those who remain outside the Christian dispensation are backward and of a lower spiritual order. This anti-Semitism on religious grounds emerges more explicitly in *The Prince of India,* published thirteen years later.

The tidal wave of popularity that greeted *Ben-Hur* was to whet the popular taste for the religious novel and bring forth at least several dozen such books in the 1880s and 1890s. In 1881 James Freeman Clarke brought out his *Legend of Thomas Didymus, the Jewish Sceptic.* His attitude toward the Jews is of special interest because he was an intimate of the Transcendentalists' and was an early popularizer of comparative religion in his widely read *Ten Great Religions* (1871, 1883). He states that one of the aims of his religious novel is to "reproduce . . . the opinions, beliefs, and prejudices of the Jewish sects and peoples,"[68] but what emerges more clearly are Clarke's own biases.

Thomas Didymus, the narrator, works his way toward a stable faith, which he ultimately finds in Christianity after he receives "proof" of Jesus' divinity through the Resurrection. He first becomes a scribe in Jerusalem, where he acquaints himself with the secret society of the Pharisees, "The Separate Ones," but rejects it. He travels, and in Alexandria he learns of a more spiritual Judaism taught by Philo. He wearies of life and joins the Essenes. Realizing that God did not intend man to be alone, he comes home and becomes aware of Jesus, meets him, and after a period of scepticism is finally converted and becomes a Christian missionary. The apparent lack of divine favor that at first seems to be the meaning of the crucifixion causes him to lose faith, but when he sees the resurrected Jesus, his faith revives, never again to falter.

However, the character of the Jews is not typified by Thomas, who tortuously works his way toward the true faith, but rather through Miriam and the Pharisees, and especially their leader, Rabbi Ben-Gamlah. Miriam, strangely beautiful and dangerously proud, has a very strong character of conflicting qualities which may be turned to good or to evil. She has the strength of biblical women like Esther or Jael, and is ruled by "pride, passion, and reverence."[69] Miriam has been the favorite wife of Herod, but through the intrigues of the Pharisees she is dismissed in favor of Herodias. She meets Jesus, who forgives her evil acts; she is converted, sloughs off her evil side, and is freed of her Jewish nature.

For Clarke, Judaism is most completely represented by the Pharisaic secret society and its head, Rabbi Ben-Gamlah. All Jews are organized under the leadership of the Pharisees, who passionately hate the Roman occupiers and long to propagate Judaism. The Jewish character is epitomized in Ben-Gamlah; he is regarded as a wise and holy man by the Jews, but he will stop at nothing to gain power:

He rules by his dark wisdom the company of the Pharisees, and they govern the Jewish people. Nothing is sacred to him which stands in the way of his purpose. He cares neither for God nor man, but only for the destruction of the Romans and the triumph of his party and people. He clothes himself in lies; and he is so false, that he could cheat Gabriel, just come from the throne of God.

For Clarke, this conception of the Jewish leader is necessary to account for the profound sinfulness of the Jews' share in the crucifixion. Ben-Gamlah is determined to "expose his [Jesus'] imposture"[70] and to crush his influence. He convinces Herod that Jesus is a menace, and the implacable opposition of the Pharisees to Jesus is set forth at length. Ben-Gamlah's cynical pursuit of power wins out in the councils of the Jews and shows the dominance of their evil side. Jewish hatred is contrasted with Christian love throughout, and the impression of Judaism left by this novel is invidious.

A few years later the Missouri clergyman William Dennes Mahan published a presumed find of firsthand contemporary accounts of experience with Jesus, memoirs of Caiaphas and Herod Antipas, Pontius Pilate's report to Rome, and similar "original" documents. Mahan hoped thereby to confirm the historicity of Jesus and to show the Jews in a more human light than did Christian tradition. The nineteenth-century character of the "documents" is obvious, such as one in which Caiaphas resigns his post in repentance for the crucifixion. Called *The Archko Volume* (1887), the work tries to humanize the main characters of the Christ drama. The anachronism of the entire book is obvious. Interestingly enough, although Christ is described as having light hair and blue eyes, "his nose is that of a Jew. In fact, he reminds me of an old-fashioned Jew in every sense of the word"[71]—"old-fashioned" meaning like the ancient Hebrews.

Mahan's fictions are unusual in that they deliberately view the rejection of Jesus without the traditional vindictiveness.

The Jews [writes Mahan in his own voice] were honest in all their dealings with Christ; they thought both he and John the Baptist were destroying their nation, and as their nation and religion were one and the same, the course Jesus was pursuing jeopardized all their hopes, religious and political. . . . Hence, much of the prejudice among Protestants against the Jews is groundless. There never was a people more honest and devoted to their country and their God than the Jews. Many Protestants in this country, and some preachers among them, think that the more they denounce the Jews and Catholics, the more they serve God. The Jews were wrong in rejecting Jesus Christ as their Saviour, and so are those who reject him now; but when a man reads this book he will come to the conclusion that the Jews had a better reason for rejecting Christ than men have today, and would it be right to abuse all who refuse Christ as bad men?[72]

A minimum of religious sentiment and a maximum of romantic feeling mark the prolific F. Marion Crawford's contribution to the biblical novel in *Zoroaster* (1885). The all-wise and kindly prophet Daniel is tutor to the young Zoroaster, who is in love with Nehushta, "last of the descendants of Johoiakim the King remaining in Media, . . . the fairest of all the women of Media, of royal blood and of more than royal beauty," in whose features "the signs of the Jewish race were all present and unmistakable." Crawford suggests that perhaps she loves the Persian Zoroaster the more because his "face was fair, and not dark like hers." While Daniel is alive, the lovers are reluctant to give him pain at Nehushta's marriage outside the faith to "a stranger and unbeliever."[73] The machinations of the favorite wife of King Darius, the wicked Atessa, who unrequitedly loves Zoroaster, separates the lovers.

This disappointment in love, as in much romantic fiction, is the occasion for Zoroaster's retirement to the wilderness. After three years he emerges as the religious leader known to history. Because of his new transcendent spirituality, he rebuffs Nehushta's efforts at reconciliation. In the fashion of the romantic tradition, he later unbends and is reunited with Nehushta at the end; then both are slain by rebels. There is no strong anti-Jewish feeling in the novel, since Crawford is engaged with the two most favorable aspects of the literary convention of the Jew: the patriarchal prophet and the beautiful woman.

Quite different is the strange fiction by the Reverend A. Stewart Walsh, in which the Victorian worship of woman as pure, unblemished, and morally superior is conjoined with a worshipful conception of the mother of Jesus as the embodiment of the Victorian womanly virtues that verges on Mariolatry. The title, *Mary: The Queen of the House of David and Mother of Jesus, the Story of Her Life* (1886), suggests a story set in the first century. One section does relate in detail the life of Mary, but the bulk of the book actually concerns a thirteenth-century crusader and his Jewish wife and family. The book's introduction, by the Reverend T. De Witt Talmage, expatiates on the quintessential Victorian qualities of woman, and the story proceeds to elevate this conception by identifying it with the character of Mary. This tendency is so pronounced that at one point the author is obliged to disclaim Mariolatry explicitly by asserting that this doctrine places Mary before Jesus, while "no friend of the Divine Son can dethrone Him by honoring her aright; indeed, as He, Himself did."[74] After their defeat in the thirteenth century in Jerusalem the crusaders had exalted Mary and in her name had preached all over Europe as missionaries of the Teutonic Knights of Saint Mary's Hospital (the Teutonic Order).

The hero of the story, Sir Charleroy de Griffin, is an English member of the Knights, and has been taken prisoner by the sheik. Ichabod, a Jew, is a fellow prisoner. The proselytizing Charleroy tells Ichabod: "Jew, thine eyes are veiled. I'll teach thee to see Him yet." Ichabod turns out to be an easy mark and is readily converted. "I offer," says Charleroy, "the true, new, refined and final Judaism." He wants to convince Ichabod that "humanity is one. The very creed

I'm trying to teach and would fain have all thy race, ay, all mankind fully understand, is full of love, joy, peace."

Ichabod soon replies: "As a dog his master, a maid her lover, so blindly I follow thee. . . . I was a dead sea. . . . I'm now refreshed and purified. . . . Would I could gather for all; for my race, so blinded! Oh, it is a tristful thought that the nearer I get to God, the further I get from them I love next after Him."[75] For the remainder of their brief association, Charleroy hardly ever calls Ichabod by his name, but always "Jew." They escape from captivity and meet the Jewish maiden Rizpah and her family, whom they escort through brigand-ridden country. When brigands attack, Ichabod is killed, but the wounded Charleroy and Rizpah and her family escape.

Charleroy convalesces at Rizpah's home in Berzah; they fall in love and wish to marry. Rizpah's father indignantly refuses permission. "I'd rather a thousand times," he tells Rizpah, "see thee lying dead by thy true Jewish mother." The lovers elope and are married by a Christian missionary. After Rizpah's father dies she inherits his fortune, and the couple live a life of pleasure and luxury.

But Rizpah begins to regret her apostasy: "The valiant English knight lured me into his Christian love and my race's hate." When their first child, a daughter, arrives, they quarrel bitterly over her name and religious upbringing. The author comments: "It was the old, old story of a difficulty seemingly easily adjusted to all, except to those who have actually met it, in this case, as usual, the two parties fanatically opposed each other. In the name of sweet religion they loyally served the devil for a time."

The couple separates, and twenty years later their daughter, Mariamne, who has been brought up by her mother as a Jew, becomes acquainted with a missionary. Despite her mother's prohibition against speaking with "that hoary-headed old wizard," Mariamne is converted. She devotes herself to missionary work, and it is her emulation of the ideal of Mary in its Victorian version that consumes much of the latter half of the book. Mariamne goes to England to find her father and win him back. In London she finds him confined in a lunatic asylum. Her ministrations restore him to sanity, and they go home to Berzah and are reconciled with Rizpah. Mariamne meets a kindred spirit in Cornelius, and together they pursue missionary work. At her death she comes to the conclusion that "this hidden truth: the sacrifices of the gentler sex work out the purification of the race."[76]

The demand for religious fiction in the next decade seemed insatiable. The Sabbath Library in Chicago for instance, claimed that its cheap editions of Florence M. Kingsley's *Titus* (1894) sold nearly one million copies within a few years. The twenty-five religious novels of the 1890s that we have examined are only a sampling. Most of these novels dealt with the period of Jesus' lifetime or shortly thereafter, but at least a quarter of them were stories of Old Testament events and people. Of the latter there occasionally is one, like Walter Kennedy's *Javan Ben Seir* (1898), that tells its story straightforwardly, without marked Christian bias, as an adventure story that happens to have occurred in the era following the death of Solomon. It has its courageous hero, its beautiful heroine, its evil villain, and a happy ending. Most, however, are distinctly christological in orientation, reading into the biblical characters intimations of the coming Christ, criticism of Jewish particularism, and anticipation of a universalistic religion. Some contain anachronistic renderings of the stereotype, and others exhibit the ambivalence that we have so often encountered.

One christological aspect of this fiction about the Old Testament is the fusion of the Hebrew patriarch and the Christian saint. Such is the figure of Daniel in *The Master of the Magicians* (c1890), by the husband-and-wife team of Elizabeth Stuart Phelps and Herbert F. Ward. Daniel, a saintly, all-wise, miracle-worshiper true to Jehovah, is described as "a dreamer." "Like Joseph of old, he had strange visions and told them to no one. This habit of communing with a world beyond the visible had given him peculiar eyes. They were un-Jewish."[77]

The patriarchal priest Nahum in Rose Porter's *Daughter of Israel* (1899) also has something of this character. The hope of Jephthah's lovely, pious daughter, Elesheba, is that she "might be honored of the Lord, and mother of the promised Messiah," but that hope is put to an end when Jephthah condemns her to virginity. Nahum pities her, and "the sympathy which shone in the priest's eyes, and sounded in his voice, was due to his possession of a spiritual outlook that . . . reached beyond the dark, mistaken belief of the age and caught a glimpse of a distant time when 'a star would come out of Jacob and a sceptre rise out of Israel.' " Jephthah, too, then extends his vision, and becomes

dimly conscious of something higher than the doctrine of paganism, and the sanguinary worship, which materialized supplication by a sequel which included propitiatory offering of fruit, bird, beast, and alas! sometimes human life. This dim consciousness was nothing less than a ray of light from the dawn of Christianity, which began to reveal God as a Spirit, to be worshipped in spirit and truth long before Jephthah's day.[78]

Anticipations of Jesus' coming, the growth of Christianity through intermarriage, and criticism of Jewish particularism are basic themes of the Reverend James Meeker Ludlow's *King of Tyre* (1891). The Hebrew patriarch Ben Yusef marries a non-Jewish wife against the injunction of Ezra, but he remains a faithful Jew. He leaves Jerusalem for Galilee to avoid harassment, but, writes Ludlow, "no quarrel with the rulers of Jerusalem could alienate his patriotism or dim his larger hopes in the coming glory of his people." Ben Yusef speaks "with prophetic rapture of the day that was sure to come, when a new King, greater than Solomon, the Lord's own gift to the people, would spread the nation from the Euphrates to the Great Sea." God is a "Father" who does not demand "suffering sacrifice from men. If sin needs atonement," adds Ben Yusef, "God's own gracious heart will make it. He wants only man's contribution and love."

Similar sentiments are expressed by Menassah, high priest of Samaria, who opposes "bigots among the Jews" because "I believe the Lord is too great a God to be confined to Jews' notions. They belittle him." Menassah protests against Nehemiah's expulsion of non-Jews from Jerusalem. For himself, he says, "I want to see the Jewish religion broadened and liberalized, until you Baalites even can worship at our altars." He reports the feelings of one Malachi: "He has impressions he cannot utter; as if he stood in the presence of some glorious being who was coming to be the King of Israel. He cannot shake off the feeling."[79] In his view of the Old Testament, Ludlow falls into a sort of dialectic of Christianity that he sees as having emerged from the conflict and contradictions within Judaism.

Perhaps most explicit in christological interpretation of the Old Testament is the Reverend George Anson Jackson's *Son of a Prophet* (1893). The author explores Carlyle's suggestion that, because of its universality, the Book of Job reads "as if it were not Hebrew." King Solomon has sent Shammah abroad as a roving trade ambassador, and this broad experience "had given him the concept of a universal religion." He has thereby "outrun the mission of his age and his people. . . . The possibilities of distant generations may exist in individuals in earlier days." Shammah's hearers are inspired by his universalistic vision of the God of Jacob as not belonging to the Jews alone but as "the God of . . . all the sons of men." But when sober second thoughts descend, writes Jackson, practicality intervenes on the council. " 'Hosanna!' cried the prophetic, the godlike; 'Crucify!' cried the earthly, calculating spirits of the same men." A thousand years had yet to pass before "the Israelitish conception of the Eternal" could be shared with all peoples. "Somewhere," writes the author, "must be developed a spiritual life, accumulated a reservoir of spiritual power, sufficient to fling out to the whole world the revelation through the Eternal Son. Such a repository was Israel."

At the hands of intriguers Shammah dies a martyr to the idea of universality, but his son, Eleazar Ben Shammah, carries his idea forward and makes it even closer to the Christian conception. The younger Shammah undergoes the trials of Job for his faith, and, though most of his family is killed by his enemies, he "trusted God." He has, concludes the author, "laid hold of something unknown to Iyob [Job]." All of Jackson's spirituality, however, does not prevent him from manifesting contemporary anti-Semitism. At the great gathering at which Shammah projects his universalistic vision, others "had spoken in a tone which gave promise only of the modern Jew, who controls the bourse of Europe. Only Shammah was more than a tradesman."[80]

An anachronistic rendering of Haman, who uses modern anti-Semitic clichés, is presented in Mrs. T. F. Black's *Hadassah* (1895), another of the many fictional versions of the Esther-Haman story. Haman tries to bribe the Jewish merchant Milalai to have his wife, who is a waiting woman to Queen Esther, poison the queen. He meets Milalai's refusal with the conventional observation: "Now I understand why Milalai hesitated to do our will. Thou knowest that the race of dogs hangs together and depends upon one another. . . . When before did a Jew refuse to do aught for money?" Haman further characterizes the Jews "as a class of merchants, they are grasping, filthy in their habits, and so *extremely humble* that they shame the poorest class of natives."

Haman engages Milalai to build a scaffold on which he expects to hang Esther's uncle, Mordecai. "How much money will it be?" asks Haman. "Charge a fair price, but don't let your Jew blood name too big a price, for I can just as well go elsewhere!" The author praises King Ahasuerus for reversing the murderous decree against the Jews, and adds her own opinion of the centuries-long persecutions and the current pogroms in Russia:

More than two thousand years have passed since that time, and the twentieth century of *christianity* is dawning upon the world, yet in what condition does it find the oppressed race so kindly delivered from persecution by a *heathen* monarch! Is there an Esther today to plead their cause? Would the most absolute monarch in the present day, as in the past, open his heart to her supplications in their behalf! Who will rise up and plead the cause of this oppressed race, now undergoing the most infamous persecution since the days of the destruction of Jerusalem.

To round out the moral of her story, Mrs. Black explains that in the final battle of the Jews against the armies of Haman's sons, the conquering Jews took no spoils, "to show that they had fought for a righteous cause alone . . . ; avarice, with which as a class they are credited, having little weight with them on this occasion."[81]

Criticism of Jewish particularism, as expressed in the implacable Jewish opposition to intermarriage in the sixth century B.C.E., is found in the altogether undistinguished novel *Shem* (1900), by J. Breckenridge Ellis. The Moabite Shem falls in love with the Hebrew Adah, whom he rescues several times, but he cannot marry her. "Love me not," Adah tells Shem, "for I am an Hebrew. Thou mayest not think to marry such as I. Put thy thoughts upon a maiden of thine own people."[82] The author could not bear to leave the reader without a happy ending, however. It is finally revealed that Shem was a changeling and is a Hebrew after all, so he may and does marry Adah. Ellis also gives us a stock character: a Hebrew usurer who threatens to dispossess Adah and her family from their lands for nonpayment of a loan.

The literary stereotype of the Jew proved useful to authors of those years, whether their setting was the sixth century B.C.E. or the seventeenth century C.E. A Jewish peddler of this ahistorical type is found in Anna May Wilson's *Days of Mohammed* (1897). Abraham of Joppa, "walking along with a pack on his back," is "the little Jew," "a craven-hearted Jew," and a "coward knave." He "knows little and cares less for religion," but this is not unusual among the Jews of Mecca, where the story is located. There are some good Jews there, like the saintly family of Nathan, but they are after all *Christian* Jews. "A few among a band of coward Jews who live in the Jewish quarter of Mecca," writes the author, "believe in One whom they call Jesus." But they are exceptional, for "the majority of them do not accept him as divine; . . . they live no better than others, and indeed, they are slurred upon by all true Meccans as cowardly dogs, perjurers and usurers."

Yusuf, a Persian priest, disillusioned with his own creed, finds religious fulfillment in conversion to Christianity by the Jewish Christians of Nathan's family. "In that little dingy room, he saw the first gleam of that radiant light which was to transform the whole of his after life." Though the Jewish quarter is a sink of "filth and vice," the Nathan family is its saving grace and shows that there is "some good in the Jewish quarter," and, indeed, that "there are some good among all peoples."

However, bad as the Jews were in the author's eyes, the Muslims were worse. After Mohammed's flight from Mecca and his wars of religious conquest, "Mohammed's hatred to the Jews began to show itself, and the awful persecution of the little Jewish band in Medina commenced."[83] All "non-submissive" Jews are expelled, and Nathan and his family, together with Yusuf, go to Palestine, where they become preachers of the gospel.

Many of the religious novels of the 1890s were more directly concerned with the life of Jesus and his influence in his own time or shortly thereafter. The popularity of this genre is attested to by the fact that even the fin-de-siècle esthete and dandy Edgar Saltus tried his hand at it in *Mary Magdalen* (1891), which was dedicated to Henry James. In Saltus's retelling of the Christ story through his interpretation of the story of Mary Magdalen, the Jews are no less blameworthy for the death of Christ or crudely ritualistic than in the versions by clergymen. But there is a difference. Harry Levin has commented that this novel is "a typical intermingling of pornography and hagiography, which reads like a collaboration between Flaubert and General Lew Wallace."[84] The novelty in this effort lies not only in the author's esthetic approach, but also in his variation of the Judas story. Mary Magdalen, a beautiful courtesan, is converted and transformed by Jesus, to whom she is devoted. Judas falls in love with her but she repulses him. Judas threatens that if she does not yield to him, he will betray Jesus to the authorities. At first she refuses, then relents in order to save Jesus. But it is too late; Judas has done the deed. Jesus is crucified, and Judas hangs himself in remorse.

In Elbridge S. Brooks's *Son of Issachar* (1890) (first published in 1889–90 as a prize story in the *Detroit Free Press*), Cheliel Bar-Asha, who is descended from Issachar, fifth son of Jacob and hence of the royal line, is an obscure camel driver. Juda Bar Simon, a fanatical believer in the coming of the secular Messiah who will conquer Rome, later betrays the spiritual Messiah. Bar Simon inspires Cheliel with the dream of reclaiming the kingship of Israel by throwing off the Roman yoke. Word of these aspirations comes to Herod's ears, and he orders Cheliel killed. But the true Messiah (the story never refers to "Jesus" or "Christ," but only to "Messiah") miraculously brings Cheliel back to life. Cheliel then vows to help the Messiah by plotting the overthrow of the Romans, and he persists in viewing the Messiah as a political king of Israel.

The spiritual concept of the Messiah is espoused by Adah, a convert whose father has been brought back to life by the Messiah. Although Adah and Cheliel are in love, she cannot bring him to accept her spiritual view of the Messiah, and he ultimately abandons her in order to advance his ambitions to become king. He and Juda undergo many adventures in promoting their plans. Juda betrays the Messiah on the theory that the arrest will precipitate armed action when the Messiah enters into Jerusalem, this forcing, as he thinks, a miracle that will result in the conquest of the Romans and investment of the Messiah as king. When he reveals to a "stranger" that he is the one who betrayed the Messiah, he is answered with "intensity of contempt. . . . 'Thou!—a Jew! Then is the world gone mad when one who cometh but to save is sold by those who are not worth the saving.' " With the failure of the revolt, Juda hangs himself in remorse.

For his part, Cheliel is now an enemy of the Messiah who has thwarted his ambition for kingship. But after the crucifixion Cheliel is converted and rejoins the forgiving Adah, saying: "I have learned to hold the wiser precepts of the Master of Men—He whom Moses' Law and our nation's blinding hate alike have slain on Calvary." Ten years later Cheliel is Stephen, the first Christian martyr, condemned to death by stoning by judgment of "the vindictive Seventy, compounded of bigotry and superstition, of jealousy and craft, who made up the great Sanhedrin of Jerusalem."[85]

Come Forth! (1891), by Elizabeth Stuart Phelps and Herbert F. Ward, is an exposition of the religious life of the Jews. This theme is the vehicle for the love story of Lazarus, depicted as an artist who resists Pharisaic rigidity and finally becomes the Lazarus of the Gospel story. The approach to the Jews is generally benign, except for the rendering of Annas the Sadducee as a ruthless, rigid, cruel man, and of Malachi the Pharisee, to whom Jesus "may prove a dangerous fellow." Before his conversion Lazarus is "a conscientious, influential Pharisee,—the progressive, protestant, the come-outer of his faith and time." His love for Zahara releases his soul, and "he ceased to be a cautious Jew." With all their deficiencies, write the authors, the Pharisees are "a party with many excellent points not always credited" to them.[86] The burden of the story, however, is the conversion of Lazarus, his family, and his friends through Jesus' miracles: the restoration of one's sight, of another's ability to walk after paralysis, and even the restoration of life to Zahara.

An intense indictment of the Jews as a rigid and deicidal people is leveled in a later novel by Elizabeth Stuart Phelps. *The Story of Jesus*

Christ (1897) is a straightforward reconstruction of the Gospel life of Jesus. "Of mercy," she writes, the Jews "knew little. Commandments carved in stone by the greatest of legislators grimly cut their ancient laws into the Hebrew instinct. . . . Moses was not a tender man. The fiat and consequences were as unornamented as Sinai, and as hard." At the trial of Jesus, Pilate is "more than ready to dismiss the complaint against the Nazarene," but he sees that he cannot deflect "the inexorable Hebrew will." The Jews set up one long sinister cry for crucifixion: "Baser was never uttered by any nation." What else could one expect from "a church dying of ceremony, rotten with hypocrisy"? How could Jesus expect acceptance of his doctrine "that they should love their neighbors as they loved themselves" by a people "whose habits of thought were stiff with the selfishness of a race to which self-protection has been for generations foremost in mind"?[87]

The contrast between Christianity and Judaism is even more sharply drawn by Edward Payson Berry in *Leah of Jerusalem* (1890), which examines the career of Paul. As the Pharisaic Saul of Tarsus, "hater of the Nazarenes" and the man who condemned Stephen to death by stoning, he has led a people from whom "fell the thick covering of their pride, and they stood forth in all their naked hideousness, the murderers of the Son of God." But Stephen has left behind some believers, like Leah (whose sight he has miraculously restored), who know "that a great revolution had taken place" in their lives. Only after being captured by bandits, which results in the death of her little son, does Leah realize how great the change is: she is no longer a Jew. " 'Thou shalt love thy neighbor and hate thine enemy,' " writes the author, "had become a maxim vacant of meaning to the noble girl. Its force had vanished. Under the guidance of that spiritual presence which was ever at her side, Leah did not know how little of a Jew she had become."[88] Her story is joined to that of Saul, become Paul, by her conversion and life under Paul's influence. For Berry, as for so many of the writers of religious fiction, the only good Jew is the converted Jew.

While most of the conversions in the novels derive from direct experience of Jesus and his miracle-making, there is no lack of conversion by remote influence as well—through secondhand accounts of miracles, eyewitness reports, and letters from the source—as in Enoch Fitch Burr's *Aleph, the Chaldean* (1891). As usual, the most positive characters are those who become converted. When news of Jesus trickles down to Alexandria, the locus of the story, the sages of the synagogue discount it. Jesus, they say, cannot be the Messiah, for he "is a mighty King and Deliverer. Jesus is plain in appearance, associates even with publicans and sinners, and has nothing of the warrior and statesman about him—in fact, says his kingdom is not of this world." The miracles of Jesus must therefore be attributed to "the Evil One." Those who are convinced of his authenticity believe that

this Messiah is not, as has commonly been supposed, a secular warrior, conquerer, and king; but a spiritual monarch ruling over willing hearts in the interests of truth and righteousness, and whose victories are salvations—that his mission in the world is one of humiliation instead of exaltation, suffering instead of pleasure, of death instead of life; and that in dying he completed a vicarious sacrifice for the sins of the world.

Neither of the two synagogues in Alexandria, and only the best individuals among the Jews, accept Jesus. The traditional synagogue is headed by Alexander, who has a "genius for honorable money-making," as well as eloquence and scientific ability. He is an admirable human being, even though he remains unconverted. But the leader of the second synagogue, called Malus, "Evil," is clandestinely a villain, rapacious and crafty. Malus is obese and pockmarked, has a "characterless expression," and is "by far the largest and most successful dealer in the city."[89] Unlike Alexander's synagogue, however, that of Malus allows freedom of interpretation of the Law, so that any adherent can reject or accept anything in the Bible according to his own lights. Thus Burr seems to equate freedom of interpretation of the Bible with evil, though he does not explain how this critical approach differs essentially from that of Jesus.

The tradition of Christian anti-Semitism because of the Jews' alleged deicide is strongly and intensely asserted in the popular tetralogy by Florence M. Kingsley: *Titus* (1894), *Stephen* (1896), *Paul* (1897), and *The Cross Triumphant* (1898). The keynote of the series is taken from 1 Thessalonians 2:15 (she does not use the King James Version), as quoted in *Paul:* The Jews "killed both the Lord Jesus and the prophets"; they are "a people displeasing to God, and enemies to all mankind."[90] At a time when anti-Semitism was rising and becoming more overt than ever in the United States, the Kingsley stories, with their enormous popularity, could only promote this tendency among pious Christians. Unmistakably, among the Jews all virtues belong to those who acknowledge Jesus as Savior, and all evil to those Jews who "believed not, for their eyes were blinded to the light, and their souls were filled with bitterness and envy."[91] The miracles performed by Jesus are abundantly used to precipitate conversion. In the first story Titus, the kidnaped son of Caiaphas, has become a member of a Jewish defense force headed by Barabbas. (This is not the robber band of the New Testament story.) They are arrested by the Romans while attempting to remove the Roman eagle from the Temple, and Titus is crucified with Jesus.

The anti-Jewish feeling that pervades *Titus* is intensified in *Stephen,* which depicts the ministry of Stephen and his death at the hands of evil Jews during the time when Paul was the relentless, cruel Pharisee Saul. Stephen has performed miracles that have brought many Jews and Arabs to Christianity. His martyrdom is brought about by Jewish manipulation, murder, and mayhem. The series continues with *Paul,* his conversion, and his ministry, and again Mrs. Kingsley underlines her conception of the Jews as evil when they do not acknowledge Jesus: "We see the breed of evil creatures, that loved darkness rather than light, bestir themselves to do him [Paul] battle." But Paul outwits the scheming Jews, and the "malignant hatred" for the Christians by anti-Christian Jews is turned into "impotent rage."

Not only do the Jews hate Paul; they fight savagely among themselves. The Sadducees and Pharisees, writes the author, are "past finding out; first they are all for beating the man [Paul] to death, then half of them turn and fight the other half like a pack of curs. Ay, curs they be, one and all." They are also called "these slippery rabbins from Jerusalem."[92] Throughout the book Jews are depicted as rigid, mechanical followers of the Law. They are also exclusivistic, refusing any contact with gentiles. Only those who accept Jesus are virtuous. And in the last volume of the tetralogy, *The Cross Triumphant,* the Jews get their comeuppance in the destruction of the Temple, which to the author is a proper, climactic punishment for their presumed deicide.

The conventional distinction, in a simple child's level of prose, between converted and unconverted Jews recurs in Mary Elizabeth Jennings's *Asa of Bethlehem* (1895). At first Asa cannot accept Jesus because he believes the Messiah will "come with pomp and power and riches," and not humbly, like the actual Jesus, preaching and healing. He is finally converted by the miracles of Jesus, and, when he is dying, he states the theme of this book (and many others): "O Israel, my nation! . . . He would forgive thee thy sins, and heal thy body of disease, yet how hast thou received the precious gift? With hate and reviling and unbelief. And now thou wouldst kill him, the

Son of God! His blood will be upon thee, and God's curse will rest upon thee and crush thee utterly and forever." Judas' treachery is attributed to disillusionment with his dream that the disciples would possess "power and greatness"[93] when Jesus ruled the Kingdom of Israel.

The ministry, as seen through the eyes of a twelve-year-old boy, Antipas, and without animus against Jews, is the subject of Louise Seymour Houghton's *Antipas, Son of Chuza* (1895). The boy at first cannot acknowledge Jesus as the Messiah because "there is a strange absence in this young man of all we have been wont to expect in the Messiah—no pomp, no majesty, no military following." Antipas becomes dangerously sick, and at Chuza's request Jesus miraculously restores Antipas to health from a distance; all are converted by this evidence of supernatural power. They perceive in him an authority that requires no support from tradition. Jesus speaks so simply that the young Antipas can understand him. The boy "had supposed that it was right for people to hate their enemies and for Jews to hate and despise Gentiles; he had supposed that God loved only good people, and it seemed very strange that Jesus taught that the Heavenly Father loves and cares for every one, whether he is good or bad, and proved that God is infinitely loving."[94] Yet this book, unlike many others of its genre, does not have the effect of promoting doctrinaire hatred of and incitement against Jews.

William Osborn Stoddard, author of some seventy books for young people, wrote several that emphasized the universalistic aspect of Christ as against the particularism of the Jews. In *The Sword-maker's Son* (1895), Ezra the swordmaker has an "aquiline" nose, but his sixteen-year-old son, Cyril, has a straight nose and "his lips were thinner." His mother was Greek but had converted to Judaism, and "in him the Hebrew and Greek races had been merged into one." Their extremely doctrinaire rabbi, Isaac Ben Nassur, leads them to expect the "promised King" who would come "to lead us against the Romans."[95] Convinced by his miracles that Jesus is the Messiah, Cyril follows him, but does not rid himself of the notion of Jesus as a military leader. Ezra, who also believes in a military Messiah, trains soldiers to be placed at Jesus' disposal at the crucial hour. The Pharisees become ever more hostile to Jesus and finally demand, and get, his crucifixion. This denouement finally convinces Ezra and Cyril that the kingdom of which Jesus preached is not of this world.

In *Ulric the Jarl* (1899) the universalistic thesis is even more pronounced. For the story is essentially about the pilgrimage of the

Viking jarl (leader) Ulric from the northland to learn more about "the Jews and their God," of whom he has heard his father speak. Ulric wishes to discover if "this Jew God hath ever met with Odin and Thor, and whether or not they are friends." On the way Ulric's ship rams a Roman vessel; Ben Ezra, a warrior, is rescued from it and becomes Ulric's friend. Ben Ezra is the typical patriarch, "tall and broad and strong and heavily bearded. His face proveth for him high intelligence, . . . a subtle man. . . . He is a man of rank among his own people, for common men are not as he is."

They journey to Judea and on the way, Ben Ezra tells Ulric that after Hannibal's defeat at Carthage, "even their gods died, being slain by the sword of Jehovah"; to which Ulric replies: "I like your god, that destroyeth his enemies." Ben Ezra also tells Ulric that his own wife and his daughters had killed themselves "rather than become the sport of the heathen."[96] Ulric replies that he would like to find a woman like that, but Ben Ezra warns him that such a one would not marry one who was not a Jew. And later, when Ulric is stunned by the beauty of Miriam in Jerusalem, she does indeed send him away because he is not a Jew. However, they are later reunited by their common conversion to Christianity.

At Mount Carmel, Ulric and Ben Ezra come upon Jesus, who looks to Ulric "not altogether like a Jew. I have seen darker Saxons. I think he is a jarl. Such as he might be a leader of men." They witness Jesus performing miracles. Ulric is impressed and offers himself to Jesus as a soldier in his service. Jesus replies: "Thou knowest not yet what thou art. . . . But the Saxons are also my people. I shall send for them." Along the way Ben Ezra runs afoul the inevitable moneylender and dealer in stolen gods, Abbas, who is a henchman of Herod and Pilate; he is characterized by Ben Ezra as being "overfond of money."[97] When Ulric hires himself out as a gladiator his legs are broken, but Jesus heals them miraculously, and Ulric reiterates his offer to be a soldier for Jesus. He is condemned as a murderer and is crucified with Jesus; only then is he fully converted. The quest of Ulric the Jarl thus becomes one episode in the preordained spread of Christianity.

The Jews are heavily berated for their rejection of Jesus in Katherine Pearson Woods's two stories, *John, a Tale of King Messiah* (1896) and *The Son of Ingar* (1897). As *John* opens the Jews collectively are credited with favorable qualities. Although "the rabbis took care to exempt themselves from taxation, their arrangements for the public education, health and welfare were far in advance of all modern legislation, and of all but the best of modern thought." But as the

Jews clash with Jesus and his movement the author's opinion changes, and she emphasizes their alleged invidious traits—excepting, of course, for those Jews who embrace Jesus. She feels it necessary to differentiate John from the Jews by making him "slightly above the average height of the small Hebrew race."

Judas receives much attention. He is a merchant who is in love with Ingar, the non-Jewish daughter of Mary. When he proposes to Ingar, she recoils from him with horror because she has a prevision of his betrayal of Jesus. In Mrs. Woods's emendation of the Judas story, Malchus, the high priest's servant (mentioned in John 18: 4–10), is the go-between in the bribery of Judas. Judas is approached by Malchus, who has a "face with the hooked nose and gleaming eyes, the face of a money-changer . . . who also had been driven from the Temple by the Lord." Malchus complains that Jesus has called the money changers "friends of the Mammon of unrighteousness," when they are only after all deriving "lawful gains which a man may win from the trade whereby he lives."

At first Judas refuses the bribe that Malchus offers him to betray Jesus, but Malchus assures him that "the offer is always open." When Judas finds he is unable to perform miracles, and believes that he has failed because "the Lord was jealous, and would not that any but himself should do powers in the sight of the multitude," he agrees to Malchus' offer. Afterward, Judas hangs himself in remorse, and the author adds an unintended farcical conclusion to the story; the branch on which Judas hangs himself breaks. "Once more," writes Mrs. Woods, "Judas had blundered, the old tree was insecurely rooted to sustain the weight. Down, down, neither living nor dead, upon the toothed rocks in the dreadful valley" Judas falls. The real victim of the crucifixion, writes the author, is not Jesus but Israel; "the tragedy centered not at Golgotha, but in Jerusalem." Her hostility to the Jews comes out in her characterizations, like that of the sheep dealer Menahem, who is "primed to the lips with malice and a knowledge of the law," and the thief Bar-Phineas, "a sinister looking fellow, with strongly Jewish features,"[98] who is crucified with Jesus.

A sequel, *The Son of Ingar,* carries the descendants of the earlier characters into the time of Paul. A number of them undergo conversion, and as usual the unconverted characters are the bad ones, even though the author acknowledges that Christianity originated among the Jews. The unconverted are associated with the devil, and the converted are intensely spiritual. The gospeler James has doubts that the Jews will ever see the light: "God be praised," he says, "that

salvation is come unto the Gentiles, but is Israel cast off forever?
. . . Unto a Gospel which is for the uncircumcised also, Israel will
never hearken." The unconverted are inexorably sharp in money
dealings. Zilpah tries to persuade Theophilus, the converted son of
Ingar and John, to renounce Christianity, but he rejects her urgings
with: "O Zilpah, thou knowest thine errand was of the devil." The
sinfulness of her petition is so profound that she expires on the spot
with her arms spread in the form of a cross. Another recalcitrant
Jewish figure, Alexander, a wealthy man from Ephesus, "lived, for
the most part quietly and uprightly, save only for a certain greed of
gain for its own sake, which had very early laid hold upon his soul."
on another occasion he "was still Israelite enough to wish to be
revenged." One cannot avoid the conclusion that the author suspects
that it is the stiff-necked nature of the Jews and their love of gain that
account for the fact that "the Jews were everywhere hated among
the nations among whom they were scattered abroad."[99]

Two religious novels published in 1896, however, do not bear
down heavily on the Jews as a whole. While they agree, as Caroline
Atwater Mason writes in *The Quiet King,* that "among the people at
large, religion had become a dry and empty thing," they do not
encourage hostility to the Jews as a deicidal people. Mason brings
out the contrast between the worldly and spiritual conceptions of the
Messiah by introducing Adriel, a boy contemporary with Jesus and
a "prince of Israel," who will rule after Herod is overthrown. The
contrasting lives of Adriel and Jesus are followed. Adriel is cruel,
selfish, dissolute to the point of self-destruction; Jesus is, of course,
perfect. After Adriel is restored to health by a miracle of Jesus, he
is converted. He is arrested for defending Jesus, escapes, and proselytizes for Jesus in Rome.

The author's judgment on the Jews after the crucifixion is straightforward and lacks the usual barb. "For the fact was simply this," she
writes. "The nation, whether Sadducee, Herodian, ecclesiastic, or
Pharisee, men who cringed to Rome or those who plotted for freedom and independence, the worldly minded or the bigoted religion-
ists, all alike, save the lower classes of society, having weighed the
claims of the Nazarene to the Messiahship, had scornfully rejected
him." On the other hand, she condemns the high priests mercilessly:
Annas, she writes, had "a cruel crafty smile" and made one grow
"dizzy before the depths of man's hideous hatred" of Jesus. The
author does not mitigate the character of Pontius Pilate, as so many
have done: he "used his power to its utmost limit of cruelty and
violence. Like all cruel men, he was cowardly."[100]

Another novel that displays no special animus toward the Jews is

Fannie E. Newberry's *Wrestler of Philippi* (1896), which is superior to most of the books of the genre in narrative skill and interest. Its purpose is to stress the universalism of Christianity and the saintliness of the early converts. As the Christian Jewish woman Elizabeth says: "There is neither Jew, nor Greek, nor Roman, either, in the sight of God—all are equal and his children." The time of the story is about a generation after the crucifixion, when Greeks, Romans, Jews are being converted by the Pauline mission and persecuted by Nero. A prosperous Jewish dyer, Lydia, is treated favorably by the author, even though she is "a Pharisee of the strictest sect, . . . [and] found it difficult to believe that any Messiah would be other than a great King and Deliverer who would restore Jerusalem, and make the Jewish nation once more a power among men."

Jewish resistance to Paul's ministry is described, and one incident reflects a reverse image of the ritual murder hoax later used against the Jews. The Jews, writes the author, "told the most shocking stories of the Christian rites and practices. The breaking of bread and drinking of wine 'in remembrance' were construed into an actual feeding upon human flesh and blood, and infants were said to be stolen for this revolting ceremony."[101] Severe as the author's criticism of the Jews may be, it does not invite hatred, as most novels in the genre do.

The influence of Christ is only vaguely and occasionally hinted at in an adventure story of the Rome of Tiberius, J. Breckenridge Ellis's *Dread and Fear of Kings* (1900), but the universalism of Christianity is emphasized. In the end, Jews, Greeks, and Romans live sainted lives as Christians in Palestine. Mary has visited Jerusalem and has been converted by Jesus. Alexis, an architect, esthete, and hedonist, has a Greek mother and a Jewish father, but conceals his Jewish origin. When he sees Mary's picture, he perceives that she is not like other Jews. He "saw that she was a Jewess. Had he not seen many Jews? But not one of them wore this look. There was here no pride in a national God not to be shared by other nations; there was here no hatred for the Gentile world." Mary tells Alexis that she speaks to him "of the only God, for there is but one; and I have seen the Son, for he liveth in Judea." When Mary is taken to Tiberius' court to be a concubine, she mars her face to avert the catastrophe, and the esthetic Alexis repudiates her. She marries the Roman soldier Caius, who falls in love with her precisely because of her heroic act, and both are converted. The couple go to "far-off Palestine, where the Christ had been crucified," and there "lived, loved, and were happy."[102]

Ellis balances "good" and "bad" among the unconverted Jews.

The "good" Jew is Zia, father of Mary; he is a Jewish slave who is heroic, clever, brave, and altogether admirable from beginning to end, even though he is never converted. Mary's uncle, called only "the Jew," is rich, ordinary, and avaricious. He wishes his niece Mary to marry a rich old Roman because of his money and status, and because the Roman might harm their family if he is rejected. The uncle drives his brother, Zia, from his door, refusing him even overnight shelter when Zia is being hunted as an escaped Roman slave.

Our sole interest in William A. Hammond's *Son of Perdition* (1898) is as an example of nineteenth-century anti-Semitism. This poorly written, overblown, and amateurish book centers on a variation of the Judas story. Here Judas is not a Jew, but stems from a noble Syrian family. He is converted to Judaism by love for Salome. The leader of a robber band, he joins Jesus in order to enhance his own power over the people. After the betrayal he kills himself. All Jews in the story who lean toward Jesus are good, all others are rigid, fanatical observers of the Law. Pilate is gently treated. Remorseful over the crucifixion, Pilate tells the Jewish priests that they caused him to "violate the first principle of justice." There is something slightly indecent in placing in the mouth of Pilate this anathema on the Jewish people: "You are a turbulent and ill-disposed set of men. The time will come when Rome will destroy your city to its uttermost foundations. You are not fit to form a nation. You will be scattered throughout the earth, and you will be despised and hated by the people among whom you dwell, for what you have done to this man, Jesus."[103]

The intention of the religiously oriented novels of this genre, as expressed in the endpaper of a volume in the Sabbath Library, was "to make the life and teachings of Jesus seem real and practical."[104] Some were written primarily for young people, but it is not always easy to distinguish these from the works for adults. Both types have essentially the same purpose and style; they are usually didactically moralistic and credulous, and are often cast in the form of adventure fiction. Hardly any can claim literary distinction. Most draw invidious comparisons between Christianity and Judaism in which the latter is criticized or condemned with varying degrees of intensity. In most of them the comparison is enforced through several recurrent themes: the "Jewish" politico-military versus the "Christian" spiritual conception of the Messiah; the negative characterization of Jews who refuse to acknowledge Christ as Savior; deicide of the Jews; facile conversion of Jews, usually under the influence of miracles; and anachronistic expressions of anti-Semitism.[105]

8

THE HISTORICAL NOVEL

Considering the vogue of the historical novel in the 1800s, the days of Scott's greatest popularity, it is not surprising that the Jew is to be found in a few of them. The novels on biblical and early Christian themes that began to pour forth in the 1830s are, of course, historical, but they focus on the religious rather than the historical aspect; hence they have been treated separately here.

James Fenimore Cooper tried his hand at the historical novel in one of his least successful books, *The Bravo,* published in 1831. In an essay on Cooper, William Cullen Bryant relates that Cooper was prompted by Lafayette to write this novel as a reply to aristocratic European critics of his native land.[1] Cooper designed the book to demonstrate that although Venice was called a republic, it was actually ruled by a despot. Whether a country is actually democratic, he asserts, depends on whether its government is based on majority consent. If a government lacks majority support and imposes its will by physical force, as in Venice, it is not a republic no matter what its form.

Cooper's plot is devised to expose the government of Venice, which is vice-ridden and in which unscrupulous Jews carry out the evil intentions of the ruling despots. His depiction of the Jewish jeweler and moneylender Hosea is in the worst tradition of the stereotype, and the novel is peppered with pejorative references to the Jews—some in the mouths of characters, and others as interjections by the author. Hosea is a "bearded old rogue," a "knave of a Jew," and "a grasping Hebrew." He has a "quick, greedy, suspicious eye," and "a manner in which habitual cupidity and subdued policy completely mastered every other feeling."[2] With fidelity to the stereotype, Hosea professes a shortage of funds when asked for a loan and like Shylock, promises to collect the sum from his fellow Jews.

Hosea is implicated in a plot to kill Don Camillo, beloved of Violetta, because the state wishes to give Violetta in marriage to Giacomo Gradenego, the villainous and profligate son of a Venetian senator. The deed is to be done by Jacopo, who purports to be a bravo (an assassin) but is really an upright young man who has actually killed no one. He has been forced by the state to acquire the reputation of a bravo and thus to shield the actual murderers for state purposes, in exchange for release of his innocent father from prison. Jacopo foils the plot, and Don Camillo and Violetta are united at the end. Jacopo is then charged with the murder of a gondolier, and although the state authorities know him to be innocent, they have him executed. Thus Cooper exposes the vice and despotism of the "republic" of Venice. Hosea's function in the plot is to hire Jacopo for the murder and to arrange payment for the deed. The murder is to take place in the Jewish cemetery, "among your despised graves," thus making it more diabolical; for this cemetery is "set apart for heretic and Jew," and to be dispatched there is "the last indignity which man can inflict on his fellow."[3]

Prior to Hosea's involvement in the murder plot, he lends money to the nefarious Giacomo, whose father strongly disapproves of their connection—"that one of the scions of thy great stock should waste his substance for the benefit of a race of unbelievers!" At the same time, the senator affirms the utility of the Jews to the state. They are financially "of good service in the republic's straits." But for encouraging Giacomo's profligacy by his loans, the senator says, "the Hebrew shall be punished, and as a solemn warning to the whole tribe, the debt confiscated to the benefit of the borrower. With such an example before their eyes, the knaves will be less ready with their sequins [gold coins]."[4] Jewish moneylending provides the occasion for numerous pejorative allusions throughout the novel, which give unrelenting support to the stereotype.

Cooper is not, however, totally insensitive to the condition of the Jews. He praises the freedom from intolerance in his own country:

We shall not endeavor to seek that deep-seated principle which renders man so callous to the most eloquent and striking appeals to liberality, but rest satisfied with being grateful that we have been born in a land, in which the interests of religion are as little as possible sullied by the vicious contamination of those of life; in which Christian humility is not exhibited beneath the purple, nor Jewish adhesion by intolerance.[5]

A few years before writing *The Bravo,* Cooper, then traveling in Europe, had proudly emphasized the successful separation of church and state at home. For instance, Mordecai M. Noah, "the sheriff of the city of New-York," he writes, "an officer elected by the people, was, a few years ago, a Jew!"[6] Unfortunately Cooper was mistaken in his facts. Noah was indeed appointed sheriff of New York in 1822 but was defeated for the office when it was made elective in 1824, and anti-Semitic charges were a factor in his defeat. Despite equality in principle, the Jews remained to some extent the target of age-old prejudice.

Cooper's goodwill leads him to account for the money obsession attributed to the Jews. Giacomo tells Hosea: "The shrewdness of thy race is its livelihood!" To which Hosea answers: "It is its sole defence against the wrongs of the oppressor, young noble. We are hunted like wolves, and it is not surprising that we sometimes show the ferocity of the beasts you take us for."[7] Despite Cooper's protestations of tolerance, he depicts Hosea as a thorough villain. Although Hosea is quite ready to participate in a murder, he advises Giacomo against it, urging that disabling rather than killing the intended victim will suit their purpose. The picture of the Jews follows the stereotype in that they are presented as a morally inferior people.

Some years later Cooper introduced a discussion of the Jewish question in a quaint, whimsical manner in *The Oak-Openings* (1848). Parson Amen, a missionary to the Indians, appears before an Indian tribal council and tries to persuade them that "the red man is a Jew; a Jew is a red man," for "Manitou has brought the scattered people of Israel to this part of the world." This belief, is, of course, the old Puritan theory that the Ten Lost Tribes of Israel wandered eastward till they settled in America. An Indian replies that a local bee-hunter had spoken to him of the Jews as "a people who do not go with the pale-faces, but live apart from them, like men with the small-pox." The millenarian preacher replies that the bee-hunter has misinterpreted the Bible, for the Jews are "the chosen people of the Great Spirit, and will one day be received back to his favour. Would I were one of them, only enlightened by the words of the New Testament!" Nevertheless, the Indian replies, "we do not wish to be Jews. . . . We think we are red men, and Injins, and not Jews."[8]

A chief asks the awkward question of whether "the pale-faces honour and show respect to Jews?" The parson is forced in truth to answer no, though really good Christians "look with friendly eyes on this dispersed and persecuted people." The council deliberates whether to accept designation as Jews, and discussions with the palefaces continue. One Indian asserts that, though he never saw a Jew, "I will own that I have a sort of grudge against them, though

I can hardly tell you why." In any case, he adds, "no man breathing should ever persuade me into the notion that *I'm* a Jew, lost or found, ten tribes or twenty." Another Indian affirms that his is a great tribe that "never was *lost*. It *cannot* be lost," since none know the paths through the woods better than they. "I never heard of these Jews before," he concludes, "I do not wish to hear of them again." Another chief is "not surprised" to hear that the Jews are lost, for "it seems to me that all pale-faces get lost. They wander from their own hunting-grounds, into those of other peoples." The Indians conclude that it is not they, but the Yankees who are lost. "The Yankees are Jews, they are lost."[9]

Possibly in order to vie with Cooper, William Gilmore Simms also attempted to write a historical novel, with scarcely greater success than his rival. Both novelists wrote their best work when basing it on indigenous materials. In *Pelayo* (1838) Simms attempted a historical romance about the eighth-century Spanish hero to whom legend has assigned the role of the founder of Spain as a nation; Jews figure importantly in it. Simms's treatment of the Jews is far more sympathetic and perceptive than Cooper's, both historically and culturally. Indeed, it would appear from this novel that anti-Jewish attitudes were remarkably absent in Simms. Though the tale is not totally free from the conventional literary image of the Jew, a superior understanding of the Jewish situation pervades his allusions to them. He opens his romance with the unpopular King Witiza's treatment of his Jewish subjects, whom he oppresses and orders expelled. As a consequence, the Jews enter into an intrigue with Witiza's enemies, the Saracens, against the king. When the plot is frustrated, the Jews are oppressed even more heavily. The lesser nobles, though they are also discontented with Witiza, further exacerbate the hardships of the Jews. Simms makes the interesting observation that "the intrigues of the oppressed Jews had opened the eyes of thousands in other classes, to their own oppression."[10] Witiza is killed in single combat with the Goth Roderick. Pelayo, Witiza's son, vows to avenge the defeat of his father, and the novel is substantially concerned with Pelayo's struggle to restore the country for the good of the people.

Pelayo meets the wealthy Jew Melchior, who proposes to ally his small Jewish army with the forces of Pelayo, even though Pelayo is "possessed of many of the prejudices common among Christians of the time, which held the Jews an odious race on many accounts, as well of trade as of religion." Simms comments: "[Pelayo's] mind was too superior to the prejudices of the period, too noble and truly chivalric not to forebear." The patriarchal Jew gives his allegiance to Pelayo as king. When Pelayo charges Melchior with disloyalty to his country for his alliance with the Saracens, Melchior replies: "And what is my country? What is the country of the Hebrew? This is not his country. The ties which thou wouldst bind him to it are the scourge and the chains, the cruel taunt and unlimited exaction. . . . The practice of the Saracen was the Christian faith—the Christian practice to the Hebrew was worthy of the name of terror and cruelty thou hast given the Saracen." Nevertheless Melchoir pledges his people's true devotion to Pelayo if the prince merits their confidence. Pelayo agrees, and Melchior pledges the service of his Jewish army of three thousand men.

The plot weaves in and out of intrigues among the rivals for power. In the final battle Pelayo arms Melchior's Jewish army, but he has misgivings. "Thy people," says Pelayo, "ceased to be warlike —they ceased to bear arms, and lost the noble exercises which make a warrior confident in his hand and weapon."[11] In the actual battle, however, the Jewish force fights well, and, together with Pelayo's army, they are victorious.

The Jews in the novel are stereotypes, not individuals. Melchior is the idealized patriarchal figure devoted above all to the freedom of his people and is an attractive figure reminiscent of Lessing's Nathan the Wise. His daughter, Thyrza, a beautiful Jewish girl, lacks a mother, as is usual in the convention. She is courted by the young Jew, Amri, a profligate and a spy for the enemy. Melchior, who knows of Amri's treachery, upbraids him, and reminds him that their struggle is "a blow for the emancipation of the Hebrews. It is thy freedom not less than ours," in accordance with Melchior's understanding with Pelayo. But Amri is incorrigible. Melchior and Thyrza refuse his offer of marriage. Later Amri's Gothic paramour poisons Amri and herself.

Thyrza is in love with Pelayo, even though of course they cannot marry. She is killed in a battle, but not before she undergoes conversion to Christianity. At one point she discusses Christianity with Melchior, who says:

It was a narrow policy in the Jewish people to seek his [Jesus'] death, for, of a certainty, he strove for the rescue of Israel from the tyrannic sway of the Romans; yet was it not so much the deed of our people as of the selfish priesthood who led them. They feared the rise of another faith which should swallow up their authority; and the Nazarene died, not because of the doctrine which he taught, but because he himself was a teacher. He was a good man, and his deeds and designs were holy; but I cannot think, my child, that he was a god, as the Christians regard him.

When Thyrza is felled by an arrow, Pelayo comes up to her and exclaims: "She died a Christian, Melchior—look! it is the holy cross which she bears within her hands!"[12]

Simms avails himself of another cliché—the luxurious living quarters of the wealthy Jew. Pelayo is led to the home of Melchior in Toledo. It is in the poorer section of the city and has an unprepossessing exterior. But after passing through a dark passage, Pelayo enters a richly furnished apartment. "It was thus," writes Simms, "that the persecuted Jew endeavoured to indulge his own eyes in these luxuries which he might not dare to expose to the eyes of others. It was thus that he strove to satisfy himself, by an extravagant crowding of his wealth around him, for the thousand privations he was compelled to undergo in his commerce with the world." Melchior offers his wealth and jewels in Pelayo's cause, for he values freedom for the Jew above all his possessions.

Melchior has won the trust of Pelayo. When they go to Archbishop Oppas to discuss their plans, that worthy recoils at an alliance with the Jew, "the slayer of his God—the foul and beastly infidel." To which Pelayo replies: "I truly say, Lord Oppas, that you, not less than this old Hebrew, are no Christian. The faith of Christ is that of liberty. It teaches that the religion of mankind must spring from each man's reason." And Simms comments ironically on Oppas: "To do murder for his cause was legitimate enough, but it was grossly unbecoming in a Christian to employ a Jew for that purpose."[13]

To account for Simms's unusually understanding and sympathetic attitude toward the Jews, it may be significant that he resided in Charleston, where the old established Jewish community was on quite good terms with their non-Jewish fellow townsmen. And perhaps the snubbing that Simms suffered from the Charleston aristocracy in his early years because of his lower-middle-class origin disposed him toward greater sympathy with the Jews than was usual. Nevertheless he was out of his depth in *Pelayo* and had to resort to the literary stereotypes in his depiction of eighth-century Spanish Jews. Nor did he rise above the stereotype in his rendering of the "exotic" Jewish woman in his short story "The Last Wager" (1843). This is a not particularly memorable tale of the Yazoo wilderness in Mississippi, set in 1824. Since Simms had traveled in Mississippi when he was eighteen, as does the youth in the story, it may embody some actual experiences of his own. The Jewish woman of the story

—a Christian at this time—is "darkly oriental . . . all beauty . . . the charm of the face before me grew out of the piercing, deep-set, and singularly black eye."[14]

Later in the century the popular novelist Amelia E. Barr depicted the Sheva and Rebecca stereotypes in her *Bow of Orange Ribbon* (1886). In the early 1770s, Jacob Cohen, a New York tradesman and moneylender, and his granddaughter, Miriam, become enmeshed in the love affair of Katherine Van Heemskirk and a British officer, Captain Hyde. Hyde, who owes Cohen money, responds contemptuously to Cohen's requests for payment. Katherine's father dislikes British officers because they are "insolent and proud men, all of them," and adds that he would like "to strike down the one [Hyde] who yesterday spurned with his spurred boot our good neighbor Jacob Cohen, for no reason but that he was a Jew." Cohen, however, is not visibly affected by Hyde's rebuffs: "There was neither anger nor impatience visible in his face." He has a shop on Pearl Street that has an unattractive exterior but is crammed with precious objects within. Cohen assures a client that he will "make my just profits—no more, no more."

Another feature of the stereotype is brought out when Cohen exhibits extraordinary medical skill—"the Holy One hath given me the power of healing," he explains—and he saves Hyde's life after the surgeon despairs of bringing Hyde back to health when he is wounded in a duel. Cohen's deed is only one, although the most important, of the services rendered to Hyde, and Hyde is led to repent of his prejudice. "Cohen," Hyde says, "few men would have been as generous, and, at this hour, as considerate as you. I have judged from tradition, and misjudged you. Whether we meet again, we part as friends."[15]

Cohen's grandchild, Miriam, is the Rebecca stereotype. Katherine's brother, Bram, is in love with the beautiful Miriam, but she promises Cohen that she will not marry Bram because he is "not of our people." Cohen explains: "If our law forbid us to sow different seeds at the same time in the same ground, or to graft one kind of fruit-tree on the stock of another, shall we dare to mingle ourselves with people alien in race and faith, and speech and customs?"[16] In his own display of prejudice, Cohen, a Sephardic Jew, would not have Miriam marry an Ashkenazic Jew from New York, and he sends to London for the Sephardic Juda Belasco as a suitable husband for Miriam. Bram's mother displays a less tolerant attitude than Bram or her husband. She believes that God is angry with the Jews, and that the Jews have even greater pride than the English or the

Dutch. Despite Barr's obvious attempt at goodwill to Jews, the characters of Cohen and Miriam are shaped by the stereotype rather than individually characterized.

Three nineteenth-century novels of the American Revolution are romans à clef containing fictional characterizations of three well-known Jewish figures: Haym Salomon, Major David S. Franks, and Rebecca Franks. All are treated with respect. The two Franks are not stereotyped and are treated no differently from sympathetic non-Jewish characters. Haym Salomon, however, is described according to the stereotyped "positive" Jewish character. His historical role in giving financial aid to the revolution leads the author to fall back on the primitive economic stereotype.

In John Richter Jones's anonymously published *The Quaker Soldier* (1858), Haym Salomon is extravagantly praised for his services to the revolution. But so little did the writer know the Jews, and so deeply ingrained was the stereotype, that the fictional Solomon Isaakski does Haym Salomon no great credit, other than to show that he is wholeheartedly committed to the cause of independence and freedom. Solomon is a short man, a "wealthy Polish Jew," a pawn-broker who speaks in stage dialect. Although he lives in a "dingy-looking edifice," behind this facade is an apartment that "could have been fitted up only in a dream, or by the gorgeous tastes of the Orient . . . a divan of some unknown, but rich and lustrous fabric, . . . burnished silver . . . a magnificent Turkish saber. . . ." The room is like a tent, arched with a "surprisingly magnificent . . . crimson cloth of cashmere . . . gathered by a golden cord of Saracenic arches." One chair is marked SACRED and never used, for Washington had once sat in it. Solomon explains to his military guests that he lives in a tentlike abode because "a curse has been on de Beni Israel since ve leave de tent and live in de house." Solomon's wife is an "exquisitely beautiful" Circassian. Solomon is "a type of oriental man—for he was energetic when roused to action, as he was luxurious in his softer hours. The outer world knew nothing of his luxury, as it knew nothing of his secret magnificence nor of his great wealth."[17]

Solomon's "face and forehead were grand; full of intellect and benevolence, with a slight seasoning of something like cunning, though not enough to impair the general effect; you could wonder what those features were doing on the shoulders of a pawnbroker." No one was "more zealous" in the cause of the revolution and "more ready to sacrifice what man held most precious. . . . His ease —no slight matter with him—his money—still more precious—was lavished unsparingly." He often "advanced the funds to carry on the war—to move the army, to equip the fleet; and . . . to the present day those loans are said to be not repaid." The pawnshop is actually a cover for Solomon's underground patriotic activities. However, Jones cannot resist adding that "possibly with his noble qualities he mingled some of the hereditary habits of his race."[18] The shop is left in the hands of a poor Jew, unflatteringly portrayed, and Solomon receives little gain from it.

In addition to his financial aid, Solomon participates in the army's intelligence activities, and his shop is a drop and channel for these operations. Solomon exclaims to his Christian comrades-in-espionage:

Oh, me friends, dis cause must not go down! It is de cause of me own race and peoples; it is mine own cause. Every vare ve Hebrews are treated as brute-beasts, not as mens; ve hab no rights, but de right to make moneys for de oppressors. If dis cause succeed ve vill see vat ve Hebrews can be. Oh, mine friends, ve vill be like oder mens . . . dis cause must not go down! Ve must fight for it till death! Meself vill fight too!

To which the Protestant minister replies that as a Puritan he too belongs to a group proscribed since the Restoration. "Side by side," he says, "we will fight the battle of proscribed and oppressed men."[19]

Rebecca Franks, so named, is a secondary character in S. Weir Mitchell's *Hugh Wynne* (1896). She was in actuality a famous beauty of the time who later married a British baronet, and Mitchell describes her as a pretty, charming young woman. Only once does he mention her Jewish origin, when, for a time, Hugh Wynne's cousin is enamored of her: "My cousin having so far shown no marked preference for any one except the elder Miss Franks, who was rich and charming enough to have many men at her feet, despite her Hebrew blood."[20] In all respects she is a romantic young beauty regarded no differently from any other.

Paul Leicester Ford's *Janice Meredith* (1899) briefly mentions Rebecca Franks's cousin, the patriot officer Major David S. Franks, who was an aide to Benedict Arnold but totally innocent of any participation in Arnold's treason. In Ford's novel Major Franks makes a brief appearance as the second to the hero, John Brereton, in a duel. His Jewishness is not alluded to, and he is treated like any other patriot officer.[21]

When Ford is not dealing with an honored Jewish figure of revolutionary history, however, he indulges in the stereotype for "comic" relief. In a tavern Brereton asks the tavern keeper to exchange a guinea for shillings. "A Jewish-looking man" offers him "dirty-two" shillings, bringing out from his purse "a batch of very soiled money." A drinker jeers: "Trust Opper to give a shilling less than it's worth." Brereton wants to buy a razor, so Opper brings a razor out of a pack, speaking "in an accent which proved his appearance did not belie his race." "You've a sharper to deal with now," says one of the company. "Now ye'll need no razor ter be shaved," says another. When Opper produces a razor he asserts: "Dot iss only dree shillings, und it iss der besd of steel." To which the "local wit" replies: "You can trust Opper to know pretty much everything 'bout steals. It's been his business for twenty years!" Brereton responds "good-naturedly, 'I want a sharp razor, not a razor sharp.' "[22]

In *Richard Carvel* (1899) the American novelist Winston Churchill tells a story of the last years of the eighteenth century, set in Maryland and England. A Jewish moneylender is introduced with undisguised contempt. The titular hero visits in England, where he mingles in aristocratic society and becomes friends with the historical Charles Fox. On a visit to Fox one day he discovers in the anteroom "a person seated with an unmistakable nose and odour of St. Giles's [a London slum district where many Jews lived]." Another friend, Fitzpatrick, enters but deliberately ignores the Jew, who is obviously trying to attract his attention to ask for repayment of a loan. Fitzpatrick tells the Jew to return the next day, and the Jew, who speaks with an accent, tells him he will return with a bailiff. After he leaves Fitzpatrick asks: "Do you have Jews in America, Mr. Carvel?" as if Jews are some kind of pestilential species.

Fox then enters and explains that he has a "Jerusalem chamber . . . where I keep my Israelites; but by Gad's life! I think they are one and all descended from Job, and not father Abraham at all. He [the Jew] must have thought me an ascetic, eh, Fitz? Did you find the benches hard? I had 'em made hard as the devil. But if they were of stone, I vow the flock could find their own straw to sit on." Fitzpatrick advises Fox to settle his accounts, for "the dog is like to snap at last." Fox replies with a laugh: "And the rest of it is not to be printed." Later in the story an allusion to the medieval notion of the devil's eye of Jews is made when Fox warns Carvel against a mean horse, who "had a devil inside him. It gleamed wickedly out of his eye. . . . 'He has a Jew nose; by all the seven tribes I bid you 'ware of him.' "[23] There is not the slightest intimation that Churchill dissents from the Jew-baiting done by his characters.

Another popular novelist of the period, Robert W. Chambers, included in *Cardigan* (1901) a Jew whom he no doubt considered a sympathetic character, since Saul Shemuel is loyal to the rebelling colonists and becomes a member of a gang of rebel guerrillas just before the Battle of Lexington; he is finally killed in an engagement with the British. But from such sympathetic characters may the Jewish people be preserved. Shemuel is an itinerant "Hebrew peddler" whose vocation is used to mask his function as courier for the rebels. Throughout he is described in the most contemptuous and condescending terms. He is "a little Hebrew man with watery, red-rimmed eyes," and he has a "red beard" and a "greasy neck." He acts with "alert obsequiousness."

When the young hero, Cardigan, meets Shemuel in Boston in the course of their preparations for revolt, "Shemuel almost rolled at my feet in ecstasy of humble delight, sniffling, writhing, breathing hard, and clawing at my sleeve in his transports at the sight of me." After Shemuel is killed by a British trooper, Cardigan delivers this dubious eulogy:

Like a doomed man the Jew had gone to his end, with what courage God had lent him. He had been a friend to me. For all his squalid weakness of limb, his natural fear of pain, his physical cowardice, he had not swerved from the service of his country, nor had he faltered or betrayed the confidence of men while peril imperilled himself. Nothing save his fidelity to us had forced him to leave the city; nothing save the love of liberty in his grotesque and dirty body had lured this errant child of Israel to risk his life in bearing messages for those who watched the weighty hours creep on towards the bloody dawn already gathering under the edges of the sleeping world.[24]

9

THE DRAMA

The Jews in the earliest American plays were American neither in nationality nor in style. They were simply a copy of the stereotypes established in British drama and solidly reinforced on the eighteenth-century British stage. With few exceptions, the traditional stereotype of the Jew persisted throughout the century in the approximately three dozen plays here examined in which he appears as a character. The reader should be cautioned, however, that this catalog of plays cannot claim to be exhaustive. For there were probably hundreds of plays written during the century that either have not survived, or exist in very rare editions or only in manuscript in obscure places. The copyright law of 1790 protected the author's rights on printed plays but not on performances. It was not until 1856 that an author's rights to royalties for presentation of his plays on the stage were protected. As a consequence, actors often bought plays outright from authors and kept them from being printed to prevent others from performing them. In this way highly successful plays by leading authors were monopolized by famous actors, who reaped a fortune from them, although the authors received only a pittance.

The stereotyped nature of the conception of the Jew in American drama is cast into relief by several considerations. First, in two highly successful plays of the century a broker and a usurer, who are not Jewish, emerge as quite different kinds of characters from the stage Jews in those same vocations. In Robert Montgomery Bird's *Broker of Bogota* (1834), reputed to be the best of his plays, the broker Febro, the central character, is a man of the highest integrity in business and in life. When the decadent and dissipated Hidalgo Cabarero (who corrupts and misleads Febro's son, Ramon, into stealing money from his father's vaults) baits Febro, there is no doubt where the sympathies of the author and the audience lie.

"Hola, you money-vender!/You reverend old blood-grater of the poor!/ . . . Come, how stand/Your vaults and money bags? Still filling, filling,/Like the horse leech's paunch, and crying 'More'?/I'll be thy customer. What rate today?/Not cent per cent, with tenth of gross for premiums?" When Febro responds: "I will not be angry,/Why should I with a rascal? Senor, base fellow,/You may go hang or drown—I'll give you naught,"[1] the audience echoes his sentiments. But if Febro had been a Jewish broker, this same taunting speech by Cabarero would make the audience laugh at Febro.

Similarly, in Nathaniel P. Willis's *Tortesa the Usurer* (1839) the non-Jewish usurer Tortesa is the hero of the piece, a wholly sympathetic and appealing character. In both plays the new middle-class character is defended against feudal attitudes, but in *Tortesa* the defense is more pronounced. The painter Angelo, Tortesa's rival for the hand of a count's daughter, challenges Tortesa to a sword fight, but Tortesa refuses and is not troubled by this violation of the feudal code of honor. "I have a use for life so far above/The stake you quarrel for, that you may choose your words to please yourself." In order to improve his social status, the wealthy Tortesa has virtually bought the count's consent to marry his daughter Isabella. "Oh, omnipotence of money!" says Tortesa. "Ha! Ha! Why, there's the haughtiest nobleman/That walks in Florence. *He!*—whom I have bearded—/Checked—made conditions to—shut up his daughter—/And all with *money!* . . . Had I been *poor,* that man/Would see me rot ere give his hand to me."[2]

But this dubious procedure turns out to be more of a reflection on the count than on Tortesa. Consider the negative intentions of the author and unsympathetic response of an audience to this speech if it had been uttered by a *Jewish* usurer. It is the decadence of the aristocrat, rather than the power of money, that is primarily criticized here. Tortesa continues to assert that he is not at all inferior to the aristocrat by a manifestation of the bourgeois sense of power. On his appointed wedding day, while awaiting the arrival of Isabella, Tortesa is greeted by a lord: "We're happy, Sir, to have you one of us." Tortesa is furious at this condescension. He asserts his independence: "What have I been *till now!*" he exclaims. "I was a man/Before I saw your faces! Where's the change?/Have I a tail since? Am I grown a monkey?" When the lords walk away Tortesa says, presumably to himself (and Jew-baiting in the process): "Here's a fellow/That, by much rubbing against better men,/Has, like a penny in a Jew's pocket,/Stolen the color of a worthier coin,/And thinks he rings like sterling courtesy./ . . . He was *'happy'*/That I should be one of them. . . . As if *till now,* I'd been a dunghill grub,/And was but just turn'd butterfly!"[3] In the end he releases Isabella to Angelo and marries Zippa, a merchant's daughter who loves him.

This treatment of the broker and the usurer significantly exposes the medieval character of the Shylock stereotype. During the Middle Ages the prohibition against Christian usury was conveniently merged with Jew-hatred, and this symbiosis of attitudes forms the base for the Shylock stereotype. But the stereotype persisted into the later period, even though the prejudice against usury, or interest-taking, had itself become obsolete. The dramatic treatment of Febro and Tortesa in extremely popular plays demonstrates that when not practiced by the Jew usury no longer bore a stigma; but it did when a Jew was a dealer in money.

The stereotyped nature of the Jew as character in drama also emerges when considered in relation to the indigenous comic types developed in the American theater during the century. The stock Jewish character is a direct imitation of his counterpart in English drama and is not American at all, except by total adoption. Indeed, the image projected is not even English but pan-European, deriving from the bogeyman the Middle Ages had made of the Jew. For about a century after the creation of the United States the drama used a ready-made comic type in the stage Jew that bore little direct relation to the Jew in American life. Indeed, as far as I have been able to discover it was not until mid-nineteenth century that an *American* Jew ever even appeared as a character in drama at all. This is in sharp contrast to fiction, for the first Jew in America to be introduced into American fiction was Achsa Fielding in part 2 of Charles Brockden Brown's *Arthur Mervyn,* in 1800.

One early play does not include a Jewish character but makes an invidious allusion to the Jews. In A. B. Lindley's *Love and Friendship* (1809), set in Charleston, the Yankee character Jonathan is searching for the captain of his ship, on "Broad-Street" of the city and says to himself:

I must keep tewe eyes bout me, or I shall be intewe King-street, and the black barded jews'll shave the hair off my teeth. Folks say they're keener than yankees for all they aynt hafe the wit; yit a poor lubberly country cracker, stands no more chance with um, 'thout he's a brother Jonathan, than a leetle Tomy cat in hall 'thout claws, or a fly skippen bout in a hot glew pot.[4]

In *Guiscard the Guerilla* (1844), H. J. Conway's romantic play set in Savoy, one of the characters takes on the disguise of a Jewish peddler to gain access to the imprisoned ladies, and thus to inform them of plans to effect their escape. He is, writes Conway, "disguised as a Jew Pedlar—Box strapped on his back and a pack before him —with repeated bows and the utmost servility." His speech is in the conventional dialect: "Got plesh your honorable ladyships and your honorable lordships! Poor Isaacs, ish all of a tremble to shtand in the preshence of such peautiful and noble pershons—. Will your lord-ships' honors choose anytings out of poor Isaacs' pack. There ish de most elegantest sword knots and de most peautifullest gloves and de most delightfullest snuff."[5]

Although there were few American plays with Jewish characters during the early period, the Jew was not absent from the American stage. The American audience became formally acquainted with the Jew on the stage in 1752. "The first play performed in America by a regular company of comedians," writes William Dunlap, first his-torian of the American theater, "was represented to a delighted audience. The piece was *The Merchant of Venice.*"[6] From this date to 1821, Edward D. Coleman has reported, eighty plays of Jewish interest were published or produced on the English stage. Of these, twenty-eight were produced also in the United States.[7] One of the most important, Cumberland's *Jew,* was staged in Boston in 1794, the same year as in England. In the next few years it was presented again in Boston and in Philadelphia, New York, Charleston, Prov-idence, and Hartford, so it was familiar to practically the entire theater audience.

The central character of the play is the classic stereotype of the "good" Jew, or counter-Shylock. However, Cumberland's good in-tentions far exceeded his power of characterization. When the moneylender Sheva is baited in the first scene as "the merest muck-worm in the city of London," he retorts with some eloquence:

We have no abiding place on earth—no country, no home. Every-body rails at us, everybody points us out for their way-game and their mockery. If your playwrights want a butt, or buffoon, or a knave to make sport of, out comes a Jew to be baited, and buffeted through five long acts, for the amusement of all good Christians. . . . How can you expect us to show kindness when, we receive none?[8]

In this negative stereotype Sheva is a character of absurd "good-ness" and a stage Jew in reverse. He is alone in the world, lacking even the usual beautiful daughter. As in the alleged poor feeding of Shylock's servant, Launcelot, he keeps his servant at the edge of starvation, though in a good cause. He and his servant barely nourish themselves in order to increase the funds available for charities to be dispensed to Christians. Anonymously and without motivation, Sheva loans a young man money to allow his marriage with a poor girl and settles ten thousand pounds on her. When Sheva discovers that the bridegroom's father had saved him years before from the Inquisition in Cadiz, he makes the young man his heir.

Sheva's appearance was welcomed. In March 1795 a reviewer, probably Dunlap, wrote in the *New York Weekly Magazine* that "the idea of vindicating the Jews and bringing forward on the stage a kind of white [!] Shylock is certainly a very happy one."[9] But the reviewer rightly bridles at the inadequacies in the characterization of the ultrabenevolent Sheva: "But why Mr. Cumberland has chosen to throw together such incongruities as make up the character of *Sheva* one cannot tell, unless the miserly traits of the Jew's character are introduced to give rise to Jabal's jokes. . . . We must confess that these are, in our opinion, very starved kind of witticisms. The serious part of the comedy is certainly deserving of praise."[10] When he discusses the production of 1795, Dunlap writes that "the comedy is deservedly praised as abounding in"—quoting a reviewer—" 'the purest morality and the most instructive lessons of disinterested virtue.' "[11]

A similar recognition of the need to redress the injustice of the Shylock stereotype is apparent in Joseph Dennie's *Port Folio* review of Thomas Dibdin's *Liberal Opinions,* produced in Philadelphia in 1801, which contains a character on the Sheva model. The reviewer thinks the play amusing, though not particularly striking "for strength of character or novelty of incident." But he adds that "we praise it for its evident tendency to obviate those unjust and illiberal prejudices which have too long been entertained in *every country except this* against that unfortunate race of men."[12]

Despite the large number of English plays with Jewish characters that were performed in the United States, few American playwrights wrote such characters into their works. As far as we have been able to discover, between 1794 and 1823 only six plays by Americans contain Jewish characters. These are Susanna Rowson's *Slaves in Algiers* (1794), William Dunlap's *Bonaparte in England* (1803), John Howard Payne's *Trial without Jury* (also titled *The Maid and the Magpie*) (1815), James Ellison's *American Captive* (1812), Jonathan B. Smith's *Siege of Algiers* (1823), and Mary Carr Clarke's *Benevolent Lawyer; or, Villainy Detected* (1823). The locus of all these plays is foreign, and none of the Jewish characters is American.

The cycle of plays about Barbary pirates of the first quarter of the century included North African Jewish bankers because in the Barbary States they in fact did negotiate with American representatives to free American citizens and ships captured by corsairs.* In pursuit of this theme, Mrs. Susanna Rowson, in her play *Slaves in Algiers,* produced in Philadelphia in 1794, was the first to introduce a modern Jewish character in American drama. Mrs. Rowson was born in England in 1762 and brought to this country at the age of six by her father, Lieut. William Haswell, a British officer. In 1778 she returned to England with him and was married. When her husband went bankrupt she wrote plays, acted, and sang to support the family. She returned to America in 1793, and in the next year her play was performed.

Slaves in Algiers, which dramatizes the attempt of a group of American captives to escape servitude, is full of melodramatic clichés and paper-thin characterizations. The Jewish characters are Ben Hassan, a London-born Jew turned Muslim to escape punishment for a crime in England, and his daughter, Fetnah, also born in London. No mother or wife is in evidence. Ben Hassan is an unmitigated villain, closer to Barabbas than to Shylock. The beautiful Fetnah is treated more gently, as the convention dictates. She is taught love of liberty by an American captive, Rebecca Constant, and wants to escape from Algiers with the Americans. Like Jessica, she wishes to become a Christian. To Frederic, the American hero of the piece, she exclaims: "I do wish, some dear, sweet Christian man would fall in love with me, break open the garden gates, and carry me off"; to which Frederic replies: "Say you so, my charmer, then I'm your man." At the end, however, the softhearted author cannot bear to have Fetnah follow in Jessica's footsteps and leave her ruined father. Fetnah gives up flight with her Christian lover and remains at home. "While my father was rich and had friends," she explains, "I did not much think about my duty; but now he is poor and forsaken, I know it too well to leave him alone in his affliction."[13]

But Mrs. Rowson is ruthless in her projection of Ben Hassan. Although born in England he speaks ungrammatically, lisps, and has the peculiar accent of the stage Jew. Fetnah, however, speaks good, unaccented English. Ben Hassan is in love with Rebecca, whom he has cheated out of the ransom money sent to her from America. When he proposes marriage, she excoriates him: "You who worship no deity but gold, who would sacrifice friendship, nay, even the ties

*On the Jews in the Barbary States, see above, chapter 1.

of nature at the shrine of your idolatry." The virtuous, she adds, "will scorn the venal wretch who barters truth for gold." Ben Hassan is bribed to arrange the escape of the American captives, but reveals to the audience in an aside that he will betray the plan. He sings a ballad relating how he came to be in Algiers and why he has become a Muslim. Beginning as a barker of petty wares in London, he went on to become a moneylender and graduated to forging bank checks.

> So, having cheated the Gentiles, as Moses commanded,
>   Oh, I began to tremble at every gibbet I saw;
> But I got on board ship, and here was safely landed,
>   In spite of the judges, counsellors, attorneys, and law.[14]

In fairness to Mrs. Rowson we should add that a footnote in the printed text informs us that this ballad was "not written by Mrs. Rowson."

Ben Hassan's betrayal does not succeed because the dashing Frederic has organized a slave revolt. The slave rebels surround Ben Hassan's house in search of Rebecca. Ben Hassan is terrified and resorts to the stage cliché of disguising himself as a woman, saying to himself: "Oh, this is a judgment fallen upon me for betraying the Christians." Thinking he is Rebecca, the slaves bring him before Frederic. When his wig falls off he is exposed and taken prisoner. The revolt overcomes the dey, and the victorious Frederic dispenses justice. "Ben Hassan," he says, "your avarice, treachery and cruelty should be severely punished; for, if any one deserves slavery, it is he who could raise his own fortunes on the misery of others." The petrified Ben Hassan then exclaims: "Oh, that I was crying old cloaths in the dirtiest alley in London." He is left to the mercy of the dey, who is repentant and wishes to be taught "how to amend all my faults." The dey promises Frederic that he will no longer abuse his power, and as a first token of reform he frees Ben Hassan.

At this point Fetnah renounces her lover and proclaims that she will remain behind with her father. The Americans depart for home, "where liberty has established her court—where the warlike Eagle extends his glittering pinions in the sunshine of prosperity . . . til the bright Eagle, united with the dove and olive branch, waves high, the acknowledged standard of the world."[15]

In view of Dunlap's welcoming the "good" Jew to the stage, it is unfortunate that we cannot evaluate his own practice when he had occasion to create a Jewish character in his farce *Bonaparte in England,* for the text of this play has never been found. The play was produced in 1803, and, reports Dunlap, "brought more applause and less money the third than the first night." However, we may assume from his own summary of the play that he did not depart from the convention.

Harwood played a German Jew broker [writes Dunlap], who, being shipwrecked on the coast of England, is taken up as Jerome Bonaparte, for whom the English government were keeping watch, and the honours paid to Shadrach, by an Irish officer, who confounds Jerome with Napoleon, and insists on treating the broker as First Consul or Emperor, constitute the *fun* of the piece.[16]

The play by Payne, the author of "Home, Sweet Home" and reputed to be the first outstanding American dramatist, was written during an English sojourn from 1813 to 1818. *Trial without Jury* is not an original play but an adaptation from the popular French drama *La Pie Voleuse,* by L. C. Caigniez and J. M. T. Baudouin. Payne's adaptation was probably never produced and lay in manuscript until publication in 1940. The plot hinges on the theft by a magpie of a silver knife owned by the mistress of the house. A duplicate of this knife is owned by the maid, Rosalie, who sells it to a Jewish peddler, Solomon Isaac, in order to obtain money to aid her father escape imprisonment for desertion from the army. Rosalie is charged with theft of her mistress's knife and is arrested with Isaac, who has already sold the knife when loss of the mistress's is discovered. When the magpie's mischief becomes known, Rosalie is freed, but we hear nothing about Isaac's release.

Isaac is the conventional stage Jew. He is first heard offstage peddling his wares: "Knifes! Fine knifes! Chewels! Fine lace! Chentlemen and ladies, come puy! Come puy!" He speaks in dialect throughout and bargains with Rosalie in the usual sharp manner of the stereotype. When he gives her six shillings for the knife, he adds in an aside: "I vas nigh do give sheven." A friend whom Rosalie tells about the sale exclaims: "I'll wager now he's got it for next to nothing. For they are so Jewish, those Jews!"[17]

Payne did not add the stereotyped and pejorative features, he merely followed the original. In the French, Isaac speaks with an accent ("mestames" for "mesdames," "pichoux" for "bijoux," "fous" for "vous"). But it is significant that other English adapters of this play did modify the treatment of Isaac. In two other versions Isaac is not jailed with the girl. In the adaptation by Isaac Pocock (*The Magpie and the Maid,* London, 1815), the role of the Jew—

called Benjamin—is changed and enlarged in the direction of the Sheva type, and he is not imprisoned. The invidious references to the Jews in the original are omitted. In Benjamin's bargaining for the knife, he voluntarily raises his offer out of compassion for the girl. He is very fond of her, if not in love with her; and when the girl is led away to jail, the stage directions inform us that "the Jew appears overwhelmed with grief." In light of the fact that Payne's grandfather was a convert from Judaism, Payne's literal following of the original takes on added interest.

James Ellison's *American Captive,* was produced in Boston in 1811. The action takes place during the war with Tripoli, in which Commodore Preble attacked the city by sea while William Eaton commanded an overland force. Ten Americans are taken off a prize ship by the corsairs and enslaved. They contrive a successful plot to gain their freedom, thanks to Immorina, niece of the reigning pasha and daughter of the former pasha, whom he had deposed. She falls in love with Anderson, the daring leader of the enslaved Americans. Immorina pities the captives, expresses strong antislavery views, and plots with Anderson to return her father to rule. If Anderson succeeds, she will see to it that the Americans are freed. The American fleet blockades the port, Anderson leads a victorious revolt, the ex-pasha is returned to power, and the Americans are freed.

As usual the Jew in the play participates in the plot treacherously. Ishmael first appears in the act of "counting his gold," as the stage directions state. His opening speech as he lovingly fondles his money is the epitome of the stereotype:

Vat smiling dogs they are! *(takes up a zequin)* Vat comely form! The world talks of *peauty,* of *voman's* peauty! Spshaw! compared with this, 'tis all *deformity!* 'tis transient, fleeting, fades upon the sight, but this! not so with this; ages pass away, and this be still the same. *Time* brings no wrinkles here! smiles ever dwell on its front; aye, it shall live in endless bloom! O Ishmael! had'st thou found a nymph, some *two-score* years ago, possessed with half de charms of this, perhaps I then had *married!* vat! *married* a *Vife!* O then my monies would have flown indeed! Ishmael! Ishmael! thou'rt a lucky dog to have no vife! no teasing, fretting, jangling, wrangling now.[18]

His Muslim servant is a caricatured imitation of the Launcelot prototype of the Jew's servant. So miserly is Ishmael that the servant is starved and must steal his food. But the servant conjectures that he will not die of starvation because "death wanted men for food for worms," and he has not flesh enough on him "to give a worm a single taste." Immorina enters to enlist the help of Ishmael to further the plot. Ishmael is her father's banker. She asks for a loan, and he responds with the usual speech; he is out of money, but may get it from one of his "tribe." Immorina reminds him that he still owes her father one thousand sequins (actually three thousand, as he tells the audience in an aside), which he denies—unsuccessfully, since she has incriminating documents. She strikes a bargain with him: if he will smuggle Anderson, disguised as a Jew, in his caravan and take him to Mecca, she will write off the debt. The plan succeeds, and all ends happily.[19]

Jonathan S. Smith's play *The Siege of Algiers* returns to the Barbary theme. It was published in Philadelphia in 1823, but is not known to have ever been performed. This is not surprising, for the play is a talky tract rather than a stage piece, as its subtitle hints: "The Downfall of Hadji-Ali-Bashaw, a political, historical and sentimental Tragi-Comedy." A tenuous dramatic thread is provided by the effort of a New England merchant, Citizen Yankoo, to sell a shipment of coffee in Algiers, a task that takes two years of intrigue to complete. The play is full of discussion, informative to the historian, of the various aspects of the foreign dealings with the dey, and of the American's relations with the British and French consuls. Smith's intention is to show, as he says in his dedication, how a "minor maritime power" like the United States demonstrated to the great European states how to end piracy and tribute by the use of force. The play stresses the rivalry among the powers in furtherance of their special interests and exposes the manipulations of each to gain advantage over the others. This wholly undramatic work is full of long, expository speeches and matter inessential to the slender dramatic thread.

The Jewish character is David Brokereye, a "money-changer of great note," who is "admitted as the organ of all commerce here." The stage directions describe Brokereye as having "a penetrating eye," a feature of the stereotype. Interestingly enough, however, he does not speak in dialect and is presented in a highly favorable light. "Here the Christian slaves all adore him," says one character, "as he is benevolent and charitable, and at all times forthcoming, when called on for ransom money—however, it is true, he fixes his own premium, and has the guarantee of some Christian consul resident at Algiers." Brokereye is apparently modeled on the merchant-banker Bacri, for he is said to be "the King of the Jews here."[20]

The Algerian prime minister plots to topple the dey and take his place. Wishing to cancel notes on him held by Brokereye, the prime minister charges that Brokereye has conveyed state secrets to the

Christian consuls. When Brokereye is brought before the dey he denies all charges with dignity, but to no avail, for the dey has him decapitated, as the historical Bacri actually was. The prime minister wishes to prevent a pogrom and looting, for "as you know, our soldiery sometimes takes advantage in such cases to plunder, as they did with the massacre of the Jews in our city a few years since." The dey confiscates Brokereye's possessions. Under prodding from the British consul, the dey orders the American consul to wind up his affairs and leave, because war with England is imminent. The dey regretfully remarks: "I shall now miss our friend David Brokereye"[21] in settling finances with the Americans. The play ends with the takeover of Algiers by the American fleet, the suicide of the dey, his replacement by the prime minister, and the conclusion of peace.

The Jewish character in Mary Carr Clarke's *Benevolent Lawyer* (1823), set in England, is the conventional grasping usurer. Named Gripe, he speaks in the usual dialect and declares he will lend Mrs. Campbell money at "ninety per cent interest." He emerges from the lady's apartment with his moneybag intact, for she has refused to pay 90 percent interest; but he assures the villain, Fairface, that "she deal vid nobody elsh but me, all her monish came from me. . . . I not know vot the devil de womish thinks, I am going to get the monish for her for nothing." Fairface advises Gripe that when she sends for him again, as she must, he should charge 100 percent interest, and Gripe agrees, saying: "Vat a good friend Mr. Fairface ish."[22]

An American Jew appeared in Jason R. Orton's *Arnold* (1854), which probably did not see production. Mordecai the moneylender is a completely stereotyped character who, true to form, at first complains to Benedict Arnold that he does not have the thousand pounds Arnold wants to borrow. "The more bright guineas, Jew, you'll let me have," jokes Arnold, "the more bright guineas, Jew, you'll get again,/With that on which you fatten—usury." The charade of the reluctant moneylender ends when Arnold assures Mordecai that he has the money coming to him from Congress. "Well," replies Mordecai, "be it so./No knowing, General, what your strait might be,/I called upon a brother, on my way,/And borrowed the sum you asked."[23]

Another play on the same subject that also probably never saw production was W. W. Lord's *André* (1856). It contains a historical Jewish figure, Major David S. Franks, one of Benedict Arnold's aides. In the play Franks is a brave and honorable, if gullible, American soldier. He is easily absolved of any part in Arnold's treason and is sent to capture Arnold. He is himself captured by the British, who release him so he can see Arnold. When Arnold asks Franks to kill him, Franks breaks the sword and tells Arnold he will die the degrading death of a traitor. What is noteworthy is the fact that Franks's Jewishness is nowhere mentioned in the play; he is presented simply as a loyal American soldier.[24]

But Lord's play is exceptional in depicting a Jew as a human being who is no less admirable than other favorable characters. James Pilgrim in *Yankee Jack; or, The Buccaneers of the Gulf* (1852)—the first American play to include an American Jew, as far as I could discover —briefly introduces "Kizer, a Jew Tavern Keeper" in his play set in New Orleans. In the drinking room of his tavern, Kizer tells the pirate company: "Here's de rum, my tears, I likes to do vots right in de way of business." The pirate, Harvey, says: "Why Jack, here's an honest Jew," and Jack replies: "Then he ought to be tarred and feathered, *(all laugh)*. Don't look blue, old Israelite. Many of our craft boast about honesty, but cruise the world over. . . . As my old Commander used to say, the greatest thief generally calls out thief first." When the pirates are drawn out of town to rescue a lady in distress, Kizer says: "Bless me, vat is de reason dat Irish girl take avay mine pusiness."[24a]

If evidence were needed of the almost universal and completely uncritical acceptance of the anti-Semitic portrait of the Jew on the American stage, one could adduce the play *The World's Own* (1857) by Julia Ward Howe, Boston bluestocking, abolitionist, and for half a century an advocate of advanced causes. This romantic play in verse, full of pompous rhetoric and melodramatic in the extreme, is set in the early nineteenth century in Piedmont, Italy. It is a tale of seduction and revenge in which the seduced Lenora hires a Gypsy, Zingara, and the moneylender Jacob to kidnap the villainous Count Lothair's child. The Jewish moneylender throughout threatens everyone with ruin unless they return borrowed money. "The moneylenders press him [Lothair] hard./These vultures circle in the van of ruin,/And fan it onward with their eager wings." In one scene Lothair enters with the dunning Jacob at his heels and then dismisses Jacob, who leaves. A courtier asks the distraught Lothair: "Are you bewitched? or does the Jew/Feed on your heart's blood?" But Lothair replies that Jacob is "a mine of shrewdness/A serviceable imp." When Zingara and Jacob plot to kidnap the child, Jacob confirms how "love of money and mischief vie/To speed us on our errand."[25] Even the lively social awareness of a Julia Ward Howe was insensitive to the prejudice inherent in the use of the stereotype.

The stage Jew straight out of the English tradition also appeared in several plays by John Brougham, a Dublin-born playwright who came to the United States in 1842, at the age of thirty-two, and, except for the Civil War years, spent the rest of his life here. His *Columbus el Filibustero* (1857) does not contain a Jewish character but does extract some anti-Semitic humor out of King Ferdinand's attempt to joke with his spiritual adviser, Rodriguez, who suggests: "You might, combining piety and pleasure,/Cook a few heretics." The king replies: "That *would* drive off the blues!/I *could* enjoy a dozen roasted Jews,/On the half-shell." Rodriguez: "Sire, I regret to say/We're out of Jews, upon your last birthday/We dressed them all." "What a burning shame!" replies the king.[26]

In Brougham's *Lottery of Life, a Story of New York* (1867), however, Mordie Solomons is an elaborate villain, a fence, moneylender, counterfeiter, and blackmailer. He is bent on revenge, increasing his hoard of money, and victimizing the innocent hero. He pursues his evil machinations in two disguises. Brougham describes the stage costume for Mordie: "Long shabby coat, derby, silk handkerchief tied round his head, old slippers, long beard, and false Jewish nose with glasses, dark trousers worn all through." Although Brougham directs that the character speak "with a strong Jewish accent," his dialogue is set down in straightforward English, leaving it to the actor to supply the "accent." When first seen on the stage, Mordie is in back of his old-clothes shop, counting his receipts: "A good week! a very good week!" No crime or treachery is too revolting for Mordie to engage in. At the end of the complicated plot, Mordie's plans have all been frustrated. Disguised as a rough sailor, he bemoans his fate: "Ruined, degraded, marked and spit upon by these children, imbeciles, miserable dotards, in this the end of my scheming—the fox set upon and cackled to death by the barn-door fowls." Finally caught, he gives his dying speech: "And all unharmed, myself the only victim after all! Cheated out of my revenge! Oh! Curse you! curse!"[27]

Brougham also exploited the vogue for burlesquing Shakespeare. In a one-acter of lighthearted absurdity with a satiric edge, *The Great Tragic Revival* (1858), Brougham introduces a miscellany of characters with Shakespearean Christian names (among them Shylock, Jessica, Romeo, and Iago) and modern surnames. Shylock Barown and his daughter are not identified as Jewish, but Shylock is a businessman. In a later burlesque, *Much Ado about a Merchant of Venice* (1868), which was extremely popular and played for several decades, Brougham is quite explicit, for Shylock and his situation are the object of a huge joke, yet at the same time he is recognized as the victim of anti-Jewish prejudice. In his dramatis personae Brougham describes Shylock as "a shamefully ill-used and persecuted Hebrew gentleman, in fact, an Israelite of other days, whose character was darkened by his Christian contemporaries simply to conceal their own nefarious transactions, victimized, as he was, by sundry unjustifiable confidence operations." Lorenzo "swindles Shylock out of his duck of a daughter, and his ducats as well," while Jessica "makes a jubilee of her Sire's sorrows, and gives a further proof that love laughs at Shylocksmiths"—an example of the outrageous puns that the play abounds in. Though the setting is Venice, the allusions are to New York, and American jargon is used. Shylock's famous speeches are burlesqued, such as his indictment of Antonio:

> He's treated me most shameful on the street.
> Told me that stocks were up when they were down; . . .
> I could forgive each jibe,
> For sufferance is the badge of all our tribe,
> Aye, every insolence without a groan,
> If he had let my Synagogue alone,
> But at our ancient faith he mocked and jeered,
> Made *barberous* jokes upon my Jewish *beard.*
> Dangled forbidden meats before my nose . . .
> If a Jew wrong a Christian, what does he?
> Why bring an action for it, so do we
> The example that they teach us we but follow,
> And in financial questions, beat him hollow![28]

The burlesque possibilities offered by *The Merchant of Venice* seem to have appealed to playwrights of the period. In 1866 George M. Baker copyrighted a play, *The Peddler of Very Nice, Burlesque of the Trial Scene in the "Merchant of Venice."* In this play Shylock is a peddler wearing "three hats, one on top of the other, in imitation of the old Jew peddlers." Antonio has pawned his coat to Shylock but cannot pay; Shylock demands its twelve brass buttons in payment, but Bassanio offers stamps instead. With ponderous humor and punning, the young lawyer Portia offers the buttons, but warns Shylock that "the law gives thee here no jot of thread."[29] Shylock then offers to take the stamps but Portia points out that the bond has no revenue stamps on it. Shylock's money and old clothes are awarded to Antonio, and Portia agrees to marry the eighty-five-year-old Shylock to avoid becoming an old maid. Though dull and heavy-handed, the play is too bland to be really unfriendly to Shylock.

The vogue for Shakespearean burlesque persisted for a few

decades, and in 1883 an elaborate burlesque by "The Larks," *The Shakespeare Water-Cure,* was copyrighted. Leading Shakespearean characters are recuperating at a water-cure spot after the ordeals through which Shakespeare has put them, and what ensues is succinctly conveyed by the argument:

Staying at a water-cure establishment are: Hamlet, for his health, with his wife Ophelia; Macbeth and Lady Macbeth, for economical reasons, in need of the needful; Mrs. Bassanio, enjoying a legal vacation. The Montagues having been disowned by both their houses, Mr. R.M. has taken to the stage, and is here with his travelling company and his wife. Shylock, wishing to possess Portia's gold, bribes Lady Macbeth to incite her husband to the murder of Bassanio, so that Shylock may marry the fair heiress. All of which is accomplished, and a wedding dinner, under the superintendence of Othello, is given by the patients to the happy bride and bridegroom.

The play is offensive not only regarding Shylock, but also Othello, who is degraded to a stage Negro, a waiter at the water cure, who speaks in dialect and plays a banjo to accompany songs. His song as he sets the table conveys the flavor:

> Othello, de gay and festive nig,
>   Who has lost his rank and title,
> And yet doesn't care a fig.
>   Othello, de military Moor,
> A-waiting on de table
>   At de Shakespeare Water-Cure.

Echoes of famous speeches are placed in ridiculous contexts. Bassanio's murder accomplished, Portia subjects Shylock to the test of the three caskets; he chooses the winning casket and invites Portia to come with him "upon the Elevated Road" to Chatham Street, where Shylock is going, "my goods to sell." After they marry the others discuss the affair, and Lady Macbeth sums it all up: "When Shylock is best he is a little worse than a man; and when he is worst, he is little better than a beast!"[30]

The traditional British treatment of the Jew appears also in the plays of Dion Boucicault, who, like John Brougham, was originally from England. He came to New York in 1853, but, also like Brougham, spent the Civil War years in England before returning in 1872. While he was abroad, however, his plays were produced in this country as well as in England, and several contain Jewish characters. His *Flying Scud* (1867)—the title is the name of a race-horse—centers on a horse race. The Jewish character, "Mo" Davis, is a crooked, unscrupulous, cowardly member of a criminal gang that schemes to fix the race and defeat Flying Scud in the Derby. But their scheme is foiled and Flying Scud wins; the chicanery and forgery of the gang is exposed, although Mo tries to wiggle out of blame for his forgery. Mo is the comic, with his occasional exclamation "Jumping Moses!" and his cockney and "Jewish" dialect speech, as well as gags like this one: when threatened with transportation he says: "Oh, dear! Oh, dear! It's a good thing my mother's dead; dis dreadful blow would have killed her. It's all through mixing with bad companionship. Vy didn't I join the 'Band of Hope' ven I was young?"[31]

A second play by Boucicault written during this period is *After Dark, a Drama of London Life in 1868,* which includes the gambling-house keeper Dicey Morris. The author advises the actor of this part "to study it up as a leading character," for "T. H. Dominick Murray's imitation of the salient peculiarities of the low-lived London Jews' speech and mannerism having strengthened his attractions and made a perceptible proportion of the audience be of that race." Dicey Morris handles the negotiations for the blackmail of Medhurst. Medhurst later confesses that, "tempted by Dicey Morris, in his gambling-house, in a fit of drunken desperation, I forged my father's name."[32] The police finally catch up with Dicey Morris and his partner in crime, Bellingham, and they go to prison. Morris is a thorough villain and is far from funny, even though his stereotyped features are intended to make him so.

The stock figure of the British stage Jew continued to be used throughout the century and made a brief appearance in Clyde Fitch's *Beau Brummel* (1890), in which he is the instrumentality for Beau's imprisonment for debt. Mr. Abrahams, who enters the play in the opening scene, is conceived in the same terms that he would have been in an eighteenth-century comedy of manners, although his speech in the printed text is without accent. He is, Fitch directs, "the typical Jew money-lender of the period, exaggerated in dress and manner." He insists on seeing Beau to demand payment on loans he has been trying to collect for four years, and for which he has now called seven times. Beau's faithful valet, Mortimer, refuses to allow Abrahams to see his master, and edges him out. When Abrahams next appears it is at the summons of Beau—not to receive payment, but to lend him more money. At first Abrahams protests he will lend no more; but he is "overcome with wonder"[33] when the prince regent's footman comes in to invite Beau to the prince's dance, and Beau dismisses Abrahams to settle the amount of the loan with

Mortimer. After several attempts by the bailiffs to collect, Beau is finally jailed for debt.

If Fitch followed one convention of the stage Jew, Steele Mackaye created a Jew in the Fagin tradition in Slink in *Money-Mad,* produced in 1890. This trashy melodrama also contains an Italian assassin and the Negro and Irish stereotypes. But Mackaye is merciless in depicting the evil, cowardly, crafty Slink, who, Fagin-like, has trained a set of criminal characters to be "the smartest gang of rogues in the whole country." One is Haskins, the society man, "de finest pointer for Jack Adams gang," who informs the gang of the location of jewels in fine houses he frequents. Tom and Jack Adams, boasts Slink, "vas the two smartest rogues I ever raised." It is not Slink who is the "money-mad" character of the title, but Cary, who literally goes mad for love of money. He is in debt to Slink and hopes to gain a fortune by marrying an heiress. The play is a succession of formula melodramatic situations that end in the exposure of the gang and the reform of one of the gang, who saves the heroine. The virtuous are rewarded and the villainous get their comeuppance. When Slink is finally trapped, he pleads: "Blease, blease, ledt me go, Chack, and I vill become a corporal-general in de Salvation army—so hellup me cracious I vill."[34] But the police arrive, and the play ends with Slink being led off to prison.

But not all Jews in the drama of the century were caricatured. A shifting of attitudes toward humane treatment of the Jew did take place, and one of the most noted examples in the century was the conception of the Jew in Augustin Daly's maiden play, which was highly successful and established him as one of the earliest dramatists of the modern American theater. Daly was born in North Carolina in 1838, and at twenty-one became a drama critic in New York. The theatrical producer H. L. Bateman wanted an acting vehicle for his nineteen-year-old daughter, Kate, and asked Daly to adapt a German play that had been called to Bateman's attention by a German friend: *Deborah.* The piece, by Salomon H. von Mosenthal, was about persecution of the Jews in an eighteenth-century Austrian village. With a keen sense for the American audience, Daly freely adapted the play and made it more dramatic than the original. Under the title *Leah, the Forsaken,* the play opened with great success in Boston in December 1862 and in New York the following month. Kate Bateman established her reputation as Leah, and appeared for many years thereafter in the part. For forty years the play held the stage, and in 1892 Sarah Bernhardt played Leah in the United States.

Audiences, both men and women, were moved to tears by the play. It was one of the great successes in the history of the American stage, as was attested to not only by its long life, but also by its performance under other names by stock companies, and—the supreme tribute— by its being burlesqued.

Leah and her children, driven from Hungary and destitute, are hiding near an Austrian village. She has a secret lover, Rudolf, a Christian who visits her in the woods at night. Both Leah and Rudolf have been freed from religious hatred by their love, and they are determined to further a "new religion, that shall teach love and brotherhood to all men." If Rudolf's father refuses permission for them to marry, they will go to the United States. Leah is discovered by the superstitious villagers, who fear that because she is a Jew she will kill their children. The most vehement enemy of Leah and her children is Nathan, a Jewish apostate whom Daly makes the villain of the piece, although in Mosenthal's original Nathan is rather a pitiful and forgiven sinner. Nathan fears exposure as a native Jew and seeks to enforce concealment of this fact, as he thinks, by inciting the villagers against Leah; he is the spokesman of anti-Semitism. When the town learns that Rudolf wishes to marry Leah, it is unanimously opposed to the marriage, and Nathan asserts that the Jews "think only of money. Do you know why they thus haunt our villages? It is to beg, to steal, or to wheedle money from the unsuspecting—it is part of their faith! . . . Are they not a soulless and a grasping race, who value more the clink of gold, than all the virtues of humanity strung together?"[35]

With Rudolf's agreement, they decide to test Leah—to tempt her to leave for money. Instead, Nathan gives the money to an old Jewish couple so they can leave for Bohemia, but says he has given it to Leah. When Leah reappears in the village, she is charged with having taken the money "joyfully," and Rudolf then repudiates her, saying: "When I learned that you, too, like all your race, hold honour, love and faith less than the pettiest coin, and have sold me, Judas-like, for a few pieces, when, had your greedy soul been patient, I would, myself, have given you hundreds, I tore away the silken sinews of your love, struck down your image here, and forgot you as if your treachery and my love had been a dream." Rudolf decides to marry Madalena, but just before the wedding he sees Leah again, realizes his error, and begs her forgiveness. However, she now is adamant in her hatred.

Some years later, Rudolf goes in contrition to the emperor to plead that Jews be allowed to live in the villages, while Nathan continues to incite the people against the Jews. The village priest, Lorenz, regrets his part in the injustice to Leah, and bemoans "this accursed hate which is handed down from father to son!" Leah reappears in the town and forgives those who had persecuted her. Nathan is arrested when he wishes to serve a warrant on her, and Leah then leaves the village for "the promised land!"[36]—that is, the United States.

It is significant that this first play of perhaps the first modern American playwright should be a melodramatic exposure of anti-Semitism, and that it should evoke the sympathies of the audience. The play emerged also at a critical turn in American history, the early years of the Civil War. The significance of the play in this historical context is drawn by George William Curtis, editor of *Harper's Weekly*. In the issue of February 28, 1863, Curtis attacks an Old Testament defense of slavery by a rabbi (most probably the famous proslavery sermon by Rabbi Morris Jacob Raphall in New York on January 4, 1861), which he argued against by drawing a parallel between Negro slavery and Jewish persecution. Jews in Europe, writes Curtis, "had no rights which any Christian man was bound to respect, because they were Jews."[37]

During the next week Curtis saw *Leah,* and writes in the next issue that in the past week's discussion of anti-Semitism, "we did not know of the powerful sermon that was nightly preached from the same text in the drama of *Leah.*" The play, he writes, "shows the deceit, the terrible crimes, the hopeless imbruting of human nature, which necessarily springs from indulgence of such hate" toward Jews. Curtis summarizes the intense anti-Semitic action of the play, and then likens the venom of Nathan the apostate to "the attitude and arguments of the reactionary leaders at the North." Their agitation, like Nathan's, is

an appeal to the popular prejudice against the outcast race. . . . Upon this hatred of race the reaction tries to found its political power in order to abase, divide, and destroy this nation. It has no other hope, no other resource, than this desperate pandering to the meanest and most inhuman prejudice. If such a course is not in itself sufficiently revolting—if its exposure in history is not appalling enough—then, whenever and wherever you can, go and see *Leah,* and have the lesson burned in upon your mind, which may help to save the national life and honor.[38]

However, *Leah* was one of only a few plays in the American theater for the rest of the century that sympathetically portrayed Jews. Nor should we pass on without noting that the center of sympathetic treatment is a Jewish *woman,* and that the Jewish woman was traditionally treated more humanely, or even idealistically— Scott's Rebecca is the prime example—than the Jewish man. Daly's villain (but not Mosenthal's) is Nathan, a Jewish man, though he is an apostate. Yet the condemnation of Jewish persecution in the play is unequivocal.

However, in a play Daly adapted from the German, *The Last Word,* which was produced in 1890, he makes the Jewish male character, Moses Mossup, into a stereotype. Mossup, says one printed prompt book, is "an overdressed and presuming person of evident Hebrew extraction." He has a "slow, oily, foreign accent," and offers his congratulations to a father at his son's engagement "with offensive slyness." When told that the engagement is still a secret, he insists, "still smiling and insinuatingly."[39] It is significant that in the prompt book which I examined at the New York Library of the Performing Arts, the phrase "of evident Hebrew extraction" was crossed out. And this phrase was also absent from another edition (both privately printed) that I later saw. In such cases, the impression that Mossup is a Jew depends on the actor's characterization. One undated review of the play states that "a neat little sketch of a Jewish character is given by Robert Middlemass." Another review, dated July 10, 1906, states that "Mr. William Humphrey's Mossup was a gem of dialect impersonation," while still another review of the same date comments that "Mr. Humphrey gave a good piece of acting as a crafty, hypocritical friend."

Although the stage Jew in the first century of the national life was not an indigenous figure, but rather the embodiment of a centuries-old tradition drawn from the British stage, a peculiarly American stage Jew did eventually emerge, as did other characters. The first distinctively American comic type was the Yankee, the shrewd, wry, provincial character created in Royall Tyler's *Contrast* (1787). This play was not only the first American play produced in this country, but also the play that projected for the first time on the stage the New England Yankee, Jonathan, as the bluff, democratic, shrewd comic figure with a wry sense of humor. He was, however, different from most comic characters—certainly from the stage Jew—in that the audience usually laughed *with* him, not *at* him. From Brother Jonathan to Uncle Sam to Jack Downing's Yankee figure, writes Constance Rourke, down to the 1880s "the country was never without a Yankee oracle or even half a dozen. . . . No character precisely like him had appeared before in the realm of the imagination."[40]

A second comic type emerged on the stage in the middle decades of the century in the New York Irish fireman, "Mose," who was a big-city character, belligerent and nationalistic.

Also deplorably and distinctively American was the stage Negro. Although Negro singers had appeared on the American stage at the end of the eighteenth century, the full-fledged stage Negro emerged in all his popularity with Thomas D. ("Jim Crow") Rice, whose sensational career in the late 1820s singing blackface versions of Negro songs and dances firmly established the stereotype, which was later elaborated in the minstrel show.

It was not until the late 1870s, when Jewish mass immigration had begun, that a distinctively American variant of the stage Jew emerged. The new stage figure was, on the whole, identified with the Jewish immigrant: with eccentricities of dress—for instance, hat over ears—and accent, together with the traditional obsession with money. When the stage Jew was added to the Yankee, Negro, and Irishman of the American comic theater and vaudeville stage, he became only one of several nationalities of immigrants whose foreign ways made them the butt of ridicule and prejudice.

The first Jewish comics are said to have been the team of Bert and Leon in the late 1870s, who are generally credited with being the first of the "Hebrew" comedians. They used rapid-fire patter and gags. They adapted familiar material to their own use—for instance, they parodied a current popular Irish song, "The Widow Dunn," in "The Widow Rosenbaum":

> Her father keeps a hock shop
> With three balls on the door,
> Where the sheeny politicians can be found.
> Her husband was a soldier
> But he got killed in the war,
> And his money went to Widow Rosenbaum.
> About three thousand mashers
> They hang around the place,
> But she's got her money buried in the ground.
> You can bet your bloody life,
> You can't get her for a wife,
> She would rather be the Widow Rosenbaum.

> Chorus: Was hast gesachta? Zu klein gemachta,
> A gang of suckers, around the town.
> The kleine kinder, looks in the winder. . . .
> Dot was sung by the Widow Rosenbaum.[41]

But it was a non-Jew, Frank Bush, who is reputed to have established the vaudeville Jew. Edward B. Marks, who writes out of personal knowledge, says of Bush that this "light-haired German

. . . imitated an East Side Hebrew of the varieties to perfection."
Marks relates how Bush came to know the type that he imitated
"with a power of mimicry that was uncanny." Like "Jim Crow"
Rice's blackface minstrel, the stereotype had a certain basis in reality.
Rice had originated his song-and-dance routine after close study of
an old crippled Negro's method of singing and dancing. Bush developed his own techniques, Marks relates, by protracted observation
of a Grand Street pawnbroker. Bush "watched him wait on customers day after day for years. As people came into the dingy shop to
pawn their belongings, Bush absorbed every story, every jest, every
bit of kindly and witty philosophy and every mannerism of the Old
Man."[42]

Does this mean that the stage characters which "Jim Crow"
Rice and Frank Bush developed are genuine character studies,
rather than stage caricatures that demean the peoples they are
meant to represent? Obviously this is not the case, since the "humor" of the representation arises out of the assumption of their
inferiority and foreignness. The spectator's laughter arises in
large measure out of a sense of superiority. The standard is the
current Anglo-Saxon mode, and divergence from this signifies an
inferior position in the scale of national values. The "type" issues
as a caricature. For the originals from which Rich and Bush
derived their stage Negro and Jew, respectively, were eccentric
figures even within their own ethnic groups. Repeated representations of such eccentrics on the stage reinforced in the public
mind their identification as typical.[43]

In Frank Bush's "original act," writes Douglas Gilbert, "he
opened in grotesque Jew make-up: tall, rusty plug hat, long black
coat, shabby pants, long beard which ran to a point, and large spec-
tacles." An early song of his went:

> Oh, my name is Solomon Moses I'm a bully Sheeny man,
> I always treat my customers the very best I can.
> I keep a clothing store 'way down on Baxter Street,
> Where you can get your clothing now I sell so awful cheap.

Chorus: Solomon, Solomon Moses
      Hast du gesehen der clotheses?
      Hast du gesehen der kleiner kinder,
      Und der sox iss in der vinder?
      I sell you for viertel dollar,
      You will say was cheap,
      Oskaploka overcoats
      For fimpf sehn dollar and half.
      My name is Isaac Levy Solomon Moses hast du ge-
      sacht?

Bush had great success with his act through the 1890s, and he also did German and Yankee impersonations as well; but, "as a pioneer Jewish single," writes Gilbert, "he made that type of comedy a staple in our variety theaters."[44]

The Jew comic, as we can see from these characteristic songs, was a variation upon the traditional stereotype, with the addition of comic "business." It was based on the new visibility of the Jew, and the strange variety among the flood of immigrants from all of Europe, and even from China. The implicit notion of Anglo-Saxon superiority made the German, Italian, and other immigrant groups, as well as the Negro, the target of ridicule. Blackface comedy in the minstrel show was ubiquitous, and Jews on the variety stage exploited blackface even before the Jew comic became popular. The comic types in vaudeville tend to confirm a comment attributed to Boucicault: "All that the Americans seem to recognize as dramatic here is the caricature of character, and that is what the successful plays are—caricatures of eccentric character set in a weak dramatic framework."[45]

That not all Jews were pleased with the attention they were getting in vaudeville is apparent from an editorial comment in 1886 in the *Jewish Messenger,* which complains that "the name of Frank Bush attached to a list of performers at a recent benefit was enough to disgust one with the programme."[46] While it is probable that there was an element of middle-class discomfort among the established Jewish community at this exhibition of the poor, unassimilated Jew, it would be an error, I believe, entirely to discount this "disgust." It was in all likelihood based in some measure on a justified resentment at the ridicule of the Jew.

Although the caricature of the Jew was on the whole founded on prejudice—not necessarily consciously so—the depiction of comic types was not in all cases unfriendly. This was true of the American master of the Irish stage genre, Edward Harrigan, whose intent was to be "as realistic as possible," even though, he said, "I use types and never individuals." Early in his career, he writes, he had

found that whenever I tried to portray a type, I was warmly applauded by the audience, and praised by the press the next day. This, in all probability, is what gave me a decided bent, and has confined all my work to certain fields. It began with the New York "boy," the Irish American, and our African brother. As these grew in popularity I added the other prominent types which go to make up life in the metropolis, and in every other large city in the Union and

Canada. These are the Irishman, Englishman, German, Low German, Chinese, Italian, Russian, and Southern darky.[47]

Harrigan was indeed the chronicler of the Irish East Side, where he himself had been born in 1845. In 1886 Howells welcomed Harrigan into the ranks of the realists. "Mr. Harrigan," writes Howells, "accurately realizes in his scenes . . . the actual life of this city . . . and he has preferred to give its rich-American phases in their rich and amusing variety, and some of its African and Teutonic phases." Yet Howells was not uncritical, for he notes that, while the "Irish aspects of life are treated affectionately . . . the colored aspects do not fare so well under his touch. . . . All the colored people are bad colored people."

In commenting on *The Leather Patch* (1886), Howells gently derides Harrigan for his rendering of the "ol' clo'" stereotype. "When the old-clothes men and women of Chatham Street join in a chorus, one perceives that the theatre has come to the top, and the poet has lapsed." Nevertheless, speaking generally, says Howells, "loving reality as we do, we cannot do less than welcome reality as we find it in Mr. Harrigan's comedies."[48] Harrigan's career began in variety shows; in 1871 he formed the phenomenally successful team of Harrigan and Hart, for which he wrote the skits, and in the mid-1870s began to produce the highly successful Mulligan Guard series of plays, in which Dan Mulligan is a continuation of the earlier "Mose," the Irish fireman type.

Like his contemporary chronicler of the Irish East Side, Stephen Crane, Harrigan apparently paid little attention to the Jews. One of the Mulligan series, *The Mulligan Guard Ball* (1879), includes a Jewish immigrant tailor, Rosenfelt, who appears briefly at the very end. He enters looking for Mulligan's house, to which he has come to collect money for the cutaway coats he supplied to the Mulligan Guard for their ball. He finds the house, and tells Mulligan he wants money for the thirty-five hired coats. "Get out of here," says Mulligan.

> *Rosenfelt:* Never, I die, but not till I get my money.
> *Mulligan:* You're a fraud sir.
> *Rosenfelt:* You're a Molly Maguire.

After this, the play ends in a "general melee and curtain."[49]

When Harrigan concentrated on the Jewish character in a single play, *Mordecai Lyons* (1882), he lost his touch, for the play was a failure. Harrigan played the central character, a pawnbroker, and his partner, Hart, played his son. But the heavy brogue of the cast could not be altogether suppressed, and the result was incongruous. The journal *Music and Drama* on October 21, 1882, shares the protest of a Jewish paper. The Jewish paper "supposes that, as usual, it [the play] will pander to the popular prejudices." With hardly an exception, the journal goes on, all plays "have represented the Jew as a sordid and contemptible character; none has painted the heroic spirit, the suffering, the patient endurance and the close family attachment of the Jewish race. . . . Will Mordecai Lyons go beyond the popular idea, the popular prejudice? It can scarcely be expected." The *Spirit of the Times,* on November 4, 1882, panned the play, remarking that Harrigan had made the Jew's harp sound like an Irish harp. When Harrigan wrote another play about a pawnbroker, his wife insisted that he make the character Irish rather than Jewish, and *Reilly and the Four Hundred* (1890) was the result. One would like to think that Mrs. Harrigan, who had a Jewish grandfather, [50] was moved by the wish to avoid the invidious stereotype; it is more likely that she had in mind the failure of *Mordecai Lyons.*

Once the vaudeville variation on the stage Jew became established, the refurbished stereotype turned up in many plays. Here and there one finds an awareness that the stage Jew is really unfriendly to the Jewish people. How little the problem was understood and how deep was the confusion over the affront to Jewish dignity is plain from the remarks of an actor and playwright, Milton Nobles, in a preface to a play, *The Phoenix,* which he first produced in Philadelphia in 1875. Nobles writes: "I may lay claim with equal justice, that I was the first to place on the stage the modern young American Jew, a jolly, up-to-date man about town, and not a Villain." His Moses Solomons, a broker from Chatham Street who speaks with an accent, is a dealer in forged checks, a gambler, and a sharp money broker—yet he is supposedly a break with the stereotype! "I have frequently found a forged signature more valuable to me than the genuine would have been, as I am an honest man," Moses explains as he cashes a forged check. He engages in what is intended to be witty banter. At a gambling house he plays number thirteen. An Irish player protests: "Tirteen! do you want to hoodoo the game?" Moses replies: "I don't care who I do, as long as I get a mazumma." When the gambling house is raided, Moses bribes a policeman to let him go. The policeman had refused a ten dollar bribe but, says Moses, his "honesty weakened in di second ten. An honest policeman is vorth twenty dollars. I'm going to introduce him to my friend Lichtenstein, who keeps a dime museum and vants to exhibit him as a freak."[51]

The line between vaudeville patter and play dialogue was narrow in such plays. For instance, at one point Moses stops the action with the following typical vaudeville story. His brother Schmule, says Solomon, "took his money along with him when he died." Where to, he is asked. "Vell," says Moses, "I'm not prepared to say where. He didn't leave any address, but he left a vill, saying dot he didn't owe a cent, unt he had tree tousand dollars in de Hebrew Savings Bank, unt he didn't vant his relations to get to fighting apout it, . . . so he said I must put it in the coffin mit him." The company asks if Moses put the money in the coffin in greenbacks, gold, or silver. "I just took de cash," Moses replies, "and put in my sheck payable to his order."

Moses then goes out on a lark with several of the characters, one of whom boasts of his lack of prejudice. "Moses is a trump," he says. "Take a Jew out of his shop, and nine times out of ten he is a jolly good fellow!" In the end Moses finally gains the will for the hero by a shady deal and saves him from a charge of forgery, and all ends happily. The play ends with a final piece of business by Moses: his "horse pistol goes off as though by accident, he drops it, and falls in comic fright."[52]

The stage Jew appears in several plays by F. E. Chase. *The Great Umbrella Case* (1881), set in Nevada, opens with a jury selection in which a man named Godolni Nozoviski talks unintelligibly. The judge, a pompous Irish politician, asks: "Is it a Bulgarian or an Oirish Jew?"[53] The man then produces a bomb marked DYNAMITE. Everyone takes cover, and the judge excuses him from jury duty.

Chase's plays exploit the antiforeign stereotypes to the hilt. In *A Ready-Made Suit* (1885) Chase once again offers a court trial. This time a woman, Arethusa Snyppe, is on trial for having married a succession of nine men without intervening divorces. Chase goes through the foreign stereotypes by making one husband a Frenchman, one an Italian, one a Cockney, and two Jews. Isaac Gutentag and Levi Cohen are the owners of a firm of "eminent Hebrew jobbers in second-hand clothes." Chase directs that they be "made up exactly alike to resemble the most pronounced Jewish types." They testify in unison and in dialect. They are, they say, "sole agents for dose fife toller und a halef New York market ofergoats, marked down from dirteen tollars and a kevorter." There is a good deal of punning on the terms of their trade, as in the following dialogue:

Prosecuting Attorney: You know the penalties you incur if you use your office to cloak villainy.

Gutentag: Gloaks vas owit of staile, dese long times. Dos Norfolk House jackets vas all de rage now.

Cohen: but Shakey, don' forget dot shob lot of soldiers gloaks—.

Gutentag: I solt dem, Ikey, a veek ago, ven you vas owit, for fife dollars.

Cohen: Gott in Himmel, you vill ruin de beesiness. Vy, dey *gost* us feefty cents.[54]

After more of this banter, Gutentag explains how they happened to marry the same woman. "Oh, vell," he says, "it vos like dis. Ikey and I, ve tink ve get married, but ve can't afford dot expense. Vell, ve vos partners in peesness, und so ve dinks uf ve can get von vife betveen us, dot vill be less oxpensive. Times vos so hard, shentlemen, und peesness so pad, dot vos reely de best ve could afford." Cohen adds that the rabbi charged half the usual fee because it was a wholesale deal, and took his pay in goods. To the judge's question about their religion, they reply: "Ve are Chews, sare." "Chews of tobacco?" "Nien, Chews of Germany." "Oh, Jews! You surprise me. Then I suppose I can absolutely depend upon your telling me the truth." "Ve nefer tell a lie ven ve can sell goots without it."[55] And so on, till the end of their interrogation.

Chase continued to write plays in vaudeville terms. In *In the Trenches* (1898), the Jewish Moses Bullheimer is in partnership with the Irish Patrick Green in swindling operations. They are "army contractors and general speculators" whose field of operations is Cuba during the 1898 war. Bullheimer speaks with a German accent, Green with a brogue. Bullheimer has fled from his wife, who has had a liaison with Green; she is now in Cuba trying to find her husband. The partners are plotting to buy an estate very cheaply by murdering the heir. The heir, who has been hidden away to save him from an earlier plot, is on the verge of being found. Bullheimer's wife catches up with her husband in Cuba and exposes Green as her paramour. In revenge, Bullheimer reveals to the United States Army that Green is about to betray their troop deployment to the Spaniards (he, too, is involved in the plot). Green is tried, while Bullheimer, now on the side of the angels, suddenly loses his accent, saying to his convicted partner: "Good-bye Green; we have rowed in the same boat, but we sha'n't be hanged by the same rope."[56]

This play well illustrates the very thin line between the Jewish character in vaudeville and in melodrama. The partners are obviously a stage Jew and a stage Irishman, who banter back and forth in vaudeville fashion. Throughout the play there is recurrent patter like this:

Bullheimer: Ugh! you Irish bog trotter.
Green: Ugh! you damned Sheeney! But I forgive you.
Bullheimer: I accept your abology.

Green: The divil take yez for a Hebrew sneak.
Bullheimer: Damnation!
Green: But I forgive you.
Bullheimer: I accept your apology.

Bullheimer; I tell you you vas a humbug.
Green: What's that, ye Sheeney divil? Oi'll pull your nose.
Bullheimer: No! You von't!
Green: Yis, I will but I forgive you.
Bullheimer: I accept your abology.[57]

It would appear that the vaudeville Jew was a staple of the popular stage for some decades after 1880. In the play *Down the Black Canyon* (1890), by Forbes Heermans, the device of disguise as a Jew is used. A character called Solomon Goldstein appears, but he is really the non-Jewish sheriff of San Juan County in Colorado. To achieve the disguise, the author directs that the actor be "dressed in 'loud' clothes; a heavy black beard, much jewelry, false nose, strong German accent." The author suggests that "this part may be done as a Spaniard, if preferred."[58] In either case the "wicked foreigner" becomes a partner of the villain, but throws off his disguise when the villain's guilt is exposed.

A particularly vicious example of the stage Jew is Solomon Isaacs, "a Jewish 'crook' " in Charles Townsend's *Jail Bird* (1893). There is no hint of restraint in Townsend's conception. The costume should be "loud and vulgar dress; checked trousers, short, black velvet coat, flashy tie, profusion of diamonds." The author leaves no room for doubt. Isaacs, he writes, "is a vulgar, brutal Jew of about forty-five. Use a dark shade of grease paint, shade the eyes, and rouge the lips so as to give them a thick, sensual look. Isaacs is a brutal, vulgar, cowardly Jew, and although a comedy part, yet the characteristics of the role must not be lost sight of." He owns a bar, and explains: "I vas too honest und respectable for de clothing business. I never have de nerve to sell a man shoddy. So I goes into dis business, vere nobody asks any questions." He sells a drink and a cigar, asks a dollar, and says, "aside, finger on nose": "Ninety-five cents clear profit on dot deal."[59] As our detective hero suspects, Isaacs's place is the center for a counterfeiting ring. He and his handyman pass a counterfeit bill to a man from the country, who gives it to the poor, starving heroine. They lure the countryman into a robbery, but the resourceful detective clears everything up. Isaacs helps plan the safe-break, but of course does not participate. He is an unmitigated, melodramatic villain.

Not content with one stage stereotype, some playwrights employ the entire arsenal in one play, and for this a jury is a convenient device. Harry E. Shelland's *Great Libel Case* (1900) has the jury members enter one by one. There is "Theodore Rosenvelt, Jew peddler, with shoe laces and suspenders on his arm"; then "George Washington (colored) . . . showy darky get-up in clothes and manner"; there are also the German stereotype, Blotwurst; and "Daniel Moriarty. Typical stage Irish costume." Rosenvelt tries to sell someone something whenever he speaks. As he enters, he offers to sell the clerk of the court some shoelaces and displays his goods to the other jurors. The judge asks each juror if he wishes to serve. When the judge asks Rosenvelt, the response is: "How much vill I get?" Then the following dialogue ensues:

> *Judge:* Three dollars a day.
> *Rosenvelt:* An, vot a skindecure is dis. The lawyers will please not hurry on my account.
> *Judge:* Take your seat over there with the jurors.
> *Rosenvelt:* Yes, I know, but ver is dot three dollars?
> *Judge:* The State pays you after the case is over.
> *Rosenvelt:* Vot State?
> *Judge.* This State, of course: the State of Kentucky.
> *Rosenvelt:* Ah vot a state I am in. How can Kentucky pay me dis? It is no human being. Please explanation dot.

Professor Socrates Rawbones testifies in a long polysyllabic, quite unintelligible speech, and Rosenvelt breaks it up with a "comic" interlude. "I vouldt like to ask vone question, Mr. Sock—Sock—vot kinds of socks haf you anyway? . . . Vell, I vouldt like to know if you can speak Yiddish?" The professor replies: "I cannot, but my brother plays on a Jew's harp." After another long bit of testimony, Rosenvelt makes a disturbance in the jury box. Says he: "I was looking for my coat." The judge comments: "I have had men in this court who have lost their whole suit without making that disturbance," to which Rosenvelt replies: "Who lost dot suit you have on?"[60]

Involvement of the stage Jew in a counterfeiting ring and a plot to swindle innocent people out of their land recurs in Frank L. Bixby's *Little Boss* (1901). Not only does the play call for Moses Solomon as a "character heavy, Jew," but it also has "character comedy, Negro" and "Irish comedy." Moses and his partner in crime, John Lydecker, plot to buy valuable land in Tennessee very cheaply, but a detective who is tracking down counterfeiters frustrates their attempt to swindle the heroine and her father out of their land. The plot is discussed:

Lydecker: I never saw you when you didn't want money.
Moses: Who, me? Vot a scantal on the name of Simons.

Their aim, says Lydecker, is to "get the land for a song." That, says Moses, is "a crate idea, Jackie tear, crate. Put I can't sing. I hafen't my nodes." Lydecker comes back: "Oh, yes, you have, plenty of them—and some of them counterfeit, too." When Moses offers to buy the land, he introduces himself as "Moses Finkelstein Simons, commission proker, and Infestor's Achent." The plot gets as far as bringing the drafts for money to the bank, and Lydecker offers to go to the bank. Moses wants to accompany him.

Lydecker: Getting leery you won't get your bit? *(Aside)* You're lucky if you do.
Moses: Vat vos id, Jackie?
Lydecker: Oh, nothing. I said, that's just like a Jew.[61]

But of course they are caught in time and both are arrested.

Several sketches by Harry L. Newton and A.S. Hoffman may serve as final examples of the vaudeville Jew. In *Glickman, the Glazier* (1904), a sketch with two characters, the "Hebrew Glazier" is to wear "Hebrew makeup," described as "black coat and white vest; coat somewhat the worse for wear; large turned-down collar and red tie; light striped trousers, narrow at the bottom and short, showing loud colored stockings; black wig and black whiskers; old derby hat on the back of his head and so large that it sets down over his ears." An irate actress, Charlotte Russe, waits in the office of a newspaper critic who has given her a bad notice, in order to scold him. Impatient and furious when he fails to arrive, she shatters his window and leaves. The glazier enters, shouting: "Glass put in! Umbrellas to mend! Goldbrick's regilted! Fires made! Fires put out! Insurance policies copied! Bad money bought!" He reads "Jewish news" from the paper, the *Dramatic Looking Glass,* until Charlotte reenters. She mistakes him for the critic, and they converse under this misapprehension. Since Glickman talks with an accent, she says in an aside: "Why he can't even talk plain English." She asks Glickman how long he's been in this business.

Glickman: De glass business?
Charlotte: Yes, the Looking Glass.
Glickman: Oh, ever since my second-hand store burned down.

Thinking Charlotte mad, Glickman plays the game. He says he's an "actorine" and she asks what parts he plays. "Jew-veniles," he replies, and goes on: "I give an imitation of a Jew." She replies: "An imitation? I thought you were a Jew." "Oh, go on," he answers, "somebody must have told you."[62]

After more banter she asks him to advise her how to become a good actress, and sets up a situation they can act out so he can instruct her. She is to be poor; she has "but one trusty negro servant. You [Glickman] are the negro servant." Glickman replies, "I'm a nigger? Alright," and sings "a coon song in burlesque manner."[63] The silly scene is worked out, and she finally gets a whip and beats him in revenge for the panning the critic gave her. He finally reveals that he is the glazier, and the sketch ends.

In *The Troubles of Rozinski* (1904), the same authors repeat the "Hebrew make-up" for the actor. The monologue is a blatant anti-union piece. When Rozinski's clothing shop goes out on strike and he is charged with being a scab, he quits. He joins the union, and several union functionaries extort money from him. He is injured in a scuffle with scabs, and he says: "I couldn't vork for six months. Dot's de unions." He relates how his friend Goldberg complained that he was punched by a bartender, and when they went to remonstrate, Rozinski was hit by the bartender. The ridicule goes on relentlessly. At the cemetery after his wife's funeral, his friend Goldberg is happy because "I got t'ree vifes buried over dere."[64]

Despite the ubiquity of the stage Jew, there was some awareness that this image was less than just to the Jews, as can be seen from Nobles's fatuous claim to have avoided it. If the reviews are to be believed, one popular play, *Sam'l of Posen*, by George H. Jessop, made an attempt to modify its objectionable features. The text that we have is one that apparently was revised by the actor M. B. Curtis and the comedian Ed Marble.[65] Although hardly literature, the play was an effective theatrical piece, judging from its great popularity over several decades. The parts of the Jews are not written in dialect, although it is obvious from the reviews that they were in fact spoken in thick dialect, and there is an occasional interjection in Yiddish. The play made a star of M. B. Curtis, a Jewish actor originally named Maurice Bertrand Strellinger, born in Detroit in mid-century.

The first production was in 1881. Curtis cannily perceived the potentialities of Jessop's play, bought it from the author, and revised it from time to time. For several decades Curtis was identified with the role of Sam'l through the course of a checkered career which included trial and acquittal for the murder of a policeman in San Francisco. As in the case of other "impersonators," Curtis once asserted in an interview that his rendering of Sam'l was based on his observation of a "drummer" in San Francisco: "There was a very funny drummer here at that time, a man named Wolf. He was, perhaps, one of the most comical men that I ever met; and for the life of me I could never refrain from giving imitations of him."[66]

Samuel Plastrick, an immigrant from Posen, comes to the jewelry shop of Mr. Winslow to sell something, and there he meets the Jewish salesgirl, Rebecca Heyman, who lives with her pawnbroker uncle, Goldstein. Samuel is recommended for a job with Winslow by the latter's nephew Jack, whose ring had been found by Sam and returned. Sam'l is, says Jack, "honest, trustworthy and industrious,"[67] and nothing in the action of the play impugns this characterization. Winslow hires Sam'l as a stock clerk and then as traveling salesman. Sam'l and Rebecca become engaged, and Sam'l is sent to New York with diamonds worth ten thousand dollars.

Meanwhile, the villain, Frank, Jack's brother, schemes for the hand of Winslow's daughter, who is engaged to Jack, so that he can become Winslow's business partner. He lures Jack to a gambling house in New York. When Sam goes there to warn Jack of the plot against him, he is drugged, and the diamonds are stolen from him. The scene shifts to Goldstein's pawnshop, where some bargaining provides an opening for comic business. The diamonds are recovered when they are brought in for sale by Frank. Jack weds Ellen and becomes the partner of Winslow, who sets Sam up in business. Sam'l is shown to be a generous person by his help in supporting an indigent Irish woman and her two children.

The portrait of Rebecca is straightforward and sympathetic. But the other Jewish characters, Sam'l and Goldstein, are stereotypes, and apparently were played as such to the hilt. In the New York *Daily Graphic* of May 17, 1881, the reviewer draws back in revulsion from the play: "From *Sam'l of Posen, the Commercial Drummer,* angels and ministers of grace defend us! It is very vile in the sense of offensiveness to any person who claims even an approach to refined feelings." As Sam'l, continues the review, Curtis "made a wonderfully realistic appearance and characterization of a miserable type of Jewish humanity. . . . The better the portrayal, the more painful it was to the refined sense." The reviewer then observes that "uproarious laughter on the part of the audience greeted his uncouth movements, his mean 'set-ups,' and his drummer cant." But this laughter, he goes on, came less from the non-Jewish than from the Jewish part of the audience, who caught meanings incomprehensible "to a refined American." The reviewer concludes that the character "is made to be gross, coarse, and vulgar throughout. Nothing can redeem this. He is offensive, and one sickens of him before the piece is ended."

Such reviews evidently moved Curtis to temper his rendering of Sam'l. A Philadelphia paper in 1890 observes that this play marks "a new order of things" in the projection of the Jew on the stage. Sam'l is now

harmless, effervescent, easy-going. Depth of character was not thought of nor aimed at; suffice it that the Jew of the stage furnish mirth. He had been raised a trifle from the standards set up for him in bygone days, and was allowed, here and there, even to score a point against the other characters. He had advanced some, a trifle, perhaps, but nevertheless he had advanced.[68]

Note that the writer cautiously records only a step of advancement, not the end of the stage Jew.

When Curtis revived the play again in 1894 it played with great success and acclaim to generally highly favorable notices all over the country. All of them note that Curtis has retained the basic plot but has brought it up to date, and that earlier crudities in the characterization of Sam'l are removed. All emphasize that Curtis's performance is hilarious. One newspaper review calls attention to the fact that

the type of Hebrew he [Curtis] presents on the stage is harmless and amusing. . . . Until Mr. Curtis took up their cause, the Hebrews of this country were fittingly represented in our drama only by *Leah, the Forsaken.* But what Dr. Mosenthal and Augustin Daly have done for the emotional and tragic sentiment of the Hebrews, M. B. Curtis has achieved for their humorous phase. Nobody, whether Jew or Gentile, could find offence in this amiable, ingenious and kind hearted young Israelite.[69]

A reviewer in a Detroit paper calls Curtis's "up-to-date *Sam'l of Posen* unquestionably the cleverest and cleanest characterization of the Hebrew ever presented on the stage."

However, the favorable response to the play, at least to the earlier version, was not unanimous. An editorial in the *American Hebrew* in

1889 alludes critically to "the Fagins and Sam'l Posen's that have served to calumniate and caricature our people."[70] A sophisticated review appeared in the *New York Times* of May 20, 1894. The piece, says the reviewer, "is not much of a play, to be sure, but it is vastly better than most of the pieces put together for comic stars." The central character, he writes, "is a purely comic personage, a caricature, in fact, though he is founded on reality." But the reviewer complains that he "does not cease to be comic when he is drugged and robbed, and the result is sadly inartistic." Curtis is extremely good in the part, he concludes: "He is undeniably and continually funny. . . . [He] will afford much wholesome merriment to the multitude." Although not altogether inoffensive, the stage Jew in this play was far less offensive than the usual rendering of the Jew in the theater at that time. But the Saint Paul *Dispatch* of August 21, 1894, observes that the play was still closer to burlesque than to comedy, and Sam'l's "character is an elaboration of the vaudeville theater."

Curtis's success with the Jewish character led him to sink much of his money in a play of his own, *The Schatchen* (The Matchmaker), produced in 1890. He employed the dramatist Charles Klein to rewrite the play for him, but the play failed. I have been unable to locate a copy, if indeed one still exists.

An intensely pro-Jewish play, in which the author virtually identifies himself with the Jews, is Edward W. Tullidge's *Ben Israel* (1875). This identification is what we should expect, for Tullidge was a Mormon and hence considered himself to be a latter-day Israelite. He was born into a Wesleyan family in England in 1829, was converted to Mormonism in 1848, and was called to the United States in 1861 to write a biography of Joseph Smith, the founder of the Mormon faith. He remained here for the rest of his life, writing also the biography of Brigham Young, histories of Utah and Salt Lake City, and plays. He was a dissident but very devoted Mormon.

His *Ben Israel*, dedicated to the "Jews of America," is so philo-Semitic that one is not surprised to read in the review of the play in New York in the *Spirit of the Times*, that the author "is reputed to be a Jew by birth and a Mormon by persuasion." The reviewer's judgment, that "this piece, whose literary merits are few, . . . has no dramatic power whatsoever,"[71] is easily borne out by a reading of this pompous, ridiculously melodramatic play about the first years following the return of the Jews to England, during the reign of Charles II. It centers on the conspiracy of several active anti-Semites to bring about a reversal of the order to allow the Jews to return to England, by falsely accusing the Jews of murder and then inciting the people to demand expulsion again. The plot is foiled, of course, and the plotters exposed. The Mormon dispensation must have lain behind the final speech of the play by the "Jewish Prince," David:

> Ay, King of England, thou shalt marvels see.
> There is a spirit in our sacred race,
> Which, fan'd, shall send a blaze o'er all the earth.
> Our seers shall rise; our psalmists sing;
> Our Solomons give wisdom to the world,
> And every land shall bless, not curse, the Jew.[72]

The Jews were sensitive to the affront they suffered in the vaudeville and stage Jew, and the English Jewish press took notice of plays that diverged from the stereotype—even when they were extremely poor. This happened in 1889, for instance, when Charles Stow, presumably a non-Jew, who was a journalist and long-time advertising agent for Barnum's Greatest Show on Earth, produced *An Iron Creed* in New York. In the most obvious stage clichés this crude, sententious melodrama unfolds the story of how an angelic Jewish daughter of a virtuous Jewish financier is duped into marriage with a scheming charmer, and the last scene is strewn with the dead bodies of all four characters. The best that could be said of the play was that in the portrait of a "Hebrew banker of noble impulses and generous hand, . . . an effort has been made to picture the successful Hebrew of this day without any of the caricature and dialect of the pawnbroker"; but the situations, adds the critic of the *New York Press* on April 18, 1889, are "tame." The *New York Dramatic Mirror* of April 3, 1889, is more candid. The aim of the author "was laudable," says the reviewer, "although the effort to achieve it failed signally." A reading of the play will confirm his comment that this "archaic" piece gives rise to an "inclination . . . to smile audibly over the dramatic portions of the piece, which several times threatened to break through the bonds of rigid politeness."

The critical faculties of the editorial writer of the *American Hebrew* were apparently in abeyance at his relief to find Jews in a play who were not caricatured.

The author [he writes] introduces several Jewish characters, but they are introduced not for the sake of mocking or laudation, ridicule or elegy, but because the exigencies of the plot itself evolve the necessity of Jewish characters. Delmont, the Jew of the play, is Jewish only so far as religion is concerned, in all else he is an American. This seems a simple thing to have done, but considering the temptation which so few playwrights seem able to withstand to have utilized the character for eccentric burlesque, Mr. Stow deserves credit for having consistently held to the dictates of truth and justice.[73]

In an urbane, mild social satire, *The Cable Car, a Howellsian Burlesque* (c1891). Clara Harriott Sherwood neatly exposes the fatuity of middle-class anti-Jewish attitudes. Several woman characters are chatting in a cable car, when the young Miss Harris drops her umbrella. Another passenger, designated only as "a Jew," picks it up and gives it to her; then he leaves the car. The umbrella falls away from Miss Harris without her realizing it; and when the ladies later realize that the umbrella is gone, Miss Harris exclaims: "That abominable, detestable Jew has taken it. He sat next to me. He and he alone could have taken it."[74] But at this point another man in the car reveals that someone else, not the Jew, took it by mistake.

Probably the most significant mark of this trend away from the vaudeville Jew at that time, however, was *Men and Women,* by Henry C. DeMille and David Belasco, first produced in New York in 1890. The play was a great hit, playing 204 performances in New York and touring the country successfully as far as San Francisco. It is difficult to separate the contributions of each author to the four plays on which they collaborated. This is how their plays were composed: DeMille would sit out front and give lines to Belasco on the stage; Belasco would then act out each part in turn, modifying the lines for maximum effect. Their aim was not literary but stage effectiveness, and *Men and Women* is actually of small literary interest. It fits smoothly into the tradition of the comedy of manners. It is contrived in the extreme, with four simultaneous love affairs, all of which turn out happily in the end. The plot was suggested by a notorious bank scandal then current in which the defendant had speculated with bank funds.

In the play, the bank cashier, on the verge of marriage to Agnes Redman but fearing that a panicky money market will deprive him of the wherewithal to marry, foolishly draws $300,000 in bank bonds for speculation. He promptly loses it all in the stock market. The president of the bank, Israel Cohen, is a cultured, high-minded Jewish character. Although he is the rejected rival of the bank cashier for the heroine of the play, he harbors no resentment, and in fact helps to save his rival from the worst consequences of his defalcation.

Cohen is not a Sheva character, but rather the typical two-dimensional man-of-virtue of the comedy of manners. He tells Agnes that he has just been offered the post of minister to Germany, and asks her to marry him and go to Germany with him. Though she says she wishes to marry the bank cashier, Will Prescott, she tells Cohen: "I have learned from others to admire you." He congratulates her on her impending marriage, and leaves. Later in the play he responds sympathetically to her plea for mercy for her delinquent fiancé.

Cohen is, moreover, a banker of great integrity. When he sees it will be necessary to close the bank, he exclaims: "I could give every drop of blood in my body to ward off the blow that will strike us, unless something is done tonight." At the very end, after all the right marriages have taken place or are about to, Cohen comes to say good-bye as he leaves to take up his post as minister to Germany: he utters this sententious homily: "Through the darkest valley a man may find his way, if there is left to him Love—and Home; Heimat und Liebe."[75]

The fact that David Belasco was a Jew and Henry C. DeMille was married to one is surely not irrelevant to the depiction of Cohen as a Jewish banker of culture, magnanimity, and integrity. David Belasco was born in San Francisco in 1853, to English Jewish parents of Portuguese origin. His family moved to Victoria, British Columbia, where from the age of seven to nine and a half he was educated at a monastery under the tutelage of a Father McGuire. This training made a deep impression upon him, and was manifested externally by his wearing a reversed collar and severe dress for many years. One may conjecture that the religious allusions at one point in the play may be accounted for by this phase of Belasco's life. Act 3 takes place in Cohen's house, and the authors direct that "above the fireplace is a niche in which is set a stained-glass picture of the Magdalen at the feet of the Savior." When Agnes comes to plead for the bank defaulter, she notices the picture and asks Cohen: "Adhering as you do to your faith, why do you keep in your house that picture?" Cohen answers: "Because of my admiration for the man. Whatever the Nazarene may have been, His treatment of mankind, His help to them, His hope for them, puts the breath of Heaven into the words of His philosophy. What picture I have in the house of a Jew is more appropriate than this picture of a Jew!"[76]

In practically the only unfavorable review of the play, the critic of the New York *Herald,* among other criticisms, questions the propriety of a Jew's having a stained-glass picture of Christ and Mary Magdalene. The scene, says the reviewer on April 12, 1892, is not only inappropriate, but is a "bit of mechanical clap-trap which necessarily weakens an otherwise impressive scene." It is altogether likely, however, that the scene reflects Belasco's own feeling about the Christ story, derived from the deep impression left upon him by Father McGuire. In a subsequent production of the play in 1898, the temptation to make the Jew foreign was apparently too great to resist. On October 10, 1898, a reviewer notes that Frederick Paulding had "acted the role to perfection" for this "type of the high class Jewish financier." Paulding "spoke with a trace of the German Jew's accent, while his make-up carried out the resemblance in every detail."

The appearance of a favorable Jewish character in this successful play was not lost on the Jewish press. The *Jewish Exponent* reprinted an article pointing out, somewhat optimistically, that with this play, "the stage . . . has at last shaken off the prejudice of the centuries and given us a Jew unsullied, untrammeled, uncaricatured." The Jew on the stage had usually been depicted with "a trickiness of disposition, a nasal twang and double-jointedness of arms, . . . the butt of every other character in the play: vengeful, grasping, unlovable." *Sam'l of Posen* had represented an "advance," but in *Men and Women* the Jewish character appears "in the guise of a living, breathing man —not a wooden prototype of a creed, but a being imbued with the same faculties, hopes, fears and ambitions as his brother Christian."[77]

It is quite likely that Belasco created this Jewish banker as an admirable character in a conscious effort to offset the vogue of the vaudeville Jew. A later theater incident is perhaps relevant here. In 1897 the San Francisco playwright Francis Powers produced *The First Born,* a play about Chinese life in that city. A Jewish peddler, played by David Belasco's brother, Walter, appears in it. So popular did the play prove that a New York production was put on in the same year by David Belasco. It is interesting that the typescript of the New York production of the play, which is in the Theater Collection of the New York Public Library, has no part for a Jewish peddler. May one speculate that Belasco dropped this character to avoid a Jewish stereotype? If so, Belasco was exceptional among Jewish producers. The *Indianapolis News* in 1901 comments that

it is a curious thought that, with the growing influence of Jews in theatrical matters, so little respect is paid on the stage to the Jewish character or the Jewish traditions. It seems curious to people of this age who see men of the Hebrew stock among the successful leaders in all branches of endeavor, that racial prejudice ever militated against those people, as a people. Everywhere, except on the stage, the Hebrew today is rated at his true worth, and it is well recognized

by thinking people that the old gibes and smears have lost their point
and force. It might be imagined that with a great preponderance of
the theatrical business of this country in the hands of the Jews, that
the frightful caricature of the Hebrew that has long served as a
buffoon for the amusement of the unthinking would disappear, but
there are no signs of any such change.[78]

However, the Jewish press was not unanimous in its condemnation of the stereotype. A New York weekly, the *Reformer and Jewish
Times,* in 1878 reflects the contempt of the uptown German Jews for
the newly arrived, poor East European immigrants, an attitude that
persisted well into the new century. The paper refuses to comply
with a correspondent's demand that it "denounce the managers of
certain variety halls in this city who have recently introduced the
character of the 'Jew clothing man' among their 'song and dance'
attractions." The caricature, the paper says editorially, "is not of the
Jew as a member of the Jewish faith, but of a peculiar class of Jews."
Only "densely ignorant people" would mistake this type for the Jews
as a people, but it would be "unreasonable" on that account to
expect theater managers to refrain from responding to public taste.
The correspondent, the paper goes on, is hypersensitive. "For ourselves, we fail to observe any general prejudice against the Jews as
a race; where prejudice exists it is against certain classes of Jews only
who find no more favor with their respectable brethren than they do
with the Gentile world." The paper does not feel it has to "take up
the cudgels in defense of the Chatham Street clothier." Like all
peoples, the paper concludes, the Jews have their upper as well as
their lower classes, which "have their peculiarities." It is "neither
reasonable nor wise" for Jews to suppose that such caricatures insult
Jews or Judaism.[79]

10

AMERICAN JOURNEYS
OF THE WANDERING JEW

In restrospect there is a certain inevitability to the legend of the
Wandering Jew. Did not the Christian world believe for centuries
—as many still do—that, in Longfellow's words, "the Jews, the tribe
accursed,/Mocked him, scourged him, crucified him"?[1] And for this
did not the Jews deserve to suffer, at least until Christ returned in
the Second Coming? And while awaiting his return and in penance
for their sin, should not the Jews wander endlessly in dispersion?

In actuality, however, it was not until in the early eighteenth
century that the Wandering Jew as a symbol of the Jewish people first
received articulation. It is Johann Jacob Schudt, in his *Judische Merk-
wurdigkeiten* (1714–18), who advances this idea as the only cogent
manner of interpreting the legend, since he argues rationally against
the historicity of the Wanderer. Schudt says that Christ was too
gentle and forgiving to impose such a cruel sentence; that neither the
Gospels nor church historians mention the legend; and that the
supposed facts concerning the Wanderer—his name, occupation,
and location—are various and inconsistent.[2] But the legend fits in
very well with the historical dispersion of the Jews and their survival
as a people, and hence can stand as a symbol for it. One can only
suppose that the symbolism must have been felt in the depths of
consciousness from the start, even if the feeling was not articulated.

In any event, the constituent germs of the legend are to be found
in the New Testament. The idea of suffering in retribution for
physical or mental violence done to Jesus derives, in fact, from
passages like John 18:4–10, 20–22. The idea of deathlessness until
Christ's Second Coming stems from a passage in Matthew 16:28:
"There be some standing here, which shall not taste of death, till
they see the Son of man coming in his kingdom"; or the several times
when Jesus enjoins a disciple to "tarry till I come" (e. g., John
21:20–22). In its developed form, then, the legend is concerned

with the notion of eternal suffering for anyone who did physical or mental violence to Jesus.

The legend was probably originally formed and transmitted orally. The first primitive written version of the legend appeared in the sixth century, but the first full-fledged story—and a primary written source for subsequent versions—is found in the *Flores Historiarum* by Roger of Wendover (1228). Roger tells of having heard the story from an Armenian archbishop who had himself talked to the Wanderer. In this version Cartaphilus is a Roman (not Jewish) doorkeeper for Pontius Pilate. He strikes Jesus on the way to the crucifixion, for which offense Jesus pronounces sentence: Cartaphilus must remain alive and must wander until Jesus returns. It is of interest that in one respect the legend resembles the source story for Shakespeare's Shylock. In Shakespeare's source—the biography of Pope Sixtus V by Gregorii Leti—the would-be wielder of the knife is a Christian and the victim is a Jew. The legend, with the aggressor/victim roles reversed, continued to proliferate in oral and written form; the Wanderer received different names and underwent various adventures; he became an eyewitness chronicler of events for a millennium and more of history.

In a version of the legend that appeared in 1602 in a German *Volksbuch, Kurtze Beschreibung und Erzehlung von einem Juden mit Namen Ahasverus,* the Wanderer is definitely launched as the Jew Ahasuerus, a shoemaker of Jerusalem, who was present at the crucifixion. As Jesus passes him, weary of bearing the cross, he leans against Ahasuerus' house. Ahasuerus drives Jesus off with curses, and Jesus, looking meaningfully at him, decrees that he must walk forever.

The legend then found its way to England as a ballad, in 1612. It flourished all over Europe in folklore and in printed form. But its entry into sophisticated literature came through the influence of the poem "Der Ewige Jude," in 1783, by the minor Enlightenment poet and critic Christian Friedrich Daniel Schubart, and thence raced through European and American literature.

Through the centuries the idea of the Wandering Jew has proved extraordinarily hardy. It derives from deep roots in the unconsciousness; it draws upon the subtle psychological unease caused by ideas of death and deathlessness; its religious origin endows it with mystery; its association with the supernatural lends magical possibilities to it; and its scope is expanded by its fusion with the Faustian legend. It may serve as an outlet for religious or secular prejudice against the Jew or tolerance toward him.

Moreover, it is susceptible of adaptation to the outlook of different periods. Under religious auspices, the legend can drive home the sacrilege of rejecting Jesus; in periods of scepticism, such as the Enlightenment, it can be given an anti-Christian connotation by expressing the Wanderer's resentment at unjust treatment, as in Schubart's version; or it may give voice to the spirit of rebellion, as in Shelley's Queen Mab, when Ahasuerus is "Resolved to wage unweariable war/With my almighty tyrant" (canto 7). In what was probably the most widely read version of the legend, Eugène Sue's *Wandering Jew* (1844–45), the Wanderer is allied with the forces of labor against the rich and their allies and applies his supernatural powers in behalf of the poor and the oppressed.

Use of the Jew in the legend is remarkable in one respect: its extreme flexibility, in contrast with that other literary prototype of the Jew, Shylock, an image that remained rigid through several centuries. Until the twentieth century the Jew was depicted in literature usually either in terms of the Shylock convention or the later improbably "good" Sheva stereotype. The character and activity of the Wandering Jew varied considerably in accordance with alterations in prevailing ideology, as became most obvious from the eighteenth century on. When Christianity came under drastic criticism, the punishment of Ahasuerus for doing violence to Christ evoked different responses. Defiance of God, as in Schubart and Shelley, took the place of total subordination, as in earlier versions.

Readers in the United States were amply supplied with European versions of the legend—works like Lewis's *Monk* (1796), Godwin's *St. Leon* (1800), and, more especially, best sellers in this country like George Croly's *Salathiel* (1829), which was the most popular version until Sue's *Wandering Jew* became a best seller everywhere,[3] including the United States, where it was published in 1845.

Nor was the Wandering Jew a literary figure only. There were periodic reports that he had actually been encountered. Horace Greeley's magazine, the *New Yorker,* reported in the late 1830s that a Wandering Jew had been seen in Europe, and there were newspaper reports in New York about his appearance. The *Deseret News* reported in 1856 that a Wandering Jew had conversed "with a rabbi in New York in Hebrew and Sanscrit, saying that he must keep wandering." The *Western Monthly Magazine* in Cincinnati published a poem in 1833, "The Wandering Jew," in which the notion is joined with the Mammon motif:

> Beneath the dreadful ban of God,
> Judea's sons are scattered now—

The blasted wreck of former days—
And to the god of mammon bows.[4]

The United States also supplied its own versions of the legend in
both folklore and literary works. So widespread and popular was the
idea that it was the rare writer who did not sooner or later make
either an allusion, or give extended treatment, to the theme or one
of its variants. In his poem "The Flying Dutchman," James Russell
Lowell indicates how several variants are associated:

Don't believe in the Flying Dutchman?
    I've known the fellow for years;
My button I've wrenched from his clutch, man
    I shudder whenever he nears.

He's a Rip Van Winkle skipper,
    A Wandering Jew of the sea,
Who sails his bedevilled slipper
    In the mind's eye, straight as a bee.[5]

A New England version of the Rip Van Winkle type of variant of
the legend was used in a story by the Boston lawyer William Austin,
Peter Rugg, the Missing Man (1824). Austin's adaptation of the legend
drops the Jewish theme but retains the notion of the suffering eternal
wanderer. Peter Rugg starts out on horseback for home in Boston
in 1770, but half a century later, when the story is being told, he is
still traveling. From several states comes word that Peter has been
seen and given directions for Boston. The unearthly nature of his
ride is signaled by the laying back of horses' ears as he passes, and
by a cloud that bursts into rain after Peter has passed. After twenty
years a neighbor reports having seen Peter passing his own house;
but everything has changed so greatly that he insists that this is not
Boston and rides away. Another says that Rugg passed his house but
was unable to stop his horse, and the houses round about shook as
he passed. All of which, as in the case of Rip Van Winkle, may
symbolize the irreversibility of the past, the futility of hoping for an
unchanging present, and the torments to which such expectations
may give rise.

Of all the major American writers of the century, only Hawthorne
used the legend in extended form. He was deeply impressed with
the legend in the version by Godwin, *St. Leon,* which he read when
he was sixteen. Peter Rugg also appears in one of three stories by
Hawthorne in which the Wandering Jew appears. The legend
figures importantly in *The Marble Faun* (1860) as well. (We have

treated these matters in chapter 5.) Herman Melville devotes one canto of his long poem *Clarel* (1876) (book 3, canto 19) to the legend. Melville makes a reverent and compassionate restatement of the plight of the eternally suffering Wandering Jew, which is retold in a masque by the monks of the Bar Saba Monastery in Palestine. But Melville did not, like Hawthorne, turn the legend to his creative purposes.

However, many minor writers exploited the legend and its variants through the century. One of these variants is that of the Wandering Jewess, who is generally depicted as Herodias, condemned to eternal life for having ordered the decapitation of John the Baptist. She appears in George Lippard's *Nazarene* (1846). The novel inveighs against "the Despotism of Banks" and is dedicated to "Stephen Girard, the [Philadelphia] Banker, who . . . never once swindled the public by a suspension of payments, and consequently never robbed the poor of their hard earnings, the widow and orphan of their crust of bread." The novel is a tract against "religious fanaticism" and political corruption in the same vein as the earlier *The Quaker City,* continuing its excoriation of the rich. When the heroine of *The Nazarene* declares that she can marry the hero even if they are both poor, he vehemently protests:

Happy without wealth? Where? In this great city [Philadelphia], where hearts are sold for gold, where money will sanctify any crime, or the want of it provoke any insult? Where to be rich is to be virtuous, to be poor, is to be dishonest and depraved? Where Justice is so holy and refined that she only draws her sword at the magic word—DOLLAR! Where you can buy beauty, intellect, righteousness, even as you buy a peddlar's ribbons, for so much per yard? Where souls cannot be saved, unless they come to the altar of Almighty God, burdened with gold, and shrouded in silks and broadcloth?[6]

The villain of *The Nazarene* is an evil banker, Calvin Wolfe, who is also the grand master of the United States L. P. O. (Loyal Protestant Order), an ancient organization committed to the extirpation of Catholicism; the story recounts the machinations of the order. Halfway through the story, without preliminaries, the reader is confronted with a shipwreck scene in which Wolfe, the grand master of the L. P. O. of the British Empire, the papal legate to America, and a beautiful Jewish actress are adrift at sea. Their food is gone, and they eye each other: who will be sacrificed to save the others? Their choice falls on the woman. However, she reveals at last that she has food; they are saved—but not without being mocked by her at their willingness to kill despite their religiosity. She then reveals that she is the Wandering Jewess and tells them her story. Lippard describes her: "A woman, who has once been beautiful, and even now in this dread hour of famine and death, wears about her darkly flowing hair, and dazzling eyes and bared bosom, some traces of that gorgeous loveliness, peculiar to the daughters of Palestine, from immemorial time."[7]

Lippard tells her story in the lush, voluptuous, melodramatic prose that his readers had come to expect. She is Herodia, wife of Herod, who, like the Wandering Jew, is cursed to live forever because she demanded the head of John the Baptist. After the reluctant Herod orders the decapitation, Herodia dances, holding the head on a plate of gold over her. It is an orgiastic scene, described in lurid, trashy prose. Then, "when she is about to sink into the incestuous embrace of Herod, the King, her flushed face is changed to the hue of a cor[p]se." She sees "a Form, pale, livid, deathly, with a flowing beard and dark eyes, that glowed like living coals. *The Murdered Prophet;* she knew him; she heard that voice that spoke to her heart without a sound." She knows the curse that has been put upon her. "Never to die! Never to grow old! Ever to feel the fire of passion burning in my veins—to be loved—worshipped—and not to love again! Never to die—oh, terrible vengeance! Never! Never! Never!" She will test the decree—she plunges a knife into her heart, but no blood flows, no death follows. She hurls herself from the parapet, but lives! "She was not permitted to taste the luxury of—Death."[8]

Another example of the Wandering Jewess in Joseph C. Heywood's interminable, overblown "dramatic" trilogy in verse: *Antonius, Herodias,* and *Salome* (1867). Kaliphilus (Cartaphilus), the Wandering Jew, who is in love with Salome, murders John the Baptist at her behest. He converses with Salome about his endless suffering. But Salome spurns him and becomes a Christian. She tells Kaliphilus that he can be saved only if he loves the Jesus whom he offended, but he refuses. The plot plods through three volumes, until at last we find Kaliphilus at the battle for Jerusalem in 70 C. E. He saves Salome from captivity and threatens to reveal that she is a Christian, but she will not accept him and he kills her, thus ending her deathlessness—which is no doubt possible for her because she has become a Christian.

The protean idea of the Wandering Jew had other expressions that did not designate the Wanderer as a Jew. The fusion of the idea with that of the Faustian bargain was made by, among others, the German writer Chamisso in his fantasy *Peter Schlemihls Wunderbare Geschichte* (1814). The hero sells his shadow to "the Gentleman in Black" for the "purse of Fortunatus," from which coins can inexhaustibly be drawn. But the Gentleman in Black wants Peter's substance as well as his shadow, and when Peter finally throws the purse into a well in defiance, he becomes invisible.

The American George Wood wrote a sequel to Chamisso's story in his *Peter Schlemihl in America* (1848), a satire on life in New York, "Babylon the Less." The book is an illustration of the variety of uses to which the supernatural personage of the Wanderer is amenable, in this case a vehicle for satire on New York society. The Gentleman in Black seeks Peter Schlemihl in order to punish him for losing the purse, a rather difficult task because of Peter's invisibility. Later in the book Peter is arrested in New York and hauled before a magistrate named Rabbi Ben Jarchi, a friend of the Gentleman in Black's. As befits a man with such associates, the rabbi is quite indifferent to considerations of justice.

The legend was used by Eliza Buckminster Lee in *Parthenia* (1857) to confirm the truth of Christianity, by demonstrating that the failure of the Emperor Julian to restore paganism bore out the prophecies of the gospel. Julian seeks to advance belief in the Roman gods by demonstrating that the Scriptures prophesied wrongly when they foretold the destruction of the Temple. In a scheme to rebuild the Temple and restore the Jews to Jerusalem, he enlists the aid of the "noble Jew" Cartaphilus, who is eventually revealed as the Wandering Jew. "I have learnt," Julian tells Cartaphilus, "that the time has come to summon the wanderers of your nation to return to their ancient Temple up on Mount Zion. . . . Are you not ready to gather again to your ancient city your oppressed and scattered people?" Cartaphilus replies: "The Jewish people are everywhere dispersed, everywhere the objects of contempt and hatred. Years must pass—." Julian then strikes a bargain: he will relieve Jews from tribute and rebuild the Temple if Cartaphilus will pray for Julian's victory in the Persian wars. The shrewd Cartaphilus knows that Julian is not really suggesting this out of love for the Jews. He is aware, writes Mrs. Lee, that "the present scattered condition of the Jews was a perpetual testimony to the truth of Christianity. Could the ancient prophesies be falsified, the whole would fall together." And of course Julian is defeated by the Persians, saying as he dies from his wounds: "The Galilean has conquered." Although Cartaphilus has agreed to aid Julian, his attempt to rebuild the Temple meets with disaster, for miracles frustrate all his efforts and the truth of Christianity survives.

In this tale Cartaphilus does not exhibit the magical powers usually attributed to the Wandering Jew, but displays only his great abilities. In the first part of the book he is pictured as a sinister character who has a thin veneer of charm. But his virtues emerge as the story proceeds, for the author observes that he "has ever been *almost* a Christian."[9] Her feeling is not friendly toward those Jews who are unwise enough to reject Jesus as Savior. She does not, however, exploit to anything like their full possibilities the fictional potentialities of the Wandering Jew.

Surely the strangest (and longest) American effort to exploit the legend is an enormous work by David Hoffman, a lawyer from Baltimore. He was professor of law at the University of Maryland and the author of several instructional books on the law and on the ethics of the profession. After a quarrel with the university he resigned, and in 1847 he went to Europe to gather material for his book on the chronicles of Cartaphilus, into which he hoped to incorporate a history of the world in the Christian period. He projected a six-volume work. By 1853, when his saga had reached the middle of the seventh century, he returned to America, and in 1854 he died of apoplexy at the age of seventy.

The first three volumes of his work, *Chronicles Selected from the Originals of Cartaphilus, the Wandering Jew,* had already been published in London in 1853–54 in eighteen hundred closely printed pages. (An American edition appeared in Baltimore in 1858.) Hoffman purported to be the editor of the manuscripts of Cartaphilus, who dedicated the *Chronicles* to "Jehovah's favorite people," hoping that they will be led to "the only revealed and True Faith," that is, Christianity.[10] The chronicles include not only Cartaphilus' account of historical events, but epistles from his friends through the centuries. These correspondents are eminent men of learning and action, and Cartaphilus plays a part in historic events throughout, even becoming Mohammed for a time. One wonders how many readers the prodigious labors of Hoffman have garnered in the more than a century since the *Chronicles* was printed.

A far less weighty treatment of the legend was offered by Mark Twain in *The Innocents Abroad* (1869). Tourists in Jerusalem, he writes, pass "the veritable house where the unhappy wretch once lived who has been celebrated in song and story for more than eighteen hundred years as the Wandering Jew." After telling the story of the encounter, Twain notes the futile efforts of the Wanderer to end his life; he places himself in the thick of the sack of

Jerusalem, betrays Mohammed during the wars of conquest, and takes part in the Crusades—all to no avail, for he cannot die. Twain adds that the Wanderer has pretty well given up hope of dying, but compensates for his desperate situation with sepulchral interests. "He has speculated some in cholera and railroads," he writes, "and has taken almost a lively interest in infernal machines and patent medicines. . . . He goes sometimes to executions, and is fond of funerals."[11]

It was to be expected that F. Marion Crawford, a romancer of exotic and foreign milieus, should try his hand at the legend of the Wandering Jew. In *A Roman Singer* (1883) he exploits both this theme and the cliché of Jewish musical talent. The putative Wandering Jew, Benoni, is a great violinist, and the usual features of the Wanderer are ascribed to him: he has a "dazzlingly white" beard, but his complexion "had all the freshness of youth"; he was once a poor shoemaker, but he has "worn out more shoes than I ever made"; he has led a wandering life as a musician, but "never stayed long" at any place, and the reason for this would be a "very long story"; when asked his age, he replies that it "is a rude question"; he has "loved several women all their lives"; he hates Rome, "but Jerusalem more"; "Never," he says, "is a great word, You do not know what it means. I do"; he will never get to heaven, he says, for "there are exceptions, you know." Like the Wandering Jew of Hawthorne's "Virtuoso's Collection," he is a materialist, for he is a dandy, loves pleasure, and believes that "money is the only thing in the world worth having."[12]

Benoni is in love with Hedwig, the daughter of a Prussian count. The count gives his consent to the marriage for pecuniary reasons, even though Hedwig hates the violinist. Nino, a talented young "Roman singer," also loves Hedwig, but labors under the handicap of being "plebian" and is rejected by the count. He pits his youth and talent against Benoni's "old age, much talent, an enormous fortune, and the benefit of the Jewish faith into the bargain." Crawford then observes: "The count winced perceptibly at the mention of Benoni's religion. No people are more insanely prejudiced against the Hebrew race than the Germans. They indeed maintain that they have greater cause than others." Crawford then adds that "it always appears to me that they are unreasonable about it. Benoni chanced to be a Jew, but his peculiarities would have been the same had he been a Christian or an American. There is only one Ahasuerus Benoni in the world." The count is adamantly opposed to a match with Nino because of his lowly origin, but Benoni blunders by insulting Hedwig, and Nino and Hedwig marry. Crawford then ends with a "rational" explanation of Benoni's intimations of immortality: the press reveals that "Baron Benoni, the wealthy banker of St. Petersburg, who was many years ago an inmate of a private lunatic asylum in Paris, is reported to be dangerously insane in Rome."[13]

The legend of Peter Rugg was brought up to date in a charming ballad by Louise Imogen Guiney in "Peter Rugg, the Bostonian" (1891). After an engaging restatement of the legend, several verses of reflection follow:

> Tho' nigh two hundred years have gone,
> Doth Peter Rugg the more
> A gentle answer and a true
> Of living lips implore:
> "Oh, show me to our town,
> And to my open door!"
>
> How shall he know his own town
> If now he clatters thro'?
> Much men and cities change that have
> Another love to woo;
> And things occult, incredible,
> They find to think and do.[14]

But the work in which this theme is most central, with the exception of *The Marble Faun,* is Lew Wallace's *Prince of India* (1893). This work did not approach the popular success of *Ben-Hur* and, indeed, is inferior to the earlier book. But Wallace's two-volume *The Prince of India* gives the legendary Wanderer full play in magical power and in evil intentions. The time is the fourteenth century and the Wanderer, described as being "of the type Rabbinical that sat with Caiaphas in judgment on the gentle Nazarene" and "undersized, slightly stoop-shouldered, thin,"[15] has acquired an immense treasure by ransacking the sarcophagus of Hiram, king of Tyre. Now, after fourteen centuries—the events of which are recorded briefly—he is the wealthy "prince of India."

His ostensible reason for coming to the Near East is to attempt to establish a unified faith for all the world by "lopping off all parasitical worship as are given to Christ and Mohammed." He offers a "compromise" between Christianity and Mohammedanism in a "Universal Religious Brotherhood with God for its ascendant principle"—a notion, current in the 1890s, of a nonsectarian religion transcending the specific faiths. But his real intention is to destroy the two religions so that Judaism may emerge as the sole remaining faith. Entwined with the execution of the prince's scheme are the love stories of two women. Lael, the young Jewish adopted daughter of the prince, is wooed by a saintly Christian, Sergius. Irene, a naval hero's daughter whom the Emperor Constantine in gratitude has made a princess, is courted by both the emperor and Mohammed, and she becomes an instrument of the prince's scheme. The development of these love affairs is enmeshed with the progress of the prince's plan.

The prince tries to persuade the emperor to adopt his new universal faith, but although the emperor is willing, his church is not. Constantine's rival for Irene's hand, Mohammed, declares war. The prince's hatred of Christianity reinforces his hatred of Sergius the Christian, the suitor of his adopted daughter; he therefore gives Mohammed the sword of Solomon, which the prince had taken possession of with the resolve "to give it to him whom the stars should elect for the overthrow of the superstitions devised by Jesus, the bastard son of Joseph the carpenter of Nazareth."[16] The prince hopes to enthrone Mohammed instead of Jesus in the Sancta Sophia. Constantine is killed in battle, Islam takes over in Constantinople, and the prince's real purpose is accomplished by the defeat of the Christian order in the Near East. The prince is left for dead on the battlefield, but he arises once again as the youth Caiaphas and loses his identity as the prince of India.

The core of this dull, bloated fiction is the Wandering Jew's hatred for Christianity as rooted in his original legendary revulsion from Jesus. When the prince discovers his adopted daughter, Lael, with Sergius, he mutters: "I will show him what all of hell there can be in one man's hate!" His lieutenant, Mohammed, says of him: "How he hates Christ and the Christians!"[17] Thus Wallace was animated by primitive Christian resentment of Jews. "I believe absolutely in the Christian conception of God," Wallace wrote later.[18] In fulfillment of this belief, he utilizes the theme of the Wandering Jew to illustrate the devious, unprincipled character of the Jews, a character that befits those who have rejected the principle of goodness. The prince's avowed purpose of achieving peace among the world's religions is a perverted subterfuge to vent hatred on Christianity and to establish Judaism as the world's religion. The prince's purpose is achieved by the overthrow of the Christian order in the Near East, and he himself is renewed once again to continue his evil career.

Lew Wallace's version is only one of a number written in the last decade of the century, though most are not so lengthy or solemn as his. A rather dull, sentimental version is given in Eugene Field's short story "The Holy Cross" (1893), in which Father Miguel, priest to Cortez's conquistadors, meets the suffering Wanderer in the Brazilian forest. As the Wanderer tells his story, Father Miguel discerns that he is genuinely repentant for his sinful act against Jesus; he feels that it is time he is forgiven and allowed to die. Through the night Miguel prays, while the Wanderer dreams that he is reenacting his crime in Jerusalem; but this time he implores forgiveness from Jesus, who bestows it, thanks to the prayers of Miguel. The Wanderer dies with a smile of peace.[19]

A rather light adaptation of the legend is *The Vizier of the Two-Horned Alexander* (1899), by Frank R. Stockton, in which the deathless one is a wealthy New York stockbroker who denies that he is the Wandering Jew. His own story, he asserts, is the basis for the Wandering Jew legend. He had been first vizier to Alexander at the time of Abraham and had then imbibed a potion that conferred immortality. In his nineteenth-century guise he saves a young man from a sinking ship, and reveals to him (and later the ex-vizier's current Quaker wife) his adventures throughout history.

The humorist Oliver Herford, writing at about the same time, continues the legend with a dash of the anti-Semitic stereotype in the poem "The Wandering Jew" (1900). An anti-Semitic drawing at the head of the poem shows a bearded, long-nosed Jew with hand extended. This poem is an interesting exhibit of the kind of stereotyping that was an acceptable form of humor until recent years:

> No Living Soul can testify
> With such authority as I
> Upon the weariness and Ache
> Of Walking just for Walking's sake;
> But ever since I undertook
> To be the Agent of your Book,
> And travelled for the sake of Trade,
> I've felt like quite a different Shade.
> Indeed, I have at last begun
> To wish my journey never done;
> Both for your good Book's sake and mine;
> Love and Percent. I thus combine—
>   And that reminds me—
>   I enclose
> My statement for the month, which shows
> The net subscriptions up to date
> (With Discount at the usual rate).
> Among subscribers you'll perceive
> The names of Cleopatra, Eve,
> Lady Godiva, Horace, Jonah,
> Lady Macbeth and Desdemona.

> They all send testimonials too,
> More later—until then, adieu.
>   P.S.
> I have (I trust with your consent)
> Deducted sixty-five per cent.[20]

The legend continued to engage writers into the twentieth century. A rather imaginative rendering is O. Henry's short story "The Door of Unrest."[21] A small-town newspaper editor interviews a visitor who passes himself off as the eternal Wanderer. He says he has been erroneously labeled a Jew named Michob Ader in a clipping which he shows the editor (based on an actual seventeenth-century report of Michob Ader, the Wandering Jew). His name is really Mike O'Bader, he says, and he then assumes the role of the chronicler of the events of centuries, relating his experiences with historical figures such as Nero, Tamerlane, Charlemagne, Joan of Arc, and others. When the editor makes inquiries the next day, he finds that there is a shoemaker named Mike O'Bader in town. He is told that Mike goes on a monthly spree and pretends to be the Wandering Jew in penitential expiation for having turned his wayward daughter away from his door thirty years before, after which she was found drowned.

Another version is Edwin Arlington Robinson's poem "The Wandering Jew,"[22] which conveys a kind of spiritual psychology of the Wanderer: the loneliness in his "endless eyes . . . remembered everything." Though a profound pity for the Wanderer's anguish pervades it, the poem's meaning is elusive. Perhaps it signifies the paradox of life, as the poet and the deathless one gaze into each other's eyes. "What life has in it to be lost" is revealed. What is good in life one does not want to lose; what is evil makes one want to lose life itself.

At the end of the nineteenth century efforts were made by several rabbis to modify the invidious aspects of the legend. An impressive effort, at least in size, was made by Herman M. Bien in *Ben-Beor, a Story of the Anti-Messiah* (1891). (Bien was then living in Vicksburg, Mississippi, having emigrated from Germany in 1854.) This was not his first venture into literature; he had published a verse drama, *Samson and Delilah* (San Francisco, 1860), while he was a rabbi in San Francisco. The play, which was actually performed in that city in 1859, was first written in German and translated by the author into dull, traditional, uninspired English verse. Bien did better in *Purim: A Series of Character Poems in Four Casts and Tableaux*, 2d rev.

ed. (Cincinnati, 1889), probably written in the early 1880s, which reads like a good *Purim-Spiel* that children can perform and witness with enjoyment.

For his 500-page novel, Bien takes his cue from Numbers 22:5–6, where Balak, king of the Moabites, summons Baalam with the call: "Behold, there is a people come out of Egypt: behold, they cover the face of the earth, and they abide ever against me; Come now, therefore, I pray thee, curse now this people; . . . that we may smite them, and that I may drive them out of the land." The story is in two parts: the first purports to be a narrative in Hebrew incised on intaglios delivered from the moon to earth in a meteorite; the second part is inscribed on palimpsest manuscripts. Baalam Ben-Beor is enamored of Pharaoh's daughter, who spurns him for Balak the Hebrew, whereupon Ben-Beor vows revenge on all women and Jews. He is transported to the moon, a kind of limbo where everyone speaks Hebrew. There he is a corrupting influence. During a stopover on the moon Elijah, messenger of God, hears of Ben-Beor's evil influence, and sends him back to earth under the curse of remaining on earth until God chooses to relieve him.

Thus we find Ben-Beor on earth as the "Wandering Gentile." He is the "Anti-Messiah," sworn to bend all his energies to the destruction of the Jews. Throughout the story his designs on women, who are reincarnations of his beloved Pharaoh's daughter, are frustrated, although in each case the women are destroyed in the process. The author does not raise, much less answer, the question of why Elijah, with all his powers, should let Ben-Beor loose upon the Jews to plan destruction upon them for several thousand years. Of course, Elijah always prevents Ben-Beor from succeeding in his mission, but not before great suffering has been inflicted on the Jews.

Elijah's curse on Ben-Beor is like the sentence upon the Wandering Jew: "Thou must wander in thy human body from generation to generation, without rest, or quiet. . . . Creep on, miserable wretch, until the measure of retribution for thy iniquity shall be full!" Elijah hints at the birth of the United States in 1776 as being the counterpart of the Second Coming of the original legend. "The time at last will come," he says, "when thou shalt stray to a country as yet unknown and undiscovered. In the morning-light of universal Freedom and religious Tolerance will there arise a new nation. Then the malediction that rests upon thee shall be changed into a blessing. . . . Thou shalt once more be permitted by God's never-ending mercy to die!"[23]

In a preface to the second part Ben-Beor writes that he began the narrative of his second life on earth in 1780 in a cave in the mountains, and recounts the chronicles of his life as the Wandering Gentile since the fall of Jerusalem. His task, he writes, was "to drive from the face of the earth the Israelites, his [Elijah's] people, whom he vaunted to have been selected as 'God's chosen' for the promulgation of the law, embodied in that book of inspired revelation called the Torah." He realizes that his antimessianic mission has failed, that if he had succeeded in annihilating the Jews, the progress that culminated in the establishment of the United States would never have taken place.

All his plans against the Jews have come to nothing.

Never before in the history of man, was the holy titled Book in the hands of such multitudes; never has it been read, studied, understood, loved and revered to the immeasurable extent by any other nation like this American. Where it formerly was but in the possession of the Israelites, a few monks, prelates and students of the Christians, here it has spread into every house, hut and tent. . . . Directly emanating from the core of its teachings, Freedom, under panoply of the whole power of a new government, is arrayed to end on this continent the last vestige of despotism. . . . Right, Truth and Tolerance will prevail! When these facts shall be officially prero gated, I, Baalam Ben-Beor, must—and let me say it, Thank God— will gladly die![24]

Ben-Beor now comprehends how futile and evil his efforts have been. With this realization comes the understanding that all the cruel acts performed in the name of Jesus were not in his spirit. On the contrary, Jesus was "the most loving, humble, humane, sympathetic and most worldly poor. Never since his coming, unto this day, has a true follower, an honest, conscientious member of his church and her ideal mission raised arm or tongue for deed or word in persecution, hatred or malignity against any other creed or race." It will take the world a long time to realize that it was Ben-Beor, the anti-Messiah, who in various guises through the centuries, "sowed the seeds of hatred and contentions, causing war, émeutes and bloody revolts; doing the work of Satan, so as to make him ultimately the primate of this globe, neutralizing, effectually combatting and thwarting the work of Moses the Teacher and Jesus the Reformer."[25]

The narrative depicts Ben-Beor starting with his alliance with Titus, as the instrument of whatever power has oppressed the Jews. He is a false Messiah; he helps the Russians destroy the Khazars in the tenth century; he helps Peter the Hermit incite the people to the

Crusades and then recruits crusaders; he originates the blood libel against the Jews in Blois in 1171; he invents gunpowder in the fourteenth century; and he turns up as a grand inquisitor, a friend and ally of Torquemada.

Ben-Beor's final effort is to become an agent for George III against the American revolutionists. It is at that point that Elijah appears to him on shipboard and deprives him of all power. For the prophesied end is approaching; Ben-Beor meets his ultimate frustration when the Declaration of Independence is signed as he lands in Philadelphia. Now he knows he is defeated. He slinks off to a cave, becomes a "Recluse of the Mountains," writes his phantasmagoric memoirs, and at last dies in the cave on the day Cornwallis surrenders.

It is not to be wondered that Rabbi Isaac Mayer Wise felt impelled in the last years of the century to deliver a lecture on the Wandering Jew. As a spokesman for a large segment of American Jewry, he probably felt it incumbent upon him to offer his own version of the legend, since everyone else was doing so. One need not take too seriously Wise's speculative "scholarship" concerning the thirteenth-century origins of the legend. Since a thirteenth-century slaughter of the Jews in Germany did not succeed in exterminating the Jews, says Wise, they were regarded as " 'the eternal Jew' . . . which meant the indestructible Jew. This outlawed, persecuted, hunted and downtrodden individual could not possible be happy, it was believed; how could a man be happy who did not believe in Jesus? He must be namelessly wretched, miserable, crushed down to despair. Why then does he not die? Because he is cursed with eternal life on earth to be miserable forever." This was the German conception, says Wise. The English and French notion was that "the Wandering Jew is the type of the Jewish character,"[26] the exponent of skepticism and doubt; but since skepticism is no longer feared, neither is the Wandering Jew.

From this point Wise rings the changes on the Wandering Jew as a symbol of a dispersed Jewish people who were bearers of monotheistic and undogmatic wisdom as they sojourned in various parts of the world. The Jew was regarded everywhere as a skeptic because he challenged the prevailing modes of thought. Together with the Greeks, the ancient Hebrews formed the basis of future Western civilization by undermining the Greco-Roman religion. "Some innocent people," says Wise, "imagine the Jews always sold clothing, new or old, handled money at low or high rates, ate no pork, and wore long beards. The Jew has a history." And he proceeds to sketch this history, mostly emphasizing their contributions to the development of Western civilization by their "skepticism," their undermining of the obsolete. Many were the contributions to Western civilization made by the Jews as they wandered and exerted their influence in Egypt, Greece, Rome, medieval and modern Europe, claims Wise. There is a need, he concludes, for the Wandering Jew to

reappear and do his work, until there shall be no more superstition, no ignorance and no intolerance, no hatred, no self-delusion and no darkness among sects. He must reappear and wander on to the end of all woe and misery in society, till the habitable earth shall be one holy land, every city a Jerusalem, every house a temple. . . . Then the curtain will drop on the grand drama of the Wandering Jew.[27]

PART THREE

THE JEWISH SELF-IMAGE

11

JEWISH WRITERS TO 1880S

During the first half of the nineteenth century the established Sephardic Jewish community produced a small number of writers: a few whose contribution was entirely negligible and a few others of some small significance in the development of an American national literature. Considering that the Jews comprised such a minute percentage of the population—about one-twentieth of one percent —the emergence of these writers is striking evidence of the rapidity with which Jews came to participate in the national life and culture under conditions of relative equality.

Several Jews had a glancing contact with the literary life of the nation in the early years of the Republic. At a time when respectable people looked down on the novel as a form with dubious literary, if not moral, value, Isaac Franks, Revolutionary War veteran of New York, defended the novel on both grounds. A hand-written statement, "On Novel Reading," dating from about 1800 and presumably written by Franks himself, was found among his papers. The essay displays a cultivated taste, and concludes: "Ignorance and malignity may decry this species of writing; but in my opinion, the names of Cervantes, Fielding, Richardson, Smollett, Roche, and Burney will and ought to command the admiration of those who possess feeling, discernment and taste."[1]

Another Jew of the period, Jacob N. Cardozo, was editor and owner of the *Southern Patriot,* of Charleston; he was a journalist, noted economist, and opponent of the southern doctrine of nullification. His essay "An Oration on the Literary Character," delivered and published in 1811, was a vacuous and pretentious tribute to the growth of culture, and is significant only as a sign of literary interest.

Isaac Gomez, Jr., was an early literary anthologist. His *Selections of a Father for the Use of His Children* was published in New York in 1820 with the approbation of John Adams, among others. "Your selections," writes Adams, "deserve a place in every family. There is not an impure or mean thought in the whole book."[2] The collection was intended to promote "virtuous" living and includes anti-slavery writing and edifying bits of philosophy, poetry, ethical writing, and science; it is wholly secular. A hint of the Jewish origin of its editor is given by the inclusion of a passage from *The History of Pope Sixtus V* (pp. 326 ff.), the source of the pound of flesh story used by Shakespeare. As we have mentioned, it reverses the characters as found in *The Merchant of Venice*—the would-be wielder of the knife is a Christian while the victim is a Jew. Gomez was obviously trying to combat the effects of the Shylock stereotype. "The following subject," says Gomez in his preface to this excerpt, "shows that Shakespeare altered the character of Shylock, making him to be of Jewish nationality, when he was not" (p. 326).

Another figure with a tangential connection with literature was Rebecca Gratz, a gracious Philadelphia personality who was the daughter of the wealthy merchant Michael Gratz. She never married, tradition has it, because she refused to marry Samuel Ewing, the Christian with whom she was in love. Her collected letters from 1808 to 1866 afford insight into the period and particularly into the Jewish community.[3] Washington Irving was an intimate friend of the family's, and Rebecca herself was a close friend of Irving's fiancée, Matilda Hoffman, whom she nursed during a fatal illness. It is interesting that, despite Irving's acquaintance with this Jewish family, there is virtually no reference to Jews in his writings. In *Salmagundi* there is a passing allusion to the Wandering Jew,[4] and the *Knickerbocker's History* offers a whimsical conjecture that the Ten Lost Tribes came to America via Greenland and settled the country.[5]

There is a probably accurate story that Irving warmly described Rebecca to Walter Scott, and that Scott modeled his Rebecca in *Ivanhoe* on the description given him by Irving. Joseph Jacobs suggests parallels between the book and Rebecca Gratz's life: a similarity of name and character; the nursing of the wounded Ivanhoe by the fictional Rebecca and Rebecca Gratz's devoted nursing of Matilda Hoffman; and, in both cases, frustrated love for a non-Jew.[6]

Scott wrote to Irving in 1819: "How do you like your Rebecca? Does the Rebecca I have pictured compare well with the pattern given?"[7] Miss Gratz herself was intrigued by her fictional counterpart. Writing to her sister-in-law Maria Gist Gratz on April 4, 1820, she asked: "Tell me what you think of my namesake Rebecca." On May 10 she wrote again, explaining Scott's failure to have Rebecca marry Ivanhoe in terms similar to those Scott was to use later:

Ivanhoes insensibility to her, you must recollect, may be accounted
to his previous attachment [to Rowena]—his prejudice was a characteristic of the age he lived in—he fought for Rebecca, tho' he despised her race—the veil that is drawn over his feelings was necessary to the fable, and the beautiful sensibility of hers, so regulated,
yet so intense might show the triumph of faith over human affection.[8]

(Was she thinking of her own experience here?) In a preface to an
1830 edition of *Ivanhoe,* Scott explains why he could not marry
Ivanhoe to Rebecca: "The prejudice of the age rendered such a
union almost impossible."[9]

Another Jewish woman of the period, the long-lived Penina
Moise, aspired to poetry writing. Her wealthy parents had fled from
the slave insurrection in Santo Domingo in 1791 and settled in
Charleston, where Penina was born. Being fervently religious, she
refused to marry outside of Judaism and remained unwed. Hymns
and devotional verse make up a large part of her poetic production
during a long life of eighty-three years. In 1833 she published
Fancy's Sketch Book, the first book of verse by a Jew, woman or man,
in the United States. The Damascus affair elicited a poem from her
in 1840. Unfortunately she lacked a poetic gift, but that did not
prevent publication of her work in a number of current literary
journals.

Most interesting is her poem "To Persecuted Foreigners," published in the *Southern Patriot* for February 23, 1820, which closely
resembles Emma Lazarus's later poem "The New Colossus," now
inscribed on a plaque in the pedestal of the Statue of Liberty. While
the imagery is rather alarming, the import is similar:

> Fly from the soil whose desolating creed,
> Outraging faith, makes human victims bleed,
> Welcome! where every Muse has reared a shrine,
> The respect of wild Freedom to refine. . . .
> Rise, then, elastic from Oppression's tread,
> Come and repose in Plenty's flowery bed.
> Oh! not as Strangers shall welcome be
> Come to the homes and bosoms of the free.[10]

A rather unpleasant, bizarre figure of this period was Samuel B.
H. Judah, a lawyer by profession who fancied himself a playwright
and satirist. His book reads like the work of an irresponsible misan-
thrope. His verse satire, *Gotham and the Gothamites* (1823), is an
unrelieved flow of vitriol poured on the heads of numerous prominent New Yorkers, including Mordecai M. Noah. Early in the book
he announces his theme:

Proud city! e'en in thy infinitude
Of pride, and loveliness, there is a stain
Of guilt upon thee, gloomy as a cloud
That veils the heaven, ere from his shroud
The snowy whirlwind springs; treach'rous and vain
Thy merchant nobles, weak and willing slaves
To gold; and wild and boundless luxury
Reign in thy halls. The giant Vice doth wave
His black vanes in the air: in place so high
But with bold pinions he hath dared to fly.[11]

Judah's satire is targeted on about one hundred figures of the city, designated by name. So clearly libelous is this presumed social satire that Judah was imprisoned for it, but then pardoned by the governor. His *Odofrieda, the Outcast, a Democratic Poem* (New York, 1822), an absolutely unreadable verse play, is a kind of reductio ad absurdum of the Faust theme. His effort at romance, *The Buccaneers,* a 650-page book published anonymously in 1827, is an exasperatingly prolix story of sixteenth-century New Amsterdam. At one point he lashes out at white hatred of the Indian and at hostility between white and white. An Indian character says: "Yet remember the white man loves not his brother, more than he loves the red Indian—ye belong to one family—ye walk the same path—ye assist not each other to bear your burdens—though ye slake your thirst out of the same spring, yet lend not unto each other your cups—brother, beware—the white people are to one another like poisonous serpents."[12]

He wrote several stale melodramas, among them *The Mountain Torrent,* produced in New York in 1820. George Odell writes that "this 'American' play, unlike those of [Mordecai M.] Noah, is but an attempt to pour sour European wine into American bottles. . . . The language is nearly the funniest I have ever seen; it is stage English of paleozoic variety."[13] Fortunately, no Jewish characters figured in his three melodramas.

However, in the 1830s Judah did write two plays on Jewish subjects, both of them verse dramas on biblical subjects. Besides being bad verse, they were vituperative attacks on biblical figures, in the deist tradition. *The Maid of Midian* (1833) deals with the massacre of Midian captives by order of Moses, as told in Numbers 31. In *David and Uriah,* published in Philadelphia by the author in 1835, Judah returns to the attack, this time on David, who is pictured as a brutal, slaughtering demon. In his preface to the play, Judah writes: "There is scarcely to be found in the records of human depravity an individual whose life has been marked with more acts of atrocity

than that of holy David." He is appealing in this play, Judah continues, to those who *"do not* acknowledge the Jewish records of ancient
ignorance, barbarism and cruelty, as the proper basis of just laws and
enlightened morality."[14]

Judah continued to blast away at religious superstition in a twelve-
page poem published anonymously in 1842 by the Beacon, a New
York press for freethinking and rationalism that also reprinted Voltaire and Tom Paine. His *Spirit of Fanaticism, a Poetical Rhapsody*
(1842) is a tirade against the fanaticism of current revivalism. In the
preface to this poem he asserts that one would "suppose that human
nature has undergone a change," if one believes that "those who
pretend to act as mediators between God and man" do not use their
influence "to promote their own power, and favour their own ag-
grandizement" (p. iii). He concludes the poem in the vein of Voltaire and Paine:

> Yes, bigotry's horrors,
> Awaken our sorrows,
> For myriads doomed by its mandates to bleed [p. 12].

He continued his crusade in the next year with another twelve-page
anonymously published poem, *The Battles of Joshua, a New Version*
(Philadelphia, 1843), in which he ridicules the miracles of the biblical story of Joshua, such as the sun standing still. In the introduction
he writes that the story of Joshua is "a series of bloody atrocities,"
and points to the contradiction between the commandment against
killing and the slaughter in the event. To reconcile these, he writes,
"is difficult for those acquainted with all the mysteries of godliness
to determine" (p. 2).

Another Jewish dramatist of the period was Jonas B. Phillips
(1805–69), a lawyer from Philadelphia. He wrote melodramas, the
best known of which is *The Evil Eye,* based on a story of the evil eye
printed in the *London Keepsake* in 1830. From its premiere in 1831
this popular play was staged off and on until 1899. His best work
is *Camillus; or, The Self-Exiled Patriot* (1833), which draws its inspiration from *Coriolanus.* His *Tales for Leisure Hours* (1827) is a collection
of a dozen conventional Gothic tales. In 1835 he published a volume
of poetry, *Zamira, Dramatic Sketch, and Other Poems,* which contains
no Jewish material.

Phillips has the dubious distinction of being the only Jewish
dramatist of the period to include a contemporary Jew in one of his
plays, *Jack Sheppard; or, The Life of a Robber!,* first performed at the

Bowery Theater in 1839. The play, which exists in a holograph copy in the Harvard Library, is one of the many adaptations of William Ainsworth's novel *Jack Sheppard.* This melodrama of crime in England includes Abraham ("Nab") Mendez (a Jewish "denizen" of the extortionist Jonathan Wild), who speaks with an accent. Mendez executes Wild's plan to throw Sir Rowland Trenchard into a well, with fatal results. However, Mendez moves quickly in and out of only one scene, and is not as prominent a character as he is in other versions. Obviously, Phillips must have been uncomfortable about this part and gave short shrift to this stage Jew.

Not all Jewish writers of this period were insignificant. Joseph L. Blau and Salo W. Baron understate the case when they write that "we may, perhaps, by an exercise of generosity, accept the few Jewish journalists as literary men."[15] While the most talented figures of the group, Mordecai M. Noah and Isaac Harby, were distinctly minor writers, they did add somewhat to the emerging American national literature. Noah's play *She Would Be a Soldier* (1819), hastily written in three days to celebrate Washington's birthday, was one of the first plays to draw upon exclusively American materials. In the preface to the play Noah writes, in a tone that anticipates Emerson's call for a literature embodying our "incomparable materials": "National plays should be encouraged. . . . We have a fine scope, and abundant materials to work with, and a noble country to justify the attempt."[16] In the same year, Noah reiterates in his book of travels the need to "establish a permanent literary character of our own."[17] Arthur Hobson Quinn regards Noah as "probably the most important playwright of this period next to James Nelson Barker"[18] as a dramatist of the American nationality.

Mordecai M. Noah had an extraordinarily varied career. Born in Philadelphia in 1785, he spent most of his adult life in New York, where he died in 1851. His was a variegated, crowded life. He was appointed United States consul to Tunis on the recommendation of Joel Barlow and served from 1813 to 1815. In 1822 he was appointed sheriff of New York, but was defeated for the office when it was made elective in 1824, the same year in which he became sachem of Tammany Hall. Besides writing plays, throughout his life he was editor of a series of newspapers and a prominent figure in the life of the city.*

---

*While reading Charles F. Briggs's *Adventures of Harry Franco* (2 vols. [New York, 1839]) in the Houghton Room of the Harvard Library, I came upon a penciled marginal note, "Major Noah," probably scribbled by a contemporary, beside a

Noah was also a leading member of the Jewish community. His fantastic project of establishing a refuge for the Jews of the world at Grand Island, in the Niagara River near Buffalo, was inaugurated with a monstrously inflated ceremony in 1825, but the project was a complete fiasco. The haven, called Ararat, was to be the temporary abode of the Jews until they could ultimately return to Palestine. Noah was prompted to project this new city to counterbalance the proliferation of societies to convert the Jews to Christianity. In 1844 he delivered a "Discourse on the Restoration of the Jews" that was an anticipation of political Zionism. He calls for support from "a free country and a liberal government . . . in the cradle of American liberty"[19] to help return the Jews to Palestine. Like Herzl after him, he discusses the rivalries for control of the Near East between Turkey and the great European powers, and suggests prophetically that Britain would seize Egypt.

Then [he writes], Palestine thus placed between the Russian possessions and Egypt, reverts to its legitimate proprietors, and for the safety of surrounding nations, a powerful, wealthy, independent, and enterprising people are placed there by and with the consent of the Christian powers, and with their aid and agency the land of Israel passes once more into the possession of the descendants of Abraham.[20]

Noah had been subjected to anti-Semitism on several occasions. He was removed as consul to Tunis in 1815 by the then secretary of state James Monroe, partly on the ground that he was Jewish, which Monroe deemed diplomatically disadvantageous. Noah was also charged with malfeasance. He vigorously protested this intolerant act and the charge, and an investigation cleared him of the charge. When he was running for sheriff of New York in 1823, his patriotism was impugned because, said his critic, a Jew did not have an absolute national allegiance to the country—an early instance of

---

description of a New York notable. The young hero of the book has been taken to the theater by an older friend, who points out to him the celebrities in the audience, among them "Major Noah": "He was an elderly gentleman, with a good-humored broad countenance, a high nose, and a pair of twinkling black eyes. 'That gentleman,' said Mr. Worhors, 'is Major Rigmaroll, the editor; he has written criticisms about the stage for the last thirty years. I knew him all to pieces. He is going to publish a book about Shakespeare, and he has published one,[21] in which he proves as plain as the nose on his face, which is plain enough, that the American Indians are descended from Shem, Ham, or Japheth, I forget which; and he claims relationship with one of them himself' " (p. 112). Briggs was himself an editor, journalist, and novelist in New York, and must have known Noah well. Briggs's own novels contain contemptible, negatively stereotyped Jews (see above, chapter 2).

the accusation of dual allegiance. But such experiences and his fervent affirmation of devotion to American freedom did not prevent him from upholding slavery.

While Noah was editor of the Whig paper, *The Union,* in 1842, he berated Horace Greeley, whom he had seen eating with two Negroes in a boardinghouse. Greeley's response is devastating:

> We choose our own company in all things, and that of our own race, but cherish little of that spirit which for eighteen centuries has held the kindred of M. M. Noah accursed of God and man, outlawed and outcast, and unfit to be the associates of Christians and Musselmen, or even self-respecting Pagans. Where there are thousands who would not eat with a Negro, there are (or lately were) tens of thousands who would not eat with a Jew. We leave to such renegades as the Judge of Israel* the stirring up of prejudices, and the prating of "usages of society," which over half the world make him an abhorrence, as they not long since would have done here.[22]

Despite Noah's assertion of Jewish identity he does not introduce a single Jew into his dozen plays. Perhaps it would be more correct to say this is *because* of his Jewishness. For when they saw a Jew on the stage the theater audience of the time expected to view a stereotype, and Noah was not prepared to satisfy this expectation. Considering his limited gift for drama, it is perhaps just as well that he did not attempt to portray a Jewish character. It was enough that after a few conventional attempts at using foreign motifs, as in *The Fortress of Sorrento* (1818) and *Paul and Alexis; or, The Orphans of the Rhine* (1812), he devoted himself to the writing of authentically American plays. He turned to American subjects in *She Would Be a Soldier; or, The Plains of Chippewa,* which was about the War of 1812, and in *Marian; or, The Hero of Lake George* (1814), a Revolutionary War play. David Grimstead has observed that in *She Would Be a Soldier,* Mordecai Noah is convinced that the Indians represented the lost tribes of Israel, and he "allowed the Indian, a very peripheral character in the play, a strong statement of his case against the whites," and gave considerable dignity to his rendering of the Indian chief.[23]

Noah's enthusiasm for the cause of Greek freedom brought forth *The Grecian Captive; or, The Fall of Athens* (1822). This play was written as a vehicle for Noah's uncle, the actor Aaron Phillips. It was a spectacular affair. Noah provided the audience with printed copies of the play, and the simultaneous turning of pages during the performance created an obvious distraction. Noah also introduced an elephant onto the stage in this play. At one point the frightened animal

*This is an allusion to the title that Noah assumed as the leader of the Grand Island project for a Jewish refuge.

gave way, as a contemporary observed, to "an unexpected hydraulic experiment to the discomfort of the musicians."[24]

An indication of the regard in which Noah was held by contemporaries is given by the fact that William Dunlap, first historian of the American theater, solicited and received from Noah a brief account of his dramatic career. Dunlap publishes Noah's letter as an appendix to his *History of the American Theatre* (New York, 1832). Noah protests that his "dramatic productions . . . constitute a sorry link in the chain of American writers . . . a kind of *amateur* performance" (p. 160). Yet, for all his hasty writing and bravura, Noah has a permanent, though minor, place in the history of American drama.

Charleston-born Isaac Harby was perhaps the most distinguished personage of the group. His death in 1828 at the age of forty cut short a career of some promise. When he had to drop his study of the law after his father died in 1805, he turned to teaching and journalism. In politics he was a Jeffersonian and a supporter of Andrew Jackson. Under his leadership the first steps toward Reform Judaism in the United States were taken in Charleston.* In 1824 under Harby's leadership forty-seven members of the Beth Elohim Congregation of Charleston signed a memorial to the governing body of the synagogue, pointing to the stagnation of religious spirit and attributing it to the outworn ritual. They offered a Reform program quite similar to the program then developing in Germany: shorter services, some prayers in English, abolition of the money offering at services, and omission of the doctrine of a personal Messiah and physical resurrection.[25] The congregation elders rejected the memorial, and Harby led the reformers out of the synagogue to found the Reformed Society of Israelites in 1825. The movement was weakened by Harby's departure for New York, and it expired in 1833.

During the few years of life left to him Harby made a deep impression. When he died in New York, he was widely mourned and eulogized in the press, and a theater performance was given for the benefit of his children. In the obituary notice in the *New York Mirror* of December 27, 1828, the writer asserts that, "as a critic, he was considered unrivalled in this country."[26]

Harby wrote his first play, a "tragedy," when he was seventeen.

---

*Jefferson's acknowledgment of receipt of Harby's discourse on Reform Judaism is an interesting echo of the underlying philosophy of the movement and its modernism. "I am little acquainted with the liturgy of the Jews or their mode of worship," writes Jefferson, "but the reformation proposed and explained in the discourse appears entirely reasonable. Nothing is wiser than that all our institutions should keep pace with the advance of time and be improved with the improvement of the human mind" (quoted in Blau and Baron, *Jews of the U.S.*, 3:704).

In 1807 he wrote a melodrama full of Gothic business, *The Gordian Knot,* which was produced in 1810. His *Alberti,* a play of fifteenth-century Florence, was produced in Charleston in 1819. His writing for the theater was less overblown and bombastic than that of most plays of the period, and had greater elegance in language and imagery. In addition to plays he wrote criticism that was highly regarded by his contemporaries. A high estimate of his quality comes from a more recent literary historian, N. Bryllion Fagin, who has written that Harby's "mind was first rate, his taste excellent, and his knowledge of his craft comprehensive, but his temperament was gentle. . . . His remarkable combination of knowledge, character, imagination, and literary skill certainly made him one of the best of America's early dramatists and critics."[27]

Harby defended the theater against Puritan prejudice. He affirmed that the drama affords more than relaxation and relief from "dull pursuits of a day of toil and business," as he writes in the New York *Evening Post* in 1828. Drama is more than this; it should be "a spectacle of life, as it is, and was, and ever shall be. A representation more vivid than any other art can create, of passion and sentiment." It is also a vehicle for satire with the power to move an audience. "It is then principally," he concludes, "as a moral lever that the statesman and philosopher should regard the stage."[28]

However, there is a peculiar lack of perception in one of his best-known critical essays, his critique of *The Merchant of Venice,* published in New York in 1827. In his vehement attempt to disown Shylock, Harby overlooks the anti-Semitism of the other characters. Most of the play, he writes, is "enchanting," but "a certain unnatural atrocity about the character of Shylock, . . . renders disgust so prevalent over our admiration, that the effect of the whole is considerably injured, if not destroyed." Shakespeare's creation of such a character of "demoniacal and black atrocity"[29] was clearly a concession to the ignorant prejudices of his audience, says Harby. In other Shakespearean plays, such as *Macbeth, King Richard II,* and *Julius Caesar,* he asserts, the evil characters are at least motivated by ambition or patriotism. But Shylock's wickedness, he holds, is totally unmotivated and hence simply atrocious.

Harby's reading of the play is in some respects obtuse. Reprehensible as Shylock's demand for a pound of Antonio's flesh is, Shakespeare clearly—indeed explicitly—establishes a motive. In response to Salerio's question as to why he would take Antonio's flesh, which is worthless, Shylock replies: "If it will feed nothing else, it will feed my revenge" (act 3, scene 3). And Shylock does indeed have much cause for wanting revenge—Antonio's anti-Semitic baiting of him and Antonio's attitude toward usury, the defection of Jessica, and her theft of his money and jewels.

Harby's obliviousness to these elements of the play is consistent with his strange insensitivity to anti-Semitic aspects of the other characters of the play. He seems unaware of the ubiquitous Jew-baiting that has gone on. He speaks with approbation of "the sadness of Antonio . . . the courageous tenderness of Jessica . . . the peculiar humour of Launcelot"—this in the face of Antonio's contemptuous anti-Semitism, Jessica's theft, Launcelot's "the Jew is the very devil incarnal" (act 2, scene 2). Harby's condemnation of the stereotype, however, in unexceptionable: "When we observe in a drama, an Irishman represented as a *rogue*, an Englishman a *sot*, a Frenchman a *monkey*, and a Jew a *usurer*, we evidently are aware, that the author's sole object is to gratify the malignant passions of mankind. And such is the viciousness of human nature, that men are rather gratified than otherwise, at these national reflections."[30] Yet he apparently does not perceive that the attitudes of Antonio, Jessica, and Launcelot issue from this same unfeeling conception of the Jew.

The quartet of dramatists in the first third of the nineteenth century—Noah, Harby, Judah, and Phillips—generally made no attempt to depict the Jews. The next group of Jewish writers, who began writing in the 1840s, devoted themselves almost entirely to Jewish themes. While the first group of Jewish writers stemmed from established Sephardic families, the second were predominantly of German origin and were mostly the products of the wave of German Jewish immigration, which gained momentum from the 1830s on. Collectively the group, except Nathan Mayer, showed little literary talent.

The launching of Jewish magazines provided a great stimulus for this writing. The first Jewish journal in this country, *The Jew*, which appeared in 1824 and lasted for two years, was devoted exclusively to polemics against the lucubrations of conversionists. This was also one of the motives for the founding of the several journals in the 1840s which launched the prolific career of Jewish journalism in the United States. Ardent efforts to convert the Jews bore negligible fruit, but Jewish leaders were unduly concerned over the threat. They were also disturbed by the false dogmatic conception of the Jews promoted by the widespread agitation of the conversionists, and the consequent reinforcement of the traditional condemnation of the Jews for refusal to accept Jesus as Savior. The comprehensive aim of the new journals was to provide a medium for Jewish religious expression, the advancement of Judaism, and the defense of the Jews.

The first general Jewish journal, *The Occident and American Jewish Advocate,* established as a monthly in April 1843, was founded and edited until his death in 1868 by the traditionalist Rabbi Isaac Leeser, who like Rabbi Isaac M. Wise, was one of the most prominent and influential Jewish figures of the period. In October 1849 *The Asmonean* appeared in New York as the journal of Orthodox Judaism; it lasted until 1858, when its editor, an English Jew named Robert Lyon, died. Then in July 1854 Rabbi Isaac Mayer Wise brought out *The Israelite* in Cincinnati as the organ of the Reform movement. All these journals followed similar editorial policies, within their sectarian viewpoints. Of primary importance was the theological material, but when the need arose considerable parts of the journals were devoted to Jewish defense against anti-Semitism and to Jewish news from the United States and all over the world. They also reprinted relevant material from periodicals at home and abroad.

The "literary" sections of these magazines consumed a large part of their space, for the editors hoped to encourage literary culture among their readers. These magazines expressed perturbation over the lack of writing by American Jews. For it was essentially true, as John Higham observes, that "in the middle of the nineteenth century there was no American Jewish literature,"[31] that is, fiction and poetry written in English by Jews about Jews. An 1855 editorial in *The Asmonean* asks: "Are the Jews of America Patrons of Literature?" and answers in the negative. The editorialist suggests several reasons for this: the heterogeneity of the immigrant Jews and their retention of "foreign" culture—German immigrants continued to use German in their publications—and the preoccupation of the Jews with business concerns.[32] It should be added that the editorialist was thinking of literature primarily as writing on Judaism. An editorial, probably by Leeser, assures Jewish writers that they would

serve their fellow-believers in the most important point, by aiding them to rise in public estimation, and to become known for something nobler than the mere acquisition of wealth, which the world believes the only pursuit in which Jews can excel. It is really a pity that a people so naturally intelligent as ours, should have furnished so small an amount of literary productions in England and America, and of this, so little towards the elucidation of our religion.[33]

To further this aim, the editorialist suggested that prizes be offered Jewish writers for literary work animated by religious feelings. An article a few months later on "Native Jewish Talent" suggests one reason why Jews of talent avoided the vocation of literature: the difficulty of earning a livelihood in a land where "commerce and the professions of law and medicine offer the easiest methods for acquiring both wealth and position."[34]

Leeser had earlier had a discouraging experience in promoting Jewish literature. In 1845 he had initiated the Jewish Publication Society, which followed upon a similar venture in London called the "Cheap Jewish Library." The society published fourteen volumes of "The Jewish Miscellany," reprints of small books issued by the London project. The first volume, *Caleb Asher*, was the sentimental story of a young English Jew who converts to Christianity in order to gain employment, but recants and reconverts to Judaism on his deathbed. Added as an appendix to this story is an address, probably by Leeser, that sounds the alarm at the "new danger,—the secret attacks and open assaults, by specious arguments, of those whose darling object it is to break down the landmarks of Judaism . . . [and risks] the loss to Israel of many precious souls who are now of our communion."[35] Other volumes in the series, nearly all sentimental and pious, included several works of fiction, accounts of ancient biblical figures, and the memoirs of Moses Mendelssohn. The project ended in 1851 with the destruction of its stock of books by fire.

The magazines did, however, elicit poetry and fiction from American and English writers, and novels by German and French Jewish authors were translated and serialized. Not an issue appeared without some poetry and fiction, mostly historical novels. Among the writers represented were parochial poets such as Celia Moss, Rebekah Hyneman, Penina Moise, and Rose Emma Salaman ("R. E. S."). Grace Aguilar's poems were reprinted from England, as well as, on occasion, those of Longfellow, Whittier, and Lowell. *The Israelite* published the famous actress Adah Isaacs Menken's poetry in the late 1850s.

The quality of the work of these Jewish poets was not high. Reviews of this poetry in *The Occident,* probably by Leeser, gently suggest this. The reviewer of a volume by Rose Emma Salaman remarks that "Miss S. has not attempted to give expression to the forceful, but mostly to the tender and devotional; hence, since feelings are, at best, but simple, especially if they may be amicable and pathetic, there is a sameness occasionally perceptible, and a recurrence here and there of the same words and thoughts which suggest them." The reviewer then offers the consoling thought that "this is far better than plagiarizing from others."[36] An equally gentle review, probably also by Leeser, of another of his regular contributors,

Mrs. Rebekah Hyneman, suggests that "she appears to excel more in mere representation of feelings, the poetry of the heart, than in invention, the poetry of the imagination."[37]

As with the poetry in *The Occident,* much of the fiction of American origin was the product of women, such as Celia Moss (later Celia Moss Laritus), Marion Hartog, and Sarah Cohen. Like the fiction translated from German, their work was mostly historical and dealt with the persecution of the Jews. The Spanish Inquisition, the persecution under Edward III in thirteenth-century England, the fifteenth-century German Jewish martyrs, and biblical tales were typical subjects of these novels. These stories are unreadable today.

For some reason the American Jewish writers of *contemporary* fiction in English in the first few decades of *The Israelite* were nearly all men, perhaps because Rabbi Isaac Mayer Wise himself was the author of a good share of the fiction and inspired other men to do likewise. In the first numbers of *The Israelite,* Wise promised his readers that, besides attempting to "unlock the mystical shrine of our ancient literature, . . . *The Israelite* will contain novels, romances and poems, gleaned from our own fields, and sheaved by our own sons and daughters."[38] While few "daughters" responded to his call, several "sons" did—including Nathan Mayer and H. M. Moos. Wise also published translations of tales by German Jews.

One of the few short stories by a non-Jewish author that Wise published was "The Saracen and the Dwarf," by the young Horatio Alger, Jr., reprinted from *The Flag of Our Union.* This story, in which Alger seems to have drawn upon Edgar Allan Poe's "Hop-Frog," is an account of how Issachar, a rich English Jew of thirteenth-century England, was helped to escape from the fort of Sir Reginald De Courey when a Saracen dwarf pushes the baron, instead of Issachar, into a pit. The fiction in these early Jewish periodicals was written unabashedly in the style of the current popular novel: sentimental, melodramatic, full of action, extolling virtue.

In response to complaints from readers that "romances" had no place in a religious magazine, Rabbi Wise took the opportunity to expound his didactic rationale for the novel.

The fine literature of a religious journal [he writes] must have a religious tendency and highly moral tone, and the fine literature of *The Israelite* must, besides all this, have an Israelitish tendency. . . . The novel offers the advantage that it unrolls in life pictures to the reader, the realized doctrines of morals and religion which in their abstract form are dry and serious; in the novel, they are incarnated, living, pleasant, attractive, and much more impressive. Good novels with a moral and religious tendency will effect more good than good treatises on these subjects; because they are read more extensively, understood more readily, and the living and acting characters impress themselves much deeper on the mind than dead words.

He then pointed to the "romances" published in the magazine dealing with Bar Kochba, Rabbi Akiba, Hillel, and other heroic figures of Jewish history which "have roused many a youthful heart, and filled it with love and admiration for Israel."[39]

Wise conceived his task at this juncture to be twofold: to promote the "Americanization" of the Jews, and at the same time to make sure that their Judaism did not disappear in their Americanism. After concluding that he could not "create an Americanizing-Judaizing literature single-handed," he decided to bend his efforts toward emphasizing in all his work "the historical mission of Israel"; bringing out "the bright side of the Jewish character" and leaving the negative side to the enemies of the Jews; popularizing and promoting respect for Jewish literature; and arousing interest, especially in the young, in "brilliant periods of Jewish history" by casting these in fictional form, thereby awakening "Jewish patriotism."[40]

For the first decade of *The Israelite,* Rabbi Wise himself supplied the fiction that was not readily forthcoming from the Reform community. In the very first issue Wise anonymously published the opening section of his novel *The Convert,* situated in contemporary Bohemia. The story revolves about fidelity to Judaism; a convert is finally saved from apostasy by emigrating to America and returning to the Jewish fold. In the next years the indefatigable rabbi also founded a German-language journal for women, *Die Deborah,* and wrote novels in German for this publication, too. His biographer notes that "altogether he [Wise] wrote eleven novels in English, sixteen in German, and also hundreds of unsigned poems."[41] His novels, first published anonymously in *The Israelite,* celebrated heroic Jewish episodes in history such as the war of Rabbi Akiba, the Maccabean revolt, the courage of Jews in the period of Hillel and Herod and the Inquisition. Instead of signing his novels with his name, Wise called himself "the American Jewish Novelist," and later admitted that his work contained "more truth than fiction, more reality than poetry."[42]

Wise published two of his novels in book form in Cincinnati, *The Combat of the People; or, Hillel and Herod* (1859) and *The First of the Maccabees* (1860). Both books were published by the newly emergent Jewish publishing house of Bloch and Co. Although his fiction is completely undistinguished and, to be candid, unreadable today, his achievement in terms of energy and industry is impressive. Considering that he arrived in the United States in 1846, the extent and facility of his fiction writing in English, which began only eight years later, is remarkable. His stilted, clichéd style is exemplified in the opening sentence of his *Combat of the People:* "Solemn and harmonious was the merry song of the winged minstrels of the air greeting the radiant herald of the rising queen of the day."[43]

While his readers probably were inspirited by his didactic, devotional tales, it cannot be said that his fiction exerted any influence on the image of the Jew presented in general American literature. Wise himself asserts his belief that "the labors of the American Jewish novelist [Wise] have reanimated the spark of patriotic sentiment, of genuine Jewish pride and self-estimation in the breasts of thousands of our co-religionists, especially the young."[44] From the historical point of view, however, it is pertinent to credit him with being one of the earliest and most productive Jewish novelists in the country. The distinction of being the very earliest probably belongs to Celia Moss, Sarah Cohen, and Marion Hartog, who wrote fiction for *The Occident* before Wise began publishing his journal.

Several young men around Rabbi Wise emulated his fictional efforts. H. M. Moos, literary editor of *The Israelite* for some time, published novels in the magazine and thereafter republished them in book form. His *Hannah; or, A Glimpse of Paradise,* which appeared serially in *The Israelite* in 1865, was reprinted in Cincinnati in 1868. It is an interminable, melodramatic, overelaborate, overwritten story of the acculturation to American life of a German Jewish immigrant peddler in Cincinnati. In 1860 Moos published a dramatization of the Mortara affair in a verse play, *Mortara; or, The Pope and His Inquisitors;* his verse in this play is as sententious, stilted, prolix, and inflated as his prose.

Another of Rabbi Wise's literary disciples was Moritz Loth. His incredibly amateurish novel, *Our Prospects* (1870), tried to affirm the literary achievement of the Jews and defend their ethical and religious tradition against the misconceptions of Christians. Loth followed up a revised edition of this novel with several others in the late 1890s.

But one of Wise's literary disciples, Dr. Nathan Mayer, was not a hopeless failure at fiction like the others. Born in Bavaria in 1838, Mayer immigrated to this country when he was ten. He graduated from Cincinnati Medical College in 1857 and continued his medical studies abroad until 1862, when he returned to serve as a surgeon in the Union army, rising to the rank of brigadier general. After the war he moved to Hartford, where he practiced medicine with distinction until a few months before he died in 1912. For forty years he also served as drama and music critic of the *Hartford Times.* His fictional productivity in the late 1850s was second only to Wise's. Beginning in 1856 he wrote poetry and five novels, which were published serially in *The Israelite.*

With the appearance of his *Count and the Jewess* in the April 18, 1856, issue, it was evident that he was far above the other Wise disciples in literary ability. The simplicity of his style and the absence of clichés and pomposity that bedeviled the others is immediately apparent. This first novel is set in sixteenth-century Prague. A Jewish girl, Esther, and a Christian, Count Hohenfels, are in love. After a series of melodramatic adventures and incidents centered upon the anti-Semitism of the time, Esther agrees to marry the count in order to save his life; but her father murders her to prevent her marriage to the Christian.

In the next few years Mayer continued to publish serialized historical fiction about Jewish life and persecution in Germany and France and during biblical times. None of these efforts, although superior to the other fiction in the magazine, was especially noteworthy.

After the Civil War, however, Mayer wrote a novel about the immediate postwar period in the United States that was by far the best work of fiction inspired by Wise. Indeed, Mayer's *Differences,* published serially in *The Israelite* in 1867 and later the same year as a book, is the first novel by an American Jew that can be at all considered to have reached the minimum literary level. Abraham H. Steinberg is right, I think, in asserting that this work "is the first novel of literary value to treat of American Jews seriously, realistically, and at length."[45] The book is surprisingly readable today, but it is on a level with the popular sentimental fiction of the time. Although Mayer himself fought on the Union side, the book does not convey militant antislavery feeling in its southern episodes, though his hero does not conceal his opposition to slavery. It manifests aristocratic German Jewish attitudes toward and ridicule of newly rich Jewish merchant families in New York.

The hero, Louis Welland, is a handsome and able Jewish university graduate who has emigrated to America after the failure of the 1848 revolution in Germany, in which he had served as a rebel captain. The story opens in June 1860, with Welland traveling to Tennessee to take up his post as state surveyor for Claibourne

County. ("A surveyor, you say? What a queer business for a Jew," says one character.) There he becomes friends with a prosperous Jewish family, the Goldmans. Mrs. Goldman is the daughter of a German Jew, granddaughter of one of Napoleon's generals, and a pretentious aspirant to aristocracy. Mr. Goldman, of German Jewish origin, is "very good-natured, very patient, a sharp, close calculator as those of his race are apt to be, and a passionate lover of music."[46]

Their daughter, Antonia, and son, Charles, are involved in the love affairs on which the story hinges. Welland has met Frank Tourtelotte, a local plantation owner, by exposing a villainous character who had cheated Tourtelotte at cards. Tourtelotte confesses love for Antonia and apparently has no objection to her Jewishness, for marriage to her would ultimately join the Goodman plantation to his own. But Welland and Antonia fall in love. The cardsharp, Hazelton, turns out to be a German named Hassel who had embezzled money captured by Welland's unit during the revolution in Germany, for which Welland had been blamed. Hazelton sets going the false rumor that Welland is an abolitionist and incites a lynch mob, forcing Welland to flee north. Antonia and Welland declare their love, and she tells him she will wait for him. He escapes to New York, where another strand of the story unwinds.

Welland stays at the Fifth Avenue home of the Reichenaus, a wealthy German family. There Emma Reichenau becomes infatuated with Welland. But Charles, son of the Goldmans, is already in love with Emma, and believes his sister, Antonia, will marry Tourtelotte. When he meets Welland at the Reichenaus, Charles asks why his sister is not already married to Tourtelotte, and Welland suggests that Antonia may have "scruples of a religious nature." Charles then reveals that in the North he has concealed his Jewishness. "I am a moral coward on this point," he tells Welland. "I can not make up my mind to face continually the charges, just or unjust, which society has been in the habit of bringing against those of the Jewish—those of my father's—those of our—faith." If he were not in love with the non-Jewish Emma, he would even marry a Jew, he says, as his parents wish. Welland replies that it is impossible for Charles to break his Jewish connection, even if he wishes to.

When Charles goes home to gain permission from his parents for marriage to Emma, they reply that they hope Emma will convert to Judaism if she marries him. Charles objects to marrying a Jewish girl, he says, because most of them "I have found to be ill-bred, tainted by the pecuniary difficulties that overshadowed their childhood, or by the coarse disposition of their parents. . . . The worth of the purse so overshadows one in the estimation of these ladies, that the husband is of secondary consideration."[47]

When Charles returns to New York to propose to Emma, she rejects him and virtually proposes instead to Welland, who rejects her because he loves Antonia. Charles returns to the South and tells Antonia that Welland is in love with Emma. In pique Antonia then promises to marry Tourtelotte. The Civil War has broken out and Charles enlists in the Confederate army. The Goldmans, especially Antonia, are intensely loyal to the South. Welland has enlisted in the northern army and rises to the rank of brigadier general before the war's end (as Mayer himself did). Welland captures Tourtelotte at the Battle of Antietam, and Hazelton-Hassel is taken also as a deserter and spy. In the course of a discussion of world views between him and Welland, Hassel remarks: "Your God is a God of aristocrats. He will look only at those with money in their pockets. Your religion is a system to protect the rich. . . . Who is ever tempted to steal? Not the millionaire, but the starving beggar." Hassel confesses to Welland his guilt for the theft of the money missing in 1848.

After the war the misunderstanding between Welland and the now impoverished Antonia is cleared up, and they marry. Charles finally marries Emma, with the reassurance of Welland that intermarriage is not forbidden by the Bible. The prohibition, he says, is only "a custom, and not a positive law," and he adds, in the vein of Lessing's Nathan: "God is God, whether adored in Jewish, Christian, or Mohammedan manner."[48] Nevertheless, Emma does convert to Judaism before marrying Charles.

A significant strain in the novel is the disdainful description of the club life and the attitudes of and toward Jewish nouveaux riches in New York. These vulgar rich are intended to stand in sharp contrast to the aristocratic Goldmans and Welland, as well as to the liberal non-Jew Reichenau, through whom the aristocratic characters are made acquainted with the arrivistes. Significantly, the liberal Reform Jew Mayer projects something close to the stereotype in depicting the mercantile newly rich Jews. Charles goes to a ball at a wealthy Jewish club at which the Jewish merchant families' members, female as well as male, are disdainfully described. Jewish merchants of all sorts—one who is in wholesale dry goods, a shirt manufacturer, a watch inspector, a men's goods dealer, and a clothing manufacturer —are all unfavorably shown. While it is true that the newly rich merchants and their families did display vulgar behavior and crass attitudes, one senses that Mayer's disapproval is reinforced by the snobbish viewpoint of the well-to-do German Jews, who felt threatened by their less polished, less "Americanized" fellow Jews.

When the Jewish merchant Merrins meets Charles in Cincinnati, he asks about Charles's career in the southern army: "Did you make much?" Charles replies that he engaged in the war for his country's sake. "Don't throw such words at me," replies Merrins. "These are phrases for the Gentile. What has a Jew to do with country or rights? . . . Because we have no country and no acknowledged rights. Yes, they pretend to give us rights here, but 'tis only because they acknowledge the principle in general, and can't make a special exception." (Note that the condition of the Negro is not remarked upon by Merrins.) Charles is shocked at this "monstrous doctrine." Merrins persists: he asks if Charles sold cotton on the side. Charles insists that he put on a uniform to fight. "Fight?" replies Merrins. "A nice occupation for a Jew." He fought, says Charles, because his rights were threatened. "But you have no rights or wrong in the affair. The only fight that has been left to us is to garner wealth, and the only wrong we can fear is to be deprived of it." Merrins tells Charles that he himself is married to "Krakowitzer and Co., Gents Clothing and Furnishing Goods, Chatham Street."[49] He has made much money smuggling goods to the South.

Mayer's novel stands as a representation in fiction of Rabbi Wise's approach to the issues of his time. Even though Mayer himself served with distinction in the Union army, and in the novel depicts the sometimes violent response of southerners to abolitionism, in effect he takes a prosouthern, a so-called neutral, stance toward the Civil War, following his mentor's lead. He offers a favorable picture of the aristocratic proslavery southern Jews without uttering a word of criticism for their fervent devotion to the slave system; at the same time he places the merchant Jews of the North in the worst possible light. In his conception of Reichenau, the liberal Christian free from anti-Jewish prejudice, who has no objection to his daughter's marriage to a Jew, Mayer at the same time conveys his own toleration of intermarriage. Reichenau declares that he—like Mayer—is "truly liberal in religious matters . . . [like] most of the educated Germans. The prejudices which they still nourish are not religious but social, and as such, as a matter of course, are out of place in this country."[50]

The novel has structural defects—the episodes that introduce the merchant Jews are not necessary to the plot, and are obviously included to extend the delineation of Jewish life in this country and expose the reputed crude commercial scheme of values of this sector of American Jewry. Mayer displays considerable skill in setting forth

—in a one-sided way to be sure—the less admirable commercial sector of the Jewish community. His description of army life during the Civil War, particularly the medical aspect, which Mayer knew from personal experience, is well done.

In sum, this novel does not deserve the almost total obscurity into which it has fallen. It has the distinction of being the first American novel by a Jew about Jews in which literary talent is exhibited, and it is more readable today than many other popular novels of its time.

For a few decades after 1850 American Jews produced a number of works, most of them of negligible value. A romantic play written in very stilted, highly artificial verse, *The Italian Bride,* is attributed to Samuel Yates Levy, a Savannah lawyer who authored a number of plays. Published anonymously in Savannah in 1856 in a privately printed edition, the play was performed at Wallack's Theater in New York the following year. It contains no Jewish characters. In San Francisco an overblown, pretentious, "Biblio-Romantic Tragedy" in verse, *Samson and Delilah,* by Herman M. Bien, appeared in 1860. Another drama, *Esther,* by Mrs. Anna S. Moses of Sheffield, Alabama, published in Cincinnati in 1887, is an amateurish, turgid play about the Esther and Haman story. The *Jewish Messenger,* which began publishing in 1857, collected seven of the short stories from its pages in a book, *Friday Night,* in 1871. All were translations from French and German authors about the most favorable aspects of Jewish life in the ghettos of Europe.

Successful resistance to conversion efforts is recounted in a pious, highly melodramatic, contrived novel by I. N. Lichtenberg: *The Widow's Son,* issued in New York in 1884. The novel is full of hocus-pocus whereby a seventeenth-century Jewish boy in the Rhine Valley overcomes harassment and the attempts to convert him and, in a complicated set of circumstances, emerges as a count and local governor.

While "literary" activity of this sort is decently buried in the archives of libraries, the work of two women poets of the period, Adah Isaacs Menken and Emma Lazarus, is still remembered, and that of the latter, at least, is still read. Both were far more sophisticated than Penina Moise, who was thirty-eight when Adah Menken was born in 1835. Both had poetic talent, which Miss Moise lacked. Yet if it were not for Adah Menken's immense reputation—perhaps notoriety would be more accurate—as a personality, siren, and sensational actress, it is doubtful that her poetry would be remembered today. Legends grew up about her life and origin, many of them promoted by herself. One of the controversial points of her biography was the claim of Jewish origin. The most recent biography, *Queen of the Plaza,* by Paul Lewis, would seem to put the question to rest, for he had access to her diary, letters, and papers. She was *not* Jewish in origin, but was converted to Judaism in 1857 in Cincinnati by the mother of her first husband, Isaac Menken, the son of a well-to-do manufacturer of textiles in that city. She assiduously studied Hebrew, could read the Old Testament in the original, and wrote poems in that language. In February 1857 she wrote to Rabbi Henry F. Grossman, of Cincinnati: "I have become convinced in the course of reading and our many conversations that I have found my true spiritual home as a Jewess. . . . With my mind as well as my heart, my heart as well as my mind, I rejoice that I may become a Jewess."[51]

Although Rabbi Grossman did officiate at her conversion, we know that Rabbi Isaac M. Wise had refused to do so. The latter's son, Leo Wise, has written that his father rejected her many requests to convert her. Though Leo Wise professed not to know why his father refused, one may conjecture that the reason may have been the rabbi's moral disapproval of her. Leo Wise writes: "With all her shortcomings she was a brilliantly gifted, warm-hearted and lovable woman, who might have made a lasting record had her strength of character been as great as her intelligence."[52] In any case, all the evidence seems to point to a serious conversion. Throughout her flamboyant public career she never relinquished her Jewish religious identity. She was buried with Jewish rites in Paris in the Jewish section of the Père Lachaise Cemetery on August 12, 1868.

Menken's life was so spectacular that it has fascinated subsequent generations. She was irresistibly attractive to men, but her marital career was checkered. She married four times, never for longer than three years. In 1856, in Texas, she married Isaac Menken, her only Jewish husband. On the mistaken assumption that Menken had divorced her, in 1859 she married the boxing champion John C. Heenan, who repudiated her when he learned that there had been no legal divorce from Menken. After she was properly divorced, she married an editor and political satirist, Robert Henry Newell, well known as "Orpheus C. Kerr," who later wrote: "Adah was a symbol of Desire Awakened to every man who set eyes on her. All who saw her wanted her, immediately."[53] In 1866, two years before her death, she married her fourth and last husband, the Confederate officer James Paul Barkley.

During her career as an actress she was noted more for her beauty and sensational behavior than for her acting ability. She played in many parts of the United States and Europe. The role for which she became most famous was that of Mazeppa, in which, strapped to a horse and dressed in flesh-colored tights that left the impression of nudity, she rode onstage up a steep runway.

She moved easily and with much favor in literary circles. While in New York she was a frequenter of Pfaff's, where she met Walt Whitman, whose genius she recognized early; he was best man at her marriage to Newell. In San Francisco she made friends with the literary men around the *Golden Era,* among them Mark Twain, Bret Harte, Artemus Ward, and Joaquin Miller. In Europe she was a friend of Charles Dickens's (to whom she dedicated her volume of poems, *Infelicia*). Dante Gabriel Rosetti thought enough of her poems to include three of them in an anthology he edited, and she was reputed to have been Algernon Swinburne's mistress. In France she was a friend of Theophile Gautier's and George Sand's, and she carried on an affair with the aged Alexandre Dumas that scandalized the public.

But it was not her sexual appeal alone that captivated literary people. After her death her one-time husband R. H. Newell wrote in his biography of her that she "had the keenest mind I ever encountered in a member of her sex. Indeed, few men were her mental equals and she could discourse fluently on matters pertaining to literature, the sciences and the latest news of the world in which we live. . . . Her erudition, coupled with her great beauty, made her the rarest of her sex."[54]

Loving poetry passionately, she steeped herself in it. Her many early poems were rejected by the New Orleans *Picayune,* and it was not until 1857 that she made her poetic debut in Rabbi Isaac M. Wise's *Israelite* with "Hear, O Israel."[55] In the next year and a half she contributed to over twenty-five issues of that journal—poems and essays on Jewish religious and secular themes and secular lyric poetry.[56]

In an essay on Shylock, originally published in the *New Orleans Sunday Delta* in September 1857 and reprinted in *The Israelite* on October 2 of that year, she optimistically asserts that the Jewish character in literature "received a truer estimate in the present time than in former days." She offers no supporting evidence, and one is at a loss to surmise what works she had in mind.

We can find [she continues], when a Jew is introduced by most of authors, he is represented as having the impulses and feelings of a man, and not devoid of higher aims than merely to amass gold or gratify an ignoble spirit of envy or revenge against his Christian fellow-men. Formerly, the Jew was portrayed as possessing little but a combination of the darkest vices and worst passions that could possibly disgrace or degrade man; pictured as a being without consideration or remorse, to whom no position was too mean to stoop to, the Jew was scarcely brought forth but as a being to be scoffed, reviled and despised.[57]

She also published essays in *The Israelite* in defense of the seating of Rothschild in Parliament after a disapproving article had appeared in the *New York Churchman*.[58] From September 1859 to mid-1862 she appeared in almost fifty issues of the *Sunday Mercury,* the New York weekly edited by her third husband, R. H. Newell. She published several poems and essays in the *Golden Era* late in 1863 and early 1864 while she was playing in the West. Her poems also appeared in other journals.

Her poetry shows that she possessed a modicum of poetic talent. Her occasional free-verse efforts were influenced by the Bible and Whitman, but lacked their poetic power. Her single volume of poems, *Infelicia,* was published in an elegant edition simultaneously in New York, London, and Paris in October 1868, two months after her death, and went through about eight editions. Of her poems from *The Israelite,* only "Hear, O Israel" was included, and most of the others were drawn from her *Sunday Mercury* items. As the title suggests, her poems are the outcry of pain of an apparently most unhappy woman. In "Drifts that Bar My Door" she writes: "Life is a lie, and Love a cheat." In "Infelix" she writes: "I can but own my life is vain/A desert void of peace."

She was capable of such ineptitudes (in "Pro Patria") as "So, blest was Columbia; the focus of Nature's/Best gifts, and the dimple where rested God's smile." But she could also hit upon a striking image. In "Working and Waiting," a poem about the exploitation of a poor seamstress, she writes: "Fly swifter, thou needle—/ Swifter, than asp on the breast of the poor." Her limited poetic gift is indicated by the fact that an effective device—a series of short lines in which the first word is repeated in each line—recurs in at least eight poems. In "Resurgam" she writes:

> So I am certainly dead.
> Dead in this beauty!
> Dead in this velvet and lace!
> Dead in these jewels of light!

> Dead in the music!
> Dead in the dance![59]

Constance Rourke's judgment is concisely appropriate: Menken's "verse must be read as passionate autobiography rather than as poetry."[60]

12

EMMA LAZARUS

Of the Jewish writers in the last half of the nineteenth century, the most talented was unquestionably Emma Lazarus. To be sure, her competition among Jewish Americans was not keen. Yet she has won a minor place in the history of American literature because she embodied a valid fusion of a genuine poetic sensibility with inspired advocacy and defense of her calumniated and persecuted people. Her career demonstrates once again that poetry enlisted in the service of a cause need not be ephemeral, but may be art in its own right. In her poetry and prose the Jewish people found an effective voice against the incoming tide of anti-Semitism abroad and at home. During a period of generally undistinguished poetic creativity, she was, as George F. Whicher writes, "contributing poetry easily distinguishable by reason of its firmness, poise, and point from that of contemporaries whose only motive was literary."[1]

Emma Lazarus was born in New York in 1849 of a long-established patrician family of Portuguese Sephardic origin. Her father, Moses, was a successful sugar-refining industrialist whose wealth freed her from the need to work for a living. A shy, sensitive, precocious child, she was so proficient in languages that she made competent translations of French and German poetry from her fourteenth year onwards. At eighteen her first volume, *Poems and Translations,* was privately published by her father; it included renderings of poems by Hugo, Dumas, Schiller, and Heine as well as original poetry. She later added Italian and Hebrew to her language repertoire. In 1871 her poetic drama on the Alcestis legend, "Admetus," appeared in her *Admetus, and Other Poems.* Despite the fact that she had had a book published at such an early age, the shy girl did not mingle in literary society until her twenties. Thomas Wentworth Higginson wrote his sisters in 1872, after meeting Emma Lazarus in Newport, where her family spent summers, that she "is rather an interesting person," adding that her family "are very rich and in fashionable society in New York, and she has never seen an author till lately. . . . It is curious to see how mentally famished a person may be in the very best society."[2]

In 1874 she published a novel, *Alide*, a fictionalized account of an episode in Goethe's life, which brought her a gratifying response from Ivan Turgenev, to whom she had sent a copy. "An author," he wrote, "who writes as you do—is not a 'pupil in art' any more; he is not far from being himself a master."[3]

Her verse drama *The Spagnoletto* (Little Spaniard), privately published in 1876, obviously borrowed from *King Lear.* The painter Ribera's daughter, Maria, is in love with the Austrian prince Don John, who persuades her to elope with him. She becomes his mistress, but he abandons her to marry a princess. The devoted father, Ribera, is irreparably bitter and unforgiving, and stabs himself to death in a nunnery in Maria's presence. His wild speeches are reminiscent of King Lear's but lack the depth of great poetry.

In 1881 she brought out her *Poems and Translations of Heinrich Heine,* which was favorably received, and are to this day regarded as among the best translations of this poet.[4] Her *Songs of a Semite,* including her stirring drama of medieval persecution of the Jews, was published in 1882. A posthumous collection, *The Poems of Emma Lazarus,* in two volumes, was brought out by her two sisters in 1889. During all these years, she published many articles and poems in the periodical press: in the 1870s in *Lippincott's Magazine* and *Scribner's Magazine,* and in the 1880s in the *American Hebrew,* the *Century Magazine,* and *The Critic,* among others.

Emma Lazarus was late in affirming and expressing her Jewish identity; she was not an adherent of Judaism in form and ritual, but was rather an Emersonian in her philosophical attitude. The recent discovery by Louis Ruchames of an 1872 poem, "Outside the Church," explicitly reveals her religious attitude. Published in *The Index,* a Boston radical religious weekly, this poem is patently autobiographical. She writes that she opened herself to belief in the church, but her experience there was frustrating in that it failed to gain for her a needed spiritual solace:

> I waited, but the message did not come;
> No voice addressed my reason, and my heart
> Shrank to itself in chill discouragement.
> To me the ancient oracles were dumb,
> The lifeless rites no comfort could impart,
> Charged with no answer for my discontent.

She did not, however, reject religious belief, but embraced the transcendental creed of the divine significance of nature:

> Here where I stand, religion seems a part
> Of all the moving, teeming, sunlit earth;
> All things are sacred, in each bush a God;
> No miracles accepts the pious heart,
> Where all is miracle; of holy worth
> Seems the plain ground our daily feet have trod.[5]

She adhered all her life to a deeply felt, nonsectarian, humanist attitude. On her deathbed, we learn from an obituary in *The Critic,* "she sent for Dr. Felix Adler [leader of the Ethical Culture movement], but not for the Rabbi of her synagogue; yet it was her wish that Jewish rites should be used at her burial. She died as she lived, as much a Christian as a Jewess—perhaps it would be better to say, neither one nor the other."[6]

Until she was in her late twenties, her interest in Judaism was at most peripheral. In their biographical introduction to the posthumous collection of her poems, her sisters write that "it was only during her childhood and earliest years that she attended the synagogue, and conformed to the prescribed rites and usages which she had now long ago abandoned as obsolete and having no bearing on modern life."[7] But they are in error in dating her passionate interest in her people in 1882. Careful inquiry into her work reveals that her interest in the Jews as a people, rather than in ritualistic Judaism, was aroused earlier.[8] This awakening was cumulative. When Rabbi Dr. Gustav Gottheil of Temple Emanu-El asked her to translate poems for a hymnal he was preparing, she complied, but her heart was not in it. She wrote Dr. Gottheil on February 6, 1877, that "the more I see of these religious poems, the more I feel that the fervor and enthusiasm requisite to their production are altogether lacking in me."[9]

Lack of fervor for Judaism, however, did not preclude identification with her people. In the same year, 1877, she wrote a poem for the rabbi of Shearith Israel, in which her family held membership, "In Memorium—Rev. J. J. Lyons," eulogizing this "good old man who wrought so well/ Upon his chosen glebe."[10] While she did not share his specific beliefs, she memorialized him because he was of her community. The feeling was weaker, however, in the poem written a decade earlier, "In the Jewish Synagogue at Newport." She expresses deep feeling for those buried there as an exiled people, but the poem is pervaded by a sense of pastness and deadness;

however, at the last it is pervaded by a sense of present reverence: "Natheless the sacred shrine is holy yet," she writes.[11] Later, in 1882, in an essay on Longellow she explicitly rejects the judgment of the deadness of the Jewish people expressed in his poem on the Newport Jewish cemetery.[12]

Her devotion to Heine, signalized by her translations of his poetry, was an early influence in surmounting her detachment from her people. The two volumes of 1866 and 1871 containing translations from Heine include not a single poem of his on a Jewish theme.[13] But a change appears in 1876, when her translation of Heine's "Donna Clara," a poem about the love between a Spanish lady and a rabbi's son, appeared in the *Jewish Messenger*. To this translation she added two poems of her own, based on Heine's notes on the sequel. In "Don Pedrillo," the son of this union vents anti-Semitic hatred on the rabbi, whom he does not know to be his father; and in "Fra Pedro" the son has become an abbot and persecutor of the Jews.[14]

Probably also under Heine's influence she became interested at this time in the medieval Spanish Hebrew poets Judah Halevy, Moses ibn Ezra, and Solomon ibn Gabirol. She did not learn Hebrew until the 1880s, but she read these poets in a German translation and published retranslations into English in the *Jewish Messenger* during 1879. She paid tribute to Heine in a fine sonnet, "Venus of the Louvre," which she wrote on a visit to Paris in the summer of 1883, in which she invokes the Greek and Hebrew sources of his inspiration:

> Here *Heine* wept! Here still he weeps anew,
> Nor ever shall his shadow lift or move,
> While mourns one ardent heart, one poet-brain,
> For vanished Hellas and Hebraic pain.[15]

For the most part, however, her work up to the late 1870s dealt with conventional themes: lyrical, abstract effusions about the virtues and tribulations of man, apostrophes to nature, themes from Greek and German mythology, and incidents from great periods of Italian and Spanish art. She wrote long poems based on the Alcestis and Tannhauser legends, and the verse drama *The Spagnoletto*. Form and structure were traditionally correct, but much of the language was artificial and "elevated," and followed the outworn tradition of poetic diction that afflicted the minor poets of the century. The total effect is one of remoteness from living reality.

William James hints at this quality in his 1882 letter on her youthful volume, *Poems and Translations,* and advises her not to be "too much professional artists at it, I mean too exclusively bound to it,— it ought to be the overflowing of a life rich in other ways." Emerson, too, sensed this abstract quality in her verse. At first he greatly admired her "Admetus," which, as he wrote her on November 19, 1868, he thought "a noble poem which I cannot enough praise." But when he wrote to her again a few months later, on January 20, 1869, he gently advised her that "high success must ever be to penetrate into and show the celestial element in the despised Present."[16]

Her acquaintance with Emerson, then an old man, probably dated from 1868, when she met him at the home of a mutual friend. She was elated and encouraged by his praise of her poetry. During the first few years of their acquaintance he served as her mentor, her "ghostly counsellor," as he wrote her. When James Russell Lowell rejected several poems submitted to the *North American Review,* Emerson wrote her that he agreed with Lowell, "if by rough judgment he can drive you to severer pruning of your verses, and mainly to a severer ear." He agreed upon rereading them that the poems needed more work. "You permit feeble lines and feeble words," he wrote, and pointed to the artificiality of her language: "You write words which you can never have spoken." But when William Dean Howells refused to publish "Admetus," which she had dedicated to Emerson, in the *Atlantic Monthly,* the sage wrote her that "I should have printed it thankfully and proudly."[17]

But Emma Lazarus experienced shock and "extreme disappointment" when she discovered that Emerson had failed to include any of her poems in his personal anthology, *Parnassus* (1874). Her letter to him on December 27, 1874, expressed her bewilderment and resentment at the omission in view of his "numerous expressions of extravagant admiration." His favorable opinion of her work, she wrote, was "confirmed by some of the best critics of England and America." She quoted back to him the several expressions of high praise he had sent her, and wonders what "panegyric" he might have expressed for some of his inclusions.[18] We do not know of any reply from Emerson to this sharp letter, but it is a tribute to the magnanimity of both that the friendship did not end. Fifteen months later Emerson invited her, on July 22, 1876, to spend a week in Concord and "correct our village narrowness."[19] During the week's visit she formed a warm relationship with Emerson's daughter, Ellen, that was sustained for years afterward.

However transient Emerson's admiration for her poetry, he had pointed to the central deficiency of her early work; her weak grasp on "the despised present" both in language and theme. With maturity, however, her language became less stilted, and—more important—her passionate preoccupation with the Jewish theme infused her work with immediacy and vitality. Heightened persecution of her people pushed her fully into the present. The tsarist pogroms, from 1879 on, were only the most exacerbated symptoms of a new period of overt anti-Semitism in the Western world, and Emma Lazarus was too sensitive a human being to be unaffected by it. Her interest after 1876 in the Jewish aspect of Heine's work may have been triggered by the awareness of a growing anti-Semitism in the United States.

Although her verse drama "The Dance to Death" was published in the *American Hebrew* in 1882, she wrote the editor that she had written the play "a few years" earlier.[20] This play was a passionate dramatization of the events in 1349 leading to the slaughter of the Jews of Nordhausen. The depth of feeling with which the play is written lends it vitality. It is interesting to observe that she uses one of the literary conventions regarding the "Jewish" heroine. Prince William is in love with Liebhaid von Orb, daughter of the wealthy Jew Susskind von Orb, but it turns out that she is an adopted daughter and a Christian, actually the daughter of Schnetzen, the anti-Semitic inciter of the slaughter of the Jews. A similar device, it will be recalled, was used in Lessing's *Nathan the Wise,* in which Nathan's "daughter" was actually a Christian adopted by Nathan as a baby. In the play the girl marries the Templar, but Emma Lazarus deepens the tragedy of her play by having Liebhaid cremated with all the Jews, despite her prior revelation to the wicked Schnetzen that she is a Christian and his daughter.

Emma Lazarus's interest in the Jewish theme was reinforced by her friendship with Edmund Clarence Stedman, who was, like Lowell, a leading critic of the period. From 1879 to 1881 Stedman lived a few doors from the Lazarus house on East Fifty-seventh Street, and Emma Lazarus was a frequent visitor at the Stedmans'. In a brief essay on Emma Lazarus, Stedman recounts a conversation with her which stimulated her interest in creating works on the Jewish theme. He asked her if she had ever thought of her Jewish heritage. "There is a wealth of tradition you are heir to," he told her, "and could use as a source of inspiration." She replied that she was "proud of my blood and heritage, but Hebrew ideals do not appeal to me." Stedman replied that he "envied her the inspiration she might derive from them."[21] This advice from Stedman, her literary mentor during this period, no doubt played a part in the decision to turn her energies and talent to the service of her people. But it was the horrifying news from Russia, the reports of pogroms beginning in 1879, that probably exerted the strongest influence on her to devote herself wholly to defense of the Jews.

By mid-1882 it was apparent that the quality of her commitment had changed. Earlier that year, in April, the *Century Magazine* published her article "Was the Earl of Beaconsfield a Representative Jew?" (her Emersonianism is reflected in her concept of "representative"). The tone of her article is still rather detached. Disraeli, she writes, was indeed a representative Jew, but he was not a "first-class man." Moses, Jesus, the prophets, Saint Paul, Spinoza, she says, were "first-class men," but centuries of oppression had narrowed the outlook of Jews, so that a Disraeli stands as representative of the Jewish national character at that time, unlike the great spiritual leaders of the past.

In the same issue of the magazine, however, an article by Madame Z. Ragozin, a Russian journalist, places the onus for the pogroms on the Jews themselves in the most rabidly anti-Semitic terms. The article charges the Jews with causing the pogroms by their presumed oppressive practices against the Russians:

The Jews [writes Mrs. Ragozin] are disliked, nay, hated in those parts of East Europe and Russia not because they believe and pray differently, but because they are a parasitic race who, producing nothing, fasten on the produce and the land and labor and live on it, choking the life out of commerce and industry as sure as the creeper throttles the tree that holds it.[22]

This article provided the spark that inflamed Emma Lazarus with an all-consuming passion for the defense of her people. In the next issue she writes a point-by-point refutation of the preposterous charges of Madame Ragozin. Thenceforth the vow of dedication by Liebhaid in "The Dance to Death" became her own:

I am all Israel's now—till this cloud pass,
I have no thought, no passion, no desire,
Save for my people.[23]

In the next few years she poured out a stream of poems and articles, informed by a knowledge of Jewish history mainly derived from Graetz and infused with pride in the prophetic heritage. She cried out against both past and present persecution, and summoned her people to battle against it.

Hard upon her reply to Madame Ragozin she wrote "The Crowing of the Red Cock," a denunciation of the tsarist pogroms.

> Where is the Hebrew's fatherland?
> The folk of Christ is sore bestead;
> The Son of Man is bruised and banned,
> Nor finds whereon to lay his head.
> His cup is gall; his meat is tears,
> His passion lasts a thousand years.
>
> Each crime that wakes in man the beast,
> Is visited upon his kind.
> The lust of mobs, the greed of priest,
> The tyranny of kings, combined
> To root his seed from earth again,
> His record is one cry of pain.[24]

In "The Banner of the Jew," published in *The Critic* of June 3, 1882, she recalled the heroism of the Maccabeans and exhorted her fellow Jews to emulate their example:

> O deem not dead that martial fire,
> Say not the mystic flame is spent!
> With Moses' law and David's lyre,
> Your ancient strength remains unbent.
> Let but an Ezra rise anew,
> To lift the *Banner of the Jew!*

The language of her poetry now became more spare and direct than in the earlier work, charged with a dynamic sense of Jewish identity and fervent commitment to the defense and welfare of the Jews. The difference between the earlier poetry and later is striking, writes George F. Whicher, "when the wrongs of her people filled her with indignation and brought her forward as the champion of an oppressed race. . . . In the literary hot house of the later nineteenth century the breath of a great cause blew through her verse with tonic effect."[25]

As an already established contributor to current periodicals like *The Century* and *The Critic,* she sought to arouse her non-Jewish compatriots, to enlighten them, and to enlist them as allies. She spoke to her own people in the poetry and prose she contributed to the *American Hebrew* of New York. In her poems she celebrates great Jewish heroes like Bar Kochba. The focus of her exhortations is not theological, but rather the past greatness of her people and their struggle for freedom. She calls for "grateful homage" to Bar Kochba, "The last Warrior Jew," who died for Jewish freedom.[26]

A pair of poems, "Raschi in Prague" and "The Death of Raschi," celebrate the intellectual beauty and wisdom of the great talmudist, and memorialize the legend of his martyrdom in Prague. "By the Waters of Babylon," the last poem published in her lifetime, is a series of eight "Little Poems in Prose," invoking episodes of Jewish history. She mourns the expulsion of the Jews from Spain in 1492: "Whither shall they turn? for the West casteth them out, and the East refuseth to receive"; she broods on the "Passion of Israel" and greets the welcome accorded to Jewish refugees from Russia by the United States; she calls on the Jews in the name of their great men from Maimonides to Heine to succor the ghetto Jews, to bring them forth to "the emancipating springtide."[27]

In her article "The Jewish Problem," published in *The Century* of February 1883, Emma Lazarus realizes what has become evident in our own time: "From the era when the monotheistic Semitic slaves of the Pharaohs made themselves hated and feared by their poly-theistic masters, till to-day when the monstrous giants Labor and Capital are arming for a supreme conflict, the Jewish question has been inextricably bound up with the deepest and gravest questions that convulse society." In this essay she sketches the history of Jewish persecution and describes the emancipation resulting from the French Revolution. Observing that in the United States Jews "en-joyed absolute civil and political freedom and equality," she qualifies this by adding, "until the past few years." She realizes realistically that even in this country,

public opinion has not yet reached that point where it absolves the race from the sin of the individual. Every Jew, however honorable or enlightened, has the humiliating knowledge that his security and reputation are, in a certain sense, bound up with those of the mean-est rascal who belongs to his tribe, and who has it in his power to jeopardize the social status of his whole nation. It has been well said that the Jew must be of gold in order to pass for silver.

She notes the spread of prejudice and social discrimination that began to assume serious proportions from the 1870s on. It is a calumny, she asserts, to hold that the Jews thirst for money, for their yearning is for knowledge. The notion that Jews are a historic "relic" is contradicted, she says, by the fact that Jews are "most frequently the pioneers of progress." The modern movement for reform and for socialism, she affirms, "has its roots in the Mosaic Code, . . . which formulated the principle of the rights of labor, denying the right of private property in land, asserting that the . . . gleanings of the harvest belonged in *justice,* not in *charity,* to the poor and the stranger. . . . In accordance with these principles we find the fathers of modern socialism to be three Jews—Ferdinand Lassalle, Karl Marx, and Johann Jacoby." Finally, she offers her conviction that *"they* [the Jews] *must establish an independent national-ity."*[28]

Emma Lazarus's enthusiasm for the creation of a national seat for the Jews in Palestine was fired by *Daniel Deronda,* by George Eliot, to whom she had dedicated "The Dance to Death" for having done "most among the artists of our day towards elevating and ennobling the spirit of Jewish nationality." Promotion of this idea forms one of the themes of "An Epistle to the Hebrews," a series of sixteen articles in the *American Hebrew* which appeared from November 3, 1882, to February 23, 1883. However, she did not project the idea of "renationalizing" the Jews in the same statist Zionism terms as did Theodor Herzl later. She propounded no theory of the inevitability of anti-Semitism, nor the "ingathering of the exiles" of Herzlian doctrine. She did not urge, she writes, "the advisability of an emigra-tion *en masse* of the whole Jewish people to a particular spot. There is not the slightest necessity for the American Jew, the free citizen of a republic, to rest his hopes upon the foundation of any other nationality soever." She envisioned Palestine as a "secure asylum" for Jews from places where they were oppressed, as in tsarist Russia. "Today," she says, "wherever we are free, we are at home."[29]

She was basically animated by the will to help *oppressed* Jews. If Eastern European Jews could escape oppression by emigration to emancipated lands, that was a good solution for them; they need not necessarily go to Palestine. But she was nevertheless inspired by the ancient prophecy of return to Palestine, as expressed in her sonnet "The New Eziekel." "The House of Israel [could] come forth and breathe afresh . . . living in your land."[30] The prophetic solution elicited a deep emotional assent, perhaps unconnected to any practi-cal or immediate motive.

She was singularly free from the prejudice and antagonism felt by most affluent and established Jews of the earlier immigrations, the Sephardic and German, toward the masses of impoverished ghetto Jews pouring into the country from Eastern Europe. Middle-class Jews generally were contemptuous of the Orthodox rigidity of the new arrivals, of their poverty and their ghetto mode of life, and disliked the transplantation to this country of the medieval life-styles and the hermetic intellectual and social conditions of the old coun-try. Already integrated into the economic life of the country, these middle-class Jews feared that the conspicuously different mode of life of their immigrant brethren, and the financial burden of settling them in their new home, might jeopardize the relatively secure status they themselves had already achieved. In order to minimize the problems of acculturating the new arrivals to the non-Jewish population, and also because they did feel the obligation to help their fellow Jews, they created institutions to locate housing and jobs for the immigrants. In an effort to establish the incoming Jews in agriculture, attempts were even made to settle some on farms, but with little success.

The motives of Emma Lazarus in speaking out for East European Jews were purer than those of most middle-class Jews. She felt none of the repugnance for her lower-class brothers and sisters and showed a deep understanding of their situation. The fourteenth section of her "Epistle to the Hebrews" is devoted to "antidoting" the "poison" of contempt as exemplified in the preface written by Barnet Phillips, a Jew who was then literary editor of the *New York Times,* to an American edition of Karl Emil Franzos's German novel of Polish ghetto life, *The Jews of Barnow.* "Comfortably entrenched in the freedom and equality of American citizenship," she writes, "Mr. Phillips looks down with enlightened contempt upon the degrading superstitions of the Polish Jews, ignoring the fact that his own better knowledge is the direct and immediate result of political enfranchisement."[31] In the first section of her "Epistle" she categorically condemns those Jews who looked down on their less affluent brothers, as "the contemptible aversion and hostility manifested between Jews of varying descent."[32]

Emma Lazarus did not confine her services to writing. She was also active in the practical work of aiding in the resettlement of the newcomers and in relieving their hardship. She met incoming immigrants at Ward's Island with food and clothing. The impression she made on immigrants is suggested in Abraham Cahan's recollections: "When I arrived [in the United States in 1882] the immigration committee included one wealthy young Jewish lady who belonged to the cream of the monied aristocracy. She was Emma Lazarus. She often visited the immigrants' camp on Ward's Island in the East River, but this never undermined her status as an aristocrat."[33] Despite this difference of class, the sincerity of her devotion is beyond doubt.

She was also active in efforts to settle immigrants in agriculture, and especially to provide vocational training for them. She was convinced that Jews would succeed in farming, as she asserted in the sixth section of her "Epistle." Considering that for many centuries during the dispersion the Jew had had to adapt to various physical and social environments, and had usually attained some measure of influence in each society, Jews *"can be whatever they will be."*[34] When a violent outbreak occurred in the immigrant refuge on Ward's Island on October 14, 1882, in protest against inadequate food, she published a letter in the *American Hebrew* for October 20 condoning the outbreak. She itemized the scandalous conditions under which the seven hundred immigrants lived, and proposed a program not only for improving their physical facilities, but also for educational and occupational activity. Under her inspiration the Hebrew Technical Institute for vocational training was founded. In "By the Waters of Babylon" she rejoices in the efforts at agricultural colonization: "The herdsmen of Canaan and the seed of Jerusalem's royal shepherd renew their youth amid the pastoral plains of Texas and the golden valleys of the Sierras." When she learned, in the spring of 1882, that a group of Russian refugees were living happily in an agricultural settlement in Texas, she celebrated their free and contented life in a poem, "In Exile":

> The martyr, granted respite from the rack,
>   The death-doomed victim pardoned from his cell,—
> Such only know the joy these exiles gain,—
> Life's sharpest rapture is surcease of pain.[35]

She was especially active in fund raising for relief of immigrants and Russian refugees. At such affairs others would read her poetry, and "In Exile" was read on one such occasion in 1882. Her most famous poem, and the one that will insure her immortality, was written expressly to raise money. In 1883 the people of France gave to the people of the United States the Bartholdi Statue of Liberty—"Mother of Exiles," as Emma Lazarus was to name it—but the immense statue lacked a pedestal. One of the devices used to raise money for the pedestal was an auction of manuscripts by famous American authors, and Emma Lazarus reluctantly agreed to contribute a poem. Much as she disliked to write occasional poems, the cause inspired the sonnet "The New Colossus," which was finally inscribed on a plaque affixed to the pedestal of the statue:

> Not like the brazen giant of Greek fame,
> With conquering limbs astride from land to land;
> Here at our sea-washed, sunset gates shall stand
> A mighty woman with a torch, whose flame

Is the imprisoned lightning, and her name
Mother of Exiles. From her beacon-hand
Glows world-wide welcome; her mild eyes command
The air-bridged harbor that twin cities frame.
"Keep, ancient lands, your storied pomp!" cries she
With silent lips. "Give me your tired, your poor,
Your huddled masses yearning to breathe free,
The wretched refuse of your teeming shore.
Send these, the homeless, tempest-tost to me,
I lift my lamp beside the golden door!"[36]

The poem has become a classic expression of the ideal of American hospitality to the oppressed and an antidote to racist prejudice. James Russell Lowell, who had fourteen years earlier rejected her poems submitted to the *North American Review,* now paid tribute to her in a letter of December 17, 1883: "I liked your sonnet about the statue much better than I like the Statue itself. But your sonnet gives its subject a *raison d'etre* which it wanted before quite as much as it wants a pedestal. You have set it on a noble one, saying admirably just the right word to be said, an achievement more arduous than that of the sculptor."[37]

Just as her poem was a universal call to the oppressed of all peoples, so her passionate involvement in the fate of Jews was not parochial, but opened her sensitivities to the problems of society in general. She possessed what she had once written Longfellow lacked: "the active energy or the passionate enthusiasm of an inspired champion in the arena of the present." She responded warmly to the teachings of William Morris and Henry George. In the summer of 1883 she spent a day with William Morris at his workshop and came away greatly impressed by his deep humanity. She describes her visit in an article in *The Century* of July 1886, when the antiradical hysteria over the Haymarket affair was in full cry, and writes appreciatively of the humane relationship between Morris and the workers in his shops. What strikes her especially is Morris's interest in art as an effort to realize beauty in the life of all people, rather than as a striving toward a "sickly and selfish aestheticism." The depths of poverty and prevailing inequality in England seem to her to account for "Mr. Morris' extreme socialistic convictions." She believed that, while the degree of opportunity in the United States tended to mitigate poverty here, thus making "extreme" doctrine inappropriate for this country, Morris's "magnanimity must command respect."[38]

Years earlier she had been profoundly moved by her reading of

Henry George's *Progress and Poverty*. She was among the many Americans disturbed by the facts of grinding poverty and exploitation revealed in the book, and she was inspired to write a sonnet, "Progress and Poverty," which was published in the *New York Times* on October 2, 1881. There she contrasts the economic achievements and social depths of modern society. A society "Richer than Cleopatra's barge of gold" is confronted with "that deep reeking hell" in which the workers slave to "feed the ravenous monster, pant and sweat,/Nor know if overhead reign night or day."[39] She sent a copy of the poem to Henry George, who responded appreciatively. In her reply on October 17, 1881, she could hardly find words to express the effect the book had had on her. George's "burning eloquence" in the book, she wrote, "takes possession of one's mind and heart to such a degree as overpowers all other voices. . . . It sets the minds of men on fire."[40] Her largeness of heart and mind prevented the absorption with her own people from shutting off her sensitivity to injustice in the larger community.

Her interest in literature was not limited to Jewish topics even after she became "all Israel's now." She was a stout advocate of an American national literature, and held views not shared by leading critics and artists at that time. In mid-1881 Stedman, in a sign of his respect for her judgment, solicited from her a criticism of the manuscript of an article on his conception of American national literature. She disagrees with his thesis that poets in the United States did not engage in longer poetic forms because the American milieu did not offer adequate material. "I have never believed," she writes, "in the *want of a theme*—wherever there is humanity, there is the theme for a great poem." She agrees with Stedman that this country had not yet produced a great national poet. However, she absolutely refused, in a letter to Thomas Wentworth Higginson on July 8, 1881, "to share the 'low-down' estimate of our national literature which the Anglo-American and half-informed Englishman are inclined to make. To my eyes, there are signs of fresh vitality in every direction."[41]

While she apparently did not recognize the full stature of Whitman, she did appreciate his modernity. She realized that Longfellow harked back in mind and poetry to an earlier generation, and she contrasted his orientation to the past with the contemporaniety of Emerson and Whitman. John Burroughs complimented her, with male condescension, on her appreciation of Whitman. "I am delighted," he wrote, "to hear that you are equal to the task of appreciating Democratic Vistas. I have not found a woman that was, and but few men."[42] Whitman himself never met her and knew little of her work, as he told Horace Traubel after her death, but he was impressed by her photograph: "a beautiful face," he said to Traubel. "I know little about her or her work: but her face is an argument." Later he remarked; "She must have had a great, sweet, unusual nature."[43]

The last few years of her short life were wracked with pain. In 1885 her beloved father died. Her attachment to him was deep, perhaps excessive. The intense devotion of father and daughter depicted in "The Spagnoletto" and "The Dance to Death" must have reflected her personal experience. She herself had been stricken with cancer the previous summer, and under the impact of her illness and devastating grief over her father's death she decided to go to Europe. The next two years she spent traveling while her illness took its destructive course. She returned home in July 1887 in grave condition and died on November 19, 1887, at the age of thirty-eight.

Her death brought forth expressions of the deepest respect for her work as writer and defender of her people from distinguished figures in England and the United States. Memorials to her were published by *The Critic* (December 10, 1887) and the *American Hebrew* (December 9, 1887, and October 5, 1888), which contained tributes from many noted contemporaries. Robert Browning cabled his condolences from London. Whittier wrote:

With no lack of rhythmic sweetness, she has often the rough strength and verbal audacity of Browning. Since Miriam sang of deliverance and triumph by the Red Sea, the Semitic race has had no braver singer. . . . Well may those of her own race and faith lament the loss of such a woman. They will not sorrow alone. Among the "mourning women" at her grave the sympathizing voice of Christian daughters will mingle with the wail of the daughters of Jerusalem.

Joseph B. Gilder, Charles Dudley Warner, Edward Eggleston, H. H. Boyesen, John Burroughs, E. L. Godkin, and Charles S. Dana paid their respects. Her literary mentor, Edmund Clarence Stedman, wrote: "Viewed merely on the literary side, her abilities were so progressive, under the quickening force of a lofty motive, that her early death is a deplorable loss in a time when so much verse, if not as sounding brass, seems to come from tinkling symbols." John Hay wrote that "her early death . . . is an irreparable loss to American literature. No where among our writers was there a talent more genuine and substantial. . . . Her place is secure among our best writers."[44]

Looked at in perspective, Emma Lazarus was a minor American poet, but she was probably the finest Jewish writer up to our century. The country had to wait several decades before it produced Jewish literary talents of major stature. The tributes from leading literary figures after her death give some indication of her quality and the deep impression she made on contemporaries. Stedman included six of her poems in his *American Anthology* (1900).[45] She achieved a permanent place in American poetry with her poem "The New Colossus," which is inscribed at the base of the Statue of Liberty.

Yet despite her sensitivity to modern currents, she never quite cast off the language of an outmoded tradition. Only in the last poem published in her lifetime, "By the Waters of Babylon," a prose poem published in *The Century* of March 1887, did she depart from traditional structure. To the end she persisted in using to excess the hyphenated adjective (e.g., "ivory-pale"). Although her language lost some of its stiffness after she became a defender of her people, traces of traditional poetic diction remained. But she so infused her later poetry with intensity of feeling and conviction as to raise it above conventionality. Deeper research needs to be done to bring her more fully to our knowledge. From what we do know, however, she merits a permanent place in American literature as a talented, humane poet.[46]

PART FOUR

FROM RECONSTRUCTION TO 1900

13

THE POPULAR NOVEL, 1870S TO 1900

The frequency with which the contemporary Jew was depicted in the nineteenth-century American novel correlates directly with the growth of his presence in the country. Before the wave of German Jewish immigration in the 1830s and 1840s, relatively few novels introduced a contemporary Jewish character. In the next few decades the contemporary Jew was still an infrequent personage in the novel.

Mass immigration in the 1870s and 1880s rendered the Jew more and more visible, however, and the rise of racist theories brought the Jew further into public discussion. A change in the intensity and overtness of anti-Semitism in the United States was symbolized by the charge that losses in the insurance business were owing to the deliberate setting of fires by Jews to collect insurance. In 1867 many insurance companies instructed their agents not to insure small Jewish businesses or to insure them only under special conditions. Arguments pro and con were aired in many newspapers all over the country, and many Jewish communities protested this discriminatory treatment.[1]

Immense social forces were coming into their own in the 1870s. The Civil War had been the watershed of American civilization, for the sudden multiplication of need for manufactured goods of every kind for war purposes brought on unprecedented industrial growth. The big moneymen succeeded in asserting their dominant power in the Republic. Reconstruction was rescinded in 1877, and the "Jim Crow" system was launched. Nativism and notions of Anglo-Saxon superiority became increasingly influential. Anti-Catholic feelings were high, Indians were herded into reservations; Chinese were denied citizenship; immigrants from Eastern and southern Europe, especially Italians, were targets of discrimination and vilification, and even violence. Labor was restive; the first national railroad strike broke out in 1877. And the political life of the nation came under control of the big business interests.

The Jews did not escape this access of bigotry and discrimination. By 1870 the German Jewish immigration had brought the Jewish population of the country to about three hundred thousand persons —still less than one percent of the total population. But by now Jews had become much more visible than before. A number had enriched themselves by manufacturing and trade during the Civil War. The erstwhile peddlers of the 1830s, 1840s, and 1850s had by now become leading retail merchants, manufacturers, and even bankers. In the 1870s, the Jewish banking houses of Seligman, Kuhn, Loeb, Lehman Brothers, and others had been established, and Jewish merchants were dispersed throughout the rapidly growing cities. Jews had now become substantial economic competitors of the established Anglo-Saxon stock.

The wealthiest Jews took the natural step of trying to enter the social world of their non-Jewish peers. But they discovered that the country had changed; the relatively relaxed attitude toward association with Jews that had prevailed in the earlier periods was over. While many of the suddenly affluent Jews no doubt displayed the crudities and vulgarities of the nouveaux riches—features that they shared with their non-Jewish counterparts—they became the scapegoats for this phenomenon. They were excluded from the resorts and clubs of the wealthy. The Seligman affair was the flashpoint of a cumulative process. The pattern of discrimination in the next few decades became general in many phases of American life. Overt anti-Jewish attitudes were to be reinforced by Anglo-Saxon racism and racist anti-Semitism imported from Europe. The Jew had advanced to the forefront of current consciousness, and consequently turned up with increasing frequency in that medium which most immediately reflects contemporary life and attitudes: the novel.

Perhaps the most virulent anti-Semitic novel of the American nineteenth century was *Gwendolen: A Sequel to George Eliot's "Daniel Deronda."* (1878). The author understandably concealed his identity behind anonymity. Within the perspective of post–Civil War United States, *Gwendolen* seems almost inevitable. In Europe a new phase of overt anti-Semitic theory and practice was coming to the fore. In response, the seeds of a Jewish nationalism in the form of Zionism were being sown, on one hand, and on the other, masses of Jews in Europe began to participate in the labor and socialist movements. With the weakening of the Turkish empire in mid-century, British imperialism was eyeing Palestine for its own. The vague theological prospect of a Second Coming, when the Jews of the world would foregather in Palestine and Christ would return, was slowly being transformed into the Jewish secular aspiration to establish Palestine as a national center.

Impetus was given to this new Jewish nationalism by George Eliot's *Daniel Deronda* (1876), which not only injected the idea of a Jewish national state into the currents of general thought, but was also among the influences that inspired Jews to advance and develop the idea that was to reach its crystallization in Herzl's *Jewish State* twenty years later. Despite its weaknesses—Daniel Deronda is, in fact, a highly sophisticated, spiritualized Sheva figure—the novel could not but make a deep impression on its time. No major literary work in English in the nineteenth century exceeded *Deronda* in the comprehensiveness of its observation of Jewish life, or in the variety of its Jewish characters, from the etherealized nationalist Mordecai, to the lower-middle-class Cohen family, to the radical Jewish workers, to the self-hating assimilationist, Deronda's mother. In the American literature of the nineteenth century only Herman Melville's long poem *Clarel* can compare, in scope of Jewish characterization, with *Deronda*.

Eliot's sympathy toward the Jews and her espousal of Jewish nationalism could not help but infuriate the anti-Semites, among them the author of *Gwendolen*. By ending with Deronda's journey to Palestine with his wife, Mirah, to regenerate the Jews, this author thinks, Eliot's novel had stopped too soon; it should have exposed what the author of *Gwendolen* considered to be the real nature of the Jews. And so he (or she?) "resumes" the story in Palestine.

Disillusionment sets in quickly. Deronda "found nothing but disappointment in the facts which were elicited by his researches after Jewish faiths and nationalities; thus tending to eliminate the spark of faith and reverence he once held." The Jewish case is based on a great deception, for Deronda "arrived at the conclusion that as a nation they had been scattered for cause, and that their habits as individuals were not such as to add glory or bring greatness to a nation consolidated of such integralities." The new Deronda no longer believes the Jews can form a viable nation, for they do not practice the variety of occupations necessary to maintain such a nation.

At present [says the author], the Jew flourishes at the expense of other people, and were they consolidated as a compact nation, it would then be necessary, in order to feed the Jews, and to preserve their business habits, to mix with them a preponderating number of Gentiles, [for] the Jews are not given to industrial or mechanical pursuits. It is upon the labor of the farmer, the mechanic, that the

Jew, with his present notions of subsistence and living must thrive.
. . . It is an absurd hallucination to indulge in the wild impossible
idea of Jews as a nation.

The author's solution for the Jewish people is assimilation. "The
only hope for the Jews is in being extirpated, by amalgamation with
the industrious and honest people of other nations; to learn new
habits; and by application to labor, strive to do for themselves that
which they now allow others to do; and which their unscrupulous
minds now feast upon."[2]

It is not the author's opposition to a Jewish national life or his
espousal of assimilationism that indicates his intense anti-Semitism,
for such views were certainly arguable and tenable in a non-anti-
Semitic context. It is rather in the total acceptance of the most
invidious concept of the Jew that underlies these views that the
author's bias is exposed. The further development of the novel fully
bears this out, for he/she remakes Deronda into an anti-Semite. In
Cairo, Deronda and his wife, Mirah, are caught in an anti-Jewish
riot. They find refuge in the "civilized household" of the British
consulate. One would suppose that a pogrom would cause Deronda
to rise to the defense of his people. On the contrary:

Again disparaging thoughts of Hebrewish ways and manners came
prominently into consideration, and so disgustingly real, and un-
wholesome in detail, that he inwardly resolved to henceforth abjure
the faith, which was permeated with the rankest vices, that coun-
tenanced the vilest means; and where co-adjuters still gloried in their
conviction of the Son of Man.

These thoughts he conceals from Mirah, but soon the author conveniently kills off Mirah in childbirth. Deronda is too much oppressed
by grief, says the author,

to at the same time sorrow for the degeneracy of those whom he had
once been proud to own as his kinspeople, but whose debased
characteristics had even rendered distasteful to him the religious
practices of his own dear Mirah. . . . [He had observed] the depravity
of nature, the paucity of honor, the unholy proclivities of those
among whom were garnered all the ancient and perfect traditions of
the race.

Deronda finally concludes that "as a nation they would only unite
gross traits, and that even as individuals they were totally unqualified
and undesirable rulers over themselves, much less over others."[3]

Deronda's rage against the Jews is intensified when he discovers that his mother's grave is unmarked because she died outside the faith. He thereupon transfers the remains of both his mother and his wife to a Christian burial ground; he curses the Jews, and vows "that from henceforward her [his mother's] persecutors were his enemies." His transformation into an anti-Semite is now complete. He goes to Germany, where he is finally converted to Christianity. To him, Christ is "the symbol of Christian salvation, represented by the Jewish ideal of torture. Christ was indeed the King of the Jews, but not being a Jew by nature or by traits of humanity, he was crucified."[4] Deronda returns to England, again meets Gwendolen, the Christian girl who loved him and whom he had rejected in Eliot's novel, and they marry. The author thereby rights the "wrong" done to Gwendolen by Deronda's error in marrying the Jewish Mirah, and Gwendolen is now "reclaimed" in marriage by Deronda.

A more conventional conception of the Jew underlies an earlier novel of the 1870s, *Joseph the Jew* (1873), by Virginia Wales Johnson. In this melodramatic story a young Danish Jew's quest for a priceless jewel stolen from his grandfather by English pirates is the means for reuniting an American family. The Rost family of diamond merchants in Denmark "avoid a display of wealth." They still try to conceal their wealth with "an hypocrisy which fear had taught," even though by mid-century "the days of heavy tribulation were past." So behind the walls of a house with an ordinary front is a secret room of oriental splendor. Writes Mrs. Johnson, letting her imagination run riot:

This state apartment had once been fitted for the reception of a prince of the Hebrew race, a great banker and statesman, who was a confidential friend of emperors, and who wore more noble orders on his breast than royalty itself. . . . Venetian mirrors, framed in silver, lined the walls; the floor was of polished wood, in mosaic patterns, with a Persian carpet laid in the centre; amber satin curtains shrouded the bed and windows; the chairs and sofas were solid ebony and amber stain, relieved by graceful festoons of lace. A chandelier of pure cut crystal held wax tapers, half-consumed. Indian vases wafted still a lingering aromatic perfume, [etc.][5]

The younger son, Joseph Rost, goes to America to recover the stolen jewel, and on the boat he meets another Jew, Reuben Wentzel, who is of a lower social class. Mrs. Johnson explains that Joseph feels "contemptuous superiority for the cringing, servile family of Wentzel," for the Jews are "a race where the distinctions between rich and poor are rigidly maintained. . . . Observe, we are not describing our Anglo-Saxon youth, bluff and honest, but the son of a people whose aims and operations have, from necessity, followed circuitous avenues of thought for ages." Joseph will not reveal his mission to the lowly Reuben, for, "if a Hebrew does not trust a Christian, still less frequently does he trust one of his own kind." Joseph is further endowed with Jewish "traits": he is obstinate, "call it bravery. . . . He possessed all the curious submissiveness of his people, united with a tenacity of purpose, a persistent adherence to one fixed aim amidst adverse buffetings." Joseph and Reuben undergo a series of adventures, together and separately, in search of the jewel, of which Reuben has learned, and both die in the quest. But they are instrumental in causing the reunion of a long-lost father and son, a consummation for which "Joseph the Jew has fulfilled his allotted task."[6]

While *Gwendolen* must mark the zenith of anti-Semitic virulence in American fiction of the century, anti-Jewish treatment of fictional characters continued unabated. One of the worst practitioners was Julian Hawthorne, son of the great artist, who published a number of novels. It might have been the better part of wisdom if Julian Hawthorne had not followed his father's vocation. "To be the son of a man of genius," Henry James wrote about him in 1874, "is at best to be born of a heritage of invidious comparisons, and the case is not bettered if one attempts to follow directly in the paternal footsteps." Julian Hawthorne, he noted, has "a hundred faults of taste to unlearn."[7] One of these lapses (whether James had this in mind I do not know, since he was himself guilty of this on occasion) was his crude treatment of his Jewish characters. Julian's father had no higher opinion of Jews than is manifested in Julian's novels, as is clear from the great Hawthorne's aforementioned description of the lord mayor of London's brother in the *English Notebooks,* but the father had the good sense and taste not to allow this prejudice to find crude expression in his fiction.

Julian Hawthorne, like most of his contemporaries, escaped criticism for this in his own time. When an editorial in the *Jewish Messenger* reported his complaint that his work was always being compared with that of his father, pleading that "it is time that he was judged by himself or let alone entirely," the editorialist utters not a word about the anti-Semitic features of his fiction.[8] But in reviewing the younger Hawthorne's books, Henry James was unsparing in his criticism, in 1876 charging Julian with "a strange immaturity of thought." His work is "unduly trivial and even rather puerile. . . . It gives us the feeling that the author has nursed his dislikes and irritations in a dark closet."[9] A reading of his work leaves the impression of a rather insufferable upper-class snob and stuffed shirt.

Jews make brief appearances in several novels. In a detective story, *An American Penman* (1887), a Dresden banker appears, one Knoup, who has a "Hebraic profile and soft voice and manner." One character says of him: "Knoup is all right, from his point of view, but his point of view is that of his own interests entirely, and therefore disregards those of other people. If you intrust your money to him, he will keep three francs of interest in it for every two francs that he gives you."[10] In an earlier novel, *Beatrix Randolph* (1884), set in New York State, the titular heroine is an aspiring singer. This provides the occasion for introducing an impresario, Moses Inigo, who has a slight Jewish accent (Jewish impresarios were in fact prominent by this time). He is said to know his business; he is "the foremost impresario and musical manager of the age," and he recognizes Beatrix as a genuine talent. Inigo is a "vulgar Jew, of uncertain nationality, whose past history and private life would not bear examination; but he knew what music and musical genius are." Faithful to the convention, Hawthorne has Inigo bemoan his poverty when he is really wealthy. Complaining that the artists he sponsors earn huge sums, Inigo adds: "And here am I, a poor man today, and they rolling in riches!" Another character responds: "Yes, for a poor and virtuous man you've done pretty well."[11]

In *Sebastian Strome* (1879), however, a young Jew from a wealthy English family is a central character, and a rather pathetic one. Set in England in mid-century, the story centers on the heiress Mary Dene, who is wooed by both Sebastian Strome and Selim Fawley, the son of a Jewish banker. Strome loses Mary to Fawley because a child was born from Strome's liaison with a servant girl, who conveniently dies in childbirth. Mary really loves Strome, and when she tells her husband, Fawley, this, he dies in a fit, and she marries Strome. The story is melodramatic and sentimental; the motivations of the characters lack plausibility. Strome is, of course, rendered as quite superior; Fawley, a weak character who is guilty of some undisclosed dishonorable act known to Strome, is baited by various characters throughout the novel.

Selim Fawley's father is represented as a crude stereotype. He is closely related to the "well-known firm of Bullion Brothers," and was married to "Miss Sarah Kugelmann, a wealthy pawnbroker's daughter, . . . who was a Jewess only on her father's side." He adheres to the crudest pecuniary values. "A true friend," he advises his son, "one to be depended on, is the man that owesh you money on good security, or money'sh worth! Now just you listen to me and don't forget it! There's two times when I know I can trust a man: when I can beggar him, and when I can shame him; and shaming is twenty per cent better than beggaring any day." When his son asks him for a loan, he offers one at 10 percent for six months; the son protests this is a little high for a paternal loan. " 'Times are very hard,' " replies the father, "rubbing his thick hands together, 'and the security is rather unsure—he, he!' " As a favor to his son, he agrees to "deduct the interest beforehand"[12] from the sum loaned.

The elder Fawley has gone to some expense, he says, to make his son "a first-class shentleman." Selim Fawley has gone to Oxford, where he graduated with high honors. "As for his Jewish proclivities, they must have been of the mildest sort. . . . [He looked] handsome, gentlemanly, and deferential and not obtrusively Judaic." But the mark is on him: "Still there was something in the play of his red lips while talking, and a Semitic humidity in his small brown eyes when smiling, and yet more when laughing, which tended to counterbalance his many solid attractions in the judgment of certain ultra-fastidious Christian critics." Hawthorne seems here to be dissociating himself from a prejudiced view. This also seems to be the case when he writes that Strome "delivered himself of various witty and ill-natured remarks upon Jews and Judaism, which were duly laughed at, but were considered to be in rather bad taste."[13] But these attempts at mitigation of prejudice are hardly borne out by the conception of Jews underlying his own allusions to them. Basic to the book is the contrast between the upstanding Anglo-Saxon Strome and the dishonorable, weak Jew Selim Fawley, not to speak of his mercenary father.

Hawthorne also contrives to throw in some remarks about the religious intolerance of Jews through Duncan, an old Scottish servant at Dene Hall, Mary's ancestral residence. When told that he is to have a Jewish master in Mary's husband, Selim, Duncan remonstrates: "I'm thinking it wad gar me feel queerly to be taking my orders frae onybody that didna bear the name o' Dene; mair by token if he's ane o' they Jew bodies (begging your ladyships's pardon) that crucified the blessed Saviour." But Mary replies that "Mr. Fawley is not a Jew exactly."[14]

Julian Hawthorne's introduction of a Jewish impresario in *Beatrix Randolph* is a sign of the widening occupational scope of the immigrants from Germany and East Europe, both as performers and managers in theater and music. A Jewish theater manager appears also in Ellen Olney Kirk's *Midsummer Madness* (1884), a story of upper-middle-class society life near Philadelphia. Some young people engage Mr. Stein to produce and direct a play written by one of the main characters. He is presented without stereotyped Jewish features of any kind, but rather those of the artistic temperament, including an unbearable temper when his amateur actors perform badly.

Mrs. Kirk's *Queen Money* (1888) centers on stock speculators, but also describes artistic circles in New York. Early in the novel a literary dinner for the author of a successful new "realistic" novel, Mr. Roth, who is not designated as Jewish but is likely to have been, takes place. The absence of any ethnic or religious allusion is an indication of a tolerance that was not prevalent among novelists of the times. This is borne out not only by her restraint in drawing Mr. Stein in *A Midsummer Madness* without falling into anti-Jewish clichés, but also by her treatment of the Jewish speculator in *Queen Money*. A group of brokers has made a killing in the market, and Jacobs suggests spending some of their money on an elaborate dinner. To a "fastidious" remonstrance, "Oh, Jacobs!" by one of the non-Jewish brokers, Otto March, hero of the novel, replies: "Oh, come now, don't be so aristocratic. We are all in the same business. I don't see why we should look down on Jacobs. He is a good fellow in his way. . . . I don't see that he is any more sordid, any more corrupt than anybody else" who reaped the rewards of the speculation. But even Mrs. Kirk cannot refrain from alluding to the Jew as "the little black-eyed, hook-nosed Jacobs."[15]

Considering the solid market value of the conventional Jew in the novel, it is not surprising that F. Marion Crawford, one of the most successful novelists of the latter years of the century, whom Alfred Kazin has characterized as one of the "cynical businessmen of letters . . . who had made a good thing of superplush fiction,"[16] introduces the Jew into half a dozen of his novels. In his day Crawford was an even greater celebrity than Henry James or Howells. He was converted to Catholicism and lived out his life in Italy after 1883. He was a protagonist of romance and a vociferous leading opponent of realism as espoused by Howells. All his novels with Jewish characters, which are also travel books in a sense, are set in Europe or farther East. Except in one novel, however, he uses the Jew more for exotic potentialities than to give the reader the conventional thrill from Jewish wickedness.

A curious use of the Jew occurs in Crawford's *Mr. Isaacs, a Tale of Modern India* (1882). The titular character is not Jewish, but adopts a Jewish name for business reasons. An American in India meets Mr. Isaacs, expresses puzzlement at his nationality, and asks how he came by the name. Mr. Isaacs replies that he is a "pure Iranian" and is a dealer in precious objects. The name, he explains, "has an attractive Semitic twang that suits my occupation, and is simpler and shorter for Englishmen to write than Abdul-Hafiz ben-Isak, which is my lawful name."[17] But the original for Mr. Isaacs was actually a Jew. While on a journey to Simla, India, in 1879, Crawford met Alexander M. Jacobs, who claimed to be a Turk, but was actually a Jew born near Constantinople. Jacobs had been the slave of a wealthy pasha who had educated and then manumitted him. Jacobs made a pilgrimage to Mecca disguised as a Muslim and finally settled in India. Why in his book Crawford should have reversed the identification of the original from an actual Jew who tried to conceal his Jewish origin to a fictional character who adopted a Jewish identity for "business reasons" is anyone's guess.

Crawford shifts the scene to Babylon for his *Zoroaster* (1885), in which the cause given for Zoroaster's three-year retirement to solitude in the wilderness (from which he emerged to found a new creed) is his frustrated love for Nehushta, "daughter of the Kings of Judah." Zoroaster is a warrior and a disciple of the prophet Daniel, who is depicted in the usual patriarchal manner. A blue-eyed, golden-haired villainess, Atossa, has deceived Nehushta into believing that Zoroaster loves Atossa. But Nehushta learns that he really loves her; they are reunited, but are slain in each other's arms by rebels.

In *Khaled* (1891) which is set in Arabia, Crawford briefly introduces a Jew, the sultan's physician; this doctor, said to be a supremely wise man, ascribes the cause of the sultan's murder to astrological movements.

The Jew receives more extended treatment in several other novels by Crawford. A novel set in Turkey, *Paul Patoff* (1887), gives Crawford the opportunity to describe the Jewish quarter and bazaars of Constantinople. While on the way to the Jew Marchetto's jewelry and rug shop in the bazaar, the Russian diplomat Paul Patoff sees "the quarter where the Spanish Jews have their shops and collect their wonderful mass of valuables, chiefly antiquities, offering them for sale in their little dens, and ever hungry for a bargain."

There is the customary allusion to an ordinary exterior concealing a rich interior:

It may now be supposed that the Jews have made large fortunes in the interval, but the fact is not apparent in any way; the uncertainty

of property in Turkey forcing them to conceal their riches, if they
have any. Their shops are fairly clean, but otherwise they are humble, and the best and most valuable objects are generally packed
carefully away in dark corners and produced only when asked for.
. . . But the Jews have almost a monopoly of everything which comes
under the head of antiquities, and it is with them that foreigners
generally deal. They are as intelligent as elsewhere, and perhaps
more so, for the traveller of today is a great cheapener of values.
Moreover, the Stamboul Jews are most often linguists. They speak
a bastard Spanish [Ladino?] among themselves; they are obliged to
know Turkish, Greek, and a little Armenian, and many of them
speak French and Italian intelligibly.[18]

The dealer in precious objects, Marchetto, is a key figure in the
plot, since it is through a watch pawned in his shop that the kidnaped
Alexander, brother of Paul Patoff, is traced. Marchetto is described
as a "fat man, with red hair and red-brown eyes." When he is pressed
to tell where he obtained Alexander's watch, he is reluctant to swear
to the truth of his reply, "for no people are so averse to making a
solemn oath as the Hebrews, as perhaps, no people are more exact
in regard to truth when so made to bind themselves." Much ado is
made about the bargaining—surely not a peculiarly Jewish tactic in
the East—and Paul Patoff's mother is led to observe: "I fear that the
traditions of his race are very strong."[19] On the whole, in this novel
Crawford deals with the Jew at a benign distance.

The Jewish pawnbroker again enters in Crawford's sentimental
novel *A Cigarette-Maker's Romance* (1890), located in Munich. The
poor heroine comes to the pawnshop to sell her samovar and the
luxurious locks of her own hair. The pawnbroker and his wife have
"profiles of an outline disquieting to Christian prejudices" and speak
to their clients "in oily undertones"; among themselves they use
"unctuous tones of Hebrew." They know their business well and
drive a hard bargain. "The Hebrew and his wife," writes Crawford,
"did their business rapidly with sharpness and precision. Either of
them would have undertaken to name the precise pawning value of
anything on earth and, possibly, of most things in heaven, provided
that the universe were brought piecemeal to their counter."[20]

Thus far we have found Crawford to assume a conventional attitude toward the Jews without much intensity of feeling one way or
the other. But in *The Witch of Prague* (1890) he swings from idealization to denigration. A central character, Israel Kafka, is a "young
man of singular beauty" who "represented the noblest type of the
Jewish race"; he is likened to a mountain eagle. He is in love with
Unorna, the "witch" of Prague, but she loves a Christian. Much
claptrap ensues, involving hypnotism and experimentation with a

postponement of death. A walk through the Jewish quarter of Prague evokes a sinister description by Crawford that might have come out of a contemporary anti-Semitic tract. Unorna and her lover walk in the Jewish quarter

through narrow and filthy streets thronged with Hebrew faces and filled with the hum of low-pitched voices chattering together, not in the language of the country, but in a base dialect of German [Yiddish?]. They were in the heart of Prague, in that dim quarter which is one of the strongholds of the Israelite, whence he directs great enterprises and sets in motion huge financial schemes, in which Israel sits, as a great spider in the midst of a dark web, dominating the whole capital with his eagle's glance and weaving the destiny of the Bohemian people to suit his intricate speculations. For throughout the length and breadth of Slavonic and German Austria the Jew rules, and rules alone.[21]

In the Jewish cemetery Unorna tries to command her beloved, under hypnotism, to love her, but she fails. Kafka, who has been a witness of the scene, cruelly laughs at her failure. Enraged, Unorna hypnotizes him and forces him to witness the martyrdom of Simon Abeles, the seventeenth-century Jew of Prague who was crucified by his fellow Jews because he became a convert to Christianity. Crawford again invokes a picture of the Jewish quarter of Prague, "a writhing mass of humanity, intoxicated by the smell of gold, mad for its possession, half-hysterical with the fear of losing it, timid, yet dangerous, poisoned to the core by the sweet sting of money, terrible in intelligence, vile in heart, contemptible in body, irresistible in the cruelty of their greed—the Jews of Prague, two hundred years ago."

In sharp contrast is the face of Simon Abeles, the martyred convert, which "had on it all the lost beauty of the Jewish race, . . . the features, noble, not vulture-like," more the biblical Hebrew than the modern Jew. When Abeles returns to the Jewish quarter, announces that he is a Christian who does not fear death, and refuses to repent, he is crucified. But he is bound to the cross, not nailed, for the Jews "hold it unlawful to shed blood," and the rabbis "smile" as they look on the dead boy. When Kafka awakes and is told what has been done to him, as "the best type of his race, his blood boiled at the insult that had been put upon him," and though he loves Unorna, he would kill her. "The modern Hebrew of Western Europe might be indifferent in such a case, . . . but the Jew of the less civilized East is a different being, and in some ways a stranger." Kafka is prevented from carrying out the murder, but if he had done so, it would have "accorded well with the fierce traditions of ancient Israel."[22]

*   *   *

So great was the insensitivity to the Jewish sensibilities in the
1880s and 1890s that juvenile fiction, intended to instill virtue in the
young, also warned them that Jews were a money-hungry people.
The fictional dealings of genteel little boys and girls with Jewish
pawnbrokers convey this instructive lesson. In Mrs. Julie P. Smith's
Blossom-Bud and Her Genteel Friends (1883), young Clovis runs away
from home. To obtain some money, he tries to pawn a fur coat and
asks a policeman to recommend a pawnbroker. Clovis is indignant
that the policeman should think his uncle is a pawnbroker—and
Jewish! "What do you see in me that puts it into your head to think
my folks are in the old clothes line?" he asks. Directed to a pawnbroker's (in a chapter entitled "Isaacs Trades Mit Bolite Beoples"),
Clovis bargains with a Jew of accented speech, and "had small patience to wait the slow counting of the greasy bills which seemed to
stick like putty to the trader's fingers."[23]

A little Irish girl, Pansey, in Evelyn Kimball Johnson's *Errand Girl:
A Romance of New York Life* (1889), is subjected to sharp practice
from a "Jew storekeeper" on the Bowery from whom she buys a
piece of calico and buttons. "The crafty Jew" cheats her out of a few
pennies. Later, when Pansey's aunt, Mrs. Maloney, dies, she must
dispose of the furniture at a secondhand store. The woman at the
store is a "coarse-looking German," her husband Jacob is "fiendish
looking" and "an inhuman wretch," and their children are "little
black demons." The drayman carting her furniture prevents these
wicked people from getting her clothing as well as the furniture for
the three dollars they give her, and Pansey thanks him "for his
interference to save the clothing from the clutches of the crafty Jew
dealer." When a doctor learns from Pansey what she has been paid
for the furniture, he exclaims: "The robber! He ought to be arrested
for taking such cowardly advantage of an unprotected orphan girl."
And lest the young reader fail to learn the lesson, the author has
Pansey conclude: "Poor Auntie used to say nobody could ever get
justice from a Jew dealer."[24]

It seems, however, that some Jews were not quite as socially
undesirable as thieves. This is one lesson that Frank R. Stockton
meant to convey to young people in his *Stories of Three Burglars*
(1889). A kidnaper relates how he once got jailed. He has been
hired to abduct a young girl from boarding school to restore her to
her father, who is divorced from her mother. He apprehends the
wrong girl, who turns out to be a "little Jew," the daughter of Mr.
Groppeltacker, who runs a corset shop on Broadway. When the
original employer discovers the mistake, he refuses to pay the kid-

naper: "Do you think I'd pay you anything for that little Jew?" The kidnaper then bargains with the girl for payment to take her home, since she doesn't want to return to school. She "bargains shrewdly," writes Stockton, and the kidnaper adds: "I was tickled to see how sharp that little Jew gal was." Bargaining again takes place with the father of the Jewish girl. He frustrates the kidnaper's attempt at robbery and contrives to have him taken by the police. "Aunt Martha," to whom the kidnaper is telling this story, then says: "Well, I don't approve the Groppeltacker sort of people, but if there were more of that kind I believe there would be fewer of your kind."[25]

An effort at a "balanced" view of the Jew is attempted in several books for young people by Columbia English professor Brander Matthews. In *A Tale of Twenty-five Hours* (1892), written by Matthews and George H. Jessop, a Columbia Law School professor, Paul Stuyvesant suspects the artist Charley, his fiancée's brother, of having stolen a Titian. Stuyvesant investigates the matter by visiting the pawnshop of Michael Zalinski, who is, he thinks, a "fence" and "dealer in stolen goods"; Zalinski is "a Polish Jew . . . not yet wholly Americanized," a "New York Fagin," who differs from the original only in that he lives under different conditions forty years later. He speaks with "a marked foreign accent, not exactly German, but not unlike it," which one may assume to be a Yiddish accent. Zalinski's face "was a perfect network of wrinkles; and a curious twitch which elevated one side of his upper lip at short intervals, after the manner of a snarling dog, whether rising from habit or infirmity, added a very peculiar character to the man's expression." Furthermore, he is thought to be "in communication with thieves in all the capitals of the world." Nevertheless, the even-handed authors remark that "he has his good points and his bad—like the rest of us."[26]

Stuyvesant finally learns that his suspicions about the robbery are unfounded. Charley has only been buying antique frames from Zalinski, and has surreptitiously copied the Titian. Despite Zalinski's innocence in this particular case, and the author's concession that he is not altogether bad, the impression left is hardly a pleasant one.

In another junior novel by Matthews, *Tom Paulding* (1892), the balance between good and bad Jews is more exact. The teenage heroes of the book are in New York to hunt down a treasure buried by a Revolutionary War ancestor. Tom Paulding and his friends find the treasure, but also discover that the buried money—which Simon Horowitz, "a newly arrived German," had paid to their ancestor in the land sale—is counterfeit. Later in the story, however, a "good" Jew is encountered. Joshua Hoffman, writes Matthews, "was once one of the richest and one of the best men in New York; a man good himself and never tired of doing good to others; a man full of public spirit and leading in noble public enterprises; a man who considered his great fortune as a trust for the benefit of those who had been less fortunate."[27] Neither of these figures is actually designated as a Jew by Matthews, but the author's intentions are obvious.

Thus the image of the Jew projected to the youth in the junior books is not appreciably different from that in the popular novel.

In William C. Hudson's detective novel, *On the Rack* (1891), a pawned watch is the key to the solution of a murder. The watch is traced to "Mandelbaum's place in Rivington Street," and the author explains, in case the reader has not guessed, that "this receiver of stolen goods was ostensibly a dealer in second-hand goods of every description." Only after Mandelbaum is threatened with jail does he offer the watch for sale, "trembling in every limb, so frightened was he." In his nasal accent, he agrees; "Vell, Mister Lowe, you half such nice vays, I can refuss you noddings." He takes them to another room, "taking care to call a dark-eyed daughter of Judah to occupy the room with them." But Mandelbaum tricks them into paying separately for the watch and its chain, and, Lowe admits, "the Jew bests me."[28]

An overcoat pawned to Isaac Zcayski in the "quarter of Polish Jews" similarly helps solve the mystery of *The Disappearance of John Longworthy* (1890), by Maurice Francis Egan. The foray into the Jewish section is a hazardous enterprise for the detective, Miles Gilligan, for he there "permitted himself to be almost torn to pieces by the proprietors of the various caves; for their favorite method is more forcible than that of a spider who wanted to entice the fly into his parlor. A man who falls into the hands of two of these old-clothes dealers will be so tattered and torn by the time they let him go that he will need new attire." He comes upon the coat of the vanished Longworthy, and, "after some haggling, he paid just half of what Isaac asked for it."[29] However, Isaac denies knowledge of how he got the coat, even after being offered bribes.

Considerable jejune theorizing about Jews appears in several stories by the prolific New York novelist Edgar Fawcett. Redress for the Jews was not included in the reforming zeal of Fawcett, whose fiction criticized the treatment of Negroes and ex-convicts, and satirized New York high society, especially the social competition of the Dutch patricians and the new plutocrats. In *The Evil that Men Do* (1889) Fawcett relates how Clara, an innocent nineteen-year-old girl from Peekskill, is victimized in New York City by "clannish" Jews. She hires a sewing machine and is employed in the clothing shop of the Rosenheims, having been recommended for the job by her Jewish landlady on Amity Street. But when her landlady's brother, who "thought himself very handsome, with his red lips and oily black curls," harasses her, she repels him. The landlady orders Clara out of her house because the brother, on whom she "dotes," has lied about Clara's behavior, "and then you've seen how Jews cling together."[30] Clara is soon after deprived of her job, because the Rosenheims are friends of the landlady, who must have influenced them to dismiss Clara.

In a later story, *New York, a Novel* (1898), Fawcett presents a deeply evil Jewish presumed brother and sister, who are later revealed as lovers. The ex-convict George Oliver gets work in a sailor's tavern on South Street, above which is a boardinghouse kept by "a Polish Jewess," Mrs. Volaski. She invites George to a party attended by Cuban sailors and has Polish Jewish girls brought in to entertain them, since non-Jewish girls refused to attend such a disreputable party. Inevitably a fierce brawl ensues, and the police are summoned. Enter Mrs. Volaski's "brother," John Lysko, who bribes the police and ends the affair.

In describing John Lysko to George, Mrs. Volaski theorizes about the Jews, no doubt reflecting Fawcett's own peculiar views. Lysko, she says,

must be awful rich. But he goes on with his junk shop on Pike Street just the same. That's the way with us Jews all over the world! That's why they can't kill us. We're a wonderful people. Any other, stamped on, spit on, as long as we've been, would have died out ages ago. My brother's a true Jew, though. He's full o' the old tough smartness; he can *smell* a dollar ten times further than I can see one.

George's own views on Lysko really complement hers. Lysko, opines George, is "a miserly, bloodless creature, in whom all the worst characteristics of his race seemed concentrated." George has not been invited to the party out of friendship, but because Lysko has a proposal to make. Lysko "spoke English almost perfectly, and with none of his sister's hissingly sharp accent. It was said of him that he had both brains and education of a superior kind, . . . [and] had amassed astonishing wealth." Lysko explains to George why he has extricated his sister from trouble with the police: "We Jews are clannish; we stick together."

The offer Lysko makes to George indicates that he is aware of

George's criminal background and lack of money. George fears the
offer is evil, because he says, Lysko is cruel. Yes, replies Lysko, "I
am cruel. I probably got my perfectly bloodless and heartless way
of looking at people, at life, from hundreds of persecuted Hebrew
ancestors. You cannot expect grapes from thistles. I dare say that I
represent the accumulated spite and rancour of many centuries."[31]
Lysko offers George ten thousand dollars if he will set fire to the
property of five people, including Lysko, so that they might collect
the insurance. This rounds out Fawcett's collection of typical Jewish
activities, since the accusations of committing arson for the purpose
of collecting insurance was one of the Jew-baiting clichés of the
period. The reformed George accepts the proposal only as a means
of exposing and finally trapping Lysko.

The unfavorable stereotyped treatment of the Jew was almost
universal during these latter years of the century. Thus a noted
immigrant writer like Hjalmar Hjorth Boyesen presented a no less
invidious picture of the Jew than was presented by the native Anglo-
Saxon. Boyesen, who had immigrated from Norway in 1869, became the editor of a Norwegian paper in Chicago; in 1873 and later
he published several novels of Norwegian immigrant life in the
United States. He also was a professor of German at Cornell and
later Columbia University. After 1891 he became a disciple of Howells's realism.

In 1883 he published anonymously a novel of New York life, *A
Daughter of the Philistines.* His rendering of a Wall Street broker,
Simon Loewenthal, is merciless, and the delineation of Simon's victi-
mized half sister, Rachel, is altogether stereotyped and patronizing.
Simon speaks with a heavy accent, has a "thick, hooked nose," and
is obsequious to non-Jews. He succeeds in deceiving the successful
Western businessman Zeke Hampton, who now lives on Fifth Ave-
nue, into investing in a spurious mining concern. The credulous
Hampton remarks: "He is an honest old soul, even though he is a
Jew."

Hampton's daughter, Alma, wants to make money, to "take a
flyer," so she goes to Simon to make an investment. She overhears
Simon say to a client: "Vell, vhen you vant gash, den Simon is your
man." She is repelled: "She never imagined that any human being
could be so repulsive as this Jew, and the idea of making a confidant
of him seemed so revolting that she wondered that she could for a
moment have harbored it." But she overcomes her disgust, and
Simon, sensing her hostility, reassures her: "Dere is koot Shews unt
pad Shews, Mees, unt Simon is von off de koot Shews."[32]

What Alma has overheard is Simon's offer to the engineer Wellingford of thirty thousand dollars' worth of stock in the mine if he will publicly endorse a favorable assay, and Wellingford's virtuous spurning of the offer. "Allow me," he tells Simon, "as a mark of my respect, to mail you a copy of the ten commandments, which you remember were given to your fathers for the rectification of their natural crookedness." Boyesen later notes that Simon did apply the Mosaic law in business "within the tribe," for "he would no more have thought of cheating a Hebrew than he would have thought of neglecting an opportunity for cheating a Christian." Wellingford tries to dissuade Alma from doing business with Simon by asserting that "every time he cheats a Gentile he performs a good action to a Jew, leaving himself, however, always a fair margin of profit."[33] Alma goes through with her investment, however. The encounter with Wellingford at Simon's eventuates in their becoming engaged.

In conformity with the formula, Simon's half sister, Rachel, is described as possessing a beautiful operatic voice; she is lovely, but not *too* Jewish: "Her features, which had an alabaster clearness, did not deny their origin, but they were yet in their first splendor of youth, when nationality only asserts itself as a hardly perceptible undertone in the purely human beauty." She had "the rich physical charm of Oriental womanhood." Simon had refused proposals of marriage to Rachel from "several gentlemen with Oriental noses" because he wished her to marry a great man of his people.

During the summer Simon sends Rachel to the same summer hotel attended by Alma. Alma is uncomfortable with her Jewish acquaintance, because "she shared to the full the fashionable prejudices, [and] she was inclined to resent this Semitic invasion as a personal affront."[34] But Alma's curiosity about the Jews leads her to speak to Rachel, and Rachel becomes an ardent admirer of Alma's. Rachel also falls under the spell of Alma's brother, Walter, but he is uncomfortable about their growing friendship and leaves.

However, Walter Hampton is too far gone in infatuation. He visits Rachel clandestinely and convinces her to elope. He succeeds in overcoming her "Jewish prejudices," and, being hopelessly in love, she consents to being married by a clergyman. The minister is not at home, and Walter sets her up in an establishment as his mistress. She does not understand his intentions, but on a yacht trip to Canada she overhears Walter make cruel remarks about her and disclaim any intent to marry. The shocked Rachel goes back to New York, where, after some adventures, she ends up as a prima donna in opera in New York.

In revenge, Simon vows to ruin Walter's father by saddling him with culpability for the spurious investment in mining that Zeke has sponsored and to send him to prison, while Simon maneuvers himself out of the debacle without a loss. Thus, notes Boyesen, Simon "gratified his desire for vengeance, without too great a risk to his pecuniary interests; and he vaguely felt, as one of the remnant of the chosen people whom the Lord had commanded to spoil the Gentiles, that he was an instrument of justice in the hands of Jehovah." But Hampton dies after he learns that the mine is worthless, and when Walter encounters Simon, he draws a gun. "Simon, in his fright, had dropped on the floor, [and] was slowly rising and trying to steal away unobserved."[35] By the time the novel ends, Boyesen has pulled out all the stops on the negative Jewish stereotype.

The fin-de-siècle dandy Edgar Saltus also made his contribution to the gallery of wicked Jews. His villainous Isaacstein in *Enthralled* (1894) suggests the medieval notion of the Jew as devil. He is "a fat man with a hook in his nose," has "red hair, squat features, and projecting teeth," and is told he has "no conscience."[36] He becomes acquainted with an adventurer, Quain, at a gambling house. Isaacstein invites Quain to elope with an heiress and offers to cooperate in poisoning her father before he can change his will, for which he demands 10 percent of the $20 million legacy Quain will receive. But it turns out that Quain is the illegitimate son of the girl's father, and consequently her half brother. The two plotters contrive to make the world believe that Quain has committed suicide, then Quain returns as Lord Cloden, with Isaacstein as his valet, after Isaacstein has arranged for him to be disguised by plastic surgery in England. As the English lord, Quain succeeds in becoming engaged to the heroine, but a detective exposes his real identity to the girl and Quain is arrested. Throughout, Isaacstein is the brains behind all the criminal activities.

Not all Jewish characters in the novels of the period were deeply evil, however, and some were even human. A few brief, friendly allusions occur in the work of the reform-minded novelist Margaret Sherwood. In her *Henry Worthington, Idealist* (1899), the young economics professor of the title decides to investigate labor conditions at the local department store in a New England town. The first saleslady he encounters is a young Jewish girl, "black-haired, black-eyed," who heatedly repulses his inquiries because she fears reprisals from her employer. The author explains that this uncooperative attitude has been caused by a previously experienced "well-meant, philanthropic wrong." Wher. Annice, the daughter of the store owner and fiancée of the professor, comes to work at the store incognito to learn for herself about conditions there, her shock is cushioned by the Jewish girl, who shares her lunch with her. This thoughtfulness and the way the girls help one another "save it all from vulgarity, that quick, instantaneous elemental kindness that she met everywhere." Later Annice's aunt goes on a philanthropic mission to the slums. She encounters a "dirty little Jewish girl," who runs out and "clasped her hand. Mrs. Appleton put her fingers under the child's chin, and raised the little face toward her, then stooped, and almost kissed it." In an unusually human description of the dealers in old clothes, "she studied, with an interest that was favorably returned, the faces of dealers in old clothes, who stood shrouded in their long beards, at their shop doors."[37]

The acceptance of Jews in Philadelphia high society, though prejudice is by no means absent, is assumed in *The Confessions of a Society Man* (1887) by Samuel Williams Cooper, a Philadelphia lawyer who published the book pseudononymously. This presumed memoir of the society life of Richard Conway involves, among many others, relations with Jack Isaacs, whose mother came of a "very good Southern family," although his father was "an Israelite of no station." "Jack inherited . . . from his mother," writes Cooper, "a gentle demeanor and an ability to dance as well as any man in society; from his father, a talent for lending money at usurious interest." Jack has inherited little money from his father, "despite his racial qualities." Jack, it appears, is a gentleman usurer; he frequents the gaming tables and has a few hundred dollars available to lend. It was, writes Cooper, "much more convenient to borrow at usurious rates from Mr. Isaacs, the gentleman, than 'Mishter Isaacs,' the uncle, at the sign of the three balls—even if the rates were a little higher."

But Jack still seems to be a regular member of society, mingling easily with the others. In fact, he is a rival for the hand of an heiress, Ann Houghton, to whom Conway gets engaged. But Conway's attentions stray, and the engagement is broken off. The persistent Jack finally succeeds in winning Ann as his wife. Jack now no longer needs to work; he spends his time at "club-room windows," remarking "on the females who pass by." Conway thinks it to Jack's credit "that as soon as he could afford it he left off his usurious trade."[38] Although Cooper's urbane "society man" is not free from prejudice and although he personally dislikes Jack Isaacs, he questions Jack's presence in the society of "gentlemen" only because Jack lends money, not because he is Jewish.

A few years after this book appeared, the Jewish Publication Society brought out Cooper's fictional biography of Moses Montefiore for young people. It may well be that the connection was made with the Jewish publishing house through Cooper's affiliation with the Philadelphia branch of the Ethical Culture Society. *Think and Thank* (1890) is mainly the story of Montefiore's youth. He experiences anti-Semitism at school, but after he wins a fight against the school bully, the boys stop baiting him and the masters recognize his quality. He is a leader in all activities. His first impulse is to be a soldier like his uncle, but his mother dissuades him. His uncle reads him a sententious lecture on the meaning of his Jewishness, which sets for him the perspective of his life:

Our people have made the world nobler and better in all its history. Our faith is the cornerstone of the Christian religion; the laws, the philosophy, the poetry of our books, have left an influence on all mankind and taught them the unity of God, purity of human life, and charity to everyone—and yet we are despised. They have put upon us the bonds of slavery; they persecute us where we try to break them, and, after taking away our rights, condemn us, because we do not become great. . . . Use your life to help your fellow-men, to rescue your race and make the name of Jew known all over the world for what he is—the most intelligent, industrious and faithful of all men.

And young Moses is adjured to follow the family motto: "Think and Thank."[39]

The ambiguous attitude in the earlier book by Cooper is not unusual—indeed, more nearly usual. Caroline McCoy Willard's *Son of Israel* (1898) is a subtle example of this dichotomy. Her hero, David Rheba, is a fine silversmith in Odessa in the 1840s. David, born in Nazareth, has "thick, long, wavy, red-gold hair and a close curling beard which showed the outline of a strong, masterful chin and finely shaped mouth. . . . The whole face was of the highest Eastern type, with its fire and mysticism." This resemblance to Jesus is intentional, as the author is at pains to point out in several places. David's hair, she writes, is "the colour some artists give to the hair of Christ," and an innkeeper's wife remarks that David's hair is like that of Christ in her icon, whereupon he replies: "I too am a Nazarene." Not only his hair, but his character is suggestive of Christ's in its spirituality.

There are other Jewish characters in the novel: the aging, sinful but ultimately self-sacrificing ballerina La Meldola; six-year-old Salome, who promises to be a great dancer; the impresario Daniel

Pereira, who is generous to genuine artists and businesslike with careerists in art; and others. But all are treated sympathetically.

On the other hand, the author's stereotyped notion of Jews creeps out perhaps unawares. The Russian aristocrat Marya Volkenoff finds David "not the type of Jew she was used to meeting in Odessa." David's English friend, John Pemberton, tells him he is not at all "like the regulation Jew." When Marya's fanatical anti-Semitic husband, Michael, sees David, he is surprised to find him unlike "the type of Jew common in Russia, with the hideous side-curls and close-cropped head."[40] When dealing directly with a Jewish character, the author is sympathetic but the unfavorable stereotype remains fixed in the back of her mind.

The author's attitude is somewhat out of the ordinary in another respect: her Christianity lacks the dogmatic basis for anti-Semitism. David holds that Jesus is not to blame for Christian persecution of the Jews. After Jesus died he was worshiped as a God, "and his beautiful creed was degraded by ritual and ceremony. . . . It was not Jesus of Nazareth who brought all these sufferings upon us; he was good." David and the Christian girl Olga may marry because David believes Jesus himself was a good man, and Olga realizes that the Christ to whom she prays was a Jew, one of David's people. "Why," she asks, "if they are his people, the people of our Lord, should they be treated so cruelly?" On the other hand, the dogmatic New Testament conception of the Jews as the accursed people who killed Jesus is articulated by the vehement anti-Semite Michael Volkenoff, who says to David: "I know your race! A race of usurers, thieves, spawn of the Evil One, with God's curse tacked to it evermore."[41] The author thus projects both Jewish and Christian characters on a non-sectarian level with a minimum of favoritism. But she is most comfortable with uncommon Jews, who are not "like the regulation Jew."

A story of the Russian persecution of Polish Jews is told in a poorly written novel, *Hernani the Jew* (1897), by A. N. Homer. The Jew Kasimir Hernani is the greatest banker in Warsaw, a financial genius, who is implicated in the Polish uprising of 1863. The governor-general of Poland, Hourko, falls in love with Hernani's ravishingly beautiful wife, Sara. Hourko uses Kasimir's plotting against the regime to threaten Sara with his imprisonment if she does not become Hourko's concubine. For his part, Kasimir suspects that Sara is having an affair with Hourko, unaware that she is considering Hourko's offer only in order to save her husband from imprisonment. She also believes that she can then persuade Hourko to give up his persecution of the Jews. After an insurrectionary engagement led by Kasimir, Sara agrees to become Hourko's mistress in exchange for Kasimir's life and freedom. Before the bargain is consummated, however, a treacherous aide of Hourko's is bribed to see Kasimir and Sara safely over the border, and they escape. Says Hernani:

The Pole has looked down upon the Jew, perhaps cursed and spat at him. What of that? The whole world has done the same. By this time we should be used to it, and yet, that same world might have learned the lesson we have tried to teach it for so long now—that it may hang, burn, and do its best to destroy us, but it will not succeed. We shall spread over the earth and flourish, for the God of Israel fights for us.[42]

The author's goodwill is patent, but his characters are drawn from a well-worn literary stock.

It was not often that a realistic balance was struck between idealization of the Jew—as exemplified in Homer's novel—and ambivalence, as displayed in Henry Gillman's novel, *Hassan: A Fellah* (1898). Gillman was an archeologist and botanist of note. In 1886 he was United States consul in Jerusalem, and the story is an ethnological study of the Muslim and Jewish societies in Palestine, embodied in a novel of six hundred pages. While he was consul, he demonstrated his conviction of the principle of equality before the law by his successful resistance of the Turkish order to expel all Jews from Palestine, and carried the consuls of other great powers with him. He alludes to this event in the novel. The retired Jewish banker, Anselmo,

received the news, from the American consul, of the abrogation of the Sultan's firman or decree regarding the expulsion of the Jews. "Praise be to God, the consul has succeeded in this great deliverance of my people! His representations and dispatches have had the effect. Of all the consuls in Jerusalem, he was the only one who refused to aid, and even resisted the Turkish government in this work. . . . He was alone, but he remained firm."[43]

The checkered love story of the young Muslims Hassan and Hilwe, who belong to antagonistic tribes, is the central subject of the story, and the adventures of the young half Jew Leone Spollato are of secondary importance. Leone is the son of an Italian nobleman and a Jewish beauty from Palestine. He is summoned to Jerusalem from Rome to live with his rich uncle, Anselmo Jacobini. From the beginning it is clear that the author makes a distinction between "common" and "uncommon" Jews, that the disability of Jewishness is mitigated by the degree of remoteness from the "typical" physiognomy and manners. Leone's Italian uncle reassures him before he departs that "you must not imagine that those" of his mother's family "were of the common sort of Jew. The Jacobinis had made more than one intermarriage with some of the better class of Italian families. . . . They bore little or no trace of the ancient people in their appearance. At any rate, in the case of your mother, I may say, you would never have imagined her being of Hebrew descent." For his part, Leone is worried about the Jewish half of his heritage: "It almost makes me hate myself," he says. On the other hand, his uncle recalls that there was hardly a titled Spanish family that was not at some time "contaminated" by the *"mala sangre*—bad blood . . . of the house of Judah."[44]

The author adds that in such remarks the uncle's "innate prejudice" has gotten the better of him. Yet the uncle's point of view is sustained in the author's own comments. For he adds in his own voice that the Jews are only what their history would lead one to expect: "Never," he writes, "had any people of their time had greater light. Never have any people so sinned against the light as they have sinned. Never have any people been so disgraced and degraded. . . . These are the stiff-necked, adulterous people, according to the description of their own prophets." Their rigid observance of Mosaic law has made them "past masters in the art of evasion." The author's description of Leone's uncle in Jerusalem, Anselmo, shows him also to have only peripherally Jewish traits: "Though the features were decidedly Jewish, they were of the best Hebrew type, and a certain refinement, perhaps of Italian origin, subdued and qualified traits which might otherwise have been of severe or unpleasing character." In contrast there is Rabbi Ben Cohen, who has "a hooked nose of monstrous proportions and shape, [which] gave an indescribably malicious aspect." The rabbi's face is not untypically Jewish, with the "sharp, piercing eyes, with acquisitive gleam, and the beak-like noses, curving over the flabby, protruded lips, [which] give an aspect of cruelty to many of their faces."[45]

The author's negative feeling toward the Jew, as manifested by differentiation among the Jews, coexists with positive attitudes. At first Leone is intensely prejudiced against his mother's relatives. But his love and respect for his admirable Uncle Anselmo and his immersion in the atmosphere of Jerusalem change him. The Jew "was

growing strong within him and gaining the ascendancy." His Jewishness had "clutched him and was impelling him—hugging him to its
heart." He perceives that his philanthropic uncle helps not only Jews
but also Turks and Muslims, and he is won over to remaining with
Anselmo as his prospective heir.

In another move away from Jewish particularism and toward universality, Gillman writes, in the words of his fictional consul, that
"though it seems strangely to be overlooked, Christ had in his veins
the blood of the ancient people of the land—Canaanites, Moabites,
Ammonites, and others, as well as Israel. I am glad of it. There is
a profound meaning in it." The vehement anti-Semitism of the Muslim Kadra is implicitly condemned by the author: "I can only despise
and loathe" Jews, says Kadra. "They are like walking dunghills.
. . . The Jew smells money as you would smell the fumes of roast
meat." Then, in a comment that has a prophetic ring of future Arab
attitudes to it, Kadra goes on: "These Jews are crowding into the
country and filling it. They say they will again possess the land. They
would deprive us of our inheritance, claiming they own it, through
an old covenant with Chalil-Abraham. . . . The Turk is bad enough.
But if the Yahoodi governed, it would be past bearing. There would
be peace for no one."[46]

If a benevolent ambiguity pervades Henry Gillman's novel, an
ambiguity that is finally resolved into deep hostility and an arrogant
sense of superiority is observable in the work of a popular and
prolific novelist of the 1890s, Richard Henry Savage. Like F. Marion
Crawford in the previous decade, Savage wrote romantic, melodramatic novels set in exotic locations—Russia, Poland, the Balkans,
the Near East—and the Jew is present in all of them as an added
exotic element. Savage had traveled widely, and we may assume that
he was drawing a self-portrait when he described, in *Delilah of Harlem* (1893), "William Maxwell, critic, author, and globe-trotter
. . . [whose] roving tastes had driven him over the world, from Corea
to Egypt, from South America to Siberia, in search of fresh pabulum
for that great reading monster—the American public."[47]

Judging from his treatment of Jews in these novels, he hardly
diverged from the conventional attitudes toward them. Indeed, he
seems to have assumed the notions of racist superiority expressed by
his aristocratic Anglo-Saxon characters. There is nothing in his books
to contradict the imperialistic-racist assertion made by a sea captain
in *A Modern Corsair* (1897) that his experience had taught him "what
all the dark-skinned races are. I learned an easy lesson in the Indian

Mutiny. I saw later the horrors of Soochow, and I had the delightful pleasure of shelling the unfaithful Chinese at Hankow in 'sixty-six.' I give no credence to any of them—these dark-skinned scoundrels —after seeing my brother Zachary wager his life upon it and lose!''[48] Negative, anti-Semitic clichés about Jews predominate in his fiction, although he does condescendingly depict a few Jews as positive characters.

Perhaps the most egregiously anti-Semitic passage in his work is his description of the shtetl (although he doesn't use that term) of Novokraina on the Bug River. This town, he writes in *The White Lady of Khaminavatka* (1898), is the "home of the trading vultures who fatten on the Russian peasant. . . . In all the squalid city of three thousand souls, were only domiciled a hundred Russian soldiery and officials—the whole population being the orthodox Polish cult of Jews who trafficked in usury and, with glib cunning, fattened upon the toil of the flaxen-haired, thick-headed Russian peasantry of a hundred and fifty square miles." Apparently all three thousand were engaged in usury, and none was productively employed. Moreover, they were, he writes,

cringing, cajoling, and insinuating, with their own secret mails— places of safe refuge and banking arrangements, herding in their synagogues and bath houses,—this pliant, docile, cowardly mass, without labor easily controlled the destinies of the Russian peasant woman's little annual marketings by usurious craft and ate up the profits of the million ruble grain crop of the haughtiest nobles. . . . Masters and tyrants of commerce,—these ruling slaves dominated a city. . . . A death-in-life—the parasite fattening—the country decaying.[49]

This description is more extended than is warranted by the minor importance of the one Jewish character, "the Jew peddler Moschka [a derisive term for Moses]," who had witnessed a murder committed by the villain of this story in the Russia of 1865. Moschka and another character are apprehended for the murder. "Poor old Moschka,—peddler, thief and pander,—despised jew outcast" is dragged off to Siberia in chains for the murder he did not commit. Savage also refers to "the powerful Jewish syndicate . . . making heavy secret presents to the War Minister. . . . The Russians of pure race secretly mutinied to see these interlopers, backed by the ubiquitous Israelites, gathering in the profits of nearly all the governmental contracts."[50]

Another story by Savage set in contemporary Russia exploits the Jewish nihilist theme we have already met with. *My Official Wife*

(1891) is an early novel, written before Savage had started to burden his stories with complicated plots and pepper every page with exclamation points—consequently this simply plotted and rapid-moving book is more readable than his later ones. Savage never misses an opportunity to attach pejorative terms to Jews, like the "filthy Polish Jews with curls and greasy gabardines, money-changers" at the border of Russia. An American traveling to Russia, Colonel Arthur Bainbridge Lenox (Savage was himself a colonel), allows Helene, a beautiful young woman, to cross into Russia by posing as his "official wife." It turns out that she is a Jewish nihilist who is plotting to assassinate the tsar. Lenox discovers the plot in time to foil it. Helene is contemptuous, upbraiding him for preventing the tsar's death, "a blow that would have given Russia perhaps freedom; a blow for the wronged, the oppressed, the down-trodden under the heel of this tyrant." Lenox replies: "You speak like a Pole or a Jewess!" "I *am both!*" she answers.[51] When her titled Polish father had married the daughter of a Jewish banker of Warsaw, both were persecuted for this; they had participated on the Polish side in the uprising of 1863–64 and were driven to their deaths by the Russians, leaving the infant Helene an orphan. After Lenox and Helene succeed in escaping from Russia, she vanishes into that mysterious limbo where one may suppose the nihilists lived.

Savage also attempted to portray several positive Jewish characters in his stories of Muslim lands. In *Lost Countess Falka* (1896) "the great diamond dealer of Constantinople," Faröe Moses, is, among other things, commander of a great network of spies used by the Russians throughout southeastern Europe and Turkey. His aid is enlisted in the rescue of the kidnaped Countess Falka. For her recovery, the reward held out to him by the villain is a Russian passport for any Jewish agent of his. Moses' men are useful for the purpose because they have developed a network of communication in Hebrew "from mouth to mouth," since "we, the despised Israelites, dare not write our secrets. The telegraph is denied to us!" Their experience in the Levant, says the author, has made them "the world's college of past masters in human duplicity."

At the same time, the American hero of the novel "easily saw that the Jew was honest! For, fear made him so!" Savage will not allow the Jew to be honest out of principle or human feeling. Nor can he be brave, but must be, as Savage has him, at least "timid." Moses is called variously "the timid old trader" or "the timid old Jew." How this trait is consistent with the hazardous occupation of spy master is not explained. Nor is it consistent with Moses' fervent pledge—quite proper for a mere Jew in the service of highborn Christians—that "the Christian maiden shall live! I swear it, even if I have to offer up my own life!" Thereat the grateful Russian count grasps the "trembling hands of the aged Hebrew jewel vender! 'We need your wisdom now, Moses! You shall have what no other man of your race has now, the right of ingress and egress all over Russia!' "[52]

Savage condescends in another novel, *In the Shadow of the Pyramids* (1897), to give a favorable character to a Jew. He is a key figure in a plot by British financiers to control the financial affairs of the Egyptian khedive, Ismail, and to get him deposed in favor of a financially more responsible Turkish viceroy or khedive. The khedive, it appears, "is in the hands of hungry Jews and base adventurers!" Zacharias, a banker, is "a slender, bright-eyed old man of sixty, whose flowing gray beard, bright eyes, well-curved nose and bent shoulders indicated the Hebrew money-changer!" When the young British hero learns that Zacharias is to be his liaison with his London employers, "the startled Briton" murmurs that "money makes strange friendships."

Gryffyth, the hero, visits Zacharias and finds the house and front rooms quite ordinary; but then he penetrates to a splendid concealed rear apartment, "replete with every modern luxury." Zacharias explains to his visitor: "Our hunted people . . . have become wise with dwelling in the courts of their enemies!" And he has another surprise for Gryffyth: "It would surprise you to know that I am a scholar, rather than a worshipper of the golden calf!" Gryffyth is impressed with the "simple dignity of the Hebrew."[53]

Zacharias thenceforth flits in and out of the story as a guide to Gryffyth's activities and as his defender in the intrigue-ridden Egyptian society. Our hero soon learns about "the wonderful nerve and sagacity of the veiled humble Jewish millionaire, 'a spider in king's palaces.' " However, when Zacharias is confronted with the responsibility of protecting the hero's life, he "clasped his trembling hands in a nervous affright!"

After the mission is successfully completed, Zacharias discusses the hardy survival of the Jewish people, in contrast to the fall of Greece and Rome and the like fate that will overtake even Western civilization, including Britain. "No nation in its gilded ages," he asserts, "ever recovers from the sway of the unbridled horrible vices of the dominant and corrupted class." Of all cultures, he goes on, "Israel—alone—has thriven in the house of the stranger, and,—never will her children disappear!" The reason for this is "the invincible family system of the Hebrew, the iron social armor of the Mosaic laws, [which] has built up in Israel, even while bending the back as servants, in a strange land!"[54]

In *A Modern Corsair* (1897) Savage returns to an anti-Semitic treatment of his Jewish characters, and his writing reeks of racist attitudes not only toward Jews, but toward nonwhite Eastern peoples. The plot is a highly melodramatic adventure story. Agents of Lloyds of London try to foil the scheme of a thoroughly wicked German Jew, Ernest Schnorr (snide wordplay on *"schnorrer"*?) who plans to collect insurance on a faked bill of lading by burning the old ship in which the cargo is supposed to have been carried. Schnorr is "red-bearded" and "master of all continental tongues and several Levantine languages" and is reputed on the London Exchange to be "a slick 'un"; he is "the greasy Hebrew." Indeed, Savage can hardly refrain from attaching the epithet "greasy" to anything Jewish. An account book is a "greasy Hebrew journal"; a "greasy smile" comes over a Jewish character's face; the Jewish woman Rebecca has a "greasy oriental beauty"; several Jews are men of "greasy magnificence." While Schnorr's ship is docked in London prior to its journey to an obscure Turkish cove, where it is to be set afire, Lloyds tries to buy part of the purported cargo from one of the presumed owners in order to gain access to the cargo, and then to expose the fraud. The "imitation cargo," says the Lloyds man, "is used by Polish Jews and fraudulent bankrupt dealers who sometimes cover the imposing stuff with a heavy fire insurance and then it strangely disappears in well-managed flames."[55]

Among the cargo owners in London whom Lloyds tries unsuccessfully to buy out is Isaac Meyer, who repairs to "Einstein's Coffee House." This kosher restaurant is presided over by a "motherly-looking Buda Pest Jewess." The place was "famed for 'Kosher' cooking, and sharp bargains, smuggled diamonds, stray jewels, shady notes, and stolen bonds often changed hands under the eyes of the portly Rebecca." Schnorr succeeds in buying up the cargoes so as to get out of London harbor with his cargo unexamined, but not before "with true Hebrew sagacity he had hastily removed all his own valuable records" from London. All to no purpose—our upright heroes, especially the young American reporter—outwit Schnorr; the ship accidentally explodes and goes down with Schnorr aboard. Toward the end of the action, which takes place in Smyrna, Savage observes that "the Turk has always been strangely tolerant of the inoffensive Jews, probably because they are not arms-bearers. And there are many worthy Israelites here!"[56]

In several stories set in the United States, Savage's American Jews are anti-Semitic stereotypes. A brief allusion to a pawnbroker is made in *Delilah of Harlem* (1893). The villain comes to the pawn-broker's shop of "the gentlemanly proprietor," Mr. Jacobs, in "the jungle of Third Avenue," to pawn a diamond necklace. Jacobs's "dark Semitic eyes flashed with joy as he fingered the rich bauble. His blue, close-shaven face purpled with the instant effort to appraise those gems to the last cent." Jacobs gives the villain a thousand dollars when he threatens to go elsewhere, and pays by drawing out "a greasy check-book."[57]

In another novel in which American Jews play a prominent part, *An Exile from London* (1896), Savage renders them as a pack of cheating villains. Not that non-Jews escape unscathed, for several of them are designated, together with their Jewish partner in a nefari-ous scheme, as "devoted worshippers of the Golden Calf"; and one other Jewish character is said to cast off his "servility" because he has discovered that "his Christian brothers could match the daring Isra-elite, and often 'go him one better' in calculating villainy!"

But these are asides. Savage concentrates with relish on his villain-ous Jews, each worse than the other. Isidor Blum, who speaks with a purely German accent, is the leader of a band of brothers who are partners on the Rothschild model, located severally in New York, New Orleans, Fort Worth, El Paso, and Tucson. Blum has risen "from a vicarious sort of cotton-grabber in the Semitic camp follow-ing Banks's army, to a New Orleans trader, then, a New York wholesaler, and now, . . . the proud head of the chain of aggregated Blums, with their tentacles firmly fixed on the effluent and refluent trade" of the cities named. Isidor Blum has amassed a fortune by trading with both sides in the Civil War, as he has done later in the Indian wars. His brothers and cousins have, "since the piping times of the war, [come] from Frankfurt, Breslau, Vienna, and Budapest, yea, even from Warsaw and Cracow, to aid in distributing all profita-bly sold articles of use or ornament over that broad zone of the United States, now tributary to the Blums and their international tribesmen." Isidor Blum's wife, Rebecca, is "that portly dame, bediamonded like Esther."[58]

Isidor Blum and his two non-Jewish partners plot to gain control dishonestly of a productive mine in Arizona, and are determined to stop at nothing—not even murder—to do so. Their executive agent is the Jewish lawyer Moses Dalman, who is no less unscrupulous than they are. In fact, each party is elaborately scheming to double-cross the others and gain possession of the mine for himself. The assimilated Dalman is "an ingraft of Jewish blood upon the Americanized German . . . a type of 'Younger New Yorker up to date!' An *élève* of the public schools, gliding eel-like through Columbia College, and then fastening, leech-like, upon a 'confidential' practice," he was already rich, though not yet forty. Not to omit current elements of the stereotype, Savage adds that Dalman has "the Semitic love for art, music, and form." He is called a "coward," and as part of his plan to cheat everyone else out of the mine, he has underworld Jewish henchman steal documents and kill an obstructive Englishman. Dalman works in league with another Jewish lawyer, Max Rosendahl. They argue on opposite sides of the same case, and then "pool the resulting creamy spoils!"

As agent for the avaricious cabal, Dalman goes to Arizona and works with the Tucson Blum, Morris, to find and kill, if necessary, another human obstacle to their plan. Morris Blum is "the head of the 'dollar-snatching movement' in southern Arizona, and the spacious halls over Blum Brothers 'Palatial Golden-Rule Bazaar.' " He has joined the Episcopal Church " 'in order to grow up with the country,' and advance the moral interests of Blum Brothers."[59]

Not surprisingly, all the scheming, cheating, plotting villains are frustrated, and the mine ends up in the possession of its valid owner: English, Christian, and virtuous. But not before Savage has exhausted his arsenal of pejoratives on the Jewish characters. They are never simply evil men. Their evil doings are usually designated as "Hebrew," "Semite," "Israelite," and the like. Isidor Blum is "the Hebrew 'operator' . . . visibly perspiring in that inner Semitic excitement which always tells of precious 'gelt' endangered." Dalman thinks he "can depend on Blum brothers keeping faith with each other. They reserve their lies for *Christians and their customers.*" The participants at a poker game are "the Semitic jeunesse dorée"; Blum is that "old Hebrew schemer," "that Samson of Judaic finance"; his brother Morris is "the trading Hebrew."[60] Quite obviously, Savage did know a good deal about the post–Civil War activity of German Jewish entrepreneurs, and equally obviously he put the worst interpretation on that activity. Quite simply, he did not like Jews.

14

THE DIME NOVEL

The technological revolution in printing and the emergence of the American working class as a market for published matter in the 1830s gave rise not only to the penny newspapers but also to a mass popular literature. The new expanded audience offered a new source of profit for printers and publishers—mass production of sensational, melodramatic, and sentimental fiction on cheap paper, with small type in double columns and paper covers. This brought these commodities within the price range of the ordinary American worker. As early as the 1840s George Lippard's highly successful series of novels, beginning with the best-selling *The Quaker City* (1844), had appeared in this cheap format.

This form of publishing gathered momentum until it reached full exploitation in the "dime novel" launched by Erastus Beadle in New York City in 1860, an enterprise emulated by other publishers. Selling at ten cents, these novels rolled off the presses in the hundreds of thousands and formed a good part of the reading of the common man in many sections of the country. Their plots dealt with adventure and knavery and stock conceptions about heroism: the American Revolution, the Civil War, frontier life, especially themes of Indian enmity and cruelty, and the more lurid aspects of urban life. Detective stories also became extremely popular. The house of Beadle and Adams and many competitors continued to pour forth these novels in the hundreds until the 1890s, when the field was taken over by numerous series of adventure stories.

As might be expected, the Jew, both male and female, figured in familiar stereotyped form in many dime novels.[1] This fiction generally fell in with the popular mood of the times: it was nationalistic, and reflected nativist attitudes toward the immigrant, the Negro, the Indian, and the Jew. Several of the most prolific authors of dime novels were nativistic leaders. Sylvanus Cobb and Edward Z. C. Judson (alias Ned Buntline) were leaders of the Know-Nothing movement. (Judson's life was hardly less adventuresome and fantastic than his stories. In New York in 1849 he led the Astor Place rioters, who demonstrated violently against the British actor W. C. Macready when he played *Macbeth* at the same time as the American Edwin Forrest.) These authors were incredibly prolific. Judson was said to have published at least four hundred novels; Prentiss Ingraham, son of J. H. Ingraham, claimed that he wrote six hundred. It will suffice here to view a very small sampling of this voluminous outpouring of claptrap.

While the depiction of Jews is not always all negative, it is, as might be expected, both stereotyped and on a primitive level of characterization. Jewish women, unsurprisingly, are usually beautiful and often sympathetic characters. In Judson's early *Ned Buntline's Life Yarn,* first published in 1849, Ned saves Miriam from drowning. "She was a Jewess, and all of her famed nation's beauty seemed combined in her," writes Judson. She falls in love with her rescuer, revealing that her father has left her wealthy; but Ned, too young to marry, goes off to sea. When he puts in at Galveston twenty chapters later, he learns that Miriam is there, and the reader is asked: "Have you forgotten Miriam the fair Jewess? The sweet beautiful, generous Miriam?"[2] But nothing comes of this in the end.

In a later novel by Judson, *Rose Seymour* (1865), another Miriam, "a beautiful, fair Jewess," appears. She is the daughter of a pawnbroker, Aaron Hass, to whom the heroine, Rose Seymour, has repaired to pawn her mother's precious locket. Aaron looks at Rose "with a disgusting leer,"[3] accuses her of stealing the locket, and imprisons her. Miriam, for her part, is the victim of a daily flogging and is killed and buried under a plank, but reappears without the author's making clear whether she is a resurrected Miriam or a new Miriam.

When Judson tries his hand at historical fiction in *Morgan* (1861), he turns to the England of Charles II, and gives us an old Jew, Solomon, and the usual daughter, Miriam, who is "of that rare and striking beauty so peculiar to the women of the Jewish race." This time, however, Solomon loves his daughter more than his gold. Their home in the Jewish quarter has the usual rundown exterior and interior of "oriental luxury." She loves the royalist Morgan, who does not return her love but protects her from the lascivious King Charles. Miriam's rescue causes Solomon to acknowledge that some Christians may shed "a tear for the sorrows of a Jew." Solomon is so inspired by his daughter's virtue that he is led to realize that "I, like my child, begin to value gold less than I once did."[4]

Judson's relatively favorable, if patronizing, treatment of those

Jewish characters confirms the fact that at this date the Jews had not yet become one of the prime targets of the nativist movement, as they were to become later in the century.

An anonymous shocker of 1853, *Startling Disclosures!* reprinted for decades later, introduces an exotic, beautiful slave girl, Naomi, daughter of a wealthy Jew and a quadroon slave. Naomi is purchased by the villainous Henry Baldwin, as part of an estate, from a wealthy Charleston Jew. She lives in luxury in a ménage à trois with Baldwin and his wife, Esther. But when Naomi bears Baldwin's child, Esther in fury dispatches mother and child down a well, whereupon Baldwin hurls Esther into a chasm. In a second anonymous shocker published in the same year, *The Beautiful Jewess,* Charles Bernard saves the beautiful Rachel Mendoza from murder in a New York village and kills the attacker. The grateful girl tells Bernard the story of her life: "My parents were Hebrews, of great wealth, in Portugal." She has been forced into marriage with her cousin, Gabriel, who has married her for her money, but she manages to escape from him on her bridal night. Gabriel has pursued her and, in fact, it is Gabriel whom Bernard has killed. Rachel, an "oriental beauty" entertains Bernard in her apartment of "dazzling splendor."[5] Although of Jewish origin, she tells him that both she and her family are of the Catholic faith. Rachel marries Bernard, and then a bewildering, complicated, gory set of adventures follows in which Henry Baldwin of *Startling Disclosures!* is introduced, thus indicating a common authorship with that novel.

One endlessly meets the unscrupulous Jewish pawnbroker in these dime novels. In the anonymous postbellum *The Gypsy of the Highland; or, The Jew and the Heir,* the pawnbroker Goldschnapp is a money-obsessed blackmailer, an exploiter of profligates who extorts the patrimonies of those in desperate straits. His shop has the usual dilapidated exterior but richly furnished interior. And his beautiful daughter is saved from a forced marriage with the villain.

The vogue of the detective story led the Jew in the dime novels into a new role, that of detective, and appropriately enough, endowed him with the favorable characteristics of the new hero in literature. One example is the hero of Prentiss Ingraham's *Jew Detective* (1891). This prolific author, whose most noted achievement was a spate of stories about Buffalo Bill, had been a Confederate officer. He may have written up to six hundred dime novels, and he included Jews in a number of them. In his extended treatment of the Jewish detective Alvan Judah, Ingraham endows him with all the ideal attributes of non-Jewish heroes. Judah is "attractive-looking in the extreme" and has "a superb physique." Although he does, after all, have "the stamp of his race indelibly traced on the features of all of his blood," they are "so toned down as not to be at first recognizable." Moreover he had "a certain look of conscious power in his face," and the influence of his "dark eyes" amounted "almost to magnetism." Judah is charged with a murder and convicted on circumstantial evidence, but he is saved at the last moment by the confession of Cora Keene. When she hears that a Jew is accused of the murder, Cora cannot believe it, because "this is not the character of that people."[6] She convinces the judge that she killed in self-defense, and both she and Judah are freed.

Judah does not believe Cora to be the murderer and is determined to discover the real culprit. He later saves Cora from a runaway horse. After this demonstration of manly courage, they of course fall in love. Judah is employed by a pawnbroker, Emanuel Gaspar, and at this point Ingraham launches into an apology for pawnbrokers. Gaspar, he writes,

belonged to that much-abused but very necessary class of business men, who, if they do charge a large price for loans, save many a family from going hungry, and others from despair, for jewelry, bric-a-brac, odds and ends, and other extravagances indulged in with a plethoric pocket-book, come in handy to "make the pot boil," when fortune shines no longer. Alvan Judah knew, as others know, that pawnbrokers were not naturally heartless, and that many an act of charity was done daily by them toward their, in many cases, stricken patrons.

While studying law, Judah manages Gaspar's shop, to which Cora repairs one day to pawn her jewels, so as to be able to extricate her profligate brother, Frank, from gambling debts. Judah, now wealthy, sends money to Cora's family. In the meantime, after many daring adventures he has discovered that it was Frank who committed the murder for which Cora has confessed. When all is cleared up, Cora declares her love and they marry.

Yes [says Cora], I love you, and have done so since I saw you, under trial for your life here. You say that you are known as Judah the Jew. Well, I have been called Cora the Convict, and though I am not a Jewess, my Christian friends deserted me in my anguish and danger, and you have been my truest, best friend through all, and to you I now turn for happiness in life, for your people shall be my people, your creed my creed, and your God my God.[7]

Ingraham's occasional treatment of Jews as positive heroes and heroines in this story and in *Jule the Jewess* (1881) are quite unusual in the dime novel genre, where the negative stereotype was felt to be more easily effective with the reading public. More characteristic are the numerous Jews in Albert W. Aiken's dime novels, who are an unrelieved series of the worst stereotypes. Not much is known of the life of this writer of dime novels, except that he was an actor who came from a family of actors. Apparently he found novel-writing more lucrative than the theater, for he produced hundreds of novels. Although many of his stories are located in New York, Aiken also exploited the romance of the southwestern and far western frontiers.

Aiken's New York Jews are mostly pawnbrokers and nearly all are rich, though they profess poverty. In *The Phantom Hand* (1870), an impoverished actor pawns all his belongings at the shop of Abal Hameleck. The actor is astonished at the plain house in which Hameleck lives: " 'What, you live here? You who can buy a square mile of New York!' 'Hush!' cried the Jew nervously, 'I ish a poor man, s'help me. Very poor.' "[8]

The tired theatrical cliché of disguise as a Jew is introduced into *The Spotter-Detective* (1878), in which an aggressive peddler with a pack appears at the door; his "strong accent betrayed that he was a Jew." After he forces his way into the room and puts the handcuffs on the villain, he is revealed to be "Campbell, the Virginian."[9] The detective disguised as Jew is again used in *The Wolves of New York* (1881), in which the detective Joe Phoenix passes himself off as Moses Solomon, a Wall Street broker; he escapes physical description, but manifests his "Jewishness" by assuming an accented speech, rubbing his hands together while discussing business, and protesting poverty. Thanks to this disguise, he is able to get a true will assigned to an heir.

Aiken also exploits the new cliché of the 1870s and after: that of the nouveau riche, ostentatious, bejeweled Jew. In *The White Witch* (1871), Aiken introduces Herman Stoll, a recently enriched Jew whose hands were "coarse and clumsy, red in color and ugly in outline—the hands of a man accustomed to rough and dirty labor, yet were covered with rings wherein shone precious stones. Diamonds and rubies, emeralds and pearls, adorned the ugly coarse fingers." At a masquerade in Newport, Stoll denies that he is Jewish, "although, after one look into his face—one quick glance at the high cheek bones, curved nose, piercing black eyes, and short, crispy curling hair—any one gifted with the skill of 'reading faces,' would surely have concluded that Herman Stoll lied when he denied" that he was Jewish. "As his enemies said," writes Aiken, Stoll is "a German Jew; as though a man's birth and parentage could be flung in his face as a disgrace."[10] Yet Aiken's actual portrait of the Jew in any of his works—like this one of Stoll as poisoner of a racehorse and as a social climber who engages in an unsavory plot to deprive the hero of his fortune and his beloved—hardly leads to a different conclusion about the Jews. In *The California Detective; or, The Witches of New York* (1878), "the well-known diamond broker, Isaac Abrams," is depicted as an unscrupulous intriguer, bon vivant, and womanizer. He is "a German Jew by birth, a short, thick-set, portly man of fifty, with little keen black eyes, a hooked nose and a bearded chin. . . . A beautiful solitaire diamond glistened on his immaculate shirt-bosom, and a heavy cluster diamond ring adorned his little finger." With heavy irony Aiken has Abrams protest his honesty: "I always gife have as much as a thing is worth and never charge more than five hundred per shent interest."[11] He is involved in intricate schemes of forgery, manipulated wills, double crosses, and double double crosses.

The criminal Jew is combined with the pugilist in *The Genteel Spotter* (1884). "Sheeny Lew" is a partner in crime with Red Barry. Sheeny Lew is "a rather undersized man, with a foxy face and a shambling way. As his name indicated, he came of the race of Israel, but was a most unworthy representative indeed of the Hebrew line" —as if, indeed, Aiken ever depicted a "worthy" representative. When not a-burgling, Lew is a pugilist. Not satisfied with only one "unworthy" exemplar, Aiken adds another, the fence Moses Cohenson, who is also "a fox-like man" with a "sneaky manner," who never "looked anybody in the eye, and who always cringed and crouched as though he was afraid someone was going to strike him. . . . He was always rubbing his hands together."[12]

When Aiken goes to Texas for his plot in *Lone Hand the Shadow* (1889), the storekeeper Abraham Goldsburg, whose business was "reported to be the largest in Greer County," is no different from his eastern counterparts. He is "a typical Hebrew with his prominent nose, bushy eyebrows, and billy-goat beard." Although Goldsburg and his "good-looking" daughter, Rebecca, have lived in Texas all their lives, they still speak with a heavy accent.

When a brigand comes to collect protection money, Goldsburg pleads poverty and is read a moral lesson by the robber: "That is the cry always with you Jews; you always make a poor mouth; if you were rolling in wealth you would swear that you didn't have a cent in the world. Why can't you speak the truth?" Goldsburg appeals to the Lone Hand to recover his money and is told that "it makes these Jews squeal when their pocket is touched." When the townspeople

surmise that Goldsburg has fabricated the story of the theft in order
to gain sympathy, Aiken offers an apologia for them in the mouth
of a cowboy: "Oh, wal, the people get prejudiced sometimes, you
know. The old Jew is a pretty tough cuss at a bargain. A man who
goes in his store to trade must expect to be skinned, every time, if
he don't keep his eyes peeled, and I reckon thar is a kind of feeling
ag'in' the Jew on that account."[13]

Another story in the "Lone Hand" series, *The Lone Hand in Texas*
(1888), is revealing in the contrast it offers between the treatment
of a non-Jewish storekeeper and moneylender, Peter Raymond, and
a Jewish storekeeper, Oppenheim. No pejorative overtones attend
the description of Raymond: "Raymond was a rather smallish man,
well on in years, with a sharp face, ornamented with a mop of
iron-gray hair, and a bristle-like beard of the same hue." Robbers
rush in on him as he lies on his bunk: "The moneylender rose to a
sitting posture, and gazed with eyes full of curiosity upon his unan-
nounced visitors."

Here, in contrast, is the description of the storekeeper Oppenheim:

Oppenheim was the typical Hebrew. He was tall, and thin as a
slipper pantaloon, dressed in a rusty, threadbare suit much too small
for him. He had a long head, an enormous nose, was very bald, and
had a gray thin beard like a billy-goat. His eyes were keen as a
hawk's. . . . He was a slippery, oily old fellow, who cringed and
rubbed his hands together whenever he talked to anyone. As more
than one rough cow-puncher had said to his teeth, he was one of the
biggest soft-sawder frauds to be found in the whole of Texas. And
when he was addressed in such terms as this, the old man would
laugh, and bow and cringe more humbly than ever, as if he considered it a compliment.

The upstanding young man, Webster, newly arrived in town and
employed as a clerk by Oppenheim, finally quits in a moral dudgeon.
"This old Jew is a rascal all the way through, and no honest man can
possibly get along with him."[14]

In a Colorado frontier mining town, Moses keeps the only store
in the settlement in Aiken's *Joe Buck of the Angels* (1881). Speaking
with the usual accent, Moses is denied the "four bits" for a drink he
has sold to a stranger. Moses takes a club to him, but the stranger
evades it and disappears from town. The vanished stranger is the talk
of the town, and "even Moses, who seldom troubled his head with
anything but matters of dollars and cents, fell to discussing the
matter." The stranger's friend, Skinner, comes in to buy a coat, puts
it on, and, pretending to grapple with a snake, rolls on the ground,

and muddies and tears the coat. The five-dollar piece he offers for the coat is counterfeit, and the crowd that has gathered to watch the Jew roars with delight. The incident is "the best joke of the season."[15]

Wherever Aiken places the Jewish shopkeeper, he is the same almost subhuman character. Aiken again protests: "Although in my time I have met with a great many Jews who were every bit as good as any Gentiles I ever ran across, yet as a rule, these gentle Jews don't flourish in a climate like this." In *Dick Talbot, the Ranch King* (1892) Aaron Mosenstein keeps a store in the Mexican province of Sonora. The wife of rancher Dick Talbot is kidnaped, and Mosenstein is in league with the kidnaper. Mosenstein is described as "a short, fat man, with bushy red hair and a beard of the same hue; his eyes were small, pig-like in their appearance and his nose was enormous in size. The man had a greasy look, and he came forward, rubbing his hands together, smirking as though he was delighted beyond measure to behold Talbot." Mosenstein gets a letter from the kidnaper asking him to arrange payment of twenty thousand dollars in ransom and an additional five hundred dollars for Mosenstein. Suspecting Mosenstein of a connection with the kidnaper, Talbot has him followed, and Mosenstein is frightened into leading Talbot's agent to the brigand. "Although the Jew could not be classed as a warrior,"[16] writes Aiken, he wears pistols—but there is no evidence that he uses them. Aiken creates opportunities for Mosenstein to protest his poverty and to reveal himself as cowardly.

In Santa Fe, in *The Fresh of Frisco at Santa Fe* (1891), "Fresh" Blake buys a half interest in the general store of "an enterprising Hebrew, one Moses Cohen." It is rumored that Blake has gotten a bad deal, but he protests that Cohen is "the honest Hebrew. . . . Cohen is a first class salesman; he can persuade a customer to buy an article that he has no more use for than a dog has for two tails as well as any man that ever stepped in shoeleather." But, adds Blake, "when it comes to war, he's got to be counted out."[17]

The low literary quality of the dime novel is obvious from the passages we have cited. What does emerge, however, is that the treatment of Jews is not significantly different from that in novels of higher literary quality; it is only less polished in diction. Considering the mass consumption of these cheap novels, the reiterated portrait of Jews in most of them—as ugly, unscrupulous, money-obsessed, and cowardly—could not fail to reinforce the traditional stereotype, especially in this period of burgeoning and overt anti-Semitism and discrimination. As a symptom and an instrument of anti-Semitism, the dime novel is a social phenomenon that cannot be ignored.

15

FROM THE FAR WEST

The enterprising spirit of the Gold Rush that prompted men to hasten to the West Coast in the 1850s and 1860s was freer and more liberal than that of many men who stayed at home. Although anti-Semitism was by no means absent, it should not surprise us to find that no harsh anti-Jewish stereotype appears in the work of such westward-tending artists as Ambrose Bierce, Joaquin Miller, Bret Harte, and Mark Twain. On the contrary, at some time or other in their careers all of them offered resistance to prejudice. All went west in the 1850s and 1860s. Of the four, only Bret Harte was an easterner, born in Albany, New York. The other three came from the Middle West: Bierce from Ohio, Miller from Indiana, and Twain from Missouri. During the 1860s they formed a brilliant literary circle in San Francisco and initiated western American literature.

If they were not familiar with Jews before they went to San Francisco, they must surely have come to know them in the city. The influx of Jews into California, and especially San Francisco, after the Gold Rush in 1849 was remarkable. Although some few came to try their luck at gold mining, most of them established themselves as merchants or shopkeepers. By the end of the 1850s the percentage of Jews in San Francisco—between 6 and 10 percent—was higher than that in New York. They came from all parts of the United States, and some were even refugees from failed revolutions in Europe. Quickly they virtually monopolized the clothing business in the state and set up stores in the mining towns.

While prejudice against them did exist, its overt forms were generally lacking, and in the relatively free atmosphere Jews quickly became integrated into the community. In the 1850s, for instance, Jews were city and state officials, and in 1853 Solomon Heydenfeldt was chief justice of the California State Supreme Court. The Shearith

Israel congregation for Polish and English Jews, and the Emanu-El congregation for German and American Jews were also established in the 1850s. There were congregations in mining towns, and Jewish cemeteries and Jewish benevolent societies were organized. Some thirty Jews were among the seven hundred vigilante defenders against outlaws in 1851.

Yet these western authors did not introduce Jews into their creative works to any great extent. Their largely unprejudiced attitudes emerged in extraliterary ways. Ambrose Bierce, for instance, rarely mentions the Jews in his poems, although he celebrated the centenary of Moses Montefiore with a poem (1884):

> One hundred years had bettered by his birth,
> And still his step was firm, his eye was bright.
>
> Before him and about him pressed a crowd.
> Each head in reverence was bared and bowed,
> And Jews and Gentiles in a hundred tongues,
> Extolled his deeds and spake his fame aloud.[1]

Bierce did, however, have personal relations with Jews, two of which merit comment. In San Francisco in the 1880s he was a friend of Dr. Adolphe Danziger's, a dentist, rabbi, lawyer, and publisher, who translated *The Monk and Hangman's Daughter,* by Richard Voss, from German. Danziger was unhappy with his translation and turned it over to Bierce for revision. Bierce, who rewrote the story, later engaged in a bitter quarrel with Danziger because he denied Danziger's claim to authorship. The faintest hint of anti-Semitism in Bierce's comments on the quarrel appears in his statement that Danziger carries a pistol, "but when invited to pull that he says it is the proudest moment of his life, but family reasons, largely hereditary [Jewish "cowardice"?] compel him to decline."[2]

On the other hand, Danziger defended Bierce against charges of anti-Semitism in *Portrait of Ambrose Bierce,* a book Danziger published under the name of Adolphe de Castro. When a youthful Pacific Coast poet, David Lesser Lezinsky, committed suicide after some particularly harsh criticism by Bierce, a relative of Lezinsky's charged that Bierce's strictures were motivated by anti-Semitism. Danziger (de Castro) denies that this was so. Further, Danziger reports that when a correspondent asked Bierce "how he could reconcile his ideas on religion with the conception of a 'Sheeny Jesus and a 'Dago Pope,' Bierce replied, 'Jesus Christ was a Jew and the Pope is an Italian; of Sheenies and Dagoes I have no knowledge.' "[3]

In the late 1890s Bierce was a close friend of Mr. and Mrs. Hirshberg of Iona, and he was very fond of their daughters. However, it appears that Bierce did not like Jewish men. Carey McWilliams reports that "it was once suggested to Mr. Bierce that he was inconsistent in liking female, but disliking male, Semitics. To this he responded, and the observation is borne out by his practice, that he 'hated Hebrews but adored Shebrews.' "[4] In his *Devil's Dictionary,* Bierce had defined "Hebrew" as "a male Jew, as distinguished from a Shebrew, an altogether superior creation."[5]

Considering the integration of Jews into the life of the West Coast, it is surprising that Jews do not appear in the genre fiction of Bret Harte. Perhaps the reason lies in the Jewish strain in Harte's ancestry. The story is curious. Bret Harte's grandfather, Bernard Hart (as he spelled the name), came to New York in 1780. Although an observant Jew, he married a non-Jew, Catherine Brett, in 1799. The marriage was dissolved before a year passed—but it was not without issue, however. Henry Hart was born in 1800 of the short-lived union, and Catherine Brett Hart lived with her son, Henry, in Schenectady until 1817. Although Bernard Hart continued to help Catherine financially until she died, his previous marriage was apparently not known to the all-Jewish family he raised after his marriage to Rebecca B. Seixas in 1806.

Henry Hart married Elizabeth Rebecca Ostrander, of Dutch descent, in Albany in 1830. Although raised in the Dutch Reformed Church, Henry Hart had become a Catholic soon after leaving college. His wife was an Episcopalian, and presumably brought up their son, Bret, in this faith. Bret's father added an "e" to his last name to avoid confusion with another Henry Hart.[6]

Bret Harte was thus one-fourth Jewish. He knew of his Jewish derivation, and it was apparently no secret to others. This we gather from a letter by Mark Twain to Howells, written from Heidelberg in 1878 and published for the first time by Bernard De Voto in 1946. Mark Twain had a low opinion of Harte, obviously, by 1878. "Harte," he wrote "is a liar, a thief, a swindler, a snob, a sot, a sponge, a coward, a Jeremy Diddler, he is brim full of treachery," and, adds Twain, "he conceals his Jewish birth as carefully as if he considered it a disgrace. How do I know? By the best of all evidence, personal observation."[7] This effort to conceal the Jew in him may account for the absence of Jews from his fiction. However, his biographer George R. Stewart, Jr., observes: "One can justifiably see the influence of his Jewish strain in the unusually sympathetic way in which his stories present characters of mixed white and Indian blood. These 'breeds' are traditionally the villains in literature, but in Harte's stories they are generally the heroes.''[8]

Once, however, Harte was led to protest anti-Jewish discrimination in the notorious Seligman affair, when on June 13, 1877, the Grand Union Hotel at Saratoga Springs refused to allow Joseph Seligman or any "Israelites" to register. The wealthy owner, retail merchant A. T. Stewart, had died and left management of the hotel to his lawyer Henry Hilton, who ordered the ban on Jewish guests. When a storm broke over Hilton's head, he tried to defend himself by offering some vague distinction between acceptable "Hebrews" and unacceptable "Jews." Bret Harte then promptly wrote a satirical poem on this "distinction," "That Ebrew Jew!" For his part, writes Harte, Stewart "had built up a fortune—the which, as it grew,/ Just ruined small traders the whole city through." But he did know one thing—that "There was a distinction/'Twixt Christian and Jew." When he died, he left his money to a lawyer (Hilton) ''who knew/A subtle distinction/'Twixt Ebrew and Jew.''

> For the Jew is a man who will make money through
> His skill, his *finesse*, and his capital, too.
> And an Ebrew's a man that we Gentiles can "do."
> So you see there's a contrast 'twixt Ebrew and Jew.

When Hilton came to manage the hotel, he ordered the manager to refuse entry to Israelites.

> Yet the manager knew,
> Between me and you,
> No other distinction
> 'Twixt Ebrew and Jew.
> You'll allow Miss McFlimsey her diamonds to wear,
> You'll permit the Van Dams at the waiters to swear,
> You'll allow Miss Decollete to flirt on the stair,
> But, as to an Israelite, pray have a care.
>   For, between me and you,
>   Though the doctrine is new,
>   There's a business distinction
>   'Twixt Ebrew and Jew.
> Now, how shall we know? Prophet, tell us, pray do,
> Where the line of the Hebrew fades into the Jew?
> Shall we keep out Disraeli and take Rothschild in?
> Or snub Meyerbeer—and think Verdi* a sin?
>   What shall we do?
>   Oh give us a few
>   Points to distinguish
>   'Twixt Ebrew and Jew.

*Giuseppe Verdi was not Jewish.

There was One—Heaven help us!—who died in man's place,
With thorns on his forehead, but love in his face;
And when "foxes had holes," and birds of the air
Had their nests in the trees, there was no spot to spare
   For this "King of the Jews."
   Did the Romans refuse
   This right to the Ebrews
   Or only to Jews?[9]

Of the far western writers, Jews figure most frequently in the creative work of the most flamboyant and least memorable of the group, Joaquin Miller. He was born, he claimed, in a covered wagon between Ohio and Indiana, to parents who were Quaker pacifists and abolitionists, thus foreshadowing his own sympathies for the oppressed. Although there may have been an element of the poseur in his championship of the underdog, it is true that he protested treatment of Mexicans and Indians in the Far West in one of his earliest writings. He strongly defended John Brown's action at Harper's Ferry, and was among the anti-imperialist dissenters during the Spanish-American War. Of one of the best of his works, the drama *The Danites of the Sierras,* he later wrote that he regretted its publication because he thought it unfair to the Mormons and Chinese. On the other hand, presumably on the theory that the Confederacy was an oppressed group, he edited a proslavery paper in Eugene, Oregon, the *Democratic Register,* which was suppressed in 1863 for its Copperhead sentiments. For a man who professed sympathy for the poor and oppressed, it is strange that he should finally have dedicated his collected works to the railroad tycoon Collis P. Huntington.

His broad, if theatrical, sympathy for groups victimized by injustice explains why the Jews figure in his creative work. A Jewish woman is a central figure of his utopian novel *The Building of the City Beautiful* (to which we shall revert in discussing the utopian novel). After a visit to Palestine he wrote a series of "Songs of the Hebrew Children," which are mostly christological in content. The Russian pogroms of the 1880s inspired several poems in defense of the Jews. "To Russia" reminds the Russians that "the Jew, the Jew, the homeless Jew tamed your Tartar blood." The biblical Jews and Christ, he recalls to them, were the civilizing influences in Russia:

Why, who but Moses shaped your course . . .
Your mighty millions all today

> The hated, homeless Jew obey.
> Who taught all poetry to you?
> The Jew, the Jew, the homeless Jew. . . .
> Who gave thee your Christian creed?
>   Yea, yea,
> Who gave your very God to you?
> Your Jew! Your Jew! your hated Jew![10]

In "To Rachel in Russia" Miller urges the persecuted Jews to flee to America:

> Rise up and set thy sad face hence.
> Rise up and come where Freedom waits. . . .
>   Then come where yellow harvests swell;
> Forsake the savage land of snows; ·
> Forget the brutal Russian's blows;
> And come where Kings of Conscience dwell.
> Oh come, Rebecca to the well![11]

In his prosy, long-winded poem "A Song of Creation," Miller introduces a philo-Semitic passage, that is, an excessively flattering conception of the Jews. During a love scene the girl adjures her lover to emulate the Jew. She says:

> The true Jew lover keeps the Way.
> For clean, serene, and contrite heart
> The bride and bridegroom kneel apart
> Before the bridal bed and pray.

She enjoins him to

> Go forth among this homeless race,
> This landless race that knows no place
> Or name or nation quite its own,
> And see their happy babes at play,
> Or palace, Ghetto, rich or poor,
> As thick as birds about the door
> At morn, some sunny Vermont May,
> Then think of Christ and these alone.
> Yet ye deride, ye jeer, ye jibe,
> To see their plenteous babes; ye say
> "Behold the Jew and all his tribe!"
>
> Yet Solomon upon his throne
> Was not more kingly crowned than they
> These Jews, these jeered Jews of today—
> More surely born to lord, to lead,
> To sow the land with Abram's seed;
> Because their babes are healthful born
> And welcomed as the welcome morn.

She then utters a warning and prophecy that contains, in benign "philo-Semitic" form, the warning of current anti-Semites: the Jews will rule the world. She goes on:

> Hear me this prophecy and heed!
> Except we cleanse us, kirk and creed,
> Except we wash us, word and deed,
> The Jew shall rule us, reign the Jew.
> And just because the Jew is true,
> Is true to nature, true to truth,
> Is clean, is chaste, as trustful Ruth
> Who stood amid the alien corn
> In tears that far, dim, doubtful morn—
> Who bore us David, Solomon—
> The Babe, that far, first Christmas dawn.

Her lover is not pleased. But the "truth" must be told.

> You shrink, are angered at my speech?
> You dare avert your doubtful face
> Because I name this chaste, strange race?
> So be it then; . . .
> I would not leave the truth untold
> To win the whole world to my side, . . .
> Bear with me, I must dare be true.
> The nation, aye, the Christian race,
> Now fronts its stern Sphinx, face to face,
> And I must say, say here to you,
> Whate'er the cost of love, of fame,
> The Christian is a thing of shame—
> Must say because you prove it true,
> The better Christian is the Jew.[12]

The idealized, sentimental notion of the Jew underlying these lines is not quite compatible with the realistic prose description of the Roman ghetto in *The One Fair Woman* (1876), Miller's novel set in Europe. The descriptive chapter takes one through the narrow crooked streets with "old clothes shops, fish stands, wine-stalls, Jew stores on every hand. . . . At the door of every little shop here sits a Jew. He is generally an old man and looks just like the pictures of that peculiar people painted centuries ago. They have all the Roman peasant's love of the picturesque. They are often dressed in a half savage, half Oriental style, and have their shops hung in all the colors of the rainbow." When the Tiber overflows, water rises as high as the waist in one day and goes down the next. Then

the people fill the streets, and steal and starve and suffer as before. But oh! The fevers now—the fevers, the sickness and the sorrows of this miserable people of the Ghetto! . . . This is the place where the Jews were fastened up and which they could not leave in the night for more than a thousand years. It looks like death in rags. It smells of the plague. Black-eyed women are looking at you. Black-hearted men are watching you. Bright-eyed children put out their pretty brown hands, lift up their wonderful eyes, half-hidden by the clouds of curly hair, and you stop and empty every penny into their dimpled, dirty little hands.[13]

Although the greatest of the group, Mark Twain, introduced Jews into few of his creative works, he had numerous points of contact with them throughout his life. He first came to know Jews as a schoolboy in Hannibal. In his autobiography he notes that he had several Jewish schoolmates, "the first Jews I had ever seen." His young mind strongly associated them with the image of the biblical Hebrews instilled in the young.

It took me a good while [he writes] to get over the awe of it. To my fancy they were clothed invisibly in the damp and cob-webby mold of antiquity. They carried me back to Egypt, and in imagination I moved among the Pharaohs and all the shadowy celebrities of that remote age. The name of [two of] the boys was Levin. We had a collective name for them which was the only really large and handsome witticism that was ever born in those premises. We called them Twenty-Two; and even when the joke was old and had been worn threadbare, we always followed it with the explanation to make sure it would be understood—Twice Levin=Twenty-Two.[14]

This was his first encounter with overt anti-Semitism, for, Twain noted, "the ground was all prepared." Sunday school teachings in the town indoctrinated the children with religious anti-Semitism, and the local press often charged Jewish merchants with sharp practice at the expense of non-Jews. Hence, Twain records in his notebook, the Levin boys made "an awful impression among us." The Levin boys were chased and stoned by their schoolmates, who even asked each other: "Shall we crucify them?" When a writer named Levering was drowned, Mark Twain notes that "it was believed the drowning . . . was a judgment on him and his parents because his great-grandmother had given the 11 (Levin) boys protection when they were being chased and stoned."[15]

One of the few allusions to the Jews in Twain's creative work is in *Life on the Mississippi.* Several planters traveling by steamboat complain of their economic plight after the Civil War. The complaint runs that one planter's relations with the blacks are chilly, and he will not convenience the blacks by having a store on his property, but leased the store to an "Israelite." The Jew, he goes on, then "encourages the thoughtless negro and wife to buy all sorts of things which they could do without—buy on credit, at big prices, month after month, credit based on the negro's share of the growing crop and at the end of the season the negro's share belongs to the Israelite, the negro is in debt besides, is discouraged, dissatisfied, restless, and both he and the planter are injured." The black then leaves and another black takes his place, who "will fatten the Israelite a season, and follow his predecessor per steamboat."[16] Twain reports this without a demurrer.

He does not again allude to the Jews in his published fiction until his later years. For him it is high praise when he says (in *Following the Equator* [1897]) that "the Jew himself is not more lavish [than the Indian Parsees] in his charities and benevolences."[17] In *The Mysterious Stranger,* begun in 1898 and published posthumously in 1916, Solomon Isaacs, a moneylender, threatens to foreclose the mortgage on the house of Father Peter and his niece, Marget. Satan contrives to fill Father Peter's wallet with money enough and more to pay the mortgage, which is repaid to Isaacs, and the additional money deposited with him. Father Peter is then charged with stealing the money, and it is reclaimed from Isaacs and left with the authorities. Isaacs's role in the story is thus quite casual and incidental, but the interesting feature of his brief appearances is that, unlike most literary allusions to Jewish moneylenders, there is not the slightest overtone of the unfavorable stereotype.[18]

Another interesting allusion to Jews occurs in a portion of *Extract from Captain Stormfield's Visit to Heaven* that was not included in the version published by Twain (1909). The captain's first encounter in heaven is with a Jew, Solomon Goldstein, from "Chatham Street." "It was a great improvement, having company," says the captain. "I was born sociable, and could never stand solitude. I was raised to a prejudice against Jews—Christians always are, you know—but such as I had was in my head, there wasn't any in my heart." We may assume that Mark Twain is being autobiographical here. What then follows is an exposure of the ways of prejudice, just as Oliver Wendell Holmes's poem "At the Pantomime" exposes a typical case of the scapegoating of Jews. For when Goldstein learns that he has been assigned to hell after all, along with the captain, he cries. Captain Stormfield is annoyed. "Just like a Jew!" he says to himself. "He has promised some hayseed or other a coat for four dollars, and now he has made up his mind that if he was back he could work off a worse one on him for five. They haven't any heart—that race— nor any principles." "Damn the coat! Drop it out of your mind," he roughly tells Goldstein, who of course knows nothing about it.

But Goldstein explains that he is weeping because his transfer to hell deprives him of his little daughter, who is in heaven. "It breaks my heart!" says Goldstein. Then Stormfield is contrite: "By God, it went through me like a knife! I wouldn't feel so mean again, and so grieved, not for a fleet of ships. And I spoke out and said what I felt; and went on damning myself for a hound till he was so distressed that I had to stop; but I wasn't half through. He begged me not to talk so, and said I oughtn't to make so much of what I had done; he said it was only a mistake, and a mistake wasn't a crime. There now —wasn't it magnanimous? I ask you—wasn't it? I think so." Twain's conclusion is satirical: "To my mind there was the stuff in him for a Christian, and I came out flat-footed and told him so. And if it hadn't been so late I would have reformed him and made him one, or died in the act."[19]

Why did he omit this Goldstein incident from the published version of the story? Perhaps Twain wished to avoid comment on the sensitive subject of anti-Jewish prejudice.

The remarkable thing about Mark Twain is not that he was totally free from prejudice, but that he recognized the residues of it in himself, and in his maturity was alert to its existence and consciously made efforts to rise above it. At eighteen, writing from Philadelphia in 1853, he had noted that several historic homes in the city were "desecrated" by Jewish occupants. In an article for the Keokuk, Iowa, *Daily Post* on April 10, 1857, he had written that in Cincinnati that winter the cold was so intense that the price of coal rose rapidly:

Gold dust warn't worth no more'n coal dust, and in course the blasted Jews got to adulterating the fuel. They mixed it up half and half—a ton of coal dust to a ton of ground pepper, and sold it for the genuine article. But they ketched them at last, and they do say that some of the indignant inhabitants took a hoss whip and casti- gated one of 'em till he warn't fit to associate with James Gordon Bennett hisself.[20]

According to Mark Twain himself, his attitude toward the Jews was decisively changed in 1860 by a story told him by the river pilot George Newhouse after a passenger "made a scurrilous general remark about Jews." Newhouse ordered the man out of the pilot house and explained why to Twain. It had been fifteen years, New-house said, "since he would allow a Jew to be abused where he was. This . . . was for the sake of one Jew, in memory of one Jew." Newhouse then told him the story of a young Jew on a riverboat who intervened when a notorious gambler tried to provoke a Louisiana planter into a duel, and himself shot the gambler in the duel. On another occasion Twain told how a similar exploit caused a banker he knew to respect the Jews for the rest of his life.[21] These stories made a deep impression on Twain because they refuted the cliché of the Jew as self-interested and cowardly.

It is clear by 1864 that Mark Twain was no longer carelessly making invidious references to Jews. For four months in 1864 he was a reporter for the San Francisco *Call*. Among the articles he wrote for that paper, collected by Edgar M. Branch, are about half a dozen items that deal with Jewish shopkeepers or pawnbrokers as lawbreakers or victims of crime. Mark Twain's reporting of these cases is entirely lacking in any overtones of prejudice. Instead, he often gives them a humorous turn that does not at all hinge on Jewishness. For instance, "Lena Kahn, otherwise known as Mother Kahn, or the Kahn of Tartary, who is famous in this community for her infatuated partiality for the Police Court as a place of recreation, was on hand again yesterday morning."[22] There was considerable justification for the characterization of Twain made to one of his friends by a Jew. Clemens "was the only great humorist who had ever written without poking some fun against a Jew."[23] This was not absolutely true, as we have seen, but it had sufficient basis to justify Twain's pride.

But it cannot be said, despite his patent goodwill, that Twain understood the situation of the Jews. He writes in his notebook (1879) that "the Jews are the only race who work wholly with their brains and never with their hands. There are no Jewish beggars, no Jew tramps, no Jew ditchers, hod-carriers, day laborers or followers of toilsome, mechanical trades."[24] This is, of course, a conventional notion. But at that very time there were, in fact, many Jewish immigrants who were not only beggars but also cigar-makers and clothing workers, who must have attracted general notice in the 1870s by their participation in strikes.

Twain was often respectful toward Jews where others were scornful. Many who saw Jews at the mineral bath resorts in Germany in the late nineteenth century made deprecating allusions to them. For instance, even Howells wrote Mark Twain from Carlsbad: "I was here before, you know, and it is duller than the ditch water one drinks; troops of yellow [jaundiced, one assumes] Jews with cork-screw curls before their ears,"[25] etc. But in an 1892 essay on "Marienbad, a Health Factory," Twain writes that among the sojourners at the resort, "almost the only striking figure is the Polish Jew. He is very frequent. He is tall and of grave countenance and wears a coat that reaches to his ankle bones, and he has a little curl or two in front of each ear. He has a prosperous look, and seems to be as much respected as anybody."[26]

Twain's mixture of openhearted goodwill and incomplete apprehension reached its most extended expression in an essay, "Concerning the Jews," which Twain published in *Harper's* in June 1899. In March of the previous year an article of his had appeared in *Harper's,* describing the stormy debate he had witnessed in the Austrian parliament on the proposal that the official language of Bohemia be Czech, rather than German. The deputies, writes Twain, "are religious men. They are earnest, sincere, devoted, and they hate the Jews." In the rioting and turbulence that followed the vote, the Jews were the targets of both sides—"in all cases the Jew had to roast, no matter what side he was on."[27] Twain received a number of letters from Jews on this article, but one letter in particular stimulated him to write an article in reply. Why, if the Jews were not really involved in the issue, were they the target of everyone's hate? In "Concerning the Jews" Twain undertakes to give his answer.

He begins by offering his credentials: "If I thought myself prejudiced against the Jew, I should hold it fairest to leave this subject to a person not crippled in that way. But I think I have no such prejudice. A few years ago a Jew observed to me that there was no uncourteous references to his people in my books, and asked how it happened. It happened because the disposition was lacking." All this was essentially true, but his intentions were better disposed than his knowledge and analytic powers were adequate, as the essay shows.

No one, Twain asserts, can complain that the Jews are not acceptable as citizens, for they are not a burden on the civic organization of society, since they are law-abiding in all respects. This was accurate enough, for it had statistical support. But Twain then goes on to set forth the Jews' "discreditable ways," and he apparently agrees with this "reputation" of the Jews for various forms of sharp practice in business, even though he adds that Jews do not have "a monopoly of them." Although there was some basis in reality for this stereotype, Twain was following the popular fallacy of identifying the whole with a part—so often the basis for prejudice. Twain adds the charge that the Jew has "an unpatriotic disinclination to stand by the flag as a soldier—like the Christian Quaker," an assertion that he was later to retract. He then strikes a "balance" of the presumed positive and negative traits of the Jews and concludes that "the Christian can claim no superiority over the Jew in the matter of good citizenship." Yet, he adds, "in all countries, from the dawn of history, the Jew has been persistently and implacably hated, and with frequency persecuted."[28]

In his effort to discover the reason for this hatred, Twain denies that "fanaticism *alone,*" i.e., religious hostility, can account for it, and proceeds in a simplistic way to argue that it was the Jews' superiority in whatever they undertook, whether it was trade, or medicine, or law (in other words, their success in competition with the non-Jew), that caused hatred and exclusion by the dominant group from one vocation after another. It is because "the Christian cannot *compete* with the Jew," rather than religious prejudice, that accounts for persecution of the Jew. The Jew's "success made the whole human race his enemy." Here Twain oversimplifies a very complex phenomenon, and underestimates the staying power that Jew-hatred because of the Jews' supposed role in the crucifixion has proved to have, even to our own day. Competition often does set off anti-Semitic feeling, but there are other factors as well. For instance, in the Austrian rioting that occasioned this article the Jew served as a scapegoat, a diversion from real problems.

Twain then criticizes the Jewish community for not organizing into political parties, so that it might defend itself, instead of letting "somebody else look after its safety." Here again, Twain underestimates the extent to which Jews have participated in government and national life where tolerance permitted. In the United States, for instance, Jews have held public office since colonial times. His assumption that Jews were passive everywhere and did not participate in revolutions that resulted in their liberation (e.g., the French Revolution) only reveals that Twain was historically beyond his depth. His suggestion that the Jews organize politically in defense of their interests did have the virtue of discerning the need to organize for defense, even if not in the forms proposed by Twain. Jews did organize in this century, following the pogroms and persecution in Eastern Europe and the rise of aggressive anti-Semitism.[29]

Twain is unduly optimistic in his belief that religious persecution has "already come to an end." True, the day of the religious auto-da-fé was over (the gas chambers of secular anti-Semitism were still to come), but the momentum of religious anti-Semitism was still far from expended, nor is it to this day. He is quite right, however, in his assertion that "on the score of race prejudice and trade," persecution will continue. He even believes that this will never end: "I suppose the race prejudice cannot be removed. . . . By his make and ways he [the Jew] is substantially a foreigner wherever he may be, and even the angels dislike a foreigner. . . . You will always be by ways and habits and predilections substantially strangers—foreigners —wherever you are, and that will probably keep the race prejudice against you alive."

He concludes the essay with an encomium on the Jews. Although Jews are "not *one per cent* of the human race," their contributions to commerce, the arts, science and learning are "away out of proportion to the weakness of [their] numbers." He concludes: "All things are mortal but the Jew: all other forces pass, but he remains. What is the secret of his immortality?"[30]

As could be anticipated, the article aroused comment and controversy in the Jewish press all over the world. While most acknowledged the goodwill behind the article, objection was made to Twain's historical allusions concerning Jewish passivity in the struggle for freedom of the countries in which they lived and for their own people, and to the imputed nonparticipation in the military. To Twain's complaint that important Jews had not fought back in the Dreyfus case, contrary evidence was given. Interestingly enough, Twain himself, in a letter from Sweden to the Jewish historiographer Simon Wolf on September 15, 1899, offered the view that "the Jews did wisely in keeping quiet during the Dreyfus agitation—the other course would have hurt Dreyfus's cause, and I see now that *nothing* could have helped it."[31] Twain thus not only negates his own criticism, but shows that he is unaware of the many protesting letters and petitions and resolutions by American Jews to President McKinley to intervene for Dreyfus. In this letter Twain thanked Wolf for his *American Jew as Patriot, Soldier and Citizen* (1895), which refutes Twain's assertions of Jewish passivity and nonparticipation.

One critique of the article which is unduly sharp because it charges the article with being "tinged with malice and prejudice," as well as "incorrect and false," is "A Rabbi's Reply to Mark Twain," by M. S. Levy, in the West Coast *Overland Monthly* for October 1899. Levy's criticisms, however, are cogent. With several pages of documentation he refutes Twain's assertions about Jewish nonparticipation, both civil and military, in American history, and goes on: "I could continue to show, by citing innumerable examples, how the Jew did patriotically stand by his flag as a soldier, for the instances above quoted are only a few out of the ten thousand, twenty-five per cent of whom died in service and in the field upholding the flag of their country."

To Twain's assertion of Jewish dominance in business, Levy properly points out that

> the Vanderbilts, Goulds, Astors, Havemeyers, Rockefellers, Mackays, Huntingtons, Armours, Carnegies, Sloanes, Whitneys, are not Jews, and yet they control and possess more than twenty-five per cent of all the accumulated wealth of the United States. . . . The tobacco, beer, sugar, oil, and beef trusts, and all the other trusts in which the commodities of life largely figure are in the hands of men who are not Jews.[32]

Mark Twain had himself given a searing picture of commercial venality and rapacity—in which no Jews were involved—in his *Gilded Age,* and should have known where financial and commercial dominance in his own day really lay.

But Twain's errors did not rise out of ill will; it was just that his talents did not run to history or social analysis. The greatness of *Huckleberry Finn* lies in his insight into character within a social context, not in social-scientific analysis of slavery and frontier life. Obviously, he did not know the Jew as well as he knew Huck and Jim; and his venture into the much-misunderstood territory of the Jewish question led to some unhappy results. When his errors were pointed out to him, he did try to make amends. He studied official figures of Jewish participation in American wars and in 1904 published his results in a widely publicized postscript to his article, under the title "The American Jew as Soldier." The "slur," he writes, "that the Jew is willing to feed on a country but not to fight for it," is false; and "ought to be pensioned off now, and retired from active service."[33]

The genuineness of his feelings about the Jews is attested to by his attitude toward the great pianist Osip Gabrilowitsch, who met Twain's daughter, Clara, at the turn of the century and married her in 1909. When Clara first became friendly with the Jewish pianist, she writes, she

> thought of my father. Since childhood I had heard him rail at the crass stupidity and barbarity of race prejudice. Oftenest, of course, he ridiculed the persecution of Jews, a member of whose race the entire world worships. . . . Father used to find it particularly laughable that so-called Christians, filled with contempt for the Jew, were themselves often the most insignificant or reprehensible members of the human race![34]

Clara Clemens earlier remarks that her father's comments on the Jews were so often repeated that he was suspected of being a Jew himself. Indeed, beginning in 1910 attempts were made in Germany to prove that he was Jewish and that his name was *Salamon* Clemens. The Nazis publicized these efforts.[35]

Twain's admiration for the Jews was reciprocated, especially by the Jews of the East Side, which he sometimes visited. This reciprocal feeling is illustrated by an incident in which two burglars were caught in an attempt to rob the Twain home, "Stormfield," in Connecticut, while Twain was out. On his return Twain talked to the would-be thieves. "So you're the two young men who called at my house last night and forgot to put your names in my guest-book? Now that was a pretty sort of business for you, wasn't it, and a nice way to treat me, after I've been down to the East side working for just such fellows as you, and after I made Police-Commissioner take back what he said about the Jews." "Excuse me," replied one of the thieves, "my parents are Jewish." "Then you're a disgrace to your race," said Twain. "Well, I guess I am," replied the burglar.[36] His feeling for the Jews as a persecuted people was one aspect of his total outlook. Wherever he saw it he condemned injustice, whether economic or racial, within the limits of his knowledge and understanding. Once he reached maturity he threw off racist attitudes toward Negroes, Jews, Chinese, and Indians. He supported trade unionism in its pioneer days in the 1880s, and was an anti-imperialist in relation to the Spanish-American War and the imperialist adventures of European powers (like Belgian King Leopold's appropriation of the Congo). Mark Twain was no social scientist and there were inconsistencies in his social attitudes, but the will for genuine equality was present in him as in few major American writers.

16

THE ARISTOCRATS: HENRY ADAMS AND HENRY JAMES

The sharp contrast in attitude toward the Jews between those who established the literature of the West—from Mark Twain to Ambrose Bierce—and the postbellum group of Brahmin literary figures —centering on Henry Adams and Henry James—is one index of the difference in their world views. The westerners were, on the whole, more democratic and generally without prejudice, thanks to the pioneering spirit and the unlimited economic enterprise in which the greatest variety of nationalities and classes participated. With a few exceptions, however, the Brahmins—representatives of a class in decline from their earlier political and social dominance—were at best condescending to the Jews and at worst, hostile. The Jew proved a convenient scapegoat for their sense of passage from center stage in American history. Anti-Semitism was expressed with varying degrees of intensity among the Brahmins, from the obsessive but relatively benign concern of James Russell Lowell, to the mild social prejudice of Henry James, to the Old World Jew-hatred of Henry Adams.

When referring to the Jews in his public writings Henry Adams was relatively discreet, but even here he could not entirely conceal the hatred that saturated his private correspondence. Born in 1838, Adams came to maturity just before the Civil War and spent the years 1861–68 as secretary to his father, Charles Francis Adams, the ambassador to England. On his return home in 1868 he sensed immediately the social changes that had accompanied the plunge of America into full-blown industrialism. The patrician merchant class was giving way to the businessman as the repository of political power, and Adams's own aspirations to national political power, which he almost assumed to be a birthright, were totally frustrated. Adams was a journalist in Washington for two years, and, after he had spent seven years in Cambridge as professor of medieval history

at Harvard and editor of the *North American Review,* the magnetism
of Washington as the center of power drew him again. But the time
of patrician kingmakers was past, and Adams was frustrated at his
impotence and repelled by the venality and corruption of politics in
the Gilded Age.

This early phase of his disillusionment with democracy, and indeed with all social establishments of his time, comes to expression
in his political novel *Democracy,* which Adams published anonymously in 1880. Like Adams himself, his heroine, the widowed Mrs.
Madelaine Lee, moves to Washington to explore national politics
and to influence its course through the powerful political figures she
gathers about her. She is devoted to the main reform effort of the
time: the institution of a civil service that would obviate the corruption of a spoils system gone rotten. As in Adams's own case, her
foray into the political scene ends in bitter disillusionment; democratic government, she concludes, is no better than any other kind.

Within Mrs. Lee's close circle of friends are Hartbeest
Schneidekoupon and his sister, Julia, who "are descended from all
the Kings of Israel, and are prouder than Solomon in all his glory."
Aside from the snide connotation of the name—did not Mrs. Lee
herself (and Adams) live by coupon-clipping?—these Jewish figures
are accepted unreservedly as members of her inner circle. Julia is a
great friend of Mrs. Lee's younger sister, Sybil. Schneidekoupon,
who is about thirty years of age, is enamored of Sybil. He is an ally
in Mrs. Lee's fight for civil service reform, a lobbyist for protection-
ism, a man who is interested in art and literature, and possibly an
aspirant for the presidency someday. When Mrs. Lee finally surrenders hope and leaves Washington, she and Sybil go to Europe "with
the Schneidekoupons, and Mr. S. has promised to send his yacht to
the Mediterranean, so that we shall sail about there after finishing
the Nile, and see Jerusalem and Gibraltar and Constantinople."[1]

This favorable treatment requires an explanation, for there is
ample evidence that before 1880 Adams was anti-Semitic. While he
was teaching school in Germany in 1859, Adams's young students
would question him about the United States. But, reports Ernest
Samuels, "there were limits to his indulgence; then he would tease
the children with fabulous stories or if greatly provoked, as once by
a Jewish boy, he would box the questioner's ears."[2] Would he have
boxed the ears of a non-Jewish pupil? When he wrote about fellow
travelers on his return from Europe, he placed "German Jews"
among the "obnoxious" ones. When the *North American Review,*
which he edited, fell on hard times in 1875, he wrote Henry Cabot

Lodge that "my terror is that it should die on my hands or go to some Jew." And before *Democracy* was published Adams journeyed to Spain; he wrote on October 24, 1879, that Madrid "is without exception the ugliest and most unredeemable capital I ever saw." Everything about it was bad, "and the people simply faded Jews."[3] His views intensified, and on December 21, 1879, he wrote: "I have now seen enough of Jews and Moors to entertain more liberal views in regard to the Inquisition, and to feel that, though the ignorant may murmur, the Spaniards saw and pursued a noble aim."[4]

How then account for the restraint in *Democracy?* Perhaps the Schneidekoupons' connection with Mrs. Lee was Adams's way of referring to his sister, Louisa Catherine, in the novel. In *The Education of Henry Adams* he had characterized Louisa as "much brighter than he ever was—though he thought himself a rather superior person,"[5] and she had married a Jew, Charles Kuhn, of Philadelphia. Although Adams writes not one word in the *Education* about Kuhn himself, he relates how in 1859 he had placed himself under Mrs. Kuhn's tutelage on a visit to Italy. She had died in 1870, and perhaps the favorable Jewish figures in *Democracy* were Adams's strange way of remarking her existence. In any event, the intensity of Adams's anti-Jewish feelings increased after his wife's suicide in 1884, and Adams wandered over the face of the earth, bereft of hope for the present and future of society. Until the end of his life he poured hatred on the Jews in his private correspondence.[6]

His published works to some measure echo this dislike. In 1903 his celebration of the thirteenth-century image of the Virgin Mary, *Mont-Saint-Michel and Chartres,* was privately published. In a seeming criticism of Mary, he remarks that, "like other queens, she had many of the failings and prejudices of her humanity. In spite of her origin, she disliked Jews, and rarely neglected a chance to maltreat them," quite as if he did not share her prejudice.

Precious medieval objects, he writes, cost too much for the likes of himself and are available for purchase "only to our betters, and almost invariably, if not to the State, to the rich Jews, whose instinctive taste has seized the whole field of art which rests on their degradation." Adams is relieved that the windows of Chartres have not been popularized so that one may absorb and study them "without much fear of being trampled upon by critics or Jew dealers in works of art."[7]

Adams easily falls into the stereotyping process that attends ethnic prejudice. If *some* Jews are critics or dealers in art, then a disagreeable thought relating to those categories immediately suggests the Jew; he is irritatedly invoked, and the resentment finds its outlet. So when Adams discusses the numerous miracles told of the Virgin Mary during the Middle Ages, he mentions a "Byzantine miracle" that was "an original version of Shylock." Shakespeare and other dramatists, he continues, "plundered the Church legends as freely as their masters plundered the Church treasuries, yet left a mass of dramatic material untouched." But Adams bridles at the thought that some of this precious material may be commercialized; the adrenalin starts flowing, and the Jews are available for relief. "One does not care to see one's Virgin put to money-making for Jew theatre-managers. One's two hundred and fifty million arithmetical ancestors shrink." Among other miracles, "for mere amusement" there is one "worth reading of the little Jew child who ignorantly joined in the Christian communion, and was thrown into a furnace by his father in consequence; but when the furnace was opened, the Virgin appeared seated in the midst of the flames, with the little child unharmed on her lap."[8] Deriving even ironic "amusement" from this story betrays the hardened anti-Semite beneath the façade of sensitive perception and intellectual subtlety.

When confronted with a Jew whom he admired, he applies the stereotype of "superiority." Sir Francis Palgrave, "the greatest of all historians of early England," is the "only one who was un-English; and the reason of his superiority lay in his name, which was Cohen, and his mind which was Cohen also." The then current stereotype of the Jew as arriviste also creeps out. "Fashion was not fashionable in London until the Americans and the Jews were let loose," Adams writes in 1864.

There was no need, however, to be circumspect in applying pejorative adjectives to the ghetto Jew. In those years there was a verbal open season on the poor Jewish immigrant or the Jew of the European ghettos, and just about every writer expressed his revulsion—as often as not without compassion or understanding. Certainly Adams expresses his revulsion unrestrainedly in *Education.* On his return home from England in 1868, Adams perceives that "his world was dead. Not a Polish Jew fresh from Warsaw or Cracow—not a furtive Jacoob or Ysaac still reeking of the Ghetto, snarling a weird Yiddish to the officers of the customs—but had a keener instinct, an intenser energy, and a freer hand than he—American of Americans." On a visit to Russia in 1901, he writes, the first sight to meet his eyes as he looked out of his sleeping car window early in the morning was a "Polish Jew . . . in all his weird horror."[9] In a letter from Warsaw on this trip, he makes the visceral comment: the Jew, he writes, "makes me creep."[10]

Adams's close friend, John Hay, although not an anti-Semite, was extensively descriptive in his recoil from the ghetto. While an official of the legation at Vienna in 1867, Hay entered a description of the city's ghetto in his notebook.

Along this unclean street [he writes] rolls an endless tide of Polish Jews, continually supplied by little rivulets running down from the Judenplatz and the *culs-de-sac* of that neighborhood, not running, but trickling down. . . . These squalid veins and arteries of impoverished and degenerate blood are very fascinating to me. I have never seen a decent person in these alleys or on those slippery stairs. But everywhere stooping, dirty figures in long, patched and oily black gabardines . . . covering the slouching, creeping forms, from the round shoulders to the splay, shuffling feet. A battered soft felt hat crowns the oblique, indolent, crafty face, and, what is most offensive of all, a pair of greasy curls dangle in front of pendulous ears. This coquetry of hideousness is most nauseous.

These Jews do not fit into the stereotype of Jews he knows in America, so a new stereotype must be created. "They have utterly revolutionized my ideas of the Hebrew," Hay continues. "In America, we always say, 'Rich as a Jew,' because even if a Jew is poor he is so brisk, so sharp and enterprising that he is sure to make money eventually. But these slouching rascals are as idle as they are ugly. . . . I suppose the curse of the nation has lit on these fellows especially."[11]

But Hay was an exception among Adams's intimates, most of whom were anti-Semites. It is likely, however, that Adams exceeded the rest in the intensity of his hatred of the Jews. As his own failure to achieve political power became apparent, and as the hated finance capitalists grew in power and influence after the 1880s, his anti-Semitism grew so strong that many of his letters, especially during the 1890s, were intensely anti-Jewish. He identified the finance capitalists, the monopolists, with the advocates of the gold standard —"gold-bugs," he called them—and reluctantly supported Bryan against McKinley in 1896. He identified the Jews with finance capitalism and never missed an opportunity to pour anathema on them. When writing to Sir Robert Cunliffe in 1896, he condemned "your Lombard Street Jews who rule you" and "your Jew crusade for gold."

It was not industrial capitalism, but rather finance capitalism that he hated. McKinley's assassination gave him the occasion to remark that, although McKinley was "a very supple and highly paid agent of the crudest capitalism," one had to give him his due: "He served industrial capital rather than the Jews,"[12] that is, finance capitalism.

Adams even descended to dialect in writing from Paris to John Hay on July 28, 1896: "Belmont will look in with five other Wall Street Jews to offer you won millione tollers do peat dose tam temocrats mit der tam Pryan."[13]

Although Adams hated the "gold-bug" capitalists, it cannot be inferred from this that he was progressive or socialist in his politics. He several times clearly expresses his preference for "the Jew"— that is, capitalism, even finance capitalism—over socialism. In 1898 he wrote his brother, Brooks, that "it is the socialist—not the capitalist—who is going to swallow us next, and of the two I prefer the Jew." Again in the next year he wrote Brooks: "I loathe the socialist, of the trade union, petite bourgeoisie, type, rather decidedly, and even more than I loathe the Jew."[14] He looked on the spread of socialist sentiment as a "logical necessity," but he nevertheless also held in 1896 that "the growth of socialism is obviously only a disintegration of society." In the late 1890s Adams was interested in the writings of Marx and the socialists, but in the end his generally reactionary outlook, his "conservative anarchy," as he characterized his view in 1896, made capitalism more tolerable to him. The depression of 1893, in which he and his family lost heavily, made a profound impression on him, and in 1896 he wrote that in our society one runs multiple risks from "the burglar, the Jew, the Czar, the socialist, and, above all, the total irremediable radical rottenness of our whole social, industrial, financial and political system."[15]

But his intensive dislike of the Jew antedated the economic crisis and it continued to the end of his life. In 1888, riding in a "vestibule train," he wrote his dear friend Elizabeth Cameron, with whom he shared much of his anti-Jewish outpourings: "I could not help a slight depression at finding that astonishing creation of man's genius and luxury to be entirely intended and used for the conveyance of Chicago German Jews." Why, he asked, should the German Jews "be the aim and end of our greatest triumphs in science and civilization?" Vienna, he wrote in 1898, bored him because it was "wholly Americanized and Judaized." Whatever or whomever he wished to denigrate, he associated with the Jews. The economic disasters that felled so many of Adams's friends, he wrote in 1900, had come like "the devil on a broomstick in the shape of a mob of howling Jews who upset my world."[16] In 1899 he wrote in a light vein: "Let's go to the Phillippines—or pull some Jews' teeth."[17] When the depression of 1893 hit and nearly destroyed some of his friends, he was in the mood to help "the London mob to pull up Harcourt and Rothschild on a lamp-post in Piccadilly." In his rage against the "gold-bugs," and for him this meant essentially the Jewish financiers, he exclaimed: "I want to put every money-lender to death."[18]

His personal relations with Jews in the 1890s and later were consistent with his attitude. The actress Elsie de Wolfe was one of his favorite "nieces," that is, young friends. But, though Jewish, she was congenial because she was "in a state of anti-Semite rebellion which is the mark of all intelligent Jews," wrote Adams.[19] His relationship with the art critic Bernard Berenson was more complex. Berenson had immigrated to the United States from Lithuania in 1875 when he was ten. While at Harvard he became an Episcopalian; later he was a Roman Catholic for a while, the better to appreciate Italian art. Adams's painter friend John La Farge suggested that Adams, "knowing your love for the race," should introduce the promising young Berenson to Washington society. Adams complied, and in the end they became friends. But it was not easy for Adams. Ernest Samuels reports that "once in Washington after Berenson and his wife left, Adams burst out, 'I *can't* bear it. There is in the Jew depreciation, something that no weary sinner ought to stand. I rarely murder. By nature I am humane. . . . Yet I did murder Berenson. . . . In my own house I ought not to have done so. I tried to do it gently, without temper or violence of manner. Alas! Murder will out!'" For his part, Berenson "turned the other cheek. . . . Berenson was to recall, 'but he could not forget that he was an Adams and was always more embarrassed than I was that I happened to be a Jew.'"

Perhaps it was his acquaintance with Berenson as much as anything that led Adams to ambiguous expressions about Jewish taste in art. He said of *Mont-Saint-Michel and Chartres* that none could read more than fifty consecutive pages of the book, "barring a few Jews."[20] On the other hand, the art at Fontainbleau "is a Jewish kind of gold-bug style, fit to express Francis I and Henry VIII, with their Field of Cloth of Gold, and their sensual appetites." In Paris, Adams wrote, there were "a thousand bric-a-brac dealers, and all have hopeless rubbish, except three or four Jews who force up prices by cornering fashions. Anything these Jews touch is in some strange way vulgarized."[21]

In light of Adams's keen awareness of the alienated character of the Jew in Christian society, an alienation that he felt intensely in his personal attitude toward them, it is extremely significant that he suggests a parallel between the Jew and himself in the opening paragraphs of *Education.* The keynote of the book is the "failure" of his education because the role of patrician leadership into which he was born, which set him apart from his fellow Americans, was obsolete. "Had he been born in Jerusalem under the shadow of the Temple and circumcised in the Synagogue by his uncle the high priest, under the name of Israel Cohen, he would scarcely have been more distinctly branded, and not much more handicapped in the races of the coming century, in running for such stakes as the century was to offer."[22] With all the differences between our own time and his, it is interesting that he should perceive the Jew as the prototype of the alienated man, as the literary figures of the 1950s and 1960s were to do after him, though he did not feel so sympathetic as they toward their prototype.

Adams's antipathy for the Jews was shared by his friends. Not only Jews, but also foreigners and immigrants from the wrong parts of Europe—its central, eastern, and southern sections— were the targets of their animosity. Their prejudice found expression in anti-immigration agitation. Henry Cabot Lodge, a friend whose biography Adams wrote, was a leading defender of Anglo-Saxon superiority in the Senate, and from the early 1890s he was the senatorial leader in the drive for restricting immigration from southern and Eastern Europe and the Orient. The Immigration Restriction League was established by young Boston aristocrats in 1894 and was supported by two of Adams's intimate friends, Henry Holt and Lodge, who led the fight for its racist principles in the Senate. Adams's brother, Brooks, equaled him in vehemence in identifying hated finance capitalism with the Jews. "I tell you," wrote Brooks, "Rome was a blessed garden of paradise beside the rotten, unsexed, swindling lying Jews, represented by Pierpont Morgan [!] and the gang who have been manipulating the country for the last four years."[23]

The Adams brothers' hatred of capitalism, Jews, labor, socialism, and reform progressivism of any kind was so radical as to cause them to repudiate democracy itself and embrace an anarchistic pessimism. Toward the end of his life, the world seemed to Adams to be coming to an end.

I prove it [he writes] by the fact that I live here in Paris, or there in Washington, at the mercy of any damned Socialist or Congressman, or Tax-assessor, and I can't enter the Port of New York without being made to roll on the deck, to be kicked and cuffed and spit upon by a dirty employee of a dirtier Jew cad who calls himself collector, and before whom the whole mass of free American citizens voluntarily kneel.

And in his latter days in 1914 he complained that the Washington "atmosphere really has become a Jew atmosphere." But at least he

could defend himself: "Our sway over what we call society is undis-
puted. We keep Jews far away, and the anti-Jew feeling is quite rabid.
We are anti-everything and we are wild uplifters; yet we somehow
seem to be more Jewish every day."[24]

In the 1890s his anti-Semitism was fortified by a reading of Drumont's anti-Semitic works, and he even recommended this French
writer to his friends. In 1896 he wrote from Paris that "I pass the
day reading Drumont's anti-Semitic ravings." To another he wrote:
"I blush to confess" that "I read with interest actually the extrava-
gance of Drumont—*France Juive, Libre Parole,* and all. Suppose you
try his *'Dernière Bataille,'* or *'Le Fin du Monde.'* " With all his embar-
rassment at the attraction Drumont's irrationality had for him, his
own hatred of the Jews was not less irrational or less callous. It was
easy to persuade Adams that Dreyfus was guilty. After the acquittal
of Esterhazy in 1898, he wrote Elizabeth Cameron from Paris that
the army trial of Esterhazy had "set its foot on the Jews and smashed
the Dreyfus intrigue into a pancake." He agreed with his old friend
from the 1870s in Washington, the former Turkish diplomat Aristar-
chi Bey, that "whether Dreyfus is guilty or not (and he [Bey] has
little doubt of the fact that he was, but this is no longer important
to him)," the campaign for Dreyfus was heightening anti-Semitism
in France as "the whole extent of the Jew scandal is realized. For no
one doubts now that the whole campaign has been one of money and
intrigue; and the French are very furious. Of course, all the English
and the Americans are with the Jews, which makes it worse."[25]

Zola's *J'accuse* displeased Adams, who was not disturbed at the
prospect of Zola's going to prison. On the contrary, if Zola "did not
deserve it for the special offense," he wrote on February 28, 1898,
"he did for his novels; and on the whole I think he had better have
joined his friend Dreyfus on the Devil's Island some time ago, with
as much more French rot as the island would hold, including most
of the press and the greater part of the theatre, with all the stock-
brokers and a Rothschild or two for example." When Zola did not
go to prison after all, Adams wrote to John Hay: "To my intense
regret, Zola has not yet been sent to the devil or his island."[26]
Adams's brother, Brooks, spoke for both when he exclaimed: "Here
are the most distinguished officers in France, day after day brought
up by a gang of dirty Jews, and badgered and insulted, and held up
to contempt with the connivance of the Government."[27]

By September 5, 1899, when he could no longer believe in the
guilt of Dreyfus he was willing to "grant the innocence of Dreyfus,
if that is wanted, without question." This did not stop his abuse of

the Dreyfusards: "Dreyfus himself is a howling Jew as you see from his portraits." Nor did he cease being an anti-Dreyfusard. Since Dreyfus was exonerated, he wrote, "I have had but one rule, which is to back the Army and Navy against everything everywhere on every occasion. That is why I am an anti-Dreyfusard." Adams then shifted the direction of his venom to the Boer War, which was to him, like the Dreyfus case, a "Jew war"—by which he meant that the British war on the Boers was in the "Jew interest,"[28] that is, for finance capitalism. So obsessive was Adams's anti-Dreyfus feeling that it was even too much for his friends. John Hay, who was indifferent to the Jews rather than anti-Semitic, was finally moved to remark that Adams "now believes the earthquake at Krakatoa was the work of Zola and when he saw Vesuvius reddening the midnight air he searched the horizon to find a Jew stoking the fire."[29]

Not all of Adams's Brahmin contemporaries shared his hatred of Jews and prejudice against foreigners, nor did they lose their faith in democracy. Thomas Wentworth Higginson, for example, was outstanding in the constancy and clarity of his democratic views and complete absence of prejudice. In 1897, when his Brahmin compatriots were agitating for restrictions on the immigration of the "inferior races" then streaming into the country, Higginson reaffirms the open door for all. In reply to the supposedly condemnatory argument about the mixed racial character of the new immigrant, he asserts that the "pure-blooded" English "represent a race so mingled and combined, so swept by successive invasions and conquests, that it can claim no purity of strain, but only the strength of composite structure." As for the Jews, he says, they "have probably a less mingled descent than most of those who deprecate their arrival." Moreover, it was not the descendants of the original settlers of the country, but the immigrants who "have made the material greatness of this country." He observes that the ancestors of the patricians of his day were plebians when they came, and this will be the case with the grandchildren of immigrants. It is wrong, he says, to assume "that any one race monopolizes all the virtues." To those who say the immigrants form a larger proportion of the prison population than natives, he replies that this is because they are poor. Furthermore, the worst criminals remain out of jail: "The eminent scoundrels, who are rich and shrewd enough to keep out of prison, are rarely foreigners." And one of these "successful swindlers," he adds, does "more real harm in the community than twenty men convicted of drunkenness or petty larceny."[30]

Henry Adams was at the opposite extreme. His anti-Semitism was a convenient outlet for his frustrated craving for power and for the perversity of a society that moved from the settled, patrician order of the eighteenth century to a finance capitalism in which power was held by upstarts, symbolized for Adams by the Jews. So Adams retreated to a nostalgic love of an idealized thirteenth century and easily took for his own the anti-Jewish feeling that prevailed then. Charles W. Eliot said in 1920: "I should like to be saved from the loss of faith in democracy as I grow old and foolish. I should be sorry to wind up as the three Adamses did. I shall not, unless I lose my mind."[31]

Others of Adams's generation, men like Edward Everett Hale as well as Thomas W. Higginson, opposed immigration restriction and antiforeignism and tended to feel sympathetic to the Jews. The restrictionists were Anglo-Saxon racists whose fear and dislike of the outsider seemed finally to center on the Jews. Alice James, sister of Henry and William, makes a tart comment in her journal for May 7, 1891, that exposes the hypocrisy of some restrictionists. "What a spectacle," she writes; "the Anglo-Saxon races addressing remonstrances to the Czar against expelling Jews from Russia, at the very moment when their governments are making laws to forbid their immigration."[32] One brother, the philosopher William James, who was as free from prejudice as any man of his generation, summarily wished that "the Anglo-Saxon race would drop its sniveling cant."[33]

For his part, their brother, Henry James, assumed the conventional social attitude to the Jews, as he amply manifests in his fiction. Leon Edel reports that Bernard Berenson once said that "he didn't get along very well with James because James didn't like Jews." Edel assigns this unfriendliness to James's lack of interest in art "expertise or connoisseurs."[34] In any case, however, his anti-Semitism did not approach in intensity or irrationality the attitude of Henry Adams. The difference is clear from their respective attitudes toward the Dreyfus case. While Adams condemned the Dreyfusards and the Jews, whether or not Dreyfus was guilty, because they were an evil force, Henry James was profoundly disgusted by the false accusations against Dreyfus. When Zola was tried in February 1898 for publishing *J'accuse,* every day James felt himself "in Paris by the side of the big, brave Zola, whom I find really a hero." After Zola's conviction, James wrote him a letter of support that has never been found.

Later that year he wrote: "What a bottomless and sinister *affaire* and in what a strange mill it is grinding. The poor French." In a letter to his friend the French novelist Paul Bourget, who was an anti-Dreyfusard, he expressed sympathy for the predicament of France, but did not retreat from his position. He couldn't quite understand the French in this matter, he wrote: "Nothing here [in England] corresponds to them [the French experience and their feelings]—neither the good relations which we maintain with the Jews, and, in sum, with one another, nor the supreme importance we attach to civil justice, nor the 'short work' which we would make of the military if they attempted to substitute their justice for it." If France refused to retry the case, he ended, "I will find her less subject for sympathy."[35]

Henry James went to visit the Bourgets in March 1899 reluctantly, for he was aware that they believed Dreyfus guilty. His solution was that "one must duck one's head and pass quickly." After delaying in Paris, he finally spent a tense week on the Riviera with the Bourgets. "I treat the *Affaire* as none of my business (as it isn't), but *its* power to make one homesick in France and the French air is not small. It is a country *en decadence.* "[36] James kept his feelings about the Dreyfus case private throughout its course; his one public allusion to it occurs in an article on the French literary situation published in the *North American Review* in October 1899. Discussing Jules Lemaitre as a critic, James regrets that his convictions were of the "ugliest" kind—"his voice was loud throughout the 'Affair' . . . in the anti-revisionist and anti-Semitic interest." While Henry James's unequivocal private feelings about the Dreyfus case are creditable, one wishes he had spoken out—as he admired Zola for doing—even if he was not French.

Leon Edel seems to conclude too much from this aspect of James's life. James, writes Edel, "had no hatred for any people. He might satirize national manners or national idiosyncracies, or use national stereotypes, but there was no touch of bigotry or racism in his make-up."[37] "Hatred" is surely too strong a word for James's attitude toward the Jews. But social condescension and an incapacity to see the Jew as an individual and not a type is evinced by his fiction, as we shall see. It is a widely held misunderstanding, here shared by Edel, that the use of a stereotype does not imply an inherent prejudice against a people, whether the prejudice is conscious or unconscious, whether the subject is aware of his attitude or not. To the degree that one does not approach a member of a group as an individual, rather than as a bundle of invidious predetermined traits, one is prejudiced. To be sure, there are varying degrees and intensities of prejudice. And as we have seen, James's attitude cannot be identified with that of Henry Adams in virulence or irrationality.

Perhaps one may say that, like so many writers of the age, his feelings were ambivalent. In his comments on Eliot's *Daniel Deronda* (1876), written in the form of a conversation between a critic and two young ladies, three attitudes toward the book are discussed. There is Pulcheria, a social anti-Semite, who remarks: "Oh, my dear, when I think what a collection of noses there must have been at that [Deronda and Miriam's] wedding." Theodora is a "philo-Semite": "I have never disliked the Jews, as some people do," she says. "I am not like Pulcheria, who sees a Jew in every bush. I wish there were one: I would cultivate shrubbery! I have known too many clever and charming Jews; I have known none that were not clever." James himself is the critic, who is unhappy with the Jewish part of the novel, he says, on artistic grounds only. "George Eliot," he writes, "takes them as a person outside Judaism—picturesquely. I don't believe that is the way they take themselves." The Jewish part, he believes, is "at bottom cold; that is my only objection."[38]

How, then, did James treat the Jew in his own creative work? From the beginning to the end of his writing career Jews and Jewishness appear in about a dozen of his works, ranging from a passing allusion to a major role. In his very first published novel, *Watch and Ward* (1871), the brief allusion is mild enough. Of a young girl he writes that she is "extremely pretty, and looked a little like a Jewess," for her nose is "a trifle too aquiline"; she "wore a diamond in each ear"; and she has "a pair of imperious dark eyes, as bright as the diamond which glittered in each of her ears, and a nervous, capricious rapidity of motion and gesture, gave her an air of girlish *brusquerie,* which was by no means without charm."[39] For James, the Jewish woman had at least a suggestion of the exotic. This pattern of reference, established early, is sustained in his subsequent writing. In *The Golden Bowl* (1904), Fanny Assingham is "neither a pampered Jewess nor a lazy Creole," despite the fact that she suggests "a creature formed by hammocks and divans, fed upon sherbets and waited upon by slaves."[40] The exotic fades into the vulgar in "Covering End" (1898), where "a matron of rich Jewish type, with small nippers in a huge nose and a face out of proportion to her little Freischutz hat" provides "humor" by asking the identity of a portrait: "Who's *dat?*" Interestingly enough, when James wrote two plays on the themes of the short stories *(Summersoft* and *The High Bid),* the Jewish character and accented speech of the stories do not appear. Perhaps the presence of Jews at theater productions prompted James tactfully to omit such condescending allusions.[41]

The case of Miriam Rooth, a leading character of *The Tragic Muse* (1889–90), is more complex. She is in some respects reminiscent of

Hawthorne's Miriam of *The Marble Fawn*. Like the earlier Miriam, she is part Jewish, and to some extent this accounts for her specific nature. Her non-Jewish mother comes from "the great ones of the earth," the British upper class; her father was "only a Jew broker in the City." The father has died early, and her mother "not having the safeguard of being herself a Hebrew," has squandered the property he left. Miriam, an ambitious actress who aspires to be the British Rachel, is indifferent to her Jewishness, except as it makes her more "interesting."

Peter Sherringham, who is in love with Miriam, discusses her acting, remarking: "You're a Jewess—I'm sure of that." James adds that "she jumped at this, as he was destined to see later she would jump at anything that might make her more interesting or striking." "I want to be the English Rachel," she tells Peter. But she leaves no doubt that the only identity she really cares about is that of actress. "My name's Jewish," she says to Peter, "but it was that of my grandmother, my father's mother. She was a baroness in Germany. That is, she was the daughter of a baron." "Put that all together," Peter replies, "and it makes you sufficiently of Rachel's tribe." Miriam then exclaims: "I don't care if I'm of her tribe artistically. I'm of the family of artists—*je me fiche* of any other!"[42] The novel traces Miriam's progress from a rather vulgar but extremely attractive and talented aspiring actress to a sophisticated, accomplished one who has made a great success.

Just as Hawthorne involves his Miriam in an exploration of his central theme, the nature of sin, so James's Miriam becomes the vehicle for expounding James's views on the nature of the artist and his alienation from ordinary society. Peter at first resists marrying Miriam because he fears it will hamper his diplomatic career, as she will not give up acting. When Peter returns to London after a period of trying to get over his infatuation, Miriam has just opened successfully in a play. He cannot resist her and proposes; but she has already married her stage manager.

A similar fidelity to art, the decision not to surrender art for another mode of life, is inherent in the relationship between Nick Dormer and his wealthy cousin, Julia Dallow. Nick aspires to be a painter, but Julia wishes him to give up painting and offers to sponsor a political career if he will marry her. But the implicit compromise of his painting, like that of Miriam's acting if she were to marry Peter, is intolerable, and the match is called off. Art is primary for both Miriam and Nick, and for its sake they surrender the social status and leisure of upper-class affluence.

The tragic muse is a severe mistress to whom Miriam and Nick subordinate themselves. Miriam's Jewishness accentuates the alienation that artistic integrity seems to call forth in an essentially philistine society. James lifts the problem he poses out of the track of ordinary, conventional human relations by calling upon the literary convention of the Jewish woman as beautiful and exotic and "interesting," though not quite socially acceptable.

Miriam's deceased father, Rudolf Roth (Mrs. Roth has added an "o" to this name to make it less Jewish), is described as a stockbroker and a dealer in antiquities: he possessed "the artistic temperament that is common, as you know, among *ces messieurs.*" Like other Jewish characters of James's, Roth makes the acquaintance of the Anglo-Saxon characters in the novel through their common interest in objets d'art. Rudolf Roth "made the most of his little opportunities and collected various pictures, tapestries, enamels, porcelains and similar gewgaws. He parted with them also, I gather, at a profit; in short, he carried on a neat little business of *brocateur.* . . . It was to this precarious traffic, conducted with extraordinary mystery and delicacy, that, five years ago, in Florence, I was indebted to my acquaintance with him." Moreover, "Rudolf Roth was very versatile, and, like most of his species, not unacquainted with the practice of music." Miriam did not derive her artistic sense and dramatic talent from her aristocratic but stodgy mother. "The Hebraic Mr. Rooth, with his love of old pots and Christian altar cloths, had supplied in the girl's composition an aesthetic element, the sense of colour and form."[43]

The Jewish male as art connoisseur with artistic temperament (but not without a keen nose for profit and an occupational involvement in finance) appears several times in James's fiction. In "Impressions of a Cousin" (1883) the Jewish Mr. Caliph is the executor of the estate of a New York heiress, a very clever man, and, says the female diarist, "really very delightful." Her flattering description of a Jew embarrasses her. "I suppose," she says, "I must write it very small; but I have an intimate conviction that he is a Jew, or of Jewish origin." Of course he has "remarkable eyes." He doesn't, however, "look like a gentleman," but he is "not in the least a bourgeois— neither is he of the artist type." She concludes that he is a Jew, "and Jews of the upper class have a style of their own." Nevertheless, the narrator later remarks that Caliph is "a Jew of the artistic, not of the commercial, type." When he tells his client Eunice to trust him, the narrator asks: "Who ever heard of a naïf Jew?" The diarist is on the point of warning Eunice that Caliph is a "Hebrew," but refrains to save Eunice the unpleasantness of the discovery.[44]

Caliph turns out, not surprisingly, to be anything but naive. Although he takes no commission for his services to Eunice's trust fund, he is indeed after Eunice's fortune. She is in love with him, and he hopes to marry her. But because he has mismanaged her estate, probably by unsuccessful speculation, she is reduced in circumstances. Her financial situation is retrieved by the agency of Caliph's non-Jewish half brother, Adrian, who also wishes to marry Eunice, but in the end marries her diarist cousin. Adrian is contrasted throughout with Caliph: he is the upright "gentleman" as against the "captivating Caliph" who is "no better than a common swindler." The diarist cousin is shocked that Eunice should be in love with "that pickpocket," but Eunice has "forgiven him for thieving," and they probably do marry. Caliph is unfathomable to the diarist: "I have seen other people who have no moral sense, but I have seen no one with that impudence, that cynicism, that remorseless cruelty."[45] Essential to the structure of the story is the corruption of the Jew, Caliph, and the integrity of his non-Jewish half brother, Adrian.

Like Henry Adams, who warned against "money-making for Jew theatre-managers" and commented on the "rich Jews, whose instinctive taste has seized the whole field of art which rests on their degradation,"[46] James returned again and again to the Jew as artist and exploiter of art. In *The Spoils of Poynton* (1896) the Gareths have gathered their precious collection of objets d'art from "their swing among the Jews" of Europe. Mrs. Gareth, "this genuine English lady," gaily proclaims "that she herself," the quintessential collector, "was the greatest Jew who ever tracked a victim,"[47]

James deals even more elaborately with Jewish art dealers in *The Golden Bowl* (1904). While in Brighton, Adam Verver and Charlotte Stant go to the Jewish art dealer Mr. Gutermann-Suess to buy some precious objects. The portrait is favorable if condescending: he is "remarkably genial, a positively lustrous young man." They are invited to visit with the dealer's family, and we are treated to a genteel version of the stereotype of the Jew as oriental and exotic. Although only about thirty years old, Gutermann-Suess already has eleven children. Charlotte observes condescendingly the "fat, earringed aunts, and the glossy, cockneyfied, familiar uncles, inimitable of accent and assumption and of an attitude of cruder intention than that of the head of the firm." After completing their purchase, they have wine and cake, "the touch of some mystic rite of old Jewry."[48]

James's depiction of the unnamed Jewish owner of the shop where the golden bowl is located has more sinister overtones. When the prince and Charlotte enter his shop, he "fixes on his visitors an extraordinary pair of eyes." Although he knows the golden bowl is cracked, he would sell it to them except that Prince Amerigo has been sharp enough to detect the crack. When Maggie Verver comes upon the bowl in the dealer's shop later in the story, he sells it to her at an exorbitant price, without revealing the existence of the flaw. Apparently he "likes" Maggie, for later he goes to her house, explains that he has overcharged her, and reveals the compromising near-purchase of the golden bowl by her husband and Charlotte just before her wedding. James is careful to explain that "the vendor of the golden bowl had acted on a scruple rare enough in vendors of any class, and almost unprecedented in the thrifty children of Israel." To Amerigo and Catherine he is "the little swindling Jew."[49] The dealer's visit to Maggie, which results in the revelation of the relationship between the prince and Charlotte, is more a requirement of the plot than a motivated action. Moreover, the symbolic function of the golden bowl as representing flawed human behavior is mediated by a Jew, thus rendering him an agency for dubious moral relations. He is subtly implicated in the commission of evil.

The presence of Jews in high society is disparagingly noted in several of James's novels. In *The Ambassadors* (1903) James assumes the tone of condescending aristocrat in describing the circle entertained in the studio of the artist Gloriani: "Oh, they're everyone—all sorts and sizes; of course, I mean within limits, though limits down, rather than up . . . —ambassadors, cabinet ministers, bankers, generals, what do I know? even Jews."[50] In *The Awkward Age* (1899), in a discussion of how many troubles can be solved by marrying for money, Mrs. Brooks refers condescendingly to one of the prize catches: "The Jew man, so gigantically rich—who is he? Baron Schack or Schmack—who has just taken Cumberland House and who has the awful stammer—or what is it? no roof to his mouth? —is to give that horrid little Algie, to do his conversation for him, four hundred a year."[51] In *What Maisie Knew* (1897) two of Lady Ida's dubious men friends are Jews. One of them, Mr. Perriam, wears on his hand "a diamond of dazzling lustre." He "comes from the City . . . and has made a mass of money."[52] In "Glasses" (1896) the vacationing hero describes Jews taking the waters at fashionable Folkestone: "There were thousands of little chairs and almost as many little Jews; and there was music in an open rotunda, over which the little Jews wagged their big noses." Of one of his female characters, who talks a great deal about herself, he writes that "she held her little court in the crowd, upon the grass, playing her light over Jews and Gentiles, completely at ease in all promiscuities."[53] On the other hand, when James wants to castigate the Moreens, a financially inestimable family appearing in "The Pupil," he calls on a reliable simile. "Who had poisoned their blood with the fifth-rate social ideal? Clever as they were they never guessed how they appeared. They were good-natured, yes—as good-natured as Jews at the doors of clothing-shops! But was that the model one wanted one's family to follow?"[54]

What would have happened to Svengali if James, rather than du Maurier, had written *Trilby?* The two close friends had discussed the plot, but James had resisted du Maurier's urging to write the story. In Henry James's subsequent comments on the phenomenally successful *Trilby* as a novel and a play, there is, as one would expect, no sensitivity to the anti-Semitic animus behind the Svengali characterization. And indeed, considering the Jewish characterizations that did occur in James's fiction, is there any reason to suppose that in his hands Svengali would have been any less heinous a libel on the Jews than du Maurier's actually was? Only the gross injustice of the Dreyfus case was unsubtle enough to affront James, to move him to opposition—if only privately.

Like most Americans, the Jews were alien to James; just how distant from them James felt is evinced in his comments on the condition of the Jewish ghetto in New York. During his last long visit to the United States in 1904–5, he was given a conducted tour of the East Side, which he recounts in *The American Scene* (1907). Of course, it was not only the Jew who was alien to the aging James. If the young James considered the cultural soil of the United States too sterile for his creativity, the older James, returning to America after two decades, found a country radically different from the one he had left and even more alien to his mentality than before. The "swarming" Jews of New York, "a Jewry that had burst all bounds," was only one aspect of the new America that repelled him. To be sure, the impression that the teeming population of the East Side made on an eye and mind unaccustomed to the sight must have been overpowering. James reports that "with the exception of some shy corner of Asia, no district in the world known to the statistician has so many inhabitants to the yard. . . ."[55]

James's response to this unprecedented sight was not humane and compassionate and comprehending, but rather disgusted and dehumanized. To James, this concentration of the Jewish population intensified the Jewishness of the individuals, in that "the unsurpassed strength of the race permits of the chopping into myriads of fine fragments without loss of race-quality." He was reminded of "small, strange animals, known to natural history, snakes or worms, I believe, who, when cut into pieces, wriggle away and live in the snippet as completely as in the whole. So the denizens of the New York Ghetto, heaped as thick as the splinters on the table of a glass-blower, had each, like the fine glass particle, his or her individual share of the whole hard glitter of Israel."[56]

The unconscious process that went into creating this striking imagery tells much of James's human distance from the Jews. Jews are "snakes or worms" and Jewry as a whole has a "hard glitter." The unfeeling images continue: the Jews "were all there for race, and not, as it were, for reason"; the old ones conveyed an "excess of lurid meaning"; the " 'ethnic' apparition" sat "like a skeleton at the feast"; James can see "the spectre grin" as he is told facts and figures about "the extent of the Hebrew conquest of New York." Everywhere, it seems to him, the faces are "insistent, defiant, unhumorous, exotic."

Easier for us to understand, even if we do not concur, is James's shock at what is happening to the English language in the ghetto. The "East-Side cafes," James writes, are "torture-rooms of the living idiom" and he despairs of the future of the language.

The Jews, finally, are a mysterious, incomprehensible, and perhaps sinister people. "Who can ever tell, moreover, in any conditions and in presence of any apparent anomaly, what the genius of Israel may, or may not, really be 'up to'?"[57]

It would not be fair to James, however, if we did not mention that when his view of the East Side leads him to think about "the poor" and the depersonalization of the individual under the operation of the "Trusts and . . . the new remorseless monopolies," he displays great social insight. He discerns that "the living unit's property in himself" comes under unconditional subjection to these "properties overwhelmingly greater." He concludes that "there is such a thing, in the United States, it is hence to be inferred, as freedom to grow up to be blighted, and it may be the only freedom in store for the smaller fry of future generations."[58] Such social insight, however, emerges after his specific discussion of the ghetto. For the Jews his response is curiosity mixed with revulsion.

17

HOWELLS AND THE REALISTS

The industrialization and urbanization of the country, which proceeded so rapidly after the Civil War, was assimilated into literature in the last few decades of the century. The new condition of the nation was expressed not only in politics—by populism and socialism —but also in literature—by realism. In terms of influence William Dean Howells was the central figure of the emergent realism, as both novelist and critic. Before the century was over Howells had welcomed many new writers to his movement, chief among them Hamlin Garland, Frank Norris, and Stephen Crane. This first realist impetus was spent by the turn of the century: by then Howells had already done his most important work; Hamlin Garland had virtually abandoned the movement; Frank Norris had died in 1902 at the age of thirty-two; and Stephen Crane, the American Chatterton-Rimbaud, died in 1900 at twenty-nine.

All of them, except perhaps Norris, leaned politically toward the Left. As might be expected from this orientation, these writers did not share the violently anti-Jewish attitudes of the aristocrats of the Henry Adams circle—but neither does one find any deep understanding of the Jews. All of them were, to a lesser or greater extent, swept along by the prejudiced or racist attitudes toward the immigrants prevalent in the latter years of the century. At best, one can say of the realists' attitude toward the Jews on the whole that it was ambivalent; at worst, in Norris's case, it was plainly anti-Semitic.

In this respect one may say that Howells stood somewhere between his close friends, Henry James on one side and Mark Twain on the other. Like Mark Twain, his early rearing was in the more tolerant West, but, like Henry James, he had close ties with aristocratic New England. From his birth in Ohio in 1837 to his departure for Venice as consul in 1861, he was formed by the pioneering Midwest. But from 1866 to 1881 his editorial association with the

Atlantic Monthly and his personal friendship with the New England Brahmins disposed him toward their ethnic attitudes, which, as we have seen, included anti-Semitism.

From his father Howells acquired a tradition of dissent—William Cooper Howells was a utopian, an abolitionist, and an anti-imperialist whose unpopular opposition to the annexation of Texas had forced the family to move from Hamilton, Ohio. This paternal influence emerged strongly when Howells began to read Tolstoy in the mid-1880s, and he became a Christian Socialist. He read William Morris, Edward Bellamy, Henry George, and especially Laurence Gronlund, a Danish immigrant who became one of the earliest American socialists, whom Howells heard lecture in Buffalo in 1887, an event that inspired his interest in and sympathy for socialism. He was a charter member of the Bellamy Nationalist Club in Boston in 1890, as were Edward Everett Hale, Thomas Wentworth Higginson, Gronlund, and Vida Scudder. When W. D. P. Bliss, one of the early Christian Socialists, gathered his Brotherhood of the Carpenters in 1900, Howells was among them. He was an anti-imperialist and opposed the Cuban War and the Philippine occupation.

In one of the most courageous actions of any American writer in the century, an act that deserves to stand alongside the defense of John Brown by Emerson and Thoreau in 1859, Howells alone among writers came out strongly in defense of the Haymarket anarchists in a letter published in the *New York Tribune* in November 1887. He later revealed that his pleas to John Greenleaf Whittier and George William Curtis to join him in this letter were rejected. For the next decade he was deeply interested in the labor movement and was much concerned with the great strikes of the period; his treatment of the streetcar strike in *A Hazard of New Fortunes* (1890) reflects this sympathetic concern. Even in his later years his social interest was sustained, though perhaps at not so high a pitch. He spoke out for prison reform and advocated woman suffrage to the extent of marching in a suffrage parade in New York in 1912.

Indeed, it is remarkable that Howells faced up to not only these problems but also the central issue of the blacks. On his seventy-fifth birthday in 1912 the *Boston Evening Transcript* published a number of tributes to Howells, among them one by W. E. B. DuBois, who singled out three acts of Howells for praise. First, his work includes "the most significant thing in the land . . . the black man."[1] DuBois was deeply impressed with the fact that Howells has a white man marry a girl even after the discovery that she is part black. The novel referred to is *An Imperative Duty* (1891), in which Rhoda Aldgate is told by her aunt that her mother was an octoroon, thus making her one-sixteenth black. Rhoda's Puritan conscience at first drives her to want to devote herself completely to the welfare of her mother's people; but her husband, Dr. Olney, persuades her that she is closer to the white community than to the black, and that the best way to help blacks is to reform the white community—a bit of advice that became familiar in the 1960s.[2]

The second ground for DuBois's tribute was Howells's recognition of and help to the black poet Paul Lawrence Dunbar. Howells, writes DuBois, "discovered Dunbar. We have had a score of artists and poets in black America, but few critics dared to call them so. . . . Howells dared to take Dunbar by the hand and say to the world not simply, here is a black artist, but here is an artist who happens to be black." Howells, he mentions, accepted Dunbar's poetry (quoting Howells) "as an evidence of the essential unity of the human race, which does not think or feel black in one and white in another, but humanly in all."[3]

Someone had given Howells a copy of Dunbar's second work of poetry, *Majors and Minors* (1895), which had no indication of publisher, place, or date of publication. So impressed was Howells with this book that he reviewed it in his "Life and Letters" pages in *Harper's Weekly,* thereby bringing Dunbar at once to national attention. Howells recognized the book's "artistic quality." He was especially struck by the success with which Dunbar used dialect, but he felt that Dunbar was "a real poet whether he speaks a dialect or whether he writes a language." Nor did he think that Dunbar fell into the "too easy pathos of the pseudo-negro poetry of the minstrel show."[4]

Howells wrote an introduction to the black poet's *Lyrics of Lowly Life* (1896), in which Howells reiterates his laudatory judgment of Dunbar. The "brilliant and unique achievement" of Dunbar, he writes, "was to have studied the American negro objectively, and to have represented him as he found him to be, with humor, with sympathy, and yet with what the reader must instinctively feel to be entire truthfulness." He considers Dunbar most successful in dialect poetry, in which the "hearts and minds" of the blacks are given, "for the first time in our tongue, literary interpretation of a very artistic completeness." Dunbar, he concludes, "has made the strongest claim for the negro in English literature that the negro has yet made."[5] Howells exerted his considerable influence to have Dunbar's work published regularly, and for Dunbar to lecture and read from his work on public platforms.

DuBois adds a third ground for his tribute to Howells: when the call went out for sponsors to help form the National Association for the Advancement of Colored People, writes DuBois, Howells "was among the first to sign." All in all, DuBois concludes, "America regardless of race and America, all-inclusive mother of all races, hastens to honor the man whose hand and brain has given his land its truest and deepest expression."[6]

Yet running counter to Howells's advanced political and social thinking were his inexorably middle-class situation and preferences. Despite his profound admiration for Tolstoy, he realized that he could not bring himself to give up his middle-class mode of life and emulate Tolstoy's vows of poverty. The socialist David Hughes in *The World of Chance* (1893) expresses some of Howells's reservations. Tolstoy is "impractical," thinks Hughes. While Tolstoy "has struck some tremendous truths," he is an "extremitist" who would remove himself from the world; but Hughes (and Howells) insist on the necessity of social commitment. More personal was Howells's confession in a letter to his father in 1890: "Elinor [Howells's wife] and I are . . . theoretical socialists, and practical aristocrats. But it is a comfort to be right theoretically, and to be ashamed of one's self practically."[7]

Despite his sympathy for labor and the working class, his grasp of labor principles must not have been very strong, judging from his praise of John Hay's palpably antilabor novel *The Bread-Winners* (1884), in which labor organizers are depicted as criminals (Hay's biographer correctly interprets the book as a defense of property against the labor movement). It is, says Howells, a book that "instills into you the belief that 'honest' Labor has nothing to complain of."[8] Howells's favorable opinion of the "realism" of the novel blunts his social judgment of its message. "It courageously expressed a fact not hitherto attempted: The fact that the working men are no better or wiser than the rich as the rich, and are quite as likely to be false and foolish." Howells does not believe that "the author was assailing them as a class."[9] Howells failed to grasp that Hay puts forward the superiority of property rights over human rights.

There can be no doubt, however, that the underlying impulse of Howells's life and work was democratic. He believed that literature should be "true to the motives, the impulses, the principles that shape the life of actual men and women."[10] In concrete terms this meant an honest representation of everyday life, especially that of ordinary people. The romanticism that Howells was combatting was both aristocratic and remote from common life. While Howells drew back from the unrestrained and ecstatic universalism of Whitman's democracy, the impulse of his work stems from the same democratic roots and in effect seeks, in mitigated form, to express in the novel what Whitman had achieved for poetry. If he himself did not face up to the full implications of the doctrine he was advocating, and was in a measure inhibited by the genteel society in which he moved, his voice was nevertheless the most influential of his time in steering the American literature away from the romantic and genteel.

In view of the various ambiguities and tensions between and within his life and his beliefs, it should not surprise us that Howells was not completely free from ethnic prejudices. In his early years in Cambridge he felt hostility toward the Irish, who were moving into the city. He experienced a "grudge . . . for the increasing presence of that race among us," though he was later to characterize that grudge as "mean and cruel."[11] In 1869 he thought he would move from Sacramento Street because "all Ireland seems to be poured out"[12] into the neighborhood.

Toward the Jews there is something of the same feeling, especially in his fiction up to the 1880s. The Jew appears as a seller of clothes who palms off on unsuspecting customers cheap, ill-fitting suits at high prices. In a short story, "A Romance of Real Life" (1870), a man from the country is described as wearing clothes in which "the poverty and ignorance of the purchaser were so apparent in their shabby newness, of which they appeared still conscious enough to have led the way to the very window, in the Semitic quarter of the city, where they had lain ticketed, 'This nobby suit for $15.' "[13]

The next year Howells elaborated this image from the presumed Jewish side in a conversation between two Jews on a Hudson River boat in *Their Wedding Journey* (1872):

"Well, as I was a-say'n', Isaac don't seem to haf no natcheral pent for the glothing business. Man gomes in and wands a goat,—" he seemed to be speaking of a garment and not a domestic animal,— "Isaac'll zell him the goat he wands him to puy, and he'll make him believe its the goat he was a lookin' for. Well, now, that's well enough as far as it goes; but *you* know and *I* know, Mr. Rosenthal, that that's no way to do business. A man gan't zugzeed that goes upon that brincible. Id's wrong. Id's easy enough to make a man puy the goat you want him to, if he wands a goat, but the thing is to *make him puy the goat that you wand to zell when he don't wand no goat at all.* You've asked me what I thought and I've dold you. Isaac'll never zugzeed in the redail glothing-business in the world!"[14]

Never again, as far as I am aware, did Howells indulge in this conventional stereotyping, complete with dialect. But the image recurs in *A Modern Instance* (1881). When the rustic Maine man, Kinney, comes to visit Bartley Hibbard in the city, he contrasts Bartley's smart clothes with his own. "I don't suppose I ever had a suit of clothes to fit me," says Kinney. "Feel kind of ashamed, you know, when I go into the store, and take the first thing the Jew wants to put off on to me." When Kinney visits Bartley later in Boston, his clothes, writes Howells, indicate that "he had evidently had one of his encounters with a cheap clothier, in which the Jew had triumphed."[15] While the situation portrayed by Howells in these passages had some basis in reality, this repetitive reference to and limited characterization of the Jew constitutes a stereotype.

Although Howells did not return to this stereotype in his subsequent work, the signs of ambiguity remain. *The Rise of Silas Lapham* (1885) is significant in this respect. When the story was first serialized in the *Century Magazine,* Howells had the Laphams discuss selling their house and moving to a "better" neighborhood. Their house, they believe, will bring less in the market because, says Lapham,

you see, they [the Jews] *have* got in—and pretty thick too—it's no use denying it. And when they get in, they send down the price of property. Of course, there ain't any sense in it; *I* think it's all dumn foolishness. It's cruel, and folks ought to be ashamed. But there it is. You tell folks that the Saviour himself was one, and the twelve apostles, and all the prophets,—I don't know but what Adam was—guess he *was,*—and it don't make a bit of difference. They send down the price of real estate. Prices begin to shade when the first one gets in.

Mrs. Lapham is not impressed. "Well, what do we care, so long as we're comfortable in our home? And they're just as nice and as good neighbors as can be," she replies. "Oh, it's all right as far as I'm concerned," Lapham agrees. It turns out that Tom Corey, the Bostonian aristocrat who is interested in the Laphams' daughter, has "stirred up" Mrs. Lapham on the matter. When Mrs. Lapham remarks that a "Mr. Liliengarten" has bought a house nearby, Lapham responds: "Well, I'm agreeable. I suppose he's got the money to pay for it." "Oh, yes, they've all got the money," she answers.[16]

These passages offended some influential Jews. An indignant editor of the *American Hebrew,* Cyrus L. Sulzberger, protested in a letter to Howells on July 12, 1885, and the letter was published in the September 4, 1885, issue of the journal, after the book appeared.

As "The Rise of Silas Lapham" is about approaching completion [wrote Sulzberger], and will, I presume, soon appear in book form,

I beg to call to your notice a slur (in Chapter II) upon a number of your readers and admirers—a slur as unmerited by the Jewish people as it is unworthy of the author. It is not alone upon the ignorant and uncultured of the Jews that you reflect, for neither "the Saviour himself" nor the twelve apostles, nor the prophets, nor even Adam, were, so far as the records show, of that class which depreciated the value of property when they "got in."

The introduction of the lines in question cannot even be excused on the ground that it serves a literary purpose, for no such end is accomplished. The sentiment is violently dragged in for no other ascertainable reason than to pander to a prejudice against which all educated and cultured Jews must battle. The literary leaders of a country have so great a power in fomenting or in repressing popular prejudice, that I make bold to hope that in the permanent form in which "Silas Lapham" will no doubt soon appear, these objectionable lines will be omitted.[17]

There is a note of impatience and irritation in the reply that Howells sent from Old Orchard, Maine, on July 17, 1885:

I thank you for your frank and manly letter. I supposed that I was writing in reprobation of the prejudice of which you justly complain, but my irony seems to have fallen short of the mark—so far short that you are not the first Hebrew to accuse me of "pandering" to the stupid and cruel feeling against your race and religion. I will not ask you to read again, in the light of this statement, the passage of my story which you object to, for I have already struck it out of my book, and it will not re-appear. In that passage I merely recognized to rebuke it, the existence of a feeling which civilized men should be ashamed of. But perhaps it is better not to recognize all the facts. Perhaps also you owe me an apology for making an unjust accusation. I leave that to you.[18]

Sulzberger did apologize in his reply on July 19. While acknowledging that he had missed the irony of the passage, he justified the "stupidity" of his interpretation by pointing out that "Silas's admission that 'they' do depreciate the value of property when they get in—a fact concerning the financial accuracy of which I have some doubts—seemed to me rather an endorsement than a rebuke of what you truly call the 'stupid and cruel feeling' against us."[19]

There is no question that Howells's condemnation of anti-Semitism was honest, and that he meant the passage to be an ironic comment. Such attitudes and beliefs as the passage expresses were no doubt prevalent. After the exchange of letters was published in the *American Hebrew* on September 4, 1885, several Jews wrote Howells dissenting from Sulzberger's view. Two correspondents, S. J. Strauss, a Wilkes-Barre, Pennsylvania, lawyer, and Nathan Mayer, of Hartford, Connecticut, drama and music critic of the Hartford

Courant and author of the Civil War novel *Differences,* discussed
earlier, assured Howells that a majority of "intelligent" and of the
"best and most advanced" Jews of the country found in the passages
a factual statement accompanied by a dissociation of Silas Lapham
and his wife from a prejudiced attitude.[20]

However, instead of grappling with the problem, Howells chose
to evade the whole issue by dropping the passage altogether. It is
likely that the circumstances of Howells's life at the time disinclined
him to delve too deeply into the problem. It will be recalled that it
was Tom Corey, Brahmin suitor of the Laphams' daughter, who put
the bee of value depreciation in Mrs. Lapham's bonnet. Howells was
beginning to suggest the real problem, namely, that the old established Boston families were starting to chafe at the incursion of
prosperous Jews into Boston society. Nearly all of Howells's friends
among the Brahmins, from James Russell Lowell to Charles Eliot
Norton, were anti-Semitic; they had succumbed to racial theories of
Anglo-Saxon or Teutonic superiority and advocated immigration
restriction. Henry Adams and Lowell were only the more obstreper-
ous Brahmin anti-Semites. To probe more deeply into the problem
would have involved Howells in a criticism of his friends that he
could not face up to. As Kermit Vanderbilt has written, although
Howells "recognized the odious face of anti-Semitism, he was tied
to Lowell, Norton, and the rest on too many other counts to allow
him to 'recognize all the facts' about these 'civilized men.' "[21]

Howells himself was deeply troubled at the time by personal
problems of social status. *Silas Lapham* is autobiographical in its
description of moving into a house on Back Bay. Howells had
bought a house on Beacon Street in the summer of 1884, and in his
concern to gain status and to establish a position for the social debut
of his daughter, Winifred, he was probably not eager to confront the
anti-Jewish prejudice of his friends. He was content to utter unequivocal denials of anti-Semitism, but he evaded discussion of the
issue.[22] This was also true in 1890, in his reply to the symposium
conducted by the *American Hebrew* on "Prejudice against the Jews"
(discussed in chapter 3). Many celebrated figures of the day, including outstanding Brahmin and national professional and church per-
sonages, responded. All of them discussed the questions asked about
anti-Semitism, but Howells answered each one with a phrase or a
sentence at most, signifying categorical rejection of anti-Semitism.
Why did he not, as did friends like Edward Everett Hale and Oliver
Wendell Holmes, make some attempt at analysis?[23]

It is likely that Howells was uncomfortable with the problem. In

A Hazard of New Fortunes (1890) he introduces Lindau, a fervent socialist, who is probably patterned after a forty-eighter of the same name, a German Jewish bookbinder, who taught Howells German in Columbus, Ohio, in the 1850s. In the book, Basil March, visiting in New York, happens to meet Lindau, said to be an antislavery man and veteran of the Berlin barricades in 1848, who had taught March German in Indianapolis. Obviously March (Howells) has the deepest respect for Lindau, even though he thinks the socialist is quixotic and impractical; March even risks his editorship to defend Lindau from being discharged from his paper because of his opinions. Lindau is also described as the model for a sculpture of Old Testament prophets and for Judas Iscariot. His suitability for these figures suggests Jewishness, yet Lindau is identified throughout as German, never as Jewish. And when Lindau dies, Howells makes his own ambiguity explicit by noting that "no one knew what Lindau's religion was, and in default they had had the Anglican burial service read over him; it seems the refuge of all the homeless dead."[24] Why could he not face in the fictional Lindau the Jewishness of the original Lindau?

At the same time, Howells exhibits a dislike of the newly rich Jews of New York. It is hard to know whether this feeling was one of dislike for the middle class or an expression of the new feeling of discrimination. In this period the Jews became the symbol of the vulgarity of the nouveaux riches, even though, of course, quick riches came to many other groups in American society in those years of rapid economic expansion, with similar social consequences. In a letter to Charles Eliot Norton from Saratoga, dated August 21, 1890, Howells commented on the large number of Jews and their inelegant manners: "There are no end of Hebrews and Hebrés; the ladies all go about bare headed at night."[25]

In *A Hazard,* Howells describes a Sunday afternoon walk on Madison Avenue. The people there, he writes, are "very homogeneous, and almost purely American; the only qualification was American Hebrew. Such a well-dressed, well-satisfied, well-fed looking crowd poured down the broad sidewalks before the handsome, stupid houses that March could easily pretend he had got among his fellow-plutocrats at last." But the whole scene is "a little dull; the men's faces were shrewd and alert, and yet they looked dull; the women were pretty and knowing, and yet dull. It was, probably, the holiday expression of the vast, prosperous commercial class, with unlimited money, and no ideals that money could not realize." March prefers the poorer sections of town, such as Mott Street, where Lindau lives. On affluent Madison Avenue poor people would be "bored to death." Earlier in the story Howells describes the crowds of shoppers on Sixth Avenue, and notes that "the most picturesque admixture" includes, besides the familiar American men and women, "the brilliant eyes and complexions of the American Hebrews, who otherwise contributed to the effect of well-clad comfort and citizen self-satisfaction of the crowd."[26]

Howells's dislike of middle- and upper-class Jews as a whole is apparent enough. But what of the poor Jews on the East Side, whose numbers were increasing so rapidly in the 1890s and later? We have seen already that he found the poorer districts of the city more interesting than the affluent ones. Like so many writers of the time, Howells took a guided tour of the East Side and registers his impressions in an essay, "An East-Side Ramble." He is, of course, shocked by the "squalor," which, he thinks, it "could not be possible to outrival any where in the life one commonly calls civilized." Nothing has happened since to alter his expectation that there would "always be tenement dwellers in New York as long as our present economical conditions endure."

He marvels at the Jews' placidity, passivity, personal cleanliness, and tidiness, and the fact that in the midst of their unsanitary surroundings, the death rate of the Jews is the lowest in the city. He has provided himself with small change to dispense during his tour but his sensitivity and respect for people checked distribution of it very soon. He soon "began to fancy an unseemliness in it, as if it were an indignity added to the hardship of their lot, and to feel that unless I gave all my worldly wealth to them I was in a manner mocking their misery." The children, who go to school and speak English, seem to him "quick and intelligent."[27]

The street markets strike him as ironies, "a sorrowfully amusing satire upon the business ideal of our plutocratic civilization." For the participants are "desperately poor, yet they preyed upon one another in their commerce." He sees "splendid types of that old Hebrew world which had the sense if not the knowledge of God when all the rest of us lay sunk in heathen darkness." The women, with "clear, dark eyes, relucent as evening pools," and bearded men convey to him "the noble profiles of their race." Despite the intolerably dense crowding, with a whole family living in one room, and the inadequate clothing and food, the Jews "did not have the look of a degraded people." He does not hold out much hope of improvement, except for a few who might escape, as long as the poor are housed "by private landlords, whose interest it is to get the greatest return of money for the money invested."[28] While he did not fore-see the extent to which the Jews would leave the teeming ghetto in the next half century, his comment is still relevant for the blacks and Puerto Ricans who have replaced the Jews in the East Side.

Howells's confrontation with the East Side evoked a far more humane response than that of Henry James in *The American Scene*. As we showed in the preceding chapter, James persistently used animal imagery to describe the East Side Jews. They were a "swarming," a multiplication of fish "in some vast sallow aquarium," like "small, strange animals, . . . snakes or worms, . . . cut into pieces," "the spaciously organized cage for the nimble class of animals in some great zoological garden," the "antlike population."[29] To Howells, however, the Jews retained their dignity as human beings despite their subhuman physical surroundings. The contrast in the respec-tive approaches to the East Side by James and Howells is an index of their attitudes toward the Jews.

Yet Howells, like James, on the whole kept public silence in the Dreyfus case, despite his private indignation at the injustice of it. Unlike William James, Howells did not speak out on the case, and it was not until he wrote an essay on Emile Zola in 1902 that he mentioned the case in print. Howells writes of Zola that "when an act of public and official atrocity disturbed the working of his mind and revolted his nature, he could not rest again until he had done his best to right it." Howells thought the heroism in "Zola's cham-pionship of the persecuted Jew"[30] was greater than that of Voltaire's defense of a Protestant.

In *Their Silver Wedding Journey* (1899), Basil March of *A Hazard*, who is now taking a European vacation with his wife, is eager to see the bust of Heine in front of his house in Hamburg. (Here Howells pays tribute to Heine, whom he had admired since his youth.) The bust is a disappointment, however, for it "proved, by an irony bit-terer than the sick, heart-breaking, brilliant Jew could have imagined in his cruelest moment, to be that of the German Milton, the respect-able Klopstock whom Heine abhorred and mocked so pitilessly." March is led to deplore "the open neglect throughout Germany of the greatest German lyricist." If the Germans found some things Heine had said about Germany "unpardonable, . . . there would always be the question whether the Jew-born Heine had even a step-fatherland in the Germany he loved so tenderly and mocked so pitilessly." Howells then adds an extremely acute observation that has a contemporary ring: March "had to own that if he were a negro poet he would not feel bound to measure terms in speaking of

America, and he would not feel that his fame was in her keeping."[31]

Rather less favorably, March observes in the streets of Carlsbad "Polish Jews in long black gabardines with cork-screw curls on their temples under their black velvet derbies." At the hotel, among the names of guests posted on the rotunda he finds those from "all nations, but there were so many New Yorkers whose names ended in *berg,* and *thal,* and *stern,* and *baum,* that he seemed to be gazing upon a cyclorama of signs on Broadway." This mode of description by suffix is uncomfortably close to anti-Jewish baiting, even if it may have been unconscious on Howells's part. We soon learn, however, that Howells is really indulging his dislike of a commercial wealthy class, for he says that the Polish Jews "seemed all well-to-do" and "what impresses one first and last at Carlsbad is that its waters are mainly for the healing of the rich!" Again, on the way home, March finds conversation with a "nice Jew" on the boat "tiresome" because he talks "only about business."[32]

On the other hand, when an anti-Semitic innuendo is uttered by Stoller, a German acquaintance of the Marches from Chicago, Howells makes his disapproval clear by his pejorative references to Stoller. On being introduced, "Stoller took his toothpick out of his mouth and bowed; then he seemed to remember, and took off his hat. 'You see Jews enough here to make you feel at home?' he asked; and he added: 'Well, we got some of 'em in Chicago, too, I guess.' " Later the Marches visit the marketplace in Frankfurt, and when they consult their Baedeker, they learn that "until the end of the last century no Jew was suffered to enter the marketplace, and they rejoiced to find from all appearances that the Jews had been making up for the unjust exclusion ever since. They were almost as numerous there as the Anglo-Saxons were everywhere else in Frankfurt. There both the English and American branches of the race prevailed in the hotel dining room."[33]

In the matter of literature, Howells unqualifiedly greeted new proponents of realism from the various parts of the country—and the East Side as well. When Abraham Cahan began publishing his short stories in the 1890s, Howells was impressed and took steps to meet the young writer. He reviewed Cahan's collection of short stories, *The Imported Bridegroom and Other Stories of the New York Ghetto,* in *Literature* in 1898 and compared it with work being done in others regions of the country, like the New England stories of Mary E. Wilkins. Howells shows remarkable insight by discerning the essence of Jewish literature of the ghetto, as of the shtetl, to be "laughter through tears." Cahan, he writes, handles his materials "so skilfully that he holds the reader between a laugh and a heartache."[34]

Many years later, in 1915, in the "Editor's Easy Chair," he makes a prescient remark in a discussion of literature emanating from New York. "Very possibly," he writes, "there may be at this moment a Russian or Polish Jew, born or bred on our East Side, who shall burst from his parental Yiddish, and from the local hydrants, as from wells of English undefiled, slake our drouth of imaginative literature."[35] Considering that Bernard Malamud was born in 1914 and Saul Bellow in 1915 (in Montreal, to be sure) and that the Jewish novel by Jewish writers has been central to American literature from the mid-twentieth century on, Howells shows striking insight into the dynamics of literary creativity in this country.

As the leader of the new realism, Howells's welcome to the young writers who followed his lead—Hamlin Garland, Stephen Crane and Frank Norris—did much to establish their reputation early. Howells did not himself break down the most resistant taboos to the depiction of social reality, and even resisted them himself, as in his squeamish rejection of Dreiser. But the decisive break with romance was achieved by him, and his followers extended that break into naturalism and the frank treatment of sex. One strong element in Howells's theory and practice of realism was the realization of the dignity of the common man and of common life. This should have entailed complete freedom from age-old prejudice and stereotyping, but, as we have seen, Howells had not totally liberated himself in this respect. There were, indeed, very few who had, as there are only a minority today who can be said to be altogether free of the conventional stereotypes. However, there can be no doubt that his concept of realism was congenial to the acceptance of Jewish life into the American reality, as his encouragement of the young Abraham Cahan signified.

Far less interest in the Jews was manifested by Hamlin Garland than by his master in realism. The young Garland was taken with Henry George's single-tax outlook, and in 1888 he tried to win Howells over to the doctrine—without success. Howells responded that "it is good as far as it goes but reforms should go further."[36] But a radical viewpoint did not necessarily preclude racialism, for Garland was influenced by current racialist ideas, as appears from his essay "Literary Masters," published in *The Forum* in 1893. In it he projects the view that in literature "the real America" has shifted to "the interior" and "from these interior spaces of the South and West, the most vivid and fearless and original utterance of the coming American democracy will come." He eschews arguments "based on the difference in races," he says, not because they are untrue, but because they will be ignored. Nevertheless, he speculates that the cause of the shift is "the quicker assimilation of the Teutonic races in the West," in contrast to "the influence of the Irish and Jews and Italians upon New York and Boston."[37]

In Garland's early work, a Jewish character appears briefly in one of his best stories, "Rose of Dutcher's Cooley" (1895), about a Wisconsin farm girl who breaks with the narrow farm life by escaping to Chicago and marrying a journalist. This break with the idyllic view of middle western farm life that is found in the work of James Whitcomb Riley and Eugene Field is Garland's contribution to the realist movement. Among the boarders at the Chicago boarding-house Rose meets a Jewish salesman, Mr. Simons, who is described as "a Jew, but he's not *too much* of a Jew." His appearance is brief; during a merry dinner, a Bostonian among the boarders asserts that civilization stops at the Hudson River, whereupon the girl replies: "Some folks' manners stop after they leave the Hudson River." At this riposte "the Jew cackled joyously." The attitude toward the Jew is here patronizing and distant. But Garland did have compassion for Jews as poor people. Rose is walking through the minorities' sections of the city: "Whether they were Italians or Jews or Bohemians she could not tell, but she could see the marks of hunger and hard work on their pallid faces."[38]

Garland met Israel Zangwill in New York in the 1890s and they remained lifelong friends. In his reminiscences Garland never alludes to Zangwill's Jewishness, and always refers to him in the warmest terms. Zangwill, he writes, "was a quaint yet powerful personality, witty and wise, and genial, and made friends wherever he went." Whenever Zangwill was in New York he met frequently with Garland, and on one of these occasions Garland introduced him to Howells. When Garland was in London he stayed with Zangwill, whose study he found "the only warm place in London."[39]

Garland attended the famous 1907 performance of a dramatization of *The Prince and the Pauper* at the Educational Alliance on the East Side, at which Mark Twain was present. Of the orchestra at the performance Garland writes: "They have a facility in music which the Anglo-Saxon does not possess." Then he adds prophetically: "That they will change the character of New York musical life in certain. These young violinists, these actors, these literary folk are to be the leaders in their lines." After the performance, Garland adds, "Mark went on the stage and was instantly surrounded by a mob of black-eyed, black-haired Orientals all eager to take his hand." (Jews were then commonly and euphemistically referred to as "Orientals.") The next year he went to a Jewish play in Chicago, "a bloody page torn out of Russian history, done with quiet art and intense earnestness." So poignant was the performance, he notes, that "many Jews in the audience uttered cries of pain as if some dreadful memory had been awakened. We all went away in vast indignation. How can such an injustice exist in a Christian land?"[40]

Several years later he spent an evening with the "Jews, Poles, Italians" on the East Side and saw only that they were "avid for success, and in single-minded pursuit of the luxuries of life. . . . It is not strange that some of their children drift into piracy in their haste to get rich. As I study them, I realize that my books have no appeal to them. They are of another world."[41]

As the years went on, Garland came more and more under the influence of racist theories. In the 1920s he discussed with Kipling the "invasion" of southern European immigrants, "Jewish and Slavic types." Garland escapes the invasion by foreigners by "back-trailing" to England for the summer, for England, he says, "is renewing herself with flaxen-haired, apple-cheeked babies just as she has done again and again for a thousand years." A few years later he again returned to England. "A part of the pleasure of my return to England lay in a natural revulsion from New York's alien population and its tabloid press. " 'After all,' I said, 'I am of English stock, with more points of contact with it than with any other race.' "[42]

Racism had a deeper hold on Frank Norris and penetrated into his creative work so deeply that he projected (in *McTeague*) one of the most anti-Semitic portrayals in American fiction. He was the most explicit and articulately racist of the realists. But he also believed that "superior" races had the obligation to raise the "inferior" ones to their level into a brotherhood of man. "The true patriotism," he writes, "is the brotherhood of man . . . and the whole world is our nation and simple humanity our countryman."[43]

Racist statements recur in his writings, and the Anglo-Saxon is held up as the ideal. In *Moran of the Lady Letty* (1898), for instance, he draws a "sharp contrast" between the sinister Mongolian and the "open" Anglo-Saxon girl:

The Mongolian, small, weazened, leather-colored, secretive—a strange, complex creature, steeped in all the obscure mystery of the East, nervous, ill at ease; and the girl, the Anglo-Saxon, daughter of the Northmen, huge, blonde, big-boned, frank, outspoken, simple of composition, open as the day, bareheaded, her great ropes of sandy hair falling over her breast and almost to the knee boots.[44]

It is no wonder that nearly all allusions to Jews in his fiction are either patronizing or pejorative. A passage that is horrifying in its naturalism in *Vandover and the Brute* (written in 1895, published in 1914) concerns a "little Jew." A rowboat has been launched from a sinking ship and is already overloaded. Suddenly, "the little Jew of the plush cap and the ear-laps" leaps into the sea and takes hold of an oar. The officer in charge refuses to take him in for fear of swamping the boat, against Vandover's plea that "you can't let him drown." The officer is adamant: "It's a matter of his life or ours; one life or forty." The passengers are divided; some throw him their life preservers, but "the Jew saw nothing, heard nothing, clinging to the oarblade, panting and stupid, his eyes wide and staring." He refuses to let go, despite the twisting of the oar, and tries to pull his way up the oar to the boat rim; the desperate officer beats his hands until he lets go. He seizes the oar again, and "the engineer clubbed his head and arms and hands till the water near by grew red. The little Jew clung to the end of the oar like a cat, writhing and grunting, his mouth open and his eyes fixed and staring," until he slides away and drowns.[45]

Jews figure only incidentally in Norris's proposed trilogy (only two books were actually written). In *The Octopus* (1901) the ruthless banker and speculator is "S. Behrman," which might be a Jewish name, although Norris never identifies him as such. In *The Pit* (1903) there is a conventional passing allusion to a pawnbroker. Sheldon Cottrell, creator of colored glass, can't tolerate any art that is popular. "But," Norris continues, "he'll go over here to some Archer Avenue pawn shop, dig up an old brass stewpan, or coffee pot that some greasy old Russian Jew has chucked away, and he'll stick it up in his studio." In describing "The Pit," the floor where wheat futures are sold, he alludes to some Jewish traders. There is "a young Jew named Hirsch," who is given no special characterization, and another Jewish trader, who is variously called "the Jew," "the little Jew," "the little Jew Grossman," and "the insignificant Grossman, a Jew who wore a flannel shirt, and to whose outcries no one ever paid the least attention." At one point he says that "Grossman [is] indignant at 't'ose monkey-doodle pizeness.' "[46]

These references to Jews are ordinary enough, but it is in his most widely read work, *McTeague* (1899), that a really vicious stereotype appears. In this novel Zolaesque naturalism is wedded to the convention of the gold-obsessed Jew. Zerkov the junk dealer is "a Polish Jew—curiously enough his hair was fiery red." Red hair immediately suggests the medieval Judas-devil stereotype.

[Zerkov] was a dry, shrivelled old man of sixty-odd. He had the thin, eager, cat-like lips of the covetous; eyes that had grown keen as those of a lynx from long searching amidst muck and debris; and claw-like, prehensile fingers—the fingers of a man who accumulates but never disburses. It was impossible to look at Zerkov and not know instantly that greed—inordinate, insatiable greed—was the dominant passion of the man. He was the Man with the Rake, groping hourly in the muck-heap of the city for gold, for gold, for gold. It was his dream, his passion; at every instant he seemed to feel the generous solid weight of the crude fat metal in his palms. The glint of it was constantly in his eyes; the jangle of it sang forever in his ears as the jangling of cymbals.[47]

A Mexican girl, Maria Macapa, is Zerkov's neighbor, and every so often she sells Zerkov junk she has collected. She tells Zerkov that her wealthy parents once possessed a set of gold dishes, and "he chose to believe it, forced himself to believe it, lashed and harassed by a pitiless greed that checked at no tale of treasure, however preposterous. The story ravished him with delight." Whenever Maria visits him with a consignment of junk, "the red-headed Polish Jew, the ragman Zerkov, stood in the doorway," and begs Maria to tell him once again the story of the golden dishes. Norris repeats "the red-headed Polish Jew" like a Homeric epithet.

Maria steals gold tape from McTeague's office and brings it to sell to Zerkov. When she produces it, his "eyes glittered on the instant —the sight of gold invariably sent a qualm all through him; try as he would, he could not repress it. His finger trembled and clawed at his mouth, his breath grew short." And again he begs for the story of the gold dishes. "The red-headed Pole was in a fever of excitement. Maria's recital had become a veritable mania with him."[48]

Zerkov, who cannot believe that the gold dishes are lost, marries Maria in the expectation that she will lead him to them at last. Maria gives birth to a sickly child, "continuing in its puny little body the blood of the Hebrew, the Pole, and the Spaniard." Childbirth cures Maria of the demented fantasy that produced the story of the dishes; Zerkov, for his part,

had come to believe in this story infallibly. He was immovably persuaded that at one time Maria or Maria's people had possessed these hundred golden dishes. In his perverted mind the hallucination had developed still further . . . it existed now, entire, intact. . . . It was somewhere, somebody had it, locked away in that leather trunk. . . . It was to be searched for and secured, to be fought for, to be gained at all hazards. Maria must know where it was. . . . Some day, if only he was persistent, he would hit upon the right suggestion that would disentangle Maria's confused recollections. . . . This service of plate had come to be Zerkov's mania.[49]

But the recovered Maria denies that she ever mentioned the dishes; she remembers nothing of it. Zerkov threatens her and beats her, but she knows nothing. He searches the house, digging up the floor and walls to no avail; he spies on Maria, thinking she might lead him to the hiding place if she believes him to be away. At last Zerkov cuts Maria's throat. "Towards midnight on the day of the murder Zerkov's body had been found floating in the bay near Black Point. No one knew whether he had drowned himself or fallen from one of the wharves. Clutched in both his hands was a sack full of old and rusty pans, tin dishes—fully a hundred of them—tin cans, and iron knives and forks, collected from some dump heap."[50]

Parallel with the murder of Maria is McTeague's brutal killing of his wife, Trina: in both cases the crime is rooted in obsessive love of gold. But the cases are quite different in a way that is exacerbated by Norris's use of the money-mad Jewish stereotype. For McTeague, the culminating event occurs in Zolaesque fashion after a period of degeneration directly caused by a change in circumstances, the authorities' forbidding McTeague to practice dentistry. For Zerkov, however, there is no comparable change. From beginning to end, Zerkov is obsessed with the desire to possess the illusory golden dishes. The only change that takes place in him is a personal degeneration, from obsession to insanity. Nothing has changed essentially— whatever happens to Maria does not and cannot affect the issue, for it is apparent that Zerkov will lapse into insanity; he will not believe in the nonexistence of the object of his passion, the golden dishes, no matter what Maria does or does not tell him. Thus Zerkov is a Zolaesque naturalistic character only superficially. He is literally a monster, who fortunately is not endowed with those subtle, individualizing features that caused Fagin to impress himself so deeply on the consciousness of society.

But of all the realists centered about Howells, the greatest was Stephen Crane, whose precocious genius, as Howells said in 1893, was that of "a writer who has sprung into life fully armed."[51] He was dead at twenty-nine, but he left a legacy of masterpieces of fiction. His realism was more profound than that of Howells, for it was permeated with dense symbolic meanings. An example is a brief allusion to Jews that conveys a deeply imaginative concentration of meaning in the great short story "The Bride Comes to Yellow Sky" (1897).

The story epitomizes the giving way of the lawless old West to the ordered, industrialized society dominated by the East. In Yellow Sky, Texas, Scratchy Wilson, an ex-outlaw who is now a helper of the town marshal, Jack Potter, tends to revert to his gun-slinging character when drunk. The marshal has returned from San Antonio with his bride, a symbol of the new order in the West, and on the way home from the station is met by a roaring drunk Scratchy. With drawn revolvers in each hand, Scratchy challenges him, although he is unarmed: "Why ain't you got a gun," sneers Scratchy. "Been to Sunday-school?" Potter explains he's just been married. Scratchy sees the woman for the first time, and is deflated; he returns his guns to their holsters and walks away. "He was not a student of chivalry," explains the author, "it was merely that in the presence of this foreign condition he was a simple child of the plains." But before this encounter Crane has prefigured the essential situation. With revolvers drawn, the drunken Scratchy "in a maroon-colored shirt, which had been purchased for the purposes of decoration, and made principally by some Jewish women in the East Side of New York, rounded a corner and walked into the middle of the main street of Yellow Sky."[52]

Otherwise, however, the Jews were quite peripheral to Crane's creative work. His writings about the East Side complement those of Abraham Cahan; while Crane restricts himself to the Irish sector of that area, Cahan pictures the Jewish ghetto. Howells calls attention to this tandem activity in his joint review of Crane's *George's Mother* and Cahan's *Yekl* in the New York *World* on July 26, 1896, under the heading, "NEW YORK LOW LIFE IN FICTION"; he declares that both have "drawn the truest pictures of East Side life." A few months later, on September 22, the Lanthorn Club, made up of writers and journalists, gave a banquet in honor of the three realists, Garland, Crane, and Cahan, thus confirming the estimation given by Howells.

In *George's Mother* Crane describes a Bleecker Street lodging house in which "a Jewish tailor lived and worked in the front parlor." In his earlier *Maggie* (1893), with the same locale, Crane describes how Maggie's drunken mother "swelled with virtuous indignation as she carried the lighter articles of household use, one by one, under the shadows of the three gilt balls, where Hebrews chained them with chains of interest."[53] Another conventional allusion occurs in a sketch of New York streets published in the New York *Tribune* on July 10, 1892. Crane describes a traffic jam at Chatham Square: amid the crowded confusion, "a Chatham Square cab fought its way along with a man inside wearing a diamond like an arc light. . . . Four Jews looked out of four different pawnshops. Pullers for three clothing stores were alert."[54]

Of the realists, Harold Frederic devoted more of his creative work to Jews than any of the others we have been discussing. However, most of this attention was paid to English Jews, for Frederic was London correspondent for the *New York Times* from 1884, when he was twenty-eight, until his death in 1898. In their last few years of life, Frederic and Crane were close friends in England.

Frederic's interest in Jews appeared in what was probably his very first published story, "The Jews' Christmas" (1882). This extremely sentimental tale relates how the kindly, pious talmudic scholar and pawnbroker Aaron Ashermeyer and his young Polish violinist friend, Paul Baleski, buy an abundance of Christmas presents for the pathetic, hard-working, impoverished, orphaned twelve-year-old Josephine, who lives in their house. When Paul first suggests to his friend Aaron that they provide the child with some necessities for Christmas, Aaron replies: "You are a Christian: I am a Jew. I do not give Christmas gifts." But after some thought he relents, and the two men go out to buy the gifts, which they set up in the little girl's room while she sleeps. At the Christmas breakfast next morning Aaron tells Josephine that she need work no longer, that she will live with him, and he explains to Paul:

You are a Christian; I am a Jew. I am not a prejudiced man. I have read the story of your faith's founder. I remember that his thoughts were always with those in need, and that he found his chief happiness in doing good among the poor. Why should a man who wishes to be just scorn to do good in honor of such a memory? Upon such common holy ground as charity we can both stand, you the Christian, I the Jew.[55]

This story is of interest because the twenty-two-year-old author's sentimental benevolence toward the Jews, on christological grounds, was later to become more realistic.

Frederic was preoccupied with Jewish characters in his later mature fiction. Evidence from his letters shows that he thought of the

Jews as a "clever" people. Writing from London in 1886, he referred to "the Jews, who were much cleverer than I am."[56]

His interest in the Jews must have been heightened by his three
weeks' tour of Russia, financed by a group of wealthy Jews, to report
on the pogroms in the *New York Times* (July 23 to August 14, 1891).
The series was published the next year as *The New Exodus: A Study
of Israel in Russia*. Frederic reports the charges hurled by the Russians: "The Jews were all usurers, moneylenders, vampires who
sucked the choicest Russian blood, promoters of dishonesty in business, etc. . . . These charges began in the imagination, but it was not
long before the Russians had persuaded themselves of their truth."
Frederic knew how false these charges were because he saw nowhere
else in Europe, not even in Ireland, "a more terrible poverty than
is the rule of their lives." Far from being exploiters, as was charged,
he writes, "it is the Jew who has been 'exploited.' "[57]

Frederic makes it clear that, while the Russian charges are false,
the Jew does have his faults. He is sensible of the appeal of a persecuted people clinging doggedly to its faith, at the greatest risks.
But that

theological-racial isolation of his, much as it may appeal to the generous imagination, has done him only harm. It has not made him broad
or tolerant; it has helped neither his mind nor his body. Its effect,
on the contrary, has been to develop unlovely and unlikable qualities
in him. It has made him selfish, fanatical, narrow-minded, ignorant
of what civilization likes and respects—in a word, unsympathetic.

As a consequence, "no nation on earth desires him as an immigrant."
It is not just his negative qualities that make the Jew undesirable, for
"even his virtues are of the unsympathetic sort." He is "temperate,"
and "a creature of tireless industry," "uniformly chaste," a "faithful
husband," "a marvellously good father," "a law-abiding citizen."
The Russian Jew "alone among the scions of his race in Europe has
produced next to nothing in art, music, or letters."[58] But the grand-
sons of Russian Jewish refugees, he predicts correctly, will reach the
cultural level of modern West European Jews.

Frederic returns to a discussion of the Jews in his masterpiece, *The
Damnation of Theron Ware* (1896), although no Jewish character
appears in the novel. There is conventional insensitivity evident in
a remark by Theron's wife: "Don't let them jew you down a solitary
cent on that sidewall." Several characters advance theories about the
Jews as an aspect of their world view. The physician, Dr. Landsmar,
believes that the development of art in a people is a sign of decay.

"All art, so-called, is decay," he says. "When a race begins to breed on the beautiful,—so-called,—it is a sign of rot, of getting ready to fall from the tree." The Jews, he continues, are an illustration of this phenomenon:

Take the Jews—these marvellous old fellows,—who were never more than a handful, yet have imposed the rule of their ideas and their gods upon us for fifteen hundred years. Why? They were forbidden by their most fundamental law to make sculptures or pictures. That was at the time when the Egyptians, when the Assyrians and other Semites, were running to artistic riot. . . . You can get the artistic remains of the Jews during that whole period into a child's wheelbarrow.

Result: the Jews survived, while all the artistic peoples have passed away. But the Jews have already passed their apogee, and now that they have taken to art, they too will decline in power and influence. "I am told," continues Dr. Landsmar, "that in the present generation in Europe the Jews are producing a lot of young painters and sculptors and actors, just as for a century they have been producing famous composers and musicians. That means the end of the Jews!"[59]

Another approach to the Jews is suggested by Celia Madden, the esthetic, Catholic, fin-de-siècle bohemian with whom the unsophisticated Theron falls in love; it is through a misunderstanding of her that Theron undergoes "damnation." Celia distinguishes two types of people, Greeks and Jews. The distinction has nothing to do with race, language, or nationality, but is based on their attitude toward art. The Greeks are the artistic ones, the Jews the philistines. Theron wants to know more about the distinction and wants to be a "Greek," if Celia is one. The Greeks, she explains, have "absolute freedom from moral bugbears, . . . the recognition that beauty is the only thing in life that is worthwhile. The courage to kick out of one's life everything that isn't worthwhile."

It is the "Jewish" element, she says, that has ruined Catholicism, when "your miserable Jeromes and Augustines and Cyrils brought in the abominable meanness and cruelties of the Jewish Old Testament, and stamped out the sane and lovely Greek elements of the Church [so] that Christians became the poor, whining cowardly egotists they are, troubling about their little tin-pot souls and scaring themselves in their little churches by skulls and crossbones." Celia would replace in her Catholicism these elements which the Jews "threw out." The Greek spirit in the church, like Jesus himself, appreciated women, but the church fathers hated women. "It was only epileptic Jews [Paul?] who could imagine a religion without sex in it."[60]

In sum, the Greek element is grace, love of life and beauty, breadth of moral outlook; the Jewish element is constriction of life, insensitivity to beauty, a dour and relentlessly rigid outlook on life.

Frederic's attitude toward English Jews emerges from his last two novels: *Gloria Mundi* and *The Market-Place*. In his last novel, *The Market-Place* (1899), one of his most successful, the speculator-hero Joel Stormont Thorpe outwits a group of Jewish stock-market speculators on the London market, and the rendering of the Jews, both by Thorpe and by the author himself, is very unflattering. It appears that the Jews have slighted Thorpe earlier, but as the novel opens he is in a position to wreak vengeance on them. His opponents, he muses, "were moulded in a family likeness, these phantom visages: they were all Jewish, all malignant, all distorted with fright. They implored him with eyes in which panic asserted itself above rage and cunning. . . . The faces were those of men he had seen, no doubt, but their persecution of him had been impersonal; his great revenge was equally so." The obliteration of the individual in the group stereotype, the archetypical anti-Semitic conception, is clear from Thorpe's comment: "I don't know them apart, hardly—they've all got names like Rhine wines—but I know the gang as a whole, and if I don't lift the roof clean off their particular synagogue, then my name is mud."[61]

The anti-Semitic aspect of Thorpe's successful stock manipulations against his Jewish antagonists is explicitly brought out by Frederic. Since those speculators worst hit by Thorpe's corner on the market are Jews, the suspicion arises that as Jews they are deliberate targets. But the fact that Thorpe allows two of the Jews, Blaustein and Ascher, to save enough money for a dowry for one of their daughters "hardly justified the theory of an implacable anti-Semitic vendetta." However, Frederic refutes this view by stating that "Blaustein and Ascher had been bled white, as Bismarck's phrase went, before they were released, whereas the five Christians had been liberated with relatively moderate fines—upon the whole, a certain odour of the *Judenhetze* clung thereafter about the 'corner' on Rubber Consols."[62]

The idea is carried further when Thorpe consults with the figurehead chairman of the board, Lord Chaldon, who says: "I've heard it mentioned that your enterprise was suspected of an anti-Semitic twist." Chaldon has just persuaded Thorpe to allow the visiting

French financier, Alexander Fromentin, to escape from Thorpe's ruinous net. After the Frenchman leaves, Thorpe complains that his release of Fromentin was "most terribly against the grain. I'd sworn to let no Jew off with an inch of hide left on him—and here three of them have been wheedled out of my grip already." Then Thorpe is told that Fromentin is not a Jew, and Lord Chaldon delivers an apologia for Jewish international financiers, which we may take to be Frederic's own response to the type of anti-Semitism practiced by Thorpe. He informs Thorpe of "the uses to which they put this vast power of theirs; his conviction that on the whole they were benefi-cent; his dread of the consequences of any organized attempt to take power away from them, and put it into other and less capable hands." But Thorpe is left unmoved; he is still determined to despoil "Rostocker, Aronson, Ganz, Rothfoere, Lewis, and Mendel of their last sixpence."[63]

Since *The Market-Place* as a whole is essentially an exposure of Thorpe's passion for power and an implicit criticism of Thorpe's character, anti-Semitism, through its practice by Thorpe, may be seen as also subjected to criticism. But Lord Chaldon's apologia, which is also Frederic's, is not a blazing declaration of tolerance. The author was sufficiently ambivalent about Jews to give them a minimal kind of justification, without separating the Jew as financier from the Jew as a member of a people composed of a variety of individuals.

A more favorable and more humane rendering of the Jews can be found in *Gloria Mundi* (1898), a novel we shall discuss in its utopian aspect in the next chapter. But here we may suggest that in the total structure of the novel, the Jew represents a revitalizing element of British society as opposed to the worn-out hereditary aristocracy of England. These two contending forces in English life—the older, decadent aristocracy and the vital renewing forces of the country—are presented by two branches of the ducal Torr family. One, who call themselves "the Christians," are thin-blooded and useless. The other side is called "the Jews" because Lord Julius Torr married a very wealthy Jewish woman from Holland. Presumably taking a leaf from their book, he has preserved the family fortune by his wise governance of money, and has actually saved the "Christian" side from bankruptcy. The old duke is dying, and his prospective heir is Christian Tower (a variant of Torr), belonging to an estranged branch of the "Christian" side of the family; Tower, who has been living in France, is summoned to England by "the Jews" to be ready to assume the estate when the duke dies.

The independent, "modern" girl, Frances Bailey, whom Christian

Tower eventually marries when he assumes the dukedom, tells Tower that Julius is the younger brother of his grandfather the duke. "Julius," she adds, "is not Jewish in blood. But he married a great heiress of the race—whole millions sterling came to him from the huge fortune of the Aronsons in Holland—and he likes Jewish people—of the right sort. . . . He and his son are good men." Frances also explains to Christian that the Jewish branch of the family "have money beyond counting, and have morals and intelligence moreover. Between these two groups no love is lost. In fact, they hate each other."[64] But Julius generously steers Christian through the shoals to the dukedom with its properties intact.

It is clear from Frederic's writings on the Jews, that, like Lord Julius, he "likes Jewish people—of the right sort." The hastily added qualification—"of the right sort"—is revealing. Behind that phrase is the ambivalence of so much of the non-Jewish world toward the Jews.

THE UTOPIAN NOVEL

When American writers began to write utopian novels in the 1880s and 1890s of the century, it was not surprising that they portrayed Jews in a number of them. For several reasons the Jews were a focus of awareness. It was not just that anti-Semitism was changing from a random, individual, verbal, low-keyed phenomenon to a more articulated, outspoken, and organized form. Mass immigration of Jews from European ghettos made them far more visible than they had ever been, and the preoccupation with money theory at a time when the house of Rothschild had been made a household byword for rapacious finance focused attention on the Jews. Socioeconomic dislocations of the time made the Jews an easy target for developing racial theories and a scapegoat for many societal evils.

Since the Civil War the country had undergone a headlong transformation into a fully industrialized society. Some indices of this development suggest how drastic these changes were, and how they necessarily created profound material and psychological problems for the population. Between 1860 and 1900 the value of manufactured products increased nearly sevenfold, and railroad mileage almost ninefold. The total population more than doubled, with about one-third of the increase coming from immigration; and the urban population also doubled between 1880 and 1900. While this explosive expansion was going on, capitalization and the factory system were becoming concentrated; in the decade between 1890 and 1900 the value of manufactured goods increased by about $2 billion to $11.5 billion, but the number of business establishments declined by about one-third.

The working class, including women and children, were ruthlessly exploited by long hours of work, wretched conditions, and near-starvation wages. The catastrophic depressions of 1873 and 1893 exacerbated the plight of the working class. Farmers were impoverished and made desperate by the fall in prices of agricultural produce. The frontier, which had in earlier years provided a safety valve for socioeconomic dislocation, was closed by the end of the century, and antagonistic classes then had to confront one another. This was the era of Henry George's influential *Progress and Poverty* (1879) and later, of the Populist movement in the West and South.

The working class was becoming class conscious, and strikes were frequent. The last two decades of the century saw the decline of the Knights of Labor and the rise of the American Federation of Labor. Government, both local and national, was generally subservient to industrial interests, and the period saw the bloody repression of great strikes and the traumatic Haymarket affair in 1886. By the end of the century the United States had also entered into the arena of imperialism with the Cuban and Philippine wars.

Profit-seeking industrialism and the consequent misery inflicted on millions of workers and farmers gave rise to reform and radical movements, from trade unionism, to Populism, to the Social Gospel, to the single tax theory, to socialism. As we have seen, in literature the developing industrial society brought forth "realism," under the leadership of William Dean Howells, and naturalism (in the case of Frank Norris), under the inspiration of Zola. In the last two decades of the century one quite indigenous genre emerged: the utopian novel, in which both literary and political figures sought solutions to the current troubled state of American society. This period was, in a sense, a renewal of the reformist impulse of the 1840s, in which utopianism played such a large part. Perhaps one reason why this literary development was more emphatic in this country than in England or on the Continent was that the utopianism of the 1840s had survived in the American consciousness—partly because actual utopian experiments had been undertaken and had become a real part of the American experience.

Several score utopian novels were published in the last few decades of the century. One study reports on the rate at which utopian fiction appeared between 1884 and 1900: one in 1884, one in 1886, one in 1888 (Bellamy's *Looking Backward*), one in 1889, five in 1890, eight in 1891, five in 1892, three in 1893, seven in 1894 (including Howells's *Traveller from Altruria*), three in 1895, one in 1896, three in 1897, five in 1898, one in 1899, and four in 1900.[1]

The most influential of all was, of course, Bellamy's *Looking Backward,* which sold 60,000 copies in its first year and 100,000 the next. A fifty-cent paperback edition was a best seller in the farm belt, and within a decade 400,000 copies had been sold, the highest circulation of a novel since *Uncle Tom's Cabin.* "Nationalist Clubs" were organized to propagate the ideas in the book, and by 1891 there were 163 of these throughout the country. The underlying idea was to establish socialism by political action, rather than direct action or violence. A more militant social doctrine was enunciated by the Reverend William D. P. Bliss, who in 1889 formed the Society of Christian Socialists. Considering the Jewish origins of primitive Christianity, upon which Christian Socialism was in part based, it is not surprising that Jews should figure in several Christian Socialist utopias.

A sort of programmatic Christian Socialist work was written by one of the earliest exponents of the social gospel, the Reverend Jesse H. Jones, whose utopian novel, *Joshua Davidson,* was completed in 1903 and published posthumously.[2] The symbolism of the story is obvious enough. Rebekah is the daughter of a German Jewish mother—said to be descended from Mordecai, Queen Esther's uncle —and a Lutheran father, a believer in Jesus. In upper New York State, Rebekah meets and marries Joseph Davidson (Joseph, "father" of Jesus), who is devoted to the ministry of the gospel. Rebekah, writes Jones, "was a Jewess; and yet she was much more than a Jewess. She was a Gentile Christian also. She knew her father's blood; she knew her mother's blood; she knew the truth of Jesus; and she knew history. . . . She was a Jewess-Gentile-Christian." At twelve years of age their son Joshua (Jesus) visits his Jewish grandfather, who tells him "that he, in whose veins the blood of Israel and Gentile ran in a mingled stream, ought to be all the more a 'son of the Law. . . . He should be a Gentile and Israelite Christian combined, and that only as he was both, could he be a complete Christian.' "[3] In accordance with Israel's "law of the Rabbi," Joshua does not begin his ministry until he is thirty years old.

For Jones, Christianity is continuous with Judaism, and Christians are latter-day Jews whose relationship to God is fulfilled through the agency of Jesus. The usual accusatory hostility toward all Jews is absent. Joshua is Jones's mouthpiece, and at thirty, Joshua begins to teach his Christian Socialist doctrine. The United States is in fact the New Jerusalem; he preaches the kingdom promised by Christ, because it is devoted to service of the people. Through the Christian church, as envisioned by the Pilgrim fathers, "the United States of America is the kingdom of the Heavens, which Jesus Christ came to establish on the earth," writes Jones. Moreover, it is the duty of this country to make the whole world Christian, to achieve "the univer-

salisation of Christianity by the Americanisation of mankind."[4] For
the rest, Joshua's ministry is an exhortation of how this is to be
achieved.

Jones becomes very concrete in his sermonizing and expounds an
advanced social viewpoint. On woman suffrage he says: "Woman
suffrage means the return of the human race to Paradise, the usher-
ing in of the golden age, and the triumph of Jesus Christ—on the
earth, . . .[who] lived on earth and died on the cross to give woman
the ballot." Joshua excoriates the wage system, which is "a crime.
. . . Every man who works for wages sells his children for slaves.
. . . The will of the wage worker is made subject to the will of the
employer, which is the essence of slavery." Joshua's support of strike
movements leads to his election to the Eight-Hour League, and he
calls on strikers for solidarity.

But this New Jerusalem does not exist; it needs to be brought
about by driving out the wage slavery of the time. When Jesus told
the Jews that "the kingdom of God shall be taken away from you,
and shall be given to a nation bringing forth the fruits thereof," he
meant that the mantle of the chosen people would be taken from the
Jews and bestowed on the United States. But before the kingdom
can be realized Mammon must be defeated. The marks of service to
Mammon, says Jones, are *"taking use money,* commonly called *interest,
. . . taking profit in trade, . . . paying wages . . .*[and] trafficking in land."
The ancient Hebrews knew that interest was evil; and because they
trafficked in "Temple offerings based on the business system of Tyre
and Sidon," Jesus condemned them. So, too, "the business system
of the world is in deadly antagonism to the true Christianity of Jesus'
church," and Jesus' condemnation today needs to be visited upon
"those who are conveying the vast commercial and financial operations of our time."[5]

It should be noted that Jones condemns the ancient Hebrews for
their service to Mammon but does not, like so many modern writers,
designate Jews in the intervening period and in his own day as
symbols of this practice in modern times. For Jones there is an
unbroken continuity between Judaism and Christianity. While it
would follow that those Jews who refuse to acknowledge this continuity are lacking in complete moral vision, it is significant that Jones
refrains from castigation. For him, Joshua is a Jewish Christian, as he
believes Jesus was devoted to the realization of the Kingdom of God
on earth.

Like Jesus, Joshua is martyred for his devotion. Joshua speaks to
a great throng of railroad strikers. The businessmen of Pittsburgh

condemn him "as subversive of the very foundations of our society."[6] He does not heed their warning; again and again he preaches in behalf of the strikers until he is lynched.

A vaguer, less concrete form of Christian Socialism is espoused in Albion W. Tourgee's *Murvale Eastman, Christian Socialist* (1889). "The function of the Church," writes Tourgee, "is only to inspire action, to provide impulse, to exalt and justify motive, to induce man to apply the Christ-spirit to collective human relations."[7] His aim was to reform attitudes in Christian terms, after which social reform would surely follow. As a judge and political leader during Reconstruction, Tourgee was very active in trying to extirpate the remnants of slavery in North Carolina. After the failure of Reconstruction, Tourgee returned to the North and turned to novel-writing, chiefly about black-white relations, in which the unequal status of the blacks is exposed. The political and social problems of Reconstruction from the radical Republican viewpoint, including a sensational exposé of Ku Klux Klanism, are set forth in *A Fool's Errand* (1879).

By the end of the 1880s Tourgee's reformist zeal was applied to the rather unideological Christian Socialism expounded in *Murvale Eastman*. The titular hero is a minister who preaches Christian Socialism, at first with trepidation, while making it clear at the same time that he is opposed to "ranters" and "disrupters of society,"[8] presumably the more militant socialists and anarchists of the time. He finally organizes the League of Christian Socialists at his church, much as W. D. P. Bliss had formed his Society of Christian Socialists.

One of the members of the league is Herman Metziger, a lawyer who is a descendant of Spanish Marranos. "I am one of those of Israelitish descent," Metziger says of himself, "who, centuries ago, during the Jewish persecution in Spain, renounced a Judaism they long perceived to be insufficient and embraced a Christianity they but half approved." His family has never affiliated with any denomination, "yet some of them have carried in their very names the evidence of an inherited faith which reaches back, in an unbroken line, to Nazareth." In the end Metziger asserts that "the principles which Christianity prescribes for the regulation and adjustment of human relations . . . constitute the only true basis of social ethics and should control and govern every relation of human life." Clearly, Tourgee himself looks upon Judaism as an inferior, superseded religion.

Metziger is introduced into the plot as a lawyer whose aid is sought for the recovery of a stolen jewel that had belonged to Metziger's ancient family—which, as is the way of fiction, also turns out to have been the family of the heroine. The ancient family were "Jewish Christians of Valladolid in the fifteenth century and believed to have been akin to Abramel, who was descended from the House of David, and so bravely withstood the Grand Inquisitor Torquemada two days before Columbus sailed to discover a new world which has been indeed a city of refuge to the persecuted children of Israel." The family fled from Spain to Holland and from there came to the United States, where they "had so long abandoned the synagogue"[9] that nobody considered them Jews, even though they joined no particular church either. Thus Tourgee introduces a Jewish believer in Christ whose Marrano descent lends an exotic aura to the tale. As Metziger is in fact a Christian Socialist, his Jewish origins add nothing substantial to the nature of the doctrine.

An even vaguer Christian Socialist projection is offered in Caroline Atwater Mason's *Woman of Yesterday* (1900). Early in life a rigidly religious young Vermont woman, Anna Mallison, decides to become a missionary and marries Keith Burgess, who will go with her to India as a missionary co-worker. His illness, however, ends this plan for both, and instead they join a "cooperative colony," Fraternia, in North Carolina, presided over by an advocate of the Social Gospel, John Gregory. The underlying principle of the colony is universal love. "Christ's inflexible law, far more rigorous than the old law of Moses, says that he that hateth his brother is a murderer." No one should be idle, but no one should overwork; all men are equal, there must be no privileged classes, nor any "aristocracy of money." All property is held in common. The motto of Fraternia is BY LOVE, SERVE ONE ANOTHER.[10]

Among the members of the colony—Germans, Scandinavians, and Americans—are two Jews, Barnabas Rosenblatt and his child, Judith. He is "a wiry little black-a-vised Jew, a quondam foreman of a New York sweat-shop," and his daughter, "a little lame girl." Both are pictured in a condescending, patronizing manner, and resemble nothing so much as humble pets of the Anglo-Saxon characters. When Anna is kind to little Judith, her father, "the swarthy Jew, looked up from the clay he was mixing with quick, instinctive gratitude. . . . He grinned, a broad, and rather hideous grin, and exclaimed in a broken dialect, 'Das ist so, kleine; shust listen to our lady!' " When Barnabas sees in Gregory's cabin a painting for which Anna had modeled, "Girlhood of the Virgin," he recognizes the original and says "(in his native tongue) she is like our lady when she prays."[11] To him, Anna is the adored Lady Bountiful.

After a bad harvest Fraternia is on the verge of collapse, and Anna works herself mercilessly, while her husband tours the country to raise money for the colony. Barnabas wants to warn Gregory that this "lady" is working too hard. He meets Gregory at the door of his cabin, and says: " 'Well, shust a minit, if Herr Gregory vas not too busy,' and the little Jew shuffled along by Gregory's side." He warns Gregory that Anna is sick, and that, " 'when she go, all go' . . . and the little man drew his shoulders quite up to his ears in a characteristic shrug strongly expressive of a thing unthinkable." Gregory then goes to Anna's cabin "while Barnabas, with the action of a waiting watch-dog, humble, yet with a due sense of responsibility, hung about near by."

Later, when Gregory and Anna realize that they love each other, Anna leaves the colony and Gregory runs away to his native England. Gregory returns to America, Anna's husband dies, and Fraternia collapses. The only ones left there are Gregory, now paralyzed by a falling log, a friend of his, and Barnabas and Judith. The Jews are like adoring servants. When Anna returns on a last visit to Gregory, she sees Barnabas and Judith at the door of Gregory's cabin. "With simple and unaffected delight they welcomed her, and then suffered her to enter the house alone." Anna and Gregory agree that Fraternia was impractical. Gregory finally feels that "the message of brotherhood, of equality, cannot be spread by such means as we tried in Fraternia," and Anna replies: "I believe that such isolated, social experiments, for many years at least, will be as ours has been, premature and ineffective."[12]

Altogether different from the well-intentioned but patronizing picture of the subservient Jews Barnabas and Judith is Miriam in *The Building of the City Beautiful* (1893), by Joaquin Miller, whose philo-Semitic poetry we have examined. If Mrs. Mason's Jewish characters are slight and one-dimensional, Miller's Jewish woman, Miriam, is hardly more human, though she is the central figure of this novel and full of sententious humanitarianism. At the opening of the story she is the secretary of Sir Moses Montefiore, who is on a visit to Jerusalem to view the buildings and colonies he has established. Miller takes the occasion to contrast the vigorous pioneer Jews from Russia after the pogroms of the 1880s with the native Jerusalem Jews: "Strange how much stronger were those of the extreme North than those who had been for generations in Jerusalem and other warm lands!" The native Jews flock around Montefiore to beg money from him. Miriam, "a young and strangely beautiful woman, silent, serene, dignified, and commanding," stands aside, hoping "in vain for some gentle soul in that multitude of loud, aggressive, and half-savage Jews." She is finally rewarded by acquaintance with "a new man of the new world,"[13] an American out of the West (Miller).

They discover that they are kindred spirits, both believing that "man is not only entitled to the pursuit of happiness, but to the attainment of happiness, real and substantial, upon earth." This improbable secretary of Montefiore's is a follower of Jesus, "the divine young Jew"; she is "a Jewess knowing more of Christ than Christians!" Miriam is "indeed a Jewess . . . as Mary, the mother of Christ, was a Jewess." Born the daughter of a Russian Jew exiled to Siberia, she came to London after his death and became employed by Montefiore in his philanthropies. But she "grew beyond the narrow limits of race creed. She came to believe in all good of all religions" and followed the rituals of each wherever she happened to be. For "she loved all peoples, and she pitied all peoples in their pitiful forms of idolatry."[14]

She is deeply disillusioned with Jerusalem, for "in the very dust and ashes of the Temple, she saw the same old hates, enmities, jealousies, narrowness, and uncleanliness of soul and body." People had learned nothing in two thousand years, and the restoration of Jerusalem would be no more fruitful. Her friend from the West has found that there, despite the plenty that surrounds him, man is still the enemy of man. Together the two friends reject the "common misery of the human race." Miriam believes that "man is good, man is almost entirely good," but is made evil by his inability to resist temptation. The solution to the problem, she believes, lies in Christ's injunction, "Lead us not into temptation."

They resolve to found a community based on the Sermon on the Mount, and the first step in this direction is to get away from the great cities, which are alien to God's intentions. They establish a community among the ruins of an old Toltec city in the American Southwest. "Let those who love the world go forth," says Miriam, "find sunny slopes and natural hills of health, and there, with God to help them, lay the cornerstone of new cities under this new order of things, for those new people who so persistently and so helplessly pour into the cities." A vaguer, more contentless Christian Socialist view can hardly be imagined. All that is required is to "let each man try to believe in man and obey the precepts of the Sermon on the Mount." In the "City Beautiful" that Miriam tries to build there will be no privilege; all will be equal; the medium of exchange will be honor, not metal; the diet will be vegetarian. The book trails off into a vaguely described community life that lacks concreteness. Miriam finally dies, with the injunction: "Take care that the emancipated toiler is not made the slave of his own creations by blind intoxicated money-changers. See to it that all toil, that none but the helpless live on the toil of others."[15]

A few Christian Socialist works contain Jewish characters who are reminiscent of early converts to the church. But they are not impressive characters, either as Jews or as persons, because their creators were of limited talent and had limited knowledge of contemporary Jews. It is interesting to note, however, that their authors were at least well-intentioned and exhibited no hostility toward the contemporary Jew. The sensitivity toward the oppressed and the desire for universal well-being that animated the Christian Socialists were not withheld from the Jews.

Not all utopias, however, could be considered socially advanced; there were reactionary utopias as well. They were utopian because they projected a desired system of society, but the nature of that system depended on the outlook of its creator or the context in which it was expounded. Of the latter sort is the feudalistic utopia in *Gloria Mundi,* which Harold Frederic, a *New York Times* correspondent in London, published in the last year of his life (1898). Frederic was tough-minded, and in this novel he hacks away at illusions regarding the British aristocracy and the exploitative sources of their wealth. The "Jewish" branch of the titled Torr family (Julius Torr had married a very wealthy Dutch Jewish woman) is less moribund than the "Christian" branch. Julius Torr's half-Jewish son, Emanuel, is the agency for disillusioning the hero, Christian Tower (a variant of Torr) about any possible idealistic use for his wealth. Emanuel, immensely wealthy, is described as a dreamy, unworldly type: he has "delicate, somewhat coldly modelled features, ivory skin and serious, musing looking eyes, and a rare smile of wonderful sweetness." He is an Oxford graduate and, in an England still under the influence of "Disraeli's remarkable individuality," has notions of "the possibilities of a new Semitic wave of inspiration and ethical stimulus."

Though aware of their Jewish origin, the family has long since abandoned Judaism. Of his cousin Emanuel, Christian thinks "that he had never seen any Jewish face which at all resembled his cousin's." Emanuel's Jewish forebears are said to be "of the blood of the immortal Spinoza." Emanuel wishes to emulate his imputed ancestor, but in a practical, not abstract philosophical, manner. He is convinced that feudalism holds out the "greatest opportunities for the higher life."[16] Like Henry Adams at about the same time, he believes that mankind has taken a wrong turning, and he wishes to put it back on the right track.

He therefore devises a system based on the feudal idea of a patriarchial relationship with the farmers and workers on his land. His land, he says, legally belongs to him, but "in practice it belongs to all my people." Each derives from it as much as is required to maintain his "station" in life, with Emanuel as lord of the estate and his tenants and workers as his retainers, in accordance with the static medieval social structure. "Whatever the surplus may be, that is devoted to objects which we all have in common." But that is not socialism—Emanuel recoils in annoyance from the word, which he regards as a "monstrous imposture. . . . I am more opposed to what is called socialism than anybody else on earth. I have elaborated the one satisfactory system, on lines absolutely opposed to it, . . . that pernicious delusion."[17]

Emanuel holds an extremely elaborate Christmas celebration on his estates, and it is suspected that he does so, "unconsciously no doubt, because the Jewish side of him felt the need of ostentation in its disavowal of theological prejudices." An estimate of the "Jewish side" of his character is made by the heroine, Frances Bailey (who in the end marries Christian Tower, now a duke) in phrases that seem to echo Frederic's own mildly prejudiced notions about Jews:

Emanuel seems to me to be a magnificent character with one extraordinary limitation. I think it must be a Jewish limitation—for I have seen it pointed out that they do not invent things. That is Emanuel's flaw; he has not an original thought in his head. He merely carries to a mathematical point of expansion and development the ready-made ideas which he finds accepted all about him. What you see in him is a triumph of the Semitic passion for working a problem to its ultimate conclusion.

She adds that his achievement is to have discovered "the smoothest possible working arrangement of the social system which his class regards as best for itself, and hence for all mankind—the system which exalts a chosen few, and keeps all the rest in subjection."

Frances Bailey goes further in her class analysis: the duke's fortune, she says, was achieved "by stealing the birthright of thousands of dumb human beasts of burden, and riveting the family collar round their necks with no more regard for their wishes or their rights than as if they had been as many puppies or colts." As for the fortune on the Jewish, the Dutch Ascarel, side of the family, it was gained by "the most frightful and blood-stained human slavery in the poisonous jungles of the Dutch East Indies—that, and on ancient family business of international usury, every dirty penny in which, if you followed it far enough, meant the flaying alive of a peasant, or the starvation of his little children." Though aware of these considerations and not entirely happy about them, she adds, Emanuel rationalizes his retention of the fortune by projecting a system he considers "not only respectable, but even profitable to the slaves as well as the master. He does not see that the systems themselves are crimes." As an emancipated woman, Frances Bailey is particularly incensed that "perpetual enslavement of woman" is "the very cornerstone"[18] of his system. The system finally fails, according to the story, because its demands on Emanuel are too great; he is obliged to give it up to save his health, and it cannot survive without him.

By the end of his life, when this novel was written, Frederic had obviously lost whatever faith he may have had in utopia, whether of a past age or an age to come. In his notes for the novel he writes: "People do not improve as the world grows."[19] His life experience had forced him to resign himself to more modest prospects. Christian Tower is speaking for him when he says, as he succeeds to the dukedom, that he aspires only to leave "things a trifle better than I found them."[20]

Frederic draws on Jewish characters to accentuate his criticism of the British aristocracy; to demonstrate what he considers Jewish prudence and competence in the handling of a fortune, as on the "Jewish" side of the Torr family; to expose the essentially "criminal" nature of great fortunes, whatever their origin, whether Jewish or non-Jewish; to express his own disillusionment with current utopian thinking by projecting a utopia devised by "Jewish" logic and lack of "inventiveness," a utopia whose Jewish author, though an admirable and well-meaning person, is unable to face the whole truth about his class position. Like most of his contemporaries, Frederic had ambivalent feelings toward the Jews, for his humanity came in conflict with conventional preconceptions about them.

There are, however, no conflicting feelings toward Jews in Alexander Craig's utopian novel *Ionia: Land of Wise Men and Fair Women* (1898). Jews are unequivocally evil, and their evil doings require nothing short of their being eliminated. The utopian society of Ionia, located in the Greek isles, is a strictly regulated order in which "duty comes first and liberty afterwards," and all actions of the individual are subordinated to the "well-being of the whole community." Marriages are selectively arranged to breed "the strongest, handsomest, and best to breed from," and all others are refused the right to reproduce.

Property may be distributed until a year before death; but at death all property reverts to the state. And this is where the Jews come in. There is in Ionia "a small colony of Jews amongst us, who lived in obscurity in the ancient capital. How they came no one knew, but as they are found in all quarters of the civilized world, it is not perhaps to be wondered at that some of them found their way even into Ionia." They took advantage of opportunities to exercise "their greed and their undoubted genius for business," and by the eighteenth century they had "increased rapidly in wealth and numbers"; presently "all the banking business of the country was in their hands," and they soon threaten to be "possessed of all the riches of the community." They have become "insolvent" and defied the laws; they have made Ionian young men their servants and young women their mistresses, and acted "as if the Greeks were born merely to be the slaves of their luxury."[21]

Furthermore, the Jews have evaded the inheritance laws by so manipulating their estates as to leave them intact, indeed increased, in the hands of their heirs. The Jewish threat to the state leads one enterprising ruler, or "archon," to deal with the problem. "To send them out of the country," writes Craig, "was impossible, as there was no way of exit, and as humanity forbade a general massacre," a humane mode of annihilation is adopted. Jews are forbidden to marry with one another, though they may marry Greeks. Naturally, "the haughty Hebrews stormed and threatened" and try bribery. When all this fails, and they are faced with extinction, the Jews have the archon assassinated. The people rise in anger and are restrained with difficulty from making "a wholesale slaughter of the hated race." However, the assassination provides the opportunity for more drastic legal measures. Some of the Jewish leaders are executed, and no Jew is allowed to marry at all, "so the whole tribe died out and passed away for ever."[22] A bloodless Final Solution!

Utopian books were written by several Jewish writers intimately connected with the Jewish community. Solomon Schindler, an enthusiastic disciple of Bellamy's, was an important figure in the development of Reform Judaism in the Boston area. He organized the Boston Federation of Jewish Charities and was a communal leader who promoted the Social Gospel in Jewish life. In 1893 he left the pulpit to become a propagandist for Bellamy. He wrote a sequel to

Looking Backward in *Young West* (Boston, 1894), in which the son of Bellamy's hero carries his father's utopianism further. However, as in Bellamy's novel, there is no Jewish character in the story.

H. Pereira Mendes, who in 1877 was called from England to officiate at the Shearith Israel synagogue in New York, was a Social Gospel preacher after his fashion, and in 1899 he published *Looking Ahead,*[23] obviously inviting the connection with *Looking Backward.* The book predicts the formation of giant federations of nations that will advance a humanitarian structure of society, though with an antilabor bias. Mendes innocently follows then-current Anglophilic forms of thinking, for he projects an "Anglo-Saxon Federation," composed of England and her colonies and the United States (which has by then absorbed Central America). But his ultimate objective is the Jewish return to Palestine, for the Anglo-Saxon Federation makes war on the Turkish Empire, and Palestine is taken from the Turks. A great council of religions takes place in which representatives of the Muslims, Roman Catholics, Greek Catholics, Protestants, and Jews each argue their claim to control the holy places of Jerusalem. At the end, all agree that the Jews have the strongest claim. *Looking Ahead* is a pedestrian work; it is hardly a novel but rather a schematic, not very perspicacious venture into a wish-fulfilling future.

Several utopian novels were written as extensions of the practical, constructive civic activity of their authors. David Lubin's *Let There Be Light* (1900) proposes the solution of social problems by a new universal religious faith. Lubin was born in Russia in 1849 and immigrated in 1855. In 1874 he opened a dry goods store in Sacramento, which prospered under a policy of honesty in advertising and one price. He became interested in farmers' problems through his relations with local farmers, and, after a visit to Palestine in 1884, launched into a second career as farmer and orchard specialist in the West. His proposals for the coordinated marketing of farm produce resulted in the organization of the California Fruit Growers' Association and then, in 1910, of an International Institute of Agriculture, of which he was the guiding spirit.

He committed to his "novel" his final speculations about the ultimate solution to man's problems. The book has a tenuous narrative line, described in the book's subtitle as "the story of a workingmen's club, its search for the causes of poverty and social inequality, its discussions, and its plan for the amelioration of existing evils." The leader of the group is a Jew, Ezra Solner, and the group includes his sister, Eva, a working-class black, an Italian, an Irishman, and even some wealthy Anglo-Saxons. From an inconclusive discussion of social issues the group moves on to a consideration of the new religious dispensation offered by Ezra, a "universal faith" in a purely spiritual God, a belief that is really a Judaism stripped of ritual, with the regulation of social activity for the betterment of humankind added. All sectarianism, Christian or Jewish, is left behind, and a new human state is to be achieved through faith in the pure creativity of Jehovah.

More interesting is the collection by Charles K. Landis, a Philadelphia lawyer and real estate promoter, of the legends that had been woven around the life of Don Luis de Carabajal y de la Cueva, a sixteenth-century Portuguese Jew who was governor of a district in Mexico for several decades. Cueva's governorship was an anticipation of Landis's own venture in Vineland, New Jersey. Landis was no ordinary land promoter. In 1861 he purchased a 32,000-acre tract of land in New Jersey, from which he "never expected or particularly wished [to realize] a large fortune," but rather wanted to "found a place which, to the greatest possible extent, might be the abode of happy, prosperous, and beautiful homes." In his own account of the founding of Vineland, he states his aims:

To lay it out upon a plan conducive to beauty and convenience, . . . establish therein the best of schools, . . . also manufactories, and different industries, and the churches of different denominations; in short, all things essential to the prosperity of mankind, . . . that the home of every man of reasonable industry might be made a sanctuary of happiness, and an abode of beauty, no matter how poor he might be.[24]

Landis does not suggest any socialist basis for the community; it is to be a beneficent community of small landowners and small industry. He sets forth some principles to govern the enterprise, such as what we might now call zoning regulations: obligatory cultivation of a few acres and prohibition of fences. The whole area is to be landscaped, with shade trees planted on each plot. The first group of colonists were native Americans, but in the late 1870s a colony of grape-growing Italian immigrants was established. In 1882 a group of Russian Jewish immigrants founded a colony in the area.

On a two-months' visit to Monterrey, Mexico, in 1894 Landis became acquainted with the Carabajal story. Perceiving the likeness of his own plans to those of Carabajal, he wrote *Carabajal, the Jew* (1894). The bare historical facts are that Carabajal, born in Portugal in 1539, was appointed governor in 1579 of a district in Mexico under an arrangement whereby he would colonize the area at his own expense and reimburse himself from the district revenues. He was allowed to take with him one hundred soldiers and sixty families, many of them Spanish Marranos. Carabajal also brought with him members of his own immediate family. In 1571 the Inquisition was introduced into the province, called the New Kingdom of León, and many Marranos, including members of Carabajal's own family, were tortured and killed for "Judaizing." Carabajal himself died about 1591.

In his fictional version of the story, presumably based on some manuscripts he had seen in Monterrey, Landis supplements the facts with details, and goes out of his way to comment favorably on the Jewish people. Since Carabajal is the son of a vastly wealthy man, writes Landis, King Philip II of Spain can milk him of a great sum of money as a "loan" in exchange for the award of the governorship of the Mexican district. Since the king knows Carabajal to be a "humanitarian," he is willing to give him one hundred of his soldiers. Carabajal's wife, writes Landis, has "all the noble and womanly qualities, which belong so intrinsically to the Jews." Carabajal himself loves music and art, and has "all the business sagacity of the race," but "without shrewdness and cunning"; he is a most generous philanthropist. Carabajal's motive for establishing the colony of New León, writes Landis, is to make a "philanthropic experiment, not in the way of charity, but that of helping people to help themselves, and to encourage his own people"—the Jews—"in a life of agriculture and stock-raising. . . . There was no gold seeking inducement held out," and those attracted do not expect to find gold mines or to enslave the Indians.

Landis quotes from what he says is Carabajal's manuscript, in which the aims of the colony were set forth, much as Landis himself had done for Vineland. The venture, says the manuscript, should not be "in a mere mercantile spirit," but rather "more in a parental spirit." Development of the colony should be both agricultural and industrial, educational and esthetic. There should be free libraries, lectures, "intellectual entertainments,"[25] dancing, calisthenics, and music. Indeed, the likeness between the principles attributed to Carabajal and those that governed Landis's conception of Vineland, set down in 1903, is unmistakable.

Landis conveys an idyllic picture of the first years of Carabajal's governorship. The Europeans do not enslave the Indians, as was usual, but are on friendly terms with them. The Indians teach the Europeans their arts of pottery, decoration, and local agriculture.

"The country," writes Landis, "was filled with industry and peace, and music was heard in every house." Many oppressed Jews from Spain and Europe come to this Eden. Carabajal and his Jewish colonists build Monterey [sic] as capital of the province, adopt Jewish sumptuary regulations, and landscape the city beautifully. Land is given to the Indians for cultivation, and they are educated in their arts.

But the hidalgos and priests are antagonistic to the enlightened administration of the colony and wish to enslave the Indians and reap treasures from the gold mines. At first their resistance to Carabajal's rule is ineffectual. Many more cities on the Monterey pattern are founded in the colony. One old Spaniard writes of the region, according to the "manuscript": "He believed that he had fallen into paradise or upon a veritable Arcadia, all was peace, every home, every street, and road was beautiful. The people were universally gentle and kind."

But Carabajal is working under a trio of fatal disabilities, writes Landis. He is "honest," he is "in advance of his time," and he is a Jew. On top of these disabilities, the aim of the Spaniards in America, "to gain wealth, gold, and slaves, not by industry, but by force, battle, and adventure,"[26] finally brings down Carabajal's paradisal colony. The hidalgos and priests succeed in overturning Carabajal's order of society. They institute the Inquisition and condemn him and his family for Judaizing and on many false charges. Under this treachery Carabajal falls dead and the aristocrats win a temporary victory. But the Indians rise up and put the inquisitors to death in a grand auto-da-fé. In fictionalizing, Landis altered the historical facts to suit his own purposes.

The utopias thus far considered run the gamut from tolerance to outright hatred *(Ionia)* and exhibit no special understanding of the Jewish people. These novels are significant as indices of current attitudes toward the Jews, but were not socially influential in the sense that *Looking Backward* was. There were novels associated with the Populist movement, however, that had deeper meaning as social symptoms and were potent influences. In recent years they have given rise to some controversy in relation to their bearing on American anti-Semitism. In the 1950s and 1960s two "consensus" historians, Oscar Handlin and Richard Hofstadter, put forward the thesis that the qualitative change that took place in anti-Semitism in the late nineteenth century was basically owing to anti-Semitic agitation by the Populists. During the 1890s, writes Handlin, "the injured groups of American society, in agony . . . scarcely guessed that the source of their trials was a change in the world in which they lived. . . . Some perceived its instrument, the Jew . . . stereotyped, involved in finance, and mysterious. . . . It was this suspicion that transformed the conception of the Jew after 1900, replaced the older images with that of the Elder of Zion." In his article Handlin displays an astonishing inclination to deny the anti-Semitic character of the most obvious anti-Semitic expressions, like the stage caricature of the Jew and the "comic" cartoons of Jews in the 1890s. And amazingly, an anti-Semitic article in the April 1882 *Century*, "Russians, Jews and Gentiles," which blames the pogroms on Jewish "persecution" of the Russian peasant—an article that Emma Lazarus found it necessary to rebut—he asserts is "as a whole not hostile"![27]

A similar charge is made against Populism by Richard Hofstadter, though much more cautiously and hedged with assertions of the progressive aspects of the movement: "It was chiefly Populist writers who expressed that identification of the Jew with the usurer and the 'international gold ring' which was the central theme of the American anti-Semitism of the age." However, adds Hofstadter, "Populist anti-Semitism was entirely verbal. It was a mode of expression, a rhetorical style, not a tactic or a program. It did not lead to exclusion laws, much less to riots or pogroms." Yet, he concludes, "it is not too much to say that the Greenback-Populist tradition activated most of what we have of modern popular anti-Semitism in the United States."[28]

In other words, both Handlin and Hofstadter argue that responsibility for the new level of overt and articulate anti-Semitism that developed in American life toward the end of the nineteenth century and into the twentieth rested primarily with the anti-Semitic agitation of the Populist movement. Let us first look at the supportive evidence for this assertion, and follow with considerations that argue against this thesis.

One of the central documents of the Populist prosilver, bimetallist movement of the 1890s was William Hope Harvey's *Coin's Financial School* (1894). It sold like wildfire, perhaps as many as one million copies. Harvey's thesis was that the gold standard—and removal of silver as a basis for money—was slipped over on the American people in 1873 as the result of a plot engineered by the British, specifically by the British house of Rothschild. A cartoon in the book pictures the Rothschild family as a great octopus with the world in the grip of its tentacles. Harvey was not content, however, with this direct exposition of his thesis, and in addition published a novel in which the thesis was dramatized. *A Tale of Two Nations* appeared in the same year, 1894, and also had considerable success in its twenty-five- and fifty-cent editions, selling probably several hundred thousand copies. The success of this novel was such that, Hofstadter remarks, "it must rank in symptomatic significance with Ignatius Donnelly's *Caesar's Column* as a fantasy in fiction that illuminates the populist mind."[29] Although Harvey's novel is not utopian, it throws light on the anti-Semitism in some Populist circles.

The "two nations" of the novel are, on one hand, the international moneyed people and, on the other, Britain and the United States—that is, those who support the gold standard and the rest, who suffer from it. The opening chapters of the story unfold the conspiracy hatched in 1869 by the British Jew Baron Rothe (Rothschild) to "demonetize silver" in the United States, thus destroying its balance of trade and ruining it economically. This is to be accomplished by bribing American legislators to pass antisilver legislation, which the moneyed people will support, says Rothe, because "money has no patriotism." A senator, John Arnold, agrees to execute the plot for a bribe of twenty-five thousand dollars a year.

In 1872 Rothe's young nephew, Victor Rogasner, arrives in the United States and sets up a lavish investment establishment (he "must be something of a sybarite") as a front for his help to Senator Arnold in getting the law passed. By this time a fellow conspirator in the House of Representatives has been duly bribed to see the legislation through that body. Rogasner also seems to revel in the thought of avenging Britain's defeat in the American Revolution. "For the wrongs and insults, for the glory of my own country, I will bury the knife deep into the heart of this nation." He will "drag them down and choke the life out of their industries and commerce."[30]

The plan succeeds when the Coinage Act of 1873 is passed, under which American coinage is reorganized and codified. This happens almost imperceptibly. Silver is demonetized by dropping the silver dollar as a coin (this aspect of the law in actuality aroused no excitement). Its meaning is realized only later in the decade, when the price of silver falls drastically in the world market. Baron Rothe's conspiracy, which also includes demonetizing silver in the countries of Europe as well, succeeds everywhere completely and irreversibly. The struggle of the free silver forces in the United States meets with irretrievable defeat.

Besides tracing the course of the conspiracy, the novel also has a narrative of sorts in which characterizations of Jews appear. Baron

Rothe's daughter, Edith, whose "black eyes and raven hair betrayed her Semitic origin," makes a brief appearance early in the book as an acute judge of men. She is called upon by her father to advise him if Senator Arnold is the suitable man to execute his American plans, and she approves after virtually one glance. A confederate of Rogasner's in his Washington operations is Jeanne Soutleffsky: "The dark, almost dusky skin glowing with the rich blood of youth and health, the full red lips disclosed teeth white and regular as nature's best. The raven eyes, and tresses black as Rogasner's own, the rather prominent, though well-moulded nose, spoke her to be of his own race, that race which had shown to the world some of the most beautiful of that type of female beauty called brunette."[31] The beauteous Jeanne returns to center stage providentially at the end.

Harvey's theory of the crucial function of money in the history of civilizations is discussed in a conversation between Victor Rogasner and his younger brother, Edward, who is "a shrewd money-maker and a good business man." Victor tells his brother that in the 1890s he expects a revolution to break out soon in the United States as a result of the harm caused by the demonetization of silver, which he has brought about. "Money," he tells Edward, "is the blood of civilization. If it is corrupted or congested, there will be sores and eruptions." The people do not understand that money is at the root of their troubles. Further, lending money at interest is a disintegrating force in society, and Victor tells his brother that "it takes men of our race" to understand this, just as Jesus Christ saw it. Victor cites about a dozen passages from both the Old and New Testaments forbidding usury and calls the roll of civilizations that fell by permitting interest-taking:

Diversion of money from the natural function as a medium for the exchange of property to one of hoarding and loaning it out . . . destroyed the empires of the Medes and Persians, the Assyrians, the Babylonians and Phoenicians. With it, Sparta and Athens drank up the sustenance of Greece, and then fell prey to the anarchy it drew upon their heads. Rome . . . fell as a nation . . . through this same system. . . . The cause can be traced to usury—the accumulation of money through the interest system.

The same thing is now happening to the United States, Victor adds, and the end "will be either a monarchy or a revolution with total disintegration of the American republic." If only the United States will abolish "the right to deal and traffic in money," there can be built here "the beginning of the grandest civilization the world ever saw."[32]

Victor Rogasner is conveying Harvey's utopian conception of a
society in which debt is voluntarily entered into on the basis of
honor, not interest, so that "the dishonest man could not do business." Edward is amazed. Surely, he asks, "this would destroy our
business?" Victor replies: "I wasn't talking about our business; I was
talking about a perfect civilization." When Edward then asks if this
does not mean that morally "we are criminals," Victor replies that
one must deal with society as one finds it.

But Victor's cynicism runs even deeper than this. He has fallen in
love with Grace Vivian, the beautiful young ward of Senator Arnold's. When he proposes she rejects him, for she prefers Jack Melwyn, the handsome young congressman from Nebraska who is
fighting for silver (the young William Jennings Bryan?). Victor believes he will win her by revealing his true identity, for she knows
him only as an investment banker.

I come [he says] from one of the oldest and wealthiest of European
families. In fact, the oldest and wealthiest in the world. Our millions
aid in controlling the affairs of nations. In influence, of all the titled
families of Europe, we are next to the crowned heads. I am one of
that family. There is nothing American about me. I am here on a
mission national, even international in importance. A title will be
mine for the asking on my return to Europe.

Grace is properly shocked and repelled at this "purely commercial
offer." "You thought to buy me!" she exclaims.[33]

When Victor tells his brother of his determination to marry Grace,
Edward replies in astonishment: "An American and a Christian? Are
there not women of our own race and faith beautiful enough and
with all grace of mind and body to fit them for any man?" But Victor
cites Scripture. "Did not our ancestors, even on the Arabian plains,
take whatever women of whatever race most pleased them?" Edward has to admit that "our family pays little attention to the letter
of the Mosaic law, anyhow." Victor believes he can still win Grace
by threatening Senator Arnold with exposure of his paid complicity
in the antisilver conspiracy if Arnold does not exact Grace's consent.
As Rogasner contemplates blackmail, Harvey cannot resist an anti-
Semitic turn of the screw. Rogasner's "race instinct," writes Harvey,
"which, ages ago, made the victorious Israelites 'harrow' the conquered, now manifested itself."

Rogasner is cruelty personified. When he confronts Arnold with
the threat of blackmail, "of human sympathy, there was no more
indicated, than is shown by one of the great cats when it has made
its first strike, and toys with its benumbed prey before the death

scene. He was not exactly smiling as he was leaving, and he was as happy as Nero was in the death agonies of his mother. The Hebrew was 'harrowing' again."[34]

Arnold has of course risen to the occasion and defied Rogasner. Rogasner then returns to his old love, Jeanne Soutleffsky. She knows of his love for Grace and his rejection by her. "She rose as he entered, and her face was a poem, a great epic of the grand old Jewish race." She is, indeed, a beautiful woman and "might have been Rebecca solicitous over Ivanhoe, so earnest, so good and gracious and beautiful and all faithfulness was she." She has helped Rogasner in all his villainies and "for a woman with the desperado instinct in her, he was a man well worth the loving."[35] Rogasner is not to carry out his threat to blackmail Arnold, however, for he is conveniently stricken with paralysis before he can do any damage. Grace marries the manly Jack Melwyn, and Jeanne Soutleffsky takes Rogasner to a sanatorium in England and devotes her life to him. But the conspiracy does not end. For another representative of the conspirators is immediately dispatched to replace Rogasner in the United States.

Is Harvey's novel anti-Semitic? Norman Pollack, who has in many respects successfully defended the Populists against the Handlin-Hofstadter thesis that they bear the main responsibility for "modern popular anti-Semitism in the United States," has written that Harvey's novel "is anti-English and not anti-Semitic, . . . but has two brief anti-Semitic remarks. . . . Jews *qua* Jews are seldom mentioned, while the dominant theme, stated time and time again, is the conflict between England and the United States for commercial supremacy."

It might indeed be argued that, granted Harvey's naive monetary thesis, he was only giving graphic representation to the prominent part that the Rothschilds and other Jewish bankers of Europe did then actually play in international finance. Britain, together with the Rothschilds, was Harvey's primary target, but the Rothschilds as Jews were too tempting a personification of money power to be resisted. For they called up the age-old stereotype of the Jew as the money-obsessed usurer and banker, and hence could be used as an effective symbol in the agitation against the gold standard. Pollack is mistaken when he asserts that Harvey describes Baron Rothe "in wholly non-stereotypic terms." It is enough to identify him as a financial manipulator and author of the plot to place him within the stereotype, even if he does not conform to it in all respects.

And Pollack also makes far too little of Victor Rogasner, who, says Pollack, is the target of "two brief anti-Semitic remarks."[36] For

Rogasner's character as a whole is conceived in anti-Semitic terms. He is utterly without scruple in conformity with his nature as a "Jew," and his ruthless attempt to blackmail Arnold is described as "the Hebrew . . . 'harrowing' again," like the biblical Jewish conquerors. In addition, the heroine, Grace Vivian, charges him with being "very wise in your commercial way, the commercial way inbred through generations."[37] While the money power of England is designated as the enemy of the United States, the only identified agencies of that power are unscrupulous Jewish men, and this fact alone casts an aura of anti-Semitism about the novel. Whether consciously or unconsciously, Harvey exploits anti-Semitism in this novel.

Harvey became aware that he might be charged with anti-Semitism, for in his *Coin's Financial School Up to Date* (1895), he attempts a disclaimer, which in fact confirms that his thinking about the Jews is stereotyped and antagonistic. They are, he writes, "the brightest race of people that inhabit the earth, and they treat each other with the greatest fairness as a rule. . . . You should not be prejudiced against any race as a race. . . . Among Jews, many became money changers; it seems to be natural with them, probably on account of their shrewdness. They see that it has advantages not possessed by any other business."

He could not disengage himself from the iron association of Jews with usury, and, believing usury the root of all evil, he exhorted the Jews to give it up and thus save the world. As late as 1920, when he published *Common Sense; or, The Clot in the Brain of the Body Politic,* he still believed that the Jews alone were responsible for moneylending, based on the famous injunction in Deuteronomy 23:19–20 that Jews may not take interest from brother Jews, but may do so from "strangers."

A stricken world cries out [to the Jews] to make public renunciation of usury and to make *restitution* by crowding into the front ranks of reformers against the sin! The Jews come of a noble race, possessing a high order of intelligence, acumen and persistency in a cause; and by recognizing that it is inconsistent with the "brotherhood of man" to wield the Sword of "Usury" against the Gentiles, they will assimilate into the activities of productive civilization, the worthy descendants of their pastoral forefathers, and will become vocationally adapted to the cultivation and rebuilding of their ancient land.[38]

Harvey's conception of the Jews is one that developed at the end of the nineteenth century: they were at once superior in intelligence and shrewd to the point of unscrupulousness. In Ignatius Donnelly's

version of this dualism in the utopian novel *Caesar's Column* (1890)
Jews are in control of the economy yet are the brains of a ruthless revolutionism against capitalism. It is on the evidence of anti-
Semitism in this novel that Handlin and Hofstadter mainly base their
thesis of the responsibility of Populism for the new level of anti-
Semitism in the United States after the 1890s. But a close examination of Donnelly's entire career introduces complexities that Handlin does not sufficiently take into account, and Hofstadter himself
suggests.

Donnelly was born in Philadelphia in 1831 and was educated
there. He moved to Minnesota in his young manhood and for the
rest of his life was identified with that state. His thinking and politics
developed along a continuum of progressive stances: he began as an
antislavery Democrat, became a Republican in the mid-1850s, and
was a Radical Republican congressman from 1863 to 1869. After his
defeat for public office, he turned in the 1870s to agrarian reform
and writing. In 1889 he was an organizer for the Minnesota Farmer's
Alliance, and in 1890 became the president of the state chapter of
the alliance. In 1892 he wrote the preamble and much of the plat-
form for the People's Party convention in Omaha and published a
Populist weekly.

It was his defeat in the election for senator in January 1889 that
prompted him to write his most successful book, *Caesar's Column*
(1890), which was a "utopian" novel in the same sense that Aldous
Huxley's *Brave New World* and Orwell's *1984* were later. For the
book registers Donnelly's profound disgust and revulsion at the
corruption and cupidity of his day, and projects what society will be
like a century later if these tendencies are permitted to develop to
their destructive logical conclusion. The book is not a prediction but
a warning. If the American people allow the current social philoso-
phies and practices of the prevailing economic arrangements to continue, they will go down to destruction. But he is confident that the
people will arrest this development, and soon. The book is in essence
an exhortation to reform. In Donnelly's conception the Jew is a
sinister figure. He provides the leadership of both implacable, mutu-
ally destructive polarized forces: money power and its destructive
revolutionary antagonists.

In his preface to the novel Donnelly disclaims "anarchism." His
aim, he writes, is "to preach into the ears of the able and rich and
powerful the great truth that neglect of the sufferings of their fellows, indifference to the great bond of brotherhood which lies at the
base of Christianity, and blind, brutal and degrading worship of

mere wealth, must—given time and pressure enough—eventuate in the overthrow of society and the destruction of civilization." He deplores the current wretched state of the poor, who are "plundered to enrich the few."[39] The novel is in the form of letters from Gabriel Weltstein, who is on a business trip to New York, to his brother, Heinrich, in Uganda.

After describing the advanced technological state of the New York of 1989, a century after the date of writing, in science fiction terms, Gabriel remarks that the people are dehumanized; they are "a race without heart or honor." Outside the purlieus of the rich, all is wretchedness and misery. On the street one day Gabriel saves a beggar from being beaten by the driver of a carriage that has nearly run over him. The carriage belongs to Prince Cabano, "the wealthiest and most vindictive man in the city," who turns out to be the Jew Jacob Isaacs—the dominating influence of the city. Donnelly informs the reader that "the aristocracy of the world is now altogether of Hebrew origin" and offers an explanation for this remarkable observation:

Christianity fell upon the Jews, originally a race of agriculturalists and shepherds, and forced them, for many centuries, through the most terrible ordeal of persecution the history of mankind bears any record of. Only the strong of body, the cunning of brain, the long-headed, the persistent, the men with capacity to live where a dog would starve, survived the awful trial. Like breeds like; and now the Christian world is paying, in tears and blood, for the suffering inflicted by their bigoted and ignorant ancestors upon a noble race. When the time came for liberty and fair play, the Jew was master of the contest with the Gentile, who hated and feared him. They are the great money-getters of the world. They rose from dealers in old clothes and peddlers of hats to merchants, to bankers, to princes. They were as merciless to the Christian as the Christian has been to them. They said, with Shylock, "The villainy you teach me I will execute; and it shall go hard, but I will better the instruction." The wheel of fortune has come full circle; and the descendants of the old peddlers now own and inhabit the palaces where their ancestors once begged at the back doors for second hand clothes; while the posterity of the former lords have been, in many cases, forced down into the swarming misery of the lower classes.[40]

The beggar saved by Gabriel throws off his disguise and turns out to be a handsome young man, Maximilian Petion, an attorney and a leader of the international revolutionary Brotherhood. He explains to Gabriel that the courts, judges, and juries are "the merest tools of the rich" and the press simply the venal "hired mouthpieces of power"; their "duty [is] to suppress or pervert the truth." The

Brotherhood is a secret political society with millions of members worldwide, whose aim is to promote "the good of mankind." The leaders are an elite who rule the Brotherhood dictatorially because the masses of the poor are ground down to joyless automatism, living at the edge of subsistence. The golden age of liberty and democratic institutions in the United States is long past. The real center of government is the meeting room of the prince. So far gone are the tyranny and oppression of the money power that "the only remedy is world-wide destruction." Society rests on a volcano, awaiting the command to destroy. The world is "a hell of injustice, ending in a holocaust of slaughter. . . . Human greed, blind, insatiable human greed,—shallow cunning, the basest, stuff-grabbing, nut-gathering, selfish instincts. These have done this work!"

Maximilian explains to Gabriel that this hopeless state of affairs is not owing to ignorance, for "a hundred years earlier [i.e., 1889], warnings were heard—and unheeded." Now nearly all farmers belong to the Brotherhood and are making ready for the holocaust. In Europe, explains Maximilian,

the real government is now a coterie of bankers, mostly Israelites; and the Kings and Queens, and so-called presidents, are mere toys and puppets in their hands. . . . The nomadic children of Abraham have fought and schemed their way, through infinite depths of persecution, from their tents on the plains of Palestine, to a power higher than the thrones of Europe. The world today is Semitized.[41]

Gabriel proposes a utopia, which would first of all do away with interest on money, which "creates a radical distinction in society. . . . Usury . . . is the cause of the first aristocracy, and out of this grew all the other aristocracies."[42] Once usury is abolished, all privilege goes with it. Transport will be nationalized; individual land ownership will be limited to between one hundred and five hundred acres; money will not be allowed to hamper development because it will be issued in paper only, without a metal base; and agriculture will be eliminated by making all food of chemicals. The world will then be guided by intellect, and love and cooperation will characterize the society in all its functions. Donnelly's ideal is not socialism but, as we would say now, a mixed economy, with strong government regulation. It is also interesting that he does not demand silver as the basis for his ideal currency, but paper money.

Rebellion is imminent, and both sides prepare. On one hand there is the Oligarchy, ruled by the prince, who is described as "a large man, somewhat corpulent; or . . . bloated. He had a Hebraic cast of countenance, . . . the nose was quite high and aquiline; . . . [with a] hard cynical and sneering expression of the mouth." His ministers were also "large, coarse, corpulent men; red-faced, brutal; decorated with vulgar taste; loud-voiced, selfish, self-assertive; cringing sycophants to all above them, slave-drivers to all below them." Their spies and informers report on the "Brotherhood of Destruction," whose membership consists of the entire American working class, irrespective of race and geography, and all southern Negroes, irrespective of class. The top leader in the three-man Executive Committee is Caesar, an Italian from South Carolina; second in command is "the brains of the organization,"[43] a Russian Jew; and the third member is a young American of wealth and ability whose father was framed by the ruling class because he was a socialist—obviously Maximilian. The only plan of the Brotherhood is to destroy the aristocracy totally. The Oligarchy in turn plans to obliterate the masses entrapped during the insurrection behind their barricades, by bombing them and poisoning them with gas.

Gabriel has learned the Oligarchy's plans and conveys them to the Brotherhood's Council of the Proletariat. This council, however, has the same appearance as that of the Oligarchy, because, says Donnelly, injustice has wrought the same effects on both groups. "High and low were alike victims—unconscious victims—of a system." Caesar, the Italian leader, is an immense brute of a man, with "the eyes of a wild beast, deep-set, sullen and glaring." The Russian Jew (not given a name!) is

old and withered. One hand seemed to be shrunken, and his head was permanently crooked to one side. The face was mean and sinister; two fangs alone remained in his mouth; his nose was hooked; the eyes were small, sharp, penetrating and restless; but the expanse of brow above them was grand and noble. . . . His person was unclean, however, and the hands and the long finger-nails were black with dirt.

After the report is given to the council a discussion takes place, including a plea by Gabriel for a revival of the Christian faith as the solution for social problems and for the assurance of eternal life for the soul. "We have inherited," says Gabriel, "Christianity without Christ; we have the painted shell of a religion," and he calls for a real religion that would enforce a "Brotherhood of Justice" through education and the ballot box. But this is rejected—it is too late for reform; society has become too rotten for any treatment but destruction. A hundred years earlier something might have been accomplished by reform, but now it is too late.

A holocaust ensues, civilization is destroyed, the prince is killed.

Caesar, depicted as a raging, bloodthirsty beast, has a column constructed ("Caesar's Column") on a pile of corpses. "The Jew" flees the country with a $100 million and "several of his own nation," and "it is rumored that he has gone to Judea; that he proposes to make himself King in Jerusalem; and, with his vast wealth, re-establish the glories of Solomon, and revive the ancient splendors of the Jewish race, in the midst of the ruins of the world."[44]

For Donnelly, the Jews were the preternaturally clever men who were both the money power and the brains of the revolutionary resistance to that power. (This was an example of the polar stereotyping that was to become more common in the twentieth century, culminating in the canard that the Jews were not only the banker-capitalists who were impoverishing the people, but also the leaders of the Bolsheviks, who were leading man into a subhuman state.) If Donnelly's whole career and writing are taken into account, the ambivalence of his attitude toward the Jews emerges clearly. This does not, of course, extenuate the undoubted anti-Semitism of *Caesar's Column,* but it does, together with other evidence, help to mitigate the charge that Populism bears primary responsibility for subsequent anti-Semitism.

As early as 1876 Donnelly denounced racial prejudice in the Saint Paul *Anti-Monopolist,* which he edited.

Give the Jew a chance [he writes]. This is their country as well as ours, and they have a right to make all out of themselves that they are capable of without [one's] shouting "Jew, Jew" after them. A great nation, like all magnificent mosaic work, has room in it for all race elements of the world. There is room for Goth and Celt and Basque and African and Jew,—yes, even for the Indians, if they can survive civilization.[45]

In the 1880s he expressed a high view of the Jews historically, as he notes in *Atlantis* (1882). In this work he affirms a belief in the existence of the legendary Atlantis, and in the idea that the concept of monotheism probably originated there. This concept was transmitted through the Egyptians to the Jews, who "took up this great truth when the Egyptians dropped it, and over the heads and over the ruins of Egypt, Chaldea, Phoenicia, Greece, Rome, and India, this handful of poor shepherds—ignorant, debased, and despised—have carried down to our own day a conception which could only have originated in the highest possible state of human society"; but "our scepticism must pause before the miracle of the continual existence of this strange people, wading through the ages, bearing on their shoulders the burden of their great trust, and pressing forward under the force of a perpetual and irresistible impulse. . . . How many nations have perished, . . . since the sublime frenzy of monotheism first seized this extraordinary people!"[46]

The anti-Semitism of *Caesar's Column* in 1890 emerged from an intensification of the antigold agitation of Populism, which regarded the house of Rothschild in England as a leading influence for the demonetization of silver in 1873. But there is much evidence that anti-Semitism was not an essential element in the Populist agitation. But Norman Pollack, underestimates the charge of anti-Semitism when he calls this charge a "myth" on the basis of his study of "primary materials in the state historical societies of Minnesota, Nebraska, Wisconsin, and Kansas, and the Library of Congress. . . . The incidence of Populist anti-Semitism was infinitesimal."[47]

In 1892 Donnelly demonstrated his goodwill toward the Jews (according to his lights) in *The Golden Bottle* (1892), a more "positive" utopian novel that embodies ideas advanced by the People's party. The hero, Ephraim Benezet, is given a "golden bottle." Anything introduced into the bottle emerges as gold. It all turns out to be a dream, but much happens before the author reveals this denouement. Benezet becomes fabulously rich, is elected president, conquers the whole world, and becomes "President and Commander-in-Chief of the Army of Liberation." All monarchies fall to the liberators, and Benezet declares the formation of "the United Republics of Europe." After Russia is conquered a millennium of peace ensues—all through the power of the golden bottle, which, writes Donnelly, "represents the power of government to create its own money. With that power it will do all you dreamed the Bottle did."[48]

Before leaving Europe for home, Benezet

restored Palestine to the Jews. . . . It seemed to me that this great race, the Israelites, from whom we had derived our religion and so much of our literature, should have some share in the awakening of the world. They are a trading, not an agricultural people; and so I told them to plant themselves in the ancient seats of commerce, at the head of the Mediterranean, between India, China, and Australia on the one hand, and Europe and America on the other, with the Mediterranean Sea for a harbor and the Suez Canal for a gateway, and revive the ancient glories of their people. I gave orders that all Jewish immigrants to the Holy Land should be carried free, with their effects, over the government railroads; that the land should be divided among them; houses built; railroads and ships constructed;

a national convention held at Jerusalem, and financial help extended to make them at once a great and prosperous people. And out from all the lands of hatred and persecution the poor afflicted Hebrews, with their wives and little ones, poured in a steady stream into the old lands of their race; wealthy Israelites helped them, and natural leaders sprung up among them; and it will be a little time until the Jews, too, shall have a nation and a flag, illustrious and honored in the world; while the smoke of their steamers should ascend from sea and every harbor on the globe, and their delegates shall hold high seats in the Congress of "The Universal Republic," respected as representatives of the race which preserved the worship of the one true God in the midst of the darkness and foulness of ages and barbarism.[49]

This anticipatory vision of present-day Israel, while it is animated by a genuine desire to redress historic wrongs against the Jewish people and recognizes the legitimacy of Jewish nationhood, ignores, as if nonexistent, the claims of the Arab people in Palestine, just as so many in the Zionist movement did. Still, Donnelly's goodwill toward the Jewish people is unmistakable in these passages.

However, in several editorials written by him in the Saint Paul *Representative* in September 1894 confusion reappears. Under the present monetary system, he writes, "in these evil conditions, made by bad laws, the Jews alone thrive,—the reason is they deal only in money." To be sure, he adds, "we must not blame the Jews. Persecution forced them into their present channels. They were denied the right to own property, and nothing was left them but dealing in money, and now their cunning, and the folly of the mud-headed Christian statesmen, have put things in such shape that man, industry, property, wealth are all the slaves of an artificial thing called money."

The next week Donnelly had second thoughts about his sweeping categorization of "the Jews."

Some Yankee said [he writes in his editorial], "There are deacons and deacons!" And so we might say, there are Jews and Jews. There are Jews that are an honor to the human race, and there are Jews that are a disgrace to it. . . . And a plutocratic Jew is no worse than a plutocratic Christian;—in fact, he is not half as bad. . . . For the Jew, for nearly 2,000 years, has been proscribed, persecuted, hunted down; fenced into the corners of towns; hounded, pelted and stoned by ignorant populations [and, returning to his *Atlantis* theme of the previous decade], whose ancestors were savage barbarians when the Jews were preserving the knowledge of the one true God. . . . Karl Marx, the Jew reformer, faces Rothschild, the Jew plutocrat. . . . No; no. We would not persecute the Jews. What we meant was that they have become conspicuous, as types of the Plutocrat, because they excel all the other people in the capacity to accumulate wealth. We are fighting Plutocracy not because it is Jewish or Christian, but because it is Plutocracy,—destructive of the world, eventually destructive even of itself.

He concludes the editorial with the universal disclaimer of prejudice: "We would be sorry to be understood as saying one word that would pander to prejudice against any man, because of his race, religion, nationality or color."[50]

Despite Donnelly's confusions, this was not an idle statement. The year after he wrote *Caesar's Column,* when the whole country, both North and South, was trying to sweep the situation of the Negro under the rug, Donnelly anonymously wrote the novel *Dr. Huguet,* a bold attack on the cruel inequalities forced on the blacks. Dr. Anthony Huguet is a white liberal South Carolinian who has begun to grasp the truth about antiblack prejudice. After seeing a vision of Christ proclaiming that the blacks too are his children, Huguet awakens to find his soul, his educated, white awareness, transplanted to the body of a Negro, while the Negro's soul is now located in the body of Dr. Huguet. Huguet is subjected to a series of violent attacks and cruel indignities that reveal to him the full burden of oppression borne by the blacks. His body and soul are finally reunited, and he devotes his life to the education and "up-building of the negro race in America—this grandest and noblest of nations." He preaches "mercy and patience . . . patience and wisdom. . . . The negro's remedy is not in violence," but he will gain his equality "with ballots for weapons." Donnelly's hero calls for a coalition of white and black under a Populist political program.

At the same time, the depth of antiblack prejudice is emphasized by Donnelly's assumptions of black inferiority; his attitude toward the black is at best ambivalent. Under the influence of current racist theories, Donnelly assumes black inferiority in all respects at the same time that he argues vigorously for Negro equality; he holds out the hope that the Negro is "civilizable" by his responsiveness to the opportunity "to imitate the best examples given them by the whites."[51]

The novel was, nevertheless, a courageous, and for the time even radical, cry for Negro rights and bears testimony to Donnelly's belief in universal equality, even if his theoretical grasp was unsure. And just as his attitude toward the blacks was ambivalent, so also was his attitude toward the Jews. *Dr. Huguet* is an argument in support of C. Vann Woodward's defense of the Populists against Handlin's and Hofstadter's attacks. While Woodward grants that the criticism of Populism, including its occasional anti-Semitism, is in part justified, he emphasizes that "in the efforts they made for racial justice and political rights they went further toward extending to the Negro political fellowship, recognition and equality than any native white movement has ever gone before or since in the South. This record is of greater historical significance and deserves more emphasis and attention than any anti-Semitic tendencies the movement manifested in that region or any other."[52]

Donnelly's basic humanity (which included his attitude toward the Jews when he was not swept up in silver campaigns) received expression again in 1899, two years before his death. In the Minneapolis *Representative* for January 18 he speaks out strongly against incidents in New York City where the beards of elderly Jews were pulled. "Let us suppress the cannibals of all races, and lift up the wretched of all races," he cries. The spread of anti-Semitism in Europe and this country as a result of the Dreyfus case shocked him into writing editorially on July 27: "The Jews are not all plutocrats. A large majority of them are the poorest people in the world. The half-starved workers of the sweatshops of London, Berlin and New York are mostly Hebrews. . . . [It is] inexplicable that a Christian people, worshipping a Jew, the son of a Jewess, should entertain such terrible bigotry against the people of his race."[53] When one considers that it was the author of *Caesar's Column* who uttered these condemnations of anti-Semitism during a period of rising feeling against the Jews, the oversimplification of the Handlin-Hofstadter thesis becomes evident.

At the same time one cannot absolve the Populists of a degree of responsibility for the rise of anti-Semitism in the 1890s, as Norman Pollack tends to do. The evidence of an editorial in the *Jewish Voice* of Saint Louis, shortly after the Populist convention was held in that city, cannot be ignored (though allowances should perhaps be made for exaggeration, which stemmed in part from understandable indignation and in part from class and political opposition to the Populists). The editorial observes that there were Jews among the Populists at the convention, but that it is "dishonorable" for any Jew who respects his Jewish origin to belong to this party because the growth of anti-Semitism "is openly and insidiously encouraged . . . by the Populist hordes." The editorial asserts that "nasty, insidious remarks" issued from "the bloodless lips of some of the delegates haunting the corridors of the hotels" during the convention. The editorial also cites a July 22, 1896, Associated Press dispatch from Saint Louis calling attention to "one of the striking things about the

Populist Convention": "the extraordinary hatred of the Jewish race. It is not possible to go into any hotel in the city without hearing the most bitter denunciation of the Jews as a class and of particular Jews who happened to have prospered in the world."[54]

The mistake of the Handlin-Hofstadter thesis lies in overlooking the presence of other significant sources of anti-Semitism, a phenomenon that was much too complex to be a side effect of Populism. (Populism was hardly accountable for the increasing discrimination against Jews in social resorts and clubs, for example.) John Higham has suggested some of this complexity by placing the problem in the context of the times, when negative attitudes toward mass immigration, Jewish and southern European, were part of the general antiforeign feeling, at a time when German Jewish businessmen were rising to affluence with astonishing rapidity. He discusses three sources of late nineteenth-century anti-Semitism: some agrarian radicals in the Populist movement, some patrician intellectuals (e.g. Henry Adams, Henry Cabot Lodge, James Russell Lowell, and many traditional American aristocrats), and some groups among the urban poor.[55]

As in the Populist utopian novels, anti-Semitism was to be found in the utopian novel generally, as it was in society as a whole. So deep-seated, refractory, and complex is the Jewish question, with its centuries of overlay of prejudice, that even those who would correct the injustices of society were unclear about this particular injustice. As we have seen, anti-Semitism erupted even in those sectors of American society that criticized the nation for its shortcomings as to freedom and democracy. The democratic impulse was not always strong enough or informed enough to overcome the psychological and social momentum of anti-Semitic stereotyping.

PART FIVE

TOWARD THE AMERICAN JEWISH NOVEL

BEGINNINGS

A number of circumstances combined to bring the Jew to the fore-front of the American people's attention from the 1870s onward. The Germans who immigrated to this country a few decades earlier rose to affluence and entered into serious economic competition with native American business enterprise. Many German Jewish peddlers of the 1840s and 1850s became leading retail merchants and manufacturers in light industry, and some even became bankers; so that by the 1870s they began to aspire to social recognition by their non-Jewish peers. Their presence had become so significant in the economic sphere that they were a force to be dealt with willy-nilly, one that could not be ignored. Under these circumstances the deep-seated, age-old prejudice came to the surface and was expressed by overt social discrimination.

By 1881 the new pattern was so clearly operative that Nina Morais, of an established Philadelphia Sephardic family, in an article, "Jewish Ostracism in America," could outline it fully:

The provident hotel-keeper avoids the contact of the Hebrew purse; the little child in school finds no room for the Jew in the game at recess; the man of business, whose relations with an Israelite have been close and honorable, gives vent to a passing feeling of displeasure in the reproach of "Jew." In social and professional clubs, the "Jew" is black-balled. "Jew" is the text of the political opposition orator. The liberal-minded host tells his guests, with an apologetic air, that the stranger among them "is a Jew, but quite a cultured man." An agreeable companion is spoken of as "a good fellow, if he is a Jew." The merchant who cheats his creditors, the criminal in the prisoner's dock, is a civil offender if he belongs to the Baptist or Episcopal denomination, but if he comes of Hebrew blood, Judaism is made responsible for fraud and theft. Jew, Jew, Jew is the one all-comprehensive charge.[1]

Miss Morais further observes that the Jew is not popularly judged as an individual but as a specimen of a species deprived of individuality. "The Jew," she writes, is said to be "an objectionable character, whose shrewdness and questionable dealings in trade enable him to wear large diamonds and flashy clothes. He raises his voice beyond the fashionable key, in a language execrable to the ears of English-speaking people. . . . His conversation rings upon the key-note of the dollar; his literature is the quotations of the market." On the other hand, she does not deny that, to some extent at least, "the Jew may be answerable for the prejudice which exists against him." She grants that the traditional and "enforced confinement to trade" resulted in the Jews mounting "too rapidly to the top of the commercial ladder."[2] Though opportunity in the United States led to pecuniary success and the resulting social potentialities, it did not always bring about commensurately discriminate use of these levers.

Miss Morais did not discern several points that John Higham has since made clear. First, intensified prejudice against the Jews was one phase of a revived nativism whose targets were "foreigners" in general. Second, social climbing was not limited to Jews; it was general. The American economy was growing with amazing rapidity, and many sections of the population were quickly rising to wealth, with its accompanying social aspirations. Because the Jews were more prominent than any other ethnic group in "the struggle for status," says Higham, "the Jews symbolized the pecuniary vices."[3] Displeasure at the pretensions and vulgarities of the nouveaux riches, which was a general American attitude at that time (see, for instance, Mark Twain and Charles Dudley Warner's *Gilded Age* [1873]), found a ready symbol in the Jews, who were conspicuous in their numbers and the speed with which they emerged to affluence. The attitudes of Anglo-Saxon America toward the new-rich German Jew at this time is conveyed by these 1880 verses from *Puck:*

In this year of Christian grace
What's your state and what's your place?
Why, you're rich and strong and gay—
Chakey Einstein, owff Broadway!
Myriad signs along the street
Israelitish names repeat.
Lichtenstein and Morgenroth
Sell the pants and sell the coat;
Minzescheimer, Isaacs, Meyer,
Levy, Lehman, Simon, Speyer—
These may just suggest a few
Specimens of Broadway Jew—
And these gentlemen have made
Quite their own the Drygootz Trade.

Surely you're on to-day,
Chakey Einstein, owff Broadway.
Fond of women, fond of song;
Fond of bad cigars, and strong;
Fond, too fond of Brighton's Race,
(Where you're wholly out of place,
For no Jew, in Time's long course,
Ever backed a winning horse;)
Fond of life, and fond of fun,
(Once your "beezness" wholly done;)
Open handed, generous, free,
Full of Christian charity;
(Far more full than him who pokes
At your avarice his jokes;)
Fond of friends, and even kind
To the sick and lame and blind;
(And, though loud you else may be,
Silent in your charity;)
Fond of Mrs. Einstein and
Her too-numerous infant band,
Ever willing they should share
Your enjoyment everywhere—
What of you is left to say,
Chakey Einstein, owff Broadway?

Well, good friend, we look at you
And behold the Conquering Jew![4]

The situation of the Jew was being profoundly affected from another direction as well. The avalanche of East European Jewry that was to alter the configuration of Jewish life began late in the 1870s. Oppressive restrictions against Jews in the tsarist Pale of Settlement and in other East European lands caused Jews to seek liberation in emigration to the "promised land." While almost 7,500 East European Jews entered the United States in the first seventy years of the century, about 40,000 came in the 1870s. Pogroms and intensified persecutions brought approximately 150,000 more in the 1880s and about 400,000 in the 1890s. A small percentage of these fanned out into the country, but most remained in New York (as did most other immigrants arriving in that city).

At the time when many German Jews of the earlier immigration were prosperous businessmen, many of these newcomers entered the American economy as skilled workers. Some took to peddling in the city with pack on back or on pushcart, and later they had food or candy stores; most found work as skilled or semiskilled artisans. The highest percentage entered the clothing industry, which by 1870 had become the leading Jewish industry. At first East European Jews manufactured clothing in sweatshops and factories, which increased rapidly in the last few decades of the century. For instance, from 1880 to 1890 the number of men's clothing factories in New York and the capital invested in them more than doubled. Technical innovations that made manufacturing more efficient and more profitable were introduced. East European Jews steadily displaced their German Jewish employers, as Abraham Cahan vividly shows in his *Rise of David Levinsky.* In this industry's new, desperately competitive environment, where not much capital investment was needed, many East European Jews became manufacturers and rose to affluence in a few decades, as the German Jews had done before them.

The high human cost of this rapid economic development was manifest in the intensely crowded, inhuman living conditions on the East Side and the intense economic exploitation of the area's immigrant population. In the subcontractor's apartment employees worked under stifling conditions from sunrise into the night for cruelly low wages. A description of an East Side sweatshop, probably not too highly colored, occurs in a popular novel of the period, Edward W. Townsend's *Daughter of the Tenements* (1895). Eleanor Hazehurst, the uptown rich girl and teacher in a mission school on the East Side, sponsors the rise of a child from the Italian quarter, Carminella, to ultimate fame as a ballerina. One winter day little Carminella takes Eleanor to the Baxter Street home of the Jewish girl, six-year-old Lena, to find out why she has been absent from school.

Eleanor is deeply shocked by what she sees.

The people, from the youngest to the oldest, were speechless and grave and hopeless-looking. Men staggered past, their bodies bent almost double under what seemed impossible loads of clothing they were carrying to and from the sweaters' and workshops-homes. Women carrying similar bundles on their heads, or perhaps a bundle of wood from some builder's waste, hurried along, not speaking to those they passed; none of the children seen was much more than a baby in years; and they were silent too, and had no games: they were in the street because while the sweaters' work went on, there was no room for them in their homes. In the dress of none was any bright color seen, and the only sounds were the occasional cry of a hurt child, the snarling of the low-browed men who solicited trade for the clothing stores; and always, as the grinding ocean surf mutters an accompaniment to all other shore sounds—always, always, always!—was heard the whining monotone of the sewing machine.

Eleanor and Carminella climb to Lena's home on the fourth floor of the tenement. There they find four men, a woman, a girl of sixteen, and two younger girls working on machines, sewing by

hand, and pressing. Lena is working among them, taking the place
of her eight-year-old sister, who is ill—with typhus, as it turns out.

Eleanor felt herself growing faint again [continues Townsend];
the air of the hot, close room was lifeless; the odors from the perspiring, unclean bodies of the workers, the fumes from the boiling
cabbage, the steam arising from the dampened shoddy under the hot
iron of the presser, the indescribable scent from the fever-scorched,
uncared-for patient, and the utter misery of it all made her weak and
dizzy.[5]

By the late 1880s and early 1890s the expansion of the Jewish
settlement of New York and the intense oppressiveness of the new
immigrants' working and living conditions finally forced themselves
on public awareness. In these early years, Lillian D. Wald notes,
"aside from its exploiters, political and economic, few people had
any knowledge" of the East Side, and, she adds, "its literary 'discovery' had just begun."[6] Since mid-century occasional articles on the
Jews had appeared in magazines, but beginning with the late 1880s
and 1890s articles on pogroms in Russia and on Jewish life in the
United States appeared with greater frequency in magazines and
newspapers. The group later to become known as the muckrakers
were particularly interested in the East Side Jews and published
many sympathetic articles about them in the 1890s.[7] The ghetto
community of the new immigrants was not only picturesque but also
steeped in problems of life and labor. A few crusading journalists
were drawn to the East Side, and among the earliest and most
influential was Jacob A. Riis, himself an immigrant from Denmark.

Animated by the reforming spirit and armed with a camera, Riis
played a large part in informing the public of the desperately bad
living conditions in the foreign quarters, especially on the East Side.
His driving journalism and civic zeal helped to ameliorate some of
the worst aspects of tenement life. His *How the Other Half Lives,*
published in 1890, was one of the earliest exposés of ghetto conditions to appear in English. He relentlessly reveals the inhuman
crowding and unlivable dwellings in "Jewtown," as he repeatedly
calls the Jewish East Side. "It is said," he writes, "that nowhere in
the world are so many people crowded together in a square mile as
here."[8] In 1890 one acre nearest the factory area contained 523.6
persons, and in 1900, 700 persons.

Genuine as was Riis's sense of the necessity for remedy, his personal attitude toward the East Side Jews was distant and not free
from conventionality. There is condescension and detachment in his

statement that "Bayard Street is the highroad to Jewtown across the Bowery, picketed from end to end with the outposts of Israel. Hebrew faces, Hebrew signs, and incessant chatter in the queer lingo that passes for Hebrew on the East Side attend the curious wanderer to the very corner of Mulberry Street." Some passages are even tinctured with anti-Semitism. Ignoring the intense cultural life found by Hutchins Hapgood, Riis writes that

thrift is the watchword of Jewtown, as of its people the world over. It is at once its strength and its fatal weakness, cardinal virtue and its foul disgrace. Become an overmastering passion with these people who came here in droves from Eastern Europe to escape persecution, from which freedom could only be bought with gold, it has enslaved them in bondage worse than that from which they fled. Money is their God. Life itself is of little value compared with the leanest bank account. In no other spot does life wear so intensely bald and materialistic an aspect as in Ludlow Street.

Riis also echoes other notions propagated by anti-Semites about Jews. "The curse of bigotry and ignorance reaches halfway across the world [from Poland and Russia] to sow its bitter seed in fertile soil of the East Side tenements. If the Jew himself was to blame for the resentment he aroused over there, he is amply punished."[9]

Another reporter-reformer, Ida M. Van Etten, writing at the same time as Riis, although not approaching him in influence, viewed the East Side Jews with a deeper knowledge and a greater sensibility. In an article in *The Forum* in 1893, she passionately describes conditions. Before unions were formed in the 1880s, she writes,

there seemed to be no limit to the extent of a day's work, except the limit of physical endurance. The conditions under which these people worked are almost indescribable to one who has never seen a sweater's den. The over-crowding and over-work, the filth and the squalor, and the horrible sanitary surroundings make a picture which must be seen to be understood. . . . They had fled from unbearable Old World conditions to sweaters' dens and tenement-houses where human beings are packed more closely than in any other quarter of the globe.[10]

She observes that many of the political exiles that came from Russia in the late 1880s were active in union organization, and she records the workers' heroic endurance through long strikes. She also discusses with considerable sympathy the radical outlook of many Russian immigrants and their effective leadership of organized labor. She alludes to their intense intellectual activity with respect to social questions, their concern for education, and their cultural interests.

In her understanding approach to the Jews and in her recognition of their cultural values Ida Van Etten to a certain extent anticipated what we now consider to be the classic treatment of the East Side of that period, Hutchins Hapgood's *Spirit of the Ghetto*. In its genuine humanity, perception of human quality and cultural values, and utter absence of anti-Jewish feeling the book is a remarkable achievement. How difficult it must have been to attain such a high degree of humanistic realism one may judge from the almost universal revulsion from, or at best condescension toward, the strange new breed pouring into the country under a dual disability. Not only were they totally foreign and abjectly poor, but they also were victims of ingrained thinking about Jews.

Hapgood overcame all this to attain a humanistic vision. It is one of the most notable achievements of Abraham Cahan that he was Hapgood's mentor in his study of the East Side during the years when both were reporters on the *Commercial Advertiser*. This study, issued as a series of articles published from 1898 to 1902, was collected as *The Spirit of the Ghetto* in 1902. In his later years Hapgood acknowledged that he could never have attempted the book if it had not been for Cahan's tutelage.

Hapgood made no pretense at a sociological analysis of the East Side. "The Jewish quarter of New York," he writes in the preface, "is generally supposed to be a place of poverty, dirt, ignorance, and immorality . . . where the people are queer and repulsive." Some writers, he goes on, "treat of it sociologically, as of a place in crying need of improvement." Such a writer, above all, was Riis, and he was very effective in exposing the social and physical ills of the area and in provoking meliorative legislative action. But Hapgood's motives are, he writes, neither "philanthropic nor sociological." He was led to write "by virtue of the charm I felt in men and things there."[11] He was intrigued with the "spirit" rather than the social condition of the ghetto. He was not yet the socialist he was later to become, and customs and culture interested him more deeply than social statistics.

By one of those lucky historical chances, he enlisted as his collaborator a young artist, Jacob Epstein, later to become one of the great sculptors of his day; Epstein illustrated the book with sketches of the East Side that are no less humane and authentic than Hapgood's text. It is a great loss to our record of the East Side in those days that hundreds of Epstein's sketches of ghetto life that were not published in the book have never been found.

Hapgood's sympathetic understanding of the East Side did not preclude telling the truth about the older Jewish generation there, but he states it accurately, without condescension or pejorative language. "In spite, therefore, of his American environment," he writes, "the old Jew of the Ghetto remains patriarchal, highly trained and educated in a narrow sectarian direction, but entirely ignorant of modern culture—medieval, in effect, submerged in old tradition and outworn forms." To this he contrasts the younger generation, who are subjected to the larger American educational and cultural influences, and in consequence come into collision with the mores and values of the shtetl. Hapgood came to know the writers, poets, artists, actors, scholars, and intellectuals of the East Side, and in this book he describes their character and aspirations— in brief, the life of the mind in the ghetto. Among the intellectuals were "the anarchists, the socialists, the editors, the writers, some of the scholars, poets, playwrights and actors of the quarter."[12]

Hapgood's underestimation of the "anarchists and socialists" among them, who, he says, "will leave nothing behind them,"[13] was owing to his lack of understanding of and hostility toward socialism at the time. For these men did indeed exert a profound influence on the future of the Jews in the country and on the nation as a whole. In a review of Hapgood's book in *The Comrade*, "J. S." (John Spargo) severely criticizes the author for "lightly estimating . . . the constructive power of the Socialist element in the life of the Ghetto"[14] and misunderstanding its political significance. The course of events has confirmed Spargo's strictures.

On the other hand, Hapgood was sensitive to the "veritable intellectual fermentation" that was going on in the ghetto, and the passionate controversy over ideas. The poets of the quarter, he says, "sing pathetically of the sweatshops, of universal brotherhood, of the abstract rights of man." He also observes "a certain number of poets, dramatists, musicians, and writers"[15] who form "the literary bohemia of the quarter," spurred on by love of art or by the need of a livelihood. Most of the book is taken up with perceptive sketches of individuals who exemplify the lively and varied intellectual life of the ghetto.

One of these, the poet Morris Rosenfeld, whom Hapgood called "a Singer of Labor," was brought to the attention of the English-speaking world through translation of his Yiddish poems into English. His status as an "American" poet was acknowledged by Edmund Clarence Stedman after Harvard instructor Leo Wiener published Rosenfeld's *Songs of the Ghetto* in an English translation. Stedman included Rosenfeld's first poem written in English, "I Know Not Why," in his *American Anthology, 1787–1900:*

I lift mine eyes against the sky
The clouds are weeping, so am I;
I lift mine eyes again on high,
The sun is smiling, so am I.
Why do I smile? Why do I weep?

I hear the sounds of autumn sigh,
They break my heart, they make me cry;
I hear the birds of lovely spring,
My hopes revive, I help them sing.
Why do I sing? Why do I cry?
It lies so deep, I know not why.[16]

The environment that produced Morris Rosenfeld was very different from the one out of which Emma Lazarus had emerged a few decades earlier. This was something new in the world of American Jews. Something of the feel of this newly created ghetto can be gained from a passage in Abraham Cahan's *Yekl* (1896):

He had to pick and nudge his way through dense swarms of bedraggled half-naked humanity; past garbage barrels rearing their overflowing contents in sickening piles, and lining the street in malicious suggestion of rows of trees; underneath tiers and tiers of fire escapes, barricaded and festooned with mattresses, pillows, and featherbeds not yet gathered in for the night. The pent-in sultry atmosphere was laden with nausea and pierced with a discordant and, as it were, plaintive buzz. Supper had been despatched in a hurry, and the teeming populations of the cyclopic tenement houses were out in full force "for fresh air," as even these people will say in mental quotation marks.

Suffolk Street is in the very thick of the battle for breath. For it lies in the heart of that part of the East Side which has within the last two or three decades become the Ghetto of the American metropolis, and, indeed, the metropolis of the Ghettos of the world. It is one of the most densely populated spots on the face of the earth—a seething human sea fed by streams, streamlets, and rills of immigration flowing from all the Yiddish-speaking centers of Europe. Hardly a block but shelters Jews from every nook and corner of Russia, Poland, Galicia, Hungary, Roumania; Lithuanian Jews, Volhynian Jews, south Russian Jews, Bessarabian Jews; Jews crowded out of the "pale of Jewish settlement"; Russified Jews expelled from Moscow, St. Petersburg, Kieff, or Saratoff; Jewish runaways from justice; Jewish refugees from crying political and economical injustice; people torn from a hard-gained foothold in life and from deep-rooted attachments by the caprice of intolerance or the wiles of demagoguery—innocent scapegoats of a guilty Government for its outraged populace to misspend its blind fury upon; students shut out of the Russian universities; and come to these shores in quest of learning; artisans, merchants, teachers, rabbis, artists, beggars—all come in search of fortune. Nor is there a tenement house but harbors in its bosom specimens of all the whimsical metamorphoses wrought upon the children of Israel of the great modern exodus by the vicissitudes of life in this their Promised Land of today. You find there Jews born to plenty, whom the new conditions have delivered up to the clutches of penury; Jews reared in the straits of need, who have here risen to prosperity; good people morally degraded in the struggle for success amid an unwonted environment; moral outcasts lifted from the mire, purified, and imbued with self-respect; educated men and women with their intellectual polish tarnished in the inclement weather of adversity; ignorant sons of toil grown enlightened—in fine, people with all sorts of antecedents, tastes, habits, inclinations, and speaking all sorts of subdialects of the same jargon, thrown pellmell into one social caldron—a human hodge-podge with its component parts changed but not yet fused into one homogeneous whole.[17]

The sheer quantitative impact of the Jews upon the country and their growing influence in trade and industry and even the cultural life of the nation, especially in entertainment and theater management, was felt not only in New York City, where the great majority settled, but also in varying degrees in many areas of the country. A limited number of immigrants fanned out into various parts of the country. The affluent and established German Jews, fearful that the flood of shtetl Jews descending on New York City with their "foreign" ways would impair their own status, set up agencies to shunt immigrants to different parts of the country. They especially wished to settle Jews on the land—not only to remove them from urban areas, but also to prove to their countrymen that Jews were not inexorably traders; they could work the land as well. Numerous agricultural colonies were established, financed by the Baron de Hirsch Fund and the contributions of wealthy German Jews like Jacob Schiff; agricultural colonies were set up in New Jersey, Texas, the Middle and Far West. But virtually all of them failed within a very short period, because of both the lack of agricultural skills among the colonists and their remoteness from centers of association with other Jews.

After these failures many of the hundreds who went out to farms moved to cities and small towns throughout the country, where they achieved success in trade and business. Jewish workers engaged in militant strikes that riveted public attention, both favorable and unfavorable, upon them. The visibility of Jews in the country rose markedly, as indicated by the numerous articles in the daily and periodical press about one aspect or another of Jewish life and immigration. As Leo Stein writes (1900): "The truth seems to be that the Jewish question is arising among us in an even more pronounced form. The Jew is becoming more numerous and prominent, and the eyes of the community are more and more fixed upon him. . . . The

Jew is an object in the landscape, and must expect to be drawn."[18]

And drawn he was, with greater frequency than ever in fiction, the drama, and other entertainment. From the 1870s on, the Jewish vaudeville comic emerged, a variant of the age-old stereotype. In this period, too, the American Jewish novel became a part of the American literary landscape.

The number of American Jews who aspired to the status of novelist at this time increased markedly, although unhappily most aspirants were inept and incompetent. However, the awareness was growing among American Jews that they should not leave the depiction of Jewish life to the non-Jewish writer. In 1888 the noted rabbi Dr. David Philipson delivered a series of lectures in Philadelphia on "The Jew in English Fiction," which were published the next year in Cincinnati in book form (enlarged editions came out in 1902 and 1911). The authors treated in the book are English, from Marlowe to Zangwill. Probably under the stimulus of these lectures, in the same year Ephraim Lederer read an essay, "The Jew in Fiction," before the Hebrew Literature Society of Philadelphia, in which he called for an American Jewish literature:

A native Jewish literature is a crying need in this country; and Jewish works of fiction, written by American Jews, can therefore with reason be included in our catalogue of wants. . . . It is high time that we native-born American Jews should contribute our proper portion to the literature of our race. It is time we should cease trading on the literary capital which our brethren, born in other lands, have provided for us.[19]

The year of Philipson's lectures, 1888, also saw the founding of the Jewish Publication Society of America. One of its earliest publications was Graetz's *History of the Jews,* and other works in Judaica followed. Several of Zangwill's works were also issued by the society. By 1900 some works of didactic junior fiction were published, two authored by non-Jews: Louis Pendleton on the young biblical Prince Almon (see above, p. 149), and Samuel W. Cooper's story about the boyhood of Moses Montefiore (see above, p. 323).

Sara Miller's *Under the Eagle's Wing* (1899) tells a story about the teenage Joseph, who is apprenticed to the brothers Moses and David Maimonides in their silversmith workshop in the Egyptian city of Fostat. Joseph is accepted by the philosopher Moses Maimonides, "the Great Eagle," as a chief disciple. While Joseph is on a dangerous mission for Maimonides, he is taken by the Muslims and threatened with imprisonment unless he renounces Judaism. He refuses, affirming that "if every Jew had been less submissive, and had shown some of the fire and courage which animated our forefathers, we should not now be a despised and persecuted people." The author also combats the stereotype of vengefulness as a Jewish characteristic by having Maimonides and his niece, Ester, dissuade the young hero from wreaking his revenge on the anti-Semitic French count, who had tortured Benjamin's father to death for refusing to give up his fortune to the count. Joseph is finally convinced that " 'Vengeance is mine, I shall avenge,' saith the Lord."[20]

Another book published by JPS was Milton Goldsmith's *Rabbi and Priest* (1891), purportedly a true story told to the author by an actual Russian Jewish immigrant in 1882. It is a melodramatic tale of two brothers separated in boyhood, one of whom becomes a great rabbi and the other an anti-Semitic priest. The latter is brought up by Christians who keep him ignorant of his Jewish origin. After becoming a priestly theorist of anti-Semitism and an inciter of pogroms, the priest meets his brother during a pogrom, recognizes him, realizes his Jewish origin, becomes remorseful for his anti-Semitism, and is then killed trying to save his brother's daughter during a pogrom.

The quality of most fiction written by Jewish authors in the last few decades of the century was generally not high. Nearly all these authors were German Jewish immigrants, and several even set their stories in Germany. A seventeenth-century Rhine Valley village is the locus of I. N. Lichtenberg's *Widow's Son* (1884), a drearily melodramatic tale of a Jewish boy who, as a nominal Christian still faithful to Judaism, becomes the governor of a province. The novel is a kind of conversion tale in reverse, for the young Jew's elevation is made possible by a Father Anselmo. The "priest" is actually a rabbi, who has taken on this identity in order to strengthen Judaism by posing as a Christian. Lichtenberg was no doubt a Reform Jew, for one of his characters is an emancipated Jew who is excommunicated from the ghetto community, but is obviously a sympathetic character. The author wishes to bring home the lesson that not all Christians are anti-Semites, for the local duke is tolerant of Jews and helpful to the Jewish hero.

Far better written is Adelina Cohnfeldt Lust's *Tent of Grace* (1899). Mrs. Lust immigrated to the United States in 1876 at the age of sixteen, and her story is located in the Germany she knew as a youth. Attitudes toward Jews, whether anti-Semitic or tolerant, are central to the story, and German Jewish prejudice against their Polish brethren also appears. The basic belief of the author, it would seem, is an adaptation of the faith of Lessing's Nathan the Wise. The pastor who takes in an orphaned Jewish girl, Jette, and allows her to live by her own faith, believes, as his son tells his Catholic friend, that "the better life beyond is our common goal. No matter by what road we travel to attain it, so long as we go about the right way to reach it. Thou as a Catholic, I as a Protestant, she as a Jewess."[21] Despite the many well-intentioned sentiments of various characters, Jewish and Christian, this novel rings the changes on anti-Semitism, religious rigidity, and intolerance on both sides, and ends in tragedy.

Jette's father dies when she is eight, and her mother remarries a Polish Jew; but he is looked down upon, for German Jews "generally stigmatized" Jews born on the Polish border. After Jette is orphaned, she is set upon by Christian children. "Fed upon superstition, local influence, and family traditions," writes the author, the children "were ready, like their elders, to let prejudice run riot, at any and every provocation." After she is orphaned, the kindly local pastor and his wife take her to live with them, seeing to it that she lives by her own religion.

Jette grows into a lovely young woman and falls in love with the pastor's son, Fritz, but they are prevented from marrying when both her rabbi and the good pastor will not countenance intermarriage, "an unnatural union," as the pastor says. But after the pastor suffers a stroke he realizes his error, and tries to persuade the rabbi to permit the marriage. The rabbi is adamant: "The Jewess cannot wed the Christian. If she does, she dies to her people; they know her no more." The pastor replies that the religious structure of the rabbi cannot survive in the future "unless it be founded on the solid rock of brotherly love." The plan of Jette and Fritz to go to the "land across the sea . . . where liberty of thought and action prevail" never comes to fruition.

Jette is charged with the ritual murder of a Christian child. When an old hag tells the anti-Semitic mob, "She has killed her, and gathered the blood that she may sprinkle it over the altar in the synagogue, for it is near Passover time,"[22] Jette is killed by the mob.

A description of the life of the wealthy banking family of Goldman and Son, of Cologne, occurs in mid-story when Jette makes their acquaintance, and Julius, the twenty-eight-year-old son of the family, falls in love with her and wishes to marry her. He has red hair, is squat and rotund, and is generally rather unattractive; seventeen-year-old Jette is repelled by him. He agrees to wait three years before asking for her hand, and in the meantime Jette shares the Goldmans' life from time to time, giving the author occasion to describe the mode of life of wealthy German Jews. The clash between Orthodox and Reform is suggested in the conflicting convictions of father and son, respectively. Jette's tentative agreement to marry Julius is negated by the love between Jette and Fritz, which in turn is frustrated by the tragic death of Jette. Mrs. Lust has packed many aspects of Jewish life in her long, literate novel, but there is no real depth in the human relations of her characters.

Other novels by Jewish writers in the 1890s are worth scant notice. A novel of the New York ghetto, *In Gold We Trust* (1898), by A. H. Frankel, a propagandist for vegetarianism, is on the level of a dime novel, with evil and angelic cardboard characters. One interesting aspect of this utterly dispensable work is its depiction of German Jews of the period ridiculing Jewish East European names, names ending in "ski." These Eastern Jews were regarded as uncouth and money-obsessed.

The novels of Moritz Loth, a faithful disciple of Rabbi Isaac Mayer Wise's, and one who responded to Wise's call in the 1850s for American Jewish writing, are only a little less poor, obvious and moralistic, sententious and sentimental. He advances a self-congratulating conception of the Jews. In *On a Higher Plane* (1899) Loth has Rabbi Mordecai (probably modeled on Rabbi Wise), "a great scholar and a benefactor to humanity" who is fluent in twenty languages, cure Squire Parker of Jew-hatred. "I considered them [the Jews]," the squire tells Mordecai, "a small, mean, grasping people, while they are in fact great, noble, and generous in thought and action." Rabbi Mordecai, says the author, "was a good and great man, whose aim in life was to lead mankind to a higher plane of perfection. And this aim we claim for this novel, 'On a Higher Plane': to lead the whole human race nearer to perfection. Perfection is the mother of happiness."[23]

A strange product of the American Jewish effort to project the "Jewish" nature is an absurd novel by Nadage Dorée, a contemporary Jewish actress and the author of several plays. Her *Gelta; or, The Czar and the Songstress* (1897) is the author's transparent effort at self-glorification, claiming supreme virtue for the Jews as a people. In reading this amateurish effort one finds it hard to understand how Israel Zangwill could say, as quoted in the endpaper, that the book "is written in a bold masterly way; it is replete with flashes of genius. . . . [It is] most skilfully constructed . . . [a] flesh and blood creation." The full-length photograph of the author in the frontispiece appears to answer the description of Gelta, her heroine, "this willowy brunette" of "perfect form."[24] Gelta, the daughter of a Hungarian father and French mother, was born in Louisiana. Now an operatic prima donna, she meets the Russian grand duke Ivan Demetrius at the British Museum. He turns out to be the heir to the throne. She is unaware of his identity, and they fall passionately in love; but she refuses to see him because he is a Christian, she is Jewish—and opposed to intermarriage.

In discussing with him the oppression of the Jews in Russia, she represents the Jews as being the fount of all virtue and knowledge. "Have they not been the means of civilizing the world? Giving it poetry, music, commerce, religion, a God." But, she continues, "what does the Christian in his ignorance do for all these splendid gifts? Persecutes the Jew, his benefactor." Curiously enough, despite Gelta's inordinate pride in her Jewish origin, she agrees when the duke tells her that she has "not a Jewish cast of features." Except, she adds, that she has Jewish eyes. "If you will observe the expression of my eyes," she says, "you will see that divine light of intelligence, reflected through Israel's daughters who glory in a race of forefathers whose benefits have ever been to benefit and uplift humanity."

Gelta's high-mindedness leads to tragedy. She has enormous success in Paris and Saint Petersburg, and her celebrity status puts her in a position to get close to the tsar. The nihilists, through the agency of a Russian count, the son of a Russian father and Jewish mother, try to recruit Gelta for an assassination attempt on him, "but no, her heart of a true Jewess, shrank from a deed so brutal, a deed of blood and murder." Instead, she obtains an audience with the tsar and pleads for her people. His answer is to expel her from Russia as a Jew. The night before her departure a bomb is due to be set off at a ball that the tsar is going to attend. Knowing this, she goes to the ball, warns the guests in time, and puts her own body between the bomb and the tsar. On her deathbed she summons a rabbi, who speculates about what will happen "when they behold the sacrifice this noble daughter of Israel had offered up to save the Czar, what sublime mercy she had shown to him, who had always been so merciless to her race! Would the Czar repent of his past cruelty?"

What the author is trying to prove by all this is expounded by Gelta to the grand duke, whom she has refused to marry: "By nobly putting into practice the divine teachings of Christ, you will save Judaism; for true Christianity is merely *transposed* Judaism, or it is nothing; both are one, and the same, and mean a pure, ideal life, to work, to help, to suffer, for the happiness of others."[25] And she reiterates this sentiment on her deathbed.

But not all American Jewish fiction writers who emerged in the 1890s concentrated on the exposition of Jewish life. Isaac Kahn Friedman's early book of short stories about Chicago life, *The Lucky Number* (1896), includes only one story about Jews among its half dozen pretentiously written tales. And "Aaron Pivansky's Picture" might equally have been written by a non-Jew, for all the light it sheds on Jewish life. Solomon Pivansky, father of the aspiring young painter Aaron, is a pawnbroker straight out of the stereotype: "His face was mean enough ordinarily, literally, as well as figuratively, without a redeeming feature,—a harsh, hard, cunning, repulsive face, a face that made it useless for the owner to deny sordidness and avarice and tyranny, a face that bore the marks of thirty years of Russian persecution, and a face that bespoke a sullen waiting for vengeance." Solomon is enraged at Aaron's "waste" of time and materials in painting until Aaron suggests that the painting might be worth money. "Money!" writes Friedman. "The word acted like the touch of a talisman, it made the whole affair appear different in Solomon's eyes."[26] When Solomon sells the painting without Aaron's knowledge, Aaron is furious; he leaves home to seek it out and recover it, finds it in a museum exhibition, and slashes it to shreds. Then he leaves the city with his artist-teacher and with his faithful love, Becky.

Friedman, a university graduate from a wealthy Chicago family, was a socialist. Walter B. Rideout has noted that his *By Bread Alone* (1901) was the "first radical novel in twentieth century America."[27] Friedman's condemnation of the anarchism of his Jewish character in his novel, Sophia Goldstein, an immigrant from Russia, is an oblique criticism of the real Emma Goldman. But Jewishness is a minor aspect of the book, as of the earlier *Poor People* (1900). This latter tale of tenement life includes among its poverty-stricken characters only one Jewish family, the Bernheimers, who are briefly described. But poor Jews were remote from the author's experience. Mr. and Mrs. Bernheimer, he writes, "look odd—the quintessence of oddness itself. He plucks at his frowzy black beard, and grins and grins, reaching the ends of his ears with gymnastic smile. His wife plucks him by the sleeve and frowns disapprovingly."[28]

Since Friedman concerns himself so little with Jews and their milieu and problems in his fiction, in what sense can he be considered an American Jewish novelist? When an American Jew like Friedman creates fiction does it necessarily follow that his work is American Jewish fiction? These are matters of definition, but it would seem that a work should be Jewish in content if it is meaningfully to be considered "American Jewish." Within this framework most of Friedman's work is simply American. Similarly, the work of the early American Jewish dramatists—Noah, Harby, Phillips, Judah—do not fall within the American Jewish category because (with the exception of Judah) they put no Jewish content in their plays. Their work is, in fact, indistinguishable from that of their non-Jewish contemporaries.

It should further be clear that Judaism, the Jewish religion, need not necessarily be considered essential to the Jewish milieu, since many Jews live as Jews without adhering to that belief or its practices. In this sense the Jewish religion is not an essential element in Jewishness. To argue otherwise, as some do, leads to the absurd conclusion that a nonreligious person of Jewish extraction who manifests the ethnic traits of the Jew—like a ghetto inhabitant or even a Zionist who rejects the Jewish religion, or any Jew who professes no religion at all—is not Jewish. It is clear that the atheistic ghetto dweller who speaks Yiddish, with its unique ethnic psychophilological makeup, is a Jew, despite any attempt to read him out of the Jewish people because he does not profess Judaism. Jewishness is a set of ethnic, or cultural, characteristics that are distinguishable from those of the dominant culture in whose midst the Jews live. It is the content of the work, not the author's religion, that supplies the criterion for American Jewish literature. Indeed, it is possible for a non-Jewish author to depict with insight the American Jewish milieu, and we shall see that this has been the case.

When Rabbi Isaac Mayer Wise called for Jewish participation in literature in the 1850s, he wished to promote writing that would deepen religious consciousness. He himself wrote stories to fulfill this need, and called himself the "American Jewish Novelist." But the setting of his fiction was mainly Europe or biblical times. The locale of his first novel, *The Convert* (1854), is Bohemia, although its oppressed Jews do escape to America. The setting of a second novel, *The Shoemaker's Family* (1854), is Austria. The half dozen other novels he wrote in English are also set in Europe or in biblical times. Wise's talents did not encompass the writing of fiction. Most of his disciples who took his call to literature seriously did attempt to write fiction about American Jewish life, but their writing was by and large negligible.

The one exception is Nathan Mayer, whose *Differences* (1867) can be regarded as the first American Jewish novel of any significance or competence. At the core of this novel, as we have seen, are the problems and mode of life of American Jews, North and South, just before and after the Civil War. Several decades were to pass before more significant American Jewish fiction was to appear. Stereotyped Jews continued to crop up in the popular novels of the decades following the Civil War.

By the 1880s the growing Jewish communities in many parts of the country brought Jews into greater visibility. The German immigrants of the middle years of the century were rapidly rising to affluence. Yet in 1872 W. M. Rosenblatt could write in *Galaxy* that, despite the tens of thousands of Jews living in New York, "the people generally know almost as little of this great Hebrew community as they do of the Brahmins in India. It is curious to see how much ignorance most of the writers who attempt to describe and discuss them exhibit. To a large share of Americans the Jew of Chatham Street is the typical Jew."[29] In the course of the next few decades the situation was to change, at least in some of its literary manifestations. While many writers continued to render the Jew in stereotype, the American Jewish novel that was emerging promised to make available to the American public literary re-creations of American Jewish life that were more or less adequate. Jewish and non-Jewish writers offered both sociological and literary contributions to the American people's knowledge of the life of their fellow Jewish Americans. By the 1880s the life of New York Jews became a subject for Henry Harland, the next significant novelist of American Jewish life after Nathan Mayer.

THE STRANGE CASE
OF HENRY HARLAND

The first novels focusing on the American Jewish milieu that were widely read by the American public came from the pen of a non-Jew, Henry Harland, and were published in the 1880s under the Jewish-sounding pseudonym Sidney Luska. Heretofore, the Jewish aspect had been secondary in fiction written by non-Jews. But with Harland it was precisely to the celebration and criticism of Jewish life that he applied himself.

He was born in Norwich, Connecticut, in 1861, but lived in New York from boyhood on. His father, Thomas Harland, was a Fourier-ist, and he and his close friend E. C. Stedman lived in a cooperative on Fourteenth Street called Unitary House, where Thomas met and married his wife. (The cooperative survived until the outbreak of the Civil War.) Stedman was Henry's godfather and later his literary mentor.

After the war the Harlands lived in the German Jewish section of the city on Beekman Street, which later provided the setting for Harland's fictional Jewish characters. In this milieu he became intensely interested in the Jews and studied their manner of life and folklore. When the Ethical Culture movement supplanted Fourier-ism as the ideology of the Harland household, Henry shared the new family interest. It is reported that he was a pupil of the leader of the movement, Felix Adler, whom he greatly admired. Adler was the son of the rabbi of Temple Emanu-El, the foremost synagogue of the time, and was expected to follow his father in the post; but instead he founded the social-minded Ethical Culture Society, a nonsectarian expression of the rising Social Gospel movement. Adler is admiringly portrayed as Raphael Grickel in Harland's autobiographical novel, *Grandison Mather.*

Harland entered the City College of New York in 1877, but dropped out in his sophomore year and was registered for one term at the Harvard Divinity School in 1881, after which he toured Europe. On his return in 1883 he renewed his association with the Ethical Culture movement, whose membership was largely Jewish, and he lived in or near the Jewish districts of the city. In her memoirs his second wife writes that "everything Jewish became of interest to Henry Harland, who was nothing if not whole-souled in his attachments. The Jewish element of New York appealed to his imagination, perpetually athirst for picturesque material; he saturated himself with the romantic traditions of the Jewish race."[1]

After his first marriage in 1884 he began writing under the tutelage of E. C. Stedman, who edited the manuscript of his first novel and arranged for its publication. *As It Was Written, a Jewish Musician's Story* was published in 1885 under the pseudonym Sidney Luska. Years later Harland told a Norwich lady that he adopted this name "because my books were about the Jews and every young Jew I ever heard of was named Sidney and Luska I thought a good name because it didn't mean anything."[2] But why conceal his authorship under a pseudonym at all? He explains why in his autobiographical novel, *Grandison Mather:* "Because if it should be a failure, I don't want to be handicapped by it. I don't want to be saddled with an unsuccessful book. But if it succeeds, I can drop the nom-de-plume, run up my true colors, and no one will be the loser."[3] Harland had reason to be apprehensive over the fate of his book. Not only was it a first novel, but its subject matter was a gamble for a fledgling novelist. Stories set in the Jewish milieu had been published by amateurish Jewish novelists whose books hardly reached the general community, but never before had a non-Jew attempted this. To be sure, the pseudonym, Harland hoped, would make the public believe the author to be Jewish, and he succeeded in taking in most of his public.[4] But Harland won his gamble: the book proved popular and eventually sold fifty thousand copies. He was launched as a writer.

The first-person narrator is Ernest Neumann, a German Jewish violinist and music teacher. He becomes engaged to the singer Veronika Pathzuol ("pronounced Patchuol," Harland explains), whose uncle, Baruch Tikulski, is a composer. Veronika's "eyes were bottomless. Far, far in their liquid depths the spirit shone like a star. All the history of Israel was in her glance. . . . All the experience of the Jewish race, all the martyrdom of the scattered hosts were hers by inheritance."[5] Shortly before they are to be married, Veronika is stabbed to death. Neumann is charged with the murder on the strength of circumstantial evidence, but no motive can be established, and he is released. He abandons music and becomes a waiter.

Other less important Jewish characters are introduced. The one non-Jewish character, the poet Daniel Merivale, who befriends Neumann, is Harland's mouthpiece for expounding his ideas about the Jews. Merivale congratulates Neumann "for belonging to the ancient and honorable race of Jews. Your ancestors were civilized and dwelt in cities and wrote poems, thousands of years ago: whereas mine at that epoch inhabited caves and dressed in bearskins and occasionally dined on a roasted neighbor. I should be proud of my lineage, were I a Jew." When Neumann reminds Merivale that Jews are generally "despised," the latter replies that "it is the fashion for a certain ignorant, stupid set of Philistines to do so—but those who pretend to the least enlightenment, on the contrary, regard the Jews as a most enviable people."

Merivale goes on to expound, in 1885, a theory about what was later to be called the melting pot (a phrase coined by Zangwill as the title of a play [1908]), and he projects his notion of the Jews' place in that scheme. Today, says Merivale, "there is no American people—or rather there are twenty American peoples—the Irish, the German, the Jewish, the English, and the Negro elements— all existing independently at the same time, and each as truly American as any of the others. Good! But in the future, after immigration has ceased, these elements will begin to amalgamate. A single people of homogeneous blood will be the consequence." But the Jews have a special part to play. They will

leaven the whole lump—color the whole mixture. The English element alone is, so to speak, pure water; the German element, one portion of *eau sucrée;* now add the Jewish—it is a dose of rich strong wine. It will give fire and flavor to the decoction. The future Americans, thanks to the Jew in them, will have passions, enthusiasms. They will paint great pictures, compose great music, write great poems, be capable of great heroism.[6]

While we may discount the hyperbole of Harland's conception, he should be credited with a certain insight, in light of the prominent part that Jews have played in the arts in America in our own century. Such an eventuality was not obvious in the early period of mass immigration of poor East European Jews, and I know of no one else who predicted at this early stage the eventual great participation of Jews in the arts.

In the latter part of the novel Neumann obtains a manuscript left him by his father, which forbids him to marry because of a family curse that for four generations has compelled the husband to kill his unfaithful wife. Under the excitement of this revelation, Neumann composes a work of music and adds, by automatic writing, an account of his murder of his betrothed, Veronika, which was perpetrated during a trance under the influence of the curse. The book ends with Neumann's decision to give himself up to the police, because "I am enough of a Jew to believe in eye for eye and tooth for tooth. . . . I shall see to it that the murderer of Veronika Pathzuol meets with the punishment which his crime demands."[7]

Considering the readability of this novel, as well as Harland's others, its success gives no cause for wonder. However, the characterization is superficial and the style rhetorically overblown. To Harland, the Jews were an object of esthetic curiosity, interesting because they were "picturesque." Merivale remarks that "New York was the most picturesque city in the world, 'thanks,' he said, 'to the presence of your people, the Jews.' "[8]

Harland was a "philo-Semite"—a term that has been used in some sociological writing as if it were the only alternative to anti-Semitism. Actually the term is the "positive" form of anti-Semitism, in that it assigns excessively good attributes to the Jews, in contrast to the bad features that the anti-Semite imposes on the Jews. In both cases, all Jews are indiscriminately endowed with traits that are imaginary—"Jewish eyes," for instance—or excessively credited with good or bad qualities. And in both cases the Jews are conceived of simply as the embodiment of some stereotype. In neither case is the Jew regarded as an individual who has a range of talents and virtues and vices like any other person. The generalizations about Jews made by a philo-Semite such as Harland are not any truer—even if they are more flattering—than those made by an anti-Semite.

The book was widely and favorably reviewed. Among others, the review in the New York *Jewish Messenger* (September 25, 1885) is duly taken in by the flattery and greets the novel with enthusiasm. Doubt about whether the author's name is "real or assumed" is expressed, but the reviewer looks forward to the next book. The novel is overpraised as showing "an originality of thought, a deftness of plot-weaving, a strength of character painting"; and its climax is said to be "equal to Poe's weirdest fantasies." The reviewer is gratified that it contains "no caricature," and he thinks that "the Jewish element is not obtruded on the reader." Finally, "a debt of gratitude" is owed to the author for "contributing more powerfully than could sermons and editorials to the genius of Judaism."

Harland was naturally pleased by this reception, and quickly supplied the *Jewish Messenger* with a short story, "A Purim Episode." He deliberately sought to confirm that he was Jewish by referring to "our co-religionists" and by explaining "for Gentile readers" that all Jews keep open house on Purim. The story relates, in a claptrap imitation of Poe's horror tales, how three merry young Jews on a Purim lark enter an undertaker's house and, after hearing a blood-curdling woman's laugh, come upon an ostensibly dead woman in an open coffin. The woman rises from the coffin and grapples with one of the youths, who bites her and draws blood. The youths flee in terror. On returning later they are told that the undertaker's daughter is insane, and "used to sleep in a coffin and make believe she was dead."[9]

Flushed by the success of his first novel, the following year Harland returned to the theme with a second novel, *Mrs. Peixada,* again under the name of Sidney Luska. All the important characters are Jewish except for the hero, Arthur Ripley, a young lawyer who is obviously the spokesman for Harland. He lives on Beekman Street with Julian Hetzel, a Jewish college teacher. Ripley is engaged by Benjamin Peixada, the head of a small insurance agency, to find his sister-in-law, Judith Peixada, who has disappeared a few years earlier after being acquitted of her husband's murder on a plea of insanity. Peixada needs to find her in order to recover the full estate of his brother, on the basis of a later will than the one probated.

Ripley becomes acquainted with some of his German Jewish neighbors and meets a beautiful young widow, Mrs. Ruth Lehmyl, who has a sweet singing voice. As the reader immediately suspects, she is the Mrs. Peixada he has been engaged to find. They fall in love and marry. Ripley, unaware of the true identity of his wife, places an unsigned personal advertisement asking Mrs. Peixada to appear at his office. He is stunned to discover that he has married a missing person, and his equally stunned fugitive-cum-bride accuses him of betraying her to Benjamin. She then reveals the true story of the murder: she had overheard her husband planning a burglary, was discovered eavesdropping, had grappled with her husband and his accomplice in an effort to escape, and had killed them both in self-defense. Once the story is known, she is exonerated by the district attorney, but Ripley is prostrated by her desertion of him. She is finally convinced of Ripley's innocence, nurses him back to health, and they live happily thereafter.

Harland's plot enables him to delineate a number of the characters of this "picturesque" people. They range from the quaint to the musically endowed to the devil stereotype. Two old Jewish matrons who speak with a German accent, Mrs. Berle and Mrs. Hart, are kindly and hospitable. To Harland, the Jews always mean music, and his heroine sings beautifully. He also meets a cellist, Mr. Lipman, who, like Veronika of the earlier novel, gives Harland occasion to expatiate on Jewish eyes: Mr. Lipman has "deep-set, coal-black eyes, with an expression in them—an anxious, eager, hopelessly hopeful expression—that told the whole story of the travail and sorrow of his race."[10] There are other minor characters: Ripley's roommate, Hetzel; Mr. Mendel, a benevolent brewer; Mr. Rimo, Mr. Peixada's nephew, who is a flighty, flirtatious dandy.

However, Mrs. Peixada's description of her late husband, Bernard, a sixty-year-old man whom she married only to save her father from utter financial ruin—she was in effect sold to him—corresponds in all details to the medieval fantasy of the Jew-devil. He had

a hawk's beak for a nose, a hawk's beak inverted for a chin; lips, two thin, blue, crooked lines across his face, with yellow fangs behind them, that shone horribly when he laughed; eyes, two black, shiny beads, deep-set beneath prominent, black, shaggy brows, with the malevolence of a demon aflame deep down in them; skull, destitute of honest hair, but kept warm by a curling, reddish wig; skin, dry and sallow as old parchment on which wrinkles were traced. . . . His voice . . . was a dry, metallic voice that grated like a file . . . which could not be forced to say a kind and human thing. . . . His hands —his claws, rather, for claws they were shaped like; and instead of fingers, they were furnished with long, brown, bony talons, terminated by black untrimmed nails.

To complete the medieval conception, she adds that "he was the Antichrist of my theology."[11]

One would suppose that a person of this description would be judged by his community for the fiend that he was. But no; he was a most respected member of society because he was rich, closed his shop on Jewish holidays, fasted at the appropriate times, attended synagogue regularly, and was over and over again elected parnas of the congregation. Harland crudely vents his dislike of the Orthodox community in this portrait of Peixada.

In a long conversation between Mrs. Lehmyl-Peixada and Ripley, Harland expounds his ideas on the Jews. Under the illusion that she is not Jewish, Ripley praises the Jews in philo-Semitic fashion. The more he knows of them, the better he likes them. He can't understand the prejudice against them. "Their past, you know, is so poetic. They have the warmth of old wine in their blood. . . . I think the

Jews are the kindest-hearted and clearest-minded people one meets hereabouts." When she tells him she is Jewish, he apologizes for his patronizing comments but reaffirms his sincerity; "The Jews are a noble and beautiful people, with a record that we Gentiles might well envy."

More of Harland's opinions emerge from the conversation. Ripley is glad that Mrs. Peixada is not Orthodox—he approves of "this tendency among the better educated Jews to cast loose from their Judaism." Ripley then puts forth a favorite theme of Harland's: "I want to see them intermarry with the Christians—amalgamate, and help form the American people of the future. That, of course, is their destiny." Although she agrees, she is a little "melancholy" that the amalgamation will take place before the Jews

could compel recognition from their persecutors, when, as a united people, they could stand forth before the world, pure and strong and upright, and exact credit for their due . . . prove that Shylock is a libel. . . . I should like him to retain the name of Jew until it has grown to be a term of honor, instead of one of reproach. . . . Now that the chance is given him, it seems a pity for him quietly to efface himself, become indistinguishable in the mass of mankind.[12]

Although Mrs. Peixada is reconciled to amalgamation and loss of Jewish identity, in this early statement of the melting pot theory she grants that "very few" Jews believe that "amalgamation is inevitable." In fact, they don't even think about it, she says. "The majority of the wealthier Jews here in America," she adds, "are epicureans. Eat, drink, be merry, and lay up a competence for the rainy day, is about their philosophy." Furthermore, she says, the older people have a strong "prejudice" against intermarriage. This view, she goes on, is "prejudice pure and simple, the offspring of superstition." Despite the fact that many Jews are indifferent to religion, they are horrified when intermarriage occurs and predict "some dire calamity for the bride and bridegroom."[13]

When the conversation turns to discrimination, Mrs. Peixada relates how she once experienced social prejudice. She and Mrs. Hart were at first socially accepted at a mountain hotel, but then, she says,

innocently enough, one day I said we were Jewesses. After that we were left severely alone. I remember, we got into an omnibus one afternoon to drive to the village. A young man and a couple of young ladies—guests at the same house—were already in it. They glared at us quite savagely, and whispered *"Jews!"* and signaled the driver to stop and let them out. So we had the conveyance to ourselves, for which we were not sorry.

Ripley responds to this story with indignation—"it makes my blood boil," he says. But she disdains even to resent the incident, for that "would lend undue importance to it."[14]

This novel, like the first, was on the whole favorably received, and Harland felt encouraged to continue to mine this new fictional vein. A dissenting voice was the review in the *New York Times,* which says with discernment that "the story of Jewish life in New York City, the true realistic one, has yet to be written." Harland "has not got 'the hang' of it."[15] But William Dean Howells greeted Harland as a promising recruit to the realism that he was propagating. The novel, he said, has "go." This is true; no doubt Harland had a gift for sustaining narrative pace, for the reader is impelled to read his books through at one sitting.

But Howells had no profound grasp of the problem—as indeed what non-Jewish artist or writer of the time did? For he went on to overpraise "Mr. Luska's mastery in the treatment of his various Israelites, in their presentation individually, and in their collective localisation here in New York. They are neither flattered nor carica-tured. They are simply portrayed with truth by a hand that is already firm and that gives promise of greater and greater skill."[16] Howells apparently overlooked Ripley's absurd philo-Semitic encomium of the Jews, and the devil image of Bernard Peixada.

Emboldened by his success, Harland launched a frontal attack on the problem of intermarriage in his next novel, *The Yoke of the Thorah* (1887). The theme of the book is epitomized by the title. Rigid adherence to the Torah, especially its prohibition of intermar-riage, is a "yoke" to be cast off by the American Jew, whose destiny is to amalgamate. The representative of an inhumanly rigid Judaism is the rabbi Dr. Gedaza, uncle of the painter Elias Bacharach, the central character of the novel. Elias has been brought up in strict Orthodoxy and has been emphatically told by his uncle that inter-marriage is the very worst sin, the unpardonable sin. Catastrophic misfortune surely overtakes an intermarried couple, says his uncle; they will "be as if touched with leprosy, shunned and despised of all men. To the Goy, they will continue to be Jews; but to the Jew they have become Goyim." The feeling of a Jew for a Christian, he says, can never be love but only the allure of the senses; you don't marry them. The rabbi makes the most extravagant assertions of superior-ity: "The blood of Israel outranks the blood royal; for the Lord our God created the heavens and the earth . . . for the special enjoyment of his chosen and much beloved people."[17] Death is preferable to marrying outside of Israel, and to the good Jew a mixed marriage is equivalent to a funeral, the rabbi admonishes his nephew.

Elias has precipitated this discussion by falling in love with a young Christian girl, Christine Redmond. He is horrified by his uncle's admonition and prays through the night to divest himself of his love for Christine, but to no avail. He declares his love to Christine, and she reciprocates it. "At a touch, it seemed, love had converted Elias Bacharach from the most reactionary sort of orthodoxy, to a rationalism, the bare contemplation of which, a few days ago, would have appalled him." Whatever view one may hold of the issue, his concluding sentence—"The man had got the better of the Jew"—is a tactless, invidious statement, an almost involuntary assertion of Jewish inferiority. When Elias tells Christine's father of their impending marriage, Redwood replies in conventionally "nonprejudiced" terms: "Well, Mr. Bacharach, though you *are* a Hebrew, you're white [sic]; and anyhow, religion doesn't worry us much in this household, and never did. . . . You're a perfect gentleman; you can't help it if you *were* born a Jew. You don't look like one, and don't act like one."[18]

A different response comes from Elias's uncle, who tells him God won't permit the marriage to go through. Terrified by the prophecy, Elias endures a night of feverish hallucination. Though he is gripped by fear, Elias is determined to marry Christine. His uncle's presence at the wedding disturbs him, and when the parson asks Elias if he will take Christine to wife, Elias falls senseless to the floor. Elias believes he has been struck down by God, but the author reveals that the uncle knows the seizure to be an epileptic fit, a fact he does not reveal to Elias.

"The God of Israel had indeed interfered," Elias is now convinced, and he determines that "I shall always be a good Jew after this." He suppresses his love for Christine and is drained of all feeling for her and her suffering. His uncle is ruthless: "She is a Christian, a Goy, despised and abominated by the Lord. She has served her purpose. Now she must bear her punishment." (Earlier in this study we encountered similar attitudes, with the roles reversed, in Henry Ruffner's "Judith Bensaddi" [1839], in which William Garame is contemplating marriage with the English Jew Judith Bensaddi. He loves her but is filled "with detestation at the very name of Jew. . . . The stiff-necked, hard-hearted race, . . . cursed and banned . . . from the pale of human society." Nevertheless, he is willing to marry her, but when he finally does, in a sequel to the story, she has been converted to Christianity. See page 72.) Christine's father is enraged by Elias's refusal to go through with the marriage, saying: "If it does kill her, I—I'd rather *have* it, by God, than have her married to you, now that I know what you are, you damn, miserable, white-livered Jew!"[19]

A new phase in Elias's life gives Harland the opportunity to depict New York's German Jews. For it is to them that Elias turns after a period of complete apathy. He enters the social life of the nouveau riche Koch family. The attitude of the established Sephardic Jews toward the recently arrived German Jews emerges in a comment by the Sephardic rabbi Gedaza: "They talk too loud, and their grammar isn't of the choicest; but they're thoroughly kind-hearted and well-meaning; and they're not wanting in brains, either, though they may be a trifle unpolished." Harland dilates on the gustatory achievements of the Koch household, where Elias dines: "After the French, the Jews are the best cooks in the world."[20] The conversation plays about the superiority of the United States and the prevailing sense of decency and honesty in business. The German Jews, they comment, are the most devoted theatergoers in the country.

Elias's uncle encourages a match between Elias and Tillie Morgenthau, a pretty girl whom Elias meets at the Kochs'. Harland never fails to emphasize the Jews' affinity for music: Tillie is a fine pianist. Tillie invites Elias to her home in Beekman Place, which she prefers to Lexington Avenue, where the Kochs live—"Jerusalem Avenue, I call it, on account of the number of Jews that live over here." Under his uncle's prodding he visits Tillie frequently, although he is apathetic and not in love with her. His uncle finally persuades him to propose, and the engagement reception brings together a microcosm of New York Jewry: "Old and young, good and bad, wise and foolish, rich and poor, savage and civilized, fat Jews and lean Jews, shabby Jews and shoddy Jews; gentlemanly Jews and rowdy Jews; petty tradesmen, banker princes, college professors, commercial travellers, doctors, lawyers, students, musicians." The wedding takes place "in the strictest orthodox style" at the Advance Club (in real life the German Jewish Harmonie Club).

After a period of humdrum married life, Elias happens to see Christine and his love returns in full force. He undergoes anguish and remorse at his desertion of her, and finally becomes disillusioned with Orthodoxy. It is, he now believes, a "delusion, a monstrous lie. . . . My superstition was the dragon, whose breath poisoned our joy, withered our world, burned out our hearts."[21] He learns that Christine is to be married and implores her to meet him in the park. When she fails to appear, he dies in the park of an epileptic fit.

As might be expected, the book created a furor in the Jewish community. Most of the Jewish press condemned it. In the review in the very first issue of the Philadelphia *Jewish Exponent* Harland's ideas on the Jews were deemed more damaging than those of Henry James, because James appealed to a limited cultivated audience, while Harland's audience was the ignorant and prejudiced. Later in the year (November 4, 1887) a writer in the same paper clears Harland of being an enemy of the Jews, but says he thinks that the book is "grossly inartistic" and "shows a spirit of friendly condescension, not to say vulgar assumption towards Jews."[22] The Christian-hating rabbi of the book, writes the reviewer, does not depict a modern rabbi, but rather one of inner Poland a century earlier. Harland, he concludes, deludes himself by thinking he is not prejudiced against the Jews, for he actually is.

Harland is also roundly criticized in *The Menorah* by the noted Reform rabbi Dr. Kaufmann Kohler, who complains that the author leaves the impression that "the Jews, as a class, lack refinement." Harland would have the Jew separate himself from "all Jewish affiliation," if he is to be a "man."[23] Harland clearly would prefer to have the Jews assimilate totally, although his target in this book is ostensibly rigid Orthodoxy. He has in fact anticipated this criticism by entering a disclaimer in a footnote: "It would seem hardly necessary, yet it is no more than fair to say that among the better-educated and more intelligent Jews in America, orthodoxy of this stripe is not common." But he adds:

Even among them, notwithstanding, it prevails to a sufficient extent; and among the ignorant classes it is the rule. It is curious circumstance, however, that, in the majority of cases, those very Jews who have cast quite loose from their Judaism, and proclaim themselves "freethinkers," "agnostics," or what not, retain their prejudice against intermarriage, and even their superstitions about its consequences.[24]

Basically, then, Dr. Kohler's complaint is justified, since Harland says that even among the "majority" of the non-Orthodox, Jews not only disapprove of intermarriage but even share apprehensions about divine retribution. Kohler makes clear his own disapproval of intermarriage, but recalls that it was the church, not the synagogue, that first introduced the prohibition. He denies that a Jew who intermarries is mourned as dead; this, he says, applies only to the renegade. Finally, says Dr. Kohler, in categorically regarding the Torah as a "yoke," Harland has ignored its socially positive aspects.

The *Jewish Messenger* discusses the book in a number of issues. The initial editorial comment criticizes *The Critic,* a literary journal, for its approving comment that the novel contrasts the Jewish "horror" of intermarriage with the Christian affirmation that only love counts. The editorialist responds with a *tu quoque:* "The Jewish 'horror' of mixed marriage is hardly more intense than the Christian horror of marriage between Catholic and Protestant." He then repeats a standard argument that mixed marriage is most likely to be unhappy because of religious and social differences. Some of his characters, he continues, are "not types but caricatures on a par with Puck's [a humor magazine] occasional creations of Jews that never were on sea or land."[25]

A few issues later an indignant reader returns to the attack. Harland's "sermon" against mixed marriages, he writes, sounds like Spinoza's excommunication. The work, he says, is an "anachronism" because the characters "are not Jewish: they are Germans, who refuse to be Americanized." He repeats the argument that intermarriage is "likely to produce disharmony in life after the first few months of romance are past." Although Harland does not intend it, the book "teaches prejudice."[26]

However, some Jews were disturbed by the onslaught on Harland. The young men's group of Rabbi Kohut's Congregation Ahaweth Chesed invited Harland to address them on his book on January 19, 1888. Several Jewish papers were critical of this gesture, but the *Jewish Messenger* disagreed, and offered a less negative estimate of the book than it had earlier. "Mr. Luska is friendly disposed," says the editorial, "and has no intention to wound anyone's feelings. If he calls a spade a spade, sensitive people must not worry on that score. His last novel was exaggerated in parts, and truthful in parts; . . . [the book] is not so radically faulty as some of his critics would assume." Some of his critics abuse him "as if he were a second Haman or Stocker." Harland is, in fact, "singularly free from prejudice." The editorialist then chides the hypersensitivity of some critics:

Even the most rabid pro-Semite . . . must recognize that some of us are not yet refined and cultured, and that we have our proportion of quite ordinary people whose wealth has not made them flawless. . . . We have no right to be blind to our own defects. . . . We voluntarily seek the ghetto, and in too many cases invite social ostracism by our prejudice. . . . Conceit is as insufferable in a race as in an individual.[27]

In a letter the next week Harland expressed his gratitude to the journal for its defense of him.[28]

Harland must have been deeply shaken by the attacks, but he did not at once abandon the Jewish theme, though it is not central to his next novel, *My Uncle Florimund* (1888), a book for boys. The hero is a Connecticut boy, Gregory, from an aristocratic French family, who is abused by his guardian, Uncle Peter. Gregory runs away to New York to seek work from a Jewish businessman, Solomon D. Marx, whose lost fishing pole Gregory has rescued from the water. Both Marx and his father-in-law, Gottlieb Finkelstein (who is "fond of music"),[29] are sentimentally represented as angelic in their goodness and are transparently patronized by the author, perhaps as a misguided attempt to show his goodwill. In its review of this book the *American Hebrew* is relieved to find that "the fantastic spirit of Mr. Harland's fancy has been moderated somewhat in the book. . . . Both [Jewish characters] are exemplary, being large-hearted and generous to a fault. The dialect of the younger man is hardly as permissible as in the case of the elder."[30]

However, Harland's fixation on the Jewish theme was loosening. His next volume was a collection of short stories, *A Latin-Quarter Courtship, and Other Stories* (1889), of which only one story, "Mr. Sonnenschein's Inheritance," deals with Jewish life. His two main Jewish characters are invidious stereotypes. Emmanuel Sonnenschein, a German Jew who lives in Tompkins Square, is a peddler and a schlemiel, defined by Harland as "one who never prospers, with whom everything goes wrong . . . [a man who is] constitutionally unsuccessful."[31] He is a kindly fool, outrageously patronized by the author. The other is the shopkeeper, Levinson, a knave of a Polish Jew. Interestingly enough, in this story Harland echoes the prejudice of German Jews against Polish Jews.

Sonnenschein inherits thirty thousand dollars from his European brother, but fears to deposit the cash in the bank. Instead, he leaves it in his neighbor Levinson's burglar-proof safe. Levinson's store burns down under suspicious circumstances, but since he has no insurance he is absolved of arson for lack of motive. However, when Levinson finally confesses that he removed the money from the safe before setting fire to the store, he is imprisoned for arson. Sonnenschein recovers his inheritance, which he finally agrees to put in the bank.

The German Jew's "goodness" is dubiously praised by the author: "Though a Jew by birth and faith, he is as good a Christian as most professing ones," for he makes some provision for Mrs. Levinson and her children. Levinson, the Polish Jew, is thoroughly bad in all respects. When the narrator asks the fire marshal if the fire was set, that worthy replies: "Whenever a fire occurs in premises occupied by a gentleman of Mr. Levinson's race, class, and profession, I may say it's suspicious. These low-class Polish Jews think no more of setting fire to a house, if they've anything to gain by it, than they do of lying." The narrator extends the characterization:

> These low-down Polish Jews . . . all look pretty much alike; there is an astonishing poverty of types among them: take the first old-clothes or glass-put-in man who comes along, and he'll answer fairly well for Mr. Levinson. . . . As for his person, it would have been base flattery to call it dirty. It was unspeakable. I could not help feeling that by its presence it soiled the atmosphere of the room.[32]

Harland's next book, *Grandison Mather* (1889), was his last incursion into New York Jewish life, and his final use of the pseudonym Sidney Luska. *Grandison Mather* is largely autobiographical. Thomas Gardner (Harland) meets and marries Rose Cartaret in Rome. They return to New York. When Tom loses his inheritance through speculation by the estate's trustee, they find a cheap place to live at the Beekman Place house of the Grickels, a German Jewish family who immigrated with the post-1848 wave. Speaking with a heavy German accent, Mrs. Grickel tells them: "Ve're Chairman Chews." Rose later comments: "Who cares about her religion, so long as she is good and kind?" Tom quite agrees with her, adding that "it doesn't correspond very well with the popular idea of the Jewish character, the way she lowered her price to suit our means. That wasn't very Jewy." Rose replies that "very likely the popular ideas of the Jews are absurd. If Mrs. Grickel is a Jewess, I'm prepared to love the whole race. And that little Jew-boy we saw as we went in —he had the face of an angel."

As always, music figures importantly in the lives of the Grickels, and they "were not strictly orthodox in point of faith." Inevitably, also, intermarriage enters the novel, this time as a minor theme. Rose brings together Tom's lawyer friend Pearse and the Grickels' daughter, Lina, and they are married. Throughout the book Harland gallantly represents Rose as the defender of the Jews against Tom's mild dubieties on the subject. When Tom complains about the mixed marriage, Rose replies: "That doesn't make any difference. Miss Lina was telling me this morning how a great many Jews were opposed to the two races intermarrying; but she said that her people felt quite the other way, and were in favor of it."[33] Apparently the hostile response to *The Yoke of the Thorah* had not yet completely shaken Harland's philo-Semitism and patronization of the Jews, nor his zest for the theme of intermarriage.

Raphael Grickel is a patent portrayal of Harland's early idol, Felix Adler. Like nearly all of Harland's favorable Jewish characters, Grickel does not look Jewish, but he does not escape Harland's obsession with "Jewish eyes." "Except for his eyes," Harland writes, "you would never have dreamed that he was a Jew; but they stamped his race unmistakably. They shone with a certain intense, wistful light, half sorrowful, half passionate, such as I have never observed in any eyes but those of a Jew or Jewess." Grickel is the leader of the "Society for Humane Culture" (Ethical Culture Society), and Harland explains the program and activities of the society in some detail; they correspond precisely with Felix Adler's innovating educational and social welfare projects. "Grickel," says Harland, "believes that we should observe literally the teachings of Christ . . . and he regards Christ as the greatest of the prophets. . . . He stands between two fires. The Christians despise him as worse than a Jew, and the Jews rate him as an apostate."[34] Tom and Rose become Grickel's disciples, just as Harland was Adler's. They attend Grickel's weekly lectures and are active in his projects.

Tom turns to writing a novel at night after work. He meets the influential literary personage Everett St. Marc (E. C. Stedman), who reads the manuscript and is favorably impressed. "I read it through yesterday at a sitting," says St. Marc, probably an authentic remark in light of the extreme readability of Harland's own novels. St. Marc arranges for publication of the book (as Stedman did for Harland's first book), and it is favorably received. Tom (Harland) writes a quite accurate self-judgment of the book: "Of course I know that it isn't a novel to set the world on fire. . . . It isn't a profound study of character or motive; and it isn't destined to become a classic on account of style. But I do believe it's an interesting story."[35] Tom gives up his job and becomes a professional writer, as Harland did after his first book was published.

Thereafter Harland abandoned the Jewish theme, although Jewish characters and allusions to them do appear fleetingly in his subsequent work. His chagrin over the vigorous denunciation of *The Yoke of the Thorah* by the Jewish press may have been a factor in his change of direction, but more basic tendencies were at work in him. His interest in the Jewish milieu around him was basically an esthetic fascination with their "picturesqueness," as his second wife declared, and as he himself said through one of his characters. His underlying inclination was toward fin-de-siècle estheticism.

A trip to Europe in 1889 that must have confirmed this inclination led him to cast off the influence of Stedman and Howells, and to adopt the estheticism of Bloomsbury and Paris. He remained in England, and there established connections with the fin-de-siècle literary figures. He began to romanticize his past falsely, somewhat in the way that Poe had. He gave out that he had been born in Saint Petersburg, said he was the illegitimate son of Emperor Franz Josef, and even lay claim to an English baronetcy, the Harlands of Sprague Hall. So successful was his deception that the *National Dictionary of Biography* records his birthplace as Saint Petersburg. This penchant for noble status had already appeared in *My Uncle Florimund*, where the boy Gregory idolizes the aristocratic French family of his mother.

In England, Harland published a series of novels from his new viewpoint and was converted to Roman Catholicism. *The Cardinal's Snuff Box*, published by John Lane in 1900, was a huge success; it is said to have sold over one hundred thousand copies in two years and earned him seventy thousand dollars. When *The Yellow Book* was founded in 1894, he became its literary editor. After the magazine expired in 1897, he lived both in England and the Continent, where he died in Italy in 1905 at the age of forty-four.[36]

His European novels are far less interesting as literary works than the Jewish stories. An insufferably self-conscious aristocratic tone, pretensions to glamour, and esthetic Catholicism pervade them. They are superficially polished in style, but thin in human substance. In *The Cardinal's Snuff Box* (1900)—the Sidney Luska pseudonym was now totally abandoned—his interest in intermarriage becomes the theme: this time a mixed marriage between Protestant and Catholic. This story of the Protestant hero's love for a Catholic lady whose uncle is a cardinal concludes happily with his fervent conversion to Catholicism. But the attitude toward the Jews becomes progressively anti-Semitic. The cardinal tells his niece, Beatrice, about an encounter on a train with a Jew, who has remarked that the cardinal looks like a Jesuit. The Jew is "a very gorgeous gentleman, with gold chains and diamonds flashing from every corner of his person. . . . He turned to me in the most affable manner, and said, 'I see, Reverend Sir, that you are a Jesuit. There should be a fellow-feeling between you and me. I am a Jew. Jews and Jesuits have an almost equally bad name!' " The cardinal refuses to tell Beatrice what he replied, but Beatrice suggests that he should have answered that "the Jews, at least, have the advantage of meriting their bad name." But the cardinal wishes he had "found a retort that would have effected the Jew's conversion."[37]

Later in the book Harland allows an anti-Semitic statement to pass altogether without comment or sign of dissent for the first time. Beatrice tells the hero the history of her estate: "The estate fell into the hands of the Jews, as everything more or less does sooner or later; and they—if you can believe me—they were going to turn the castle into an hotel, into one of those monstrous modern hotels, for other Jews to come to, when I happened to hear of it, and bought it. Fancy turning that splendid old castle into a Jew-infested hotel!"[38]

In subsequent novels anti-Semitic comments also go unchallenged. In *My Friend Prospero* (1904), the story of an heir to an English title living in Italy, there is a single reference to Jews. The hero's aunt discourses on the desirability of living in London. She remarks that this city is not only beautiful, but "the only place where there are any people." He replies: "Yes, but, as at Nice and Hamburg, too many of them are English. And there's a liberal scattering, I've heard, of Jews?" " 'Oh, Jews are all right when they aren't Jewy,' said Lady Blanchemain, with magnanimity. 'I know some very nice ones.' "[39]

Finally, in *The Royal Road* there is the association of the devil with the Jew.

Look here [says one character], the devil has been acquiring souls continuously for the past five thousand years. Practice has made him a perfect dab [expert] at the process—and he was born a perfect Jew. You may be sure he doesn't go about paying the first price asked— not he. He waits till he catches you in a scrape, or desperately hard up, or drunk, or out of your proper cool wits with anger, pride, lust, whichever of the seven deadly impulses you will, and then he grinds you like a money-lender. . . . Oh, trust the devil. He knows his trade.[40]

So we have come full circle. The philo-Semite, in the sense in which it is properly to be understood, does not accept Jews as equal human beings, whether or not his intentions are good. The evidence in Harland's case shows an ambiguous attitude from the start: idealization of Jews as well as acceptance of the negative stereotype. He never really understood them—the discerning *New York Times* reviewer of *Mrs. Peixada* is right in saying that Harland "has not got 'the hang' " of Jewish life in New York. When his esthetic interest in Jews as "picturesque" faded, his earlier admiration disappeared too and he fell in with the anti-Semitism of the aristocrats, whom he emulated. It is another irony of Jewish history that the first writer for the general public to give fictional currency to the life of New York Jews—to the life of American Jews, for that matter—was not only non-Jewish, but eventually an anti-Semite.

21

EARLY AMERICAN JEWISH NOVELS

By the 1890s American Jewish writers had emerged on both coasts and in the central states. The New York and San Francisco works have some literary interest; those of the central states have interest only as indications of the growing Jewish physical and literary presence in the country.

The discovery of gold in California in 1848 and the Gold Rush boom and excitement of the following years attracted numbers of Jews from the East and from Europe, and many soon became important members of the young pioneer communities. By the 1890s there were a number of affluent, well-established, and respected Jewish families in San Francisco. One contemporary local writer notes that "nowhere on this continent, probably, is there a more cordial feeling between Jew and Christian."[1]

But the unusually good relations prevalent in the open pioneer community by no means precluded the existence of tensions between Jews and non-Jews, as the novels of Emma Wolf show. She was born in San Francisco in 1865 of parents who had immigrated from France. Her fiction, set in San Francisco, shows her to be a gentle, intelligent, dignified, strong-minded, but rather genteel young Jewish woman brought up in a middle-class Jewish family, as indeed she was. Her work attracted attention after her first novel, *Other Things Being Equal* (1892), appeared. An omnibus fiction review in *Overland* asserts that it is "the most notable novel . . . by a local writer."[2] A reading of the work does reveal a competent, though minor, writer. All the central characters but one are Jewish, and the theme is Jewish-Christian relations as they develop in the course of a proposed intermarriage. Like the author's own family, the family of the novel is of recent French origin, affluent, cultivated, and sophisticated. Although they are on easy social terms with the non-Jewish community, the marriageable daughter's susceptibilities for non-Jewish young men are strictly controlled lest intermarriage threaten.

The only non-Jewish character in the book is Dr. Herbert Kemp, a Unitarian. A friend of the retired Jules Levice's, he finally becomes acquainted with the lovely twenty-two-year-old daughter, Ruth, through his attendance on her sick mother. Kemp, who is tall and handsome, quickly falls in love with Ruth, and she reciprocates his feelings. When Ruth tells her father of her wish to marry Kemp, Levice strenuously disapproves—despite his high estimate of Kemp as a man, notwithstanding his liberal religious views and his social sophistication—but does not forbid the marriage. "I can never bring myself to approve of a marriage between you and a Christian," he tells Ruth. "There can be no true happiness in such a union." Kemp seeks an explanation from Levice: "You are not orthodox," he says. "I am intensely Jewish," Levice replies, and some aspects of the union, he adds, "are all powerful obstacles to your happiness." Most people on *both* sides, he says, will ostracize the couple, even though each clings to his or her own religion. Ruth and Kemp affirm that each will respect the other's religion. When Kemp says that he loves to celebrate one holiday, Christmas, Ruth astounds her father by revealing that

so far as Christmas is concerned, I am a Christian also. . . . Christ has been to me the loveliest and one of the best men that ever lived. . . . When I had read "The Sermon on the Mount," I grew to see that what he preached was beautiful. It did not change my religion; it made me no less a Jewess in the true sense. . . . As a teacher of brotherly love, he is sublime. So I may call myself a christian, though I spell it with a small letter.

Her father sadly replies that he did not think she could "leap thus far."[3]

It becomes clear in the end, however, that Ruth expresses the author's views. At first Ruth breaks off the engagement because she cannot endure to think of the suffering her marriage would cause her father. But he in turn observes her torment over the separation. He becomes mortally ill and from his new perspective gains insight into his "narrowness" in upholding "a vanishing restriction." On his deathbed he tells Ruth and Kemp that he and his wife now believe "that our child will be happy only as your wife, and that nothing should stand in the way of the consummation of this happiness." The couple acquiesce in his wish that they be married in his sickroom before he dies.

Contrasted to the emancipated attitude of the Levice family is that of their more parochial, conventional cousin, Mrs. Jennie Lewis, "a smiling, plump young woman, sparkling of eye, rosy of cheek, and glistening with jewels and silk." Mrs. Lewis hardly approves of the Levice's close association with non-Jews or Ruth's belief that all people are essentially the same, because she feels that others look down upon Jews and do not care to associate with them. Nor does she approve of Ruth's being seen in public alone with Kemp, for this is an infraction of the social code of the affluent Jewish community. Ruth believes her cousin to be one of those Jews "with diseased imaginations [who] take every remark on the race as a personal calumny."[4]

One is led to question whether Ruth (and the author) have not themselves, to some extent and quite unconsciously, become insensitive. When Dr. Kemp comments on lack of "controlled appetites" of some of his patients, he adds: "Jewish appetite is known to dote on the fat of the land." Ruth does not take offense, but her joking response causes Kemp to recognize that he may have committed a faux pas and he adds: "I hope I was not rude." He affirms that "as a race, most of their characteristics redound to their honor."

Though Ruth does not always recognize stereotyping, there is no doubt of her wholehearted acceptance of her Jewish identity. This emerges, for instance, from her discussion of Shylock with Kemp after viewing Edwin Booth in the role. Booth's interpretation, she thinks, had "no exaggeration,—it was quite natural." But she has been unable to enjoy the merriment and poetry of the last scene after Shylock's heartrending exit from the court, for her "heart was sobbing with that lonely old man." She has "detested" Jessica. "I was not ashamed of Shylock," she later explains. "If his vengeance was distorted, the cause distorted it. . . . After all, his punishment was as fiendish as his guilt."[5]

By 1900 the new, more intense quality of anti-Semitism in the United States was well advanced, and Emma Wolf's *Heirs of Yesterday* (1900) makes a frontal attack on it and the rejection of Jewish identity that was its by-product among some of the second generation. The story unfolds in her home city, San Francisco, in the last few years of the outgoing century, and most of the characters are Jewish. The central figure is the lovely young Jean Willard, mouthpiece of the author, who fiercely clings to her Jewish identity in an ethnic, rather than a religious, sense. In the words of one character, "the Jew is no longer a religion apart—only a race apart." In contrast to Jean there is Dr. Philip May, the son of a wealthy real estate broker who started as an immigrant peddler and still speaks ungrammatical, Yiddish-accented English. Philip, who has been away from the city for fifteen years at Harvard and Leipzig, has finally returned to the city as a promising surgeon to become a professor of medicine. He has long since passed for a non-Jew and intends to continue doing so, if he can get away with it. "Frankly," he says, "beyond the blood I was born with, pretty nearly all the Jew has been knocked out of me. . . . I have discovered that, to be a Jew, turn wheresoever you will, is to be socially handicapped for life," and he is determined to avoid the "handicap," if he can.[6]

Although Jean and Philip are attracted to each other, Jean rejects him with contempt because of his renunciation of Jewish identity. He causes his old father intense suffering when he refuses to join the local Jewish club and, in speaking of his career, he cuts his father to the quick by telling the old man: "You see I should be making a move in the wrong direction were I to identify myself unnecessarily with any Jewish club, Jewish anything, or Jewish anybody." Instead, he has applied for admission to the local Christian club under the sponsorship of his friend Otis, who assumes that Philip is a Christian. An old schoolmate of Philip's, the talented but anti-Semitic painter Stephen Forrest, has been since his youth envious of Philip's superiority in intellect and achievement. Forrest, a member of the club, reveals Philip's Jewish origin, and Philip is blackballed. When Otis asks Philip for a denial of this "damned preposterous libel," Philip's awakening to reality begins. "Why damned—why preposterous?" he asks. Otis does not reply, but Philip's admission of the truth brings forth the charge from Otis that Philip is a "hypocrite." "We out here," he says, "are still unregenerate enough to damn the hypocrite with the lowest of criminals." Philip's further questioning drives Otis to the admission that the notion of democratic equality is a "shibboleth"[7] in social life.

Following this scene at Otis's home, several other men enter, including Forrest, who recalls his school acquaintance with Philip. Despite his obvious anti-Semitism, Forrest has been attracted to Jean Willard. Early in the story he has revealed his anti-Semitic feelings to Jean, prompted by his resentment over the fact that in relation to Jean, as in everything, he is inferior to Philip. Forrest now confronts Philip at Otis's house; his bigoted resentment smoulders throughout a card game until, after he loses a hand, he charges Philip with cheating. They fight and Philip wins.

Yet Jean's alienation from Philip continues because of his denial of his Jewishness; she is unaware that his recent experiences have taught him the futility of his effort to suppress his Jewish origin. He continues his distinguished career as a surgeon, finds some consolation in music—he is an accomplished pianist—and engages in much thought and discussion about Jews and Judaism. At the end the Spanish-American War has broken out, and Philip enlists as a surgeon. Before he leaves he meets Jean accidentally, and it is clear that Jean has now changed her mind—she wishes to be reconciled. He tells her: "I decided I would not be fate's social cripple linked by an invisible chain to a slavish past. *I resolved to break that chain.*" But, he adds: "I discovered, *you can never break the chain.*" At last he has accepted his Jewish identity, not because he wants to, but because he must. And finally the lover speaks: "If you are Jewish, must I not too be Jew?"[8] No doubt they will marry when the war is over.

As in Emma Wolf's earlier novel, middle-class Jewish life in San Francisco, various characters in that community and their Reform Judaism, and indications of non-Jewish response to the Jewish community are depicted with sensitivity but not great depth. The enthusiasm felt by most Jews toward participation in the Spanish-American War is conveyed.[9] But by this time Emma Wolf must have undergone disillusioning experiences with non-Jews, for her conclusions in this last novel are rather pessimistic. At the wedding of a friend Jean encounters a Miss Goyne [Goy?] who, while "an old classmate and intimate friend of the bride," suggests by her attitude to Jean a " 'citizen' speaking of the 'stranger.' " When they discuss Philip May, Miss Goyne remarks that "he has none of the characteristics —," but Jean corrects her: "Caricaturistics."[10] In her first novel the responsibility for Jewish-Christian tensions, particularly on the issue of intermarriage, lies with the Jewish side; in her last novel, on the larger issue of non-Jewish attitudes toward the Jew, she seems to have reached the conclusion that the Christian world regards Jewishness as an ineradicable stigma.

The 1890s yielded other novelists of American Jewish fiction, less talented than Emma Wolf, in the Middle West. The Peoria journalist and editor Eugene F. Baldwin collaborated with the Jewish writer Maurice Eisenberg to produce *Doctor Cavallo* (1895), which attempts to paint a broad panorama of Jewish life in the Middle West. It touches on all aspects of the Jewish question in a middle western city in the course of its involved plot. The story introduces Reform and Orthodox Jews, idealistic and unscrupulous Jews, and anti-Semitic and unprejudiced non-Jews. The writing is banal and stilted, the characterization simpleminded and heavy-handed, as are also the social commentary on Jews and others; but the story has interest as a reflection of the then current attitudes on Jewish identity and anti-Semitism. The central figure, Dr. Cavallo, is described as a splendid specimen of a man physically and mentally. At first he conceals his Jewish identity from his friends and patients, the non-Jewish Lawrences. In the course of a discussion of anti-Semitism, Lawrence condemns "outrages against the Russian Jews" and the scapegoating of Jews in repressive Germany. Still without revealing his Jewish origin, Dr. Cavallo launches into an encomium on Jewish virtues, making excessive claims for Jewish eminence in world history. "The Jew," he says, "has been in all ages the Messiah to humanity and he has been rewarded by the fagot and the torch." He has given the world, says Cavallo, banking, exchange, medicine, law, modern science, and the modern university. Dr. Cavallo later berates himself for denying "my race and creed. . . . It is not a crime to be a Jew but it is a terrible misfortune."[11] He fears that a confession will cut him off from friendship with the Lawrences, and especially from the fair young Margaret Lawrence.

On another occasion Margaret's father assures Dr. Cavallo that the Jews will at last acknowledge Christ, gather again in Jerusalem, and create "the greatest spiritual government on earth." Margaret shares her father's enthusiasm for the Jews and explains: "If I were a Jewish maiden, I should be proud of such a glorious race. . . . To be ashamed of this heritage, as were some of my Jewish classmates, is to be ashamed of all that is greatest and best in history, to be ashamed of the influences that have blessed the world, and given rise to the greatest prophets and the greatest law-givers, the wisest statesmen, and the loftiest poets!" Cavallo reveals that he is a Jew and gives his friends a glowing account of Judaism as an open, rational, supremely moral religion, the only one "that matches the scientific facts . . . and [is] consistent with the broadest humanitarianism." Margaret sympathizes with Cavallo's exalted notions. After he leaves, however, Mr. Lawrence remarks that Dr. Cavallo is a fine fellow, but that it is "a great pity . . . that he is a Jew"[12] —although protesting that he is himself indifferent to this fact, an attitude in which Margaret concurs.

Cavallo is a high-minded civic leader, and as a doctor he condemns a row of tenements owned by the anti-Semitic Mr. Abbott, who charges that Cavallo's efforts at reform are "a Jew trick, . . . to get hold of that property cheap. . . . You sneaking and infernal Jew, you outcast and worthless fag-end of a detested race, you talk of trying to help your fellows, when you are simply arranging to steal my property. . . . I will publish you . . . to the world as a Jew. . . . I will destroy your practice, I will drive you from town." Despite support for Abbott from the clergy and politicians, the Board of Health condemns the tenements, and Dr. Cavallo persuades the wealthy Jewish philanthropist Bernheim to buy the land and organize a housing project. When Cavallo is offered as a reform candidate for Congress, an anti-Semitic campaign is waged against him, in part supported by Seidel, a dishonest Jewish speculator; Jew-baiting provocation leads to violence. But Dr. Cavallo wins, Seidel's fraud is exposed, and he disappears. At the end Margaret Lawrence accepts Cavallo's proposal of marriage. The authors sententiously conclude: "What is race prejudice, what religious differences, to two such souls as these, through whose every aspiration breathes the fervor of religious poetry, and whose souls pulsate in unison for the uplifting of their fellow men."[13]

Jews of various types are introduced in the course of the story. Traditional Orthodoxy is represented by Dr. Cavallo's uncle, Abraham Mendez, from London, who is shocked at Cavallo's heterodox religious views, especially his view that there is no essential difference between a Jew and a Christian, since men should be judged by their acts alone. There is the corrupt Seidel, who began as a bacteriology student of Dr. Cavallo's but, cynical atheist that he is, has abandoned science after striking it rich selling mining stocks (Seidel is subsequently exposed as dishonest speculator). A Russian immigrant who is portrayed, Jacob Kinofsy, speaks with a heavy accent and opposes modernizing revisions of the prayer book. Mrs. Nagle literally hates "her race." "I simply detest it," she says, "and I wonder how you can bear to identify yourself with this people, who are so gross, so coarse. I threw them overboard years ago."[14]

A second American Jewish novel of the Middle West, Horace J. Rollin's *Yetta Segal* (1898), does not attempt as much as *Doctor Cavallo* and achieves even less. It is pompous, pretentious, and ridden with rhetoric. The book purports to advance the thesis that an evolutionary process of "race-blending" is under way. The wisest course for Jews, therefore, is to abandon their tendency to be "exclusive" and different, and to lend themselves to the natural development of the blending of all human types. The titular heroine, born in Illinois and orphaned at the age of five, has been brought up by a Mrs. Schwartz in Cincinnati. Her features are "somewhat of Jewish accentuation," but not sufficiently marked to prompt "any kind of prejudice." She is not a strict Jew, and her contact with fellow Jews is limited. She rejects several Jewish suitors "looking in her direction with characteristic enterprise"; one she turned away because he was excessively strict in religious observance.

The scene shifts to Chattanooga, where Yetta, now a painter, is visiting with her friend Mrs. Franks. There she meets and becomes engaged to Alvarez Lanning, though he is a non-Jew. Lanning suddenly falls heir to a fortune, and at the same time learns that his fraternal grandfather had married a woman with some Negro blood. He then determines to end his engagement to Yetta, but their mutual friend, John Skoopman, an anthropologist, dissuades him by propounding to the couple his theory of the blending of races. Skoopman says that Yetta is an example of this tendency, for although her "lineage" is "strictly Jewish," she has escaped: "The great Jehovah has not been powerful enough to enforce conformity. You have escaped, soul and body—I congratulate you."

According to Skoopman's theory, he points out, a return of the Jews to Palestine would be a "retrogression," for the Jew's best course is to become "a citizen of the wide world." Consequently, reasons the author, "the isolation of any type of humanity, at a time when its best members show a fitness for general association, would be a retrogression."[15] The author then combines a pseudoscientific theory of foreshortened "race-blending" with its logically sequential social corollary of national nihilism, or denial of actual ethnic differences. In light of the stubborn persistence of anti-Semitism, this self-deception is reassuring to those who wish to attain greater social eligibility by blending with the dominant nationality.

When we turn to New York for the American Jewish novel of the 1890s (reserving Abraham Cahan for special consideration later), we find that, just as the best fiction of the German Jewish immigrant generations in the 1870s was written by the non-Jewish Henry Harland, so the outstanding novel of the Russian immigration and its life on the East Side in the 1890s was written by the non-Jewish Edward King. His *Joseph Zalmonah* (1893), a roman à clef in which the hero is closely patterned on the Jewish trade unionist Joseph Barondess, reveals an intimate knowledge of the labor movement and deep observation of the intellectual and cultural life of the East Side.[16]

King was born in Massachusetts in 1848 and became a reporter for the *Springfield Republican* at sixteen. He continued as a journalist and editor, and in 1870 he went abroad to report on the Franco-Prussian War and the Paris Commune. After he returned to New York he was extremely active in the late 1880s and 1890s as a civil libertarian. He died in 1896.

Anyone acquainted only with King's schematic depiction of Jews in two novels published in the early 1880s, during his European sojourn, could not have predicted his deep, sympathetic involvement in the New York ghetto a few years later, or the view of Jewish life presented in *Joseph Zalmonah*. In his first novel, *The Gentle Savage* (1883), the theme is Indian resentment of injustice at the hands of the whites. The novel traces the change in attitude toward the whites of a half-Cherokee Indian, Pleasant Merrinott, who harbors deep antagonism toward whites because of the injustice done to his people. At the start he is determined to promote the recovery of lands and reparations for his tribe, and to enforce separatism from the white United States. He is vehemently opposed by the Bluelot Indians, a neighboring tribe that preaches assimilation into the white community. On a mission to Europe for his tribe, he falls in love with a white American girl, Alice Harrelston. After a series of adventures in Europe he returns to the United States, where he is reunited with Alice and gives up his intransigent separatism. "Love," he romantically concludes, "is worth more than everything else in the world; worth more than race, or country, or home, or friends."[17]

In Europe Pleasant meets the pianist Stanislas and his "sister," Vera (later revealed to be his fiancée), who are both Jewish nihilists and see in him a potential fellow conspirator. "He will not betray us," says Stanislas, "because, like each of you, he is a victim of the injustice of society and government." They try to recruit Pleasant into their conspiracy to destroy the tsarist regime by terrorism. "Why," urges Vera, "should you submit to the extermination of your race? As society is at present constituted you can make no successful resistance within its limits to the sort of injustice of which you complain."

They are aided in instructing Merrinott in Bakuninism by Ignatius, a Polish Jew who "spoke passionately, and his eyes lighted up his face." Ignatius is later described as that "patriarchical conspirator, . . . [with] scarred and wrinkled face, the gray beard, the sparkling eyes, the expression of mingled malice and mournful disappointment." He tells Pleasant that he has spent his life inventing an infernal machine that will destroy Russian society. Vera tells Pleasant: "You, Indian, victim of society in America, I, victim of society in Russia, can gain little by protesting. . . . We can undermine it and blow it into fragments—such minute fragments that they can never be found and put together again."[18] But Pleasant is not won over. Vera dies of tuberculosis, and Ignatius and Stanislas are killed by an accidental explosion of the infernal machine.

To this stereotype of the Jewish nihilist, Edward King adds that of the evil Jewish moneylender in his *Golden Spike* (1886). In this poorly written novel the brother of the hero is victimized by a swindling Jew "who had charged sixty per cent for discounting" a loan "in irregular fashion." After the sudden death of the brother, a second note with a forged signature is found, and the hero is threatened with the exposure of his purported forgery if he does not redeem the note. But this second note is found to have been forged by the Jewish moneylender himself and used for blackmail. Again and again, "the Jew" gives vent to a laugh that makes our hero's "blood run cold" and makes his "flesh creep."[19] "The Jew" is at last exposed, and our hero's innocence established.

These novels hardly seem an auspicious prelude to *Joseph Zalmonah* (1893), which is the fruit of King's journalism about the Jewish East Side community. The action takes place wholly in the Jewish ghetto, and all the characters are Jewish. King bases his story on the actual career of Joseph Barondess, and his life is closely paralleled in the story. Barondess offered a congenial model for the novelist, for he was a flamboyant personality whose career was sensational. In addition, at the time the story was written Barondess was in sharp opposition to the socialists, with whom King also did not agree. King gives them harsh treatment in the book. The story encompasses the entire range of East Side life: economic, cultural, religious, and social. The outcome is an interesting work that may still be read with interest today, especially for the flavor it conveys of the ghetto community of its time.

Barondess arrived in the United States in 1888 at the age of twenty-three. It was only a few years later that he became the charismatic leader of the Yiddish-speaking workers' movement in New York. He was idolized by the workers in a way that recalls the German workers' adulation of Ferdinand Lassalle a few decades earlier. The events of *Joseph Zalmonah* center around a fight against a lockout that was led by Barondess in 1891. His strength lay not so much in a talent for strategy and tactics as in a magnetism and warmth of personality, joined to the reputation he had gained by early successes in leading strikers to victory.

Although the Barondess figure, Joseph Zalmonah, is at the core of the story, the range and richness of East Side life illuminated by the novel can be gauged from some of the chapter headings: "Land of Promise," "The World Is a Wedding," "Night March," "Pig Market," "Poet of the People," "Wonder-Rabbi," "White Fast (Yom Kippur)," "Purim in the 'Colony,' " "Passover Supper." The

early days of East Side Yiddish theater are vividly represented
through the character of David, a playwright and theater producer,
"temperate, honest, pure, and stocked with stage lore and a knowledge of archaic music so common in the Jewish theatre." There is
also the charming figure of the twelve-year-old Miryam, who worships Joseph. An entire chapter is devoted to a detailed account of
a performance of the Yiddish opera "Judith and Holofernes" at
David's theater on the Bowery. The gallery audience is obviously
described from firsthand observation: "From the sole gallery came
rustling and murmurs, interspersed with occasional laughter and
guttural remarks in jargon, which proclaimed the presence of a
strong contingent of juvenile cloakmakers. These pallid, sharp-eyed,
thick-lipped, lean and scrawny slaves of the needle managed to
scrape from their miserable pittances money enough to see most of
David's new plays."[20]

As a writer of popular novels King tends to melodramatize his
characters even though they are modeled on actual people. Bathsheba, the socialist in love with Joseph, who is assigned the task of
winning him over to the socialist position in current labor disputes,
is a beauty, "exquisitely proportioned, and with the full and rounded
outlines so common to Jewish beauty." Her role is that of a femme
fatale who almost succeeds at a crucial point in winning Joseph over
to the socialist side. But her love for Joseph overcomes her loyalty
to the socialists, and she warns Joseph that he is in mortal danger
from them.

Another striking figure is Mordecai Menzer, "Poet of the People," who may have been modeled on the folk poet Eliakim Zunser,
who had come to this country in 1889. King represents Menzer as
disillusioned by America, the promised land, where he found only
starvation. He wrote, says King, "a bitterly satirical ballad tinged
with socialism, in which he ridiculed the United States as the land
of promise, but not one of performance." Zunser had in fact published a bitter poem on the front page of the *Freie Arbeiter Shtimme*
in 1890. Menzer is represented as believing in the imminence of
social revolution; he had written a ballad of "the cloak-makers'
tortures" which was "a new Marseillaise of the poor."[21]

As for Joseph Zalmonah, the career of Joseph Barondess was in
itself sensational enough to lend itself easily to melodrama. King also
suggests a parallel to both Christ and Moses. Joseph, he writes, "bore
a resemblance to an old print which he had once seen of the crucified
Nazarene." A later chapter, in which Joseph is framed on an extortion charge and is on his way to jail, is called "Carrying the Cross."

On his way, Joseph sees what appear to him to be the contented wealthy and their children, and he says to himself: " 'Our people will be like that some day—when I have suffered enough for them.' He took up his cross and went on." On another occasion, at a great meeting celebrating the settlement of the strike, "the young leader was fairly worshipped by the mothers and wives who recognized in him the deliverer leading their sons and husbands out of the land of Egypt." The workers exclaim: "Joseph, our Joseph, will give us bread!"[22] King's portrait of Joseph as an autocratic leader is not far from the truth, for Barondess's arbitrary leadership aroused adoring faith among the workers in real life.

The leader of the socialist forces ranged against Zalmonah's leadership of the union is Rudolf Baumeister, a stereotyped caricature of a socialist. Although the socialists did oppose Barondess during this period, in the novel King does not accurately convey the reason for the opposition, which was actually an attempt to wrest leadership from the anarchists with whom Barondess was allied, rather than Barondess himself. Baumeister is represented as a satanic villain, who "looked as black as the Devil deprived of his prey" when Joseph refuses to join his "party of force." On occasion he gives "a mocking laugh, which had a Mephistophelian ring to it." He is, moreover, "profoundly egotistical, without knowing it, while professing to serve others."[23] He will stop at neither the murder of Joseph (in the deluded belief that the revolution will thereby be precipitated), nor an attempt to burn to death, as living encumbrances, his recently arrived immigrant wife and child. He is finally adjudged insane. The portrayal of this conventional, cardboard villain is the most serious defect of the book, which in several respects is among the best of the early East Side novels.

Baumeister's direct appeals and indirect stratagems, using the lure of Bathsheba and the scheme of the poet Menzer to win Joseph over to the socialist side, all fail. When the socialists attempt to discredit Joseph at mass meetings and demonstrations, the crowd rejects them, shouting: "Yes, yes, down with the Socialists!"[24] They reject the doctrine of "force," which was not in fact the view of Barondess's actual opposition. Solidarity of the workers in the face of a lockout finally wins victory for them, as they demonstrate the determination and strength of united action against the bosses. Several mass marches based on actual events are vividly described. One of the lockout bosses tries to bribe Joseph with money for his return to Russia, if he wishes, or to pursue a college education in America —in exchange for giving up his union leadership. Of course Zalmonah scornfully rejects the offer. The bosses finally surrender and give Zalmonah a check for one hundred dollars for the union. (This was a customary mode of "reparation" levied against employers as a part of the strike settlement.) Since the union has no bank account, the check is made out to Zalmonah personally. After the lockout is over the boss charges Zalmonah with "extortion" on the evidence of the check, as actually happened to Barondess. During the appeal following his conviction, Bathsheba begs Zalmonah to escape imprisonment by fleeing to Canada with her. The strongly tempted man refuses in the end. The real Joseph did flee to Canada after his conviction, but soon returned to serve his term. The outcome in the novel and in real life is the same: a petition signed by thousands to the governor wins a pardon for Joseph in a short time.

This novel gains stature in that it was one of the earliest works of American fiction to depict Jews with sympathy and a degree of understanding, without condescension. This is probably attributable to the fact that so much of the novel was woven out of King's personal experience, even though he was not Jewish. His novel covers an even broader range of experience than Hutchins Hapgood's classic work. Its novelistic form accounts for both its positive and negative aspects as a faithful picture of East Side life. On the negative side, the conventions of the popular novel, reinforced by King's personal ideas, tend to distort some of the characterizations, especially that of Baumeister; and on the positive side, the literary form brings out the best of King's talent in a vivid presentation of the life he knew so well from his own experience.

22

FICTION IN ENGLISH BY ABRAHAM CAHAN

Abraham Cahan began to publish short stories, novellas, and novels in the 1890s. The themes and character types adumbrated through Cahan's fiction reached their mature development in 1917 in *The Rise of David Levinsky,* the most important fictional work about American Jewry up to that time by any American writer, Jewish or non-Jewish.

The depth of Cahan's fiction, both as social drama and as a personal statement, raises complex questions and invites interpretation on several levels. Part of these complexities and subtleties arise from the fact that Cahan was personally involved in and helped effect the transformation of the immigrant Jewish community from a poverty-stricken, densely packed mass in the ghetto to a highly significant force in much of American life. The fact that this milieu was Yiddish has made the materials for a thorough and comprehensive interpretation of Cahan's life and work almost inaccessible to most English-speaking critics and biographers. An adequately analytical biography of Cahan and a just evaluation of the positive and negative aspects of his life and work remain to be written. His work, indeed his life, was tied up with the Yiddish language and culture of the American ghetto, a culture from which virtually all writers in English were sealed off. Such a work would require an immersion in the passionately lived Yiddish milieu, which lasted from the 1880s to the 1940s —and in the Yiddish language.

Most critical writing on Cahan has been distorted by political or personal predisposition. The changes that occurred in both the Jewish community and Cahan's response to these changes, from the radicalism of his earliest years to his abandonment of socialism and the obsessive anticommunism of his last years, render it exceedingly hard to make a just evaluation. He has been considered as a central positive influence in the acculturation of the Jewish mass immigration and as a "misfortune" *(umglik)* for the Jewish people. Whatever judgment history may make on Cahan, it seems likely that his *David Levinsky* will be deemed a permanent contribution to American literature and will continue to be read as a social novel of permanent interest.

The essential facts of Cahan's life convey the remarkable scope of his activity and influence.[1] He was born in a Lithuanian shtetl in 1860, and his father began to give him instruction in Hebrew when he was four. The family moved to Vilna when he was six and he continued his education at a yeshiva, until he persuaded his parents to allow him to go to a government school at thirteen. He began to read Russian writers and lost his faith in Judaism. He went on to the free government Jewish teachers college at seventeen, and was attracted to and joined the peasant-oriented, nihilist Narodnaya Volya movement when he was nineteen. Following graduation in 1881 he taught at a Jewish school in Velizh, where he joined a local revolutionary circle. During the ensuing repression after the assassination of Alexander II, Cahan narrowly eluded arrest, and fled to the United States in June 1882. After several months of work in a cigar factory and a tin shop in New York, he had learned English sufficiently well to earn a living by giving private English lessons to immigrants.

Cahan became deeply involved in socialist activity soon after his arrival in the United States and quickly became a noted speaker, especially in Yiddish. He had his first article in English published in the New York *World* only six months after his entry into this country, and within two years was writing regularly for the New York *Sun* and other papers. He edited and wrote for the Yiddish socialist press until 1897, when he participated in the founding of the socialist *Forward (Forverts)*, a paper which he edited for a few months until a dispute about his journalistic methods caused him to resign. For five years thereafter he worked wholly in English as a reporter for the New York press and wrote articles and short stories for national magazines. During this period he was not only a colleague of Lincoln Steffens and Norman and Hutchins Hapgood on the daily New York *Commercial Advertiser,* but also published two volumes of fiction, *Yekl* (1896) and *The Imported Bridegroom and Other Stories of the New York Ghetto* (1898), as well as short stories in magazines.

In 1902 he returned to the editorship of the *Forward,* and, except for a few months, ruled that daily with absolute, dictatorial authority until his late years. When he took over the *Forward* in 1902 its circulation was about six thousand: at its height in the late 1920s circulation was said to be almost a quarter of a million. In its earlier years especially, it was the organizing center of union and socialist activity and was a driving force for the organization of the Socialist party and Jewish unions and the propagation of labor fraternalism. Cahan himself was at the center of this activity, and there can be no doubt that he was personally a significant influence in all aspects of the acculturation of the immigrant masses in their earliest years. A properly balanced, comprehensive judgment of the precise nature of this influence, it seems to me, has yet to be made.

Interpretation of Cahan's fiction can contribute substantially to an understanding of the man. At the core of his personality was a set of contradictions, a conflict, hints of which are discernible in his fiction and appear most clearly in *David Levinsky*. The central conflict was between fidelity to his intellectual, social, and esthetic convictions and his capitulation to expedience and the lure of success. At one pole was his fiction, in which his esthetic taste, founded on the realism of Turgenev and Tolstoy, and his social and intellectual integrity are expressed. At the opposite pole was the *Forward*, through which he carried on a campaign of vulgarized "Americanization" of the immigrant masses and the vulgarization and finally abandonment of socialism. Cahan's career as a fiction writer in English and as the journalist who dominated the *Forward* are distinct, and indeed opposite, because each was a path antagonistic to the other.

What were the sources of the contradictions within Cahan?

He had extraordinary talent. This was recognized early, when Lincoln Steffens hired him as a reporter for the New York *Commercial Advertiser* in 1897. Steffens had just taken over this stodgy daily, dismissed most of the staff, and hired a group of young writers fresh out of college—among them Norman and Hutchins Hapgood—to present the news in terms of its warm human significance, rather than as dry fact or sensationalism. He wanted, Steffens writes, "writers," men who "could see and express the beauty in the mean streets of a hard, beautiful city." He was interested in the motives behind deeds. A murder, he thought, should not be reported as a "bloody hacked-up crime," but rather "as a tragedy," and he instructed Cahan to write in this way. Steffens was himself deeply interested in the ghetto, and at that time, as he writes, he was himself "almost a Jew, . . . and nailed a mezuza on my office door. I went to the synagogue on all the great Jewish holy days." He reports that Cahan was the catalyst of much serious discussion in the paper's editorial rooms on the nature of art and realism, and under Cahan's influence the paper reported on the Yiddish theater of the time. "Whether it was Cahan and the Ghetto or my encouragement," Steffens concludes, "the *Commercial* city room had ideals and flaunted them openly."[2] Cahan's full-time occupation as a journalist in English ended in 1901, when he resigned from the *Commercial* after Steffens left for *McClure's* and muckraking.

When Cahan was asked to become editor of the *Forward* in 1902, he agreed on the condition that he be given absolute editorial control. He differed from colleagues like Morris Winchevsky and Michael Zametkin in his conception of a socialist paper for the immigrant masses, and in some respects he was probably right in trying to make the paper more palatable to the nonsocialists in order to bring them closer to socialism. We can perceive from our present perspective that he was right in eschewing the open and offensive flouting of Orthodox Judaism that was then common among socialists. Although it is generally acknowledged that theoretical analysis was not among his talents, he had a great talent for popularization. However, he carried a sound approach too far, from popular journalism to vulgarized journalism.

He undertook to publish material new to the *Forward*—stressing a vulgarized lower-middle-class view of women and marriage that verged on sensationalism. The classic instance is the *Forward*'s method of promoting the Yiddish translation of August Bebel's *Woman Under Socialism* in 1912 by advertising that it would throw light on "Why Were Women in the Past More Beautiful Than Today?"; tell why "Moslem Women Are Not Allowed to See a Doctor"; reveal that "Solomon Had a Thousand Wives and That Was No Sin"—all ending, "Read August Bebel's Book." It was said at the time that this type of advertising was stopped by the intervention of Bebel himself.[3]

From the start Cahan rejected *"Daitchmerish,"* a stilted Germanified form of Yiddish, and supervised the use of "Yiddish Yiddish" in a simple, *"pleiner"* (plain) Yiddish easily understandable by the immigrant masses. At the same time, he followed the current usage of incorporating incorrectly pronounced English words into Yiddish. Cahan composed a sentence to illustrate this, as he notes in his autobiography, ending "Ich vel scrobbin dem floor, klinen die vindes, un polishen dem stov."[4] Those who loved the Yiddish language charged him with vulgarizing and corrupting it. Cahan was a popularizer in the negative sense; he pandered to the inferior tastes of the uneducated, instead of combining simplicity with linguistic and literary integrity. The noted Yiddish writer Joseph Opatashu says of Cahan that he "spit on our language."[5] Cahan was the promoter of *shund,* an untranslatable Yiddish word whose approximate meaning is a fusion of vulgarity, sentimentality, and banality, in language and literature. After Cahan assumed his dictatorial editorship of the *Forward,* there were vain protests by some of his socialist colleagues against the vulgarization of socialism, which the paper was perpetuating, and many left the newspaper and Cahan's wing of the movement. Cahan notes in his autobiography that his "intelligent *chaverim"* charged him with "cheapening the Jewish word." To such complaints, Cahan made the telling reply: "My policies don't please you. But the circulation which they bring is welcome. I used to say this in a joking tone. But in my heart I knew it was really so."

The rising circulation and the profit-making that came with it did indeed induce a toleration of whatever Cahan did. When it was charged in debates over the paper's policies that he stooped to the masses instead of raising them up, he replied: "If you want to lift up a child from the ground, you must first bend down to him. If not, how will you reach him?"[6] The trouble was, however, that he did not lift the child.

The fact was that in the end Cahan was closer to the Hearst press than to the more responsible wing of the American daily press. Moses Rischin leaves an erroneous impression in his article on Cahan's apprenticeship in journalism at the *Commercial Advertiser.* In a fully documented account of Cahan's relationship with the paper, Rischin concludes that his employment there was "a seminal period in his journalistic apprenticeship," and asserts at the end that Cahan "carried back with him to the *Forward* the refreshing liberal American spirit that animated that paper."[7] One would never guess from Rischin's article that the *Forward* approximated the Hearst press more nearly than the *Commercial.* Several other writers with a more personal, intimate working knowledge of the *Forward* do not make this mistake. Melech Epstein, who worked for the *Forward,* observes that Steffens's training "stood Cahan in good stead in building the *Forward* into a powerful medium. It must also be noted that Joseph Pulitzer and William R. Hearst shared with Steffens in guiding the course of editor Cahan."[8]

Cahan's *Forward* differed in essential respects from the *Commercial.* While Steffens sought writers and individuality of writing, Cahan expected something quite different from his staff. Lamed Shapiro, who worked on the *Forward* in 1907, has written that Cahan considered the editorial room his "shop," and used to say to his staff men:

"I don't need any writers here, only 'hands.' "[9] (David Levinsky, in the novel, several times alludes to the workers in his shop as "hands.") Cahan succeeded in alienating many, if not most, of the leading Yiddish writers of his time by his insulting behavior and insistence on promoting *shund*. Even a partial list of the men whom Cahan offended or forced out of the *Forward* reads like a roster of the outstanding figures of the East Side: Jacob Gordin, Michael Zametkin, Morris Winchevsky, Abraham Liessin, Isaac Hourwich, Morris Rosenfeld, Lamed Shapiro, Leon Kobrin, and Sh. Niger. So passionately did some Yiddish writers feel the culture-corrupting influence of Cahan to be that one of them, David Pinski, was led to exclaim that "the *Forward* is the greatest misfortune to befall the Jewish people since the destruction of Jerusalem."[10]

Cahan exercised arbitrary personal judgment by simply excluding from mention, let alone review, certain Yiddish writers and intellectuals, so that a reader of the *Forward* alone would be unacquainted with leading figures and writers and movements in the Yiddish-speaking community. He did not tolerate dissent in the paper.

Furthermore, nothing could be farther from the "refreshing liberal American spirit" of the *Commercial* than the obsessive anticommunism that gripped Cahan and the *Forward* after 1922, and especially during the McCarthy period. Melech Epstein relates one reason why Cahan refused to employ him during the early years of World War II: Epstein, who had recently broken with the Communist party and the *Morgen Freiheit*, refused "to write pieces of 'inside information' on the workings of the Communist Party" and refused "to appear before the Committee on Un-American Activities, headed by Congressman Martin Dies."[11] On the other hand, Cahan readily employed informers against the Left.

Another phase of Cahan's inner conflict resulted in his gradual abandonment of socialism. In organizing and propagandizing for socialism in the earlier years of his career, his contributions to the unionization of the Yiddish-speaking workers were such that even his severest critics acknowledge that he was among the "pioneers." Paul Novick writes that "Ab. Cahan was one of the pioneers of the Jewish worker-movement in America. He took part in the founding of unions, socialist organizations and was a leader in the movement to found the *Forward*." Novick adds that, because the *Forward* was the sole labor daily in Yiddish until 1922 (when the *Freiheit* was established), it was indispensable for the labor and socialist movement; but Cahan converted it into a "necessary evil."[12]

It is probable that Cahan's contributions were more positive in his earlier days, for it should be recalled that his participation in the socialist movement dates from shortly after his arrival in this country in 1882. But with the success of the *Forward* came the degeneration of his social thought. His socialism was so watered down in the last few decades of his life that it became imperceptible. Furthermore, his affinities in the labor movement early proved to be with the labor bureaucrats, just as was the case with Samuel Gompers, who was his ally. When the rank and file of the United Garment Workers refused to follow their leaders' settlement of a strike in 1913, the *Forward* supported the settlement, and irate workers broke windows at the *Forward*. In 1905 the typesetters on the *Forward* struck, and the impartial arbitrators concluded that the *Forward* used "capitalist methods" in fighting the strike. In 1909, 1917, and 1946 the staff writers of the *Forward* struck. There were occasions when a strike was reported on page one and an advertisement for scabs to break the same strike appeared on another page.

Philip Foner has succinctly stated the relation of the *Forward* to the labor movement:

In the opening years of the twentieth century, the *Forward* had helped the Jewish workers in their struggles to organize unions and conduct strikes for better conditions. As a result, the majority of Jewish immigrants read the paper. Before many years had passed, however, the character of the *Forward* changed sharply. As its circulation soared and its revenue from advertisements increased, the *Forward* became a wealthy and powerful organization. The interests of the *Forward* were paramount to any other consideration. Those trade unionists who "played ball" with the paper were assured of its powerful support. Those who dared to take issue with Abraham Cahan, head of the Forward Association and editor of the paper, would be attacked as enemies of the labor movement.[13]

Cahan's promotion of the Americanization of his readers was another source of inner conflict. His notion of the function of the *Forward* was to speed the Americanization of the uneducated Jewish immigrant masses. But his concept lacked perspective and was limited to striving toward the prevailing code of manners and Anglo-Saxon mores—the use of a handkerchief instead of the sleeve, proper table etiquette—and minimizing external differences from the "Americans," like not using hand gestures while talking.

That Cahan's actual communication through the *Forward* did not exceed this elementary level of acculturation is indicated by Bezalel Sherman. One year before Cahan died, Sherman wrote an article for the *Yiddisher Kemfer* on the occasion of Cahan's ninetieth birthday in which he says that Cahan taught the largely uneducated masses of the pre-1905 immigration their ABC's, but never carried them further once they learned the elements. Thus, Sherman continues, Cahan did not respond to the needs of the more highly educated, liberal, and revolutionary immigrants who came after the 1905 revolution. Cahan was in error, says Sherman, when he tried to dictate the taste and social attitudes of these newer but more sophisticated Yiddish-speaking immigrants, as he had done for the earlier immigration.[14]

Cahan's efforts to Americanize these Jewish masses were replete with personal contradictions. On one hand, Cahan was convinced that Yiddish was a dying language. He repeatedly prophesied that it had five or ten years more to live. Furthermore, he opposed efforts at Jewish education because he was an assimilationist, believing that the best course for the Jews was to become indistinguishable from their non-Jewish fellow Americans. At the same time, hardly any Jewish leader of his time was more deeply rooted in Yiddish and Jewish life than Cahan. Considering Cahan's well-known contempt for the immigrant masses, it is not surprising that his method of weaning them away from Yiddish and Jewishness was to exploit the less admirable potentialities of the masses of men in the Hearstian manner of the yellow press, through its Yiddish counterpart, *shund.* There was an inner conflict between the Cahan who was most at home in the Yiddish-speaking milieu and the Cahan who willed himself to live on the conscious level as closely as possible to the Anglo-Saxon American ideal. The mass of contradictions that we have tried to set forth provides the key to the meaning of Cahan's fiction. In these stories he writes out a kind of spiritual autobiography, whose fullest expression comes in *David Levinsky.* These unresolved conflicts largely explain the pervasive tone of dissatisfaction, longing, "yearning" (a recurring word in his fiction), and frustration of his main characters.

Cahan quite consciously adopted a different attitude toward the literary and journalistic work written before he took over the *Forward* and his work on the *Forward* itself. He was a socialist and an artist of integrity in the former, and in the latter he was essentially an opportunist whose objective was to increase circulation. He subordinated his ambitions to his socialist conscience in his early years, as he explains in his autobiography. In those pre-*Forward* days, he writes, he "felt that there were limitations to what a socialist could write in the capitalist press. Frequently I would refuse to write on subjects editors tried to assign to me . . . because I thought it improper."[15] He later realized that he was "naive" in turning these down, but his scruples indicate the strength of his integrity in those early years.

Moreover, he was uncompromising in his condemnation of the new sensational journalism—which he was later to emulate—of Pulitzer's New York *World*. He relates how in 1898 the Sunday editor of the *World* asked if he could reprint several chapters of his novel *Yekl* with a sensational layout, and Cahan refused on the advice of his literary mentor, W. D. Howells. When the *World*'s managing editor asked Cahan to write regular feuilletons about life in the various New York immigrant sections, Cahan refused the flattering and lucrative offer. For it appeared, writes Cahan, "that he meant them to be cheap, sentimental stories, fancied up with 'local color.' " Cahan's attitude toward his literary work was similarly austere, and it persisted, but his journalistic standards deteriorated steadily. "I expected," he writes, "no financial rewards [*gliken*] from my literary career. One could earn money from writing stories, romances, or pieces of the cheaper sort, and that kind of literature I could not think of doing." And, he added, "today, only *shund*-writers are rich."[16] Although he promoted *shund* in the *Forward*, he was not himself a *"shund*-writer" in his own fiction.

Cahan's activity as a literary figure in English was largely concentrated in the decade between 1895 and 1905. In addition to several novels and short stories, his articles on Russian literary figures, on Zangwill, on Russian revolutionary politics, and on Russian Jews in this country appeared in leading national magazines.[17] As a youth in Vilna, Cahan had started to read the great Russian authors of the century with enthusiasm and adopted their literary creed, as he understood it, in his theory of realism. He particularly admired Turgenev and Tolstoy, and delivered a lecture on "Realism" in 1889 that was published in the *Workmen's Advocate*, the Socialist Labor party weekly, on April 6 of that year. Cahan had read Herbert Spencer, and he attempted to give his literary theory of realism a Spencerian philosophical foundation. More concretely, he discussed realism in terms of the socialist-oriented painting of Vassily Vereshchagin, a contemporary Russian who had exhibited in New York a year earlier, and most particularly in terms of the work of Leo Tolstoy, whom Cahan regarded as "the greatest of realists." Cahan looked upon Henry James as a realist, and evidence that he had read James is found rather quaintly in his repeated use in *David Levinsky* of James's revival of the Elizabethan phrase "as who should say."

But it was Howells to whom Cahan looked as the prime American advocate and exemplar of realism, as indeed he was. Because of Howells's devotion to the American reality, writes Cahan, his "pen makes a more dangerous assault on the present system than the most eloquent speeches of the most rabid 'foreign socialist.' " Cahan criticizes the then current view that "the beautiful" is the sole aim of art. An honest depiction of human reality is also art, and hence inevitably leads to social criticism. "The rottenness of capitalist society," he writes, "inevitably lends color to every work of realistic fiction."[18]

Cahan was a devoted reader of Howells's work even before they became acquainted. Cahan was thrilled when Howells sought him out in 1892 as a union activist, a "walking delegate," and Howells was amazed and pleased to learn that Cahan had read his novels.

When Howells read Cahan's first published short story in English, "A Providential Match," in *Short Stories* for February 1895, he invited Cahan for a talk. Howells did not think the story was a "serious thing," he added, "but it convinces me that you can write. It is your duty to write."[19] The story is a harsh depiction of Rouvke, an ignorant immigrant who works his way up from nothing to prosperity as a peddler, and thinks it time he enhanced his social position with marriage. After communication with his shtetl, a match is arranged with the daughter of his former wealthy employer, who is now bankrupt and accedes to the match out of desperation. Money for Hannah's journey to America is sent. When Rouvke and the shadchen (matchmaker) meet her boat on arrival, they learn to their fury and frustration that Hannah is engaged to a young student she met on the boat. The plot is amply filled with East Side lore.

One can understand why Howells urged Cahan to write: as a first effort the story is remarkably good. From the perspective of his entire work several features stand out. Already he has sounded the note of yearning, a theme that was to pervade his fiction. In his first few months in America, Rouvke yearns after his shtetl; after Hannah's father loses his money, the unmarried girl's "soul would be yearning and longing, she knew not after what." The syndrome of yearning and longing was in one form or another to afflict many of Cahan's fictional creations. Another recurrent feature is frustrated relations with women, as in Hannah's rejection of Rouvke.

One feature of this story he was to drop shortly afterward from his literary arsenal—his use of dialect. American literature is strewn with the Jewish stereotype who speaks a heavily accented, ungrammatical English, and the use of dialect in Cahan's story awakens the feelings aroused by the stereotype. Set in the context of Rouvke's vulgar ignorance and Cahan's palpable contempt for this type of character, some phrases attributed to Rouvke—"bishness is bishness"; "buy a teecket for a ball, veel you? A ball fi'sht clesh"; "I vant my hoondered an fifty dollar!"[20]—verge on the anti-Semitic.

Cahan obeyed Howells's injunction to write, and after he finished a novel Howells read it and offered to see to its publication. *Harper's Weekly* rejected the manuscript because, the editor wrote, "the life of the Jewish East Side would not interest the American reader." Another rejection, Cahan recalls, offered the opinion that the magazine's men and women readers wanted romances about "richly-clothed cavaliers and women, about love that unfolds on the playing fields of golf. How then can they be interested in a story about a Jewish immigrant blacksmith who became a tailor here and his ignorant wife?" In a conversation, the editor of *McClure's*, who also rejected the novel, recommended that Cahan use his talent "to create art, by which he meant that I should write about 'beautiful things.' "[21] Discouraged by these rejections, Cahan published his Yiddish translation of the novel in the *Arbeiter Zeitung*, which he was editing at the time (1895). However, Howells could finally report that Appleton and Company would publish the book, which appeared in 1896.

As in "The Providential Match," Cahan had not yet achieved a tone that would carry his fiction beyond the thin line that separates the anti-Semitic from the naturalistic in fiction about Jews. His as yet insecure taste emerges from his discussion with Howells about the title of the book, as he recalls in his autobiography. Cahan suggested "Yankel the Yankee." Howells gently chided Cahan with the comment that such a title "would be appropriate for a vaudeville, but not for such a story as yours," and they finally agreed on *Yekl.*

Cahan's taste was insecure in another important respect: he makes Yekl talk in an extremely ugly dialect throughout the story, and, as was the case with the earlier Rouvke, Cahan's contempt for his character is patent. Leon Kobrin, the Yiddish short-story writer, who was working with Cahan on the *Arbeiter Zeitung* at the time, reports that Cahan would read the Yiddish translation of *Yekl* to him. Kobrin once remarked that the Jewish character was "a little caricatured,"[22] a criticism Cahan made Kobrin suffer for and for which he never forgave him. Cahan reports that while some reviewers praised his use of dialect because, they said, it reflected real life, the reviewer in the *Commercial Advertiser* expressed some impatience with the addition of Yiddish dialect to the already existing Irish and Negro dialects; he felt that though dialect may be necessary on occasion, it was not needed so constantly. Cahan then realized that the frequent use of dialect is "no more than a cheap bit of comedy." He then and there determined that he would "henceforth avoid such 'dialect' in my subsequent English stories."[23]

As with other contemporary followers of Howells's realism, like Stephen Crane, the quality of much of Cahan's fiction—and this is especially true of *Yekl*—is naturalistic. Unlike Frank Norris, who was a devoted disciple of Zola's, Cahan did not read Zola or other naturalists, as far as we know. Perhaps Cahan's tough-minded attitude toward the ignorance and squalor and unpleasing realities of East Side life, together with his low opinion of the immigrant masses, led him by a logical process to naturalism. Yekl has been a blacksmith in the shtetl, but becomes a sweatshop worker in New York who emulates the "Yankees" by displaying his knowledge of boxing and baseball in conversation with his shopmates. Three years earlier he has left his wife, Gitl, and their six-month-old son in Povodye, expecting to send them their steamship tickets when he has saved enough. Yekl, or Jake, as he now calls himself, lives the free life of the single man, associates with several women without letting them know he is married and without being especially attached to one, and loses his incentive to bring over his wife and child, though he sends them a monthly allowance. Cahan describes Yekl's visit to a dance hall on Suffolk Street and the several women who figure in his life; the story is replete with authentic details of ghetto life.

Yekl's course takes a sudden turn when he learns that his father has died. He borrows money for steamship tickets, and Gitl and his son arrive several weeks later. When they meet, Jake's "swell attire" makes him look to Gitl like a *poritz,* or nobleman, while Jake's "heart sank at the sight of his wife's uncouth and un-American appearance." Jake is ashamed of his wife's Old World manners and Orthodoxy, her appearance, and her lack of English. The couple follow the East Side practice of taking in a boarder, Bernstein, Jake's shopmate, "a rabbinical-looking man" and a reader of English books, to help pay the rent. Jake has not told his several girl friends that he is married, but when one of them, the perfumed Mamie Fein, comes to visit him after his long absence, she discovers this fact. Gitl is thrown into doubt about her husband's fidelity. For his part, Jake finds Gitl less and less tolerable, and Mamie more attractive. In a fit of jealousy another former girl friend of Jake's informs Gitl of her husband's infatuation with Mamie.

Gitl and Jake are divorced. Gitl marries the quiet Bernstein, and they open a grocery story with the divorce settlement from Jake. On his way to City Hall to marry Mamie, Jake feels that "he had emerged, after the rabbinical divorce, from the rabbi's house the victim of an ignominious defeat." His own future now "loomed dark and impenetrable." Life with Mamie is not really what he wants. "Each time the car came to a halt he wished the pause could be prolonged indefinitely; and when it resumed its progress, the violent lurch it gave was accompanied by a corresponding sensation in his heart."[24]

The central character's frustrating relation with women and his vulgarized Americanization that results in unhappiness for him— Cahan was setting forth themes here that were to become more and more pronounced as his work matured. And herein lies one of the main contradictions of Cahan's life and work: Cahan, the Americanizer of the ghetto, projected the frustrations and unhappiness that issue from Americanization.

Although *Yekl* earned little money for Cahan, it did immediately project him onto the American literary scene. While it was generally reviewed favorably, the positive response was not unanimous. Nancy Huston Banks's review in *The Bookman* notes that the book has been "unreservedly praised" by the best critics, but she is dubious about the wisdom of publishing such a work. While granting that the story is "realism in the narrowest sense of the term," the book reveals "not a gleam of spirituality, unselfishness, or nobility. . . . It is a hideous showing, and repels the reader." Does Cahan wish the reader to believe, she asks, that the characters and ghetto mode of life depicted in the work "are truly representative of his race?" If this is so, "was it wise to develop the pictures? . . . Are such books ever worth while? . . . *are* they literature?"[25] This reviewer was no doubt reflecting the conventional genteel conception of literature that led to rejection of the manuscript by several editors. But not entirely. For as we have seen, Cahan later realized that his taste was not yet secure, and the reviewer's observations were therefore not altogether lacking in penetration.

But Howells's review jointly of Cahan's *Yekl* and Stephen Crane's *George's Mother* in the Sunday, July 26, 1896, edition of the New York *World*, under the title "NEW YORK LOW LIFE IN FICTION," literally catapulted Cahan into public attention, for the review appeared on posters all over the city, advertising in its text that Howells had discovered a great new writer. The headline over the review read: "The Great Novelist Hails Abraham Cahan, the Author of 'Yekl,' as a New Star of Realism, and Says That He and Stephen Crane Have Drawn the Truest Pictures of East Side Life."

Howells calls the story "intensely realistic." Cahan's "sense of character is as broad as his sense of human nature is subtle and deep," and he will "do honor to American letters. . . . He sees things with American eyes, and he brings in aid of his vision the far and rich perceptions of his Hebraic race." Howells sees in the book "its promise of future work."[26]

The review stimulated great interest in Cahan on the part of the public and the press. A long biographical article was published in the *Boston Sunday Post* on September 27, 1896. In addition, Cahan came to know Stephen Crane. On September 22, 1896, a dinner in honor of three young "realists," Hamlin Garland, Stephen Crane, and Abraham Cahan, was given at the Lanthorn Club, a Bohemian group of artists and writers.

The temptation for Cahan to adopt the vocation of American writer must have been very strong. But his roots in the Jewish community were too deep and his devotion to socialism too intense at the time to permit him to sever his ties with Yiddish journalism. As we have mentioned, in 1897 he was one of the founders and an editor of the *Forward (Forverts)*, but he resigned a few months later because his colleagues would not accept his proposals for popularization of the paper. The next five years, until he assumed the autocratic editorship of the paper, were consumed in writing essays and short stories in English. He continued to write short stories until 1901, and in 1905 he published a long novel, *The White Terror and the Red.*

By 1898 Cahan had five more short stories, several already published, for a second volume of fiction, *The Imported Bridegroom and Other Stories of the New York Ghetto.* In addition to "A Providential Match," the group included "A Sweatshop Romance," which the eager editor of *Short Stories* published in the June 1895 issue. The scene is a vividly etched picture of a subcontractor's sweatshop in his tenement apartment. Typical immigrants people the scene: Leizer Lipman, the ruthlessly aspiring boss subcontractor; his wife, Zlate, shrewish and ridiculously pretentious; the operator Heyman, miserly, clinging to his job in fear of his boss's displeasure; the girl he loves, Beile, the young finisher who awaits his proposal of marriage; David, the baster, also in love with Beile. When Zlate orders Beile to go to the store for soda for some visitors Zlate wishes to impress, David urges Beile not to do the personal errand. Zlate fires Beile without demur from Heyman, who is loath to risk his job; and David walks out with Beile. Heyman is ashamed and does not attempt to see Beile for two weeks. When he does approach her house, he hears a wedding celebration in progress—the wedding of Beile and David. The story serves to highlight the dehumanizing and oppressive sweatshop conditions. But the stamp of the Cahan outlook is on Heyman's frustrated love for Beile.

The milieu of the immigrant Russian Jewish intellectual in which Cahan moved was first put in his fiction in "Circumstances," which *Cosmopolitan* published in April 1897. Tanya, the daughter of a Jewish merchant and Hebrew writer from Kiev, and her husband, Boris, who has studied law at a Russian university, live in hardship because Boris earns a pittance in a button factory and refuses to allow Tanya to work. To make ends meet, especially during the dreaded "slack season," Tanya reluctantly agrees to take in their mutual friend Dalsky, a medical student and English teacher, as a boarder. After a few months Tanya becomes increasingly wearied of her work-sodden husband and attracted to the lively young student, until she succumbs to love for Dalsky. First the atmosphere of irritation between husband and wife, and then small hints in her behavior lead Dalsky to realize her feelings for him, and he invents a reason to move. Tanya, finding life with Boris intolerable, leaves him and takes a job as a sewing-machine operator. Boris is heartbroken, and everything ends quite unhappily. Once more, frustrated love is the theme, and the hard life of intellectual immigrants unable to pursue their professions in the new land is depicted.

Cahan returned to the life of the uneducated immigrant workers in "A Ghetto Wedding," which appeared in the *Atlantic* in February 1898. Goldy and Nathan, living in the Grand Street area, wish to marry, but have not saved enough out of their pitiably meager earnings in the shop for the "respectable wedding" Goldy insists upon. After many delays, Goldy suggests that they spend all their money on a "respectable wedding" as a device to get an appropriately rich return in presents which will furnish them with money for their married life. Unfortunately the wedding occurs during a period of severe unemployment. Very few of the invited guests come because they cannot afford presents, and very few presents arrive. Goldy and Nathan walk home to their barren rooms. On the way home they are harassed by anti-Semitic hooligans; Goldy restrains Nathan from fighting back and they go home, drawn more closely together by the event, and warmly happy in each other. While love itself is not frustrated in this story, Cahan cannot avoid the element of frustration, which applies in this instance to their wedding plans.

The story was so well liked by Walter H. Page, editor of the *Atlantic,* that he asked Cahan for another story. The novella that

Cahan submitted, "The Imported Bridegroom," was too long for the magazine, but was published as the title story of a collection of his short stories. This novella was Cahan's most mature work so far. The range of material was broader, and the contradictions in Cahan's views and feelings were becoming more distinct. His themes exhibit how with seeming inevitability desired aims are frustrated.

Asriel Stroon has amassed a fortune in bakeries and real estate. Now in retirement thirty-five years after his arrival in this country from the shtetl of Pravly, he yearns to see the old home again and experiences a religious reawakening, partly out of fear of retribution for his sins after death. He goes to Europe to renew the link with his old home. His daughter, Flora, is a superficially educated, Americanized girl who aspires to marry a doctor, an alliance most desired by socially ambitious girls. In his hometown, which has changed little in the interim, Asriel refreshes his memories of people and the old life, and he realizes that he could buy up the town. In the synagogue he outbids Reb Lippe, the richest man in town, in the auction for the reading of the Pentatuch, but Reb Lippe is called nevertheless. Asriel makes a shocking scene in the synagogue to claim his right to the reading, but is prevailed upon to yield and apologize. That evening, Shaya, a talmudic prodigy, is to be claimed by Rep Lippe for his daughter, but Asriel's far more alluring bid, including an income for life in America, wins Shaya for Asriel's daughter, Flora.

Before presenting Shaya to Flora, Asriel bedecks Shaya in elegant American clothes. But Flora will not hear of accepting Shaya, brilliant as he may be in talmudic learning. She is determined to marry a doctor, certainly not an Orthodox rabbi. She consents to tolerate Shaya's presence in the household, however, and Asriel does not give up hope. After a few months Flora discovers that Shaya has been bootlegging secular learning at the Astor Library, thanks to the stimulus of the English teacher hired by Asriel. She proposes to Shaya that if he will study medicine and become a doctor, she will marry him, to which he agrees.

Asriel is overjoyed that Flora will have Shaya, but of course he is ignorant of the real state of affairs. Shaya not only studies profane subjects, but abandons his faith and violates the dietary laws—he is an *appikoros,* a nonbeliever. When Asriel learns the truth he forbids Flora to marry Shaya. But she now cannot live without him. They are married in a civil marriage; then Asriel capitulates and the pair are married in a Jewish wedding ceremony. Asriel gives Flora half his property and sells the rest, marries his housekeeper, and goes to Jerusalem to end his days.

But Flora soon faces an unhappy truth. Her husband is completely absorbed in his intellectual activities. He is now a member of a discussion group that is studying Auguste Comte. Flora accompanies him, but comes to realize that she is alien to these men and their interests. The scene

impressed her as the haunt of queer individuals, meeting for some sinister purpose. It was anything but the world of intellectual and physical elegance into which she had dreamed to be introduced by marriage to a doctor. Any society of "custom peddlers" was better dressed than these men. . . . She had a sense of having been kidnapped into the den of some terrible creatures, and felt like crying for help. . . . A nightmare of desolation and jealousy choked her . . . of the whole excited crowd, and of Shaya's entire future from which she seemed excluded.[27]

Cahan's basic themes are developed in the story. Asriel's yearning and longing for the familiar and essentially congenial life of the old country reflect one form of Cahan's perpetual dissatisfaction with the present, and were probably experienced also by the author. The theme of frustration takes several forms in this story, in which Americanization turns out to be a disillusioning experience. Asriel's desire to unite his daughter to a learned talmudist and to have a son-in-law to say kaddish for his memory are frustrated by Shaya's Americanization. And Flora's Americanized longings for a doctor husband, and the respectable, exalted life she envisions as its concomitant, are thwarted by her own actions. Despite Cahan's own efforts in behalf of Americanization of the immigrant masses, his own deep roots in Yiddish life and his Russian childhood aroused in him ambivalent feelings toward Americanization, and all that it implied. In "The Imported Bridegroom," both the results of Americanization as they affect Asriel and Flora and the tribulations entailed by the transition are exposed.

Between publication of "The Imported Bridegroom" and 1901 Cahan published half a dozen stories which have not been reprinted or collected. In "The Apostate of Chego-Chegg," (*Century,* November 1899) Cahan continues to explore the theme of apostasy that was opened in the earlier story. The Jewish woman Michalina is married to a Polish Christian immigrant, Wincas, and is a *meshumedeste,* a convert to her husband's faith. Cahan describes the horror with which the Jews traditionally look upon apostasy: "Years of religious persecution and enforced clannishness had taught them to look upon the Jew who deserts his faith with a horror and loathing which the Gentile brain could not conceive." It was even worse than atheism:

"Atheism would have been a malady; *shmad* (conversion to a Gentile creed) was far worse than death."

Michalina and her husband live in a Long Island village whose name, "Chego-Chegg," was bestowed by a politician as the closest approximation he could make to the Polish name of the village. Michalina expresses various forms of yearning: "She was yearning for her Gentile husband, and their common birthplace, and she was yearning for her father's house and her Jewish past." In the opening of the story Cahan thus enunciates the contradictions by which his characters (and he himself?) are riven, longing for the old home while in America, longing for the Jewish traditional past while repudiating it in practice. Near Michalina is a Jewish town, which her longing directs her to despite its rejection of her. She bears a daughter, but she is mocked by her Gentile townswomen as the "Jew woman."[28]

Rabbi Nehemiah of the Jewish town had been horrified by Michalina's conversion earlier, but he is now a peddler, an atheist "cured of my idiocy." They now share contempt for the Jewish community. Nehemiah complains: "The one thing that gives me pain is this: The same fellows who used to break my bones for preaching religion now beat me because I expose its idiocies." America, he adds, wipes out all distinctions: "All are noblemen here, and all are brothers." Michalina longs for the devout Jewish world that he brings close to her, and clings to him as a "fellow-outcast" —she cannot resolve her contradictory longings. She persuades her husband to give up his farm and move closer to the Jewish town; she does her shopping there. Nehemiah agitates in the town for assimilation, while Michalina condemns herself for her doomed soul and for her apostasy.

Nehemiah tells her that in the eyes of the Talmud her marriage to a non-Jew is nonexistent. A venerable rabbi on the East Side whom she consults advises her that if she is genuinely repentant and properly marries a Jew, she will be that man's wife. The reformed Michalina, now called by the Jewish name of Rieva, is welcomed in the Jewish town; she plans a Jewish marriage ceremony with Nehemiah in London. They are about to leave for New York and the boat to Europe when Wincas appears. Michalina is torn between her Jewish roots and her love for Wincas, and she chooses the latter. "I know that I am doomed to have no rest," she cries, "either in this world or the other, but I cannot leave him—I cannot."[29] Is Cahan torn between his Jewish roots and his American assimilationism, unsettled by his unquiet, unresolved acceptance of the latter?

His next story was free of these concerns. "Rabbi Eliezer's Christmas," published in the December 1899 issue of *Scribner's,* is, as Cahan said, "a light, humorous story."[30] Pious old Eliezer had been a sopher (a Pentateuch scribe) in the old country, but has had to resort to a newspaper stand in New York. During the pre-Christmas period, Miss Bemis, headworker of the College Settlement, and the philanthropic Miss Colton notice Eliezer during their tour of "deserving cases," and learn from him that with a few dollars he could bring his stock up to standard. Miss Bemis gives him a twenty-dollar bill. His neighboring peddlers tease and terrify him by suggesting that the money is a Christmas gift. After much soul-searching, Eliezer decides to return the money to the settlement worker. Miss Bemis assures him that the money was not a Christmas present, suggesting that he return the money to her for presentation to him later as "a fresh present."[31] While he is reassured that he has not sinned, he is torn with anxiety as to whether Miss Bemis will really give him the money. Cahan exhibits considerable depth of sympathy for the displaced, lonely, unhappy old man, whose skill in fine lettering is obsolete in technologically advanced America. The pathos of the story gives it deeper meaning than Cahan's characterization of it as "light, humorous" would indicate.

Perhaps it was in response to Howells's remark in his review of *The Imported Bridegroom*—"It will be interesting to see whether Mr. Cahan will pass beyond his present environment into a larger American world"[32] —that Cahan attempted several non-Jewish stories in the next few years. As if to proceed by gradual steps, these stories deal with the life of non-Jewish immigrants. But after this first step he did not explore the American non-Jewish milieu any further. These short stories are less interesting than his others, and it is apparent that he was at his best in writing of the world that he knew to the marrow.

Frustrated love continues to play its part in the non-Jewish stories. "A Marriage by Proxy," perhaps the least interesting of his tales, published in *Everybody's Magazine* for December 1900, is concerned with Italian immigrant life. An immigrant Italian barber sends his brother to Italy to marry a girl by proxy and to bring her to New York. The girl, Philomena, finds the barber not to her liking and wants to return to Italy, but her landlady advises her to go to the "wine-lady" for advice. The "wine-lady" shrewdly awakens jealousy in Philomena by making her believe that her husband will marry another girl, and Philomena returns to her husband and is contented.

In a second story, "Dumitru and Sigrid," published in *Cosmopolitan* in March 1901, Romanian Dumitru and Swedish Sigrid are immigrants awaiting clearance at Castle Garden, the admissions depot at that time. Neither knows the other's language, but they communicate through dictionaries, and Dumitru falls in love with Sigrid. She is taken away by a relative, and for several years, while he gains a foothold in American life, Dumitru nurses his love for her. Walking in the uptown East Side one day, he sees Sigrid on the steps of a tenement building with a baby in her lap. "Her maidenly comeliness of yore was gone only to make room for the good looks and the ripe loveliness of young motherhood." As they converse, her husband comes out. She introduces him to Dumitru and says: " 'Dis is de gentleman vat mashed me in Castle Garden.' . . . Husband and wife smiled as at a good joke." Dumitru finds the little family of three "equally uninteresting and incomprehensible to him, and he hastened to take his departure."[33] The long-held illusion is shattered.

The third story with a non-Jewish background, "Tzinchadzi of the Catskills," published in the *Atlantic* for August 1901, is important in Cahan's development because it brings into explicit focus the connection between his perpetual yearning and the failure of Americanization to set his mind at peace. The first-person narrator encounters a Circassian nobleman in the Catskills, and they chat in Russian. Tzinchadzi, the Georgian nobleman, still wears his native dress. He tells his story: after he lost his beloved to a rival in the Caucasus, he was persuaded by the American consul at Batum to ride a horse at the World's Fair in Chicago. Later he sold Caucasian goods, and "a Jew" had suggested selling them in the Catskills. He is unhappy; he makes plenty of money, but that cannot bring back his lost beloved or the Caucasus.

Six years later the narrator meets him in New York. He is dressed in the American style; his name is now Jones; he has a good business and owns real estate. Then follows a passage that casts revealing light on Cahan and his work:

"Shall I tell you the real truth?" he asked. . . . "I have money and I have friends, but you want to know whether I am happy, and that I am not, sir. Why? Because I yearn neither for my country nor for Zelaya, nor for anything else. I have thought it all out, and I have come to the conclusion that a man's heart cannot be happy unless it has somebody or something to yearn for. Do you remember how my soul was while we were in the Catskills? Well, there was a wound in me at that time, and the wound rankled with bitters mixed with sweets. Yes, sir. My heart ached, but its pain was pleasure, whereas now—alas! I have nothing, nothing! . . . It amounts to this: I do enjoy life; only I am yearning for—what shall I call it?" "For your old yearnings," I was tempted to prompt him. . . . He finally said, . . . "if you want to think of a happy man, think of Tzinchadzi of the Catskills, not of Jones of New York."[34]

In other words, the desired mode of life for Cahan does not consist in a settled contentment, but rather in unresolved conflict. His ambivalence toward traditional Jewish life, assimilation, and Americanization would thus appear to be what at bottom he desired. A decisive break with one or the other would render life stale and unprofitable. For him, the essence of life was indeed this tension.

The successful but lonely and yearning manufacturer, who was to receive fullest treatment in *David Levinsky,* is prefigured by Aaron Zalkin in "The Daughter of Reb Avrom Leib," published in *Cosmopolitan* in May 1900. After twenty years in business, the prosperous, nonreligious, unmarried Zalkin has "a great feeling of loneliness" and begins to "yearn for the Jewish quarter, his old home." He goes to an East Side synagogue, where his attention is caught by Sophie, the daughter of the cantor Reb Avrom Leib; Leib is also a composer whose work consists of "Hebraized snatches of popular operas and recent street music." Drawn by Sophie, Zalkin comes often to the synagogue and finally sends a shadchen to Reb Avrom. Zalkin impresses Reb Avrom with his talmudic learning and wins him over. Sophie and Zalkin are betrothed, but she is unresponsive and confesses that she is ambivalent about the marriage. He breaks off the engagement, but after a time he renews his suit and they are engaged again. Sophie is still indifferent, and again the engagement is broken.

Meanwhile, Reb Avrom dies; his final wish is that Sophie be reunited with Zalkin, who returns to the synagogue on Yom Kippur in longing for her. In common sorrow at the death of Reb Avrom, whom Zalkin had loved, Sophie gladly agrees to marry him. Yes, she will love Zalkin—and, "as if afraid lest morning might bring better counsel, she hastened to find herself by adding, with a tremor in her voice: 'I swear by my father that I will.' "[35] Ever distrustful of a satisfactory outcome for a love relationship, Cahan cannot help but introduce a nagging element of doubt in this "happy ending."

Cahan's fiction met with a mixed reception. W. D. Howells continued to welcome Cahan's work as it appeared. In a review of *The Imported Bridegroom,* Howells places Cahan among the regional realists, like Mary E. Wilkins Freeman of New England. "No American fiction of the year," writes Howells, "merits recognition more than this Russian's stories of Yiddish life, which are so entirely of our time and place, and so foreign to our race and civilization." Howells seems to me to be stretching the point when he calls Cahan a "humourist"; "ironist" would perhaps be closer. Cahan, he continues, "does not spare the sordid and uncouth aspects of the character whose pathos he so tenderly reveals. . . . Of a Jew, who is also a Russian, what artistic triumph may not we expect?"[36] The severest criticism, however, issued from the American Jewish press. Cahan reports in his autobiography how the *American Israelite* was indignant at "The Apostate of Chego-Chegg" because, they held, the story was mistaken in asserting that marriage with a non-Jew is not recognized by Judaism. The paper asserts that Jewish law does not teach one to violate the law of the land, and says that "Cahan is prepared to sell the Jews for the price given him for a story." Cahan notes that "the 'Yahudim' are forever afraid that one might say they were not loyal Americans." He insists that his story is accurate, for he has conferred with two Orthodox rabbis. The established German Jews, the "Yahudim," he concludes, have "denied the law 'in the interests of Judaism.' "[37]

Complaints by the Yahudim against both fiction and descriptive stories about immigrant East Side life were frequent. They were embarrassed and even a little apprehensive that the emphatic differences between the Jewish immigrants and the Americans, of whom they considered themselves an inseparable part, might jeopardize their status and might even arouse anti-Semitism. The Reverend Rudolph Grossman, a Reform rabbi, charges in the *American Hebrew* of March 18, 1892, that "nothing has contributed so much toward keeping alive the old prejudices against the Jew, as these productions of fiction that place them before the reader, not only in the most unfavorable but in the most ludicrous and false light." It turns out, however, that the author includes among these "caricatures" articles "that represent the Jews of New York as observing the ceremonies and superstitions of the ghetto. . . . These garbled and misleading accounts of the Jew and Judaism . . . foster not only ignorance but prejudice and hatred." Apparently wishing the East Side ghetto out of existence, or else believing it only decent that one should be quiet about it, the rabbi points out that the Jew—that is, the assimilated German Jew—is different "in one respect only . . . from the generality of men—in his religion."[38] To him, and to so many German Jews, the East European Jew of the ghetto was no more a valid subject for literature than the caricature and stereotype.

Displeasure of the Yahudim at Lincoln Steffens's feature stories in the New York *Post* about Orthodox East Side Jews was so great that in a letter to the editor one indignant "socially prominent Jewish lady" decried the great amount of space given "to the ridiculous performances of the ignorant, foreign East Side Jews and none to the uptown Hebrews."[39] After Steffens called on her and defended his stories, she tried to get him fired. Since the paper was at the time campaigning against exclusion of Jews from clubs, the Jews could hardly insist on the firing.

Cahan's stories especially drew protest from the Yahudim. *The Bookman* came to Cahan's defense editorially: "To judge from the attitudes assumed by some of the Jewish newspapers, any attempt by a member of that race to depict the life of the Ghetto in a frankly realistic manner constitutes an offence only slightly less heinous than treason." Zangwill's and Cahan's work were targets of this protest, and a boycott of their works was threatened. The *American Israelite* is quoted as being

convinced that this fellow Cahan has intentionally exaggerated what is worst among his own class of people. A man who is capable of painting the people from whom he comes in such vile colours would be enough of a scoundrel to lie about them for the sake of a few dollars. . . . It is infinitely better for Jews to buy books and other publications which advocate their cause, than to give through vulgar curiosity financial support and encouragement to writers and publishers who do harm to the cause of Judaism and to the Jews.[40]

The Bookman editorially replies that such criticism increases the market value of Cahan's work and observes that Cahan is far too much the genuine artist and student of human life to allow such criticisms to inhibit him from further work.

These comments prompted one daughter of the Sephardic aristocracy, Annie Nathan Meyer, a cousin of Emma Lazarus's and a founder of Barnard College, to write her views; while rejecting the threat of boycott and personal abuse, she complains that "the Americanized Hebrew is denied *in toto* the luxury of pointing to any literature that pretends to describe him seriously." The exotic ghetto Jew is more interesting to the non-Jewish reader "than the Talmudically ignorant Americanized Hebrew," who is in turn getting tired of seeing these exotic Jews in print. She notes that in a world of discrimination, persecution, and anti-Semitism, "the Jew is asking himself is it wise, is it expedient, to hold up in literature all that is foreign, all that is strange, all that is exceptional in the Jew?" Is it any wonder that the Jew has a thin skin, she concludes?

In the same issue Martin B. Ellis replies to the Jews who threaten to boycott Cahan's stories, relating that he himself sees much beauty in the religious observances and way of life in the ghetto, while the uptown Jews seem not unlike the Christians. "The rich, Philistine, semi-Christianized Jews of the uptown or Golden Ghetto," he writes, "—I believed they are ashamed of Israel. . . . He is trying to become just like everybody else."[41]

The bitter attacks by the Yahudim must have reinforced Cahan's intention to write a novel about a Russian immigrant that would, for one thing, show the deep gulf between the East Side Jews and their prosperous uptown German Jewish brethren. The theme he chose was the barriers placed in the way of intermarriage between children of the two groups. Cahan must have discussed this novel, *The Chasm,* at some length with *The Bookman*'s editor, who mentions that it is "nearly finished." *The Chasm* promised to be an epic of the post-1882 Russian immigration: it would show how the immigrant life of the time was a superimposition of second-century life on the nineteenth; would maintain that the struggle to abolish the sweatshop was an internal Jewish class struggle between the Jewish workers and Jewish bosses; and would point out the deep incompatibility between the two Jewish communities of New York. The editor notes that although Cahan grants the material aid bestowed upon the immigrants by the uptown Jews, their cultural differences "explained the half-veiled superciliousness, the unspoken animosity"[42] of the uptown Jews. The irony of this is that Cahan himself was guilty of a like condescension toward the immigrant masses whom he was ostensibly raising up.

As it turned out, *The Chasm* was never finished. Instead, Cahan published a long novel, *The White Terror and the Red* (1905), which does not deal with the subjective themes that run through his other fiction. There is not yearning love—only militant revolutionary activity. The novel is, in fact, a fictionalized account of the related themes of the revolutionary movement in Russia, Jewish participation in it, and the counterrevolutionary pogroms that figured in Cahan's article "Jewish Massacres and the Revolutionary Movement in Russia," in the *North American Review* for July 1903.

The bulk of the revolutionary army is made up of Gentiles [he writes], not of Jews. . . . But it is true that the Jews have more than their quota among the men and women who defy the isolated prison-cell and the gallows in their devotion to the cause of liberty; . . . they take an exceptionally active part in the dissemination of Western ideas; and this is another reason why an anti-Jewish outbreak, on the eve of the proposed May demonstrations, would have been an advantage to the government in troublesome times like those. When the news of the Kishineff horrors spread, and the panic-stricken Jews of other towns begged the authorities to protect them in case of an anti-Semitic attack, they were given to understand, through their "official" rabbis, that full protection would be guaranteed to them provided they undertook to prevail upon the revolutionists of their faith to stay away from the prospective demonstration. The result was that in several cities the May parade was abandoned.[43]

While the novel dramatizes these themes, as well as the revolutionary movement in general, it also adds in analytic detail attitudes of the Jews to the revolutionary movement and to their Jewish identity, and those of the revolutionaries to the Jews. The writing, though competent, is uninspired and lacks the vitality of his other fiction. It is not surprising that the book has almost completely dropped from attention. From the historical point of view, however, it is of interest in its depiction of the nihilistic attitude of the Jewish revolutionaries to their Jewishness and to their fellow Jews.

Cahan had experienced some of these attitudes in 1891, when he went to Zurich as delegate from the United Hebrew Trades to the Second Congress of the Second International. He insisted upon placing a resolution about anti-Semitism on the agenda. He discovered considerable antagonism to his proposal, for the current agitation against Jewish bankers—especially the Rothschilds—was popular on class grounds and was reinforced by traditional anti-Semitism. Furthermore, there was a disproportion of Jews among the socialist leaders. An unqualified condemnation of anti-Semitism, it was feared, might tend to confirm the identification of Jews and socialists that anti-Semites insisted upon (as Chief Rabbi Dreyfus of Brussels tried without success to convince Cahan). Austrian socialist leader Viktor Adler tried to dissuade Cahan from pressing the resolution with the argument that it would lead the anti-Semites to call the congress a Jewish affair. But Cahan was adamant, and was shocked when the best that the congress could come up with was a condemnation of *both* anti-Semitism and philo-Semitism; then it passed on to the next order of business because the congress was not considered to be the proper place for consideration of the question.[44] The ambiguous attitude toward anti-Semites in the context of the Russian revolutionary movement among both Jews and non-Jews is brought out in the novel in connection with the pogroms.

The locus of the novel is Russia of the 1870s and early 1880s. The activity centers about the love story of a young nobleman, Pavel Boulatoff, a leader of the revolutionary movement, and Clara

Yavner, a Jew and leading revolutionary activist. Other significant Jewish figures are Clara's cousin, Volodia, an educated assimilationist; Elkin, "an underfed Jewish youth, with an anaemic chalky face and a cold intelligent look,"[45] a revolutionary who finally becomes a Jewish nationalist after disillusionment with his comrades' attitude toward the Jews; Makar, a brilliant medical student and talmudic scholar who is a revolutionary. The plot carries these characters through their interactions in revolutionary activity. At the end Pavel and Clara are married, and all but Volodia are thrown in the tsarist jail during the repression that follows the assassination of the tsar, Alexander II, in 1881.

Clara moves from an initial indifference to the Jewish question, to a disturbed feeling that all is not well with her comrades' attitude after she experiences a pogrom. Early in the story Cahan shows that her conceptions about the peasants are "so many literary images" and are quite distinct from the world of "Jewish realities." Thus when she discusses the hanging of four Jewish revolutionaries with her educated, assimilated, bourgeois cousin, Volodia, he complains that the execution does the Jewish people no good. Clara replies: "What else would you have Jews do? Roll on feather-beds and collect usury? Would that do 'the Jewish people' good?" Volodia replies: "You talk like an anti-Semite, Clara." Clara answers that she is proud of the four and then challenges him: "Since when have *you* been a champion of 'the Jewish people'—you who have taught me to keep away from everything Jewish, you who are shocked by the very sound of Yiddish, by the very sight of a wig or a pair of sidelocks; you who are continually boasting of the Gentiles you are chumming with; you who would give all the Jews in the world for one handshake of a Christian?" Volodia replies that his attitude toward Yiddish and earlocks harms no one. "If all Jews dropped their antediluvian ways and became assimilated with the Russian population half of the unfortunate Jewish question would be solved."

Clara chides Volodia for "worrying over the Jewish question" at a time when the "whole country is choking for breath." She further taunts him, as an assimilationist, on his interest in the question. Volodia insists that Jews have a right to protest because they are the target of "unnatural oppression." Clara replies that Jews should participate in the struggle, since they will participate in the ensuing freedom from *all* oppression. The argument goes back and forth, Clara charging Volodia with total indifference to the Jews and insisting that, when the revolutionaries have succeeded, "there won't be any such thing as a Jewish, Polish or Hottentot question." Volodia replies that Clara's "golden mist of that glorious future"[46] does not negate enforcement of equal rights in the present. The argument ends in an unfriendly impasse.

This exchange has a certain irony, for each represents one side of Cahan's own views: he was both an assimilationist and a socialist. His assimilationism, though, was troubled by his actual immersion in the Yiddish-speaking community, and his socialism included a specific concern for the Jewish question (although many of his comrades, both nationally and internationally, believed with Clara that Jewish issues would automatically be resolved with the victory of socialism).

Volodia's dilemma is carried further. When he visits a Russian princess, he manifests great love for Russia and its literature. She is both surprised and bored—"I had an idea," she says, "Hebrews were only interested in money matters"—and dismisses him. He agonizes over this rebuff and this challenge to his "right" to love "Gogol, Turgeneff, Dostoyevski." Volodia's father, an enlightened Jew who is learned in both secular and talmudic thought, calms him with the thought that the princess, a "penniless spendthrift," is like a pig who knows only the backyard of a mansion: it is quite natural that "she should mistake a handful of usurers for the whole Jewish population." A "Gentile reprobate"[47] would have no occasion to go to any other kind of Jew because the latter has no money to lend.

As for Clara, she comes to the realization at last—after the pogroms have begun, and her party shows insensitivity at best and anti-Semitism to the slaughter and persecution of the Jews at worst —that all is not well on the Jewish issue among her comrades. She is now married to Pavel. An issue of the *Will of the People,*[48] the organ of the Narodnaya Volya (People's Will party), comments on the anti-Jewish riots in a manner "as puerile as it was heartless." Clara resents this position. "As long as it does not concern the Jews they have all the human sympathy and tact in the world. . . . The moment there is a Jew in the case they become cruel, short-sighted and stupid —everything that is bad and ridiculous." Even of her husband, she thinks to herself that "he is a Gentile after all. . . . There is a strain of anti-Semitism in the best of them." Her conclusion is that she must endure.

For Pavel, his love for Clara has given the problem immediacy. On one hand, he shares the view of his party that if the peasants "can attack Jewish usurers, I don't see why they could not turn upon the government some day." But he feels uneasy and guilty about his view in relation to Clara, for he knows on reflection that the Jewish poor and workers are the targets of the pogroms at the hands of those whom his party aims to liberate. At the same time, the cult of the Russian peasant projects him under a "golden halo," so that "if the Russian masses were rioting, could there be a better indication of a revolutionary awakening? And if the victims of these riots happened to be Jews, then the Jews were evidently enemies of the people."[49]

In a proclamation the revolutionary party has at first joined the Jews with the tsar and landlords as enemies of the people, but protests by both Jews and non-Jews have forced withdrawal of the proclamation. Despite the generally unsympathetic attitude of the nihilists toward the Jews, writes Cahan, "so far as the higher strata of the movement were concerned, the personal relations between Jew and Gentile were not affected by this circumstance in the slightest degree." Most Jewish comrades, moreover, greet the pogroms as "a popular revolutionary protest." Makar, the gifted student and erstwhile talmudic scholar, sees nothing new in persecution of the Jews: "One might as well stay away from the *Will of the People*" he says, "because, forsooth, Jews were burned by Gentiles in the 15th century." Clara is not at this stage occupied with the threat to Jews in general, but concerned for the safety of her parents in Miroslav, her hometown. She has gone there to be with them, and the loving Pavel ardently hopes for her sake that the Jews of Miroslav will be spared. Moreover, Pavel realizes that his uncle, who is governor of the province, might be able to stop the pogrom if he wishes, and since "he is in league with his fellow-fleecers, the Jewish usurers, . . . he simply cannot afford an anti-Jewish demonstration, the old bribe-taker."[50]

The pogrom does take place after the peasants are incited by false rumors. Pavel, now in Miroslav, observes the whipping up of a pogrom spirit, and he is inspired by the thought of the French Revolution. "So our people are *not* incapable of rising!" he thinks to himself. The nihilists decide that during the riots they will try to divert the mob away from the Jews and aim their fury at the tsar and his officials. One revolutionary shouts to the pogromists: "Don't drink too much boys! Don't befog your minds! For this is a great historical moment! Only why attack the Jews alone? Behold, the Czar is at the head of all the blood-suckers of the land!" The crowd accuses him of having been sent by the Jews with such talk, and they rush at him. After it is all over, the revolutionaries still do not understand the counterrevolutionary nature of the pogroms. They are mesmerized by the prospect of an actual mass rising, mistaken by them for a sign of revolutionary awakening against economic oppression, which the masses identifies with the Jews. Even Clara finally works herself into approval of this view of the matter, regarding her earlier doubts as a relapse into "racial predilections."[51]

The effect of the pogroms on Elkin, who had become a revolutionary earlier than Clara or Pavel and is the original organizer of the Miroslav group, is different. He now decides that his loyalty to the Jewish people transcends the claim of Russia upon him. He still believes in socialism, but his tactic now is to organize communistic colonies and to emigrate to the United States with them. In a conversation with Elkin, Pavel is angered by what he conceives to be Elkin's attempt "to mix socialism with Jewish chauvinism." Elkin's retort is: "Can socialism be mixed with . . . the welfare of the Russian people with a pailful or two of Jewish blood thrown in; in plainer language, socialism can only be mixed with anti-Semitism. Is that it?"

Pavel's reply is that there are other Jews in the movement on whom the pogrom does not have the same effect that it does on Elkin. The feeling on both sides grows bitter, and Elkin leaves. The gist of the conversation is that "no effort should be spared to keep the mob from attacking the Jewish poor," but that an attempt should be made to divert the pogromists to attack the tsar, "to lend the disturbance a revolutionary character."[52] Elkin and Volodia are in the Jewish defense force, and during the pogrom the nihilists and Elkin are on opposite sides. After the pogrom, Clara's efforts to win Elkin back to the revolutionaries are unsuccessful, nor does he convince her to join his emigrating colonists. Before he can leave, however, the repression has imprisoned him, Clara, Pavel, and their other comrades. At the novel's end they communicate with one another by a wall-tapping code.

What makes *The White Terror and the Red* distinctive from the rest of Cahan's English fiction is that it is his most objective work, in which typical attitudes toward the Jews, especially among revolutionaries, are set forth. His purpose in the novel, as in the *North American Review* article, is to convey the truth about the Russian revolutionary movement, especially as regards Jews in general and Jews within the movement in particular. No single character represents his own view, but each of them manifests what he considers valid or invalid aspects of the movement. The characters are treated very sympathetically, with less sense of personal tragedy than in his other works. In sum, the novel is virtually his sole effort at sociopolitical realism in fiction divorced from his personal ambivalences.

*   *   *

When Cahan was again offered the editorship of the *Forward* in 1902, he faced a dilemma. The reception his fiction had received forecast a promising career as an American writer in English. At the same time, he was assured absolute control of the *Forward,* subject only to confirmation each year by the Forward Association. At first Cahan thought that he could pursue both his writing career and his editorship by leaving the paper at two o'clock each day and returning home to write. But the press of editorial work was too heavy to allow for afternoon writing sessions. Nevertheless, for a few years Cahan did turn out fiction in English, as we have seen. After *The White Terror* was published in 1905 no more fiction in English appeared until 1913, and this at a significant point in his life which helps account, at least in a symbolic sense, for the underlying meaning of *David Levinsky.* Since Cahan had taken over the *Forward* a decade earlier the paper had prospered mightily: its circulation had risen to over a hundred thousand, and in 1910 the *Forward* started to build a ten-story building that towered over the Lower East Side. As the sole Yiddish labor paper it was looked to by the Jewish workers for support of their trade union struggles.

In 1912 the United Garment Workers, with a membership of only about five thousand, struck against oppressive conditions, but about fifty thousand workers followed the strike call. By this time the *Forward* had developed vested interests in certain unions and union leaders, and Tom Rickert, president of the UGW was one of these. After nine weeks of a bitter strike, Rickert reached an agreement with the bosses and settled the strike without consulting the workers. On March 1, 1913, the workers read the banner headline in the *Forward:* "THE STRIKE IS SETTLED—BRAVO, CUTTERS!" The workers were enraged at what they regarded as a sellout. They stormed the *Forward* building in protest and broke its windows. When Cahan came out to address them, he collapsed and was rushed to the hospital for an emergency abdominal operation. As a result of this strike and its settlement, the union was weakened and its leaders were rejected. In December 1914 the Amalgamated Clothing Workers of America was formed.

This incident is a striking manifestation of one of the central contradictions within Cahan—between his labor socialist convictions, and his vested interest in a successful newspaper and sociopolitical expedience. By 1913 Cahan not only had absolute authority over the *Forward,* he exercised this power tyrannically. He had already established himself as the enemy of Yiddish culture, language, and literature, and as the foremost exponent of *shund* in

Yiddish journalism and literature. He had employed and then alienated, as he was to continue to do, outstanding Yiddish writers. As
Bezalel Sherman has written, while one must recognize Cahan's
early pioneering work for socialism among the masses, one cannot
deny "his dilution and vulgarization of socialism."[53] The contradictions in Cahan's life and career form the basis for his culminating
work in English, *David Levinsky*.

The first form of this story was published in 1913. Cahan was
asked by *McClure's* to write some articles on the sensational successes
in the economic world achieved by erstwhile Jewish immigrants.
Cahan responded with two articles in the form of a fictional autobiography of a successful garment manufacturer. *McClure's* was delighted with them and asked for more. Before Cahan could comply
he was involved in the United Garment Workers strike, which as we
have seen ended in collapse for him. During his convalescence he
supplied two more parts, and the whole was published serially in
McClure's from April to July 1913. This early version was amplified
in the novel published four years later as *The Rise of David
Levinsky*.[54]

Like all his English fiction, Cahan's novel is a vivid, perceptive
document of aspects of Jewish life on the East Side between the
1880s and World War I, the heyday of Yiddish-speaking immigrant
life in New York. No single work of fiction can capture all the
features of the richly varied life of that community. Later works of
permanent value like Mike Gold's *Jews without Money* and Henry
Roth's *Call It Sleep* provide different angles of vision on East Side
life. But Cahan's sensitive, tough-minded rendering of that life pre-
serves for posterity a vision by one who was himself immersed in the
community. By placing his central character in the garment industry,
in which the largest portion of the Jewish immigrants were engaged
as boss or worker—a sector of economic life Cahan was intimately
familiar with, both as observer and labor organizer—Cahan was able
to picture the growth of that industry.

It is a matter of history that the garment manufacturers in the
1870s and 1880s were mainly German Jews, and that they were
pushed out by the newer East European immigrants. This process is
portrayed by Cahan through his depiction of the "rise" of Levinsky
as garment manufacturer. John Higham has observed that *David
Levinsky* is "among the best novels of American business." He further notes that other novelists of the period, like Dreiser and Frank
Norris, present business tycoons and show, as Cahan does, "the
conquests of the market-place as morally debasing." But Cahan does

more. "Whereas Dreiser and others concentrated on the business-man's personal style of life, Cahan also wrote, in the guise of fiction, a critically important chapter in American social history."[55]

Cahan himself writes in *David Levinsky:*

The time I speak of, the late 80's and the early 90's, is connected with an important and interesting chapter in the history of the American cloak business. Hitherto in control of German Jews, it is now beginning to pass into the hands of their Russian co-religionists, the change being effected under peculiar conditions that were destined to lead to a stupendous development of the industry. If the average American woman is today dressed infinitely better than she was a quarter of a century ago, and if she is now easily the best-dressed average woman in the world, the fact is due, in large measure, to the change I refer to.

The talent of the pioneer German manufacturers in an industry "scarcely twenty years old" was primarily mercantile, while the workers in the shops, the East European immigrants, knew tailoring and practiced better product control. As he is trying to obtain an order from an influential non-Jewish Chicago buyer, Levinsky explains the reasons why the rising Russian Jewish manufacturers were displacing the German Jewish ones:

The Russian cloak-manufacturers operated on a basis of much lower profits and figured down expenses to a point never dreamed of before; . . . the German American cloak-manufacturer was primarily a merchant, not a tailor; . . . he was compelled to leave things to his designer and foreman, whereas his Russian competitor was a tailor or cloak-operator himself, and was, therefore, able to economize in ways that never occurred to the heads of the old houses.[56]

Levinsky's ascent of the economic ladder is pictured in detail. Beginning on a shoestring as a shopworker, he parlays his small capital into success as a small manufacturer. Finally, through skillful manipulation and good luck, he works his way up and uptown from the sweatshops of Division Street, via Broadway, to the pinnacle of Twenty-third Street and Fifth Avenue. It is obvious from Cahan's account that the survival and growth of Levinsky's business would never have occurred without his resorting to a series of deceptions and to antiunion manipulation of his workers. These were the classical business methods of the laissez-faire age, as the histories of the great corporations attest, and Levinsky is an astute practitioner of them. He is able to get started in business by deceiving his designer as to the extent of his capital. When he is in dire need of capital, he proposes marriage to a fellow worker, a "homely" girl who has saved money to attract a prospective husband in lieu of physical beauty. Possessed of great common sense, she rejects his offer.

But his greatest resource for undercutting his competitors is to employ cheap nonunion labor. This did not mean inferior workers. Levinsky runs an informal shop in which the workers feel at home, and he permits them to observe the Saturday Sabbath and work on Sunday instead. Although his piecework rates are low, his workers operate at greater speed and work longer hours than in other shops, so that they draw more pay. Furthermore, Levinsky cuts his profit margins below those of established firms. When the union is strong enough to require his shop to become a union shop, his workers still continue to work on a nonunion basis. He betrays not only the union, but his fellow manufacturers. When they lock out the workers, he formally agrees to follow suit but clandestinely continues to operate his shop. He even subcontracts to established firms during the lockout. His deception is exposed, and the labor paper calls him a "cockroach manufacturer." When the strike is won, his workers receive the union wage but are forced to kick back the difference between the union and his own scale of wages. "The lockout and the absolute triumph of the union," he says, "was practically the making of me."[57]

The designer who has made possible the beginning of Levinsky's business has continued in his old job with the understanding that he is to become Levinsky's partner when the firm is established. But when his business expands, Levinsky gets rid of the talented designer: why share his profits when he can hire a designer? Another reason he no longer needs the designer is that he knows an employee of a large shop who agrees to let him steal the designs of the shop. This practice of copying designs from the big firms soon becomes a regular practice in the trade.

In addition to his antiunion practices, the shrewd Levinsky helps form a "Levinsky Antomir Benefit Society," composed of immigrants from Levinsky's hometown. Most of his workers are members of the society, thus affording him a cosy personal connection with them that virtually assures him of freedom from "labor troubles." Levinsky uses a "shadchen," a bought shop chairman who cheats the union in the employer's favor, and stool pigeons to report any union agitation.

Levinsky has come to the United States with four cents in his pocket; thirty years later he is worth several millions. Cahan shows how this was done by what is in essence a vivid case history. Along the way Cahan depicts many East Side characters: Anna Tevkin, the young woman with whom Levinsky is desperately in love at the novel's end, her socialist sisters and brothers, and her father, a Hebrew poet of declining reputation who is employed as a real estate broker. Tevkin and other characters participate in the speculative real estate boom in the first decade of the century, in which many Jews lost or gained a fortune. Various types of workers and employees are encountered. The kind of Americanization that Cahan tried to teach the Yiddish masses is illustrated, both in its more admirable aspects as a road to a cultured and useful life, and as a vulgarized emulation of the dominant culture. We meet once again the themes and types of characters that Cahan had broached in the short stories. The novel is, in objective terms, a remarkable microcosm of the East Side.

But these objective features do not at all exhaust the content of the novel. For it is also Cahan's personal testament, and thus derives added interest and significance, in light of the important role played by Cahan in the life of the Jewish immigrant community for more than three decades. The dominant mood of the novel is one of melancholy and yearning. Besides occurring in so many of Cahan's stories, this word itself is used more than two dozen times in the course of the novel. What is David Levinsky to Cahan? Above all, Cahan was a realist and Levinsky, the enemy of the socialists, is the ruthless capitalist boss worshiping at the shrine of the bitch goddess Success. The evidence points to this: Levinsky is a thinly disguised Abraham Cahan.

The import of this first-person novel is announced in its first paragraph, and reiterated in the final paragraphs.

Sometimes, when I think of my past in a superficial, casual way, the metamorphosis I have gone through strikes me as nothing short of a miracle. I was born and reared in the lowest depths of poverty and I arrived in America—in 1885—with four cents in my pocket. I am now worth more than two million dollars and recognized as one of the two or three leading men in the cloak-and-suit trade in the United States. And yet when I take a look at my inner identity it impresses me as being precisely the same as it was thirty or forty years ago. My present station, power, the amount of worldly happiness at my command, and the rest of it, seem void of significance.

At the end of the novel, as he contemplates his lonely, luxurious mode of life, he says to himself: "There are cases when success is a tragedy." He was born to live the life of the mind; he would have preferred to gain distinction in the professions or sciences instead of business, where many successful men "have no brains."

How did Levinsky happen to traduce his own best instincts? In the novel Cahan improbably attributes the choice to an "accident." In his first few years in this country Levinsky determines to save enough money by working in a shop to take him through college, and thence to the intellectual life. He is working in the shop of Jeff Manheimer, a native American of German Jewish origin, who treats his immigrant workers with contempt. One day a bottle of milk slips out of Levinsky's hands onto the floor and spills on some silk coats. Manheimer rages against him and says that the cost of the soiled garments will be charged against Levinsky, who then "became breathless with hate."[58] He will get revenge by inducing Ansel Chaikin, Manheimer's talented designer and the soul of the business, to enter a partnership with Levinsky himself. The more he thinks of the scheme the less revenge figures in it, and the more the vision of himself as a rich man challenges him. From these beginnings develop the structure of his power and wealth. So Levinsky's manufacturing career has not been wholly an accident after all, but more deeply an expression of a commanding strain of his character.

How, then, can we demonstrate the essential identicalness of Levinsky with Cahan himself? In writing the original sketches that resulted in this novel, Cahan was fulfilling the *McClure* editorial request to present the success story of Jewish business. But Cahan himself represented one such success story, with his conversion of a socialist paper of limited circulation into a popular Yiddish paper with the highest circulation of any Yiddish paper in the world. What Cahan did (with what degree of awareness we do not know) was to invest his own qualities, minus his socialist convictions, in Levinsky, as if Cahan had been himself in Levinsky's situation. There is some truth in H. W. Boynton's observation: "The disconcerting thing is that we cannot make out whether Mr. Cahan appreciates the spiritual obscenity of the creature he has made; embodiment of all the contemptible qualities an enemy of the Yiddish Jew could charge him with."[59] If Boynton implies that Levinsky is a stereotype, he seems to me mistaken, since Levinsky is a complex individual and a credible character. But it is true that in a subtle way Levinsky and his deceptions are presented so sympathetically as to justify Boynton's perception of an ambiguity in Cahan's own feeling toward Levinsky.

Like Levinsky, Cahan went through a critical period of deciding which course to follow: that of his higher inclination or the one which promised personal power and success. For Cahan, the choice was between continuing as a man of letters in English ("the ideal of my personal life") or being a journalist in Yiddish. In his autobiography he records his internal debate as to whether to reassume the editorial post of the *Forward* in 1902. One could make money as a writer only by writing "pieces of the cheaper sort."[60] While *shund*-writers were rich, a real writer like Theodore Dreiser earned very little in the first few decades of his writing—only with *An American Tragedy* in 1925 did he achieve financial success. Life as a writer could yield deep spiritual satisfaction but a meager livelihood. At the same time, the prospect of building the *Forward* attracted him.

Cahan's decision was—as Levinsky told himself when he decided to plunge into manufacturing, and at the same time to continue his college education—"again performing the trick of eating the cake and having it. I would picture myself building up a great cloak business and somehow contriving, at the same time, to go to college."[61] Although when he resumed the editorship it was understood that Cahan would be free after two o'clock to work on his writing, he was no more able to pursue both careers—except, of course, to write the masterpiece that gave expression to his lifelong dilemma—than Levinsky was able both to be a manufacturer and to pursue a college career. That this conflict was one source of Cahan's yearning is attested to by a comment made by Hillel Rogoff, who succeeded Cahan on the *Forward*. Rogoff was reported in an obituary article to have said that "Cahan did not follow the profession of his choice. He wanted, and in all probability was intended to be, a novelist and a writer of short stories."[62] And Cahan has Levinsky muse at the end of the novel: "I think that I should be much happier as a scientist or writer, perhaps. I should then be in my natural element."[63]

Furthermore, there is a similarity, within limits, between the actual careers of Cahan and Levinsky and their desired vocations: writer and college-educated man (a doctor, perhaps.) Both Cahan and his fictional hero were huge successes in their chosen work. When Levinsky moves into his Fifth Avenue establishment occupying five floors of a great building, he is aware of how he is regarded. "Success! Success! Success! It was the almighty goddess of the hour. Thousands of new fortunes were advertising her gaudy splendors. Newspapers, magazines, and public speeches were full of her glory, and he who found favor in her eyes found favor in the eyes of man."[64] At about the same time that Cahan reached a peak of success with the *Forward* he moved into the new ten-story building, and was the object of interviews and magazine articles in recognition of his success.

By this time, too, the dilution and vulgarization of his socialist views were apparent in the *Forward,* as we have indicated, and the decades that followed saw the end of even any pretense of a socialist approach and the adoption of some of the worst features of yellow journalism. When Cahan came to write *David Levinsky,* the contrast between the intellectual and personal integrity of himself as writer, on one hand, and as master journalist who stooped to the level of the uneducated and unenlightened masses and, so to speak, held them down at that level, on the other, must have been one source of the dissatisfaction he felt and transferred to his fictional hero.

In his personal life, too, Levinsky is unhappy, full of yearning and frustration, especially in his relations with women. Of Levinsky's relationships with five women with whom he is in love or who wish to marry him, none is stable or satisfactory. From beginning to end, Levinsky courts only women whom he cannot marry for one reason or other. I do not know to what extent this frustration reflects Cahan's life, since I know of no biography that conveys such intimate information about him. However, it is known that he was an unhappy man and that his marriage in 1885 to Anna Bronstein (Levinsky's last love in the novel is also called Anna), an intellectual Russian, was not altogether satisfactory. The obituary article cited earlier states that "in his personal life Cahan was a lonely and unhappy man. He had few friends and many enemies. He was respected by almost all, but loved by few." This real-life statement is close to Levinsky's lament at the end of the novel: "Am I happy? . . . I am lonely. Amid the pandemonium of my six hundred sewing machines and the jingle of gold which they pour into my lap I feel the deadly silence of solitude."[65] What Cahan himself would have said about the circumstances and meaning of *David Levinsky,* as he promised to do in volume 5 of the *Bleter* (page 288), might have proved revealing, but Cahan never completed his autobiography.

The reception of *David Levinsky* was mixed. W. D. Howells, now eighty years old, was repelled by the love scenes, which he thought "too sensual." In a letter on September 20, 1917, he wrote: "Abraham Cahan has done a pretty good autobiographical novel, but it is too sensual in its facts, though he is a good man."[66] Some assimilationists among the Jews were unhappy with the novel because they regarded an American Jewish novel as an invalid concept altogether. As one said of the early version of the novel in *McClure's:* "There is no more reason for Abraham Cahan to write the autobiography of an American Jew [the title of the series in *McClure's*] than there would be in Domenick Petro writing an autobiography of an

American Catholic, or of Tommy Atkins writing of an American
Anglican. There ought to be organized a society among the Jews
. . . to compel both Jews and Christians to look upon the Jew as a
human being and full grown."[67] In this passage the assimilationist's
insistence that the Jew is, or should be, regarded as different from
all others *only* in religion, arising from the wish to obliterate differences he disapproves of or fears, is exposed in all its blindness to
actual distinctions. On the other hand, the critic and scholar Isaac
Goldberg, writing in *The Call,* the Socialist party organ, on September 23, 1917, hails the book as being "unique among the books
published not only this year, but during the past decade. . . . This
book is more than a literary event; it is a permanent addition to
American letters."

Howells's genteel revulsion from the naturalism of the novel was
shared by Kate Holladay Claghorn in *The Survey.* The novel, she
writes, "reveals with crude and unashamed realism the growing
ascendancy of the sensual over the spiritual, the material over the
ideal, in the narrator's own life. . . . The people we are introduced
to are in varying combinations crude, selfish, sensual, tasteless—
above all, tasteless!—foolish, ignorant, ambitious and egotistical."
The rendering of the Jews in the novel is so utterly negative, she
believes, that if a Jewish author had not written it, if it had been
published anonymously, "we might have taken it for a cruel caricature of a hated race by some anti-Semite." She exposes her limited
comprehension of the book by calling it a "campaign poster," calling
on the "non-socialist, non-union sinners of the household to repent." She assures her readers that this novel is not "a picture of
Jewish life in general. There are some admirable traits in the character of even the business Jew."[68]

She was not alone in warning of the anti-Semitic effect of the book.
Cahan's own colleague on the *Forward,* Hillel Rogoff, reviewing the
book in that paper on September 28, 1917, is unhappy with the
naturalistic rendering of Jews in the novel. He says he wishes that
Cahan had omitted some chapters "which portray the swamps of the
former East Side and vulgarities and superficialities of the 'allright-
niks.' First, these aspects are superfluous; secondly, they make a bad
impression on the non-Jewish readers because the portrayals are
one-sided and sometimes over-spiced. The East Side of the 90's had
a lofty, beautiful, idealistic spiritual life, which the book does not
mention."[69]

The charge that the novel, and specifically the portrait of Levinsky,
damages "the public concept" of the Jew has been maintained in

recent years by Morris U. Schappes. He does not challenge the portrait of Levinsky as such, but he maintains that "more of the truth is required." The piratical business ethics of Levinsky are not peculiarly Jewish but those of American free enterprise. Therefore, Schappes holds, by isolating Levinsky and his fellow Russian Jewish clothing manufacturers and by not depicting "elements of the Jewish working class, that idealistic, militant, heroic and often noble working class," and the "non-Jewish rapacious American business man, alongside of and in contact with and in fact 'inspiring' the Levinskys," he has left the reader with "a partial truth." Such partial truths are dangerous for the Jews because "anti-Semitism is a staple in the system in which we live."

Had Cahan indeed done what John Macy in a review in *The Dial* claims for the novel, the hazards would have been avoided. "The portrait of David Levinsky," writes Macy, "is a portrait of a society, not simply of the Jewish section of it, or of New York, but of American business. And business is business, whether done by Jew or Gentile. If Levinsky is a triumphant failure, he is so because American business, which shaped him to its ends, is, viewed from any decent regard for humanity, a miserable monster of success." As Schappes notes, "the few non-Jewish business men who appear in the volume fleetingly are all paragons of business virtue, of etiquette, of manners, of personal morality and of English speech."[70] Only the Jewish businessmen in the book are represented as less than scrupulous in both business and their private lives. It is apparent to the reader that Cahan was like Levinsky in his awe and emulation of "American" status and manners; his chary, almost reverent treatment of the non-Jewish businessmen in the novel is a manifestation of Cahan's contempt for the immigrant.

It will not do to dismiss these considerations. When the book was first published, there remained a huge mass of recently arrived shtetl Jews living in the teeming tenements. Racist theories of Anglo-Saxon or Teutonic superiority were quite respectable and the movement for immigration restriction was strong, so that the apprehensions of some Jews and non-Jewish liberals were not groundless. It should be recalled that the anti-Semitic atmosphere in 1915 permitted Leo Frank to be lynched in Georgia after conviction on a false charge of murdering a Christian girl. Under such conditions, a candid portrayal of ruthless pursuit of profit by a Jew in a totally Jewish milieu, as *David Levinsky* is, might readily serve to reinforce prejudiced attitudes. Since the end of World War II, however, the Jew has become such an accepted and familiar figure of American litera-

ture that Cahan's novel may be grasped as a trenchant depiction of
a talented, conflicted Jew who succumbs to the lure of money and
power at a given juncture in the development of industry in the
United States. The hazards to the "public image" of the Jew may
perhaps always be present in some degree, but the novel must be
recognized as the most talented contribution by a Jew to American
literature up to that time, a work of permanent interest.

A large degree of truth inheres in the judgment of Cahan's fiction
made in 1900 by Leo Stein, the brother of Gertrude Stein and a
student of esthetics. While Stein may have somewhat exaggerated
Cahan's "disinterested" attitude toward the fictional Jew, on the
whole his statement is precise.

> In the work of an American writer, Abraham Cahan [writes Stein]
> we have finally what we may call the disinterested attitude toward
> the Jew in fiction. By this I mean that the author writes about the
> Jew not because the Jew is more admirable than others or more
> interesting, but because the writer is interested in the delineation of
> human character in imaginative form, and deals with the Jew be-
> cause, having been born and bred in the ghetto, he knows the Jew
> better than he knows other kinds of men.[71]

This is, at the least, an objective judgment. But the novel is more:
it is Cahan's fictionalized evaluation of himself as a conflicted person
who chose success over integrity, a career as an exploiter and rein-
forcer of inferior journalism over a career as a writer devoted to
maintaining human dignity and integrity. It must be remembered by
those who would rush to his defense that this is Cahan's own judgment as revealed in the novel. But all was not lost—the best part of
Cahan must have derived great artistic satisfaction and comfort from
the awareness that he had produced the finest American Jewish
novel of the first century and a half of the American nation.

NOTES

INTRODUCTION

1 Morris U. Schappes, ed., *A Documentary History of the Jews in the United States, 1654–1875* (New York, 1950, 1971), p. 79.

2 Charles I. Glicksberg, "Anti-Semitism in American Literature," *Chicago Jewish Forum* 5, no. 3 (Spring 1947): 159,160.

3 Oscar Handlin, "How U. S. Anti-Semitism Really Began," *Commentary* 11 (1951):542; the same material appears in Handlin's *Adventures in Freedom: Three Hundred Years of Jewish Life in America* (New York, 1954), pp. 178–79, and in his "American Views of the Jews at the Opening of the Twentieth Century," *Publications of the American Jewish Historical Society* 40, pt. 4 (June 1951):326–27.

4 Charles Follen Adams, *Leedle Yawcob Strauss and Other Poems* (Boston and New York, 1878), pp. 50–52.

5 Handlin, *Commentary* 11: 542–43.

6 Isaac M. Wise, *Reminiscences,* trans. and ed. David Philipson (Cincinnati, 1901), p. 272.

7 Edgar Rosenberg has clearly enunciated this cogent idea in his *From Shylock to Svengali: Jewish Stereotypes in English Fiction* (Palo Alto, Cal., 1960), pp. 262–63, and passim.

8 Montagu Frank Modder, *The Jew in the Literature of England to the End of the Nineteenth Century* (Philadelphia, 1939), p. v. This book was reprinted in a paperback edition by Meridian Books (New York, 1960).

9 Rosenberg, *Shylock to Svengali,* p. 14.

10 Ibid., pp. 188, 15.

11 Cited in ibid., p. 18; emphasis added.

12 Lafcadio Hearn, *Occidental Gleanings,* ed. Albert Mordell, 2 vols. (New York, 1925) 2:170–89.

13 Lafcadio Hearn, *The Japanese Letters of Lafcadio Hearn,* ed. Elizabeth Bisland (Boston and New York, 1960), pp. 55, 374.

14 Elizabeth Larocque Tinker, *Lafcadio Hearn's American Days* (New York, 1924), pp. 366–70.

15 Sol Liptzin, *The Jew in American Literature* (New York, 1966), pp. 82–83.

16 Eleanor E. Simpson, "Melville and the Negro: From *Typee* to 'Benito Cereno'" *American Literature* 41, no. 1 (March 1969):19–38, passim.

17 F. O. Matthiessen, *American Renaissance* (New York, 1941), p. xv.

CHAPTER 1

1 Jacob Rader Marcus, *Early American Jewry, 1655–1790,* 2 vols. (Philadelphia, 1953), 2:524.
2 Sidney Kaplan, *The Black Presence in the Era of the American Revolution, 1770–1800* (Washington, D.C., 1973), p. 110.
3 Hannah Adams, *The History of the Jews from the Destruction of Jerusalem to the Nineteenth Century,* 2 vols. (Boston, 1812), 2:221.
4 Morris U. Schappes, ed., *A Documentary History of the Jews in the United States, 1654–1875* (New York, 1950), pp. 83, 80, 79.
5 Joseph L. Blau and Salo W. Baron, eds., *The Jews of the United States, 1790–1840: A Documentary History,* 3 vols. (New York, 1963), 1:12, 11.
6 Schappes, *Documentary History,* pp. 156, 92.
7 Henry James Pye, *The Democrat; or, Intrigues and Adventures of Jean Le Noir . . . ,* 2 vols. (New York, 1795), 1:vii; reprinted in Schappes, *Documentary History,* pp. 84–85.
8 Morris U. Schappes, "Anti-Semitism and Reaction, 1795–1800," *Publications of the American Jewish Historical Society* 38, pt. 2 (December 1948): 118; also in Schappes, *Documentary History,* p. 89.
9 Schappes, *PAJHS* 38:130.
10 Schappes, *Documentary History,* p. 73.
11 Isaac E. Barzilay, "The Jew in the Literature of the Enlightenment," *Jewish Social Studies* 18, no. 8 (October 1956): 251.
12 Arthur Hertzberg, *The French Enlightenment and the Jews* (New York, 1968), p. 303.
13 Thomas Jefferson, *The Complete Jefferson,* ed. Saul Padover (New York, 1943), pp. 950, 951, n. 2.
14 Thomas Paine, *The Complete Writings of Tom Paine,* Philip S. Foner, ed., 2 vols. (New York, 1945), 2:737. In contrast with the deistic condemnation is Emerson's more liberal and imaginative approach. "What would be base, or even obscene to the obscene," he said, "becomes illustrious spoken in a new connection of thought. The piety of the Hebrew prophets purges their grossness: the circumcision is an example of the power of poetry to raise the low and offensive" (cited in David Hirsch, "Jewish Identity and Jewish Suffering in Bellow, Malamud, and Philip Roth," *Jewish Book Annual* [New York, 1971–72], 29:17).
15 Paine, *Complete Writings,* p. 837.
16 W. E. Woodward, *Tom Paine, America's Godfather, 1737–1809* (New York, 1945), p. 264.
17 Thomas Paine, *Representative Selections,* ed. Harry Hayden Clark (New York, 1944), p. xxx, n. 77.
18 Edmund Wilson, "The Jews," *A Piece of My Mind* (New York, 1956), pp. 90 ff.
19 M. J. K[ohler], "Daniel Webster and the Jews," *Publications of the American Jewish Historical Society* 11 (1903): 187.

20 Diary entry for June 8, 1782, in Morris Jastrow, "References to Jews in the Diary of Ezra Stiles," *Publications of the American Jewish Historical Society* 10 (1902):16.

21 Quoted in Adams, *History of the Jews,* 2:214–15.

22 Benjamin Rush, *Letters of Benjamin Rush,* ed. L. H. Butterfield, 2 vols. (Princeton, 1951), 1:431.

23 Quoted in Rabbi David Max Eichhorn, "A History of Christian Attempts to Convert the Jews of the United States and Canada" (Ph.D. diss., Hebrew Union College, 1938), p. 64. Rabbi Eichhorn kindly permitted me to consult his copy of this work.

24 Adams, *History of the Jews,* 2:325–26.

25 *Israel Vindicated; Being a Refutation of the Calumnies Propagated Respecting the Jewish Nation, in Which the Objects and Views of the American Society for Meliorating the Conditions of the Jews Are Investigated,* by an Israelite (New York, 1820), p. vi.

26 Quoted in Blau and Baron, *Jews of the U.S.,* 1:677–79.

27 John Pierpont, *Airs of Palestine and Other Poems* (Boston, 1840), pp. 44, 334.

28 Ibid., pp. 188–89.

29 Robert Treat Paine, Jr., *The Works, in Verse and Prose, of Robert Treat Paine, Jr.* (Boston, 1812), p. 292.

30 Philip Freneau, *The Poems of Philip Freneau,* ed. Fred Lewis Pattee, 3 vols. (Princeton, 1902), 1:3–14, 28, 41.

31 Ibid., pp. 75, 53, 54, 56.

32 Ibid., p. 126; 2:267.

33 Philip Freneau, *The Prose of Philip Freneau,* ed. Philip M. Marsh (New Brunswick, N. J., 1955), p. 265.

34 Ibid., p. 199.

35 Robert Slender, O.S.M. [Philip Freneau], *Letters on Various and Important Subjects, . . .* (Philadelphia, 1799), p. 76.

36 Marsh, *Prose of Philip Freneau,* p. 435.

37 Pattee, *Poems of Philip Freneau,* 3:78; 2:185, 186, 187, 199; 3:129.

38 Ibid., 3:110; 2:174, 177.

39 On the history of United States relations with the Barbary States, see Louis B. Wright and Julia H. MacLeod, *First Americans in North Africa* (Princeton, 1945).

40 *Naval Documents Relating to the United States War with the Barbary Powers* (Washington, D. C., 1939), 1:337, 570.

41 Wright and MacLeod, *First Americans in North Africa,* p. 42.

42 Mordecai M. Noah, *Travels in England, France, Spain, and the Barbary States in the Years 1813–14 and 15* (New York, 1819), pp. 157–58.

43 Ibid., pp. 1, 309–10.

44 Ibid., p. 309.

45 Royall Tyler, *Four Lost Plays,* ed. A. W. Peach and G. F. Newbrough (Princeton, 1941).

46 Royall Tyler, *The Algerine Captive; or, The Life and Adventures of Doctor Updike Underhill, Six Years a Prisoner among the Algerines,* 2 vols. (London, 1802), 1:xii, 166, 189.

47 Ibid., 2:182.

48 Ibid., pp. 183, 184, 186.

49 Ibid., pp. 133, 169, 170.

50 Ibid., pp. 148, 216, 227.

51 James Butler, *Fortune's Football: or, The Adventures of Mercutio, Founded on Matters of Fact,* 2 vols. (Harrisburg, Pa., 1797–98), 1:27.

52 Ibid., 2:142.

53 Ibid., pp. 142, 157.

54 Charles Brockden Brown, *Arthur Mervyn; or, Memoirs of the Year 1783* (New York, 1962), p. 417.

55 Ibid., p. 416.

56 David Lee Clark, *Charles Brockden Brown, Pioneer Voice of America* (Durham, N.C., 1952), pp. 181, 195.

57 Harry R. Werfel, *Charles Brockden Brown, American Gothic Novelist* (Gainesville, Fla., 1949), p. 96.

58 Brown, *Arthur Mervyn,* p. 397.

59 Ibid., pp. 116–17, 399.

60 Ibid., p. 398.

61 Ibid., pp. 398–99.

62 Ibid., p. 400.

63 Hugh Henry Brackenridge, *Modern Chivalry; or, The Adventures of Captain John Farrago and Teague O'Regan His Servant,* ed. C. M. Nesolin (New York, 1937), pp. 762, 570, 782.

64 Washington Irving, *Salmagundi; or, The Whim-Whams and Opinions of Launcelot Langstaff, Esq. and Others* (New York, 1905), p. 431.

65 Washington Irving, *Knickerbocker's History of New York* (New York, 1883), pp. 51, 60.

CHAPTER 2

1 John Higham, "Social Discrimination against Jews in America, 1830–1930," *Publications of the American Jewish Historical Society* 47, no. 1 (September 1957):3.

2 Cornelius Matthews, "The Ghost of New York," *The Spirit of the Times* 14 (January 11, 1845) 1844/45):544; reprinted from *The Democratic Review* (January 1845).

3 See Joseph Jackson, "George Lippard: Misunderstood Man of Letters," *Pennsylvania Magazine of History and Biography* 59, no. 4 (October 1935):376–91; "George Lippard," *Dictionary of American Biography;* Alexander Cowie, *The Rise of the American Novel* (New York, 1948), pp. 319–26. Leslie Fiedler has applied his imaginative talents to an apologia for George Lippard in an essay, "The Male Novel" (*Partisan Review* 27, no. 1 [1970]:74–89). He makes several careless assertions about Lippard, it seems to me. His notion that Lippard's "very existence was kept a secret in the official histories of the novel" (p. 74) until Alexander Cowie mentioned him in 1948 seems to me dubious. Lippard was only one of innumerable popular novelists who went unmentioned in the histories of American literature until the appearance in recent years of more comprehensive works of literary scholarship. If Lippard has been deliberately suppressed, how does Fiedler

explain the fact that the *Dictionary of American Biography* includes him, while no mention is made of Mrs. E. D. E. N. Southworth, who was a far better-selling novelist than Lippard, and a proper Victorian to boot? If Fiedler believes Lippard "an immensely attractive figure" (p. 74), he is entitled to his judgment of taste. But one must challenge his designation of Lippard as a "convinced socialist" (p. 79) who has been overlooked by "Marxist critics" because he was not a "properly pious Socialist" (p. 75). It is true that Lippard hated the rich and urged a class war by labor. But the mumbo-jumbo secret organization that he formed and his general excesses identify him as a crackpot, rather than a serious socialist influence.

4 George Lippard, *The Quaker City; or, The Monks of Monk Hall, a Romance of Philadelphia, Life, Mystery, and Crime*, 2 vols. in 1, 27th ed. (Philadelphia, 1849), p. 4.

5 Cowie, *American Novel*, p. 319.

6 Lippard, *Quaker City*, p. 30.

7 Ibid., pp. 149, 202, 413.

8 George Lippard, *The Empire City; or, New York by Night and Day. Its Aristocracy and Its Dollars* (Philadelphia, 1864), p. 205.

9 Charles F. Briggs, *The Adventures of Harry Franco, a Tale of the Great Panic*, 2 vols. (New York, 1839), 1:49, 50.

10 Harry Franco [Charles F. Briggs], *Bankrupt Stories* (running title, *The Haunted Merchant*) (New York, 1843), pp. 188, 310.

11 B. C. F. [Charles F. Briggs], *Working a Passage; or, Life in a Liner* (New York, 1844), title page.

12 Ibid., pp. 48, 50.

13 Luke Shortfield [John Beauchamp Jones], *The Western Merchant, a narrative containing useful instruction for the Western man of business who makes his purchases in the East; also, information for the Eastern man whose customers are in the West: Otherwise, hints for those who design emigrating to the West; deduced from actual experience* (Philadelphia, 1849), pp. 128, 133, 134, 143.

14 Ibid., pp. 183, 184.

15 John Beauchamp Jones, *Life and Adventures of a Country Merchant, a narrative of his exploits at home, during his travels, and in the cities, designed to amuse and instruct* (Philadelphia, 1877 [c1854], p. 337.

16 Ibid., pp. 366, 369, 371–72, 347.

17 John Beauchamp Jones, *The Winkles; or, The Merry Monomaniacs* (New York, 1855), pp. 33, 34, 40, 169, 170, 392.

18 John Beauchamp Jones, *Border War: A Tale of Disunion* (New York, 1859), pp. 74, 157, 159. This novel was also published in Philadelphia in 1859 under the title *Wild Southern Scenes. A Tale of Disunion and Border War.*

19 George G. Foster, *New York by Gaslight* (New York, 1850), pp. 58, 59.

20 Peter Hamilton Myers, *The Miser's Heir; or, The Young Millionaire* (Philadelphia, 1854), pp. 90, 91, 92.

21 Samuel Longfellow, *The Life of Henry Wadsworth Longfellow, with extracts from his journals and correspondence*, 3 vols. (Boston, 1891), 1:312; 2:35.

22 *Knickerbocker* 30 (1847):556.

23 J. H. Ingraham, *Moloch, the Money-Lender; or, The Beautiful Jewess,* De Witt's Ten Cent Romances no. 38 (New York, 1869 [c1843]), pp. 17, 20, 59, 63, 18, 21, 24, 32. Also published under the title *The Clipper-Yacht; or, Moloch, the Money-Lender: A Tale of London and the Thames* (Boston, 1845).

24 Ibid., pp. 35, 96, 39.

25 Ibid., pp. 61, 63, 64, 94, 100.

26 J. H. Ingraham, *Romero* (New York, 1869), p. 90.

27 [J. H. Ingraham], *The Sunny South; or, The Southerner at Home, embracing five years of experience in the land of sugar and cotton* (Philadelphia, 1860), pp. 5, 59. This novel was reprinted in 1880 under the new title *Not "A Fool's Errand," Life and Experiences of a Northern Governess in the Sunny South,* as a kind of reply to Albion Tourgee's, *A Fool's Errand* (New York, 1879), which was a relentless exposure of the anti-Negro forces in the South, such as the Ku Klux Klan, which frustrated Reconstruction.

28 Ibid., pp. 307–8.

29 Ibid., pp. 400–401

30 Ibid., p. 401.

31 Ibid., pp. 401–4.

32 Mrs. E. D. E. N. Southworth, *The Bridal Eve* (Philadelphia, 1864), pp. 383, 384.

33 Mrs. E. D. E. N. Southworth, *Allworth Abbey* (Philadelphia, 1865), pp. 143, 144.

34 Mrs. E. D. E. N. Southworth, *Miriam, the Avenger; or, The Missing Bride* (Philadelphia, n.d. [1854–55]), pp. 630, 85, 119, 184, 454.

35 Frank Luther Mott, *Golden Multitudes: The Story of Best Sellers in the United States* (New York, 1947), p. 136.

36 Mrs. E. D. E. N. Southworth, *Ishmael; or, In the Depths* (Philadelphia, 1884 [c1864]), pp. 154, 155, 191, 194, 202, 204.

37 Mrs. E. D. E. N. Southworth, *Self-Raised; or, From the Depths* (New York 1884 [c1865]), pp. 38, 434.

38 Fitz-James O'Brien, "The Diamond Lens," *The Diamond Lens and Other Stories* (New York, 1885), pp. 10, 21. The story first appeared in the *Atlantic Monthly* for January 1858.

39 William Barrett [Joseph A. Scoville], *Vigor* (New York, 1864), pp. 47, 33, 34. This novel was also published in London in 1864 under the title *Marion* and the pen name "Manhattan." During the 1860s Scoville published at least four volumes under the title *The Old Merchants of New York City,* authored by the pseudonymous William Barrett.

40 Ibid., pp. 295, 297, 200–201.

41 Nathaniel Parker Willis, "The Gypsy of Sardis," *Inklings of Adventure,* 2 vols. (New York, 1836), 2:26, 44, 37, 26.

42 Nathaniel Parker Willis, *Poems, Sacred, Passionate, and Humorous* (New York, 1850).

43 [John Lothrop Motley], *Morton's Hope; or, Memoirs of a Young Provincial,* 2 vols. (New York, 1839), 1:197, 198.

44 S. B. Beckett, "The Jewess of Cairo," *Ladies Home Companion* 14 (1840–41):276.

45 B. Parley Poore [Sylvanus Cobb], *The Mameluke; or, The Sign of the Mystic Tie: A Tale of the Camp and Court of Bonaparte* (Boston, 1852), pp. 9, 27, 22, 53.

46 [Theodore Sedgwick Fay], *The Countess Ida, a Tale of Berlin,* 2 vols. (New York, 1840), 1:91; 2:248.

47 [Theodore Sedgwick Fay], *Sidney Clifton; or, Vicissitudes in Both Hemispheres. A Tale of the Nineteenth Century,* 2 vols. (New York, 1839), 1:140–41.

48 Ibid., pp. 142, 143, 146, 147.

49 Ibid., pp. 156, 164, 166–67; 2:136–37.

50 Joseph Jonas, "The Jews of Ohio," *Occident,* 1844, pp. 143–47; cited in Morris U. Schappes, *A Documentary History of the Jews in the United States, 1654–1875* (New York, 1950), p. 231.

51 Leopold Mayer, "Recollections of Chicago in 1850–1851," *Chicago Journal,* November 14, 1899, p. 5; cited in Schappes, *Documentary History,* p. 310.

52 Israel T. Naamani, "Gold Rush Days," *Commentary* 6, no. 3 (September 1948):265.

53 Higham, *PAJHS* 47:5.

54 "Present State of the Jewish People in Learning and Culture," *North American Review* 83 (1856):368.

55 Mrs. Sarah Hall, "Miss Edgeworth and the Jews," *Selections from the Writings of Mrs. Sarah Hall* (Philadelphia, 1833) pp. 57–60; cited in Joseph L. Blau and Salo W. Baron, eds., *The Jews of the United States, 1790–1840: A Documentary History,* 3 vols. (New York, 1963), 2:682, 683, 682.

56 For material relevant to the story and its author, see Curtis Carroll Davis, "*Judith Bensaddi* and the Reverend Doctor Henry Ruffner," *Publications of the American Jewish Historical Society* 39, pt. 2 (December 1949): 115–42. In my treatment I am indebted to Davis's article.

57 [Henry Ruffner], "Judith Bensaddi: A Tale, Second edition, revised and enlarged by the author," *Southern Literary Messenger* 5, no. 7 (July 1839):471.

58 Ibid., pp. 485, 491.

59 Ibid., p. 491.

60 Ibid., pp. 493, 498.

61 Ibid., pp. 499, 500, 501, 505.

62 [Henry Ruffner], "Seclusavel; or, the Sequel to the Tale of 'Judith Bensaddi,' " *Southern Literary Messenger* 5 (1839):638–63.

63 Davis, *PAJHS* 39:137, 138, n. 58.

64 Maxwell Whiteman, "Notions, Dry Goods, and Clothing: An Introduction to the Study of the Cincinnati Peddler," *Jewish Quarterly Review* 53 (1963):307.

65 Rudolf Glanz, "Notes on Early Jewish Peddling in America," *Jewish Social Studies* 7, no. 2 (April 1945):120.

66 Otto Ruppius, *The Peddler, a Romance of American Life* (Cincinnati, 1887 [c1857]), pp. 8, 12, 19, 27.

67 Bertram W. Korn, "Jews and Negro Slavery in the Old South, 1789–1865," *Publications of the American Jewish Historical Society* 50, no. 3 (March 1961):191, 200. However, Louis Ruchames shows in his

article "The Abolitionists and the Jews," ibid. 52, no. 2 (December 1952):131–55, that Dr. Korn distorts both the character of the abolitionists and their attitude toward the Jews in his book *American Jewry and the Civil War* (Philadelphia, 1951).

68 This modification occurs in the paperback edition of Korn's book (Meridian, 1961), p. xx.

69 *Occident* 18 (November 8, 1860):197; 19 (September 1861):253.

70 *Israelite* 7 (February 6, 1861):244.

71 Cited in Schappes, *Documentary History,* p. 438.

72 Kate E. R. Packard, *The Kidnapped and the Ransomed* (New York, 1941 [c1856]), pp. 166, 167, 172. A facsimile edition of this book was published by the Jewish Publication Society in 1970 with a long introduction by Maxwell Whiteman, which recounts the relations of Jews with the antislavery movement. See criticism of Mr. Whiteman's introduction by Morris U. Schappes, *Jewish Currents,* September 1971, pp. 22–23; and the review by Louis Ruchames in *American Jewish Historical Quarterly* 60, no. 4 (July 1971).

73 Packard, *The Kidnapped and the Ransomed,* pp. 177, 178.

74 "The Jews," *Boston Journal,* reprinted in *Jewish Intelligencer,* June 1837; cited in Lee M. Friedman, *The American Society for Meliorating the Condition of the Jews and Joseph S. C. F. Frey, Its Missionary* (Boston, 1925), pp. 19, 20 (pamphlet).

CHAPTER 3

1 Sol Liptzin, *The Jew in American Literature* (New York, 1966), p. 52.

2 William Cullen Bryant, *Prose Writings of William Cullen Bryant,* ed. Parke Goodwin, 2 vols. (New York, 1884), 2:357, 358.

3 William Cullen Bryant, *Letters of a Traveller* (New York, 1850), p. 407.

4 William Cullen Bryant, "Bryant's Criticism on Shylock as Portrayed by Edwin Booth," *Israelite* 12, no. 52 (June 29, 1866):410–11. This appearance of the article was a reprint, but I have been unable to locate the original source. The same review is cited by Toby Lelyveld, *Shylock on the Stage* (Cleveland, 1960), p. 75, as "an unidentified clipping in Edwin Booth's prompt-book, Folger Shakespeare Library."

5 Ibid.

6 Ibid.

7 John Greenleaf Whittier, *The Poetical Works of John Greenleaf Whittier* (Boston and New York, 1892), pp. 413, 255, 257, 256, 257, 70.

8 Ibid., pp. 84, 86, 83.

9 Liptzin, *The Jew in American Literature,* p. 49.

10 Whittier, *Poetical Works,* p. 334.

11 Oliver Wendell Holmes, *The Poetical Works of Oliver Wendell Holmes* (Boston, 1895), p. 28.

12 Cited in Oscar Kraines, "The Holmes Tradition," *Publications of the American Jewish Historical Society* 42, no. 4 (June 1953):346. See also Leon Huhner, *The Life of Judah Touro* (Philadelphia, 1946), pp. 62–63; 162–63.

13 Holmes, *Poetical Works,* pp. 152, 312–14.

14 *American Hebrew* 42, no. 9 (April 4, 1890):169, 193, 194.

15 Ibid., p. 193.

16 Quoted in Kraines, *PAJHS* 42:345.

17 Oliver Wendell Holmes, *Papers from an Old Volume of Life: A Collection of Essays, 1857–1881* (Boston, 1892), p. 47 (vol. 8 of *The Writings of Oliver Wendell Holmes* [Cambridge, Mass., 1871]).

18 Oliver Wendell Holmes, *Over the Teacups* (Boston, 1892), pp. 194, 195, 197 (vol. 4 of the *Writings*).

19 Holmes, *Poetical Works,* pp. 245–46.

20 John J. Appel, "Henry Wadsworth Longfellow's Presentation of the Spanish Jews," *Publications of the American Jewish Historical Society* 45, no. 1 (September 1955):23.

21 Emma Lazarus, *Emma Lazarus: Selections from Her Poetry and Prose,* ed. Morris U. Schappes, 3d ed. (New York, 1967), p. 99. Reprinted from Emma Lazarus, "Henry Wadsworth Longfellow," *American Hebrew,* April 14, 1882.

22 Cited in Appel, *PAJHS* 45:22.

23 Henry Wadsworth Longfellow, *The Complete Poetical Works of Henry Wadsworth Longfellow* (Boston, 1902), p. 189.

24 Ibid., p. 522.

25 Samuel Longfellow, *The Life of Henry Wadsworth Longfellow with extracts from his journals and correspondence,* 3 vols. (Boston, 1891), 2:239.

26 John J. Appel's interpretation of this line strikes me as unconvincing: "Longfellow's prediction that a Jewish nation would not rise again was perhaps as much a tribute to the idea of universal brotherhood and world amity, resulting in the eventual elimination and extinction of national differences, as the denial of the Jews' ability to reconstruct their nationhood" (p. 26). Longfellow obviously took no stock in the current millenarian ideas of an imminent Second Coming, and there is no evidence that he thought of the Jews in the political sense suggested by Appel. On the contrary, in an early version of the poem he ended with a stanza foretelling that, after long wandering, the Jews "only from the hillock of the grave,/ With dying eyes beheld the Promised Land" (Appel, p. 27).

27 Longfellow, *Complete Poetical Works,* pp. 235–36.

28 Cited in Appel, p. 27, from Henry Wadsworth Longfellow Dana, "The Hebrew Cemetery," *Touro Synagogue of Congregation Jeshuat Israel,* The Society of the Friends of Touro Synagogue (Newport, R.I., 1948), p. 44.

29 Longfellow, *Complete Poetical Works,* p. 464. I am informed that this is not true: Hebrew *does* have a present tense.

30 Longfellow, *Life of Henry Wadsworth Longfellow,* 2:162.

31 Longfellow, *Complete Poetical Works,* pp. 246–47.

32 Ibid., p. 861, note to p. 251.

33 Ibid., pp. 254, 307, 254.

34 Ibid., p. 312.

35 [James Russell Lowell], "D'Israeli's *Tancred,*" *North American Review* 65 (1847): 212–13, 213.

36 James Russell Lowell, *The Complete Poetical Works of James Russell Lowell* (Boston, 1896), pp. 158, 99.

37 James Russell Lowell, *Complete Writings of James Russell Lowell,* 16 vols. (Boston, 1904), 16:29, 60.

38 *Atlantic Monthly* 179 (January 1897): 128. The writer has been identified as Sarah Butler Wister, mother of Owen Wister.

39 Lowell, *Complete Writings,* 7:15–16.

40 Leslie Stephen to Charles Eliot Norton, February 11, 1892, in ibid., 16:335, 336.

41 *Atlantic Monthly* 179 (January 1897): 128, 129.

CHAPTER 4

1 Bliss Perry, *Life and Letters of Henry Lee Higginson* (Boston, 1921), p. 125.

2 Ralph L. Rusk, *The Life of Ralph Waldo Emerson* (New York, 1949), p. 180. It is an indication of how little the Jew in American literature has been studied that Alfred Kazin could write that, when Emerson first met Emma Lazarus in 1868, she was "the first Jew" he "ever met" (*The Ghetto and Beyond,* ed. Peter I. Rose [New York, 1969], p. 421).

3 Henry D. Thoreau, *The Journals of Henry D. Thoreau,* ed. B. Torray and F. H. Allen, 14 vols. (Boston, 1949), 2:471.

4 Emily Dickinson, *The Complete Poems of Emily Dickinson,* ed. Thomas H. Johnson (Boston, 1960), pp. 102–3, 113, 143–44, 140–41, poems number 223, 247, 304, 299.

5 Mason Wade, *Margaret Fuller: Whetstone of Genius* (New York, 1940), p. 163.

6 Margaret Fuller, *Margaret Fuller, American Romantic: A Selection from her Writings and Correspondence,* ed. Perry Miller (New York, 1963), p. 202.

7 Cited in Wade, *Margaret Fuller,* p. 180.

8 Ralph Waldo Emerson, *The Letters of Ralph Waldo Emerson,* ed. Ralph L. Rusk, 6 vols. (New York, 1939), 1:227, 327.

9 Ralph Waldo Emerson, *The Journals and Miscellaneous Notebooks of Ralph Waldo Emerson* (Cambridge, Mass., 1960–69), 7:221–22.

10 Ralph Waldo Emerson, *The Complete Works of Ralph Waldo Emerson,* 12 vols. (Boston, 1921), 7:35.

11 Emerson, *Journals,* 4:156, 181–82; 3:8, 61.

12 Emerson, *Complete Works,* 11:490.

13 Philip L. Nicoloff, *Emerson on Race and History* (New York, 1961), p. 130.

14 Emerson, *Complete Works,* 6:16.

15 Ralph Waldo Emerson, *Journals of Ralph Waldo Emerson,* ed. Edward Waldo Emerson and Waldo Emerson Forbes (Boston and New York, 1914), 10:199.

16 Walt Whitman, *The Complete Poetry and Prose of Walt Whitman, as Prepared by Him for the Deathbed Edition* [1892], 2 vols. in 1 (New York, 1954), 2:397.

17 Ibid., 1:172, 174.

18 Ibid., 2:396; 1:106, 94.

19 Walt Whitman, *New York Dissected* (New York, 1936), p. 123.

20 The story is renamed "One Single Impulse" in Walt Whitman, *The Early Poems and Fiction.* This book is volume 2 of the *Collected Writings of Walt Whitman* (New York, 1963). Citations are from pp. 311, 313, 314.

21 Whitman, *Complete Poetry,* 1:155, 233; 2:490.

CHAPTER 5

1 Nathaniel Hawthorne, *Passages from the American Notebooks* (Boston and New York, 1896), p. 31.

2 Cited in Edmund Clarence Stedman, ed., *An American Anthology, 1787–1900* (Boston and New York, 1900), p. 191. The poem was originally published in an annual, *Scenes in the Life of Our Saviour by the Poets and Painters,* ed. R. W. Griswold (1845).

3 Nathaniel Hawthorne, *Passages from the French and Italian Notebooks of Nathaniel Hawthorne* (Boston, 1899), pp. 54, 89.

4 Nathaniel Hawthorne, *The Marble Faun,* in *The Complete Novels and Selected Tales* (New York, 1937), p. 813. This one-volume edition is hereafter cited as *Complete Novels.*

5 Ibid., p. 602.

6 Nathaniel Hawthorne, *The English Notebooks,* ed. Randall Stewart (New York, 1941), p. 321.

7 Ibid.

8 Nathaniel Hawthorne, *Our Old Home,* vol. 5 of the Centenary Edition (Columbus, O., 1970), pp. 336, 337.

9 Nathaniel Hawthorne, "A Select Party," *Mosses from an Old Manse,* 2 vols. in 1 (Boston, 1894), 1:70.

10 Nathaniel Hawthorne, "A Virtuoso's Collection," ibid., 2:276.

11 Ibid., pp. 270, 277.

12 Hawthorne, *Complete Novels,* pp. 1194, 1189.

13 Ibid., pp. 1191, 1192, In the *American Notebooks* Hawthorne describes an encounter with a traveling "old Dutchman" (p. 56) who speaks with "a strange, outlandish accent" (p. 58) and exhibits a diorama. The traveling man *may* have been Jewish, for in those days German Jews were often not distinguished from non-Jewish German immigrants. But Hawthorne makes no explicit suggestion that the "Dutchman" was Jewish.

14 Hawthorne, *Complete Novels,* pp. 617, 609.

15 Ibid., pp. 837, 617.

16 Ibid., p. 837.

17 Ibid., pp. 606, 607, 608, 609.

18 Ibid., p. 710.

19 Ibid., pp. 753, 854.

20 Nathaniel Hawthorne, *Septimius Felton,* vol. 11 in *Hawthorne's Works* (Boston and New York, 1883), pp. 242, 269, 275.

21 Hawthorne, *American Notebooks,* p. 117.

CHAPTER 6

1 Nathalia Wright, *Melville's Use of the Bible* (Durham, N. C., 1949), p. 16.

2 Leon Howard, *Herman Melville* (Berkeley, 1951), p. 37.

3 Herman Melville, *Journal of a Visit to London and the Continent,* ed. Eleanor M. Metcalf (Cambridge, Mass., 1948), pp. 27–28; see also p. 74.

4 Jay Leyda, *The Melville Log,* 2 vols. (New York, 1951), 2:756. I owe this speculation, as well as the possibility that David Davidson may have been Jewish, to Jay Leyda (letter to this writer).

5 Herman Melville, *Redburn,* ch. 4. Citations from Melville's novels will hereafter be made by chapter number.

6 Ibid., ch. 40.

7 Herman Melville, *Omoo,* ch. 14.

8 Melville, *Redburn,* ch. 56.

9 Herman Melville, *White Jacket,* chs. 31, 36.

10 Herman Melville, *Moby Dick,* ch. 92.

11 Herman Melville, *The Confidence Man,* ch. 22.

12 Herman Melville, *Mardi,* ch. 19.

13 Herman Melville, *Pierre,* bk. 1, sec. 3.

14 Melville, *Redburn,* ch. 33.

15 Melville, *The Confidence Man,* ch. 26.

16 Heinrich Heine, *Complete Poems,* trans. Edgar Alfred Bowring (London, 1861), p. xix.

17 Leyda, *Melville Log,* 2:760.

18 Nathaniel Hawthorne, *The English Notebooks,* ed. Randall Stewart (New York, 1941), pp. 432–33.

19 Herman Melville, *Clarel, a Poem and a Pilgrimage in the Holy Land,* ed. Walter E. Bezanson (New York, 1960), 1.31.37–38; 4.35.27, 30, 33–34. All citations from *Clarel* will be made from this edition. I am indebted to Professor Bezanson for his informative notes.

20 Ibid., 1.8.23–25, 27–29.

21 Herman Melville, *Journal of a Visit to Europe and the Levant, October 11–May 6, 1857,* ed. Howard C. Horsford (Princeton, 1955), p. 154. Hereafter cited as Horsford.

22 *Clarel,* 1.33.57–59.

23 Horsford, pp. 157, 159.

24 *Clarel,* 1.16.78; 3.21.278.

25 Horsford, pp. 119, 118, 123–34, 151.

26 In *Pierre,* Melville had already expressed his view of Judaism's inferiority to Christianity. The Plinlimmon Pamphlet asserts that "the reason why his [Christ's] teachings seemed folly to the Jews, was because he carried that Heaven's time in Jerusalem, while the Jews carried Jerusalem time there" (bk. 14, sec. 3).

27 *Clarel,* 1.41.42–43; 4.9.130–36.

28 Even in *Clarel* Melville occasionally slips into cliché, as when the abbot of Mar Saba monastery allows Derwent to see the precious jewels of the place. The monk, writes Melville, "felt of them lovingly . . ./ While fondling them (in a way, alack, of Jew his coins)" (3.23.90, 94–95).

29 Ibid., 1.24.30–31.
30 Ibid., 2.21.37, 38, 11; 2.27.189; 2.39.123.
31 Ibid., 1.24.32–34; 2.20.91–96.
32 Ibid., 2.20.12–20.
33 Ibid., 2.22.6–7, 28–30, 107, 133.
34 Ibid., 1.17.230–31, 265–66.
35 Horsford, p. 16.
36 Ibid., p. 143.
37 For Cresson's career, see Abraham J. Karp, "The Zionism of Warder Cresson," in *Early History of American Zionism,* ed. Isidore S. Meyer (New York, 1958), pp. 1–20; and Warder Cresson, *The Key of David* (Philadelphia, 1852).
38 *Clarel,* 1.16.178; p. 546.
39 Ibid., 1.16.163–65; 1.24.59–60, 81–82; 1.27.100–101.
40 Horsford, p. 157.
41 *Clarel,* 1.27.21–23, 72–73; p. 530.
42 Ibid., 4.35.26.
43 Ibid., 1.2.84–85, 74.
44 Ibid., 1.2.3–4.
45 Horsford, p. 132.
46 *Clarel,* 4.26.21, 29–31, 216–17, 235–37, 247–48.
47 Ibid., 4.28.126, 128, 144–49.

CHAPTER 7

1 Edmund Clarence Stedman, ed., *An American Anthology, 1787–1900* (New York, 1900), p. 19.
2 On the relations of Jews and Mormons, see Rudolf Glanz, *Jew and Mormon, Historic Group Relations and Religious Outlook* (New York, 1963).
3 Edward W. Tullidge, *Ben Israel; or, From under the Curse: A Jewish Play* (Salt Lake City, 1887 [c1875]).
4 A Unitarian Christian, "Letter to the Jews of This Country," *Christian Examiner and General Review* 15 (September 1833): 39.
5 "On Judah's Hill," *Western Cincinnati Journal,* 1836, p. 365; cited in Glanz, *Jew and Mormon,* p. 97.
6 From Rufus Wilmot Griswold, ed., *The Poets and Poetry of America,* additions by R. H. Stoddard (New York, 1873), p. 320.
7 Lydia Maria Child, *Letters from New York* (New York, 1843), pp. 25, 25–26, 28, 31, 33.
8 Lydia Maria Child, *The Progress of Religious Ideas,* 3 vols. (New York, 1855), 2:152–53, 153.
9 Jones Very, *Poems and Essays,* rev. ed., (Boston, 1886), p. 88.
10 Johnson Pierson, *The Judiad; a poem: detailing the rise and decline of the Jews from the Exodus from Egypt to the Destruction of their Temple by the Romans* (Saint Louis, 1844), pp. vii, ix, 101.
11 Henry James, *William Wetmore Story and His Friends, from letters, diaries, and recollections,* 2 vols. (Edinburgh and London, 1903), 1:303, 304.
12 William Wetmore Story, *Poems,* 2 vols. (Boston, 1886), 1:28, 37, 40, 46, 47, 49.

13 Ibid., pp. 58, 59, 60, 61, 62.

14 Ibid., pp. 65, 77, 80, 81.

15 Van Wyck Brooks, *The Flowering of New England* (New York, 1936), p. 476.

16 William W. Story, *Roba di Roma,* 2 vols. (London, 1866 [1st ed., 1862]), 2:106, 110–11.

17 Ibid., pp. 114, 115, 152.

18 Story, *Poems,* 2:257.

19 Mrs. Crawford, "The Crusader's Song to the Hebrew Maiden," and "The Hebrew Maiden's Answer," in *The Jews of the United States, 1790–1840: A Documentary History,* ed. Joseph L. Blau and Salo W. Baron, 3 vols. (New York, 1963), 3:679–80; reprinted from *The Ladies Garland* 2, no. 3 (1839):76.

20 Phoebe A. Hanaford, *From Shore to Shore, and Other Poems* (Boston, 1870), pp. 256, 256–57.

21 Winthrop S. Hudson, *Religion in America* (New York, 1965), p. 129.

22 Quoted in A. Stewart Walsh, *Mary: The Queen of the House of David and the Mother of Jesus, the Story of Her Life* (New York, 1886), p. v.

23 James A. Hillhouse, *Dramas, Discourses, and Other Pieces,* 2 vols. (Boston, 1839), 2:81, 82–83, 88–89.

24 Ibid., pp. 88–89.

25 Maria T. Richards, *Life in Israel; or, Portraitures of Hebrew Character* (New York, 1857), pp. vii, viii.

26 American Sunday School Union, *Hadassah, the Jewish Orphan* (Philadelphia, 1834), pp. 24–25, 106, 112.

27 Jarvis Gregg, *Selumiel; or, A Visit to Jerusalem; and the Most Interesting Scenes in and around It* (Philadelphia, 1833), pp. 80–81, 100.

28 *Iddo, An Historical Sketch Illustrating Jewish History During the Time of the Maccabees, B.C., 167–150* (Philadelphia, 1841), p. 181.

29 B.E.E. [Emma Elizabeth Brown], *From Night to Light* (Boston, 1872), p. 56.

30 [Samuel] Duffield Osborne, *The Spell of Ashteroth* (New York, 1888), p. 77.

31 Aunt Friendly [Mrs. Sarah Schoonmaker (Tuthill) Baker], *The Jewish Twins* (New York, 1860), pp. 33, 159, 54, 134.

32 Ibid., pp. 184, 205.

33 C. A. O[gden], *Into the Light; or, The Jewess* (Boston, 1899 [c1867]), p. 291.

34 Ibid., pp. 5, 52, 300, 322.

35 Aunt Hattie [Harriette Newell Baker], *Lost but Found; or, The Jewish Home* (Boston, 1871 [c1866]), pp. 36, 41, 43, 44, 45.

36 Ibid., p. 231.

37 Mrs. Madeline Leslie [Harriette Newell Baker], *Rebecca the Jewess* (Boston, 1879), p. 157.

38 Susan Warner, *The House in Town* (New York, 1872 [c1871]), pp. 40, 193, 233.

39 Annie Fellows Johnston, *In League with Israel, a Tale of the Chattanooga Conference* (New York and Cincinnati, 1896), pp. 32, 34, 134, 187, 188, 197, 73, 303.

40 S. Jane [Picken] Cohen, *Henry Luria; or, The Little Jewish Convert; Being Contained in the Memoir of Mrs. S. J. Cohen, Relict of the Reverend Doctor A. H. Cohen, Late Rabbi of the Synagogue of Richmond, Va.* (New York, 1860), pp. 51, 75, 87. For a brief historical account of this actual mixed marriage, see Edwin Wolf, 2nd, and Maxwell Whiteman, *The History of the Jews of Philadelphia from Colonial Times to the Age of Jackson* (Philadelphia, 1957), pp. 237–38.

41 Cohen, *Henry Luria*, pp. 89, 118, 136–37.

42 William Ware, *Zenobia; or, The Fall of Palmyra*, 2 vols. (New York and Boston, 1843), 1:7, 10, 11, 13. In its first appearance in 1837 this book came out under the title *Letters from Piso*, and it was later published as *The Last Days and Fall of Palmyra*.

43 Ibid., pp. 72, 75, 77.

44 Ibid., pp. 203; 2:51, 54, 55, 56.

45 William Ware, *Probus; or, Rome in the Third Century, in Letters of Lucius M. Piso from Rome, to Fausta, the Daughter of Gracchus, at Palmyra*, 2 vols. (New York, 1838), 1:14, 211. This book was later published as *Aurelian*.

46 Ibid., pp. 215, 216.

47 Ibid., pp. 220, 218, 22, 226.

48 William Ware, *Julian; or, Scenes in Judea*, 2 vols. (New York, 1841), 1:5, 6, 15, 16, 29, 35, 57.

49 Ibid., pp. 173, 230.

50 Don B. Seitz, "A Prince of Best Sellers," *Publisher's Weekly* 119 (February 21, 1931): 940. James O. Noyes in *Knickerbocker* 53 (1859): 639, remarks that Ingraham must have corrected "more than fifteen hundred anachronisms, historical errors, and the like" in the second edition of *The Prince of the House of David*.

51 Joseph Holt Ingraham, *The Prince of the House of David; or, Three Years in the Holy City* . . . (Philadelphia, 1861 [c1855]), pp. vii, ix-x.

52 Joseph Holt Ingraham, *The Pillar of Fire; or, Israel in Bondage* . . . (New York, 1859), p. 3.

53 Joseph Holt Ingraham, *The Throne of David* . . . (Boston, 1867 [c1860]), n. p.

54 Ibid., pp. 41, 51, 52, 112.

55 Ingraham, *The Prince*, p. 90.

56 Ibid., pp. 105, 127, 350, 134, 136.

57 Ibid., pp. 400, 23.

58 Maria T. Richards, *Life in Judea; or, Glimpses of the First Christian Age* (Philadelphia, 1854), p. 169.

59 Richards, *Life in Israel*, pp. vii, viii.

60 Alfred Duke, "The Fortunes of Esther," *Southern Literary Messenger* 13 (1847):419–20, 420.

61 Elizabeth Harriet Siddons Mair, *Mariamne; or, The Queen's Fate. A Tale of the Days of Herod* (New York, 1859), pp. 40, 5.

62 Lew Wallace, *Ben-Hur, a Tale of the Christ* (New York, 1933 [c1880]), pp. 527, 531, 544–45.

63 Ibid., pp. 75, 86, 82, 161, 201, 484.

64 Ibid., pp. 328, 233, 404–5.

65 Ibid., pp. 465, 538, 552.

66 Ibid., pp. 498, 264, 443, 490–91.

67 Ibid., pp. 39, 78, 108, 463.

68 James Freeman Clarke, *Legend of Thomas Didymus, the Jewish Sceptic* (Boston and New York, 1881), p. v.

69 Ibid., p. 25.

70 Ibid., pp. 109, 240.

71 [William Dennes Mahan], *The Archko Volume; or, The Archeological Writings of the Sanhedrin and Talmuds of the Jews* (Philadelphia, 1887 [c1884]), p. 11.

72 Ibid., pp. 16–17.

73 Francis Marion Crawford, *Zoroaster* (New York, 1885), pp. 17, 36.

74 Walsh, *Mary*, p. 555.

75 Ibid., pp. 89, 91, 92, 94, 96.

76 Ibid., pp. 189, 203, 235, 334, 613.

77 Elizabeth Stuart Phelps [Ward] and Herbert F. Ward, *The Master of the Magicians* (Boston and New York, 1899), p. 31.

78 Rose Porter, *A Daughter of Israel* (New York, 1899), pp. 83, 82, 83.

79 James Meeker Ludlow, *A King of Tyre, a Tale of the Time of Ezra and Nehemiah* (New York, 1891), pp. 111, 113, 115, 172, 173, 174.

80 George Anson Jackson, *The Son of a Prophet* (Boston and New York, 1893), pp. vi, 74, 75, 76, 77, 297, 383, 74.

81 Mrs. T. F. [Margaret S.] Black, *Hadassah; or, Esther, Queen to Ahasuerus* (Chicago, 1895), pp. 110, 131, 144, 174, 196, 207.

82 J. Breckenridge Ellis, *Shem, a Story of the Captivity* (Saint Louis, 1900), p. 299.

83 Anna May Wilson, *The Days of Mohammed* (Elgin Ill., 1897), pp. 6, 7, 12, 19, 49 (originally published in Sabbath Library, vol. 10, no. 295 [October 1, 1897]).

84 Robert E. Spiller et al., ed. *Literary History of the United States*, 3d ed. rev. (New York, 1963), p. 1074.

85 Elbridge S. Brooks, *A Son of Issachar, a Romance of the Days of the Messias* (New York, 1890), pp. 245, 276, 292.

86 Elizabeth Stuart Phelps [Ward] and Herbert F. Ward, *Come Forth!* (Boston and New York, 1891), pp. 7–8, 18, 5, 54.

87 Elizabeth Stuart Phelps, *The Story of Jesus Christ, an Interpretation* (Boston and New York, 1898 [c1897]), pp. 170, 375, 382, 174, 173.

88 Edward Payson Berry, *Leah of Jerusalem: A Story of the Time of Paul* (New York, 1890), pp. 27, 44, 162.

89 E[noch] F[itch] Burr, *Aleph, the Chaldean; or, The Messiah as Seen from Alexandria* (New York, 1891), pp. 67, 401, 60, 117.

90 Florence Moore Kingsley, *Paul, a Herald of the Cross* (New York, 1897), p. 348.

91 Florence Moore Kingsley, *Titus, a Comrade of the Cross,* Sabbath Library 7, no. 234 (December 25, 1894):66.

92 Kingsley, *Paul,* pp. vi, 274, 280, 394, 408.

93 Mary Elizabeth Jennings, *Asa of Bethlehem and His Household, B.C., IV–A.D. XXX* (New York, 1895), pp. 108, 179, 203.

94 Louise Seymour Houghton, *Antipas, Son of Chuza, and Others Whom Jesus Loved* (New York, 1895), pp. 79, 104.

95 William O. Stoddard, *The Swordsman's Son, a Story of the Year 30 A.D.* (New York, 1896 [c1895]), pp. 2, 24.

96 William O. Stoddard, *Ulric the Jarl: A Story of a Penitent Thief* (New York and Chicago, 1899), pp. 48, 49, 149–50, 173, 184.

97 Ibid., pp. 231, 235, 289.

98 Katherine Pearson Woods, *John, a Tale of King Messiah* (New York, 1896), pp. 15, 8–9, 193, 197, 199, 204, 317, 326, 117, 140.

99 Katherine Pearson Woods, *The Son of Ingar* (New York, 1897), pp. 31, 273, 184, 143, 123, 187.

100 Caroline Atwater Mason, *The Quiet King, a Story of Christ* (Philadelphia, 1896), pp. 35, 212–13, 299, 131.

101 Fannie E. Newberry, *The Wrestler of Philippi*, rev. ed. (Elgin, Ill., 1914), pp. 6, 18, 80 (originally published in Sabbath Library, vol. 9, no. 291 [1896]).

102 J. Breckenridge Ellis, *The Dread and Fear of Kings* (Chicago, 1900), pp. 74, 91, 360.

103 William A. Hammond, *The Son of Perdition* (Chicago, 1898), p. 491.

104 Newberry, *Wrestler of Philippi*.

105 In light of the evidence assembled in this chapter, one may doubt the accuracy of Oscar Handlin's observation in his *Adventures in Freedom: Three Hundred Years of Jewish Life in America* (New York, 1954), pp. 176–77, that among the large number of "popular novels with biblical settings . . . Jewish characters appeared in a variety of forms, generally sympathetically portrayed." This statement would be closer to the truth if it were qualified to read, "generally sympathetically portrayed, if they were converted to Christianity."

CHAPTER 8

1 William Cullen Bryant, *Prose Writings of William Cullen Bryant*, ed. Parke Goodwin, 2 vols. (New York, 1884), 1:315. Bryant concluded that *The Bravo* "is written with all the vigor and spirit of his best novels" (ibid.).

2 James Fenimore Cooper, *The Bravo: A Tale*, 2 vols. (New York, 1852 [c1831]), 1:21, 37, 95, 100.

3 Ibid., 2:35, 31.

4 Ibid., 1:90, 89.

5 Ibid., 2:31.

6 James Fenimore Cooper, *The Travelling Bachelor; or, Notions of America*, 2 vols. (New York, 1852 [c1828]), 2:246.

7 Cooper, *The Bravo*, 2:78.

8 James Fenimore Cooper, *The Oak-Openings; or, The Bee-Hunter* (New York, 1855 [c1848]), pp. 251, 259.

9 Ibid., pp. 265, 270, 324, 325, 327.

10 William Gilmore Simms, *Pelayo: A Story of the Goth*, 2 vols. (New York, 1838), 1:17.

11 Ibid., 1:84, 86; 2:263.

12 Ibid., 2:33, 270, 281.

13 Ibid., 1:94, 97, 99, 98.

14 William Gilmore Simms, "The Last Wager; or, The Gamester of the

Mississippi," *The Wigwam and the Cabin* (New York, 1882 [c1845]), p. 77.

15 Amelia E. Barr, *The Bow of Orange Ribbon: A Romance of New York* (New York, 1886), pp. 29, 42, 43, 93, 79.

16 Ibid., p. 173.

17 [John Richter Jones], *The Quaker Soldier; or, The British in Philadelphia, a Historical Novel* (Philadelphia, 1858), pp. 98, 96, 104, 105, 106, 109, 109–10.

18 Ibid., pp. 98, 99. Here Jones makes use of the legendary, discredited tradition that Salomon helped finance the revolution. Morris U. Schappes has written that "Haym Salomon himself is in no way responsible" for such "unsubstantiated statements. . . . Salomon, although an energetic, patriotic broker selling government securities, did not himself lend money to the government, and never claimed that he did" (Morris U. Schappes, ed., *A Documentary History of the Jews in the United States, 1654–1875* [New York, 1950], p. 579).

19 Ibid., p. 107. Whether Salomon did in fact engage in spying, we do not know. What is a fact is that he was arrested in New York by the British "as a Spy," as he wrote in a memorandum to the Continental Congress (Schappes, *Documentary History*, p. 52).

20 S. Weir Mitchell, *Hugh Wynne: Free Quaker* (Boston and New York, 1896), p. 166. For the historical Rebecca Franks, see Max J. Kohler, *Rebecca Franks* (New York, 1894) (pamphlet).

21 In an article, " 'Janice Meredith,' by Paul Leicester Ford," *Jewish Comment* (October 13, 1899), p. 7, the Jewish historical scholar Max J. Kohler suggests that the character of Janice Meredith herself is based on Rebecca Franks.

22 Paul Leicester Ford, *Janice Meredith: A Story of the American Revolution* (New York, 1899), pp. 31, 32.

23 Winston Churchill, *Richard Carvel* (New York, 1899), pp. 293, 294, 295, 336.

24 Robert W. Chambers, *Cardigan* (New York and London, 1901), pp. 159, 150, 162, 163, 294, 442, 458.

CHAPTER 9

1 Robert Montgomery Bird, "The Broker of Bogota," in *Representative American Plays,* ed. Arthur Hobson Quinn, 7th rev. ed. (New York, 1953), p. 206.

2 Nathaniel Parker Willis, "Tortesa the Usurer," in ibid., pp. 258, 243.

3 Ibid., pp. 265, 266.

4 A. B. Lindley, *Love and Friendship; or, Yankee Notions* (New York, 1809), pp. 36–37.

5 H. J. Conway, *Guiscard the Guerilla; or, A Brother's Revenge* (1844), holograph copy in Theater Collection at Harvard College Library.

6 William Dunlap, *A History of the American Theater* (New York, 1832), p. 8.

7 Edward D. Coleman, "Plays of Jewish Interest on the American Stage, 1752–1821," *Publications of the American Jewish Historical Society* 33 (1934):172.

8 Richard Cumberland, *The Jew: A Comedy* (London, 1794), pp. 6–7 (act 1, scene 1).

9 Coleman, *PAJHS* 33:183, n. 20.

10 Ibid.

11 Dunlap, *History of the American Theater*, p. 195.

12 Coleman, *PAJHS* 33:187, n. 35.

13 Susanna Haswell Rowson, *Slaves in Algiers; or, A Struggle for Freedom* (Philadelphia, 1794), pp. 51, 71.

14 Ibid., pp. 14, 17.

15 Ibid., pp. 53, 71, 72.

16 Dunlap, *History of the American Theater*, p. 322.

17 John Howard Payne, *Trial without Jury and Other Lost Plays*, ed. Codman Hislop and W. R. Richardson, American Lost Plays Series, vol. 5 (Princeton, 1940), pp. 13, 25.

18 James Ellison, *The American Captive; or, The Siege of Tripoli* (Boston, 1812), p. 29.

19 Ibid., p. 30. In an earlier play by Jones quite similar to Ellison's *American Captive*, entitled *The Adventure; or, Yankees in Tripoli* (1835), the Jewish character, El Hassan, is no longer the evil stereotype of Ellison's original. Jones's Jewish character is not a renegade; he is generous, opposed to tyranny, and participates in Anderson's plot out of principle, not for money. In 1842 Jones produced still another version of Ellison's play, *The Usurpers; or, Americans in Tripoli*, which dropped all mention of El Hassan as a Jew; he is now simply "an old slave merchant." *The Usurpers* was first published in *Metamora and Other Plays*, ed. Eugene R. Page, America's Lost Play Series, vol. 14 (Princeton, 1941).

20 Jonathan S. Smith, *The Siege of Algiers; or, The Downfall of Hadji-Ali-Bashaw* (Philadelphia, 1823), pp. 7, 11, 23, 24–25, 25.

21 Ibid., pp. 75, 95.

22 M[ary Carr] Clarke, *The Benevolent Lawyer; or, Villainy Detected* (Philadelphia, 1823), pp. 11, 30.

23 Jason R. Orton, *Arnold, and Other Poems* (New York, 1854), p. 85.

24 William Wilberforce Lord, *André, a tragedy in five acts* (New York, 1856).

24a James Pilgrim, *Yankee Jack; or, The Buccaneers of the Gulf*, in manuscript, n.p., in New York Public Library Theater Collection, act 3, scene 3.

25 Julia Ward Howe, *The World's Own* (Boston, 1857), pp. 104, 105, 107.

26 John Brougham, *Columbus el Filibustero* (New York, 1857), p. 20.

27 John Brougham, *The Lottery of Life, a Story of New York* (New York, n.d. [c1867]), pp. 42, 6, 40, 41.

28 John Brougham, *Much Ado about a Merchant of Venice* (New York, n.d. [1868]), pp. 2, 8, 9, 16.

29 George M. Baker, "The Peddler of Very Nice, a Burlesque of the Trial Scene in 'The Merchant of Venice,'" *American Dramas* (Boston, 1894), pp. 201, 212.

30 The Larks, *The Shakespeare Water-Cure* (New York, n.d. [c1883, c1897]), pp. 4, 32, 20, 35.

31 Dion Boucicault, "Flying Scud," *Forbidden Fruit and Other Plays*, ed. Allardyce Nicoll and F. Theodore Cloak (Princeton, 1940), p. 227.

32 Dion Boucicault, *After Dark, a Drama of London Life in 1868,* Dewitt's Acting Plays (n.d., [1868]), pp. 7, 27.

33 Clyde Fitch, "Beau Brummel," *Plays,* 4 vols. (Boston, 1915), 4:14, 39.

34 Steele Mackaye, *Money-Mad,* typewritten prompt book in Theater Collection at Harvard College Library, n.d., pp. 5, 4, 5, 14.

35 Augustin Daly, *Leah, the Forsaken* (New York, n.d. [c1862]), pp. 14, 20, 21.

36 Ibid., pp. 29, 38, 44.

37 *Harper's Weekly* 7 (February 28, 1863):130.

38 Ibid. 7 (March 7, 1863):146.

39 Augustin Daly, *The Last Word,* from the German of Franz von Schoenthan, privately printed (1891), p. 9.

40 Constance Rourke, *American Humor* (New York, 1931), pp. 32, 35.

41 Cited in Douglas Gilbert, *American Vaudeville, Its Life and Times* (New York, 1940), p. 73.

42 Edward B. Marks, *They All Sang,* (New York, 1934), pp. 13, 14.

43 This idea is set forth in Harold E. Adams, "Minority Caricatures on the American Stage," in *Studies in the Science of Society,* ed. G. P. Murdock (New Haven, 1937), pp. 24–25.

44 Gilbert, *American Vaudeville,* pp. 288, 290.

45 Quoted in Montrose J. Moses, *The American Dramatist* (Boston, 1911), p. 49.

46 *Jewish Messenger* 60, no. 20 (November 12, 1886):1.

47 "Mr. Edward Harrigan Speaks," *Harper's Weekly* 33 (February 12, 1889):97.

48 William Dean Howells, "Editor's Study," *Harper's Monthly* 73 (July 1886):315, 316.

49 Edward Harrigan, "The Mulligan Guard Ball," in *Dramas from the American Stage, 1762–1909,* ed. Richard Moody (Cleveland, 1966), p. 565.

50 Harrigan's wife was the daughter of the song composer David Braham. Braham's father, John Braham, was a Jew and a noted English singer who had married an Episcopalian. The David Braham children were all Catholics (letter to this writer from Nedda Harrigan [Mrs. Joshua] Logan, April 17, 1972).

51 Milton Nobles, *The Phoenix* (Chicago, 1900 [c1875, c1900]), pp. 4, 64, 105. The play was originally titled *Jim Bledsoe; or, Bohemians and Detectives.*

52 Ibid., pp. 106, 107, 139.

53 F. E. Chase, *The Great Umbrella Case, a Mock Trial* (Boston, n.d. [c1881, c1883]), p. 8.

54 F. E. Chase, *A Ready-Made Suit, a Mock Trial* (Boston, n.d. [c1885]), pp. 21, 21–22.

55 Ibid., p. 23.

56 F. E. Chase, *In the Trenches, a Drama of the Cuban War* (Boston, n.d. [c1898]), pp. 2, 37.

57 Ibid., pp. 14, 21, 29–30.

58 Forbes Heermans, *Down the Black Canyon; or, The Silent Witness, a Drama of the Rocky Mountains,* Dewitt's Acting Plays no. 357 (New York, [c1890]), p. 4.

59 Charles Townsend, *The Jail Bird* (New York, n.d. [c1893]), pp. 4, 7, 9, 10.

60 Harry E. Shelland, *The Great Libel Case* (New York, 1900), pp. 3, 12, 24, 29.

61 Frank L. Bixby, *The Little Boss* (New York, 1901), pp. 2, 6, 18, 38.

62 Harry L. Newton and A. S. Hoffman, *Glickman, the Glazier* (Chicago, 1904), pp. 3, 5, 6, 7.

63 Ibid., p. 8.

64 Harry L. Newton and A. S. Hoffman, *The Troubles of Rozinski* (Chicago, 1904), pp. 6, 10.

65 Introduction to George H. Jessop, "Sam'l of Posen; or, The Commercial Drummer," in *Davy Crockett and Other Plays,* ed. Isaac Goldberg and Hubert Heffner, America's Lost Plays Series, vol. 4 (Bloomington, Ind., 1963 [c1940]), pp. xx–xxi. Jessop copyrighted the play in 1880, and Curtis then bought it from him and revised it in subsequent productions.

66 Unidentified, undated clipping in Theater Collection at Harvard College Library.

67 Jessop, "Sam'l of Posen," p. 161.

68 C. B., Jr., "The Advancement of the Stage Jew," in the Philadelphia *Sunday Mirror;* reprinted in *Jewish Exponent* 8 (1890):8.

69 In the clipping of this newspaper review in the New York Public Library Theater Collection only the year, 1894, is identified.

70 "A New Stage Jew," *American Hebrew* 28, no. 9 (April 5, 1889):130.

71 *Spirit of the Times* 19, no. 5 (March 11, 1876):115.

72 Edward W. Tullidge, *Ben Israel; or, From under the Curse: A Jewish Play* (Salt Lake City, 1887 [c1875]), p. 53.

73 "New Stage Jew," loc. cit.

74 Clara Harriott Sherwood, *The Cable Car, a Howellsian Burlesque* (New York, n.d. [c1891]), p. 5.

75 Henry C. DeMille and David Belasco, "Men and Women," *Plays,* ed. Robert Hamilton Hall, America's Lost Play Series, vol. 17 (Princeton, 1941), pp. 276, 304, 342.

76 Ibid., pp. 313, 314.

77 "Advancement of the Stage Jew," loc. cit.

78 "Stage Characters of the Jews," *American Israelite* 47, no. 40 (April 4, 1901):1; reprinted from the *Indianapolis News.*

79 "The Jew on the Stage," *The Reformer and Jewish Times* 10 (April 5, 1878):4.

CHAPTER 10

1 Henry Wadsworth Longfellow, "Hiawatha," *The Poetical Works of Henry Wadsworth Longfellow* (Boston and New York, 1883), p. 189.

2 George W. Anderson, *The Legend of the Wandering Jew,* (Providence, 1970 [c1965]), p. 123. I am indebted to this book for much information in the present chapter, especially bibliographical data on American versions of the legend. However, Anderson does not treat the use of the legend in Hawthorne's *Marble Faun,* Melville's *Clarel,* George

Lippard's *Nazarene,* George Wood's *Peter Schlemihl in America,* or Eliza
Buckminster Lee's *Parthenia.*

3 When Longfellow read *The Wandering Jew,* he noted in his journal:

> Shall we ever get through
> This mighty ado,
> The old and the new,
> The false and the true,
> In the volumes two
> of *The Wandering Jew*
> by Eugène Sue?

John J. Appel, "Henry Wadsworth Longfellow's Presentation of the
Spanish Jews," *Publications of the American Jewish Historical Society* 45,
no. 1 (September 1955):21.

4 These and other allusions are noted in Rudolf Glanz, *The Jew in American
Folklore* (New York, 1961), pp. 193, 32–33, 36.

5 James Russell Lowell, *The Complete Poetical Works of James Russell Lowell*
(Boston, 1896), p. 422.

6 George Lippard, *The Nazarene; or, The Last of the Washingtons, a Revelation
of Philadelphia, New York, and Washington, in the Year 1844* (Philadelphia, 1846), pp. 4, 3, 88.

7 Ibid., p. 210.

8 Ibid., pp. 230–31, 231, 232.

9 Eliza Buckminster Lee, *Parthenia, or, The Last Days of Paganism* (Boston,
1857), pp. 367, 369, 314.

10 David Hoffman, *Chronicles Selected from the Originals of Cartaphilus, the
Wandering Jew, embracing a period of XIX Centuries now first revealed to,
and edited by David Hoffman, in two series, each of three volumes, Series the
First,* 3 vols. (London, 1853–54). For greater detail about the content
of this work, see Anderson, *Legend of the Wandering Jew,* pp. 153–60.

11 Mark Twain, *The Innocents Abroad,* 2 vols. in 1 (New York and London,
1911), 2:350, 352.

12 F. Marion Crawford, *A Roman Singer* (New York, 1894 [c1883, 1884,
1893]), pp. 150, 160, 161, 180, 185, 183, 166, 163. Henry James
was disgusted with this novel. In a letter to Howells, he called it
"contemptibly bad and ignoble . . . a piece of sixpenny humbug,
. . . shamelessly bad, seems to me to dishonour the novelist's art that
is absolutely not to be forgiven" (quoted in John Pilkington, Jr.,
Francis Marion Crawford [New York, 1964], p. 103).

13 Crawford, *Roman Singer,* pp. 259, 345.

14 Louise Imogen Guiney, "Peter Rugg, the Bostonian," *A Roadside Harp*
(Boston and New York, 1893), p. 6.

15 Lew Wallace, *The Prince of India; or, Why Constantinople Fell,* 2 vols. (New
York, 1893), 1:6.

16 Ibid., p. 60; 2:383.

17 Ibid., 2:530, 387.

18 Lew Wallace, *An Autobiography,* 2 vols. (New York, 1906), 1:1.

19 Eugene Field, *The Holy Cross, and Other Stories* (New York, 1899).

20 Oliver Herford, "The Wandering Jew," *Overheard in a Garden, et Cetera*

(New York, 1900), pp. 88–90. In Anderson's brief allusion to this poem he does not call attention to its anti-Semitic overtones, but calls it "a typical piece of Herfordian fluff" (*Legend of the Wandering Jew,* p. 340).

21 O. Henry, "The Door of Unrest," *Sixes and Sevens* (New York, 1911).

22 Edwin Arlington Robinson, "The Wandering Jew," *Collected Poems* (New York, 1929), pp. 456–59.

23 Herman M. Bien, *Ben-Beor, a Story of the Anti-Messiah, in Two Divisions: Part I—Lunar Intaglios, the Man in the Moon, a Counterpart of "Ben-Hur." Part II—Historical Phantasmagoria, a Wandering Gentile, a Companion Romance to Sue's "Wandering Jew,"* (Vicksburg, Miss., and Baltimore, 1891), pp. 58, 58–59.

24 Ibid., pp. 75, 76, 77.

25 Ibid., pp. 78, 79.

26 Isaac M. Wise, *The Wandering Jew* (n.p., n.d. [pamphlet, circa 1899]), p. 2.

27 Ibid., pp. 4. 12.

CHAPTER 11

1 Isaac Franks, "On Novel Reading," *American Jewish Archives* 12, no. 2 (October 1959):124.

2 Cited in Joseph L. Blau and Salo W. Baron, eds., *The Jews of the United States, 1790–1840: A Documentary History,* 3 vols. (New York, 1963), 2:441.

3 Rebecca Gratz, *Letters of Rebecca Gratz,* ed. Rabbi David Philipson (Philadelphia, 1929).

4 Washington Irving, *Salmagundi; or, The Whim-Whams and Opinions of Launcelot Langstaff Esq. and Others* (New York, 1905), p. 431.

5 Washington Irving, *Knickerbocker's History of New York* (New York, 1883), p. 60.

6 Joseph Jacobs, "The Original of Scott's Rebecca," *Publications of the American Jewish Historical Society* 22 (1914):53–60.

7 Gratz, *Letters,* p. xx.

8 Ibid., pp. 29, 32.

9 Montagu Frank Modder, *The Jew in the Literature of England to the End of the Nineteenth Century* (Philadelphia, 1939), p. 143.

10 Penina Moise, *Secular and Religious Works of Penina Moise* (Charleston, 1911), p. 177.

11 Samuel B. H. Judah, *Gotham and the Gothamites* (New York, 1823), pp. 6–7.

12 [Samuel B. H. Judah], *The Buccaneers: A romance of our own country, in its ancient day from the settlement of Nieuw Nederlandts until the times of the famous Richard Kid,* 2 vols., 2d ed. (New York, 1827), 1:263.

13 George C. D. Odell, *Annals of the New York Stage,* 15 vols. (New York, 1927–29), 2:557.

14 Samuel B. H. Judah, *David and Uriah* (Philadelphia, 1835), pp. iii, iv.

15 Blau and Baron, *Jews of the U.S.,* 1:xxxiv.

16 Mordecai M. Noah, preface to "She Would Be a Soldier," in *Representa-*

tive Plays by American Dramatists, ed. Montrose J. Moses (New York, 1918), p. 641.

17 Mordecai M. Noah, *Travels in England, France, Spain, and the Barbary States in the Years 1813–14 and 15* (New York, 1819), p. vi.

18 Arthur Hobson Quinn, *A History of the American Drama from the Beginning to the Civil War,* 2d ed. (New York, 1943), p. 151.

19 Quoted in Morris U. Schappes, ed., *A Documentary History of the Jews in the United States, 1654–1875* (New York, 1950), p. 247.

20 Ibid., pp. 249–50.

21 Noah had collaborated on a work in which the texts of the sources of Shakespeare's plays are reprinted: *Shakespeare Illustrated: or, The Novels and Histories on which the Plays of Shakespeare are Founded, collected and translated from the Originals by Mrs. [Charlotte Ramsey] Lenox, with critical remarks and biographical sketches of the writers,* by M. M. Noah, 2 vols. (Philadelphia, 1809). In his comments on *Othello,* Noah derides the practice of rendering Othello as "complexionally pleasant." Shakespeare made it clear, argues Noah, that Othello was "a real black" (1:76).

22 Quoted in Isaac Goldberg, *Major Noah: American Jewish Pioneer* (Philadelphia, 1936), p. 252.

23 David Grimstead, *Melodrama Unveiled: American Theater and Culture, 1800–1850* (Chicago, 1968), p. 217, 44n.

24 Lee M. Friedman, "Mordecai M. Noah as Playwright," *Historia Judaica* 4, no. 2 (October 1942):160.

25 For the full text of the memorial, see Schappes, *Documentary History,* pp. 171–77.

26 Cited in Max J. Kohler, "Isaac Harby, Jewish Religious Leader and Man of Letters," *Publications of the American Jewish Historical Society,* no. 32 (1931):44.

27 N. Bryllon Fagin, "Isaac Harby and the Early American Theatre," *American Jewish Archives* 8, no. 1 (January 1956):12, 13.

28 Quoted in Blau and Baron, *Jews of the U.S.,* 2:409, 406, 408.

29 Isaac Harby, *A Selection from the Miscellaneous Writings of the Late Isaac Harby, Esq.,* ed. Hugh L. Pinckney and Abraham Moise (Charleston, 1829), p. 262.

30 Ibid., pp. 267, 262.

31 John Higham, "Social Discrimination against Jews in America, 1830–1930," *Publications of the American Jewish Historical Society* 47, no. 1 (September 1957):8.

32 *Asmonean* 11, no. 19 (February 23, 1855):148.

33 *Occident and American Jewish Advocate* 10, no. 7 (October 1852):351.

34 Ibid., no. 10 (January 1853):501.

35 *Caleb Asher,* The Jewish Miscellany, no. 1 (Philadelphia, 1845), pp. 1–2.

36 *Occident* 11, no. 10 (January 1854):516.

37 Ibid., no. 5 (August 1853):267.

38 *Israelite* 1, no. 1 (July 15, 1854):4.

39 Ibid. 6, no. 17 (October 28, 1859):132.

40 Isaac M. Wise, *Reminiscences,* trans. and ed. David Philipson (Cincinnati, 1901), p. 332.

41 James G. Heller, *Isaac M. Wise, His Life, Work, and Thought* (New York, 1965), p. 661.

42 *Israelite* 6, no. 16 (October 21, 1859):121.

43 Isaac M. Wise, *The Combat of the People: or, Hillel and and Herod, a Historical Romance of the Time of Herod I* (Cincinnati, 1859), p. 3.

44 *Israelite* 3, no. 52 (July 3, 1857):409.

45 Abraham H. Steinberg, "Jewish Characters in the American Novel to 1900" (Ph.D. diss., New York University, 1956), p. 259.

46 Nathan Mayer, *Differences* (Cincinnati, 1867), pp. 80, 34.

47 Ibid., pp. 218, 219, 228.

48 Ibid., pp. 357, 452, 453.

49 Ibid., pp. 376, 377, 377–78, 378.

50 Ibid., p. 404.

51 Quoted in Paul Lewis, *Queen of the Plaza: A Biography of Adah Isaacs Menken* (New York, 1964), p. 59.

52 Leo Wise, "Israelite Personalities," *American Israelite* 50, no. 53 (June 30, 1904):14. Leo Wise writes: "Mrs. Menken was of Christian parentage, and while she did not have a drop of 'Semitic' blood in her veins, she was in faith and ideals an ardent Jewess. . . . She most ardently desired to become one, and often requested Dr. Wise to receive her into the fold, going so far at one time as to implore him on her knees . . . to accept her as a convert. For some reason unknown to me he steadfastly refused to do this." Sol Liptzin asserts categorically, in his *Jew in American Literature* (New York, 1966), that "in reality she [Menken] was born to a young Jewish couple" (p. 54), apparently either unaware of or rejecting the evidence in Leo Wise's article or Lewis's book on this point. From Liptzin's citation of Allen Lesser's *Enchanting Rebel: The Secret of Adah Isaacs Menken* (New York, 1947), one may assume that he based his assertion on that unreliable book. See Morris U. Schappes's critical review of Lesser in *Jewish Life* 2, no. 11 (September 1948):29–30.

53 Quoted in Lewis, *Queen of the Plaza*, p. 17.

54 Cited in ibid., p. 128.

55 Adah Isaacs Menken, "Hear, O Israel," *Israelite,* March 1857. Paul Lewis is in error when he writes that "only her first poem was devoted to a religious theme" (p. 60). For instance, in the issue of April 15, 1859, she appeared with "The Sabbath," and on April 22, 1859, with "Passover."

56 A checklist of Menken's poems and essays, though not exhaustive, is to be found in Lesser, *Enchanting Rebel,* pp. 265–69.

57 *Israelite* 4, no. 13 (October 2, 1857): 101.

58 Adah Isaacs Menken, "The Jew in Parliament," *Israelite* 5, no. 9 (September 2, 1859):68–69.

59 Adah Isaacs Menken, *Infelicia* (Philadelphia, 1888), pp. 69, 125, 92, 25, 10.

60 Constance Rourke, *Troupers of the Gold Coast; or, The Rise of Lotta Crabtree* (New York, 1928), p. 179.

CHAPTER 12

1 George F. Whicher, "Poetry after the Civil War," in *American Writers on American Literature,* ed. John Macy (New York, 1934), p. 382.

2 Emma Lazarus, *The Letters of Emma Lazarus, 1868–1885,* ed. Morris U. Schappes (New York, 1949), p. 18, n. 35 (hereafter cited as "Schappes, *Letters*").

3 Cited in Ralph L. Rusk, ed., *Letters to Emma Lazarus* (New York, 1939), p. 17 (hereafter cited as "Rusk, *Letters*").

4 Many of Emma Lazarus's translations of Heine are represented in Heinrich Heine, *The Poetry and Prose of Heinrich Heine,* ed. Frederic Ewen (New York, 1948), and Heinrich Heine, *Lyric Poems and Ballads,* trans. Ernest Fiene (with thirty-one translated by Emma Lazarus) (Pittsburgh, 1961).

5 Louis Ruchames, "New Light on the Religious Development of Emma Lazarus," *Publications of the American Jewish Historical Society* 42, no. 1 (September 1952):87–88. "Outside the Church" was originally published in *Index* 3 (December 14, 1872):399.

6 "Miss Lazarus's Life and Literary Work," *Critic,* December 10, 1887, p. 294.

7 Emma Lazarus, *The Poems of Emma Lazarus,* 2 vols. (Boston and New York 1889), p. 19 (hereafter cited as "*Poems*").

8 Morris U. Schappes has established this earlier interest in the Jews in his edition of *Emma Lazarus: Selections from Her Poetry and Prose,* 3d ed. rev. and enl. (New York, 1967) (hereafter cited as "*Selections*").

9 Schappes, *Letters,* p. 20.

10 *Poems,* 2:8.

11 *Selections,* pp. 32–33.

12 Emma Lazarus, "Henry Wadsworth Longfellow," *American Hebrew,* April 14, 1882; reprinted in *Selections,* pp. 99–100.

13 On the relation of Heine to Emma Lazarus, see Aaron Kramer, "The Link between Heinrich Heine and Emma Lazarus," *Publications of the American Jewish Historical Society* 45, no. 4 (June 1956):248–57.

14 *Jewish Messenger,* February 18, 1876.

15 *Selections,* p. 31. This poem was originally published at the head of Emma Lazarus's article "The Poet Heine," *Century Magazine,* December 1884, p. 210.

16 Rusk, *Letters,* pp. 48, 9, 10.

17 Ibid., pp. 7, 11, 12, 13.

18 Schappes, *Letters,* pp. 11, 11–12, 13. Schappes quotes from favorable comments on her work in American and English reviews, p. 12, n. 17. It has been suggested by Max I. Baym ("Emma Lazarus and Emerson," *Publications of the American Jewish Historical Society,* no. 38, pt. 4 [June 1949]:281–87) that the shock of Emerson's failure to include any of her poems in his *Parnassus* accounts for her subsequent turn and devotion to the Jewish cause. Baym supports his position mainly with the views of Emma Lazarus's sister, Mrs. Anne Humphrey Johnston, who was converted to Roman Catholicism. The evidence, both documentary and psychological, completely undermines this view. See

Schappes, *Selections*, passim; Albert Mordell, "Some Final Words on Emma Lazarus," *Publications of the American Jewish Historical Society*, no. 39 (1949–50):324; and Kramer, *PAJHS* 45:255, n. 27.

19 Rusk, *Letters*, p. 16.

20 Schappes, *Letters*, p. 35.

21 Edmund Clarence Stedman, *Genius and Other Essays* (New York, 1911), pp. 265–67.

22 Z. Ragozin, "Russian Jews and Gentiles," *Century Magazine* 23 (1882):-919.

23 *Poems*, 2:134.

24 *Selections*, pp. 38–39.

25 Whicher, "Poetry," p. 382.

26 *Selections*, p. 49.

27 *Poems*, 2:25–44, 58–66.

28 *Selections*, pp. 74, 76, 77, 78, 79.

29 Ibid., pp. 53, 89, 89.

30 *Poems*, 2:14–15.

31 Schappes, *Letters*, pp. 51, 51, n. 138.

32 *Selections*, p. 79.

33 Abraham Cahan, *The Education of Abraham Cahan*, trans. Leon Stein, Abraham P. Conan, and Lynn Davison (Philadelphia, 1969), p. 354.

34 *Selections*, p. 86.

35 *Poems*, 2:64, 6; *Selections*, pp. 40–41.

36 *Selections*, pp. 48.

37 Rusk, *Letters*, p. 74.

38 *Selections*, pp. 96–97.

39 The poem is reproduced in Eve Merriam, *Emma Lazarus: Woman with a Torch* (New York, 1956), p. 97.

40 This letter was first published by Morris U. Schappes in *Selections*, pp. 104–5, and later in Schappes, *Letters*, pp. 31–33.

41 Schappes, *Letters*, pp. 67–68, 29.

42 Rusk, *Letters*, p. 25.

43 Quoted by Horace Traubel, *With Whitman in Camden, July 16, 1888–October 31, 1888* (New York, 1908), pp. 456, 459.

44 *American Hebrew*, December 9, 1887, p. 3.

45 Edmund Clarence Stedman, ed., *An American Anthology, 1787–1900* (Boston and New York, 1900), pp. 518–20. The six poems were "On the Proposal to Erect a Monument in England to Lord Byron," "Venus of the Louvre," "The Graves of Ibycus," "The Banner of the Jew," "The Crowing of the Red Cock," and "The New Ezekiel."

46 The revival of interest in Emma Lazarus in recent years owes much to the pioneering work of Morris U. Schappes, whose *Emma Lazarus: Selections from Her Poetry and Prose*, first published in 1944, helped recall her to public attention.

CHAPTER 13

1 Morris U. Schappes, ed., *A Documentary History of the Jews in the United States, 1654–1875*, new and rev. ed. (New York, 1971), pp. 510 ff.

2 *Gwendolen: A Sequel to George Eliot's "Daniel Deronda"* (Boston, 1878), pp. 27–28, 28–29.

3 Ibid., pp. 30, 64.

4 Ibid., pp. 74, 153.

5 [Virginia Wales Johnson], *Joseph the Jew, the Story of an Old House* (New York, 1873), pp. 14, 13.

6 Ibid., pp. 21, 29, 131.

7 Henry James, *Literary Reviews and Essays,* ed. Albert Mordell (New York, 1957), pp. 247, 252.

8 *Jewish Messenger* 57, no. 1 (January 2, 1885):1.

9 James, *Reviews and Essays,* pp. 255, 258.

10 Julian Hawthorne, *An American Penman: From the Diary of Inspector Byrnes* (New York, 1887), pp. 192, 207.

11 Julian Hawthorne, *Beatrix Randolph, a Story* (New York, 1884), pp. 73, 70, 31.

12 Julian Hawthorne, *Sebastian Strome, a Novel* (New York, 1880 [c1879]), pp. 78, 79, 80, 83.

13 Ibid., pp. 81, 31, 79.

14 Ibid., p. 124.

15 [Ellen W. Olney Kirk], *Queen Money* (Boston, 1888), pp. 394, 406.

16 Alfred Kazin, *On Native Grounds* (New York, 1956; paperback), p. 10. Crawford himself defined the novel as a "marketable commodity, of the class collectively termed 'luxuries,' as not contributing directly to the support of life or the maintenance of health. . . . The novel is an intellectual artistic luxury" (*The Novel: What It Is* [New York, 1893], pp. 8–9; cited in John Pilkington, Jr., *Francis Marion Crawford* [New York, 1964], p. 111).

17 F. Marion Crawford, *Mr. Isaacs, a Tale of Modern India* (New York, 1902 [c1882]), p. 17.

18 F. Marion Crawford, *Paul Patoff* (Boston and New York, 1887), pp. 238, 405–6.

19 Ibid., pp. 241, 409.

20 F. Marion Crawford, *A Cigarette-Maker's Romance* [c1890] and *Khaled* [c1891] (New York, 1901), pp. 189, 190.

21 F. Marion Crawford, *The Witch of Prague, a Fantastic Tale* (London, 1890), pp. 47, 199.

22 Ibid., pp. 227, 228, 240, 253, 255.

23 Mrs. Julie P. Smith, *Blossom-Bud and Her Genteel Friends* (New York, 1883), pp. 119–20, 127.

24 Evelyn Kimball Johnson, *An Errand Girl: A Romance of New York Life* (New York, 1889), pp. 74, 112, 113, 114, 116, 119.

25 Frank R. Stockton, *The Stories of Three Burglars* (New York, 1889), pp. 89, 94, 102.

26 Brander Matthews and George H. Jessop, *A Tale of Twenty-five Hours* (New York, 1892), pp. 64, 66, 89, 96, 93–94, 130, 66.

27 Brander Matthews, *Tom Paulding* (New York, 1892), pp. 56, 96.

28 William C. Hudson, *On the Rack, a Novel* (New York, 1891), pp. 178, 179, 180, 181.

29 Maurice Francis Egan, *The Disappearance of John Longworthy* (Notre Dame, Ind., 1890), pp. 12, 15.

30 Edgar Fawcett, *The Evil that Men Do* (New York, 1889), p. 35. The contemporary critic Henry Stoddard became bored with the endless flow of Fawcett's novels and at length exclaimed: "Won't somebody shut this Fawcett off?" *(Dictionary of American Biography).*

31 Edgar Fawcett, *New York, a Novel* (New York, 1898), pp. 61–62, 62, 68, 73, 78.

32 [Hjalmar Hjorth Boyesen], *A Daughter of the Philistines* (Boston, 1883), pp. 31, 40, 41.

33 Ibid., pp. 46, 176, 49.

34 Ibid., pp. 43, 175, 184.

35 Ibid., pp. 239, 287, 296.

36 Edgar Saltus, *Enthralled, a Story of International Life . . .* (London, 1894), unpaged.

37 Margaret Sherwood, *Henry Worthington, Idealist* (New York, 1899), pp. 94, 116, 246, 245.

38 Blanche Conscience [Samuel Williams Cooper], ed., *The Confessions of a Society Man* (New York and Chicago, 1887), pp. 14, 15, 242.

39 Samuel Williams Cooper, *Think and Thank* (Philadelphia, 1890), pp. 114, 115.

40 [Caroline McCoy Willard], *A Son of Israel, an Original Story* (Philadelphia, 1898 [c1897]), pp. 6, 108, 227, 22, 9, 108.

41 Ibid., pp. 29–30, 43, 111.

42 A. N. Homer, *Hernani the Jew, a Story of Russian Oppression* (Chicago and New York, 1897), p. 27.

43 Henry Gillman, *Hassan: A Fellah, a Romance of Palestine* (Boston, 1898), pp. 105–6.

44 Ibid., pp. 46, 47.

45 Ibid., pp. 50, 52–53, 62, 56, 65, 55.

46 Ibid., pp. 78, 52, 428.

47 Richard Henry Savage, *Delilah of Harlem, a Story of New York City Today* (New York, 1893), pp. 7, 10, 11.

48 Richard Henry Savage, *A Modern Corsair* (Chicago and New York, 1897), p. 24.

49 Richard Henry Savage, *The White Lady of Khaminavatka, a Story of the Ukraine* (Chicago and New York, 1898), p. 13.

50 Ibid., pp. 59, 270, 309–10.

51 Richard Henry Savage, *My Official Wife, a Novel* (New York, 1891), pp. 13, 189, 190.

52 Richard Henry Savage, *Lost Countess Falka, a Story of the Orient* (Chicago and New York, 1896), pp. 120, 70, 69, 43, 70, 120.

53 Richard Henry Savage, *In the Shadow of the Pyramids, the Last Days of Ismail Khedive. 1879. A Novel* (Chicago and New York, 1898 [c1897]), pp. 122, 136, 137, 139.

54 Ibid., pp. 177, 217, 331.

55 Savage, *Modern Corsair,* pp. 194, 185, 190, 196, 198, 225, 194, 193.

56 Ibid., pp. 195, 255, 252.

57 Savage, *Delilah of Harlem,* pp. 34, 40.

58 Richard Henry Savage, *An Exile from London, a Novel* (New York, 1896), pp. 5, 56, 8, 28.

59 Ibid., pp. 10, 86, 59, 49, 9.
60 Ibid., pp. 37, 51, 56, 113, 115, 131.

CHAPTER 14

1 See Abraham H. Steinberg, "Jewish Characters in Fugitive American Novels of the Nineteenth Century," *YIVO Annual* (1956/57), 10: 105 ff.

2 Edward Z. C. Judson, *Ned Buntline's Life Yarn* (New York, 1849), pp. 14, 123–24.

3 [Edward Z. C. Judson], *Rose Seymour; or, The Ballet Girl's Revenge, a Tale of New-York Drama* (New York, [1865]), p. 43.

4 Edward Z. C. Judson, *Morgan; or, The Knight of the Black Flag. A Strange Story of By-Gone Times* (New York, 1861), pp. 16, 15, 116, 187.

5 *The Beautiful Jewess, Rachel Mendoza, her memorable connection with the dark and eventful career of Charles Bernard, otherwise called "Prince Charles"* (New York, 1853), pp. 14, 18, 17.

6 Prentiss Ingraham, *The Jew Detective; or, The Beautiful Convict*, Beadle's New York Dime Library no. 662 (New York, 1891), pp. 2, 3.

7 Ibid., pp. 14, 27.

8 Albert W. Aiken, *The Phantom Hand; or, The Heiress of Fifth Avenue*, Beadle and Adams 20 Cent Novel no. 23 (New York, 1870), p. 26.

9 Albert W. Aiken, *The Spotter-Detective; or, The Girls of New York*, Beadle's New York Dime Library no. 27 (New York, 1878), p. 23.

10 Albert W. Aiken, *The White Witch; or, The League of Three*, Beadle and Adams 20 Cent Novel (New York, 1871), pp. 10, 11.

11 Albert W. Aiken, *The California Detective; or, The Witches of New York*, Beadle's New York Dime Library no. 42 (New York, 1878), p. 8.

12 Albert W. Aiken, *The Genteel Spotter; or, The Night Hawks of New York*, Beadle's New York Dime Library no. 320 (New York, 1884), pp. 6, 11.

13 Albert W. Aiken, *Lone Hand the Shadow; or, The Master of Triangle Ranch*, Beadle's New York Dime Library no. 562 (New York, 1889), pp. 2, 7, 13.

14 Albert W. Aiken, *The Lone Hand in Texas; or, The Red Gloved Raiders of the Rio Grande*, Beadle's New York Dime Library no. 490 (New York, 1888), pp. 2, 12, 28.

15 Albert W. Aiken, *Joe Buck of the Angels and His Boy Pard Paul Powderhorn*, Beadle's Half-Dime Library no. 233 (New York, 1881), pp. 12, 13.

16 Albert W. Aiken, *Dick Talbot, the Ranch King*, Beadle's New York Dime Library no. 733 (New York, 1892), pp. 16, 21.

17 Albert W. Aiken, *The Fresh of Frisco at Santa Fe; or, The Stranger Sharp*, Beadle's New York Dime Library no. 647 (New York, 1891), pp. 23, 24.

CHAPTER 15

1 Edmund Clarence Stedman, ed., *An American Anthology, 1787–1900* (Boston and New York, 1900), p. 444.

2 Quoted in Carey McWilliams, *Ambrose Bierce, a Biography* (New York, 1929), p. 217.

3 Adolphe de Castro [Adolphe Danziger], *Portrait of Ambrose Bierce* (New York, 1929), pp. 194, 180.

4 McWilliams, *Ambrose Bierce,* p. 250.

5 Ambrose Bierce, *The Enlarged Devil's Dictionary,* ed. Ernest Jerome Hopkins (New York, 1967), p. 132.

6 For a full account of Bret Harte's Jewish ancestry, see Helen I. Davis, "Bret Harte and His Jewish Ancestor, Bernard Hart," *Publications of the American Jewish Historical Society* 32 (1931):99–111. Bernard Hart, who died in 1855, was a respected member of the New York business community and was secretary of the New York Stock Exchange from 1831 to 1853.

7 Mark Twain, *The Portable Mark Twain,* ed. Bernard De Voto (New York, 1946), p. 752. The letter is also reprinted in *Mark Twain–Howells Letters,* ed. Henry Nash Smith and William M. Gibson, 2 vols. (Cambridge, Mass., 1960), 1:235.

8 George R. Stewart, Jr., *Bret Harte, Argonaut and Exile* (Boston and New York, 1931), p. 16.

9 Bret Harte, *Bret Harte's Complete Works* (Boston, 1929), 9:392–95. The poem is reprinted in Sol Liptzin, *The Jew in American Literature* (New York, 1966), pp. 74–77.

10 Joaquin Miller, *The Poetical Works of Joaquin Miller,* ed. Stuart P. Sherman (New York, 1923), p. 309.

11 Ibid., pp. 309–10.

12 Ibid., pp. 528–29.

13 Joaquin Miller, *The One Fair Woman* (New York, 1876), pp. 145, 146, 149.

14 Mark Twain, *The Autobiography of Mark Twain,* ed. Charles Neider (New York, 1959), p. 77.

15 Philip S. Foner, *Mark Twain: Social Critic* (New York, 1958), p. 222. I am indebted to this book for its reports of Twain's unpublished material relating to Jews.

16 Mark Twain, *Life on the Mississippi* (New York, 1917), pp. 290–91.

17 Mark Twain, *Following the Equator,* 2 vols. (New York, 1899), 2:59.

18 Mark Twain, *The Complete Stories of Mark Twain,* ed. Charles Neider (New York, 1957), pp. 605, 618, 621, 622.

19 Mark Twain, *Mark Twain on the Damned Human Race,* ed. Janet Smith (New York, 1962), pp. 178–80.

20 Quoted in Foner, *Mark Twain,* p. 222.

21 Ibid., pp. 223–25. These stories are among Twain's unpublished manuscripts.

22 Mark Twain, *Clemens of "The Call": Mark Twain in San Francisco,* ed. Edgar M. Branch (Berkeley and Los Angeles, 1969), p. 210.

23 *Twain-Howells Letters,* 1:555.

24 Foner, *Mark Twain,* p. 225.

25 *Twain-Howells Letters,* 2:847.

26 Mark Twain, *The Complete Essays of Mark Twain,* ed. Charles Neider (New York, 1963), p. 101.

27 Mark Twain, *How to Tell a Story, and Other Essays,* vol. 22 of *The Writings of Mark Twain* (New York, 1899), pp. 228–29, 249.

28 Mark Twain, "Concerning the Jews," *Harper's Monthly Magazine* 99 (June 1899):528, 529, 530.

29 Ibid., pp. 530, 532.

30 Ibid., p. 535.

31 This unpublished letter is in the American Jewish Archives in Cincinnati.

32 M. S. Levy, "A Rabbi's Reply to Mark Twain," *Overland Monthly* 34 (October 1899):364, 366.

33 Mark Twain, "The American Jew as Soldier," Twain, *On the Damned Human Race,* pp. 177–78.

34 Clara Clemens, *My Husband, Gabrilowitsch* (New York, 1938), pp. 6–7.

35 Edgar M. Hemminghaus, *Mark Twain in Germany* (New York, 1939), p. 144, cited in Twain, *On the Damned Human Race,* p. 159.

36 Quoted in Caroline Thomas Harnsberger, *Mark Twain: Family Man* (New York, 1960), pp. 246–47.

CHAPTER 16

1 [Henry Adams], *Democracy: An American Novel* (New York, 1880), pp. 44, 373.

2 Ernest Samuels, *The Young Henry Adams* (Cambridge, Mass., 1965), p. 60. Barbara M. Solomon asserts that Adams first met a Jew in Germany in 1858 (*Ancestors and Immigrants* [Cambridge, Mass., 1956], p. 38).

3 Henry Adams, *Letters of Henry Adams,* ed. Worthington Chauncey Ford, 2 vols. (Boston and New York, 1930 and 1938), 1:255, 267, 315.

4 Ernest Samuels, *Henry Adams, the Middle Years* (Cambridge, Mass., 1958), p. 115.

5 Henry Adams, *The Education of Henry Adams* (New York, 1918), p. 85.

6 For a detailed, documented analysis of Adams's anti-Semitism, see Edward N. Saveth, *American Historians and European Immigrants* (New York, 1948). ch. 3.

7 Henry Adams, *Mont-Saint-Michel and Chartres* (Boston and New York, 1933), pp. 263, 105, 179.

8 Ibid., pp. 277–78, 278.

9 Adams, *Education,* pp. 214, 195, 238, 408.

10 Adams, *Letters,* 2:338.

11 William Roscoe Thayer, *The Life and Letters of John Hay,* 2 vols. (Boston and New York, 1915), 1:293, 294.

12 Adams, *Letters,* 2:98, 356.

13 Harold Dean Cater, ed., *Henry Adams and His Friends: A Collection of Unpublished Letters* (Cambridge, Mass., 1947), p. 376.

14 Ibid., pp. 438, 467.

15 Adams, *Letters,* 2:178, 111, 106, 111.

16 Ibid., 1:388; 2:178*n,* 258.

17 Cater, ed., *Henry Adams and His Friends,* p. 478.

18 Adams, *Letters,* 2:33, 35.

19 Ibid., p. 311.

20 Ernest Samuels, *Henry Adams, the Major Phase* (Cambridge, Mass., 1964), pp. 425, 426–27, 266.

21 Adams, *Letters,* 2:81, 233.
22 Adams, *Education,* p. 3.
23 Quoted in Samuels, *The Major Phase,* p. 169.
24 Adams, *Letters,* 2:540–41, 620.
25 Ibid., pp. 110, 116, 144, 145.
26 Ibid., pp. 150–51, 179.
27 Quoted in Samuels, *The Major Phase,* pp. 182–83.
28 Adams, *Letters,* 2:239, 238, 240, 238, 234.
29 Quoted in Samuels, *The Major Phase,* p. 184. For John Hay's attitude toward the Jews, see Kenton J. Clymer, "Anti-Semitism in the Late Nineteenth Century: The Case of John Hay," *American Jewish Historical Quarterly* 60, no. 4 (June 1971):344–54.
30 T. W. Higginson, "More Mingled Races," *Book and Heart, Essays on Literature and Life* (New York, 1897), pp. 155, 158, 159.
31 Quoted in Solomon, *Ancestors and Immigrants,* p. 176.
32 Anna Robeson Burr, ed., *Alice James, Her Brother, Her Journal* (New York, 1934), p. 227.
33 Quoted in Solomon, *Ancestors and Immigrants,* p. 181.
34 Leon Edel, *Henry James, the Master* (New York, 1972), p. 378.
35 Quoted in Leon Edel, *Henry James, the Treacherous Years* (Philadelphia and New York, 1969), pp. 274, 275.
36 Quoted in ibid., pp. 276, 279, 280. Paul Bourget's novel *Cosmopolis* contains a sufficiently vicious Jewish character to have won the praise of Edouard Drumont (Moses Debré, *The Image of the Jew in French Literature from 1800 to 1908,* trans. Gertrude Hirschler [New York, 1970], p. 33).
37 Edel, *Treacherous Years,* p. 275.
38 Henry James, "Daniel Deronda: A Conversation," *Atlantic Monthly* 38 (December 1876):684, 687, 690.
39 Cited in Leo B. Levy, "Henry James and the Jews," *Commentary* 25, no. 3 (September 1958):245.
40 Henry James, *The Golden Bowl,* 2 vols. (New York, 1904), 1:35.
41 Henry James, "The Covering End," *Two Magics* (New York, 1898), p. 393.
42 Henry James, *The Tragic Muse,* 2 vols. (New York, 1936), 1:61, 204–5.
43 Ibid., pp. 61, 61–62, 63, 220. James later probably makes a veiled allusion to James Russell Lowell's obsession with the Jews. When Mrs. Rooth, who is not Jewish, visited Nick's studio, writes James, Nick imagined her to be Jewish "on the general theory, so strictly held by several clever people, that few of us are not under suspicion" (2:305).
44 Henry James, "Impressions of a Cousin," *Tales of Three Cities* (Boston, 1887), pp. 23, 24, 58, 28, 29.
45 Ibid., pp. 78, 82, 83, 89.
46 Adams, *Mont-Saint-Michel and Chartres,* pp. 278, 105.
47 Henry James, *The Spoils of Poynton* (Boston and New York, 1896), p. 14.
48 James, *Golden Bowl,* 1:215, 216, 219.
49 Ibid., p. 108; 2:228, 367, 368.
50 Henry James, *The Ambassadors* (New York, 1903), pt. 5, ch. 10.
51 Henry James, *The Awkward Age* (New York, 1899), p. 272.
52 Henry James, *What Maisie Knew* (New York, 1923 [c1897]), p. 91.

53 Henry James, "Glasses," *Embarrassments* (New York, 1896), pp. 93, 86.

54 Henry James, "The Pupil," *Lesson of the Master* (New York, 1892), p. 159.

55 Henry James, *The American Scene* (New York, 1907), pp. 127, 128.

56 Ibid., p. 128. Abraham Cahan imputes the entomological analogy suggested by East Side life to a philanthropic "uptown" lady in a short story in 1899. In conversation with an impoverished old peddler in the ghetto, "Miss Bemis was tingling with compassion and with something very like the sensation of an entomologist come upon a rare insect" ("Rabbi Eliezer's Christmas," *Scribner's* 26, no. 6 [December 1899]:664).

57 James, *American Scene*, pp. 129, 131, 135, 132.

58 Ibid., p. 133.

CHAPTER 17

1 *Boston Evening Transcript,* December 24, 1912, pt. 3, p. 22.

2 See Thomas W. Ford, "Howells and the American Negro," *Texas Studies in Literature and Languages* 5, no. 4 (Winter 1964):530–37.

3 *Boston Evening Transcript,* loc. cit.

4 William Dean Howells, "Life and Letters," *Harper's Weekly* 40, pt. 1 (June 20, 1896):630.

5 William Dean Howells, introduction to Paul Lawrence Dunbar, *Lyrics of Lowly Life* (New York, 1897), pp. xvi–xvii, xix, xx.

6 *Boston Evening Transcript,* loc. cit.

7 William Dean Howells, *Life in Letters of William Dean Howells,* ed. Mildred Howells, 2 vols. (New York, 1928), 2:1.

8 William Roscoe Thayer, *The Life and Letters of John Hay,* 2 vols. (Boston and New York, 1915), 2:14.

9 Howells, *Life in Letters,* 1:357–58. In *The Bread-Winners* the leading character attends a meeting of the "labor" organization. This is Hay's description of the workers attending: "The faces he recognized were those of the laziest and most incapable workmen in the town—men whose weekly wages were habitually docked for drunkenness, late hours, and botchy work. As the room gradually filled, it seemed like a roll-call of the shirks" (John Hay, *The Bread-Winners* [New York, 1884], p. 82). The chief organizer of the "Bread-Winners" was "Andrew Jackson Offitt—a name which, in the West, is an unconscious brand. It generally shows that the person bearing it is the son of illiterate parents, with no family pride or affections, but filled with a bitter and savage partisanship which found its expression in servile worship of the most injurious personality in American history" (pp. 89–90). Offitt, a thorough scoundrel and a thief, attempts a murder.

10 William Dean Howells, *William Dean Howells: Representative Selections,* ed. C. M. Kirk and R. Kirk (New York, 1950), p. 363.

11 William Dean Howells, *Literary Friends and Acquaintances* (New York, 1900), p. 219.

12 Howells, *Life in Letters,* 1:142.

13 William Dean Howells, "A Romance of Real Life," *Atlantic Monthly* 25 (March 1870):305.

14 William Dean Howells, *Their Wedding Journey* (New York, 1872), pp. 67–68.

15 William Dean Howells, *A Modern Instance* (New York, 1881), pp. 123, 347.

16 William Dean Howells, "The Rise of Silas Lapham," *Century Magazine* 29, no. 1 (November 1884):22–23, 25.

17 Cyrus L. Sulzberger, "Silas Lapham and the Jews," *American Hebrew* 24 (September 4, 1885):50.

18 Ibid., 50–51.

19 Ibid., 51.

20 The letters are in the Houghton Library at Harvard.

21 Kermit Vanderbilt, "Howells among the Brahmins," *New England Quarterly* 35 (September 1962):306.

22 George Arms and William M. Gibson, in " 'Silas Lapham,' 'Daisy Miller,' and the Jews," *New England Quarterly* 16, no. 1 (March 1943):122, criticize Howells for omitting this passage from the book version of *Silas Lapham:* "We may wish that Howells had considered more acutely the possibility of not yielding to a pressure group, even when he deserved every praise for his sympathetic consideration of that group's over-sensitivity." However, it seems to me that Kermit Vanderbilt explored the problem more deeply in his article (note 21, above). He comments that for Howells to delete "these passages out of sympathy for Jewish feeling was one thing. But one strongly suspects that Howells may have been willing to avoid, thereby, an issue on which his own feelings were probably not clear to himself" (p. 306). What may be considered support for Vanderbilt's view in analogous circumstances comes from Abraham Cahan, who was acquainted with Howells in the 1890s. In his autobiography Cahan remarks that most American critics at that time tended to be snobbish. "Howells," writes Cahan, "that noble soul who was inspired by the socialist ideal, was too soft and too weak to put himself in opposition to this tendency," that is, the undemocratic snobbery of literary men. "Instead of trying to overcome it, he was conquered by it" (Abraham Cahan, *Bleter fun Mein Leben,* 5 vols. (New York, 1926–31), 4:217, 218).

23 "Prejudice against the Jews," *American Hebrew* (April 4, 1890), p. 194.

24 William Dean Howells, *A Hazard of New Fortunes,* 2 vols. (New York, 1890), 2:275.

25 Quoted in Kermit Vanderbilt, *William Dean Howells, a Reinterpretation* (Princeton, 1968), pp. 188–89.

26 Howells, *Hazard,* 2:69, 70; 1:241. Prosperous Jews are again referred to in *The Cosmopolitan* (December 15, 1893), where Howells describes "foreign restaurants in all parts of the town,—French, German, Italian, Spanish. . . . The Hebrews, who are so large and prosperous an element in the commercial body of New York, have restaurants of this sort, where they incur no peril of pork, or meat of any kind that is not *kosher.* Signs in Hebrew give them warrant of the fact that nothing unclean, or that has been rendered unlawful by hanging from a nail, is served within; and the Christian, if he sits down at a table, is warned that he can have neither milk nor butter with his meat, since this is against their ancient and most wholesome law" (William Dean

Howells, *Letters of an Altrurian Traveller,* a facsimile reproduction from *The Cosmopolitan,* ed. C. M. Kirk and R. Kirk [Gainesville, Fla., 1961], p. 108).

27 William Dean Howells, "An East-Side Ramble," *Impressions and Experiences* (New York, 1896), pp. 143, 145, 146.

28 Ibid., pp. 146, 147, 148, 149.

29 Henry James, *The American Scene* (New York, 1907), pp. 127, 128, 130.

30 William Dean Howells, "Emile Zola," *North American Review* 175 (November 1902); reprinted in Howells, *Representative Selections,* pp. 378, 379.

31 William Dean Howells, *Their Silver Wedding Journey,* 2 vols. (New York, 1899), 1:197; 2:401.

32 Ibid., 1:247, 269; 2:454.

33 Ibid., 1:250; 2:364–65. While visiting Carlsbad, Howells wrote Mark Twain on August 25, 1909: "I was here before, you know, and it is duller than the dishwater one drinks, troops of yellow Jews with corkscrew curls before their ears" (*Mark Twain–Howells Letters,* ed. Henry Nash Smith and William M. Gibson, 2 vols. [Cambridge, Mass., 1960], 2:847).

34 William Dean Howells, "Some Books of Short Stories," *Literature* 3 (December 31, 1898):629.

35 William Dean Howells, "Editor's Easy Chair," *Harper's Monthly Magazine* 130 (May 1915):958.

36 Howells, *Life in Letters,* 1:407.

37 Hamlin Garland, *Crumbling Idols, Twelve Essays in Art Dealing Chiefly with Literature, Painting and the Drama,* ed. Jane Johnson (Cambridge, Mass., 1960), p. 134.

38 Hamlin Garland, *Rose of Dutcher's Cooley* (New York, 1899 [c1895]), pp. 162, 171, 196.

39 Hamlin Garland, *A Daughter of the Middle Border* (New York, 1921), pp. 77, 92.

40 Hamlin Garland, *Companions on the Trail, a Literary Chronicle* (New York, 1931), pp. 393, 394.

41 Ibid., pp. 439–40.

42 Hamlin Garland, *Back-Trailers from the Middle Border* (New York, 1928), pp. 188, 283–84.

43 Quoted in Warren French, *Frank Norris* (New York, 1962), p. 40.

44 Frank Norris, *Moran of the Lady Letty* (New York, 1928 [c1898]), p. 148. For other examples of racist characterizations, see French, *Frank Norris,* pp. 39–41.

45 Frank Norris, *Vandover and the Brute* (New York, 1914 [c1895]), pp. 136–40.

46 Frank Norris, *The Pit, a Story of Chicago* (New York, 1903), pp. 56–57, 89, 96–97, 103, 102.

47 Frank Norris, *McTeague, a Story of San Francisco* (New York, 1960 [c1899]; paperback), p. 37.

48 Ibid., pp. 40, 50, 92, 93.

49 Ibid., pp. 168, 169.

50 Ibid., pp. 222–23.

51 Quoted in R. W. Stallman, *Stephen Crane, a Biography* (New York, 1968), p. 34.

52 Stephen Crane, "The Bride Comes to Yellow Sky," in *An Omnibus*, ed. Robert Wooster Stallman (New York, 1952), pp. 498, 494.

53 "Maggie," in *An Omnibus*, pp. 134, 69. It is interesting to note that Thomas Beer, in his *Stephen Crane* (New York, 1923), writes concerning *Maggie* that "Maggie is a pretty girl who goes to work for a Jew in a collar factory at five dollars a week rather than go on the streets" (p. 85). But Crane does not designate Maggie's employer as Jewish. After Maggie runs away with Pete, she thinks back on her job and "the eternal moan of the proprietor: 'What een hale do you sink I pie fife dolla a week for? Play? No, by tamn!' " (*An Omnibus*, p. 85). But the boss could be German as easily as a German Jew.

54 Stephen Crane, *The Complete Stories and Sketches*, ed. Thomas A. Gullison (New York, 1963), p. 72.

55 Harold Frederic, "The Jew's Christmas," Albany *Evening Journal* (December 23, 1882), p. 4. Publication of this story was discovered by Professor Stanton Garner, of the University of Texas at Arlington (letter from Professor Garner to this writer, May 18, 1972), to whose efforts I am indebted for a copy of the printed text of the story. Paul Haines, in "Harold Frederic," (diss., New York University, 1945), p. 27, states that this story by Frederic was unpublished. Similarly, Thomas F. O'Donnell and Hoyt C. Franchere, in *Harold Frederic* (New York, 1961), write that Frederic probably wrote this story in 1874, and they add: "Whether or not Frederic ever tried to find a publisher for the story is not known; the fact that he carefully saved it, however, is significant" (pp. 37–38). For a more realistic, quite unsentimental treatment of a traditional Orthodox Jew's abhorrence of Christmas, see Abraham Cahan's "Rabbi Eliezer's Christmas," *Scribner's* 26, no. 6 (December 1899):661–68.

56 Quoted in Haines, "Harold Frederic," letter of August 14, 1886.

57 Harold Frederic, *The New Exodus: A Study of Israel in Russia* (London, 1892), pp. 17, 26, 67.

58 Ibid., pp. 81–82, 83.

59 Harold Frederic, *The Damnation of Theron Ware* (New York, 1924 [c1896], pp. 37, 122, 122–23, 123.

60 Ibid., pp. 300, 357–58, 383, 384.

61 Harold Frederic, *The Market-Place* (New York, 1899), pp. 1–2, 9.

62 Ibid., pp. 228, 228–29.

63 Ibid., pp. 240, 242.

64 Harold Frederic, *Gloria Mundi* (Chicago and New York, 1898), pp. 37, 38.

CHAPTER 18

1 Allyn B. Forbes, "The Literary Quest for Utopia, 1880–1900," *Social Forces* 6 (1927):188–89; see also Vernon Louis Parrington, Jr., *American Dreams: A Study of American Utopias* (Providence, R.I., 1947).

Forbes's list is not exhaustive, as is evident from the fact that several of the works discussed herein are not listed by him.

2 Jesse H. Jones, *Joshua Davidson, the story of the life of one who, in the nineteenth century, was "like unto Christ," as told by his body-servant,* ed. Halah H. Loud (New York, 1907).

3 Ibid., pp. 11, 21.

4 Ibid., pp. 35, 36.

5 Ibid., pp. 53–54, 127, 185, 203–4, 212, 213.

6 Ibid., p. 299.

7 Albion W. Tourgee, *Murvale Eastman, Christian Socialist* (New York, 1889), p. 273.

8 Ibid., p. 123.

9 Ibid., pp. 279, 280, 421–22, 426.

10 Caroline Atwater Mason, *A Woman of Yesterday* (New York, 1900), pp. 228, 241, 228, 229.

11 Ibid., pp. 262, 263–64, 275.

12 Ibid., pp. 304, 305, 359, 364.

13 Joaquin Miller, *The Building of the City Beautiful* (Cambridge, Mass. and Chicago, 1893), pp. 2, 3, 4, 6.

14 Ibid., pp. 12, 10, 12, 13.

15 Ibid., pp. 13, 20, 24, 27, 33, 34, 195.

16 Harold Frederic, *Gloria Mundi* (Chicago and New York, 1898), pp. 178, 207, 179, 220.

17 Ibid., p. 240.

18 Ibid., pp. 274, 403–4, 405.

19 Quoted in Thomas F. O'Donnell and Hoyt C. Franchere, *Harold Frederic* (New York, 1961), p. 122.

20 Frederic, *Gloria Mundi,* p. 571.

21 Alexander Craig, *Ionia: Land of Wise Men and Fair Women* (Chicago, 1898), pp. 216, 215, 220, 221.

22 Ibid., pp. 221, 222.

23 H. Pereira Mendes, *Looking Ahead, Twentieth Century Happenings* (London, New York, and Chicago, 1899).

24 Charles K[line] Landis, *The Founding of Vineland as Told by the Founder* (Vineland, N. J., 1903), p. 7.

25 Charles K. Landis, *Carabajal, the Jew: A Legend of Monterey* [sic] (Vineland, N. J., 1894), pp. 2, 3, 25.

26 Ibid., pp. 3, 14, 15.

27 Oscar Handlin, "American Views of the Jews at the Opening of the Twentieth Century," *Publications of the American Jewish Historical Society* 40, pt. 4 (June 1951):343–44, 335, n. 51.

28 Richard Hofstadter, *The Age of Reform, from Bryan to F.D.R.* (New York, 1955), pp. 78, 80.

29 Richard Hofstadter, "Free Silver and the Mind of 'Coin' Harvey," *The Paranoid Style in American Politics* (New York, 1966), p. 293.

30 William Hope Harvey, *A Tale of Two Nations* (Chicago, 1894), pp. 13, 17, 65, 69.

31 Ibid., pp. 21, 96.

32 Ibid., pp. 217, 219, 223, 224, 225, 226.

33 Ibid., pp. 226, 227, 257, 258.

34 Ibid., pp. 265, 277, 287.

35 Ibid., pp. 295, 293, 295.

36 Norman Pollack, "Handlin on Anti-Semitism: A Critique of 'American Views of the Jew,' " *Journal of American History* 2, no. 3 (December 1964):397, n. 25. As evidence of the non-anti-Semitic character of the novel, Pollack comments that Rothe's daughter is portrayed "quite favorably" and that Rogasner's Jewish girl is "warmly" depicted, but he seems unaware that the stereotype of the Jewish woman is not just favorable but flattering.

37 Harvey, *Tale of Two Nations,* pp. 287, 289.

38 Quoted in Hofstadter, *Paranoid Style,* pp. 301, 302.

39 Ignatius Donnelly, *Caesar's Column, a Story of the Twentieth Century,* ed. Walter B. Rideout (Cambridge, Mass., 1960 [c1890]), pp. 3, 4.

40 Ibid., pp. 15, 27, 32.

41 Ibid., pp. 28, 33, 69, 71, 72, 97, 98.

42 Ibid., pp. 101, 103.

43 Ibid., pp. 117, 118, 127.

44 Ibid., pp. 149, 149–50, 169, 170, 283.

45 Quoted in Martin Ridge, *Ignatius Donnelly, the Portrait of a Politician* (Chicago, 1962), p. 264, n. 3.

46 Ignatius Donnelly, *Atlantis: The Antediluvian World* (New York, 1882), pp. 212–13.

47 Norman Pollack, "The Myth of Populist Anti-Semitism," *American Historical Review* 68, no. 1 (October 1962):76.

48 Ignatius Donnelly, *The Golden Bottle* (New York and London, 1968 [c1892]), pp. 221, 246, 308.

49 Ibid., pp. 280–81.

50 Pollack, "The Myth," pp. 77, 78, 78, n. 10.

51 Edmund Boisguilbert, M.D. [Ignatius Donnelly], *Doctor Huguet, a Novel* (Chicago, 1891; Arno Press facsimile edition, New York, 1969), pp. 308, 287, 289, 214. The ambiguities in this novel are carefully analyzed by John S. Patterson, "Alliance and Antipathy: Ignatius Donnelly's Ambivalent Vision in *Doctor Huguet,*" *American Quarterly* 22, no. 4 (Winter 1970):824–45.

52 C. Vann Woodward, "The Populist Heritage and the Intellectual," *American Scholar* 29, no. 1 (Winter 1959–60):66.

53 Quoted in Ridge, *Ignatius Donnelly,* pp. 396, 395.

54 "Are the Populists Anti-Semitic?" *Jewish Voice* (Saint Louis) 21, no. 7 (August 14, 1896).

55 John Higham, "Anti-Semitism in the Gilded Age: A Reinterpretation," *Mississippi Valley Historical Review,* 43, no. 4 (March 1957):559–78. See also the two articles by Norman Pollack cited above and his "Hofstadter on Populism: A Critique of 'The Age of Reform,' " *Journal of Southern History* 26, no. 4 (November 1960):478–500, and Woodward, *American Scholar* 29.

CHAPTER 19

1 Nina Morais, "Jewish Ostracism in America," *North American Review* 133 (1881):269–70.

2 Ibid., pp. 269, 270.

3 John Higham, "Social Discrimination against Jews in America, 1830–1930," *Publications of the American Jewish Historical Society* 47, no. 1 (September 1957):11. See also John Higham's "Anti-Semitism in the Gilded Age: A Reinterpretation," *Mississippi Valley Historical Review* 43, no. 4 (March 1957):566–67, 570.

4 *Puck* 29:362, cited in Rudolf Glanz, "German Jews in New York City in the Nineteenth Century," *Studies in Judaica Americana* (New York, 1970), pp. 150–51.

5 Edward W. Townsend, *A Daughter of the Tenements* (New York, 1895), pp. 61, 68.

6 Lillian D. Wald, *The House on Henry Street* (New York, 1915), p. 2.

7 See Rudolf Glanz,"Jewish Social Conditions as Seen by the Muckrakers," op. cit., pp. 384–407. Glanz quotes Louis Filler as noting that "the muckrakers were deeply infatuated with the Jews" (p. 385).

8 Jacob A. Riis, *How the Other Half Lives, Studies among Tenements in New York* (New York, 1957 [c1890]), p. 77.

9 Ibid., pp. 48, 78–79, 90.

10 Ida Van Etten, "Russian Jews as Desirable Immigrants," *Forum* 15 (1893):174.

11 Hutchins Hapgood, *The Spirit of the Ghetto, Studies of the Jewish Quarter of New York* (New York, 1965 [c1902]).

12 Ibid., pp. 20, 47.

13 Ibid., p. 48.

14 J[ohn] S[pargo], review of *The Spirit of the Ghetto, Comrade* 2, no. 3 (December 1902):56.

15 Hapgood, *Spirit of the Ghetto,* pp. 48, 49.

16 Morris Rosenfeld, "I Know Not Why," in *An American Anthology, 1787–1900,* ed. Edmund Clarence Stedman (Boston and New York, 1900), p. 772.

17 Abraham Cahan, *Yekl and the Imported Bridegroom* (New York, 1970; paperback), pp. 13–14.

18 Leo Stein, "The Jew in Fiction," *Jewish Comment* 11, no. 5 (May 18, 1900):8.

19 Ephraim Lederer, "The Jew in Fiction," *Jewish Exponent,* March 11, 1888. Lederer was admitted to the Bar in 1883.

20 Sara Miller, *Under the Eagle's Wing* (Philadelphia, 1899), pp. 17, 90, 211.

21 Adelina Cohnfeldt Lust, *A Tent of Grace* (Boston and New York, 1899), p. 58.

22 Ibid., pp. 21, 8, 355, 379, 383, 366, 396.

23 Moritz Loth, *On a Higher Plane* (Cincinnati, 1899), pp. 44, 112, 175. Loth rushed into print with *Our Prospects: A Tale of Real Life* (Cincinnati, 1870) before he had mastered English. He later published a somewhat corrected version of this novel as *The Great Bottwell, the Great American Novel* (Cincinnati, 1896). A sequel, *The Forgiving Kiss; or, Our Destiny, a Novel* (Cincinnati, 1896), contrasts the ancient lineage of Jews with the pretensions of non-Jewish settlers. Throughout his books Loth has one Jewish character who is a paragon of virtue and wisdom; this personage represents Rabbi Isaac Mayer Wise.

24 Nadage Dorée, *Gelta; or, The Czar and the Songtress, a Novel,* 3d rev. ed. (New York, Chicago, and London, 1897), p. 73. A search failed to reveal the place and date of the first edition. The book was reprinted a number of times in New York and London as late as 1906.

25 Ibid., pp. 15, 17, 88, 227, 169.

26 I[saac] K[ahn] Friedman, "Aaron Pivansky's Picture," *The Lucky Number* (Chicago, 1896), pp. 183, 187.

27 Walter B. Rideout, "O Workers' Revolution . . . The True Messiah: The Jew as Author and Subject in the American Novel," *American Jewish Archives* 11, no. 2 (October 1959):158.

28 Isaac Kahn Friedman, *Poor People* (Boston, 1900), p. 134.

29 W. M. Rosenblatt, "The Jews: What Are They Coming To?" *Galaxy* 13, no. 1 (January 1872):47.

CHAPTER 20

1 Quoted in John James Clarke, "Henry Harland, a Critical Biography," (Ph.D. diss., Brown University, 1957), p. 35. This is the only book-length treatment of Harland. See also Albert Parry, "Henry Harland, Expatriate," *Bookman* 76, no. 1 (January 1933):1–10.

2 Quoted in Clarke, "Henry Harland," p. 41.

3 Sidney Luska (Henry Harland), *Grandison Mather; or, An Account of the Fortunes of Mr. and Mrs. Thomas Gardner* (New York, 1889), p. 288. By this time Luska's identity was known, and both names of the author appear on the title page.

4 So deep was the impression that "Sidney Luska" was Jewish, that we find Hamlin Garland in 1903 referring to Harland as "of Jewish birth" (Hamlin Garland, *Companions on the Trail, a Literary Chronicle* [New York, 1931], p. 179). Even such a well-informed scholar as Kermit Vanderbilt couples "Sidney Luska" with Abraham Cahan as examples of the "generous support" that Howells gave "to the individual Jewish writer" (Kermit Vanderbilt, *The Achievement of William Dean Howells* [Princeton, 1968], p. 188).

5 Sidney Luska [Henry Harland], *As It Was Written, a Jewish Musician's Story* (New York, 1885), pp. 12, 24.

6 Ibid., pp. 104, 105–6.

7 Ibid., pp. 252–53. In his pamphlet *The Jew in the American Novel* (New York, 1959), Leslie Fiedler again exhibits his excessive zeal by committing a factual distortion to strengthen a thesis. For Harland, he writes, "the new Jewish-American proposed as a symbol of assimilation, of the mating of the Jewish and American psyche, ends by killing his Gentile bride and proves capable only of destruction" (p. 12). In the novel, however, the bride he kills is Jewish.

8 Harland, *As It Was Written,* p. 142.

9 Sidney Luska [Henry Harland], "A Purim Episode," *Jewish Messenger* 58, no. 24 (December 11, 1885):9.

10 Sidney Luska [Henry Harland], *Mrs. Peixada* (New York, 1886), p. 95.

11 Ibid., pp. 252, 253, 255.

12 Ibid., pp. 100–101, 102–3.

13 Ibid., pp. 103, 104.

14 Ibid., pp. 106, 107.

15 *New York Times,* April 5, 1886, p. 3; cited in Clarke, "Henry Harland," pp. 59–60.

16 "The Editor's Study," *Harper's Magazine* 73 (1886):314; cited in Clarke, "Henry Harland," p. 62.

17 Sidney Luska [Henry Harland], *The Yoke of the Thorah* (New York, 1887), pp. 58, 63.

18 Ibid., pp. 83, 85.

19 Ibid., pp. 163, 167, 171, 177.

20 Ibid., pp. 200, 204.

21 Ibid., pp. 256–57, 282.

22 M. S., " 'Sidney Luska' and the Jews," *Jewish Exponent* 2, no. 4 (November 4, 1887):4.

23 K[aufmann] Kohler, " 'The Yoke of the Thorah,' a Critique and a Protest," *Menorah* 3, no. 3 (September 1887):143–44.

24 Harland, *Yoke of the Thorah,* pp. 64–65n.

25 *Jewish Messenger* 62, no. 2 (July 8, 1887):4.

26 Ibid., no. 4 (July 22, 1887):1.

27 Ibid., no. 18, (October 28, 1887):1, 4.

28 Ibid., no. 19 (November 4, 1887):4.

29 Sidney Luska (Henry Harland), *My Uncle Florimund* (Boston, 1888), p. 92.

30 *American Hebrew,* October 5, 1888, p. 134.

31 Sidney Luska (Henry Harland) *A Latin-Quarter Courtship, and Other Stories* (New York, 1889), p. 191.

32 Ibid., pp. 216, 218.

33 [Harland], *Grandison Mather,* pp. 106, 106–7, 128, 144.

34 Ibid., pp. 124–25, 136, 139.

35 Ibid., pp. 319, 293.

36 Hamlin Garland was amused by Harland's attempted Anglicization; he became acquainted with Harland through Howells in 1903, when Harland visited this country. Garland records that "Henry Harland was at the National Institute dinner last night, and his 'extraoinary' English accent was comical. He spoke quite like the caricatured Englishman of our comedy stage. He is completely expatriated now and unpleasantly aggressive in his defense of England and English ways" (Garland, *Companions on the Trail,* pp. 212–13).

37 Henry Harland, *The Cardinal's Snuff Box* (New York, n. d. [c1900]), pp. 127, 128.

38 Ibid., p. 311.

39 Henry Harland, *My Friend Prospero* (New York, 1904), p. 231.

40 Henry Harland, *The Royal Road, a Romance* (Toronto, n.d.) p. 129.

CHAPTER 21

1 Quoted in Ella Stirling Cummins [Mighels], *The Story of the Files, a Review of California Writers and Literature* (San Francisco, n.d. [189–]), p. 356.

2 Ibid.

3 Emma Wolf, *Other Things Being Equal* (Chicago, 1892), pp. 163, 174, 180–81.

4 Ibid., pp. 257, 258, 7, 54.

5 Ibid., pp. 54, 79, 86.

6 Emma Wolf, *Heirs of Yesterday* (Chicago, 1900), pp. 284, 31, 35.

7 Ibid., pp. 36, 125, 126, 128.

8 Ibid., pp. 283, 285.

9 A contemporary comment on common Jewish attitudes toward the Spanish-American War is found in Abraham Cahan's essay "The Russian Jew in America": "The Jewish immigrants look upon the United States as their country, and now that it is engaged in war they do not shirk their duty. They have contributed three times their quota of volunteers to the army, and they had their representatives among the first martyrs of the campaign" (*Atlantic* 82 [1898]:138). There was opposition to the war, however, from sections of the Jewish labor and socialist movements, and some Jewish liberals participated in the Anti-Imperialist League.

10 Wolf, *Heirs of Yesterday*, pp. 191, 192, 193.

11 Eugene F. Baldwin and Maurice Eisenberg, *Doctor Cavallo* (Peoria, Ill., 1895), pp. 19, 20, 25.

12 Ibid., pp. 27, 31–32, 39–40, 43.

13 Ibid., pp. 97–98, 316.

14 Ibid., p. 150.

15 Horace J. Rollin, *Yetta Segal* (New York, 1898), pp. 160, 10, 27, 131, 158.

16 Two contemporaneous Edward Kings who were connected with the East Side during the nineties should be distinguished: Edward Smith King, journalist and author of *Joseph Zalmonah*, among other novels, and Edward King, Scottish Comtean, labor organizer, and friend of Abraham Cahan. For the two Kings, see Milton Hindus, "Edward Smith King and the Old East Side," *American Jewish Historical Quarterly*, LXIV, No. 4 (June 1975), 321–30. Cahan wrote of labor organizer King that "he became a kind of patriarchical uncle in our little world of Russian Jewish immigrants"(*The Education of Abraham Kahn*, trans. L. Stein, A.D. Conan, and L. Davison, Phila., 1969, p. 266).

17 Edward King, *The Gentle Savage* (Boston, 1883), p. 263.

18 Ibid., pp. 133, 136, 137, 395, 161.

19 Edward King, *The Golden Spike: Fantasie in Prose* (Boston, 1886), pp. 253, 387, 388.

20 Edward King, *Joseph Zalmonah* (Englewood, N. J., 1968 [c1893]), pp. 7, 49.

21 Ibid., pp. 46, 110, 115, 124, 126.

22 Ibid., pp. 12, 340, 348, 244, 63.

23 Ibid., pp. 35, 33, 64, 31.

24 Ibid., p. 63.

CHAPTER 22

1 The main source for Abraham Cahan's biography is his five-volume autobiography in Yiddish, *Bleter fun Mein Leben* (New York, 1926–31), which stops with World War I. The first two volumes have appeared in English as *The Education of Abraham Cahan,* trans. Leon Stein, Abraham P. Conan, and Lynn Davison (Philadelphia, 1969), and a translation of the other volumes is in preparation. The fullest biographical account in English, although the period after 1914 is only briefly summarized, is Ronald Sanders's *The Downtown Jews: Portraits of an Immigrant Generation* (New York, 1969). A long interview with Cahan by Dexter Marshall, "Life of A. Cahan, Novelist," was published in the *Boston Sunday Post* on September 27, 1896, and gives an account of Cahan's life up to that date mainly in his own words; this interview was reprinted as an appendix to "Abraham Cahan and William Dean Howells, the Story of a Friendship," by Rudolf Kirk and Clara M. Kirk (*American Jewish Historical Quarterly* 52, no. 1 [September 1962]:44–61). The story is carried up to 1911 in an interview with the novelist Ernest Poole, "Abraham Cahan—Socialist—Journalist—Friend of the Ghetto," *Outlook* 99 (October 28, 1911):467–78. An article concentrating on Cahan as editor of the *Forward,* apparently not written from inside the Yiddish-speaking community, is Leon Wexelstein's "Abraham Cahan," *American Mercury* 9 (September 1929): 88–94. A well-informed, critical, candid, though finally favorable essay forms the section on Cahan in Melech Epstein's *Profiles of Eleven* (Detroit, 1965). Several important estimates from the left are Moissays Olgin's pamphlet *Ab. Cahan, Ver Is Er? Vemen Fartret Er?* (New York, 1935), and a series of obituary articles by Paul Novick in the *Morgen Freiheit* on September 9 (p. 9), September 16 (p. 9), and September 23 (p. 5), 1951. Novick also summarized his estimate of Cahan in English in "Abraham Cahan and the 'Forward,' " *Jewish Life* 6, no. 1 (November 1951):14–16. Olgin and Novick were successively editors of the *Freiheit.* The Yiddish journalist B. Z. Goldberg attempted to deflate what he called the myths that have gathered around Cahan's name in two articles in *Yiddishe Kultur:* "Ab. Cahan, der Historisher Emes," October 1951, pp. 3–11; and "Ab. Cahan un di Yiddishe Literatur," February 1952, pp. 17–25. These two articles were reprinted in the same journal in June–July 1972, pp. 4–13, and August–September 1972, pp. 45–53.

2 Lincoln Steffens, *The Autobiography of Lincoln Steffens,* 1evol. ed. (New York, 1931), pp. 316, 317, 244, 318.

3 Paul Novick, "Ab. Cahan un dos Idishe Vort," *Morgen Freiheit,* September 28, 1951, p. 5.

4 Cahan, *Education,* p. 356.

5 Quoted in Paul Novick, *Morgen Freiheit,* May 21, 1967, p. 5.

6 Cahan, *Bleter,* 4:285, 299, 301.

7 Moses Rischin, "Abraham Cahan and the New York 'Commercial Advertiser': A Study in Acculturation," *Publications of the American Jewish Historical Society* 43, no. 1 (September 1953):10, 36.

8 Epstein, *Profiles of Eleven,* p. 82. Ronald Sanders in *Downtown Jews* agrees with Epstein in this regard, and writes that Cahan "had begun to move imperceptibly from the liberal frame of reference of Steffens or the Hapgood brothers to the demagogic one of those other journalistic contemporaries of his, William Randolph Hearst and Joseph Pulitzer" (p. 262).

9 Quoted in Lamed Shapiro, "Yoel Entin," *Yiddishe Kultur,* June 1947, p. 39.

10 Quoted in Novick, *Morgen Freiheit,* May 21, 1967, p. 5.

11 Epstein, *Profiles of Eleven,* p. 95n.

12 Paul Novick, *Morgen Freiheit,* September 16, 1951, p. 6.

13 Philip Foner, *The Fur and Leather Workers Union* (Newark, 1950), p. 125.

14 Bezalel Sherman, "Ab. Cahan," *Yiddisher Kemfer,* September 22, 1950, pp. 5–6, 12. See also Sherman's article "Abe Cahan," in *Jewish Frontier,* August 1961, pp. 14–16, in which essentially the same estimate of Cahan is given.

15 Cahan, *Education,* p. 360. For a specific example of Cahan's socialist scruples, see Rischin, *PAJHS* 43:13.

16 Cahan, *Bleter,* 4:225, 341.

17 The following are articles published by Cahan: "The Younger Russian Writers," *Forum* 28 (September 1899):119–28; "The Mantle of Tolstoy," *Bookman* 16 (December 1902): 328–33; "Maxim Gorky's 'The Spy,'" *Bookman* 29 (March 1904):90–92; "Russian Nihilism of Today," *Forum* 31 (June 1901):413–22; "Jewish Massacres and the Revolutionary Movement in Russia," *North American Review* 177 (July 1903):49–62; "The Russian Jew in America," *Atlantic Monthly* 82 (1898):128–39; "Zangwill's Play: 'The Children of the Ghetto,'" *Forum* 28 (December 1899):503–12; "Zangwill's 'The Grey Wig,'" *Bookman* 17 (May 1903):256–57; "The Late Rabbi Joseph, Hebrew Patriarch of New York," *Review of Reviews* 27 (September 1902): 311–14.

18 *Workmen's Advocate,* April 6, 1889; also quoted in Kirk and Kirk, *AJHQ* 52:29.

19 Quoted in Cahan, *Bleter,* 4:29.

20 Abraham Cahan, "A Providential Match," *Yekl and the Imported Bridegroom* (New York, 1970; paperback), pp. 182, 164, 170, 186.

21 Quoted in Cahan, *Bleter,* 4:38, 39.

22 Leon Kobrin, "Der Veg fun Ab. Cahan," from *Meine Fiftzig Yor in Amerika,* in *Morgen Freiheit,* March 17, 1946.

23 Cahan, *Bleter,* 4:54.

24 Cahan, *Yekl,* pp. 33, 34, 4, 89.

25 Nancy Huston Banks, *Bookman* 4 (October 1896):157, 158.

26 W. D. Howells, New York *World,* July 26, 1896; reprinted in part in Kirk and Kirk, *AJHQ* 52, app. 2, pp. 51–52.

27 Cahan, "The Imported Bridegroom," *Yekl,* pp. 161, 162.

28 Abraham Cahan, "The Apostate of Chego-Chegg," *Century,* n.s. 37 (November 1899):94, 99.

29 Ibid., pp. 100, 104.

30 Cahan, *Bleter,* 4:208.

31 Abraham Cahan, "Rabbi Eliezer's Christmas," *Scribner's* 26, no. 6 (December 1899):661, 668. Miss Bemis, in conversing with Eliezer, "was tingling with compassion and with something very like the sensation of an entomologist come upon a rare insect" (p. 664). It will be recalled that when Henry James came to describe the East Side in *The American Scene,* he also used entomological metaphors to describe the density of population.

32 W. D. Howells, "Some Books of Short Stories," *Literature* (London) 3, no. 63 (December 31, 1898):629; also reprinted in Kirk and Kirk, *AJHQ* 52:41.

33 Abraham Cahan, "Dumitru and Sigrid," *Cosmopolitan* 30, no. 5 (March 1901):501.

34 Abraham Cahan, "Tzinchadzi of the Catskills," *Atlantic Monthly* 88 (August 1901):226.

35 Abraham Cahan, "The Daughter of Reb Avrom Leib," *Cosmopolitan* 29, no. 1 (May 1900):53, 54, 64.

36 Howells, *Literature* 3, no. 63.

37 Cahan, *Bleter,* 4:202.

38 Rev. Rudolph Grossman, "The Jew in Novels," *American Hebrew* 40, no. 7 (March 18, 1892):123.

39 Steffens, *Autobiography,* p. 243.

40 *Bookman* 10 (1900):428, 429.

41 Ibid., pp. 533, 534.

42 Ibid., pp. 429, 430. The editor had already called attention to the presumed forthcoming novel on which, he writes, Cahan "was putting the finishing touches" (October 1899, pp. 101–2).

43 Cahan, *North American Review* 177:60.

44 The proposition passed by the congress ended with the statement that "the congress, 'while condemning anti-Semitic and philo-Semitic incitation as one of the manoeuvers by which the capitalist class and government reaction seek to divert the socialist movement and to divide the workers; decides that this is not the occasion (qu'il n'y a pas lieu) to take the question proposed by the delegation of Yiddish-speaking American socialists, and passes on to the next order of business.' " (*Congrès International Ouvrier Socialiste, Tenue à Bruxelles du 16 au 23 Août 1891, Rapport* [Bruxelles, 1893], p. 44).

45 Abraham Cahan, *The White Terror and the Red* (New York, 1905), p. 35.

46 Ibid., pp. 138, 143–44, 144, 145.

47 Ibid., pp. 220, 223, 224.

48 In its issue of September 1, 1881, the *Narodnaya Volya* did "appeal for a pogrom against 'the Tsar, the nobles, and the Jews' " (George Lichtheim, *Collected Essays* [New York, 1973], p. 414).

49 Cahan, *White Terror and the Red,* pp. 405, 314, 315.

50 Ibid., pp. 342, 343, 358.

51 Ibid., pp. 367, 374, 406.

52 Ibid., pp. 360, 362, 363.

53 Sherman, "Ab. Cahan," p. 5.

54 The likeness of Cahan's title to W. D. Howells's *The Rise of Silas Lapham* is obvious. In *Bleter* (4:16) Cahan writes that he had bought a copy

of Howells's novel when he could ill afford it. Incidentally, he calls the book *The Career [Kariere] of Silas Lapham.*

55 John Higham, introduction to the paperback edition of *The Rise of David Levinsky* (New York, 1960), p. viii. All page references are to this edition.

56 Ibid., pp. 201, 337.

57 Ibid., p. 285.

58 Ibid., pp. 3, 529, 188.

59 H. W. Boynton, "Outstanding Novels of the Year," *Nation* 105 (November 29, 1917):600.

60 Cahan, *Bleter,* 4:341.

61 Cahan, *David Levinsky,* p. 190.

62 "Abraham Cahan's Death Removes Last Giant of Giant Generation," *American Jewish Review,* September 25, 1951.

63 Cahan, *David Levinsky,* p. 529.

64 Ibid., p. 445.

65 Ibid., pp. 525, 526.

66 William Dean Howells, *Life in Letters of William Dean Howells,* ed. Mildred Howells, 2 vols. (New York, 1928), 2:375.

67 "Symposium on 'The Jew in Literature and on the Stage,'" *Jewish Exponent* 58, no. 9 (December 5, 1913): 8.

68 Kate Holladay Claghorn, review of *The Rise of David Levinsky, Survey,* December 1, 1917, pp. 260, 262.

69 Quoted in Morris U. Schappes, "Anatomy of 'David Levinsky,'" *Jewish Life* 8, no. 10 (August 1954): 23.

70 Ibid., pp. 23, 24.

71 Leo Stein, "The Jew in Fiction," *Jewish Comment* 11, no. 5 (May 18, 1900): 8.

INDEX